AMERICAN NIETZSCHE

# American

# NIETZSCHE

A HISTORY OF AN
ICON AND HIS IDEAS

**JENNIFER RATNER-ROSENHAGEN** is the Merle Curti
Associate Professor of History at the University of Wisconsin–
Madison.

The University of Chicago Press, Chicago 60637
The University of Chicago Press, Ltd., London
© 2012 by The University of Chicago
All rights reserved. Published 2012.
Printed in the United States of America

21  20  19  18  17  16  15  14  13  12      2  3  4  5

ISBN-13: 978-0-226-70581-1 (cloth)
ISBN-10: 0-226-70581-1 (cloth)

A subvention for this publication has been awarded through a
competitive grant from the University of Wisconsin–Madison
Provost's Office and the Graduate School. Graduate School
funding has been provided by the Wisconsin Alumni Research
Foundation (WARF) with income generated by patents filed
through WARF by UW–Madison faculty and staff.

Library of Congress Cataloging-in-Publication Data

Ratner-Rosenhagen, Jennifer.
    American Nietzsche : a history of an icon and his ideas /
Jennifer Ratner-Rosenhagen.
       p. cm.
    Includes bibliographical references and index.
    ISBN-13: 978-0-226-70581-1 (hardcover : alk. paper)
    ISBN-10: 0-226-70581-1 (hardcover : alk. paper) 1. Nietzsche,
Friedrich Wilhelm, 1844–1900. 2. Nietzsche, Friedrich
Wilhelm, 1844–1900—Influence. 3. United States—
Civilization—German influences. 4. Philosophy, American.
5. United States—Intellectual life. I. Title.
    B3317.R338 2012
    193—dc22

                                          2011011189

♾ This paper meets the requirements of ANSI/NISO
Z39.48-1992 (Permanence of Paper).

*For My Parents*

# Transatlantic Crossings

## *The Aboriginal Intellect Abroad*

> Truly speaking, it is not instruction, but provocation, that I can receive from another soul.
> RALPH WALDO EMERSON, "Divinity School Address" (1838)

> I profit from a philosopher only insofar as he can be an example.
> FRIEDRICH NIETZSCHE, "Schopenhauer as Educator" (1874), in *Untimely Meditations*

If book sales are a measure of literary achievement, Friedrich Wilhelm Nietzsche in 1881 was a positive failure. His first work, *The Birth of Tragedy* (1872), caused quite a stir among a small circle of Wagnerians and philologists, but failed to catch the attention of the broader literary press and reading public. And yet this was his best-selling book during his lifetime; after that it was all downhill. The next year, "David Strauss, the Confessor and the Writer" (1873), the first of Nietzsche's *Untimely Meditations*, received some initial attention but then quickly faded from view. The works that followed, *Human, All Too Human* (1878) and *Daybreak* (1881), went virtually unnoticed. Nietzsche never tired of contemplating the travails of the untimely genius. In a letter to a friend in August 1881, he bristled about an indifferent reading public, which let him starve on silence:

> If I were unable to draw strength from myself, if I had to wait for applause, encouragement, consolation, where would I be? what would I be? There were certainly moments and whole periods in my life . . . when a robust word of encouragement, a hand-clasp of agreement would have been the refreshment of refreshments—and it was just then that everybody left me in the lurch.[1]

But a few months later, as the protracted neglect exacerbated Nietzsche's frustration, three admirers from Baltimore, Maryland, Elise Fincke, her husband, and a friend, sent him an epistolary lifeline:

> Esteemed Herr Doctor, Perhaps it is of little concern to you that here in America three people ... often sit together and allow Nietzsche's writings to edify them at their most intimate [*auf's Innigste erbauen*]—but I don't see why we shouldn't at least tell you so once. We are counting on the fact that due to the depth of your thoughts and [your] sublime diction, we ... will never be able or want to read anything else ever again.[2]

Nietzsche's response to Fincke, both muted and arrogant, makes it difficult to appreciate how delighted he was to receive her praise. He informed her that he was now writing even more-challenging works, and that she and her companions should be duly forewarned: "Who knows? who knows? perhaps you too won't be able to stand it and will come to say what some others have already said: He can run wherever he pleases and break his own neck when it pleases him too."[3]

Such nonchalance, however, belied a deep sense of gratitude. His handwritten note to himself—written on the back of Fincke's letter—tells a different story. Clearly pleased, he marked the occasion: "Erster *amerikanischer* Brief. *initium gloriae mundi*."[4] Finally, it seemed, the world was waking to his genius.

In the ensuing months, however, silence settled back in. Nevertheless, Nietzsche found the inner resources to press ahead with his next book project. As he enjoyed a stretch of exuberant productivity, a second letter arrived from America, this time from a professional violinist named Gustav Dannreuther living in Boston. He wrote to express, as he put it, "my most humble thanks for the benefit I have derived from your works, and the wish (which I have long entertained) to possess a likeness, be it ever so small, of the man I have learned to adore for the greatness of his mind and the sincerity of his utterances." Dannreuther also took the opportunity to tell Nietzsche of his admiration for his "Inopportune Reflections" ("Unzeitgemässe Betrachtungen") and to inform him that he had translated his essay on Schopenhauer

> no less than three times, not so much with a view to publishing my feeble reproduction, as to that of becoming more intimate with your work ....

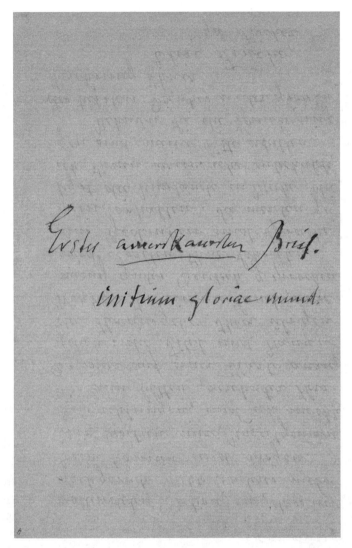

Nietzsche's note to himself, written on the back of his first fan letter from the United States, 1881. Used by permission of the Klassik Stiftung Weimar, Goethe- und Schiller-Archiv, Weimar, Germany.

But in spite of my efforts, my version fell so far short of an adequate rendition of the original, that I was only too glad for the sake of *your* reputation to keep the manuscript in my desk. Since then I have quite destroyed it, but the memory of exalted moments remains, and I am sure that my work was at least not wasted upon myself.[5]

We have no record of Nietzsche's response. But one suspects that he might have figured that though the cultural philistines of Germany were unwilling or unable to recognize genius, in America, at least, there were people with ears to hear his untimely message. Two letters from America weren't much, but given the paltry response to his writings at home, this surely seemed like an auspicious beginning. Could it be that the dawn of his philosophy was breaking in the West?

Nietzsche was barely informed about America. He made relatively few comments about it in his writings, and those that exist simply echo the commonplace enthusiasms and aversions of his day. Though Nietzsche's "America" provided him with a symbolic field on which to imagine the curious forms— the "new human flora and fauna," as he put it—a modernized culture might produce, his characterizations are but conventional romantic stereotypes.[6] He described American culture as youthful and innocent, unburdened by calcified traditions. "The American way of laughing does me good," he wrote after reading *Die Abenteuer Tom Sawyers*, "especially this sort of sturdy seaman like Marc [*sic*] Twain. I have been unable to laugh anymore at anything German." He preferred American "silliness more than German cleverness," and found the playful American spirit of "naiveté and letting-oneself-go" physically and psychically regenerative: "Even villainous acts acquire a form of completeness and the closeness to the wild, and gunshots and marinas result in good health."[7] Though he appreciated how Americans seemed free from the weight of entombing memories, he regretted that their freedom from the past yielded a hasty pursuit of the here and now. In their "lust for gold; and the breathless haste with which they work," they were infected with "the distinctive vice of the new world"[8]—"modern restlessness."[9] If these romantic tropes were the only terms in which Nietzsche thought about America, it would be hard to imagine that the fan letters suggested to him that America might be a future home for his philosophy.

And yet this is not all Nietzsche imagined as he contemplated the New World. Indeed, when he thought about American intellect in particular, he thought about one specific American *Man Thinking*. By the time the letters arrived, Nietzsche had spent the last twenty years engaged in an imaginative dialogue with an American whom he regarded as his "Brother-Soul."[10] It was not at home but across the Atlantic that he discovered an exemplar of the aboriginal intellect, a man who refused to think secondhand, bow to

4

dead gods, or deny the inner sting of his conscience. It was America that provided Nietzsche with a mentor who had counseled him through dark times, a thinker to think with, and a philosopher who had taught him what philosophy could make possible. How fitting, then, that the culture across the Atlantic that produced the philosopher to whom he would turn repeatedly as companion and guide might provide Nietzsche with readers who would turn to him for the same. In fact, Dannreuther's letter of May 1882 arrived just as Nietzsche had decided to title his current book project *The Gay Science (Die Fröhliche Wissenschaft)*—a nod to his mentor's self-reference as a "professor of the Joyous Science"[11]—and to use one of this author's quotations as the book's epigraph: "To the poet and sage, all things are friendly and hallowed, all experiences are profitable, all days holy, all men divine."[12] Was it sheer coincidence that Dannreuther's letter should arrive from Massachusetts, the very native ground of the Sage of Concord? Perhaps the letters made perfect sense to Nietzsche: they came from the land of Ralph Waldo Emerson.

For Nietzsche, Emerson represented a new flora and fauna of thought. He discovered in this American essayist and poet a new kind of thinker who believed that ontology and epistemology were useful only insofar as they addressed the fundamental question of philosophy: not *What is the nature of being? What are the conditions of knowledge?* or *How do I know?* but rather, as Emerson put it, "How shall I live?"[13] Nietzsche admired the ease with which Emerson made philosophy an ally of, rather than a retreat from or a corrective to, one's own experiences and longings. He referred to him as "the excellent [*treffliche*] Emerson," largely because he had shown Nietzsche how one can make philosophy "friends with life."[14] "Nietzsche loved Emerson," observes Harold Bloom, who regards Nietzsche's characterization of Emerson "the best comment, that I know, upon the American sage."[15] Nietzsche remarked in the *Twilight of the Idols* (1889) that "Emerson possesses that good-natured and quick-witted cheerfulness that discourages all earnestness; he has absolutely no idea how old he is or how young he [is still yet to] be."[16] He regarded Emerson as not only one of the nineteenth century's "masters of prose," but also its leading light: "the most fertile author of this century has so far been an American." Indeed, one of the rare discouraging remarks he made about Emerson was that he wished he were perhaps a little more American, or at least less "beclouded" by the obfuscating "milk glass" of "German philosophy."[17] One thing was clear to Nietzsche: this new *Man Thinking*—this aspirational, liberated, and *relevant* intellect—was (so far, at least) an impossibility in Germany.

Nietzsche scholars tend to divide his body of work into three periods—an "early" critical/polemical (1872–76), a "middle" positivistic/aphoristic (1876–82), and a "late" rhapsodic/dithyrambic phase (1882–88).[18] A consideration of Nietzsche's ongoing engagements with Emerson over the course of twenty-six years suggests that his entire oeuvre might plausibly be characterized as belonging to his "Emerson" period.[19] With the exception of the four years between his appointment to a professorship at Basel in 1869 until the dust settled after the critical reception of *The Birth of Tragedy* in 1872–73, Nietzsche read Emerson every year, sometimes more, throughout his entire productive intellectual life. Nietzsche's four volumes of Emerson's essays (and one *Atlantic Monthly* article) in German translation—worn from repeated use, their texts scarred with underlines, and covers, margins, and even flyleaves crowded with notations—document the history of his fascination with the American philosopher.[20]

Nietzsche's Emerson volumes are the most heavily annotated books in his personal library.[21] His marginalia are almost exclusively eruptions of approval: "Bravo!" "Ja!" "Sehr Gut!" "Herrlich!" "Das ist wahr!" He often brought his Emerson volumes with him on vacation, as he did in 1862 in order to write "a sketch of the book for my friends" of "his wise American reflections."[22] Sometimes they didn't make it back with him, as was the case in the summer of 1874 when, on a return trip from the mountain village of Bergün, Switzerland, his suitcase containing his copy of Emerson's *Essays* was stolen from a train platform.[23] Unwilling or unable to go without it, Nietzsche promptly purchased another copy, and resumed his dialogue with his American interlocutor, as the well-worn, heavily annotated replacement volume testifies.

Perhaps because the margins of his Emerson texts became too congested with annotations, sometime in late 1881 or early 1882 Nietzsche purchased a black notebook, which he devoted exclusively to excerpting forty passages from Emerson's *Essays*. Some of the passages are transcribed verbatim, while others show minor modifications. However, it is the passages in which Nietzsche turned a quotation from the original third person into first person that reveal his deep absorption in, and identification with, Emerson.[24] Perhaps it is not surprising that such slippages occurred. After all, Nietzsche read Emerson a lot. But according to George Kateb, we can say a bit more than

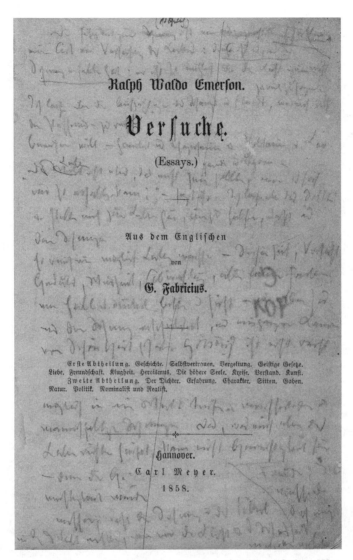

Nietzsche's copy of Emerson's *Essays*. Used by permission of the Klassik Stiftung Weimar, Herzogin Anna Amalia Bibliothek, Weimar, Germany.

that. "In important respects," Kateb argues, "Nietzsche was Emerson's best reader."[25] Indeed, as Herwig Friedl has shown, Nietzsche read Emerson in an Emersonian sense.[26] Following Emerson's counsel in the "Uses of Great Men" (*Representative Men* [1850]): "Other men are lenses through which we read our own minds."[27] Nietzsche read his way through Emerson to his own

Nietzsche's notebook with his transcribed Emerson quotations. Used by permission of the Klassik Stiftung Weimar, Goethe- und Schiller-Archiv, Weimar, Germany.

ideas about the intellectual free spirit who must break the chain of history, of tradition, and of convention. Over time, he came to identify himself as a sovereign self who refused to exalt inherited ideals. But as his reading of Emerson also shows, even sovereign selves must, from time to time, draw their inspiration from others.

---

Nietzsche discovered Emerson's philosophy in 1862 as a seventeen-year-old gymnasium (secondary school) student at the prestigious boarding school Schulpforta. His first encounter with Emerson occurred during a crisis in his studies. Four years earlier, Nietzsche had entered the gates of Schulpforta as a scholarship student, and though an obedient and compliant pupil who excelled in his studies, he had a difficult adjustment to the school's grinding regimentation and austere discipline. The sequestered and routinized program eroded rather than enriched his belief in institutional intellectual life. Nietzsche later described "the uniformizing discipline of an orderly" education at Schulpforta as "that almost military compulsion, which, because it aims to affect the mass, treats individuality coldly and superficially."[28] Young Nietzsche bristled under the regime, causing him to wonder whether Schulpforta drilled in scholarly knowledge while it drowned out self-directed intellectual exploration in equal parts.[29]

While the regimentation and impersonality of Schulpforta caused him to question his studies, his studies caused him to question his religious beliefs. Nietzsche had entered the gymnasium at age fourteen with an ardent Lutheran faith as his trusty companion. He came from a line of Lutheran clergy—both his paternal and maternal grandfathers had been ministers, as was his beloved father, Ludwig. Nietzsche had spent his early childhood in the parsonage of his father's church in Röcken, and after his father's death when Nietzsche was four years old, his mother continued to raise him and his younger sister, Elisabeth, in an environment imbued with her affirming Christian piety. At Schulpforta he received training in historical criticism to work with Greek and Latin texts, but he saw its value for humanistic studies in general. Though he still thought religion was the "solid foundation of all knowledge [*Grundveste alles Wissens*]," historical science was beginning to shake that foundation.[30] His faith provided succor during bouts of homesickness. However, Nietzsche's theological studies and daily worship at Schulpforta did nothing to help him as his ardent faith began to give way.[31]

Nietzsche's poetry of 1862 testifies to the increased sense of intellectual waywardness and spiritual crisis:

> I know not what I love,
> I have neither peace nor rest,
> I know not what to believe,
> what life am I living, why?[32]

Nietzsche's growing dissatisfaction with Schulpforta's mass regime and
his feelings of spiritual estrangement, as he put it, "led me back to myself,"
causing him to seek intellectual stimulation and emotional relief outside his
formal studies. Together with his friends, Wilhelm Pinder and Gustav Krug,
he sought escape in the form of a literary fraternity, Germania, which the
three students founded in 1860 in order to pursue their intellectual curiosi-
ties and foster their creative self-expression. The boys set the ground rules for
membership: each was expected to produce a work of criticism, poetry, a musical composition, or some original research, for critical analysis during their
quarterly "synods." For the next three years, the boys met to review one another's contributions, draft critical rebuttals, drink wine, and contemplate the
universe. As the most zealous Germanian of the three, Nietzsche delighted
in his extracurricular discoveries, churning out musical compositions, poems,
and essays on Cicero, Byron, and Napoleon. As Carl Pletsch has shown, he
would come to regard his Germania experiences—this learning outside of
learning, this self-directed study—as his true education: "I saved my private
inclinations and longings from the uniform law, I lived a concealed cult of
certain arts, I occupied myself with a hypersensitive addiction to universal
knowledge and pleasure to break the rigidity of a legalistic [time schedule]."[33]
While time with Germania satisfied this striving, it also fostered a conviction
that true knowledge cannot be found within an institutional setting, but is
rather achieved through creative aspiration on one's own terms.

And so it was in this period of personal turmoil that Nietzsche, age seventeen, first got his hands on a translation of Emerson's *The Conduct of Life*
(1860) and first got an idea of what philosophy could make possible. It was
during one of his "concealed" extracurricular forays for Germania in April 1862
that he began reading Emerson. This was his true education. This was also
Nietzsche's first contact with philosophy—it wasn't until the following year
that he expressed interest in Plato and another two years until he discovered

Nietzsche, age sixteen (*left*), with a classmate in front of the Schulpforta church, circa summer 1861. Used by permission of the Klassik Stiftung Weimar, Goethe- und Schiller-Archiv, Weimar, Germany.

Schopenhauer.[34] It was Emerson who first instructed Nietzsche "about philosophy in life."[35] Enlivened by his discovery, Nietzsche penned his very first philosophical texts as a Germanian in direct response to his reading of Emerson. During his Easter vacation from school while friends and family around him were celebrating Christ's resurrection, he took the occasion to question the veracity and relevance of Christianity. Modifying Emerson's title "Fate" to "Fate and History: Thoughts" (1862), Nietzsche showed what the world could look like when read through eyes of "great philosopher-prophets" like Emerson.[36] If, as Emerson had said, "there is no pure originality. All minds quote," and that "only an inventor knows how to borrow," then Nietzsche proved to be quite inventive in his appropriation of Emerson's ideas and images to wrestle with his doubts about religion.[37]

"Fate and History: Thoughts," and his follow-up essay, "Freedom of Will and Fate," though pieces of Nietzsche's juvenilia, sketch in embryonic form many of the major leitmotifs of his mature philosophy, and foreshadow his uses of Emerson for decades to come.[38] In these essays, Nietzsche put Emerson's imagery and arguments to work to answer Emersonian questions about the relationship between human agency and the external forces that work to constrain it. The Christian faith topped his list. What would it take, Nietzsche mused, to come out from under the "yoke of custom and prejudice," and achieve a "freer standpoint" from which to consider the balance of power between freedom and fate? He recognized that "it is entirely impertinent to want to solve philosophical problems over which a conflict of opinion has waged for many millennia." And yet, what he found more disturbing was the "question whether mankind hasn't been deceived for two thousand years by a phantom." It worried Nietzsche that the quest for a freer standpoint from which to consider human reality might cause "great revolutions once the masses finally realize that the totality of Christianity is grounded in presuppositions; the existence of God, immortality, Biblical authority, inspiration, and other doctrines will always remain problems."[39]

But Emerson's essay reminded young Nietzsche that religious faith was not the only force that limited an individual's will and intellect. Indeed, Emerson impressed on him that there are all sorts of influences—historical, physiological, even familial—that condition the individual's experiences and limit his perspectives. The plain fact, Nietzsche came to realize, is that as human beings, we inherit so much of who we are that the distinction between the aboriginal and the adopted, between freedom and necessity, might itself be a phantom. In "Fate," Emerson wondered about the influences that tyrannize one's temperament: "Ask the doctors, ask Quetelet, if temperaments decide nothing? or if there be anything they do not decide?"[40] In "Fate and History," Nietzsche likewise wondered what role temperament plays in the individual's freedom to apprehend and affect his world, reformulating Emerson's questions as "Is not our temperament, as it were, the coloration of events? Do we not encounter everything in the mirror of our personality? . . . Ask gifted doctors, Emerson says, how much temperament decides, and what . . . it does not decide."[41] The individual may seek release from that which has formed him, but Emerson expressed doubt whether this was fully possible. As he argued, "The menagerie, or forms and powers of the spine, is a book of fate: the bill of the bird, the skull of the snake, determines tyrannically its limits. . . . How shall a man escape from his ancestors, or draw off from his veins the black drop which he drew from his father's or his mother's life?"[42] In direct dialogue with Emerson on this question, Nietzsche asked, "What is it that pulls the soul of so many men of power down to the commonplace, thereby hindering a higher flight of ideas? A fatalistic structure of skull and spine; the condition and nature of their parents; . . . their environment; even . . . their homeland." For Nietzsche, it was disturbing to consider the sheer range of external forces, "stifling the capacity of the soul through force of habit." What troubled him was not simply that "we have been influenced," but that we are so blind to influences that we cannot tell the differ-ence between our self and the world, our independence and our inheritance.[43]

Though emboldened by Emerson's challenge to external forces that con-strain individual autonomy, he was nevertheless chastened by Emerson's de-scription of the consequences of a world without limits on the will and intel-lect. As Emerson formulated the problem, "If we thought men were free in the sense, that, in a single exception one fantastical will could prevail over the law of things, . . . as if a child's hand could pull down the sun. If, in the least particular, one could derange the order of nature,—who would accept the gift of life?"[44] This gave young Nietzsche reason to worry, as we see in his formulation of the problem: "If it became possible completely to demolish the entire past through a strong will, we would immediately be transported into the realm of autono-mous gods, and world history would suddenly be for us nothing but a dreamy self-deception: the curtain falls, and man finds himself like a child playing with worlds, like a child who awakens at the glow of dawn and, laughing, wipes the terrible dreams from his brow."[45] With Emerson's cautions, Nietzsche recoiled from an image of autonomy so complete that there were no checks on the ag-grandized self. Emerson insisted that he was "sure, that, though we know not how, necessity does comport with liberty, the individual with the world, my polarity with the spirit of the times."[46] But just how they did was the problem facing the philosopher. Nietzsche agreed: "Here lies every important, unend-ing problem: the question of justifying the individual to the people, the people to mankind, and of mankind to the world. And here, too, is the fundamental relationship of *fate* and *history*."[47] In "Fate and History," we see young Nietz-sche thinking with Emerson about how to reconcile the self with the world, human agency with, as Emerson put it, "Beautiful Necessity."[48]

Though Emerson raised more questions for Nietzsche than he offered answers, he nevertheless impressed on him that the act of questioning is both the activity of the philosopher and an example of free will at work. Emerson argued that the active intellect could achieve a "double consciousness," which negotiates the competing desires for freedom and for limitations on that free-dom. According to him, fate is nothing more than "a name for facts not yet passed under the fire of thought;—for causes which are unpenetrated. But every jet of chaos which threatens to exterminate us, is convertible by intel-lect into wholesome force." By likening fate to "unpenetrated causes" and the work of intellect to mastery over them, Emerson taught Nietzsche to think about what thinking makes possible.[49]

In a second attempt at philosophical writing a month after composing "Fate and History," Nietzsche, in "Freedom of Will and Fate," made his debt to the American philosopher explicit. He argued that "*Freedom of will*, [is] in itself nothing but freedom of thought," and that "free will is only an abstraction indicating the capacity to act consciously; whereas by fate we understand the principle that we are under the sway of unconscious acts." It was "Emmerson" [*sic*] who suggested to him that "thought is always compatible with the thing that is apparent as its expression."[50] So when Emerson concluded his essay with the exclamation "Let us build altars to the Beautiful Necessity," Nietzsche understood this simply as an affirmation of the active intellect passing facts under the fire of thought.[51] In imagining the self as author of its experiences, young Nietzsche imagined the power of the thinker to negotiate freedom and fate, self and history, creative will and beautiful necessity.

Nietzsche's discovery of Emerson in 1862 seems to have been the turning point when he decided he would try to go it alone without his religious faith. His first philosophical writings suggest that even as a teenager, he knew this wouldn't be easy. Clearly more hesitant than zealous, Nietzsche confessed,

> How could one destroy the authority of two millennia and the security of the most perceptive men of all time as a consequence of youthful pondering? How could one dismiss all the sorrows and blessings of a religious development so deeply influential on world history by means of fantasies and immature ideas? . . . I have attempted to deny everything: Oh, pulling down is easy; but rebuilding! And pulling down seems easier than it is.

It was Emerson who taught Nietzsche a way forward, a way to begin imagining life as a process of thought, thought as possibility, and possibility as a conception of being as "eternal becoming" (anticipating his later discovery of Emerson's notion that "the soul *becomes*").[52] Emerson bathed Nietzsche in images of the intellectual life as life on the open sea, as circles of waves emanating outward from the active intellect. As Nietzsche described the image Emerson had seared into his imagination, "A struggling and undulating of the most diverse currents, ebbing and flowing, all to the eternal ocean. Everything revolves around one another in monstrous, ever expanding circles. Man is one of the innermost circles." Emerson also provided warnings that while life on the open waters without inherited truths promises ever becoming, it also threatens to pull one under. In leading a life of inquiry and exploration on "the sea of doubt without compass and guide[,] most will be driven off course by storms; only very few discover new lands. Out in the middle of the immense ocean of ideas one often longs to return to firm land."[53] It was Emerson who first instructed Nietzsche about the joys and terrors of the intellectual life without firm land beneath one's feet, of life on the open waters of indeterminacy without compass or guide.

And so it was that in 1862 Nietzsche discovered in Emerson a thinker to think with. While the American author impressed on his young German pupil that the life of the philosopher is a life on the open sea, he also taught him that no other thinker can tell him where he's heading or where to find firm land. He simply works by "provocation" along the way.

And provoke Nietzsche, Emerson did. Nietzsche continued to read Emerson intensively throughout 1863, later noting that of all the books he "read the most," Emerson's topped the list.[54] And this was just the beginning. From the age of seventeen up until his mental breakdown at the age of forty-four; from his days as a gymnasium student through his graduate studies, his professorship, and then his years as an itinerant writer; and from the safe harbor of Christian faith to the tumultuous seas of indeterminacy, Friedrich Nietzsche turned repeatedly to Emerson, who then pushed him forward. In time, many others would propel Nietzsche's thinking—Plato, Kant, Goethe, Lange, Schopenhauer, and Wagner—but none survived his penchant for slaying his own intellectual gods. He never sought to slay Emerson, however; the enthusiasm he expressed for him as a teenager reappeared in his essays, journals, and letters, over the course of his entire intellectual career. Emerson's influence on Nietzsche was unmistakable even to Nietzsche himself. As he thought about himself while writing an early draft of his autobiography, he couldn't help but think of Emerson. Indeed, it was a rereading of Emerson's "Spiritual Laws" (1841) that suggested "Ecce Homo" as an appropriate title for his autobiography.[55] As he reflected on his intellectual path, he couldn't help but reflect warmly on Emerson's company along the way: "Emerson, with his Essays, has been a good friend and someone who has cheered me up even in dark times: he possesses so much skepsis, so many 'possibilities,' that with him even virtue becomes spiritual."[56]

Yet Nietzsche's ideas are not carbon copies of Emerson's. If they were, his uses of Emerson would be a lot less interesting than they are. The sheer fact that he read Emerson in translation reminds us that Nietzsche had a lifelong rela-

121

und du sitzest still.' Wenn es erforderlich ist, finde ich das Still-
sitzen so gut wie das Handeln. Epaminondas, wenn er der
Mann ist, für den ich ihn halte, würde mit Freuden still gesessen
und der Ruhe genossen haben, wenn ihm mein Loos zugefallen
wäre. Der Himmel ist groß und gewährt Raum für jede Art
der Liebe und Kraft. Warum sollten wir unruhige Köpfe und
übertrieben dienstfertig sein? Thätigkeit und Unthätigkeit sind
eigentlich gleich. Aus einem Theil des Baumes ist ein Wetter-
hahn geworden, aus dem andern der Querbalken zu einer Brücke;
die Tugend des Waldes ist in beiden erkennbar.

Ich möchte nicht gern den Geist erniedrigt haben. Die That-
sache meines Hierseins zeigt mir ganz klar, daß der Geist auf
dieser Stelle eines Organs bedurfte. Soll ich den Posten nicht
annehmen? Soll ich mich verstecken, Winkelzüge machen und
mich ducken mit meinen unpassenden Entschuldigungen und meiner
falschen Bescheidenheit, und mir einbilden, mein Hiersein wäre
unschicklich? weniger schicklich als das des Epaminondas und
des Homer dort? und der Geist kenne nicht seine eignen Bedürf-
nisse? Außerdem, ganz abgesehen von der Sache, bin ich nicht
unzufrieden. Der gute Geist giebt mir allezeit Nahrung, erschließt
mir jeden Tag neue Kraft und neue Freude. Ich will nicht auf
unedle Art dieses unendlich Gute von mir weisen, weil ich gehört
habe, daß es Andern in anderer Gestalt gekommen ist.

Außerdem, warum sollten wir uns von dem Namen 'Handlung' einschüchtern lassen? Sie ist eine Eigenthümlichkeit der
Sinne, — nichts weiter. Wir wissen, daß der Stammvater jeder
Handlung ein Gedanke ist. Die arme Seele scheint sich selbst
nichts zu sein, wenn sie nicht ein äußeres Kennzeichen hat, —
vielleicht die Lebensweise des Hindu, oder den Rock des Quäkers,
Calvinistische Zusammenkünfte zum Gebet, oder philanthropische
Gesellschaften, oder eine große Schenkung, oder ein hohes Amt, oder
irgend eine scharf contrastirende Handlung, um zu bezeugen, daß
sie etwas ist. Die reiche Seele liegt in der Sonne und schläft,
und ist Natur. Denken ist Handeln.

Nietzsche's marginalia in Emerson's "Spiritual Laws" ("Geistige Gesetze"). Used by permission of the Klassik Stiftung Weimar, Herzogin Anna Amalia Bibliothek, Weimar, Germany.

tionship with a highly mediated Emerson. Even accounting for linguistic variations, though, the similarities are striking enough that the additional awareness that Nietzsche "loved Emerson from first to last," as Walter Kaufmann
put it, has made many, like Kaufmann himself, insist that nevertheless, "one
would never mistake a whole page of Emerson for a page of Nietzsche."[57]

Perhaps. One might take Kaufmann up on the challenge and place a Nietzsche quotation, image, or broad concern alongside its Emersonian counterpart and see how easy or difficult it is to drive a wedge between the two. One could juxtapose their criticism of barren scholarship; their concern that excessive reverence for the past makes us "fatalists," as Emerson believed, and makes the past our "gravedigger," as Nietzsche had; or their anxiety over belatedness, which fostered a longing in Emerson to be "born again," and a fear in Nietzsche of being "late-born."[58] One could examine how both authors expressed an abiding interest in power. While Emerson averred that "life is a search after power," Nietzsche came to believe that "life simply *is* will to power."[59] Both emphasized a conception of power as something striving, pressing onward. For Emerson, "Life only avails, not the having lived. Power ceases in the instant of repose; it resides in the moment of transition from a past to a new state."[60] Nietzsche celebrated "plastic power," which he described as "the capacity to develop out of oneself in one's own way, to transform and incorporate into oneself what is past and foreign, to heal wounds, to replace what has been lost, to recreate broken molds."[61] It might be of no consequence that Nietzsche was rereading Emerson in 1881–82 while preparing the *Gay Science* and *Thus Spoke Zarathustra* (1883–85). What is noteworthy, nonetheless, is the philosophers' shared aversion to the view of revelation as something historical, rather than ongoing, and to any belief in a divinity outside the self. Emerson believed this created a bankrupt spirituality, "as if God were dead," to which Nietzsche had his madman announce in the affirmative that "God is dead."[62] Someone well versed in Emerson and Nietzsche might never mistake Emerson's line from "Compensation," "In general, every evil to which we do not succumb, is a benefactor," with Nietzsche's from *Twilight of the Idols*, "What does not kill me makes me stronger."[63] But at least it is worth noting that Emerson's line in Nietzsche's personal copy is heavily underlined.[64]

Whether we look for affinities or influences, the parallels between Emerson and Nietzsche mount. But we miss what Emerson meant to Nietzsche if we fail to consider how Nietzsche used Emerson not to get closer to him but to get closer to *himself*. For Nietzsche, Emerson provided an image of the philosopher willing to go it alone without inherited faith, without institutional affiliation, without rock or refuge for his truth claims. As Nietzsche made his way from spiritually-adrift teenager, to philology professor, to freelance philosopher, Emerson's image of the philosopher, and his approach to philosophy as a way of life, proved essential to his self-definition. Emerson gave

Nietzsche a way of describing himself to himself, as we see in his letter of 1866 to an old friend, Carl von Gersdorff. In it, Nietzsche dreamily imagined himself "as Emerson so excellently describes [it] . . . pure, contemplative, impartial eye."[65] It was Emerson who imparted to Nietzsche the image of philosophy as a spirit of play, laughter, and dancing. Nietzsche repeatedly employed this image of levity and joyousness when he considered his own thinking. In the aphorism "Learning to *think*," Nietzsche complained, "our schools no longer have any idea what this means. . . . Thinking has to be learned . . . *as* a form of dancing. . . . Who among Germans still knows from experience that subtle thrill . . . of intellectual *light feet* [?]"[66] It was Emerson's characterization of the liberated thinker as "intellectual nomad" that helped Nietzsche to imagine himself as a "free spirit" in a quest for truths of his own making.[67] Likewise it was Emerson who impressed on Nietzsche the power of the oppositional intellect to make the world anew. "Let an American tell them what a great thinker who arrives on this earth signifies as a new centre of tremendous forces," affirmed Nietzsche in "Schopenhauer as Educator" (1874). Quoting this American's essay "Circles" (1841), Nietzsche affirmed, "'Beware,' says Emerson, 'when the great God lets loose a thinker on this planet. Then all things are at risk. It is as when a conflagration has broken out in a great city, and no man knows what is safe, or where it will end.'"[68]

But of all the uses Nietzsche had for Emerson, it was his notion that a philosopher without foundations works by provocation, not instruction, as an "exemplar," not a guide, which most vividly suggested to Nietzsche the possibilities of his own philosophy. The philosopher is useful insofar as he helps carry one to one's self. "No one can construct for you the bridge upon which precisely you must cross the stream of life, no one but you yourself alone," Nietzsche insisted. "There exists in the world a single path along which no one can go except you: whither does it lead? Do not ask, go along it." Nietzsche found confirmation in another quotation from Emerson's "Circles": "A man never rises higher than when he does not know whither his path [will] lead him."[69] If Emerson sent Nietzsche on the path of philosophy without absolutes, on a path to become who he was, he also reminded him that he would not be waiting for him upon his arrival.

———

Throughout the 1880s Nietzsche sent manuscript after manuscript to his publisher, and his publisher, in turn, sent them off as books to a German reading public as yet indifferent to his ideas. Nietzsche never forgave his German contemporaries for leaving him in the lurch. Undaunted, he spent most of the final year of his productive intellectual life, though struggling with illness, swept up in a euphoric mood. It was during what would become his final sprint of productivity that a third fan letter arrived from America, this time from Karl Knortz, a Prussian-born freelance writer in New York, who wrote to express his admiration for *Thus Spoke Zarathustra*. Nietzsche now had reason to believe that the praise it contained truly signaled that his dawn was finally breaking, for just a few months earlier the prominent Danish literary critic Georg Brandes had delivered a series of high-profile lectures on him in Copenhagen, at long last drawing attention to his genius. In his letter, Knortz, a translator of American authors into German and a promoter of German literature for American readers, also relayed his desire to promote Nietzsche to American audiences.[70]

But in order to do that, Knortz would need Nietzsche's help. So he asked the German author for a description of himself and a characterization of his oeuvre. Nietzsche gladly obliged. In a letter of reply dated June 21, 1888, he sketched a portrait of his work and himself for his would-be American audience:

> The task of giving you some picture of myself, as a thinker, or as a writer and poet, seems to me extraordinarily difficult. . . . The thought of advertising myself is utterly alien to me personally; I have not lifted a finger with that end in view. Of my *Zarathustra*, I tend to think that it is the profoundest work in the German tongue, also the most perfect in its language. But for others to feel this will require whole generations to *catch up with* the inner experiences from which that work could arise.[71]

Nietzsche may have thought that his philosophy awaited an audience of readers yet unborn, but given Knortz's enthusiasm, he had reason to suspect that he might first find that audience in America. In a letter to his publisher asking for his assistance in facilitating Knortz's propaganda, he speculated about the value of securing a readership across the Atlantic. "In principle all my experiences show that my influence begins on the periphery and only from there will the currents ripple back to the 'Fatherland.'" That summer, Nietzsche sent off a flurry of letters to friends telling them that he had "admirers in North America." Soon Americans would learn, he enthused, that

"I am the most independent spirit of Europe and the only German writer—that's something!—."[72]

Though Nietzsche liked the image of himself as an intellectual nomad, and though he long ago decided that the thinker without foundations must go not only without compass or guide, but also without a final destination, his desire for freedom never fully subdued his longing for an intellectual home. He knew from his own experiences that a feeling of refuge—while fleeting—is necessary even for the free spirit. He likewise knew from his own experiences reading Emerson that sometimes it is abroad that the aboriginal intellect finds a home.

A home in America for Nietzsche's philosophy? After almost three decades with Emerson's writings, the prospect seemed likely indeed. After all, it was America that had created the thinker with whom he thought as he came to terms with himself and his world. It was the American Emerson who showed Nietzsche the possibilities of thought beyond the good and evil of Christian piety. It was the American Emerson who critiqued sterile ideas and made philosophy a friend to life. It was the American Emerson who understood that philosophical inquiry in a world without absolutes works by example and provocation only. And it was the American Emerson who Nietzsche believed never could have been produced within the suffocating philistinism of his native German culture. Nietzsche did not know much about America, but he did know—or at least he believed—that with one exception (himself), Germany could never have given birth to such a dynamic thinker. He summed up his feelings for Emerson this way: "*Emerson*. Never have I felt so much at home in a book, and in *my* home as—I shouldn't praise it, it is too close to me."[73]

Nietzsche understood what it meant to travel imaginatively through time and space in order to find a thinker to think with. Just as he had to travel to the mental and moral world of a mid-nineteenth-century American philosopher en route to himself, twentieth-century American readers would now turn to him for the same. They would look across the Atlantic for an example of the perils and possibilities of the aboriginal intellect. They would look to a nineteenth-century German thinker in order to feel at home.

We Americans have our Emerson; why, then, should we dote on Nietzsche?
CHARLES GRAY SHAW, "Emerson the Nihilist" (1914)

The rest of this book tells the story given in the prologue, only in reverse. Nietzsche's use of Emerson in his quest for intellectual independence, his longing for a philosophical "home" without foundations, his desire for a philosophy that educates by example only, and his felt need to look across the Atlantic to critique what he perceived to be his own culture's hostility to the critical intellect all foreshadow the major themes of the history of Nietzsche's ideas and image in twentieth-century American thought and culture.

Thirty years after Nietzsche's discovery of Emerson, his own philosophy began to make its way to American shores. Turn-of-the-century commentators did not characterize the arrival of his philosophy as a homecoming. None regarded his entrance into American intellectual and cultural life as the return of a prodigal son. Despite the traces of Emerson in Nietzsche's philosophy, most American commentators either failed to notice the connection or, when they perceived similarities, stressed differences. In other words, what most struck American interpreters of the period was Nietzsche's exoticism. He came from *Europe*.

In the opening years of the twentieth century, a growing number of American political radicals, literary critics, academic philosophers, theologians, and journalists took an interest in the German philosopher who in recent years had been taking Europe by storm. With curiosity and confusion, fascination and frustration, they sought to make sense of a thinker who one writer in 1900 described as "the most radical philosopher of the century, and one of the most picturesquely eccentric figures in all literature."[1] Interest in Nietzsche grew so rapidly that by the 1910s observers could, without hyperbole, refer to the American "Nietzsche vogue." But as fascination with Nietzsche escalated, so too did the apparent incongruity of it all. Commentators puzzled over what they perceived to be the incommensurability between Nietzsche's aristocratic radicalism and the democratic culture in which it found a home.

Observers then could not help but wonder: What is the philosophy of an anti-Christian, antidemocratic madman doing in a culture like ours? Why Nietzsche? Why in America?

For over a century, generations of American readers have encountered anew Nietzsche's bold claim that if a culture were teetering on the edge of collapse, one might as well give it a final push and get it over with. That's exactly what he tried to do. In book after book, this "philosopher with a hammer" (as he called himself) whacked away at Western ideals he regarded as petrified human artifacts. First on his list was the notion of eternal truth. He sought to demonstrate that no values are inherently good or evil but rather are culturally and historically contingent. Likewise, he argued that all claims to moral truth were nothing more than "human, all-too-human" desires for a particular vision of the good life, but not mirrors of extrahuman reality. While Nietzsche sought to dismantle the notion of universal truth and goodness, so too did he try to discredit his readers' faith in God. With the declaration that "God is dead," he sought to call an end to the Christian faith in the Divine. God had not created man in his image; rather *man* created an image of God in order to give life meaning, purpose, and a moral center. According to Nietzsche, modern Western culture was founded on a pack of lies: truth, universal morality, God. These were mere fictions, products of human imagination, which had no basis in the real world.

This book examines what American readers were drawn to in this philosophy and its author, and what, in turn, they drew from them.[2] It analyzes the dynamic history of how Nietzsche's antifoundationalism (the denial of universal truth), together with his sustained critiques of Christian morality, Enlightenment rationality, and democracy, has compelled many Americans to question their religious ideals, moral certainties, and democratic principles.[3] Turn-of-the-last-century scholars, writers, political radicals, and ministers form the first generation of Americans whose confrontation with his thought compelled them to reevaluate their inherited values in light of his criticisms. Though they had grown up in a world still confident in universals, Nietzsche's "genealogy of morals" caused them to question the *value* of their values. In his concept of the "Übermensch," Americans found a convenient vehicle to assess the forces confronting the individual in an age of growing dislocation and anonymity associated with mass politics and mass markets. In his tragic biography they discovered a cautionary tale about the perilous course of the great man in the democratic era and the soul of man under secularism.

American readers were drawn as well to his new language for morality. It was at this time when Nietzsche's concepts such as "transvaluation of all values," "slave morality," and "will to power," and the newly minted term *Nietzschean*, made their debut in American English. Since then, American commentators have referred to their moral universe as a world "after Nietzsche." This history of the transformation of modern American thought reveals that their new language signals a dramatic development in both the style and the substance of moral inquiry. Where once the moral life was couched in terms of foundations, now, "after Nietzsche," thinkers and writers imagined it as life on the open sea.[4]

As the intense interest in Nietzsche's radical ideas has always been accompanied by an insatiable appetite for his life story, the career of the Nietzsche trope in America is a central theme of this study.[5] I argue that readers consistently looked to Nietzsche to make sense of themselves and their America. From the details about his struggles as an itinerant intellectual, his neglect by his contemporaries, and his physical torments, they spun narratives about heroic striving, the fate of genius, achievement, and failure in modern American life. For some, Nietzsche's erudition seemed to be a product of German esteem for *Bildung*, which they thought was missing on this side of the Atlantic. They worried that the cultural conditions of their own capitalist and democratic society were inhospitable for producing great minds. However, others looked to Nietzsche's oversized ego, with his exaltation of "master morality" and his disdain for the masses, as a vestige of a decaying European aristocratic society, which had no place in a modern pluralistic democracy. No aspect of Nietzsche's personal history was more compelling, though, than his insanity. It signaled to those both enthusiastic and skeptical about his philosophy the costs of the strenuous quest for self-sovereignty in a world without absolutes.[6]

*American Nietzsche* seeks to demonstrate that reception history can be more ambitious than simply enumerating the varieties of uses of a thinker or a body of thought in a new national context.[7] While it shows that a multitude of "American Nietzsches" have appeared over the course of the century, it is not content with exposing sheer variety. Rather, this study argues that confrontations with Nietzsche laid bare a fundamental concern driving modern American thought: namely, the question of the *grounds*, or foundations, for modern American thought and culture itself. First, it shows how American encounters with Nietzsche ignited and revealed larger anxieties about the source and authority of truth and values in a modern pluralist society. Second, it demonstrates how Americans' engagement with Nietzsche incited and exposed long-standing concerns about the conditions of American culture for intellectual life. Reading Nietzsche encouraged readers to question the vitality of the American cultural soil for nourishing intellects of its own, and to question whether it was hospitable for those transplanted from Europe. Thus, encounters with Nietzsche's philosophy and persona provided an opportunity for observers to examine their ideas about truth and values in a world without foundations, as well as to rehearse persistent fears about the cultural poverty of American native grounds.

Nietzsche did not just encourage Americans to rethink the moral and cultural grounds of themselves and their modern America, he helped them to *feel* the thrill and the terror of his challenges to foundationalism. Americans' century-long engagements with Nietzsche testify to the strong affective dimension involved in the transfer of ideas. As this history shows, reading Nietzsche, in particular, has never been a neutral transmission of arguments and concepts. Because his ideas and radical image evoked strong feelings in his American readers, virtually every document in which a discussion of Nietzsche appears—whether a letter to a friend, marginalia in a Nietzsche text, an academic philosophical monograph, or an essay for a popular magazine—provides a view to the emotional circuitry involved in intellectual exchange. Thus, all the sources are more than records of American ideas, they are crucial historical testimonies of American longing. Whether yearning for a world of certainty after the death of God or striving to free American culture from its esteem for European intellectual exports, the many different uses of Nietzsche in this study—each in their own way—are historical accounts of both intellectual enchantment and disenchantment. They are also records of the somatic experience of ideas. Nietzsche's American readers document, often in lush detail, how he made their hearts race, their jaws clench, their knuckles whiten, and their blood boil. If part of the historian's task is to recapture the lived experience of historical persons—then a great place to start is to listen to the pathos, fear, revulsion, and titillation involved in intellectual exchange. In this regard, the task of the cultural historian of ideas is not to adjudicate Nietzsche claims but to listen to how American engagements with Nietzsche are records of their longings and reveal their moral worlds.[8]

Nietzsche was a rare thinker whose impact on America encourages historians to rethink their categories of analysis. In particular, the history of the thought and image of this so-called German (or European) philosopher in America yields a richer understanding of the ways in which Americans have often understood themselves through the lenses of others. A history that seeks to deprovincialize the study of American thought and culture, *American Nietzsche* demonstrates that the intellectual and cultural forces shaping twentieth-century American life have not stopped at national borders.[9]

However, this history reveals how readers used Nietzsche's thought to reconstitute borders as well. When commentators wondered what Nietzsche's thought was doing in America, invocations of his "German" heritage or his "European" sensibility were never far behind. For some, the associations gave him capital. Like Nietzsche, who believed a German Emerson was an impossibility, many appreciative American readers worried that the culture of American democracy and capitalism conspired against the cultivation of Nietzschean genius.[10] Others, however, argued that Nietzsche's philosophy carried the unhappy traces of German historicism, pessimism, and aristocratism, and thus bitterly protested making room alongside America's organic ideals of human equality and justice for a belligerent German import. Both those drawn to and repelled by Nietzsche's thought wondered what he did for America that her native intellects—in particular Ralph Waldo Emerson and William James—could or would not. So as we have seen with Nietzsche, who could not foresee a German Emerson, when Nietzsche's philosophy came to the United States, readers similarly freighted his ideas with essentialist notions of "America" and "Europe," "us" and "them," "organic" and "foreign." Thus, the uses of Nietzsche in twentieth-century American thought enable us to consider how the reception of "German" (or "European") philosophy both ruptured and remade old ideas about American intellectual exceptionalism.

Because questions about the distinctiveness (or lack thereof) of American thought and culture have been deeply bound up *in* the American Nietzsche reception itself, it makes for an awkward pivot to ask those same kinds of questions *of* the reception. The sheer international scope of Nietzsche's influence in the twentieth century invites such questions, however, for his philosophy had a deep impact not only in Germany and America but throughout the European continent, including France, Austria, Spain, and Italy as well as Russia, Britain, and Scandinavia.[11] The American Nietzsche reception set against the broader historiography of his international reception demonstrates how many dominant features of the American uses of Nietzschean philosophy—in particular, interest in his rejection of Christian altruism and asceticism, bourgeois liberalism, the ethics of economic collectivism, democratic, socialist, and feminist egalitarianism—were common features of transnational Nietzsche interpretations. And yet what distinguishes the American interest in Nietzsche is that those elements never became bundled into visions of *Die Grosse Politik* in America. Whereas in Germany, Italy, and Russia, especially, Nietzscheanism filtered much more deeply into the frameworks of political life, so that Germans, Italians, and Russians spiritualized Nietzschean political discourse and employed it to imagine their leaders as long-awaited *Übermenschen*, in America, aside from the occasional invocation of the term to describe Theodore Roosevelt (as a term of praise) or Franklin Delano Roosevelt (as a term of derision), Nietzschean engagements fundamentally eschewed using Nietzsche to spiritualize politics. To be sure, Nietzsche played as important a role in what is commonly identified as "political" discourse—anarchism in the 1890s, prewar socialism, Black Power in the 1960s, neoconservatism in the 1980s. However, he was enlisted as a moralist and cultural critic. Overwhelmingly, Americans took an interest in Nietzsche's criticism of democratic equality, in his *cultural* insights about democratic man. When Nietzsche appeared in American political thought, he did so as a thinker about the human culture American democracy fosters.

If Nietzsche's influence crossed the perceived intellectual borders between America and Europe, it also traversed the borders traditionally thought to divide "elite" from "average" Americans. By investigating the responses to and appropriations of Nietzsche's thought across a wide spectrum of readers, this history shows the porosity of "highbrow," "middlebrow," and "popular" culture.[12] For one, it demonstrates that moral inquiry and reverence for ideas were not reserved for professional intellectuals and that anti-intellectualism was not exclusively a feature of mass culture. Likewise, interest in Nietzsche moved easily between the intellectual worlds of twentieth-century Americans with otherwise very different political leanings, cultural commitments, and spiritual affiliations. Over the course of the century, Progressives and anarchists, Christians and atheists, provincials and cosmopolitans, hawks and doves, academic scholars and armchair philosophers discovered in Nietzsche a thinker to think with. Thus, by examining Nietzsche's travels across political divides and cultural sensibilities, we are encouraged to rethink the imagined communities of readers contributing to twentieth-century American intellectual life.[13]

Developments in the career of Nietzsche's philosophy and persona demonstrate that moral inquiry in America has never taken place in a vacuum. The following chapters examine how readers enlisted Nietzsche to think about concerns that, though ongoing, they felt to be particular to their own time and place. When early twentieth-century Christian clergy sparred with Nietzsche over the role of the church in modern culture, when literary radicals employed Nietzsche to imagine themselves as freelance intellectuals during the teens and twenties, when midcentury philosophers worried about the vitality of American liberal democracy and humanist commitment amid the specter of totalitarianism, and when postmodern thinkers enlisted Nietzsche to examine the role of philosophy in a world after foundations, they were responding to a particular set of social, cultural, and political circumstances in either America or the wider world, and sometimes both. Therefore, in order to understand why American readers identified as necessary Nietzsche's challenge to foundations and his own efforts to thrive without them, we must first understand the social circumstances in which such thinking took place.

That Nietzsche's American interpreters have put his philosophy and persona to use to think about American thinking does not mean that they went running with open arms into an unbounded ethical antifoundationalism. This is not a history of American "Nietzscheans." It is a history of American readers making their way to their views of themselves and their modern America by thinking through, against, and around Nietzsche's stark challenges. Throughout the century, there were indeed those who claimed that in Nietzsche they had found their intellectual "savior," while others found Nietzsche's ideas, and indeed his person, repellent. For some, reading Nietzsche was a summons to discard traditional concepts of the good life. For others, the confrontation with Nietzsche's ideas served only to strengthen their commitment to democracy, God, or unified truth. But both enthusiastic and enraged responses serve as a point of entry for the historian seeking to recapture moral outlooks of the past. This book, then, is neither a hagiography of, nor a screed about, Nietzsche. It is not even a book about Nietzsche. It is a story about his crucial role in the ever-dynamic remaking of modern American thought.

# The Making of the
# American Nietzsche

I tunneled into the foundations, I commenced an investigation and digging out of an ancient *faith*, one upon which we philosophers have for a couple of millennia been accustomed to build as if upon the firmest of foundations—and have continued to do so even though every building hitherto erected on them has fallen down: I commenced to undermine our *faith in morality*.

FRIEDRICH NIETZSCHE, *Daybreak* (1881)

The uncovering of Christian morality is an event without parallel. He that is enlightened about that . . . breaks the history of mankind in two. One lives before him, or one lives after him.

FRIEDRICH NIETZSCHE, "Why I Am a Destiny," in *Ecce Homo* (1908[1888])

"I shall never forget the long night in which I read through the *Genealogy of Morals*," remarked Wilbur Urban, recalling the summer of 1897 in Jena, Germany, when he read Friedrich Nietzsche's book from cover to cover. "It was, I believe, the greatest single spiritual adventure of my life." Urban had not come to Germany for spiritual adventures; he had come, like so many other American students at the turn of the last century, to obtain his doctoral degree in philosophy. He did not learn about Nietzsche's work in philosophy seminars, though; he stumbled across it "almost by accident" while rummaging through the densely packed shelves in a Jena bookshop. Intrigued by what he had found, Urban purchased the book, took it home with him, and read it voraciously through the night. "In the grey light of the morning," he recalled, "I found myself surveying the wreckage of my beliefs in a curious mood—one in which a profound sense of loss was not unmixed with that unholy *Schaden-freude* in which the naturally destructive instincts of youth so often find satisfaction." As the bright morning sun began to filter into his room, the "curious" mixture of terror and delight that marked his all-night vigil with Nietzsche lingered. Though still enlivened and bewildered by what he had read, though his mind continued to race with new ideas, one thing was certain: Urban knew immediately that he had encountered a thinker who would forever change his view of himself and his world. "I knew from that moment that, not only was [Nietzsche's] problem of values *my* problem, but also that it was destined to be the key problem of the epoch in which I was to live." In the course of a single night, by his later recollection, Urban had parted ways with the moral world of the nineteenth century and entered Nietzsche's universe.[1]

Shortly after his first encounter with Nietzsche's *Genealogy*, Urban passed his doctoral examinations at the University of Leipzig in 1897. He returned home to America to launch a distinguished career as an analytic philosopher with an interest in value and language, securing professorships at Trinity College, Dartmouth College, and Yale University, and a term as president of the American Philosophical Association from 1925 to 1926. Like countless other young aspiring scholars at the turn of the last century, Urban found that his studies at German universities had started him on the road to professional success in the American academy.[2] But when later asked to recall the origins of his intellectual biography—the psychological reasons as well as the philosophical concerns that guided his scholarly pursuits—Urban's memories hovered around his first encounter with Nietzsche's philosophy. It was this contact with Nietzsche that would, as Urban put it, "start all that was individual in my thinking."[3] Time at the university had provided him with encyclopedic learning and a proper pedigree, but it was his stolen moment of ecstasy during his late-night session with Nietzsche's philosophy that put Urban on the course toward himself.

When Urban sat down to read Nietzsche on that fateful night, he did so in what he described as "the most unphilosophical atmosphere the world has ever seen."[4] At the time of his studies, Continental and Anglo-American thought were saturated in a scientific positivism that sought to banish metaphysics from the realm of philosophical inquiry.[5] Since the mid-nineteenth century, virtually all fields of thought were moving toward scientific verification and away from speculative thought. It was this rigidly positivistic atmosphere that Nietzsche's writings in the 1870s and 1880s stridently opposed. However, the thinker who Urban discovered in the pages of *Genealogy* did not advise returning philosophy to the speculative realm of metaphysics. Metaphysics and positivism represented, for Nietzsche, opposing sides of the same coin: both were grounded in the principle of universal truth. Metaphysics rested on the belief in timeless foundations of universal values, whereas positivism assumed the universality of the scientific method and objectivity. Nietzsche posed his philosophical anthropology in opposition to both the older and the newer trends in thought. Urban discovered in Nietzsche a thinker who rejected the search for both the metaphysical and the natural foundations of truth and values, and sought instead to examine the human origins, cultural genealogy, and *value* of values.

As Urban read Nietzsche, he embarked on an excursion into the history of Judeo-Christian morality, which, since his childhood as the son of an Episcopal priest, he had assumed to reflect transcendent moral imperatives. Following Nietzsche's lead, Urban began not only to excavate the tangled trajectory of Western moral thought but also to rethink the standard against which he would judge all claims to universal truth. As Urban noted, "The problem widened out for me, as it did for Nietzsche himself . . . into the problem of values at large, including the values of knowledge and logic." Over the course of the night, Urban had discovered in Nietzsche the "*enfant terrible* of modernism," a thinker who was "not only the most incisive intellect of our time, but [also] the epitome of . . . the spirit of modernism."[6]

As Urban felt himself inexorably drawn into the dawn of a new moral era, the philosopher who made that possible was sinking deeper into his twilight. While the young American experienced his moral awakening that night in Jena in 1897, Nietzsche lay slowly dying in Weimar, a mere thirty kilometers away. After struggling his entire adult life with a battery of debilitating illnesses, including degenerative myopia, severe migraines, excruciating digestive problems, and periods of depression, Nietzsche entered the final phase of his illness in 1888. These chronic symptoms had already plagued him as a teenager at Schulpforta, accompanying him through graduate school, military training, and his professorship in Basel; and they had continued to torment him during the years in which he sought relief from one health retreat to the next. Pain was Nietzsche's constant companion during the sixteen-year period between 1872 and 1888, in which he produced all his major works.[7]

For the duration of Nietzsche's productive years, most of his work received little attention from readers beyond his circles of friends and colleagues. After the modest success of his earliest works—*The Birth of Tragedy* (*Geburt der Tragödie* [1872]) and *Untimely Meditations* (*Unzeitgemässe Betrachtungen* [1873–76])—the books that followed—*Human, All Too Human* (*Menschli-*

*ches, Allzumenschliches* [1878]), *The Wanderer and His Shadow* (*Der Wanderer und Sein Schatten* [1879]), *Daybreak* (*Morgenröthe* [1881]), and *The Gay Science* (*Die Fröhliche Wissenschaft* [1882])—sold so few copies that they were a serious drain on his publisher. Nietzsche was convinced that with *Thus Spoke Zarathustra: Book One* (*Also Sprach Zarathustra*), a prose poem he divined in ten days of feverish exhilaration in January 1883, he had finally realized the masterwork that would command an audience. In a letter enclosed with the manuscript, he assured his Leipzig publisher, Ernst Schmeitzner, that "my little work—not even a hundred pages" is "far and away the most serious and also the gayest of my products, and accessible to everyone," trying to convince him that this book would surely have the broad appeal that had eluded his earlier works. More to the point, he assured Schmeitzner that he had penned the "fifth gospel." Schmeitzner may have agreed, but he clearly thought the first four Gospels still took precedence over the fifth: The press temporarily shelved production of *Zarathustra* in order to print a rush job of 500,000 church hymnals in time for Easter. Not only did the announcement of God's death have to wait until after the anniversary of his (re-)birth, but Nietzsche's prediction that this would be his breakout book was wrong. A full year after publication, only 85 copies had been sold.[8]

In the years that followed, Nietzsche forged ahead with the subsequent *Zarathustra* books, *Beyond Good and Evil* (*Jenseits von Gut und Böse* [1886]) and *On the Genealogy of Morals* (*Zur Genealogie der Moral* [1887]), still with little recognition for his work. But in 1887 he became aware that a small readership among radical groups and fringe literary societies had begun to take an interest in his philosophy.[9] It was not until 1888, when the prominent Danish literary critic Georg Brandes gave a series of lectures on Nietzsche at the University of Copenhagen, that Nietzsche's work started to attract a broader audience throughout Europe.[10] Brandes, a well-known commentator on major European literary developments,[11] had discovered Nietzsche a year earlier, and in November 1887 had written him to praise "the breath of a new and original spirit" he encountered in his writings. Brandes lauded Nietzsche's contempt for asceticism, his "deep indignation against democratic mediocrity," and what Brandes referred to as his "aristocratic radicalism." He confessed to Nietzsche that he did "not always know towards what issue you are headed," but, given the elegance and brilliance of his writings, he would willingly follow him on the journey. Clearly flattered by the attention of a major critic, Nietzsche replied in a letter to Brandes a month later that he, too, didn't always know where his thinking would take him, but he did know it would open up a new moral universe for himself and his readers. "Just how far this mode of thought has brought me, how far it will still carry me—I almost dread to imagine. But there are paths that do not allow one to turn back; and so I go forward, because forward I *must*."[12]

And so it was in 1888 that Nietzsche's philosophy began its march toward international fame. It was also in 1888 that Nietzsche felt himself to be reaching the zenith of his intellectual life. And with good reason. In the course of a single year, he produced a flurry of works, including *The Twilight of the Idols* (*Götzen-Dämmerung* [1889]), *The Antichrist* (1895), *Nietzsche Contra Wagner* (1895), and *Ecce Homo* (1908). But it was also during this year of growing recognition and productivity that Nietzsche's sicknesses and his mania escalated dramatically. In his writings, his language became more strident and yet more crystalline and poetic as he "philosophize[d] with a hammer," sparing no idol.[13] With an unprecedented jubilance, elegance, and vitriol he tore into the sacred personalities of Jesus, Luther, Kant, Rousseau, and Wagner, ravaging modern Western ideals of Christian humanitarianism, scientific materialism, and democratic and socialist egalitarianism. As his disdain for the decadence of Western culture grew, so too did his estimation of himself and his enterprise. In his autobiography, *Ecce Homo*, Nietzsche proclaimed himself an opponent of Jesus, referred to his own unmasking of Christian morality as an "event without parallel," and likened himself to a "*force majeure*" whose philosophy "breaks the history of mankind in two."[14]

By the end of the year, it had become clear to Nietzsche's friends and family that his robust sense of self had ruptured the acceptable bounds of a healthy ego. Shortly after Christmas, Nietzsche wrote his friend Peter Gast, suggesting that he had crossed the "Rubicon," and in the first days of January 1889, he sent to a number of his friends wild postcards signed "Nietzsche Caesar," "Dionysus," and "The Crucified."[15] These were among the last words he would ever write. On January 4, he collapsed on the Piazza Carlo Alberto in Turin, Italy. He had been taking one of his daily strolls when he came upon a coachman beating his horse. Horrified by the brutal sight, he lunged to throw his arms around the neck of the horse and collapsed on the pavement. Nietzsche lost consciousness and had to be carried back to his lodgings. A few days later, Franz Overbeck came to Turin to retrieve his deranged friend, whom he discovered in a state of delirium, slumped in the corner of a couch while chewing and reading proofs of *Nietzsche Contra Wagner*. Nietzsche leapt up to passionately embrace Overbeck before collapsing once again onto the couch in a convulsive "stream of tears."[16] After Nietzsche stayed briefly in clinics in Basel and Jena, his sister, Elisabeth Förster-Nietzsche, moved him to his childhood home in Naumburg and then to a villa in Weimar. There, atop the Nietzsche Archive founded by Förster-Nietzsche (now his self-appointed literary executor), Nietzsche would spend the last three years of his life completely mad.[17] His days of intellectual ecstasy and agony were over, along with his ability to read, write, or even recollect that he was once an avid reader and prolific writer.

The terrible irony of Nietzsche's life—one noted by virtually all Nietzsche scholars—is that his works began to be appreciated by a broader audience only after his mental collapse. Shortly after Brandes's famous lectures in 1888, the German philosopher started to gain a significant following in northern Europe within aesthetically and politically radical circles. Interest in his work spread so rapidly that by the early 1890s, observers could refer meaningfully to Nietzsche "cults" and the widespread "Nietzsche vogue." The most prominent readers fascinated with Nietzsche's work came from left-leaning liberationist, progressive circles, including anarchists, socialists, feminists—both hard-boiled Marxist materialists and more aesthetically inclined romantic radicals. However, the early fascination with Nietzsche cut across the political spectrum, as right-leaning cultural conservatives were also drawn to his writings.[18] Yet the one divide that the Nietzsche enthusiasm did not traverse in any meaningful way in the initial years of its European vogue was the gulf between the worlds of radical cultural politics and the German academy. With few exceptions, the closest Nietzsche's philosophy came to the academy was in the form of goods smuggled into the lecture hall. Charles Bakewell, a newly minted Harvard philosophy Ph.D. who had studied under William James, Josiah Royce, and George Santayana,[19] later recalled his days as a postdoctoral student at the University of Berlin: "It was quite the usual thing to observe the German student enter the class room with a small volume under his arm, which he would open whenever the lecture failed to interest him. In every case, it was a volume of Nietzsche."[20]

Because few academic philosophers had taken Nietzsche into serious consideration, young Americans like Bakewell and Urban who learned about him while studying abroad in the closing years of the nineteenth century did so either by hearing German friends toss his name around in a smoke-filled *Kaffeehaus*, stumbling across one of his books in a secondhand bookshop, or seeing a well-worn copy of his *Zarathustra* peeking out of the pockets of their classmates' leather *Schultaschen*. It was because their first contact with Nietzsche's philosophy almost always occurred on the periphery of their formal studies that they described their initial encounter with it as a discovery, and their experience reading his works as a forbidden adventure.

For Urban, Nietzsche's absence from the sanctioned canon of philosophical thinkers that he had come to study as well as Nietzsche's dominance within the avant-garde cultural scene surely added to his allure. But these would only have confirmed that what Urban experienced as his moral awakening that night in Jena was intimately personal, generational, and yet broadly cultural. Urban, like so many others after him, came to mark his own intellectual development according to that first contact with Nietzsche. For him it was an event, which marked nothing less than the beginning of his "self-conscious purposive thinking."[21] He, like Nietzsche himself, wasn't sure where it was going to lead him, but he was certain where it would lead him from. He confronted the stark awareness that both the speculative and materialist philosophy of his training, and the Christian conceptions of good and evil of his upbringing—in short, the sturdy foundations of everything he had come to know and believe back in America—would no longer be waiting for him upon his return. Now, after Nietzsche, he must return home, but this time to a new New World. In Europe, in a German text, Urban discovered the dawn of his American modernity.

## Nietzsche and the European Axis of American Cosmopolitanism

While young Americans studying in Europe were witnessing the burgeoning "Nietzsche vogue" firsthand, a small but growing number of American radicals were participating in it from afar. The earliest US importers of Nietzsche's philosophy were anarchists, leftist romantic radicals, and literary cosmopolitans of varying political persuasions who tracked developments in European intellectual life in real time. As Nietzsche's fame grew in Europe during the early 1890s, these radical writers broke the story in their publications. Though small in numbers, they were instrumental in bringing avant-garde European intellectual and cultural movements to America, and the first to incorporate Nietzsche's philosophy into their campaigns to promote "advanced" thought at home. So it was in Robert Reitzel's radical weekly newspaper *Der Arme*

*Teufel* (*The Poor Devil*) that Emma Goldman first learned of Nietzsche.[22] It was in the anarchist publisher and Manhattan bookstore proprietor Benjamin Tucker's Unique Book Shop that the seventeen-year-old Eugene O'Neill first encountered Nietzsche.[23] And it was through the literary critic James Huneker's tireless promotion of Nietzsche in his *Musical Courier* articles and collections of essays that the young Baltimore newspaper reporter H. L. Mencken became acquainted with the thinker who would come to dominate his own intellectual biography.[24] Although their political commitments varied, American anarchists, romantic radicals, and literary cosmopolitans celebrated Nietzsche's philosophical assault on modern slavishness and his emphasis on the unfettered ego as a source of human progress. They exalted Nietzsche as an exemplar of the freethinker who was pious only to his own liberated self. And like Urban, they recognized in Nietzsche a transformative thinker who had ushered in a new era of moral philosophy. Their interest in and uses of Nietzsche also reflect a long-standing Eurocentrism in American radical thought. Though committed to a notion of intellectual cosmopolitanism, by emphasizing Nietzsche's European context and influence they suggested that advanced thought was something exclusive to Europe. In doing so, they questioned whether Nietzsche's philosophical dawn would ever break in the United States.

Nietzsche's philosophy made its first significant debut in American literature in September 1892 in Robert Reitzel's German-language, leftist newspaper, *Der Arme Teufel*. Reitzel, a German-born, defrocked Reformed minister, made a career as an essayist, poet, and prominent speaker on the free-thought lecture circuit before founding his newspaper as his new pulpit in 1884.[25] Until his death fourteen years later, Reitzel's newspaper became the organ of his aspirational anarchism—a unique blend of political liberalism, literary romanticism, religious free thought, and proletarianism—as well as a major forum for excerpts from and exegesis of avant-garde European writers. Indeed, Reitzel's newspaper was such a well-recognized forum for radical thought in the 1880s and 1890s, that he was one of the featured eulogists at the burial of five of the executed Haymarket anarchists in 1887.[26] In Nietzsche, Reitzel discovered a thinker who blended a merciless realism about the unholy authority of institutionalized religion with the romantic prophecy of a future liberated selfhood. He regarded Nietzsche's combination of thought as so unprecedented and necessary for an aspirational anarchism that he returned to his old form—the sermon—to preach the new gospel of Nietzsche to his readers.

In his eleven-part series, "Sermons from the New Bible: *Thus Spoke Zarathustra*," Reitzel characterized Nietzsche's *Zarathustra* as a modern work of sacred scripture. Unlike the New Testament, though, Nietzsche's bible "made a stoic appeal to the working for *reality*." Combining excerpts with exegesis, Reitzel informed his readers that Nietzsche prophesied a world beyond the supernaturalism and pessimism of institutional Christianity, a world in which enlightened souls would find the sources of redemption in themselves. He affirmed that Nietzsche's call for a self-initiated deliverance from every trace of ethical otherworldliness and a redemption self-achieved could help his anarchist readers articulate their as-yet hazy longings for a world free of institutional authority. However, he confessed his hesitation in presenting a philosophy so unforgiving in its anticlericism and yet so demanding of human self-reliance, since it might as yet only encourage "self-flagellation" among his readers. Though a "unified work for eternity," he warned that it was also "an apocalypse from which today's sick draw resources without getting cured." Nevertheless, he encouraged his readers to bear Nietzsche's hard truths and resist the temptation to "apologize . . . that we are not yet Übermenschen." Though Reitzel and his readers might not witness a time when "healthy people" shorn of supernaturalism "will bathe" in Nietzsche's philosophy "like . . . in an ocean wave," at least they could praise their fate to have heard Nietzsche's good tidings, and to have witnessed the birth of the philosophy of the future.[27]

Like Reitzel's *Arme Teufel*, Benjamin Tucker's individualist anarchist newspaper, *Liberty*, was instrumental in bringing new literature to American radicals in real time. In keeping with the spirit of his anarchism, which opposed the state and recognized no national boundaries (political, literary, or otherwise), Tucker strove to make his newspaper the clearinghouse for egoist philosophy, political radicalism, and avant-garde literature from around the world. In his estimation, the role of anarchism was above all to foster individual freethinking and advance ideas that fostered a liberated mindset.[28] Learning of European anarchists' growing fascination with Nietzsche, Tucker began publishing selections of Nietzsche's writings in English for the newspaper in 1892, making it the first American periodical to carry serialized translations of Nietzsche's philosophy "and thus make Liberty the means of introducing to America another great Egoist."[29] He included Nietzsche's writings among the corpus of canonical radical works he sold in his Sixth Avenue Unique Book Shop in New York City.[30] For over a decade, he was instrumental in introducing American political radicals to this important "new influence in the world of thought."[31]

Tucker's first step in building a Nietzsche industry for anarchists was to commission George Schumm, a fellow individualist anarchist and editor of the short-lived German-language version of *Liberty*, to translate Nietzsche's writings for the newspaper.[32] With Schumm's assistance, *Liberty* carried the first of many Nietzsche aphorisms and excerpts published between 1892 and 1899 on themes of interest to American anarchists. Schumm's selections introduced *Liberty* readers to a sampling of the range of Nietzsche's literary voices—expository and impressionistic, reasoned and prophetic—while providing them with a treasure of egoistic zingers for the anarchist convinced of the poverty of inherited ideals and the need for self-sovereignty. The excerpts showed Nietzsche at work unmasking the unwholesome egoism of altruism, dismantling the authority of decrepit philosophies that prevent free thought, and making the case that the dictates of duty are not the voice of reason but rather a fearful culture shouting down one's conscience. Schumm's Nietzsche advocated the "*creation of new tables of values of our own*" and reminded anarchists that their prime objective must be to shed false authority and to "*become those that we are,*—the new, the singular, the incomparable, self-lawgivers, self-creators!"[33] His translations showed a thinker who made familiar criticisms of the state and organized religion unfamiliar by providing new insights about their interdependence. Nietzsche instructed,

> As long as the State, or rather the government, regards itself as the guardian of the minor masses, and [on] their behalf considers the question whether religion shall be maintained or abolished, it will most probably always decide in favor of the maintenance of religion. . . . [For] when the necessary or accidental shortcomings of government . . . become apparent to the intelligent, and fill them with the sentiment of hostility, the unintelligent will fancy they see the fingers of God, and patiently submit to the commands from *above*.[34]

Throughout the 1890s, as regular installments of Nietzsche aphorisms appeared in *Liberty*, so too did the ideas therein about pity as a form of self-aggrandizement, the workings of external authority on the individual's psychology, and self-knowledge as the only basis of morality begin to make their way into American anarchists' writings.[35]

Aware of Nietzsche's importance for European anarchists, Tucker's relationship with Nietzsche's ideas, nevertheless, was not always an easy one. He appreciated how Nietzsche explained that true freedom requires that no states of belonging—whether religious, economic, political, or even moral—be compulsory. And yet he objected to elements of Nietzsche's egoism when they seemed predatory. Nietzsche was right to insist on an ethics of expediency, Tucker argued, but not if expediency required the exploitation he detected in Nietzsche's writings. Similarly, Nietzsche's Übermensch appealed to Tucker's ideal of the liberated ego, but not if it meant that in order for someone to be over, someone else must be under. Tucker confessed that the predatory quality he detected in Nietzsche's writings struck him as a "dreadful weakness" and made him "hate Nietzsche at times."[36] Still, Nietzsche was an important resource for anarchists, so long as they properly "exploit this would-be exploiter." He may be utilized "profitably," but not "prophetably."[37]

Nietzsche's prominence in Tucker's pantheon of vanguard thinkers nevertheless demonstrated his identification of Nietzsche's contribution to anarchism. Tucker saw Nietzsche himself as a *philosophical* anarchist and argued that anarchism, properly understood, was a philosophy of life, not a political program. He thus peppered the pages of *Liberty* with Nietzschean aphorisms that suggested anarchism as an intellectual movement: "We are entering upon the age of *Anarchy*: which is at the same time the age of the most intellectual and freest individuals. Immense mental force is being put in motion. The age of geniuses: hitherto delayed by custom, morality, etc."[38] In Nietzsche, Tucker recognized a fellow philosopher who understood freedom as a state of mind, as well as the power of the mind when freed from the state.

Tucker insisted that anarchism was perfectly consistent with American ideals of freedom, and should be familiar to any "unterrified Jeffersonian Democrats" who understood that the only government which governed by the consent of the governed was no government at all.[39] If the ideals of Tucker's individualist anarchism were American, Nietzsche's presence in *Liberty*'s pages nevertheless suggested that its best theorists and spokespeople were European. With a Pierre-Joseph Proudhon quotation on *Liberty*'s masthead[40] and its pages promoting Nietzsche, Stirner, Shaw, and Ibsen, Tucker's worldly iconoclasm revealed a common tension among Eurocentric American cosmopolitans. They recognized Nietzsche's philosophy for its contribution to radical thought by making "morality itself a problem."[41] But given the prominence of European thinkers in the canon of anarchist thought, and the marginalization of anarchists in America especially after the Haymarket affair, Nietzsche's role in *Liberty* raised the specter that Tucker's America might not yet be ready for advanced thought, or to make morality a problem.

Schumm, however, believed that America was ready for its Nietzschean dawn, and he invoked Nietzsche's affinity with Emerson to prove it. In an 1896 appreciation of Nietzsche's philosophy, Schumm sought to expose a general readership to the German philosopher by describing him as an exemplar of the liberated cosmopolitan intellect. His Nietzsche knew no national home precisely because he recognized the transitory nature of all states of belonging. He quoted Nietzsche from *Human, All Too Human*, noting, "Whoso has attained even only in a degree to the freedom of reason cannot feel himself other than as a wanderer on the earth—even if not as a traveller *toward* a final destination: for there is none." He argued that Nietzsche represented a new kind of intellect whose inspiration pointed neither east nor west, but rather encouraged the circumnavigation "of that inner world called 'man.'" Nietzsche's primary focus on the inner grandeur of the individual should be familiar to American readers, Schumm argued, because it recalled "the gentle sage of Concord." Both thinkers were "pronounced individualists" who rejected outworn creeds, and were "experimenter[s]" who sought, as Nietzsche put it, "*Life as a means of knowledge.*" Likewise both fought the "dead level of mediocrity," the hollow Christian and egalitarian chants of the age, which threaten, in Emerson's words, to "melt the world into a lump." Though Schumm made no claim for influence, he noted the strong affinity between the two authors, thus observing that if America could produce an Emerson, so too might she have ears to hear his insights repeated by Nietzsche. Schumm argued that Nietzsche's problems would become America's problems in the new century. Thus, resisting the Eurocentrism of American cosmopolitanism, he argued that thanks to Emerson, America *was* ready for Nietzsche and to make the crossing to a new world: the *true* inner world of man.[42]

Of all the turn-of-the-century cosmopolitan commentators persuaded that America should offer refuge to Nietzsche but convinced that it would not, none sounded this theme more than the arts critic James Gibbons Huneker. Huneker portrayed Nietzsche as a thoroughly European thinker, wholly alien to the American mind. From the early 1890s, Huneker had made himself a reputation for introducing European trends in thought and the arts to American audiences as a music editor, literary critic, essayist, and novelist. His discovery of Nietzsche in 1888, when he first read *Richard Wagner at Bayreuth* (1876), marked the beginning of his career-long fascination with the German philosopher.[43] In his enthusiasm for everything Nietzschean, Huneker visited Elisabeth Förster-Nietzsche in Weimar in 1904 and wrote her to boast of his important role in introducing Americans to her brother's philosophy.[44] H. L. Mencken later praised Huneker's intellectual trailblazing by insisting that "if the United States is in any sort of contact . . . with what is aesthetically going on in the more civilized countries, . . . there is surely no man who can claim a larger share of credit for preparing the way."[45] Mencken considered Huneker not only America's "official" ambassador for European philosophy and aesthetics but also, more significantly, the "first [in America] to sense the true stature of Nietzsche."[46]

Over the course of his three-decade-plus engagement with Nietzsche's philosophy, Huneker promoted a thinker who stripped himself of "all metaphysical baggage" and "dared to be naked" of every vestige of speculative thought.[47] He described him as a titanic naysayer who decried the entire fund of nineteenth-century morality—from Christian sentimentalism to secular humanism, scientific socialism, and democratic idealism—as confessions of a Western civilization in precipitous decline. Unlike other iconoclasts, however, Nietzsche's rejections expressed no morbid pessimism but rather a robust and unafraid "love of earth" shorn of all inherited psychic props.[48] Like Reitzel and Tucker before him, Huneker insisted that Nietzsche's freethinking egoism was committed to no doctrine, no ideology, nor did it advance a "formal philosophy." It was, quite simply, "a powerful critical mode of viewing the universe." Having divested himself of all outworn moral baggage of the millennia, Nietzsche had become the "greatest individualist since Adam."[49] Huneker's Nietzsche thus marked a new epoch in thought: a freethinker's freethinker with no history at his back.

Huneker's writings on Continental thought and aesthetics drew from Nietzsche's conception of the sui-generis genius. Though well known for bringing avant-garde thought to America, Huneker wasn't interested in intellectual movements, only intellectual movers. Indeed, Nietzsche confirmed his contention that great thought does not belong to a movement or even to a moment, but is singular to the solitary genius. When writing about European composers such as Wagner and Schumann, European dramatists, including

Ibsen and Strindberg, and European writers like Stendahl and Baudelaire, he argued that their accomplishments were self-achieved. "There are no 'schools' in art or literature, only good writers and artists; there are not types, only individuals."[50] The titles of Huneker's books reveal his focus on titanic selfhood, and bear Nietzsche's imprint on his aesthetic imagination. He wrote of *Iconoclasts* (1905), *Visionaries* (1905), and *Egoists* (subtitled *A Book of Supermen* [1909]), and even took Nietzsche's phrase "pathos of distance" as the title for his 1913 book of reminisces.[51] However, despite Huneker's insistence that genius knows no movements, no moments, and no homeland, his dominating Eurocentrism suggested that the real pathos of distance that genius required was from American culture. According to Huneker, "the best music comes from Germany[,] the best prose from Paris, the best poets from England."[52] Nietzsche's intellectually explosive and aesthetically fertile genius knew no state of belonging other than to itself, but it was a state of self-belonging that belonged to *Europe*.

While Huneker devoted his earliest discussions of Nietzsche to celebrating his growing influence in Europe, his ambivalence about it mounted as he came to believe it was indiscriminate. Nietzsche's effort to turn all that was sacred profane was no clever parlor trick, Huneker argued; it was an awesome feat that only the rare reader could appreciate and the rarer intellect accomplish. Huneker blanched at how Nietzsche's "revolutionary" ideas "were impudently annexed" by the very herd he took as his enemy. The genius doesn't write for others "but to free his own soul," he argued. By insisting that only genius can understand genius, he made it his self-appointed role to publicize Nietzsche, and then to insist that the public would get him wrong. Later seeking to redact the adjective "Nietzschian," which he helped to popularize in America, Huneker asserted, "The only Christian, he was fond of saying, died on the Cross. The only Nietzschian, one might reply, passed away when crumbled the brilliant brain of Nietzsche."[53]

If Huneker had doubts that his publicity for Nietzsche would yield the same influence for him in America as in Europe, he at least found fellowship with another Eurocentric cosmopolitan who wanted to give it a shot. In 1895 Huneker teamed up with Vance Thompson, a former drama critic for the *Commercial Advertiser* and Parisian correspondent for the *Musical Courier*. Together they channeled their zeal for avant-garde European literature into *M'lle New York* (1895–98), a biweekly magazine modeled on the arch aestheticism of the Parisian literary scene, with the aim of introducing foreign literature to America.[54] Of all the new figures that filled their snappy opinion pieces, including D'Annunzio, Maeterlink, Strindberg, and Flaubert, Nietzsche most embodied the spirit of their literary enterprise. Huneker later described *M'lle New York* as a "safety-valve for our rank egotism and radicalism."[55] Indeed, the publication, replete with irreverent commentaries and risqué caricatures, has all the appearances of two rowdy boys having some fun. Like Huneker, Thompson promoted a thinker whose radical quest for intellectual self-definition and self-sovereignty marked his pathos of distance from an America he regarded as "a country singularly provincial."[56]

Thompson similarly saw Nietzsche as a solitary, singular genius whose influence had come to dominate late nineteenth-century European avant-garde literature. However, he also disparaged that influence, arguing how belated even the "advanced" belles letters of fin-de-siècle Europe had become. Nietzsche stood for "independence in thought, hardy self-esteem," and yet his philosophy proved so ineluctable that thinkers in his wake merely mimicked his intellectual autonomy. But by turning this "Nietzschean attitude" into just another "ism" with an attitude, "no one, even among the best of us, seems to see that true culture begins precisely . . . at the point of untrammeled personality, original, fecund in ideas." He thus noted the irony of the quest for innovation after Nietzsche. According to Thompson, it was Nietzsche whose voice called out "Anarch and Autolatrist, I am illustriously Myself!" And yet the radical critic who longs for originality does so by dressing in "Nietzsche's cast-off clothing." If Nietzsche bequeathed an intellectual temperament that moderns were prone to ape, at least his name provided an adjective, "Nietzschean," to describe the original quest for intellectual originality.[57] And yet in doing so, Nietzsche made Thompson wonder whether American "advanced" efforts to move into a new universe of art, intellect, and morality—indeed to become modern—would be belated to him.

Though initially more aesthetic than political, Thompson's jaundiced assessment of American democratic pluralism increasingly colored the magazine's commentaries. Unlike Reitzel and Tucker, who employed Nietzsche for their anarchism of the Left, Thompson utilized Nietzsche for his aristocratism of the Right. He argued that America must be "ruled by . . . the strong man" lest it become "eaten alive by parasites." He thus used his canon of cosmopolitan thinkers to criticize cosmopolitan realities in America.[58] Nietzsche confirmed his belief that America was a "doomed republic," for it operated under the "monstrous fallacy that all men are born free and equal." The problem with modern democracy is that it mistakes "plutocracy" for leadership and "ballotocracy" for public order. Critical of the leveling tendencies in modern life, and of its assault on the natural "intellectual aristocracy," Thompson made his debt to Nietzsche explicit:[59]

> And *M'lle New York* sees the democratic hatred of the individual that is the chief mark of this drab, commercial civilization. Always democracy has irksomely groomed the rough-coated horse. Always democracy has hated the individual; always it has made it its business to castrate the thinkers. . . .
>
> The social good is not the work of the masses, but the work of the few. It is only by the few and the superior that a nation counts in history and in the life of humanity. The hypocrisy of liberalism, the ignominy of democracy, the meaner baseness of socialism are futile and discarded modes of thought. Only in an aristocracy—an aristocracy of the sparkling sword and the dominant mind—is there a germ of progress, a desire of ascension.[60]

Thompson employed Nietzsche as a fellow patrician pessimist whose philosophy confirmed that America would remain a "bankrupt" democracy as long as it mistook equality for necessity, feared individuality as a threat to order, and denatured its thinkers in order to keep the masses ignorant and content.[61]

None of the other early cosmopolitan promoters of Nietzsche shared Thompson's disdain for the masses and his hostility to the democratic ideal, but they did share his underlying critique of American commercialism, provincialism, and anti-intellectualism. Thompson's radical conservatism, however, demonstrates how Nietzsche began his American career sliding easily along the political register as radicals from the Far Left to the Far Right feared the intellectually deadening forces of modern capitalism and democracy. Though their Nietzsches spoke in different keys, all revealed a thinker who divested himself of illusory states of belonging and external authority—either to a supernatural religion, the state, metaphysical philosophy, a market economy, or a pluralist society—in order to experience the liberation of a modern self-begotten self. All turned to Nietzsche as evidence that modern individuality can only be achieved, not inherited, and that it is the product of a free mind, not a free market.

Likewise, what united Nietzsche's American cosmopolitans was their characterization of his challenge to all external authority as a transformative event in the history of morals and in the cultural life of Europe. They described Nietzsche's philosophy as marking a new era of thought. Having challenged the foundations of all external authority, Nietzsche demonstrated that the intellect, once it frees itself of all binding illusions philosophical, religious, and cultural, knows no piety, no party, and no platform. However, though committed to a notion of intellectual cosmopolitanism, by emphasizing Nietzsche's importance for *European* thought, these cosmopolitans helped establish an American impression of Nietzsche as a *European* event—a theme that would be picked up by subsequent commentators in the popular press. In advocating Nietzsche's role in advancing modern thought, by employing him as the poster child of their Eurocentric cosmopolitanism, they suggested that the advanced thought does know a home, *Europe*.

## The Nietzsche Vogue

Friedrich Nietzsche's death on August 25, 1900, drew the attention of, but no fanfare from, the mainstream American press. Major periodicals printed obituaries noting the passing of an intellectual curiosity, a writer of great talents, but questioning whether he would prove to be a thinker of lasting significance. *Bookman* mourned the loss of a "brilliant mind" and a wonderful stylist, but complained nevertheless that he "raved and gibbered of his firm belief that he had built up a new world-philosophy."[62] *Popular Science Monthly* characterized Nietzsche as a "Darwinian" thinker who "trampled like a bull," while *Outlook* dismissed him as a run-of-the-mill "pessimist," unlikely to be "counted among the serious thinkers of his time."[63] One thing the obituaries did agree on, however, was that Nietzsche's philosophy, over the course of the last decade, had a "profound influence . . . throughout the civilized world."[64]

Here it was, 1900, and from the introductory quality of the obituaries it was evident that beyond the small circles of radical cosmopolitans, America neither felt Nietzsche's profound influence on its own intellectual life, nor knew what to make of it abroad. But the characterization of Nietzsche's impact on the civilized world begged the question: wasn't *America* part of the civilized world? Perhaps not, confessed the writer of Nietzsche's obituary for the *New York Times Saturday Review*, as he wondered why Americans should pay their respects to the "dead lunatic" from Germany: "Nobody denies that he said a good many striking things. . . . But the man was a madman, and what possible value attaches to the blasphemies of a mad atheist?"[65] The answer was anything but clear. Was this Friedrich Wilhelm Nietzsche a curious thinker of the age, or one for the ages? If Nietzsche's influence never reached American shores, would its culture be better off without it?

While not yet ready to answer the questions, a growing number of intellectual commentators in the United States felt it was high time to pose them. In the years following the 1896 publication of the first English translations of Nietzsche's writings, appraisals of his work took on increasing prominence in mainstream newspapers and magazines, literary reviews, and academic journals. Now the English versions of *Thus Spoke Zarathustra* and *The Case of Wagner* (including *The Twilight of the Idols*, *Nietzsche Contra Wagner*, and *The Antichrist*), published by Henry & Co. of Britain and translated by two Darwinians—Scottish translator and critic Thomas Common and Alexander Tille, a German lecturer at Glasgow University—made it possible to consider the work of a thinker who since the early 1890s had gained a significant following abroad.[66]

The first wave of reviews and articles played a central role in introducing American readers to Nietzsche's work and in creating a climate of opinion in which he would be read. They introduced not only Nietzsche the writer but also, as one reviewer in 1896 put it, Nietzsche the European "phenomenon."[67] If Nietzsche's philosophy was a curiosity, so too was the widespread "vogue" for it across the Atlantic.[68] The earliest American appraisals of Nietzsche's thought catalogued his growing presence in Continental revolts against foundationalism in social thought, formalism in the arts, and progressive liberalism in religion. Though exhibiting varying degrees of interest and differences in analysis of the ideas themselves, all agreed about the importance of his philosophy for the intellectual currents across the Atlantic: "His shadow has fallen over half of Europe."[69] Commentators sympathetic and critical could agree that Nietzsche was more than a thinker; he was a major cultural event, in fact "The Greatest European Event since Goethe."[70]

An early press release for the English translations made this very point. It noted that because Nietzsche enjoyed "world-wide repute," his work warranted serious appraisal by American readers. That publicity for a new author would stress his intellectual importance is unsurprising. But to emphasize that that importance lay in its *influence* reveals the dominant preoccupation in this first wave of mainstream and scholarly American interest in Nietzsche. It was because his philosophy "sums up and expresses so much that is modern in thought" that it could no longer be "neglected by English readers of culture who would keep abreast with tendencies of the time."[71] From all the rage on the Continent, there was no reason to doubt, as two writers for the *Monist* in 1899 put it, that "he who will know the *Zeitgeist* must know Nietzsche."[72]

The widespread curiosity about Nietzsche's European vogue reveals not some heretofore unknown turn-of-the-century interest in the sociology of knowledge but rather a concern whether Nietzsche's ideas would have a future in America. Reviewers used Nietzsche's popularity in Europe and relative obscurity in America as a way to study their comparative intellectual cultures. They wondered whether America would be—indeed should be— similarly hospitable to his philosophy. From the start, Nietzsche interpretations were something more than a transparent analysis of the philosopher's ideas. They were always freighted with broader concerns about the relationship between European and American thought and culture. Expressing the mixed sentiments of worry and longing about the implications of Nietzsche for American culture, one reviewer wondered, "Will Nietzsche Come into Vogue in America?"[73]

In their efforts to determine whether Nietzsche would gain a US audience, the first wave of reviewers analyzed the translations of his works available in English. With regret they noted that most American readers would have access to him only in translation, especially the awkward and stilted English of the Tille and Common editions. As a number of reviewers observed, a key problem with them was the books Tille and Common chose to translate. Havelock Ellis, the renowned British sex psychologist whose writings had a broad readership in America, agreed that the translations made available only those writings that already showed traces of Nietzsche's mental decompensation. He argued that "the English publishers exclusively brought forward the latest, the most extravagant, the most insane portions of his work," failing to publish the earlier texts, which were the "sanest and most truly characteristic" of his philosophy.[74] Thus, American readers who could not read Nietzsche in the original had access only to his later works, including *Zarathustra* and *Antichrist*, which Nietzsche had written as he was approaching the "Rubicon" of his mental life.

Also troubling to English-language reviewers was the quality of the translations themselves. Most agreed with the reviewer for the *Nation* who lamented that the translations failed "to reach a fluent and idiomatic English rendering," often becoming "unintelligible."[75] On the whole, critics thought the 1908 series of translations under the editorship of Oscar Levy were a significant improvement, but they, too, still had their concerns. At issue was not just how to capture the lyricism of Nietzsche's prose and avoid the halting awkwardness of literal English renderings of the German syntax. The meaning was also at stake. Especially consternating was the proper translation of his major concepts. Was *Wille zur Macht* best translated as "will to be powerful," "will for power," or "will to be strong"? "Eternal repetition" loses the music of *ewige Wiederkehr*, but is it more accurate than "eternal return"? Even comparatively straightforward phrases like *Die Fröhliche Wissenschaft* could take on various guises in English: "gay knowledge," "happy knowledge," and "joyous science." Commentators agreed that "to translate Nietzsche well would be a task of no small skill."[76] But was it even possible? Some expressed their doubts, like the reviewer who asserted, "To be properly appreciated [Nietzsche] must, like Carlyle or Emerson, be read in the original. The character of his German cannot be reproduced in English; it is something foreign to English thought."[77] Of concern to reviewers was whether there was an inherent incommensurability between the German language and the English language, between the German intellect and the American mind.

Critics eager to stress Nietzsche's exoticism argued that his intellectual style would be less alien were it *more*, not less, German. They surmised that his mindset suggested an inheritance more exotic that his Saxon upbringing. There is, of course, a logic to these assertions: Given the dominance of German philosophers in the American canon of major thinkers, the increased presence of German-modeled research universities in American higher education, and the cachet of a German academic training, a German Nietzsche wouldn't help explain the foreignness of his mind. Slavic emotionalism, however, would. As a result, one explanation for Nietzsche's unfamiliar intellectual temperament that readers found persuasive was his alleged Polish origins. Though Förster-Nietzsche chuckled at her brother's unfounded boasting that the Nietzsches of Saxony descended from Polish aristocrats, this version of his family lineage was one that American commentators were more than happy to recite. F. C. S. Schiller, a noted British- and American-trained German pragmatist who was a major early reviewer of Nietzsche, thought his claims to Polishness were plausible, given Nietzsche's "obviously Slavonic name (niëzky)" and the significant population of people of Slavonic origins in eastern Germany where Nietzsche grew up. He also found it useful for explaining why "Nietzsche's mind and temper" exhibited such passion and histrionics. It could only be due to his "undeniably Slavonic" inheritance.[78] Others agreed, suggesting that Nietzsche's philosophy bespoke the intellectual distemper of Polish nobility, unable to find their way, like the Anglo-Saxons, to a healthy balance between liberty and order.[79] Nietzsche's exotic "Polishness" took on a special significance for reviewers who were eager to show that Nietzscheism would not, and should not, flourish in America.

American reviewers noted the obvious appeal of a writer who railed against the pretentions of tired orthodoxies in an age clamoring for revolt against inherited authority. But the power of his critique, they recognized, was in the varieties of emancipation it promised. The sheer range of Nietzschean liberation could be mapped by the geography of the battles: at home against the stifling ethics and aesthetics of bourgeois parents, at the university against the sterility and scholasticism of the professors, at church against an ethics deemed purely disciplinary, and in the public square against the easy evasions of progressive thought. What had yet to be determined, though, was the native value of Nietzsche's philosophy. Did the "unflagging interest in Nietzsche and his work on the other side of the Atlantic" bespeak nothing more than a "*succès de scandale*," and Nietzsche's ideas merely the "hollowest cant of a canting age"?[80] Were Nietzsche's ideas just some "good horse-play," or evidence of the "greatness" of a thinker "who laid down his life for his work"?[81]

Though none argued that Nietzsche's European vogue disqualified him as a serious philosopher, the hoopla surrounding his philosophy sometimes made it tempting to do so. Initially, a small but growing number of academic philosophers sought to weigh in on the debates, and likewise questioned whether Nietzsche's philosophy was simply another "ism" of modern thought, or a devastating critique of its entire philosophical grounds. In the first doctoral dissertation on Nietzsche in the United States, Cornell University philosophy student Grace Neal Dolson agreed that the Nietzsche vogue hardly justified scholarly interest in him, or warranted a philosophy dissertation on him. But she argued that to reckon with Nietzsche was simply to confront head on "the general intellectual movement of the past decades. . . . In one sense, he was inevitable." Nietzsche had observed how the increasingly naturalistic view of the universe made a mockery of moral commitments. His point, Dolson averred, was not that moderns fall short of their ideals but that their ideals fall short of reality. By questioning the *value* of values, Nietzsche offered crucial insights to Americans. "In an age whose watchword in politics is democracy, and in ethics self-sacrifice," she argued, it was important to recognize that "self-sacrifice, if consistently adhered to, results in a personality that ought to be sacrificed, and the sooner the better." Dolson maintained that Nietzsche likewise forced Americans to question their utilitarian ethics; "general comfort" was no compensation for a culture of weak personalities. Nietzsche's egoism made clear "that pain is not so bad as the want of power to endure it."[82] Thus, Nietzsche's challenge to the universality of ideals of democracy and self-sacrifice forced a serious reappraisal of those values themselves. In doing so, Dolson concluded, Nietzsche simply anticipated where philosophy in the next century was heading; his questions would become the questions of all modern thought.

The value of Nietzsche's philosophy, for many US observers, was its foreignness to American thought. As one writer for the *New York Times* put it, Nietzsche's challenge to the "facile liberalism" of "Americanism," and his "Hellenic, aesthetic" intellect posed against the "Hebraic, ascetic" American mentality, offered a crucial perspective "hitherto unrepresented by American thinkers."[83] But according to Benjamin Tucker's fellow anarchist and regular contributor to *Liberty*, Victor S. Yarros, while Nietzsche's philosophy might *seem* foreign to American thought, it was wholly consonant with American practice. It was important, therefore, to distinguish between "Theoretical and Practical Nietzscheism." Unlike other anarchists who found Nietzsche's challenge to universal morality liberating, Yarros found his ethics of expediency a frightful guide to human conduct. Because Nietzsche's "aristocratic" ideas would justifiably be so repellent to Americans, Yarros speculated in 1901 that "probably no sound thinker entertains the faintest fear of the spread of Friedrich Nietzsche's amazing gospel" in America. But that wasn't the point. While they might reject "*theoretical* Nietzscheism," they had long ago embraced it in practice. Commercialism, greed, laissez-faire, the quest for empire: these were the cornerstones of American life. Americans, he speculated, would very well find "theoretical Nietzscheism" abhorrent, precisely *because* it so accurately laid bare their ethics. Americans thus had no use for Nietzsche because they had been Nietzscheans all along.[84]

The fascination with Nietzsche's European vogue was no simple prelude to the American reception. It reflects rather one of the dominant leitmotifs of Nietzsche's initial presence in American thought. The earliest popular and scholarly commentators who had a hand in constructing his American reception did so first by making him a European "event." Nietzsche not only belonged to Europe, he belonged to a new modern mindset he helped create. By wrangling with the specter of "Nietzscheism," Americans sought to come to terms with an as yet ill-defined modernity and its implications for their moral lives. The question for American observers apprehensive about whether Nietzsche would come to America was whether America would experience intellectual modernity too.

Nietzsche's spectacular influence abroad and his relative obscurity in the United States also became a way for observers to consider the comparative intellectual cultures of America and continental Europe. Though not all agreed that a "Nietzschean deluge" could mean only that "the very culture-philistines he . . . despised" had co-opted him, commentators roundly concurred that his radical ideas were an odd fit with the American mind.[85] Though not all agreed that it was such a bad thing that America was less "sensitive to new ideas than modern Germany,"[86] none questioned the sentiment. The narratives spun rehearsed the same themes: while the European mind was shaped by discontent, striving, and curiosity, the American mind was sunny, confident, practical, not theoretical. Europe does thought, America does commerce. While Europeans scaled the upper regions of the mind, Americans were busy scouring a new continent. Nietzsche enjoyed a vogue in Europe because Europe takes seriously, if too seriously, the work of its thinkers. But the question of whether America was or should be capable of the same was a matter of dispute. In order to answer that question, American commentators looked to the curious figure at the center of the European storm. In order to come to terms with Nietzsche's implications for American thought, they sought to know Nietzsche himself.

## The Persona of Nietzsche

The earliest American commentators who had a hand in rendering Nietzsche a European event also helped transform him into an American celebrity. They examined in great detail his dramatic life story, his personal idiosyncrasies, and the circumstances leading to his mental collapse in an effort to understand the man behind the philosophy. Many had speculated whether Nietzsche's appeal lay not in what he thought but in "what he suffered." Schiller did not have to look far for confirmation: he too provided lush details about Nietzsche's chronic physical ailments that culminated in his mental breakdown in 1888. While reviewers repeatedly criticized prurient interest in Nietzsche's pathologies, they argued that it was legitimate to interpret his thought in light of the curious circumstances of his life and illness. Scrutiny of Nietzsche's personality and emotional problems, they insisted, reflected no unguarded voyeurism on their part. Indeed, as Schiller put it, it was "unusually justifiable in this case, for the mark of his emotional personality, the shadow of his approaching eclipse, is over everything that he wrote."[87] The overwhelming attention to Nietzsche's persona thus demonstrates how reviewers interpreted his philosophy through the lens of his biography. They did not simply use Nietzsche portraiture to adorn their textual interpretations; they offered portraiture itself as philosophical exegesis.[88]

Nietzsche's physical appearance captivated a number of his earliest American interpreters. Photographs and drawings of him circulated in the popular press and scholarly journals, documenting virtually every stage of his life for US audiences. American publications reproduced the 1861 photograph of Nietzsche as a boy, standing in the Napoleon pose with his right hand tucked into the breast of his suit jacket, which was taken shortly before his confirmation. Then there was the photograph of Nietzsche as a young professor in Basel, with round cheeks, a finely manicured mustache, and dark eyes partly hidden by tiny silver spectacles. Two of the most popular photographs were the profile portraits taken in 1882 by the photographer Gustav Schultze in Naumburg, Germany, when Nietzsche was thirty-eight years old. In both images, Nietzsche's thick, dark hair is swept neatly off his high forehead, and his mouth is hidden under a huge but finely groomed mustache; he is dressed in a smart jacket, a white high-collared shirt, and a black tie. One picture is a bust portrait of Nietzsche. The other portrays the philosopher with furrowed brow, head supported by his fist, which would become the iconographic image of Nietzsche as contemplative thinker.

American publications also reproduced photographs of sculptures and drawings of the philosopher that testified to an already burgeoning industry in Nietzsche iconography abroad. There were reproductions of the 1894 Curt Stoeving oil painting of Nietzsche seated on a veranda, dressed in a black jacket, his neck draped in a white ascot, with his hands folded feebly in his lap. American publications reproduced the 1899 Hans Olde etching *Small Nietzsche Head*, and photographs of the popular Max Klinger bust of Nietzsche. The reproductions of Nietzsche artwork—the oil paintings, the marble sculptures, and the woodcut prints of the philosopher—visually reinforced the existence of a Nietzsche vogue in Europe. But more important, the tendency to publish images of Nietzsche from the years of his insanity, like the first English

Friedrich Nietzsche at age thirty-eight, 1882. Photographer: Gustav Schultze. Reprinted in
F. C. S. Schiller, "Nietzsche and His Philosophy," *Book Buyer*, August 1896.

translations of his last works, ensured that Americans' first exposure to him
was of the post-Rubicon Nietzsche.

Where there were no images to draw on, reviewers used superlatives to
captivate readers. Nietzsche was not simply a great thinker, he was "the most
radical philosopher of the century."[89] His philosophy was more than novel, it
was "the most revolutionary system of thought ever presented to men."[90] The
superlatives often overshot the mark, however, as American commentators
struggled to find ways to describe a thinker who had, appropriately, referred
to himself as a "nuance."[91]

No author did more to establish the persona of Friedrich Nietzsche in
America than H. L. Mencken. His 1908 study, *The Philosophy of Friedrich
Nietzsche*—the first full-length English-language book written for a general
audience in America—offered a rollicking master narrative about Nietzsche's
religious upbringing, his intellectual path from parsonage to public enemy,
his battle with poor health, and his warfare on the slave morality of modern
Christianity. Nietzsche's dramatic life story and personality were for Mencken
no sideline attractions: they were relevant for understanding the pulsating "will

53

"Nietzsche—The Antichrist!" *Current Literature*, April 1908.

to power" marking every page of his writings. Mencken's Nietzsche "hurled his javelin" at the "authority" of God, of transcendent morality, and of universal truth. He brought his own "assertive '*ich*'" to the center of his reality, and onto the pages of his books. Mencken tried to ventriloquize Nietzsche's voice: "*I* condemn Christianity. *I* have given to mankind. . . . *I* think. . . . *I* say. . . .

54

Max Klinger, sculpture of Nietzsche, as reproduced in "The Most Revolutionary System of Thought Ever Presented to Men," *Current Literature*, March 1906.

*I* do. . . ."[92] According to Mencken, because Nietzsche's books revealed his assumption of authority in the first person, each could be read as a personal confession of their author.[93]

Mencken's monograph, which he wrote when he was twenty-seven years old, was just the beginning of his Nietzscheana. He continued to write extensively about him—in his 1910 compendium of Nietzsche's aphorisms, *The Gist of Nietzsche*, his 1920 translation of *The Antichrist*, and in countless essays and articles on him for the *Baltimore Sun*, *Atlantic Monthly*, and the two journals under his editorship, *The Smart Set* and *American Mercury*. When Mencken was not writing about Nietzsche, he was borrowing liberally from his artillery of concepts, peppering his own texts with "slave morality," "herd morality," "*ressentiment*," and "will to power" in order to articulate his displeasure with American democratic culture. Nietzsche's inventive use of language emboldened Mencken to manufacture some terms of his own, most famously "booboisie" and "boobus Americanus." Nietzsche's philological criticism inspired his own linguistic genealogy, *The American Language* (1919), and his last work, *Minority Report* (1956), shows the inspiration of Nietzsche's aphoristic warfare. Throughout his career, he also drew on Nietzsche's model of the oppositional intellect. Nietzsche's ideas and image were for Mencken gifts that kept on giving—his exaltation of the Übermensch, his warning about the perils of democracy, and his insights about the "slave morality" inherent in Christianity would animate Mencken's own intellectual biography.

As he later told a friend, the ideas that would become part of his sustained assault on American culture "were plainly *based* on Nietzsche; without him, I'd never have come to them."[94] In addition, Mencken remarked that he had learned a new style of thought by working on his Nietzsche book. "After that I was a critic of ideas," he wrote, "and I have remained one ever since."[95]

Mencken never imagined or believed that the German author who played such a dominant role in his own intellectual biography could also become fashionable in America. And yet it was his own crucial contributions to the making of Nietzsche's American persona that ensured that he would. Mencken first discovered Nietzsche in Huneker's *New York Sun* essays while writing his first book—a study of George Bernard Shaw's plays—in 1905.[96] When the positive reviews of his book started coming in, Mencken's publisher, Harrison Hale Schaff, suggested that he follow up by introducing American readers to another controversial European thinker: Friedrich Nietzsche. Initially, Mencken rejected the idea, believing that his passion for Nietzsche in no way compensated for his lack of the scholarly training (he had only a high-school education) and proficiency in German necessary for the project. But even more, it seemed to Mencken so unlikely that a difficult and revolutionary European thinker like Nietzsche could ever be naturalized into the American pantheon of greats. But the appeal of long nights reading Nietzsche's *Sämtliche Werke*, of studying at close range a master wordsmith, and of achieving a proprietary stake in the memory of the towering genius emboldened him to take on the project.

What emerged was Mencken's extended analysis of Nietzsche's life and thought, in which he laid out all the major features of the Nietzsche persona he would work with in future decades. Mencken discovered in Nietzsche traits in abundance that he believed were in short supply in modern America: fearless independence and fierce intelligence. From a young age, "Nietzsche did not belong to the majority."[97] He broke from the crowd by breaking into their truths, exposing them as misty sentimentalisms. Unlike other nineteenth-century revolutionaries who preached what they regarded as universal ideas to the universal in man, Nietzsche explicitly rejected "men in the mass," directing himself only to "the small minority of exceptional men—not to those who live by obeying, but to those who live by commanding—not to the race as a race, but only to its masters."[98] The masters Mencken's Nietzsche had in mind, however, were neither broad-shouldered warriors nor captains of industry. Mencken himself did not worship brute force, nor did he worship markets. But he did revere what he regarded as Nietzsche's "worship of the actual"—an unforgiving, searing, independent style of thought that exhibits a fearless intimacy with unadorned reality and a "pathos of distance" from the crowd.[99]

Mencken's treatment of Nietzsche's life highlighted aspects of the philosopher's biography and personality that reflected his own. He described Nietzsche's German Lutheran piety as similar to his upbringing in Baltimore, in which Mencken was "brought up in the fear of the Lord" as "ideal training for sham-smashers and freethinkers." He described Nietzsche's longing for a masculine intellect beyond the reach of the "maternal apron-string" of home, while he continued to live with his mother. Though Nietzsche broke out on his own, the strings would, in the end, pull him back: "[There] is something poignantly pathetic in the picture of this valiant fighter–this arrogant *Ja-sager*—this foe of men, gods and devils—being nursed and coddled like a little child" in his closing years. Mencken, a bachelor for most of his life, also described Nietzsche's need to resist the apron strings of matrimony as essential to his intellectual freedom: "A wife's constant presence, day in and day out, would have irritated him beyond measure or reduced him to a state of compliance and sloth. . . . The ideal state for a philosopher, indeed, is celibacy tempered by polygamy." One wonders where Mencken conjured up polygamy, but the notion that "a venture into matrimony" was unthinkable for the masculine intellect reinforced his own extended bachelorhood as a condition necessary for liberated intelligence.[100]

Mencken not only first encountered Nietzsche's philosophy in Huneker's writings, he also discovered how his persona could be used to explain it. Revealing his own preference for Nietzschean biography over philosophy, Huneker consistently crowded his essays with details of Nietzsche's physical and psychic torments. From every bout of dyspepsia, crushing migraine, and insomnia, Huneker drew a different morality tale about the travails of genius. In his treatments, visions of damnation—"[Nietzsche] lived in an inferno, mental and physical"—competed with images of martyrdom—"Nietzsche bore a terrible cross" in "his sick soul and body."[101] In his narration, every part of Nietzsche's anatomy had a story to tell, but none more so than his brain. Nietzsche's brain wasn't simply the seat of his cognition, it was the focal point of a morality tale about the penalty of genius. It was not only Nietzsche's "fury and craving after universal knowledge" that caused him to smash "his own brain," but also his being condemned to live in "a century of indifference" that "burnt" it up. Though

Huneker insisted that it was intellectually slack "to point at Nietzsche's end as the moral tag of his life," he admitted that it was his dramatic persona and his catastrophic collapse that made Nietzsche so ineluctably seductive.[102]

Huneker's fascination with Nietzsche's insanity and his genius reflects what would become the dominant features of American commentary about Nietzsche. "Was Nietzsche a Madman or a Genius?"[103] Nietzsche's relevance for America hinged on the answer. His perceived mental endowments and deficits dominated his US coverage. Titles like that used for an 1898 *New York Times* article, "Interesting Revolutionary Theories from a Writer Now in a Madhouse," helped establish the centrality of his mental state for assessing his philosophy.[104] Nietzsche's mental collapse transfigured easily into object lessons on alternately the sufferings of genius in American democratic culture or the healthy American suspicion of Continental intellectualism. One could resolve the tension by describing Nietzsche as a mad genius, but that did not answer the question of whether his philosophical challenges should be criticized as romantic excess or condoned as the stark revelations of a heroic thinker that modern values were empty.

Huneker rallied hard to characterize Nietzsche's madness as a romantic confirmation of his genius, but he faced stiff competition with the dominant image of Nietzsche as a stark raving lunatic, which had already been established in 1895 by Hungarian physician, essayist, and social critic Max Nordau. Indeed, it was the spectacular success of Nordau's *Degeneration* (*Entartung*), a literary sensation in Europe in 1892/93 and a best seller when the English translation appeared in 1895, that put Nietzsche's madness at the center of American interpretations.[105] Published a full year before the English translations of Nietzsche's works were available, Nordau's infamous book offered a raging denunciation of modern art, literature, and thought as evidence of the degeneracy of fin-de-siècle European culture, using Nietzsche's writings as confirmation of modernism's intellectual bankruptcy and moral depravity. Though American critics like William James dismissed *Degeneration* as a "pathological book on a pathological subject" and Nordau himself as a "degenerate of the worst sort," his book is nonetheless incomparable testimony to the felt moral urgency surrounding the intellectual revolts of the late nineteenth century.[106] Described by George Mosse as "one of the most important documents of the *fin de siècle*," Nordau's text displays the psychic dislocations between the confident bourgeois liberalism, positivism, and progressivism of his own nineteenth-century era and the emergent modernist "sensibilities of a searching and disillusioned generation."[107]

Nordau's critique of Nietzsche's madness hinged not on one man's insanity but on a damaged fin-de-siècle culture that helped create him and handed him an audience. Nevertheless, he felt that in Nietzsche, the degeneracy of modern thought was so complete that he devoted a lengthy chapter to him, assigning Nietzsche top billing as the philosopher of modern "ego-mania." A disciple and friend of the famous Italian physician and criminologist Cesare Lombroso, Nordau drew on the ideas of his *Genius and Insanity* (*Genio e Follio* [1863]) to argue for an organic, not philosophical, basis of Nietzsche's intellectual rebellion. Nordau believed that Nietzsche's critique of an ordered universe was nothing more than the perversions of a disordered mind. Not only did Nietzsche fetishize his own upending of rationality simply because he could not finish a thought, he worshipped power to sanction his own sexual deviance and sadism. According to Nordau, no "image of wickedness and crime can arise without exciting him sexually, and he is unable to experience any sexual stimulation without the immediate appearance in his consciousness of an image of some deed of violence and blood." Nordau's Nietzsche was a wild man from cradle to grave: "From the first to the last page of Nietzsche's writings the careful reader seems to hear a madman, with flashing eyes, wild gestures, and foaming mouth, spouting forth deafening bombast; and through it all, now breaking out into frenzied laughter, [and] . . . now skipping about in a giddily agile dance." Nordau's frantic critique described Nietzsche's followers as imbeciles duped by his false originality: he directed his assaults "against doors that stand open." The fascination with Nietzsche's philosophy, Nordau argued, thus bespoke the intellectual poverty of modern thought. It may move the masses, but the ideas themselves could not "withstand the faintest puff of breath."[108]

Nordau's critique enjoyed an early advantage in the making of Nietzsche's American persona, but other interpreters from abroad rushed to offer counternarratives. Initially, none of them were deemed more authoritative than the philosopher's sister, Elisabeth Förster-Nietzsche, who made it her mission not only to oversee her brother's translations and publications but also to publicize his image as the saintly genius. In the same year that Nordau's *Degeneration* appeared in English, Förster-Nietzsche published her two-volume biography, which was later translated into English in 1912 and 1915.[109] She offered the "scrupulous accuracy" of firsthand testimony that only a devoted family member could provide.[110] She described the "Young and Happy Nietzsche" as a "thoroughly healthy," "tender," and "obedient" boy with impeccable manners, a love of "swimming and skating," and a religiosity and "earnestness" that put him at odds with the crude compromises of the commonplace. She also described a young man who, throughout adulthood, exhibited a deep reverence and capacity for friendship. Nietzsche had very pleasant relations with women, whom he treated with "a tender, almost paternal care," she went on. Although he was capable of romantic attachments and befriended many handsome women, he forsook deeper relations only because he was so singularly faithful to his calling. As the illnesses mounted, Nietzsche greeted them with magnanimity, regretting only that they kept him from his mission. In Förster-Nietzsche's retelling, Nietzsche's life from birth to death was impeccable and upright, and was a heroic example of sacrifice and service. And yet it posed a riddle:

> For it *is* a problem that Friedrich Nietzsche, who denied our present moral values, or at least traced them to sources absolutely unsuspected hitherto— this Transvaluer of all Values—should himself have fulfilled all the loftiest and most subtle demands made by the morality now preached among us. And he did not do this because of any moral imperative, but from a perfectly cheerful inability to act otherwise. I leave it to others to solve this problem.[111]

Although Förster-Nietzsche catalogued in rich detail the peaceful, good-natured, and temperate younger Fritz turned lonely, sacrificing scholar-saint thoroughly at odds with both Nordau's googly-eyed jester and Mencken's manly, javelin-throwing "Ich," she agreed that it was her brother's life and persona that had lasting relevance for those who came after him. In an effort to win him an audience, she sanctioned philosophical exegesis by way of biography and personality, establishing Nietzsche the man as a problem to be solved.

One prominent interpreter who was more than happy to solve the problem posed by Friedrich Nietzsche's life was the German-born philosopher Paul Carus, editor of *The Open Court* and *The Monist*, and author of over two dozen books on philosophy and religion. Appreciative of scientific contributions to

THE "FRANCONIA" STUDENT CORPS IN BONN UNIVERSITY. SUMMER, 1865.
(Nietzsche in the middle, leaning on his hand.)

Nietzsche, age twenty, before he rejected the "beer materialism" of his Franconia Fraternity. As documented in Elisabeth Förster-Nietzsche, *The Young Nietzsche* (1912).

humanistic inquiry and likewise critical of the turn-of-the-century modernist assault on foundations, Carus sought to defend the idea of "philosophy [as] an objective science" against Nietzsche's "anti-scientific tendencies."[112] While Carus's commitment to monism and rationalism in a period of philosophical pragmatism signaled his resistance to current trends in philosophy and won him few supporters in the academy, it gave him a clear platform for attacking both American and Continental antifoundationalism and gained him a reputation as one of Nietzsche's foremost American critics.[113]

Like other Nietzsche interpreters, Carus played the role of amateur psychologist, examining the connections between Nietzsche's philosophy and his insanity. He argued that Nietzsche's instability mirrored the intellectual frailty of his philosophy. The problem with Nietzsche's antifoundationalism was that it denied the authority of reason, science, God, and truth as anchors of the self, and instead exalted the individual as his own arbiter of the good life. Carus warned that "he who rejects truth cuts himself loose from the fountain-head of the waters of life. He may deify selfhood, but his self will die of its own self-apotheosis. His divinity is not a true God-incarnation, it is mere assumption and self-exaltation of a pretender."[114] Carus argued that Nietzsche's madness was an object lesson for moderns who thought that "truth" was a fiction.

Carus moonlighted not only as Nietzsche's psychologist but also as a phrenologist offering interpretations of Nietzsche's appearance and bearing as evidence of the madness of his philosophy. In his 1899 *Monist* review, Carus presented two photographs of Nietzsche side by side under the suggestive heading "A Protest Against Himself."[115] The image to the left is the 1861 photograph of young Nietzsche in the Napoleon pose. Instead of mentioning that the photograph had been taken shortly before his confirmation, Carus simply noted that it was a photo of young Nietzsche as a schoolboy. What is lost in the omission is Nietzsche's robust faith in God; instead we see only a precocious youngster with a robust sense of self. Carus's description of the photograph to the right takes even greater interpretive liberties. It is a photograph of Nietzsche in military attire posing with a drawn sword, taken in 1868, when he served as a volunteer in the German artillery. Carus used these images to demonstrate that Nietzsche's philosophy was a "protest" against his own frailty. "Nietzsche's philosophy forms a strange contrast to his own habits of life," Carus wrote. "Himself a model of virtue, he made himself the advocate of vice, and gloried in it." Carus then described the photograph itself:

> He makes a good soldier, and, in spite of his denunciations of posing, displays theatrical vanity in having himself photographed with drawn sword (the scabbard is missing). His martial mustache almost anticipates the tonsorial art of the imperial barber of the present Kaiser; and yet his spectacled eyes and good-natured features betray the peacefulness of his intentions. He plays the soldier only, and would have found difficulty in killing even a fly.[116]

What Carus failed to mention was that a sword was a standard prop in military photographs and that Nietzsche wore a style of mustache considered fashionable in Germany at the time. Instead, Carus suggested that Nietzsche's imperial facial hair served as a metaphor for his will-to-power philosophy, while his tender features revealed his true delicate constitution. Carus stressed the contrast between Nietzsche the man and the Nietzschean philosophy, implicitly encouraging his readers to snicker at the alleged incongruity.

Carus's use of Nietzschean iconography in his analyses of his philosophy

Nietzsche's "Protest against Himself." *Left*: "As a Pupil in Schulpforta, 1861." *Right*: "As a Volunteer in the German Artillery, 1868." From Paul Carus, "Immorality as a Philosophic Principle," *Monist*, July 1899.

signals how essential the visual image of Nietzsche was to interpreting the implications of his thought.[117] The precocious youngster, the maturing young professor with the "imperial" mustache, the madman with the blank stare—all these figures set the tone for reading his words. Nietzsche entered American culture as a European event and a translated text, of course, but he also came as a collection of personal features. By relying on dramatic visual and textual presentations of his physiognomy, American treatments of Nietzsche communicated to readers that the thinker had significance apart from his thought. This is especially apparent in Carus's 1907 *Monist* article, "Friedrich Nietzsche," which carried a photograph of a statue of the philosopher by M. Klein. In it, Nietzsche sits in a chair, draped in a robe, with his head slightly lowered as he stares intently downward. Carus observed how Nietzsche representations would seek to portray him as a "tragic figure" but insisted that they simply document the pathos of a terribly damaged human being.[118]

Carus may have stridently rejected Nietzsche's challenge to philosophical and moral foundations, but he was not indifferent to the philosopher's suffering. Even here, though, he argued for a particular understanding of Nietzsche's woes, one that had pedagogical value for his American readers.

M. Klein, statue of Nietzsche, as reproduced in Paul Carus, "Friedrich Nietzsche," *Monist*, April 1907.

In Carus's estimation, Nietzsche suffered from the "contradiction between his theories and his habits of life.... He was like the bird in the cage who sings of liberty.... Never was craving for power more closely united with impotence!"[119] Carus mixed pity and mockery as he repeatedly stressed the contrast between Nietzsche's strident and muscular language and his wracked health and modest, even self-effacing, temperament:

> If there was a flaw in Nietzsche's moral character, it was goody-goodyness; and his philosophy is a protest against the principles of his own nature. While boldly calling himself the "the first unmoralist," justifying even license itself and defending the coarsest lust, his own life might have earned him the name of sissy, and he shrank in disgust from moral filth wherever he met with it in practical life.

For Carus, the irony of Nietzsche's life was that his philosophical bravado was nothing more than a psychological denial of his "oversensitive" and "tender" nature.[120]

Carus's postmortem psychoanalysis of Nietzsche might be simply a noteworthy curiosity were it not such a commonplace feature of the earliest American interest in Nietzsche. His emphasis on the incongruity between Nietzsche's imperial thought and his impotent life drew on turn-of-the-century gendered discourses of health, which sought connections between physiological vigor and psychic well-being. Even readers like Carus, who were hostile to Nietzsche's diagnosis of the moral sources of modern degeneracy, agreed with his sentiment that all judgments about life reflect the state of the health of the men and women who made them. That the first dissertation on Nietzsche in America was written by a woman who addressed these very issues demonstrates how gendered ideas about modern moral flaccidity, and anxieties about the feminization of intellect and virtue, worried thinkers both male and female. Though she did not refer to Nietzsche as a "sissy" or discuss his interpersonal "impotence," she argued that his ideas of the physiology of truth showed the lost promise of martial virtues.

A dissertation on Nietzsche a decade later by Johannes Broene, a Clark University doctoral student under the direction of the pioneering American psychologist G. Stanley Hall, showed how widespread this fascination with Nietzsche's contributions to, and own demonstration of, the physiological basis of philosophy had become. Now with the benefit of new Freudian psychology, introduced to him by Hall, the host and sponsor of Freud's first lectures in America in 1909 at Clark,[121] Broene offered a psychoanalytic read of Nietzsche's life and thought. He argued that Nietzsche's philosophy was no work of genius but the confessions of a mind crippled by gender confusions originating in early childhood trauma. According to Broene, Nietzsche suffered from the absence of a strong male presence after the early death of his father. "Growing up as he did in a family of women," and longing for the "strong, controlling hand of a father," he developed a "changeableness, a mutability" that explained his inability to make commitments both emotional and intellectual. In Broene's estimation, Nietzsche's philosophical antifoundationalism was the direct result of his feminized psychology. In addition, Nietzsche grew to adulthood without "the least possible connection" to the real world, Broene noted. "He never married, and, though a scholar by profession, spent most of his life without any duties." In Broene's opinion, a little bit of the conventional life—the healthy manly obligations that Nietzsche found so distasteful—would have done him some good. Instead, he got caught between his tender, feminine temperament and his rowdy, masculine philosophical persona, suffering from an overly extreme dissonance.[122]

The causal relationship between Nietzsche's sickness and his philosophy inspired an industry of speculation, always with an eye toward Nietzsche's relevance to the American mind. Whether Nietzsche was a madman or a genius was used both to recommend him to, and to distance him from, American readers. In terms now common within American Nietzsche commentary, the translator and literary critic Louise Collier Willcox described Nietzsche as "a terrible sufferer . . . profoundly wounded by life"; she insisted, however, that his sickness resulted from his acute sensitivity to a damaged modern culture, which failed to nourish great souls and great visions. But Nietzsche's psychic dislocations were valuable, she argued, precisely because they reflected a *healthy* protest against the diminution of man in the modern world. Modern forces might be seeking to make life more comfortable, but Nietzsche, Willcox argued, thought that "life was to be made bearable, not by making it easier or by diminishing the sum of suffering, but by enlarging our conceptions of life, by conceiving it as more intense, more grandiose, more imposingly beautiful." Nietzsche's psychic suffering reflected his heroic effort to reject both the easy comforts of a despiritualized Christianity and the meaninglessness of nihilism. Insofar as he examined that need and modeled that quest in his own life, he was an invaluable "doctor for sick souls" of modernity.[123]

If Nietzsche's protests against the modern diminution of man made him a stranger in his native Germany, it made him especially alien to American culture. He saw how the "progressive" intellectual, cultural, and material forces of modern life were having a regressive influence on modern man. Nietzsche suffered, not because he made the crossing into a new moral world, but because he *couldn't* make the crossing; he *refused* the human consequences of optimistic, democratic, and progressive impulses in modern culture. While his longing for man's grandeur, for his individuality, for an expansive vision of life put him at odds with nineteenth-century Germany, it was altogether "unnecessary to point out how alien [was] Nietzsche's whole attitude of mind to the American temper." America may worship individualism, but a deep reverence for human individuality was something altogether different. Nietzsche understood that, and for that reason his ideas would never make an easy transfer to the United States. The Nietzsche vogue would likely never reach American shores because he was too subtle, too complicated, too much a mad genius for the cheerful, optimistic American mind.[124]

## Launching "Nietzschean" and "Nietzscheism" into American English

Students abroad, scholars at home, literary cosmopolitans both left and right, women and men, scientists, popular writers, translators, and Victorian custodians of culture all had a hand in making the American Nietzsche at the turn of the last century. By identifying Nietzsche as the "dawn" of modern thought and a watershed "event" in European history, and by turning him into a celebrity, these earliest American interpreters established the German philosopher in their culture as an intellectual sensation. In doing so, they helped launch "Nietzschean" and "Nietzscheism" into American English; the terms came to serve as both rough-and-ready catchwords for godlessness, nihilism, romanticism, and naturalism and as synonyms for the modern challenges confronting American democracy and Christian morality. Because of the range of uses, "Nietzschean" and "Nietzscheism" were seized upon—here as an epithet, there as a statement of self-definition—but always as essential terms in the American moral vocabulary.

The prognostication about whether America would experience a Nietzsche vogue was no neutral estimation about the transatlantic flow of ideas. On the contrary, it served as a way for commentators to assess the vitality of turn-of-the-century American intellectual life and the health of American democratic culture. Readers of Nietzsche both critical and appreciative shared the belief that his genius, his madness, his "Polish" emotionalism, and his literary inventiveness all made him an unlikely fit for American readers. Amid the contestations, a consensus emerged that Americans were too confident in the universal value of their bourgeois Christian worldviews to have any meaningful use for such a radically antifoundational, antireligious, antidemocratic thinker. And yet, by invoking Nietzsche in superlatives, highlighting his European influence, debating his persona, and showing the use-value of his name as adjective and "ism," his earliest American commentators unwittingly answered their own question. In persistently asking "Will Nietzsche Come into Vogue in America?" they demonstrated that in fact, the vogue was already under way. It wasn't long before the questions gave way to affirmations, like one by a writer in 1910 who observed that "the neurotic but strangely fascinating 'philosopher with the hammer,' Friedrich Nietzsche, has begun to invade this country. . . . The slow but persistent growth of [his] fame is one of the intellectual romances of our time."[125]

Expressing a sentiment shared by the first wave of American Nietzsche interpreters, Wilbur Urban in 1897 described Nietzsche's works as the beginning of a new era in morality. In Nietzsche, he discovered the assault on foundations that would define modern thinking and therefore define a new purpose for his own. Twenty years later, that sense of both awe and trepidation about the consequences of a Nietzschean moral world lingered. As Urban wrote in 1917, "Precisely in his eternal seeking and questioning, in the contradictions of his moods and intuitions, in his very self-tormenting, [Nietzsche] becomes for us the mirror of our own souls. . . . He is indeed a résumé of modernity, but in that he has epitomized it, he has perhaps at the same time completed it and may help us to go beyond it. So at least we may hope."[126] In Nietzschean thought and Nietzscheism, Urban, like so many others at the turn of the last century, discovered the moral problems that would define the century ahead; and in Nietzsche he discovered a human, all-too-human modern persona struggling with them. But as Urban's own unresolved engagement demonstrates, Nietzsche posed moral problems that one cannot necessarily work through but rather must learn to live with.

# The Soul of Man
# under Modernity

"Whither is God? . . . I will tell you. *We have killed him*—you and I. All of us are his murderers. . . . Do we hear nothing as yet of the noise of the gravediggers who are burying God? Do we smell nothing as yet of the divine decomposition? . . . What was holiest and mightiest of all that the world has yet owned has bled to death under our knives: who will wipe this blood off us? What water is there for us to clean ourselves? What festivals of atonement, what sacred games shall we have to invent? Is not the greatness of this deed too great for us? Must we ourselves not become gods simply to appear worthy of it? There has never been a greater deed; and whoever is born after us—for the sake of this deed he will belong to a higher history than all history hitherto."
    FRIEDRICH NIETZSCHE, *The Gay Science* (1882)

They have got rid of the Christian God, and now feel obliged to cling all the more firmly to Christian morality. . . . When one gives up Christian belief one thereby deprives oneself of the right to Christian morality.
    FRIEDRICH NIETZSCHE, *Twilight of the Idols* (1889)

There is *master-morality* and *slave-morality*. . . . In the first case, when it is the rulers who determine the conception "good," it is the exalted, proud disposition which is regarded as the distinguishing feature, and that which determines the order of rank. . . . The noble type of man regards *himself* as a determiner of values; he does not require to be approved of; he passes the judgment: . . . . He is a *creator of values*. . . . It is otherwise with the second type of morality, *slave-morality*. Supposing that the abused, the oppressed, the suffering, the unemancipated, the weary, and those uncertain of themselves should moralize, what will be the common element in their moral estimates? Probably a pessimistic suspicion with regard to the entire situation of man will find expression. The slave has an unfavourable eye for the virtues of the powerful; he has a skepticism and distrust, . . . he would fain persuade himself that the very happiness there is not genuine. On the other hand, *those* qualities which serve to alleviate the existence of sufferers are brought into prominence and flooded with light; it is here that sympathy, the kind, helping hand, the warm heart, patience, diligence, humility, and friendliness attain to honour; for here these are the most useful qualities, and almost the only means of supporting the burden of existence. Slave-morality is essentially the morality of utility.

FRIEDRICH NIETZSCHE, *Beyond Good and Evil* (1886)

Friedrich Nietzsche is remembered today as a thinker whose condemnations of modern Christianity brought the simmering tensions between nineteenth-century religious faith and secular knowledge to the boiling point. Conventional wisdom casts him as an unapologetic atheist unafraid to do the dirty work of post-Enlightenment thought. With ruthless glee, he rushed in where Kant and Darwin feared to tread, reaching skyward to pull God from his celestial throne, and ensuring that His falling corpse brought down with it the entire moral, spiritual, and psychic apparatus of institutional Christianity as it somersaulted to earth.

Nietzsche speculated about his posthumous reputation in much the same terms. He recognized that in his own day few had ears to hear his glad tidings of liberation from Christianity, "mankind's greatest misfortune," with its "conception of God" "pitiable, absurd, harmful, not merely an error but a *crime against life.*" Particularly deaf were his contemporaries who embraced modern knowledge but not its consequences for their faith. It was pious moderns who had yet to realize that "what was formerly merely morbid" had become "indecent—it is indecent to be a Christian today." But he also insisted that their time, *his* time, would come. "If there is today still no lack of those" who had yet to realize that Christianity had overstayed its welcome in "the modern age," Nietzsche averred, "well, they will know it tomorrow."[1] When they did, he insisted, they would recognize his philosophy as a monumental event in human history, and his name the designation of a new era: "I know my fate. One day my name will be associated with the memory of something tremendous—a crisis without equal on earth, the most profound collision of conscience," a historic rupture with "everything that had been believed, demanded, hallowed so far."[2]

If Nietzsche expected to be memorialized as an unrivaled force against Christianity, and his philosophy a watershed event in the history of morals, his religious American readers fulfilled his expectations. In the first decades of the twentieth century, diverse Christian observers—Protestant and Catholic, liberal and orthodox, clergy and laity—participated in a heated discourse about the implications of Nietzsche's dramatic critique of their faith and its prospects at the dawn of a new century. Readily appropriating the dramatic terms with which Nietzsche characterized himself and his "immoralism," religious commentators cast him as the modern believer's bête noir, and his philosophy as the most potent intellectual threat to faith to emerge from the nineteenth century. Quick to recognize Nietzsche's growing following, Christian theologians and clergy were zealous about deflecting his power to seduce the faithful from the safe harbor of Christian living. As traditional arbiters of the moral life, they felt that they were particularly well poised to diagnose Nietzsche's appeal in the broader culture.[3] Together they wondered: Why were Americans trying to find meaning in Nietzsche's frenzied texts when all the keys to life's riches could be found in the Bible? Why were moderns joining Nietzsche's restless search for truth when in Jesus it had already been found?

Religious observers feigned no amazement that Nietzsche had found adherents among Americans who had drifted from Christianity. In their zeal to profile Nietzsche's American followers, they surveyed the modern social types for whom religion had lost its moral force. They singled out the university professoriate, natural scientists, bohemian artists, liberated women, and captains of industry for promoting Nietzsche's dangerous wares. But by surveying the intellectual and cultural domains where an indifference, even hostility, to Christian teaching and practice was thought to dwell, Christian commentators illuminated only the most obvious sources of the American Nietzsche vogue. In their vigilance to identify secular sources of American Nietzscheism, theologians and clerics failed to appreciate their own roles in spreading his gospel.

In the opening years of the twentieth century, Methodist, Unitarian, Presbyterian, Baptist, Lutheran, Anglican, and Roman Catholic commentators contributed significantly to the growing discussion about Nietzsche in religious magazines, books, and theological journals, and some clergy even devoted sermons to his life and thought. He provided them with a language to talk about the conditions of modern faith. He offered new concepts, such as "slave and master morality" and "*ressentiment*," while breathing new life into old ones, such as "asceticism," and in doing so provided them with analytically robust, rhetorically powerful, and, most important, exceedingly porous terms to articulate their concerns. Sometimes symbolic, more often literal, here as heartless misanthrope, there as brutal intellect, Nietzsche's multivalent image proved to be an indispensable resource for religious moderns to come to terms with the warring moral impulses both within their faith and between Christianity and secular culture. He gave them an opportunity to dust off what for many had become an artifact of primitive Christianity—the Antichrist—and use it to describe his menacing image for modern society. Nietzsche's religious readers invoked him as an unavoidable foe in modern life, and in doing so, unwittingly contributed to the Nietzsche fascination in the United States. By acknowledging Nietzsche's significance—however pernicious—for modern thought and morality, his religious interpreters helped secure what might have been a passing intellectual fashion as an authoritative philosophy.

The diverse uses of Nietzsche's image and ideas established a vibrant interpretive field for religious moderns to articulate their concerns about the prospects for Christianity in the new century. Turn-of-the-century Christians encountered Nietzsche's philosophy during a period of institutional and intellectual ferment in American churches. Their writings testify to a growing concern about the church's diminishing sphere of influence in a modernizing society. Industrialization, urbanization, and immigration created economic and social upheaval, which even the most liberal church leaders were slow to comprehend. A growing capitalist leisure economy offered department stores and dance halls as spaces for fellowship and recreation that competed with church services and social clubs.[4] Adding to Christian observers' concerns about the shrinking realm of the church's social relevance was the prospect that Christian cosmology might prove unable to fulfill the new psychic and intellectual demands of modern Americans. Amid the growing influence of evolutionary theories on social thought, which contributed to a picture of a dynamic world and its humanity in constant flux and transformation, Christians of all denominations were pressed to articulate the permanence of Christian truth in a seemingly impermanent universe.[5] How to demonstrate that a two-thousand-year-old gospel was no artifact of an ancient morality but a transcendent source of living values and wisdom for people in the present? Speaking for "custodians of . . . faith" who sought to demonstrate the continued relevance of Christianity, Shailer Mathews, dean of the University of Chicago Divinity School and advocate of the Social Gospel movement, warned, "A religion that cannot meet the deepest longings of restless hearts, . . . that makes respectability its morality, that would muzzle scientific inquiry will be ignored by a world that has outgrown it." Mathews understood that moderns hungry for spiritual and psychic nourishment, and a new ethics to address new realities, could no longer be satisfied with the spiritual "crusts of yesterday."[6]

Nietzsche gave custodians of faith good reason to worry about the diminished authority of and prospects for the church in the new century. His sustained attacks on their inherited religious beliefs provided a disturbing picture of a world in which their settled truths were merely human strategies for ordering a disordered universe. In book after book, he presented an account of a faith that located universals where none existed. His genealogical treatment of Christian cosmology suggested that all its foundations—its belief in an omniscient, all-powerful God, the divinity of Jesus, the premise of otherworldly redemption and resurrection—were products of human invention and imagination, creations to meet the psychic needs of man. Likewise he claimed that the entire ethical basis of Christian belief, animated by the principle of love of neighbor, had human, not divine, origins. Christian belief, piety, and practice, he stressed repeatedly and stridently, were simply historical inventions that had calcified over the millennia into cultural conventions. Long before Einstein inadvertently gave religious moderns reason to worry that God played dice with the universe simply by insisting that He didn't, Nietzsche haunted them with a picture of a topsy-turvy, indeterminate world absent a God altogether.

As we shall see, early twentieth-century American religious engagement with Nietzsche encourages a reappraisal of Protestant religiosity of the period as one awash in liberal, progressive sanguinity. Given the dominance of Protestant liberal theology at the major divinity schools and seminaries, and the prominence of the Social Gospel movement in Progressive-Era America, scholars have argued that a buoyant optimism marked mainstream Protestant theology at least until 1917 and thrived until the ascendance of a chastened Neo-Orthodoxy in the Depression years. And indeed, as we look across denominational lines, it is undeniable that both liberals and conservatives increasingly disavowed older conceptions of original sin and biblical infallibility, and conceived of the Kingdom of God in sociological and ethical rather than in millennial terms.[7] However, Protestants' sometimes vexed, sometimes appreciative, always uncomfortable relationship with Nietzsche reveals their doubts, if not latent pessimism, about their insistence on an immanent God whose will unfolds in the evolution of human affairs, and could be examined with the aid of secular knowledge. Nietzsche forced even the most liberal, worldly-minded Protestants to reconsider their own receptivity to secular knowledge and culture.

And yet, as one minister writing for *Bibliotheca Sacra* put it, the "bewitching power" of Nietzsche's frontal assault on Christian fundamentals captured the imagination of religious people, even "in spite of [Nietzsche's] pronounced irreligion." He concurred with a fellow commentator who stated, "No one can think, and escape Nietzsche."[8] The power of the philosopher's ideas was everywhere apparent, and religious commentators agreed that if any institution could put an end to what another religious observer called the "Nietzsche madness," it was the church.[9] But in their effort to call a halt to the Nietzsche epidemic that they believed had taken hold of nonreligious and antireligious Americans, religious commentators became unwitting carriers of the disease. Indeed, Nietzsche's ideas found entry into the American moral imagination through the most unlikely of promoters: men of the cloth.[10]

Both Protestant and Catholic custodians of faith worried about the dangers of a writer armed with a bracing intellect, savage wit, pitch-perfect historical sense, and haunting prophetic voice who wanted nothing less than to annihilate their religion. However, if Nietzsche's philosophy was a poison to Christian hegemony in the modern world, it could also serve as a balm that might help strengthen and revitalize the core of Christian belief. They reasoned that if Nietzsche forced them to identify inconsistencies in and outmoded aspects of Christianity, then he had surely done them an inestimable favor.

However, as useful as Nietzsche's philosophy was in enabling them to contemplate the conditions of their faith, none was willing to dispense with the Christian life that he so despised. To the contrary (and despite their own understanding of Nietzsche as a threat to modern Christianity), they creatively appropriated his ideas to defend the very object of his greatest scorn. Thus, the religious uses of Nietzsche are less a study of how his ideas transformed religious thought than a story of how religious readers imaginatively appropriated, adapted, and domesticated his ideas in their effort to reassert their flagging moral authority in modernizing America. Nietzsche's philosophy made important contributions to turn-of-the-century Christian apologetics in America, and thus proved itself a crucial if unlikely resource for strengthening religious commitments and overcoming the crises facing institutional religion as it backed its way into a new century.

## Nietzsche and the Problems of Modern Thought

Though assessments of Nietzsche's ideas ranged widely among his religious interpreters, all agreed that his philosophy represented alternately a herald, exemplar, or symptom of the problems of modern secular knowledge. They cast Nietzsche in the role of the "*enfant terrible* of modern thought," the most demanding of the "modern critics of Christianity," and "the most radical thinker of modern times."[11] The adjective *modern* wafted around invocations of Nietzsche like a smoky veil, and yet there was little agreement as to just what, both in theory and in practice, being modern actually meant. Was it defined by the rejection of Christian values, or simply the absence of them? Was modern man pessimistic and nihilistic? Or was he naively optimistic about an unbounded moral universe and thus too immature to accept the incongruities of human existence? The dramatically varying definitions of "modern man" and the "modern age" expressed by pious Americans in the early twentieth century demonstrate the degree to which the meaning of modernity was far from a settled fact.[12] What they could agree on, however, was that Nietzsche represented "more than a mere name, he is a system of thought, a 'Weltanschauung,' an intellectual power," whose philosophy presented challenges more sweeping than other secular philosophies that sought to strip Christian cosmology of its authority.[13] Indeed, his writings carried the logic of this de-divinizing impulse to its extreme, challenging not only the transcendence of God but also all scientific and moral claims to universality. The contested ways in which religious thinkers enlisted Nietzsche to come to terms with "modernity" reveal their shared sense that they were being drawn into a new moral universe. Nietzsche's philosophy enabled Christian commentators to articulate their uncertainty about their inherited customs, beliefs, and institutions and to contemplate their future prospects as authorities on the good life. Though they were not always sure how to make sense of the phenomenon of modernity, the arrival of Nietzsche's philosophy in America signaled that they would have to act fast to shore up the church's ruins if they wanted it to survive and indeed prosper in the twentieth century.

The ambiguities about the constitutive elements of modern thought are reflected in discussions of Nietzsche's philosophy. Religious commentators wrestled over the appropriate philosophical label for his philosophy. His thought was described alternatively as materialistic, subjective, relativistic, positivistic, historicist, nominalistic, phenomenological, monistic, romantic, atheistic, immoralist, pragmatist, hedonistic, epicurean, ascetic, and stoic, and sometimes several of the above, even in the same discussion. However, there was general agreement that Nietzsche's philosophy embodied the naturalistic impulse of the nineteenth-century secular philosophies and sciences, which forced a dramatic reassessment of biblical authority in modern life. The wrestling over terminology reveals that while many commentators understood *modern* as a moral rather than a temporal designation, there was little consensus about what constituted its oppositional features. Though Protestant commentators from all the mainline denominations debated the intellectual dimensions of modernity, it was conservative Protestant theologians who sought to define with greater precision how Nietzsche exemplified the troubling features of secular knowledge.

Efforts to incorporate Nietzsche's philosophy into the Protestant worldview reflect a long tradition within Reformed theology of drawing insights from the natural and human sciences for the purpose of doctrinal and ethical reform.[14] Since the early modern period, the Reformed theological tradition had emphasized the importance of individual sensory experience and reason to investigate the divine design of the universe. In the nineteenth century, developments in biblical criticism reflected liberal Protestants' continued efforts to make advances in philosophy serviceable to their faith.[15] This amicability toward secular knowledge continued into the twentieth century as Protestant commentators attempted to incorporate Nietzsche's thought into their religious worldview. And yet conservative Protestants, in particular, used Nietzsche as a way to question that long-standing amicability.

Conservative Protestants argued that Nietzsche's historicism and naturalism characterized the tendencies in modern thought that sought to breach the authority of scriptural revelation. George S. Patton, professor of moral philosophy at Princeton University and regular contributor to the bulwark of conservative Presbyterian theology, the *Princeton Theological Review*, argued that while theologians must not subject Christianity to the fanciful intellectual demands of the age, "orthodox theologians" could not ignore the implications of this "*Modephilosoph der Zeit.*" As the son of Francis Landey Patton, the conservative theologian and former president of Princeton University who was persuaded to resign due to his poor administrative skills by the university's nonclerical trustees (and replaced by the layman Woodrow Wilson), the younger Patton sought to carry on his father's tradition of fighting liberalizing forces in theology. Nietzsche's significance for theologians, Patton suggested, was not his hostility to Christianity as such but rather his questioning of Christian moral standards. Patton pointed to Nietzsche's discussion of the origin of Christian values in *On the Genealogy of Morals* as an example of how historicism, pushed to its logical conclusion, enabled him to "impugn the validity of all moral ideas by tracing their origin." The problem with Nietzsche, as with all those caught up in this genealogical impulse, is that he employed it not to better understand scriptural authority but to undermine it. By arguing that divine ideals had a human origin, Nietzsche sought not simply to criticize Christian moral values but to *"put in question the value of these values."* Having stripped Christian values of any divine authorship, Nietzsche had no recourse but to fall either back onto a biological basis of morality, or forward into the abyss of no morality at all. Though Patton argued that it was important for conservative theologians to keep attuned to developments in modern secular thought, Nietzsche's example showed why they should avoid the mistake of liberal Protestants, who sought to incorporate it.[16]

A number of Nietzsche's religious readers recognized that his radical historicist impulse presented intractable epistemological and ethical challenges for those who engaged it. Even liberal Protestants, like Unitarian Charles C. Everett, dean of Harvard's nondenominational divinity school, normally eager to keep theology apace with developments in other arenas of moral and natural inquiry, argued that Nietzsche's philosophy made things difficult for the would-be accommodating theologian. After all, Nietzsche was no run-of-the-mill atheist: "to deny the *ideals* of morality which have commanded the reverence if not the obedience of men for so many ages is something different." Nietzsche's troubling innovation was not his challenge to the notion that one people or religion has a lock on the "Absolute"—a notion which, given his sensitivity to interdenominationalism, he was predisposed to appreciate—but rather his challenge to the "Absolute" as such. "It is this recognition of an Absolute that allies philosophy with religion. The Absolute of the philosopher and the God of Religion are different forms of the same thing." But in Nietzsche, even science is denied its universality; he described it as just another version of monotheism, which believes that truth is One. Thus, by cutting both religion and science loose from all divine and material necessity, he not only denied them their coercive powers for the moral life, he also asserted that no realm of inquiry could furnish any "absolute truth" on which a mutual moral life might be built.[17]

On this liberals and conservatives could agree: the church may have had her enemies over the centuries, but none had threatened the very foundations of the Christian life as had Nietzsche. His claims were alarming: once religious belief goes, so goes its ethics. Identifying Nietzsche as the spokesperson for modern critics "who have seen that Christian ethics have no rock-basis apart from Christian dogma," a writer for the *Living Age* argued that Nietzsche had it right: without belief in Jesus Christ as savior, the morals of Christianity made no sense. As Nietzsche observed, secular moderns sought to exalt the ideals of humanitarianism and democracy while forsaking the Christian faith from which they sprang. Thus, it was liberal moderns who proved to be even more timid than religious fundamentalists, for their whole ethical worldview was now founded on a lie: they had dropped the metaphysics of Christianity but not its ethics, assuming them to be universal. Nietzsche's antifoundationalism wasn't cheery, but at least it was logically consistent: Christian ethics without Christian faith is unsustainable.[18]

Religious critics reasoned that if Nietzsche were the standard-bearer of developments in modern thought, then there was clearly little to recommend it to the Christian mind. Southern Presbyterian minister and theologian Thomas Cary Johnson identified "Nietzscheism" as a seductive but degenerate "modern ism," which mistakenly substituted the husks of secular knowledge for the core of biblical revelation. Nietzsche's problem, Johnson argued, was that he was shadowboxing with a fictive Christianity, a "caricature" of God and Christian ethics he inherited from "soulless externalities" of German higher criticism. Nietzsche rightly condemned his own tradition of intellectualized ethics apart from faith, but his mistake was to assume that the modernized Christianity of twentieth-century liberal Protestantism contained any of the truths of scripture. So while Johnson argued that "Nietzsche is the apostle of positive ungodliness," he also saw in him a helpful "foe" to the "negative ungodliness" of "enlightened" modern ethics, preferring the German God-baiter to the latter. Nietzsche's mistake, however, was to inject his godless will to power in the place of "enlightened" Christianity, thereby showing that even modern thought at its most challenging defaults to a crude pessimism. The value of Nietzsche's lesson, then, was to show Christians the slippery slope of modern thought, demonstrating once and for all why "the Church and the world should be clearly demarked."[19]

Despite the picture of early twentieth-century progressive optimism among mainline Protestants, the religious interest in Nietzsche among conservatives and, as we shall see, liberals, demonstrates a persistent ambivalence about the place of secular knowledge in modern Protestant theology. Nietzsche's extreme example of the atheistic pull of historicism and naturalism thus contributed to a growing critique from both without and within early twentieth-century Protestantism's efforts to naturalize Christian ethics. But as the debates around Nietzsche suggest, the religious dilemma facing modern Protestants was not only the tension between religion and the secular world but the competing psychic appeal of theological orthodoxy and liberalism within Protestantism itself. While orthodoxy's commitment to the impervious truth of dogma proved increasingly incongruous with modern views of a dynamic material world, liberalism overvalued the freedom that comes with a world-in-process, and failed to appreciate the psychic benefits of belief in a stable moral universe. While religious moderns sought the assurances of fundamental truths found in orthodoxy and the permissiveness found in liberal Protestantism, the two seemed increasingly difficult to reconcile. As Nietzsche's religious readers demonstrate, they may have yearned for modern freedom more than truth, but they were coming to wonder whether they needed truth more than freedom.

Nietzsche's Catholic and liberal Protestant readers also shared the concern about his influence on modern theology. Despite the spectrum of interpretations, Nietzsche's religious readers' responses to his philosophy exhibited an increasingly chastened view of the implications of the historicist and materialist impulses in modern thought. And yet they also agreed that Nietzsche's critiques could not go unanswered. As Patton recognized, Nietzsche gladly "touch[ed] the ark without fear, and without reverence penetrate[d] into the holy of holies. He will not be repressed or silenced." If modern Christianity hoped to weather his boundless assaults, then Nietzsche "must in the first place be understood, and not ignored or refuted." Patton added, "Nietzsche himself says [that] 'one refutes a thing by laying it respectfully on ice. . . .' But one cannot refute Nietzsche by laying him respectfully on ice . . . [because] he has far too much vitality to freeze to death."[20] American ministers and theologians thus grudgingly agreed with Nietzsche's assertion that "what does not kill me makes me stronger," accepting his challenges to their faith as an opportunity to reinvigorate it.[21] But they also agreed that the battle for the modern American soul was a zero-sum game: moderns would cleave their spirits and moral imagination either to Nietzsche or to Christ.

## Unapologetic Catholic Apologetics

Although Nietzsche's reception among religious readers did not track neatly along denominational lines, his early twentieth-century Catholic commentators tended to be deeply critical of, though comparatively untroubled by, his attacks on Christianity. Like many of their Protestant counterparts, they accused Nietzsche of being a false prophet whose seductive philosophy could wreak havoc on innocent minds, and a modern Mephistopheles who made bargains with marginal Christians willing to forgo the eternal for a life of earthly pleasures. However, they found his philosophy more useful than threatening, for it exemplified the misguided impulses of naturalism and relativism in modern speculative thought hostile to Catholic teachings. Though comparatively limited in scope, Catholic engagement with Nietzsche's thought shared a concern about the implications of modern thought for religious piety and practice, as well as a concern about the prospects for Roman Catholicism in modernizing America.

Like Nietzsche's pious Protestant readers, Catholic interpreters focused on his assertions about the outmoded nature of Christianity in the modern world. "Is dogma out of date?" asked a Catholic commentator responding to challenges from "fashionable notions of the present day," which viewed religious creeds and dogmas as "belated survivals" of a premodern world well lost.[22] Though not indifferent to the challenges of modernity for Roman Catholicism, they argued that the question of theological relevance itself reflected the destructive tendency in modern thought to view knowledge and values as mutable, variable, and progressive. The problem for Catholics was not that their faith was outsized by modern problems but that moderns were too willing to substitute natural philosophy for supernatural religion, and the winds of speculation for the Rock of Ages. They took delight in Nietzsche's own insistence that a despiritualized Christianity was too flimsy a foundation for Christian ethics, and thus used Nietzsche to critique liberalizing tendencies in Protestantism to divorce ethics from religion. As one writer for the *American Catholic Quarterly Review* put it, the "Broad, Liberal attitude," that in "every denomination there is a certain residuum of basic dogma common to all, which suffices. . . . This all sounds very charitable and tolerant, the main objection to it being that it is utter nonsense."[23] Nietzsche's Catholic interpreters insisted that only those who are captivated by the mystique of historicism and naturalism fall prey to the challenge that religious truth cannot have permanent validity. Their message was plain: if you adhere to the one true church, Nietzsche's critiques were no problem.

American Catholic commentators on Nietzsche argued that the premise of his philosophy reflected the fundamental flaw of nineteenth-century secular thought: the belief in a world in flux. By granting a variable universe, and by expecting that moral problems could be resolved through man's immanent intellectual powers rather than their transcendent source, liberal moderns opened themselves to the problems of competing moral codes which lacked legislative force. Expressing widespread sentiment among Catholic leadership, the writer and priest Thomas J. Gerrard equated "Modern Theories" with "Moral Disaster," likening them to a "radical disease" tearing moderns from their moral and intellectual anchors.[24] Nietzsche's Catholic interpreters thus overwhelmingly asserted that only religious moderns who accept the heresy of a changing universe feel the pressure to bring their theology up to date. They leave themselves open to moral relativism and thus have no response to Nietzsche, who would gladly "clear away" Christianity as the mere "'accumulated rubbish' of the centuries." "Modernity" loses both its glamour and its terror once the searching soul recognizes what has long ago been found in the "One, World-wide, Infallible, Indestructible," unchanging firmament of unified truth: the Catholic Church.[25]

There were Catholic dissenters from the dominant critique of Nietzschean subjectivity, though, and none as controversial as Maude D. Petre. In a series of six widely read articles on Nietzsche in 1905 and 1906 for the New Jersey–based Paulist periodical *The Catholic World*, Petre, a British Roman Catholic nun and prolific author, offered an appreciative assessment of his philosophy for practicing Christians.[26] Her analyses of Nietzsche's view of religion, art, morality, and human character, as well as his personal character and literary style, form the earliest and also the most atypical Catholic analyses of Nietzsche, and won her the attention and admiration of religious and nonreligious American readers alike. Even the atheist H. L. Mencken praised her effort to "rescue Nietzsche from the misunderstandings of Christian critics," noting that her analyses were some of the "best" he had "ever encountered."[27] Petre's studied interest in Nietzsche continued as she translated poetry in the 1910 English edition of his *Joyful Wisdom* under the editorship of Oscar Levy. Indeed, Nietzsche continued to shape her religious imagination as she went on to write extensively about the Roman Catholic faith and its relationship to the modern sciences, political thought, and moral inquiry.

Her essays are significant not only for their analysis of Nietzsche's moral vision but also because they illuminate why his Catholic opponents recoiled from his philosophy.

In her analysis of Nietzsche's "anti-moralism," Petre recognized the features of his thought so threatening to pious moderns. For one, Nietzsche's philosophy advocated a complete departure from unified truth. He argued for the relativity of knowledge, characterizing it as partial, provisional, and even arbitrary. By stripping God and truth of their prestige, so too did Nietzsche challenge the Christian notion of a world endowed with divine intention, historical telos, moral purpose, and even causality. With his rejection of causality, Nietzsche also dispensed with the "whole system of objective morality," for man's limited perception prevents him from distinguishing "when we move ourselves, and when it is other objects that are moving." Nietzsche described a world where human objectivity and moral universality were fictions of the Christian worldview that masked the will to power—the sole agent of history and the defining feature of the human condition. Petre characterized his theory of master morality as one defined by "naked egoism," a "denial of responsibility, guilt, and sin," for "he believed that the highest natures create their own precedents, and are, consequently, incapable of sin."[28] By challenging the existence of God, unified truth, and moral purpose, Nietzsche seemed to have nothing left of the Christian worldview.

Petre's studies detailing Nietzsche's philosophical assault on Christianity were published just before the "modernist controversy" erupted in the Catholic Church internationally. Her articles highlighted precisely those aspects of modern thought that had so raised the hackles of Catholics at the turn of the century. Her interest in Nietzsche's value for Catholic moderns demonstrates their restlessness with scholastic thought, and their eagerness to blend religious thinking with new forms of scientific knowledge. A prominent figure in Catholic modernism internationally, Petre was a friend and biographer of two of the most important figures in the movement, Alfred Loisy of France and George Tyrrell of England, and herself a leading force in trying to reconcile Roman Catholic theology with insights from biblical criticism, Darwinism, and pragmatism. The modernists pressed for a reformulation of doctrine which, contrary to scholastic doctrine, asserted that church dogmas are not of divine origins but are the products of human interpretation of the scriptures. In addition, they stressed the importance of sensory experience over doctrinal authority as a fund for religious insight, an idea that put them perilously close to liberal Protestant theology. Nietzsche's radical historicism exemplified the very features of modern thought condemned in Pope Pius X's 1907 encyclical letter, *Pascendi dominici gregis*, in which he chastised the "doctrine of the Modernists" as the "synthesis of all heresies," and ushered in a campaign to prevent members of the church from incorporating secular falsehoods into the Catholic faith.[29] The pope's encyclical evoked a positive response among American Catholics, who praised its rejection of modernist influences as "a recovery of our brightest Catholic tradition," and its protection of the wisdom of Catholicism from the intellectual "dangers that beset it."[30]

Petre's commitment to Roman Catholicism combined with her openness to mental and moral subjectivism formed a rare alchemy among early twentieth-century Catholics. Her exposure to thinkers like Nietzsche did not strip her of her faith. She argued that despite Nietzsche's professed atheism, his life and thought offered much for Catholics to admire. His was a "strenuous," "suffering," "unselfish" "life militant" marked by "purity, integrity, [and] utter unworldliness."[31] Despite being the sweetheart of libertine artists and writers, Nietzsche criticized the decadence and pessimism of modern aesthetics. Likewise, the goal of his celebration of free will and his critique of sin was not an orgiastic "self-abandonment, but . . . strong self-possession; a mastering of one's own life and conduct" and a recognition that true contrition is not legislated from without but cultivated from within a deep reverence for the "mysterious laws of our being." Petre insisted that in Nietzsche, Catholics could find a fellow seeker of moral strenuousness: "There is to be here no dilettantism, but sheer hard work."[32]

That a Catholic nun would turn to an "anti-Christian," "anti-feminist" thinker for moral inspiration would be a novel curiosity, were her uses of Nietzsche exceptional. However, when we examine her strategies for reading Nietzsche's criticisms of women and feminism as subtle endorsements of them, we see an approach that was increasingly common among appreciative feminists for making Nietzsche a prophet for women, and a fellow freedom fighter rattling the gilded cage of domesticity. In her essay "Nietzsche the Anti-Feminist," Petre admitted that Nietzsche had plenty of nasty things to say about women, but he did so to air more general grievances with modern society, ones which his female readers shared. Nietzsche despised feminism, she argued, much in the same way he hated all forms of human development, which are legislated from without. "The highest freedom is that which we win for ourselves and which no other can win for us," she declared. "Freedom is not a stereotyped, material possession," discharged from external authority, but the acquisition of "self-activity." Petre subtly acknowledged that Nietzsche "overlooked" the fact that society plays an important role in training individuals, making available or denying opportunities for them to exercise this "self-activity." But she suggested that to quibble about social structures, though important, missed Nietzsche's insight, that "it is the greatest mistake to confound liberty with the possession of certain external privileges," and that doing so often makes the weak beholden to the very oppressors whom they asked to grant them. Similarly, Nietzsche's criticisms of romantic love, Petre argued, were important for modern women who think it an unalloyed good. When Nietzsche wrote, for example, that "sexual love betray[s] itself as an impulse of appropriation," he was not mistaken in his estimation that oftentimes what passes for love is really the desire to possess, an instinctual form of *ressentiment* that women would do well to recognize.[33] It is, of course, interesting that a nun would turn to a philosopher who likely had very few sexual relationships for insights on sex—but again, this simply shows an exaggerated version of the gerrymandering involved in a variety of Nietzsche appropriations made by commentators of the period.

In Petre's estimation, both male and female Catholics could benefit from "the anti-Christian" Nietzsche as "our enemy and yet our friend," for his moral insights, properly utilized, required not the abandonment of Catholicism but an experimental rethinking of its nature and meaning.[34] She quickly learned, however, that her efforts to enhance her Catholic faith with modern philosophical inquiry were unwelcome with church authorities. A year after publishing her Nietzsche studies, she was refused the sacraments in her diocese, and thus discovered that her effort to incorporate Nietzschean intellectual independence into her faith was a Sisyphean task.[35]

Despite Petre's openness to Nietzsche's philosophy, most American Catholic commentators used it as evidence of both the spiritual and the psychic dangers of modern thought. In their view, none were more susceptible to dangerous secular theories like Nietzsche's than Protestants, in part because his mistakes reflected the long-standing errors of Protestant thinking. But Nietzsche's misguidedness offered salutary lessons about the failures of Protestantism. His failures demonstrated how Protestantism's rationalist approach to the Word of the Bible and its historical openness to scientific thinking stretched biblical authority too thin. By hoisting will above Word, and by failing to appreciate human intellect as a finite and imperfect faculty, Luther had sent early modern theology along a dangerous course that led straight to Nietzsche. What they both failed to realize, and what the Roman Catholic Church had always stressed, is that *true* free will is not intellect unhindered but human will working in cooperation with God's grace. Catholic interpreters thus felt compelled to highlight the *Protestant* roots of Nietzsche's errors, employing his philosophy as evidence of the dangerous worldliness of the liberal Protestantism that dominated American public life during the Progressive Era.[36]

Assured that Nietzsche's emphasis on free will and subjective truth was nothing more than the bitter fruit of Protestantism, American Catholic commentators could offer their sympathy for the wayward Protestant thinker. In a 1916 lengthy critique of Nietzsche's philosophy in *American Catholic Quarterly Review*, Joseph B. Jacobi lamented that "Nietzsche joined that throng of disorderly pilgrims who have substituted inquiry for belief and become seekers after the unknown." Nietzsche's titanic soul struggles, his groping after truth unaided by the light of the Lord, Jacobi assured his readers, brought him to that critical moment when "the authority of Catholic teaching" could have saved him from his descent into madness. Echoing a sentiment common to Catholic interpretations of Nietzsche's philosophy and biography, Jacobi noted how both were the results of a tragic accident of birth: "Had he not been the son of a Protestant clergyman, but rather the son of Catholic parents, and had his education been Catholic, the spirit of revolt against Christianity would have been changed to admiration of Catholic philosophy and theology, and there would have been a different story to tell." It was Nietzsche's bad fortune that he was nursed on the milk of Protestant individualism and not nourished by "the bosom of that [Catholic] Church the structure of which has in very truth been built upon the foundation of the impregnable and imperishable rock." Nietzsche's insanity thus served as an important reminder for modern Protestants: truth is one, timeless, and universal, and need not be sought but rather found in the one true church.[37]

Nietzsche's wider and more favorable reception among Protestants exasperated Catholic readers who saw it as yet another sign of Protestantism's all-too-worldly conception of the Christian faith. It was folly, they argued, to read fanciful metaphysics into Nietzsche, or to soften the blow of his blasphemous critiques by viewing them as poetic license. According to James Martin Gillis, a Paulist priest and prominent conservative editor of the *Catholic World* from 1922 to 1948, too many "Christian writers, curiously sympathetic with Nietzsche, after explaining that he is easily misunderstood, have

attempted to read into his attack upon morality a plea for a higher morality."
In "False Prophets," a series of lectures on the misguided heralds of modernity delivered at St. Paul's Cathedral in New York City, Gillis sought to
set the record straight. In his view, Nietzschean godlessness represented all
that was sick and morally depraved in modern life. Nietzsche advocated a
topsy-turvy moral universe, and thus underscored the gross licentiousness
and libertinism of modern culture. For Gillis, Nietzsche's haunting vision
of a post-Christian world required no interpretation. While true Christians
aimed to build a common life based on the Golden Rule, Nietzsche sought to
free the aristocratic superman to trample on the weak and to run roughshod
on all bonds of human love and obligation. Gillis criticized liberal Protestant
readers who tried to tease a religious message out of Nietzsche's philosophy:
"Any attempt to make immoralism moral can result only in a *tour de force*."[38]

Even Catholic theologians like Gillis, who were among Nietzsche's
staunchest and most visible American opponents, stressed that Nietzsche's
philosophy did not signal the closing of the accounts for religion. Nietzsche
forced all moderns to make a critical choice between the Christian and the
"Christiano-pagan" view of man's existence. But Gillis added the caveat that
while "true faith" was incompatible with secular knowledge, it was not "anti-
modern." To the contrary, Roman Catholicism was compatible with modernity. Catholics, he argued, were able to accept the stresses and strains of
modern civilization, because "the basis of our confidence is . . . spiritual and
supernatural." While the modern sciences had "made the colossal blunder of
attempting to exile God," Catholicism understood that "morality and social
progress" must have their "foundation in religion, or they will have no foundation at all. And when I say religion, I do not mean a devitalized 'natural'
religion [that is, "Christiano-pagan" Protestantism]. I mean faith in God and
in a supernatural relationship between God and Man." Nietzsche's philosophy was therefore useful insofar as it provided Gillis with the perfect artillery
as he railed against liberal Protestantism. He argued that the consistency
with which Nietzsche denounced the church made him a worthier foe than
Protestants who sought to dilute the gospel of Christ with their liberal, ac-
commodationist sensibilities. Voicing a sentiment dominant among Catholic interpreters of Nietzsche, Gillis insisted that while Christ's gospel of love
pointed to the great eternal hereafter, Nietzsche's life-denying paganism led
inexorably to spiritual castration. The option for modern Americans, Gillis
concluded, came down to a simple choice between "Christ . . . or Chaos."[39]

While Catholics typically employed Nietzsche to distinguish Catholicism from an all-too-worldly Protestantism, both Catholics and Protestants agreed that Nietzsche's assaults on Christianity helped the faith more than they hurt it. Even the modernist-friendly critic Petre argued that Nietzsche's supreme contribution was his facilitation of a reaffirmation of religious faith: "we can learn from [Nietzsche] something that will enrich the truths we already possess."[40] Nietzsche thus identified and exemplified the problems of secular philosophy as a source of values and meanings. He demonstrated that philosophy was no substitute for religion, man no substitute for God; and in doing so, that religion still had a future in modern America.

## The Social Gospel and the Practicability of Christianity

Among turn-of-the-century Christians who worried about the modern forces undermining religious faith and practice, none addressed the question of Christianity's relevance for the problems of modern living as consistently and forcefully as did the theologians, clergy, and lay activists drawn to the Social Gospel movement. In the words of William R. Hutchison, a "sharpened note of 'crisis'" characterizes the writings of these socially progressive and politically engaged liberal Protestants, eager to see their faith realized in the social realm.[41] Propelled by a sense of urgency about the increasingly menacing social problems posed by industrial capitalism, they sought to reformulate liberal theology and practice to address new social and economic realities of modern life. The generation of reformers had come of age when the massive problems of industrialization and urbanization dwarfed the bland reassurances of quietist Victorian-era liberal theology, which suggested that material progress of the era reflected its moral ascendance. As their engagement with Nietzsche's philosophy demonstrates, their urgent tone also reflects their growing self-awareness of liberalism as a coherent theology, but one that required greater articulation. Encounters with Nietzsche's critiques of Christianity alternately chastened and emboldened them as they sought to carry their convictions from the pulpit to the public square, and from a supernatural religion to a social ethics.

Social Gospelers might have found Nietzsche's claims about the death of God distasteful and extreme, but it was his attack on Christian ethics, not theology, that most concerned them. Their use of Nietzsche suggests the ways in which their sense of crisis was focused on social and economic conditions rather than on intellectual problems within liberal theology itself. Theology, they argued, was their realm of intellectual engagement only insofar as it addressed "the social problem." Theology was important as long as it fostered an understanding that spiritual salvation was a social affair, made possible by reform of, not retreat from, unjust economic and social structures. They looked to soup kitchens and relief agencies, not the church sanctuary or seminary, as they sought to reformulate Christian ethics. As a result, the impulse to modernize their theology came, not from intellectual dilemmas internal to it or to its relationship to secular ideas, but from problems of their modern America: overcrowded cities, underfunded schools, and poor sanitation. As they observed the growing ranks of the poor and disinherited and a Victorian theology unable to combat it, Social Gospelers employed Nietzsche's philosophy as a symbol of the negative individualistic ethics undermining social solidarity. As William Adams Brown, professor of systematic theology at Union Theological Seminary, asked, "Is Christ to be the ultimate conqueror or the Superman of Nietzsche?" stressing that "this is the question of questions" of the modern era.[42]

In Nietzsche's philosophy, Social Gospelers discovered an advocate for the overweening individualism and materialism that they believed were undermining modern Americans' sense of communal fellowship and responsibility. They specifically called out Nietzsche and his attacks on Christian "slave morality" as an expression of the ethics of expediency they were up against. According to Shailer Mathews, a leading light of the Chicago School's liberal theology, "In [the] contrast between the teaching of Jesus and the teaching of Nietzsche we are confronting the fundamental antithesis that lies in the world of values."[43] In *Christianity and the Social Crisis* (1907), Walter Rauschenbusch likewise described Nietzsche's philosophy as the "direct outgrowth" of the social world of industrialization, speculating that there exists "an intimate causal connection between the industrial system which evolves the modern captain of industry and the philosophy of Nietzsche which justifies and glorifies him." This was the only way Rauschenbusch could explain why the "philosophy of Nietzsche," which "scouts the Christian virtues as the qualities of slaves" and "glorifies the strong man's self-assertion which treads underfoot whatever hinders him from living out his life to the full," was "deeply affecting the ethical thought of the modern world."[44] Reflecting on the consistent sentiment animating his theology and social activism, he argued that his "social point of view" and his "Christian social convictions" were "the direct negation of Nietzsche."[45]

That pious thinkers committed to social solidarity would turn to an atheist thinker who had nothing good to say about man in the aggregate demonstrates how quickly Nietzsche had become crucial for formulating the moral problems of the day, and his image and ideas important elements of the changing American Christian lexicon. But in their willingness to wrestle with Nietzsche's challenges to their meliorism, they also reveal a concern about intractable evil in human affairs. It is because they viewed the Gospels as blueprints for social harmony that their critics have tended to dismiss their vision of the Kingdom of God as innocent and their faith as a form of despiritualized ethics. As H. Richard Niebuhr lamented, they offered "a God without wrath [who] brought men without sin into a kingdom without judgment through the ministrations of a Christ without a cross."[46] However, in their efforts to address Nietzsche's criticisms of their faith, the Social Gospelers exhibit a conscience more agonized than previously thought. Though they rejected Nietzsche's advocacy of a self beyond the good and evil of his fellow men, they agreed with him that the test of religion is the human beings it produces, as well the social arrangements it informs. They also shared with Nietzsche an intense distaste for otherworldliness. They rejected Nietzsche's earthly Übermensch as an alternative to the God of the Bible, but they emphasized that God's Kingdom was of this world and not of the next. For those seeking to "live a truly Christian life" in the modern world, Rauschenbusch contended, the "ascetic departure from the world is dead."[47] They therefore found common cause with Nietzsche, who had insisted that it is folly to view redemption as something that awaits the individual after death. The Kingdom of Heaven is available here on earth to those who help create it.

It was, however, Nietzsche's critique of Christianity's bankruptcy in the modern world that most reflected Social Gospelers' own concerns. Like Nietzsche, they wanted a kingdom here on earth, but not complacency and compromises with a compromised world. Nietzsche confirmed their fears that if Christians were unable to find the resonance of biblical words in their modern world, Christianity would indeed prove itself unfit for the modern course. The prospect that "the Christian character has become an impracticable dream," argued Unitarian minister and Harvard professor of Christian ethics Francis Peabody, "shakes the very pillars of Christian loyalty, and leaves of Christian ethics nothing more than a picturesque ruin, overthrown by the earthquakes of modern change."[48] This concern about the "practicability" of Christianity thus fronted their essays and books: Peabody worried about the "Practicability of the Christian Life," Lyman Abbott asked, "Are the Ethics of Jesus Practicable?" and William Adams Brown wondered, "*Is Christianity Practicable?*"[49] According to Shailer Mathews, "The gospel must not appear to be merely tenable; it must be seen to have power.... Verification means experiment, the demonstration of practicability. If the gospel is to be a message of deliverance, it must deliver."[50] A Christianity mute in the face of the problems of modern life was a religion without resonance, and therefore a religion without a future.

As the most liberal of liberal Protestants, Social Gospelers had problems with Nietzsche precisely because they cared about the question of modern Christianity's relevance, as he had. They shared with Nietzsche a vision of a world in flux, and yet by granting a dynamic universe they were pressed to answer why a two-thousand-year-old doctrine remained a source of values. In a dynamic universe, answers to the "social question" could be neither fixed nor final. According to Peabody, modern Christians are not interested in recovering a worldview of a dead race: that is archaeology. Nietzsche's mistake was to assume that historicism, because it shows how values have changed over time, demands ethical relativism. Expressing a sentiment common to the Social Gospelers, he argued that one can embrace a dynamic universe while accepting the Gospels as transcendental truths guiding human affairs. For Peabody, historicism simply helps distinguish the timeless from the particular, the transcendent from the immanent. Peabody was ready to admit that the Gospels' ethical ideals must be worked out in accordance to the particular needs of each age. And yet, he believed, that does not mean that *truth* changes, just the ways of apprehending it.[51]

Though Social Gospelers posed the Gospels against the struggle for existence as the law of the universe, they believed that evolution, properly understood, reflects the working out of divine revelation. Evolution, they argued, is simply God's mechanism for realizing a higher humanity and a perfected ethics. But the question remained: was there a kind of ethics that helped foster that evolutionary process? According to Lyman Abbott, Congregationalist minister and editor of *Outlook,* the "two contrasted principles"— Nietzsche's "self-seeking" versus Jesus's "altruistic" ethics—reflected the two competing answers between which moderns must choose:

According to one conception, the end of life is the development of a type—what Friedrich Nietzsche calls "the beyond man;" according to the other conception, the end of life is the development of a race organized in a new social order—what Jesus calls "the kingdom of heaven;" according to the one conception, the method is self-service and the sacrifice of others; according to the other, the method is self-sacrifice and the service of others.

If Nietzsche got his facts about evolution wrong—namely, that it works toward not an isolated human "type" but rather toward the creation of an elevated human "race"—then he was likewise mistaken in thinking that the moral exemplar is the isolated individual and not man in the aggregate. Though Abbott argued for a developmental model of ethics, he insisted that it is one guided by Jesus's message of self-sacrifice and service. The ethics of nurturing others, not the ethics of tooth and claw, abides by the true laws of the universe. Such a message, he argued, is not only practicable in the modern world, it is the only ethics that fosters the development of a worthy race.[52]

Social Gospelers surely felt the awkwardness of agreeing with a thinker who took their ethics as his enemy. But they readily agreed with him that the value of beliefs is proved by the quality of human types they foster. Nietzsche's assaults on Christianity as an "anaemic survival" of a world well lost were justified, they reasoned, if all Christianity is capable of creating is a debased modern personality. In trying to assess the "personal consequences of the Christian character," Peabody thus sought to respond to Nietzsche's contentions regarding the "unfitness of Christianity for modern life." He laid out for his readers a catalogue of Nietzsche's attacks from *Beyond Good and Evil, Twilight of the Idols,* and *Thus Spoke Zarathustra,* which held that "the Christian ideal, gentle, compassionate, ascetic, is to be frankly regarded, not only as antiquated, but as repulsive to the modern mind":

> Christianity is "a religion of decadence." "Every instinct which is benefi-cent or contributory to life . . . is mistrusted.". . . Virtue must be freed from "moralic acid." Ethics has been hitherto tedious and soporific, and morality a weariness (*eine Langweiligkeit*). . . . ["]Morality is the negation of life."[53]

Peabody characterized the "modern and virile teaching of Nietzsche" as "un-flinching Egoism" in its most extreme form. It was Nietzsche, then, who showed how egoists uniformly fall into a trap of their own design: "The more resolutely . . . the egoist sets his face to his predetermined end, the more likely he is to find no pleasure there." An aggrandized self as source of values and goal of life fails to offer a redeemed humanity and instead yields a godless self "adrift in a trackless world."[54]

While Social Gospelers agreed that human character is the evidence of Christianity's practicability for modern life, they maintained that it is not the solitary self but rather social selves to which one must look. Nietzsche, they insisted, had missed the social nature of human personality. The "fundamental objection" to modern Christianity "to which Nietzsche has given vogue," argued Mathews, was his critique of a social morality, which yoked the individual to the herd.[55] However, Mathews stated that Nietzsche's mistake was to think that morality could ever be a solitary affair. Morals that are neither regulatory nor social, he argued, were meaningless.

Much like other contributors to the Social Gospel movement, Vida Scudder was simultaneously sympathetic to Nietzsche's critique of Christian asceticism and repelled by his endorsement of the egotism that Social Gospelers believed was undermining social justice in industrial America. But Scudder more than others found common cause with Nietzsche, insisting that his "discontent with civilization" mirrored her own. In her major work of religiously inspired economic criticism, *Socialism and Character* (1912), Scudder, a Wellesley English professor, settlement worker, and leading voice of Christian Socialism in America, believed that she was witnessing the evolution of modern society from individualism toward an age of consolidation: a "socialized order." Neither Christianity nor socialism alone, however, inspired her. While Christianity's "moral idealism" appeared "invested with unreality" when pressed to respond concretely to the social problems of the age, socialism was too materialistic in its worldview. For Scudder, secular socialism failed to appreciate that "the individual soul is the only matter of real consequence in the world."[56]

Scudder described Nietzsche as one of the nineteenth-century "guides" of her youth who had burrowed his way into her moral imagination, demanding answers to his protests.[57] She had discovered in Ruskin an important critic of the ethical and aesthetic dislocations of the modern political economy, and in Tolstoy and Marx the conviction that private ethics must be socially realized.[58] But it was in Nietzsche that she found a fellow "seeker" dissatisfied with an ineffectual moral idealism, worried about the psychic bewilderment of modernity, and longing for human personality worthy of reverence. She agreed with his attacks on "the smug assumptions of a nominal democracy and a faded Christianity" and with his belief that moderns could do better. Nietzsche's "brutally potent and poetic revulsion" of modern humanity in its decrepit state had ineluctable appeal for her and helped her articulate her own discontent. She paraphrased Nietzsche approvingly:

> For here is where we are: the leveling and diminishing of man in Europe conceals our greatest danger. . . . Nothing incites us to become greater to-day: we foresee that everything is humbling itself, to be reduced more and more to something more inoffensive, slighter, more prudent, more medio-cre, till the superlative insignificance of the Christian virtues is reached. . . . There is the fatal doom of Europe: having ceased to fear man, we have ceased to love him, to venerate him, to hope in him, to will with him. The very aspect of man bores us to-day. *We are tired of humanity.*

The problem that Nietzsche left her with, however, was the recognition that while socialistic revolts of the nineteenth century were untenable, so too were ideals animating the individualistic counterrevolts. "Indeed, the indict-ment of modern life from [Nietzsche's] new point of view was even more heart-racking than from the old," she lamented.[59] Though Nietzsche did not resolve these tensions, he captured the dilemma facing moderns seeking a way to remake both self and society.

According to Scudder, though Nietzsche failed to adjudicate the warring imperatives of egoism and altruism, his philosophy remained a necessary resource for modern Christians and socialists. Rereading Nietzsche, "the fa-miliar pages gain a new significance in addition to their old charm" for the clarity with which they helped her see the interdependence of Christianity and socialism. But the *value* of that mutuality Nietzsche got wrong. He failed to realize that the two *together* were a balm, not a poison, to the modern soul longing for a more meaningful spirituality. In isolation neither could inspire. But in loving tandem they showed what Nietzsche could not see: that "true liberty is positive, not negative, dealing less with the removal of restriction than with the imparting of power." Had Nietzsche understood, to borrow Wordsworth's phrase, that one is "free because imbound," he would have realized that it is in "the socialist state we hope that the way will be open for all of us to become supermen, and we may advance on the road thither with solemn gayety [*sic*] equal to that of Zarathustra."[60]

Though Scudder found Nietzsche more sympathetic than did other Social Gospelers, all agreed with her estimation of his value for modern religious thought and practice. For the theologians, clergy, and lay activists drawn to the Social Gospel, Nietzsche gave moderns good reason to question the reasonableness and practicability of Christianity. To deny religious doubt or to cast it as sinful, Mathews stressed, only allowed a greater rift between the church and the world. Doubt, he insisted, was vital to "the process of theological reconstruction," for it challenged the gospel to keep apace with modern realities. Social Gospelers therefore recognized Nietzsche—sometimes as fellow seeker, more often as challenging doubter, but always as instrumental for refitting their faith to the modern world.[61]

## Nietzsche's Service to Christianity

Though religious interpretations of Nietzsche differed dramatically even among those of the same Christian denomination, it was his mainline liberal Protestant readers who argued that his philosophy helped modern Christianity more than it hurt it. While Social Gospelers did the most to give the concern about Christianity's practicability its visibility, it was a concern shared among all turn-of-the-century liberal Protestants. Congregational minister and writer Edwin Dodge Hardin spoke for a number of religious interpreters when he argued that it was high time that practicing Christians acknowledged Nietzsche's service to Christianity. Ministers who believed that Nietzsche aided Christians in their search for a more meaningful spirituality argued with Hardin that challenges to the faith from a critic of Nietzsche's "intellectual caliber" could only be a "tonic in its effects."[62] In a series of sermons on Nietzsche for the First Unitarian Church of Milwaukee in 1919, Rev. Robert Loring preached that "Nietzsche is more like strong medicine than like pleasant food. . . . Like many old-fashioned tonics they often leave a bitter taste in the mouth. There seems, however, to be this difference; while the old-fashioned tonic had printed on the bottle, 'Shake before Taking,' in the case of Nietzsche you first take, and then you shake."[63] In Nietzsche's bracing writings on religion, liberal Protestant ministers and theologians discovered a valuable moral stimulant that would energize Christians and an intellectual astringent that would enable them to do some long-overdue spiritual, ethical, and liturgical housecleaning.

While Catholics argued that engagements with secular philosophies like

Nietzsche's compromised the Christian faith, liberal Protestants typically argued that such intellectual engagement was essential if the church wished to remain relevant to modern affairs. Catholic commentators typically blamed Protestants' accommodation to the secular world for the softening, as Joseph Jacobi put it, of "our Christianity [which] should be virile." Conservative Catholics contended that in the modern age of ecumenicalism and religious liberalism, it was harder, not easier, to be a "real" Christian. Jacobi transformed Nietzsche's call for the strenuous life into a call for robust religious types: "We need the heroic faith of the martyrs and confessors." He granted Nietzsche's charge against lukewarm believers and combined it with a call for Nietzschean vitalism in the church: "We want less tepid Christians.... The day of the spiritual dilettante is at an end. Men have died for the faith; the hour has struck when men must live for the faith."[64]

On this point, Nietzsche's Catholic and Protestant readers could agree. As Jackson Lears has observed, many turn-of-the-century Protestants, feeling plagued by the "weightlessness" of modern experience, became attracted to the medieval asceticism in Catholicism. For Protestants of late Victorian and Progressive America who felt "overfed" and "overcivilized" by modern culture, the self-denying strain of the Catholic martyr appealed to their longing for intense bodily experience, a mystical "release" from secular anomie, and a righteous stoicism in the face of a degenerate and decadent world.[65] The comforts of modern life and the secular millennialism of modern culture, Catholics and Protestants could agree, had an influence on modern faith's making religion too easy, too soft, too feminine.

But Nietzsche's calls for strenuousness of the spirit unnerved liberal Protestants, especially those who felt that their religion was awash in feminine sentimentality. Over the course of the nineteenth century, as Reformed theology moved steadily away from orthodox Calvinism, female worshippers began to outnumber males in the pews, and feminine iconography and language, which emphasized Christian sympathy and sentimentality, began to replace the martial ethos in church sermons and religious visual culture. As historians of Gilded Age and Progressive Era American Protestantism have noted, liberal Protestant men at the turn of the last century began to recoil from the feminine qualities that they perceived were plaguing the faith and longed to (re-)create "muscular" forms of Christian piety.[66]

Nietzsche's service to modern Christianity, then, lay in his willingness to rough it up. Like a playground bully who toughens the scrawny kid with his taunts and jeers, Nietzsche pressed a feminized spirituality to demonstrate its psychic and spiritual muscularity. In a series of lectures on Nietzsche delivered in May 1915 at Lake Forest College in Illinois, and widely read in reprinted form, British Anglican minister and theologian John Neville Figgis argued that Nietzsche offered Christians a philosophy of "Alpine heights of danger and triumph"—a welcome antidote to the facile "optimism of inevitable progress, with its gospel of the sofa-millennium." Figgis discovered in Nietzsche's critique of nineteenth-century religious modernism in Germany a vision of the neurasthenic Christianity they had inherited. He lamented a softening religious worldview in which believers substituted a "pretty picture of the eternal grandmother" for "the enthralling spectacle of God as Father," for Nietzsche had signaled to them that their modern civilization had become what Figgis described as "the apotheosis of vulgarity": "a milk-and-water sentimentalism [which has] usurped the once austere name of Christian piety." He agreed with Nietzsche that modern Christian practice had degenerated into a despiritualized humanitarianism and a commitment to good manners.[67]

Nietzsche's "bitter tonic," Figgis contended, was necessary insofar as it showed the bad faith of liberal faith. Nietzsche reminded modern Christians that any life worth living comes at a cost, and any faith worth having is a faith which demands something of the believer. Nietzsche had performed a "direct service to the Christian, and is far less antagonistic than he supposed," for he helped retrieve the true meaning of Christian living from those tendencies in modern life that were cheapening it. Why call Nietzsche an enemy for demonstrating that the modern church was increasingly peopled with half-hearted believers who used their Christianity as a moral conceit? Let the all-too-human masses have their easy comforts, their blind faith in progress, their delight in breezy entertainments, and their romantic attachment to moral platitudes. But those who recognize the "tremendous greatness of life" understood with Nietzsche that true Christian faith is intractably difficult. Likewise, any God worthy of belief must be a God worthy of awe. Nietzsche had shown that "life is tragic, and that man needs redemption." Impressed by his commitment to martial virtues, Figgis affirmed that "the price for the world's ransom must be paid in blood. The world would not be worth redeeming could it be paid in any lower coinage."[68]

A number of Protestant commentators thus found in Nietzsche's method of religious critique a resource for testing the value of their faith's coinage. Religious readers recognized that Nietzsche was more than just a critic; he was also a social scientist who had articulated a new approach to the study of religion. He offered a new approach to ethics: not as moral legislation, but as a set of beliefs to be tested. Because he believed that there existed no timeless, universal methods for validating meaning, he ruled out all metaphysical and transcendental foundations for religious beliefs. However, he didn't rule out believing itself. Nietzsche had stressed that valuations are still possible. But rather than grounding the study of religion in universal claims, the value of its beliefs was demonstrated by their human uses, not their purported divine origins. Instead of asking if a belief is true, Nietzsche asked what benefits come to those who held such beliefs.

Religious readers noted increasingly that Nietzsche's novel approach to the study of religion and ethics sounded familiar. It sounded, as one commentator put it, "strikingly anticipatory of William James."[69] In a 1909 *Harvard Theological Review* essay on Nietzsche, Williams College professor of philosophy and German John Warbeke agreed, noting, "Doubtless it will be an interesting surprise to many American and English pragmatists to learn that Nietzsche has anticipated all their principle [*sic*] doctrines." Warbeke argued for affinities between Nietzsche's and the American philosophers' challenge to absolute morality and their pragmatic approach to testing beliefs. They sought to dispense with questions of first principles and philosophical absolutes, and to examine instead the benefits that a particular religious belief brought the believer. Nietzsche had summoned men to ask of their beliefs not whether they were "good" or "evil" but rather, whether they inspired. He had insisted that moderns drop their notion of truth as revealed religion and instead ask whether their beliefs yielded beautiful human types worthy of admiration and emulation. As Warbeke put it, Nietzsche's study of truth and meaning posed "pragmatic" questions, to which the "only answer is the testing."[70]

Taking their cues from the "pragmatist" Nietzsche, liberal Protestant readers attempted to revisit their ideas of the moral life as dynamic cultural creations rather than as timeless facts. Though none sought to appropriate the wholesale relativism they detected in his writing, many were willing to put aside their metaphysical differences with Nietzsche and to subject their Christian morality to his "pragmatic" test. What would happen, they wondered, if Nietzsche were right in his claim that there existed no solid ground, no privileged place from which to assess morality? What would Christians discover if they stopped trying to justify the truthfulness of their belief in nature as revealed religion and instead tried to determine the value of such a belief? According to Hardin, Christians had grown too timid to ask such demanding questions of their faith: "The Christianity which Nietzsche attacks is an incomplete, hesitating, illogical movement, most of whose followers are afraid to see it through to the finish. We fear the latent possibilities of the faith that we confess, and accordingly we are diligent to refrain from being unduly and perhaps painfully consistent."[71] Nietzsche's philosophy presented a timely challenge to them by proposing an experimental approach to religious faith and practice. At the very least, such an experiment would let Christians know whether an honest, thoroughgoing living of the Word was possible in the modern world.

In keeping with their tradition's openness toward the secular sciences, liberal Protestant readers attempted to incorporate Nietzsche's philosophical method as a way to explore new avenues for religious inquiry. Liberal Protestant theologians and clergy, especially, demonstrated a curiosity in approaching their religious beliefs as propositions about the moral life. Eager to enjoin his parishioners in the "pragmatic" testing of Christian orthodoxies, Unitarian minister Loring used his 1919 sermons on Nietzsche to invite his congregants to investigate the value of their values. As Loring put it to his parishioners, "Let us, with Nietzsche, avoid speculative questions about how far the stock Christian dogmas are historically or philosophically true" and instead "let us ask the modern practical pragmatic question;—How far are the old, stock dogmas of the churches morally or socially useful?"[72]

Loring wondered how well the church would fare if subjected to such a test. In doing so, he turned the Sunday morning service into a laboratory of ideas. He asked his parishioners whether they thought that human life was somehow more dignified if the Christian, upon taking Communion, believed that he was eating the actual body and blood of Christ. He encouraged them to consider whether it strengthened man's character and his sense of personal responsibility to believe that Jesus died for his sins. Similarly, he pressed his parishioners to examine whether it exalted romantic love and matrimony to believe that "when God wished to visit the earth he had to be born of a pure virgin in order to escape the awful [*sic*] contamination of sex." If moderns were to subject these beliefs to Nietzsche's scientific method, Loring concluded, very little of the "old church dogmas would be left unchanged."[73]

Nietzsche's liberal Protestant readers who appreciated his critical service to their faith argued that modern Christianity was failing the Nietzschean test. They surveyed the other-worldly beliefs still dominant in modern spirituality and concluded that worn-out notions of salvation and redemption stood in the way of social progress. The American political and intellectual landscape showed signs of mental and moral decay. Liberal Protestants detected an unwholesome emphasis in modern America on the life of the group at the cost of human individuality. Drawing on the tone and the substance of Nietzsche's critiques, Loring, for example, described modern democracy as a safe haven for mediocrity, socialism as a holding pen for the herd, and modern art and literature as narcotics which anesthetized men and women from feeling the harsh realities of life. But many couldn't help but wonder whether Christianity was part of the problem. "The Christian ethics and democracy," Warbeke noted, "are one in this emphasis of the commonplace, the lame, the passable, the merely existing, the many-too-many."[74] Christian observers confessed their belief that the vital qualities of individuality, ingenuity, and intelligence were the very agents of human progress that were being sacrificed on the altar of democratic equality and solidarity. Nietzsche gave his religious readers reason to protest against, as Loring put it, this modern "half-hearted kind of world, half-hearted in work and thought and ideals."[75]

Nietzsche's protests against Christianity as an ascetic, feeble denial of the strenuous life resonated, however uncomfortably, with his pious American readers. His criticism of Christianity concerned liberal Protestants eager to see their theology keep apace with modernity, but also worried that in doing so they were making too many compromises with a compromised world. Nietzsche encouraged them to test the features of their faith to see which ones still offered a meaningful account of the universe, but he also pressed them to reject a Protestantism so liberal that it amounted to nothing more than despiritualized ethics. His exaltation of spiritual strenuousness persuaded them that majesty, wonder, and struggle in achieving ideals are vital if those ideals are worth having.

## Jesus of Nazareth, Nietzsche of Naumburg

Early twentieth-century religious commentators who believed that Nietzsche provided a vital service to Christianity detected something familiar in his calls for the strenuous life and his criticism of conventional morality. Though Nietzsche referred to himself as an "immoralist" and the "Antichrist," crucial aspects of his philosophy seemed to resonate with the very Christian doctrine he assailed. Religious readers likened his strident attacks on the slackening morals of his contemporaries to the prophecies of the Old Testament, and his call for a higher humanity to the moral vision of the New Testament. Though they noted strange parallels between Nietzsche's philosophy and the religion he condemned, it was his uncanny affinity with Jesus that sparked interest, if not controversy.

Liberal Protestant readers suggested that Nietzsche's biography and philosophy were best understood as modern parallels to Jesus's life and teachings. His noble vision of the value of sacrifice and hardship for the strengthening of the self recalled, for Figgis, "a doctrine precisely similar to that of our Lord: 'Whoso loseth his life shall save it.' It is, in fact, the doctrine of the Cross, little as Nietzsche seems aware of this."[76] For others, the messianic Übermensch represented a modern corollary to Jesus's emphasis on the redemptive power of human personality. Hardin noted that "it is a far cry from Nietzsche to Christ," but conceded that "the German philosopher's bold love for reality and scorn for self-delusion and hypocrisy" recalled the "attitude of [Jesus] who had no possible common ground with the Pharisees." Like Jesus, Nietzsche preached the message that individual conscience must come before social convention; both had insisted that social regeneration was possible only through individual regeneration. In Nietzsche's teachings, Hardin concluded, "we find a gospel which has much in common with the spirit of Christianity."[77] Similarly, Warbeke detected in Nietzsche "the passionate poet of a higher humanity" who had affinities to the original "transvaluator of all values," another moral rebel who had "prophesied for personalities, for independent thinkers, for men who feared no law as such." Like Jesus two thousand years earlier, Nietzsche "can but add new values to our lives."[78]

Religious commentators adopted a number of strategies for rechanneling Nietzsche's attacks on Christian decadence and slave morality into a critique of secular culture and a defense of their faith. One way they took possession of Nietzsche's philosophy was to smuggle his Übermensch out of the broader context of his thought and into Christian theology, and thus transform Jesus into the "Christian Superman" and the "Strong Son of God."[79] In addition, Nietzsche's religious readers drew analogies between his philosophy and the original gospel of the historical Jesus. They argued that Nietzsche not only reformulated Jesus's emphasis on the value of human personality but also wanted belief to be less rule-bound and yet more spiritually demanding. Nietzsche rejected the dogmas, the priests, and the scholasticism for a truer gospel of life, just as Jesus had rejected the formal religion of the Pharisees. Nietzsche's philosophy thus hoisted Jesus above ecclesiastical Christianity, just as Jesus had himself raised the bar of spirituality above the rigid dogmas and practices of early Judaism.[80] Moreover, the religious readers incorporated Nietzsche's challenges against Christian altruism and sentimentalism in their retelling of a muscular Jesus as they sought to distance "true" Christianity from the feminizing aspects of modern Protestantism. Such a move lead Figgis, for one, to argue that altruism played no role in Christian doctrine: "[Altruistic] the Christian ethic never was and never will be."[81] Such a claim may have raised eyebrows, but his rendering of Jesus into a muscular Übermensch and Nietzsche into a model Christian would not have. Figgis's characterizations of a Nietzschean Jesus were not the transgressions of a modern apostate but evidence of an increasingly familiar strategy for putting Nietzsche's philosophy to work in religious discourse.

For all the religious readers' interest in using Nietzsche to envision a modern martial Jesus who would challenge American decadence by bringing new life to a despiritualized Christianity, they never addressed the possibility that by making Nietzsche safe for Christianity, they were likewise helping to invest him with a spiritual authority that could rival Jesus's. They did not address the possibility that a serious-minded theologian and practicing Christian would use Nietzsche not to affirm but to question Jesus's moral authority. And yet this is precisely what the most thoroughgoing Nietzschean theologian of the period, Baptist minister and University of Chicago scholar George Burman Foster, would come to do. Though unique in the degree to which he absorbed Nietzsche's ideas in his reconceptualization of modern faith, Foster's integration of Nietzsche's philosophy into his theology represented a consummation of, not an aberration from, the varieties of early twentieth-century Nietzschean religious appropriation. Foster was unique, though, in recognizing the full implications of welcoming Nietzsche into his thought. Once moderns could find in Nietzsche reasons to doubt the absoluteness of Christianity as well as an antidote to disenchantment accompanying that doubt, it would be difficult to return to Jesus as rock and refuge: "we cannot lead [our] age back to Jesus, which has grown out beyond him."[82]

George Burman Foster stands out among religious thinkers, in that he accepted Nietzsche's ideas of a fully de-divinized Jesus.[83] Trained in Berlin and Göttingen, Germany, he spent his years in Chicago teaching a radicalized version of the historicist theology he had learned abroad and preaching it from pulpits in both Baptist and Unitarian churches. Heavily influenced by Nietzsche, Foster adopted what he would come to identify as a "functionalist" view of religious belief and practice. In his scholarly books, he sought to move Christianity away from its history as an "authority-religion," which understood itself as the sole and final arbiter of meaning and truth. For Foster, the "conviction of the finality [that is, absoluteness] of the Christian religion" could no longer be reconciled in a world "where the fixed has yielded to flux, being to becoming, absoluteness to relativity, force to ideals." The question facing moderns whose intellects could not be tricked by theological dodges of modern science or their spiritual longings assuaged by secular forms of enchantment was how to make a meaningful life when a "God outside the cosmos is dead."[84]

Foster's challenging reappraisals of Christianity took shape at the center of modernist liberal theology, the University of Chicago Divinity School. He joined the faculty in 1895, much to the enthusiasm of the university's president, William Rainey Harper, who considered him the "greatest living thinker in his line."[85] He brought with him a fluency in modern German theology spoken with a deep West Virginia drawl, a disarming earnestness, and a subtlety of mind matched by an engaging personality at the pulpit and lectern. Foster's writings bear no evidence of an intellectual provocateur, but do reflect the mind of a spiritually striving moralist hoping that a thoroughly naturalized approach to religion would salvage "the maximum of Christianity that could be retained by the modern mind."[86] But in addition to being a penetrating thinker, he had a positive genius for striking more than a few nerves with his heretical theology. Both his major books, *The Finality of the Christian Religion* (1906) and *The Function of Religion in Man's Struggle for Existence* (1909), ignited controversy within the Baptist leadership, the university administration, and the popular press. If, as we shall see, "death of God" theology scandalized confessing Christians in the 1960s, then Foster's post-theistic Nietzschean excursions were downright blasphemous over a half century earlier.

Foster's *Finality of the Christian Religion* rattled the Protestant theological world when it appeared in 1906. In it, he maintained that Christians cannot make claims to absolutes outside human history. While historicism and naturalism appropriately challenge theological orthodoxies, Nietzsche had shown that both limit man's horizon of possibilities, with one crushing him under the burden of historical knowledge and the other deadening him with determinism:

Against all this Nietzsche thundered in the interest of *personality*. He ridiculed science as folly, denied every objective norm, preached the right of passion as against logic, instinct as against *Dressur,* the wilderness as against the schoolroom, heroism as against utility-morals, greatness as against philistinism, and the intoxicating poesy of life as against its regulation. And in all this, barring the exaggerations of the poet, he was right fundamentally. We have cause to thank Nietzsche. He broke down ramparts against which we were too weak. He would give back the deep again to man and awaken a great yearning.

For Foster, the yearning Nietzsche awakened in moderns is the redemption not found in belief in miracles, in sacred scripture; it is created ever anew in the dynamic exchange of personality with personality. While Nietzsche rejected a Jesus as founder of "authority religion" who stands outside human history, his own yearning for personality helped awaken moderns to the personality of the historical Jesus. "As fire kindles fire, and not some theory about the nature of flame, so persons save persons."[87] The language Foster used to describe Jesus here mirrors how Nietzsche worked on him, and how he might work for other searching moderns. Nietzsche brought moderns back to the Jesus as flame of personality.

Foster's daring mind enjoyed the esteem of his colleagues, and while they shared his Baptist belief in the autonomy and competency of the individual believer, his challenges to Christian authority pushed that Baptist sensibility too far. His provocative theology had already put his faculty position at the university at risk in 1905, and he was duly transferred from the Divinity School to the Department of Comparative Religion in Arts and Sciences. Now, after the publication of *Finality,* the Baptist Ministers' Conference voted to adopt a resolution declaring that Foster's teachings were "subversive" and "contrary to scripture."[88]

Though Foster carried on, weathering a barrage of calls to have him dismissed from not only his professorship but also the ministry, in 1909 he sought to follow up with a clarification of his ideas in his *The Function of Religion in Man's Struggle for Existence.* Despite his claims that he hoped the book would show how he "cleave[d] to the sunnier side of doubt," his underlying assertion that all religious ideals and concepts of the divine are human expressions of the longing for absolutes revealed the unmistakable Nietzschean overtones in his developing religious perspective. "We can never be satisfied with this

Jesus religion as a finality," he argued. "We must pass on from faith in a man to faith in a new eternal Messiah—*our* Messiah, . . . a creation of the spirit of modern humanity. . . . And this Messiah will be to us—what he really was to every people that created or adopted him—our Ideal."[89] From the viewpoint of Foster's fellow clergy, his "sunnier" affirmation that Christ the Messiah was a figment of human imagination only made matters worse. In another meeting of the Baptist Ministers' Conference, they voted to "eject" him, leading to another firestorm of controversy that brought Foster's outrages to the attention of the national press. As the *New York Times* reported in 1909, "Baptists after Row Expel Prof. Foster; Ministers' Conference in Chicago Indulges in Hissing and Yelling before Voting."[90]

Though elements of Foster's religious functionalism and naturalism harmonized with broader moves in liberal theology, he found himself repeatedly running afoul of traditional custodians of religion and culture, who were eager to keep the Nietzschean pastor from cultivating a flock. In addition to the attempts of fellow clerics to strip him of his ordination, public libraries nervously shied away from purchasing his heretical books for their readers.[91] Even so, Foster eventually found an audience eager for his Nietzschean gospel. Margaret Anderson, a fellow Chicagoan and Nietzschean enthusiast, invited Foster in 1914 to write a series of articles on Nietzsche for her readers. He accepted, and beginning with the first issue of *The Little Review* in March 1914, Foster contributed an article each month over the course of two years, cultivating new audiences for his Nietzschean religion.

In his *Little Review* pieces, Foster sought to inspire a younger generation of secular readers with the promises of Nietzschean post-theistic spirituality. What is striking is that in his move from a 518-page scholarly theological tome to short essays such as "The New Loyalty," "The Nietzschean Love of Eternity," and "Longing" for a secular readership, none of the Nietzschean elements of his original message were lost in translation. He simply calibrated his writing to an audience of young seekers, not those he believed were already sated. Foster argued that while no religion is a finality, all express a unifying experience of humankind, namely, the longing for divinity. "God is but another human name for Eternal Yearning," he explained.[92] It was Nietzsche who recognized the peculiarly desperate nature of modern man's spirituality. Modern science successfully challenged the toppled absolutes of religion, showing God to be a "human fantasy," but not the ultimate absolute in man: a yearning for transcendence.[93] Drawing on language from *Zarathustra*, Foster argued that Nietzsche showed the perilousness of moderns' longing to believe and their inability to do so, leaving themselves adrift in the "melancholy mood of modernity."[94]

While Nietzsche diagnosed the predicament of modern longing, he also showed the personality capable of overcoming it. Foster introduced Nietzsche as "the Prophet of a New Culture" whose life and thought heralded an exalted image of modern man. "Man as the goal, beauty as the form, life as the law, eternity as the content of our new day—this is Nietzsche's message to the modern man." He stressed that the path to higher spirituality cannot look "*backward*" to inherited traditions, but must look "*forward*" to a new imagined world of creative invention and discovery. He proclaimed, "A man is coming to be leader—a man who, as no other, embodies in himself all the pain and all the pleasure, all the sickness and all the convalescence, all the age and all the youth, of our tumultuous and tortured times: *Friedrich Nietzsche!*" Nietzsche's message, which called for the man of the future, was gaining converts as quickly as the traditional churches were losing them: "unlike most preachers, his congregation grows from year to year," Foster maintained.[95]

Foster suggested that Jesus could still be a spiritual source for searching moderns, but only as a model of this "*Sehnsucht*" (longing).[96] Moderns could not simply duplicate the forms in which his yearning took two thousand years earlier: "Were he alive today he would not copy the Jesus of that time and place. To copy even him is to kill the soul." Thus, Foster employed Jesus to make an explicitly Nietzschean point: every man must create his own forms of faith, his own God. Without recourse in timeless foundations, however, these new faiths would have to be "inspirational rather than regulative, dynamic rather than static, creative and nourishing rather than statutory and repressive."[97] Because Nietzsche had demonstrated the efficacy of the proposition that "truth moves, and, moving, demolishes thrones and altars," he understood that "*self-changing* . . . is the life task of man."[98] Paraphrasing Nietzsche, Foster argued that "the only prayer we have a moral right to pray is precisely the prayer which after all we ourselves must answer."[99]

For Foster, Nietzsche had shown that modern man should not try to deny his messianic urges, but instead become an Übermensch worthy of them. Though the "preaching of Superman might be called Messianic," Nietzsche taught that this savior is in each one of us.[100] Foster argued, then, that in coming to Nietzsche, one comes closer to himself: Nietzsche as one's inner messiah. He stressed that even those readers who were not yet familiar with "the great personality of Nietzsche" knew him, "for a part of him is in your own heart and hope. If you have ever thought seriously about yourself . . . you have taken up into yourself a part of Nietzsche as you have so thought. Even without your knowledge or intention, you have passed into the world of thought for which the name of Nietzsche stands."[101] Thus, his invocation of a messianic Nietzsche is one who is not the object of prayer but the underwriter of man's search for self. He is the only kind of savior who can stand at the bar of the modern mind: a saviour who teaches man to find the saviour in himself.

While preaching his Nietzschean gospel to a young secular readership in the *Little Review* in 1914–15, Foster continued to lecture on him to students in his religion courses at the University of Chicago.[102] Though his lectures, including "Nietzsche and Science," "Nietzsche and Religion," and "Nietzsche and Jesus," were fitted with scholarly discourse and had their messianic language toned down, he presented a similar Nietzsche to his audiences: the religious critic, the theologian, and, above all, the spiritual visionary. His use of Nietzsche shows how thoroughly he integrated his ideas, not simply to understand or even endorse a liberalized Christianity, but to imagine surpassing its finality altogether. But even for Foster, the theologian who most thoroughly integrated Nietzsche's philosophy, this position did not require abandoning the personality of Jesus. Indeed, his lectures made affirmations expressive of the broader appropriations of Nietzsche when they considered, as Foster put it, how "Jesus was a revaluator of values," how "Jesus 'lived dangerously,'" and how, despite Nietzsche's hatred for Christianity, "in some ways Nietzsche and Jesus would have been good friends."[103]

Foster's claims for a Nietzschean Jesus were neither bland affirmations of Jesus's spiritual authority nor efforts to use Jesus to invest Nietzsche with his. Rather, they were expressions of the modern seeker, still finding his way— cautiously, hesitantly, and uncertainly—between a supernatural religion and a naturalized one, God the Father and the divinity of the self, faith and doubt— with Jesus and Nietzsche as guides. Though Foster was exceptional in the degree to which he reckoned with the full implications of Nietzsche for his faith, he did so as part of his vocation as minister, theologian, and professing Christian. He struggled bitterly with the meaning behind his speculation of a Jesus-Nietzsche friendship, and he was not alone in his understanding of their affinities. He, like so many other early twentieth-century liberal Protestants, enlisted Nietzsche to come to terms with what his own Christianity meant to him.

────────

"What is Christianity going to do with Nietzsche?" asked Congregational minister W. C. A. Wallar in 1915 as he sought to make sense of Nietzsche's increasing dominance in American life. There was no alternative for pious moderns but to "take him in hand . . . and thus suck the strength of our living enemy, as well as eat honey from the carcass of the dead lion."[104] And gorge on the honey they did. Though transforming Nietzsche's scathing critique into an endorsement of the faith was no easy feat, early twentieth-century religious commentators developed twin strategies for making his philosophy serviceable to the Christian life. They simultaneously mined his writings and appropriated his phrases and concepts in their campaign to demonstrate the power and possibility of faith in modern times, while they sought to prove that his secular philosophy alone could not provide the spiritual rock and refuge of the original Gospel. However, by using Nietzsche's philosophy as a way of retrieving Christian fundamentals, religious interpreters demonstrated Nietzsche's value for modern piety. Each in their own way, Protestant and Catholic interpreters of Nietzsche agreed that his philosophy had provided a service to modern Christianity, for it emphasized anew the importance of spiritual strenuousness, the human need for transcendence, and the value of personality. They agreed that Nietzsche had helped to identify problems of the spiritual life in the modern world.

However their admission of Nietzsche's contribution to modern Christianity was no unqualified endorsement of his ideas. Nietzsche's Protestant interpreters admitted to being drawn to his longing for a higher humanity, but stressed that an elevated human personality was possible only in accordance with scripture. Nietzsche had rightly criticized the leveling tendencies of modern democracy, but they argued that only through Jesus could moderns rise above the money-getting and material comforts of mass culture. For all of the similarities between Nietzsche and Jesus, religious readers maintained that the prophet of Naumburg could never replace the divine personality of Nazareth. After forays into Nietzsche's antifoundationalism, Christian commentators returned to the foundation of Christ.

Wallar provides insight into the strange beginnings of Nietzsche's career in American religious thought: "It is the history of mind: first a slavish burden-bearer of others' wares, then a devouring appropriator of possessions in one's own right, then oblivion and a new beginning, a prime-motor at the game of creating."[105] And so it was with the early twentieth-century religious reception of Nietzsche's philosophy. Once Christian theologians and clergy began to describe Jesus as a model Nietzschean, once they referred to him as the true Übermensch and transvaluator of all values, once ministers could play with Nietzsche's language and call for Christian "will to freedom" and "will to love," they had put their seal and confirmation, albeit unwittingly, on Nietzsche's significance for the spiritual life in America.[106] By arguing that Nietzsche was a model ascetic, by likening him to a Hebrew prophet, and by finding parallels between his philosophy and Christian theology, they thus paved the way for moderns to understand Nietzsche as a viable substitute—a secular savior.

# The American Naturalization of the Übermensch

Once one said God when one gazed upon distant seas; but now I have taught you to say: Übermensch.

FRIEDRICH NIETZSCHE, *Thus Spoke Zarathustra* (1883–85)

We stumble on; the über-menschen plant a foot where there is no certain hold; & in the struggle that follows, the whole of us get dragged up.

WILLIAM JAMES, unpublished note (ca. 1900–1901)

In *Ecce Homo*, Nietzsche recalled that fateful day in August 1881 when he first came up with the idea for *Thus Spoke Zarathustra* while walking through the woods near his Swiss summer retreat. It was surely a momentous experience. But the figure realized in that moment of inspiration—the Übermensch—did not make its first appearance there. In fact, it debuted in modern literary history neither in the Swiss Alps, nor in 1881, nor in Friedrich Nietzsche's moral imagination. In order to retrace its origins, we must instead shift our attention northeastward to Weimar, rewind the historical frame to 1806 (thirty-eight years before Nietzsche was born), and enter the study of a beautiful baroque house on Frauenplan Street, where we find Johann Wolfgang von Goethe completing his masterpiece, *Faust: A Tragedy*. For it was in Goethe's *Faust* (part 1, 1808), not in Nietzsche's *Thus Spoke Zarathustra*, that the Übermensch came into being in modern literature.

Throughout the nineteenth century, American readers were intimately familiar with Goethe's epic tragedy, which retold the legend of a brilliant young scholar longing to grasp the true meaning of the universe.[1] Restless with his era's unshakable faith in the divine order of things, Faust craves truth unobstructed by superstition. He crams himself with all forms of academic knowledge—philosophy, jurisprudence, and medicine—in order to know "endless Nature." But to no avail. A spirit from heaven hears Faust's desperate pleas for a glimpse of the Eternal, and asks, "What vexes you, oh Übermensch!" (Welch erbärmlich Grauen Fasst Übermenschen dich!)[2] Although the term was used only this one time in *Faust*, the image and implications of a superhuman longing for knowledge and mastery is woven throughout the entire play. And it was the themes of heroic self-exertion and psychic and spiritual longing that served as the leitmotif of so much of Goethe's corpus.

And yet throughout the nineteenth century, despite the multiple English-language editions of *Faust*, its prominent place in American libraries and family parlors, its story set to stage in small communities and in big city theaters, the Übermensch made neither a deep nor a lasting impression on American thought. In fact, in many of the major translations it made no impression at all. Perhaps finding the image too ineffable, Samuel Taylor Coleridge skipped it altogether in his 1821 English translation: "What pitiful weakness has seized on thee now?"[3] Abraham Hayward's 1838 translation offered what would become a more familiar translation: "demigod."[4] Bayard Taylor's 1871 translation tried to give it life with "superhuman."[5] But even this rendering ignited no controversy or enthusiasm. Quite simply, Goethe's Übermensch may have resided in the United States throughout the nineteenth century, but it was not naturalized into American moral discourse. It was here, but it never ventured beyond the pages of his *Faust*.

However, when Nietzsche's Übermensch—translated as "beyond man" in the Tille and Common editions of *Thus Spoke Zarathustra*—made its way to America at the turn of the last century, commentators there took notice immediately. It was at that time that Nietzsche's image of a higher human being ignited a firestorm of interest in US radical weeklies, literary magazines, and journals of opinion. In Nietzsche's poetic and prophetic writings about the Übermensch, early twentieth-century writers, philosophers, literary scholars, and editorialists seized on a concept that helped express the persistent conflict between self and society, autonomy and solidarity in modern America.

These tensions were not new to the period; nor was individual striving, nor was the term itself. That Nietzsche's Übermensch arrived *after* Darwin and Spencer is significant. But Goethe's Faust also had been read in America, at a time when ideas about evolution were sweeping through Victorian culture. Nietzsche worked with the term much more extensively, however, devoting an entire book, *Thus Spoke Zarathustra*, to heralding its arrival. And yet as American interpreters then observed, even in *Zarathustra* Nietzsche's characterizations of the Übermensch were poetic, even prophetic, but certainly not clear. In the most extensive description of the Übermensch, Nietzsche wrote,

> *God is dead!* . . . [Behold] *I teach you the* [*Übermensch*]. Man is something that shall be overcome. . . . All beings so far have created something beyond themselves . . . . What is the ape to man? A laughingstock or a painful embarrassment. And man shall be just that for the [Übermensch]: a laughingstock or a painful embarrassment. . . . The [Übermensch] is the meaning of the earth. . . . I beseech you, my brothers, *remain faithful to the earth*, and do not believe those who speak to you of otherworldly hopes![6]

Though American interpreters were frustrated with how little they had to go on, one thing was striking: the Übermensch arrived in a world after God. In Goethe's poem, it is a spirit who refers to Faust as an Übermensch. Goethe may have been a self-proclaimed pagan, but in *Faust* heaven is still a sacred canopy. In Nietzsche's work, however, it is an earthly Zarathustra who heralds the Übermensch in the wake of the death of God.[7]

Of all Nietzsche's concepts, the Übermensch received the most intense interest while also posing some of the most difficult interpretive problems for American readers. Contestations over interpretation erupted even among those of the same political affiliation, religious denomination, and literary sensibility. Although some readers were baffled that Nietzsche's "imperialist," "elitist," "nihilist" concept had found so many enthusiasts in democratic and religious America, others believed that the self-sovereign Übermensch had found his natural habitat in that nation's culture of possessive individualism.

Both outside the academy and within, American readers turned to the Übermensch as a concept essential for understanding modern selfhood. Whereas popular authors, journalists, and social reformers typically cast the figure as an aggrandized self at war with society, philosophers, humanists, and social scientists within the academy understood the Übermensch as the self at war with itself. While few scholars thought it a salutary image of modern selfhood, they nevertheless recognized its value for testing the moral discourses of romanticism, naturalism, liberalism, and pragmatism. Rather than celebrate Nietzsche's exalted figure, they enlisted it for analyzing the conditions of morality after foundationalism.

With the onslaught of World War I, these questions took on new urgency, especially as critics on both sides of the Atlantic accused Nietzsche's philosophy of being the inspiration for and sanction of German militarism. Reports from the front lines did not substantively alter but instead heightened the urgency of prewar debates: Was it possible or even desirable to have a fully realized humanity that stays faithful to the earth? Can the individual pull down the afterworld without pulling up the underworld? The horrors of war raised the stakes as American interpreters sought to examine the sources of the self in a world without foundations.

## The Übermensch in the Popular Imagination

The concept of the Übermensch entered the American scene at a time when observers were seeking to comprehend not just the content but also the *ideals* of modern democracy, laissez-faire capitalism, and American social and spiritual life. Periodicals and books with titles such as "The Tyranny of the Average Man," *Democracy and the Overman*, and *The Menace of the Underman* popularized variations of the übermenschian theme by sounding the alarm over the retrograde moral, social, and political developments in American life.[8] For observers of the early twentieth-century United States, the image of the Übermensch served as a vivid flashpoint by which they could test and reformulate their understanding of the perils confronting the individual in an age of growing dislocation and anonymity.

In the years leading up to World War I, the question that vexed most American interpreters was whether Nietzsche's talk of mastery and transcendence was directed against the lower instincts of the self or against the "slave morality" of modern society. They likewise wondered whether it represented an endorsement of, or a delivery from, the isolating tendencies of modern democracy and industrial capitalism. Was Nietzsche an ally or an antagonist in the campaign to overcome atomistic individualism in American public life?

In the first decades of the century, many of the Übermensch's most vocal enthusiasts were socialists. In the quest for social harmony, their Übermensch embodied the strong self pitted not against others but rather against the lingering grip of stifling bourgeois ethics and aesthetics in modern society. In 1905, American audiences could witness this abstract concept take on clear (super-) human form onstage as the anarchist philosopher John Tanner in George Bernard Shaw's *Man and Superman*. Shaw's protagonist helped popularize the image of the Übermensch as a vitalist hero flouting Victorian morality by challenging repressive sex roles and mocking the institution of marriage.[9] Jack London's naturalist novels, including *Sea-Wolf*, *Iron Heel*, and *Martin Eden*, similarly promoted a Darwinian vision of the Übermensch as one who clawed against outworn ideals of possessive individualism and helped remake a strong socialist society.[10] Like Shaw and London, the socialist critic Max Eastman saw in Nietzsche's Übermensch a prototype of the new individual who would lead in the radical reorganization of American political, economic, and social life. In all three interpretations, the enemies of the Übermensch were the retrograde aspects of modern life: laissez-faire economics, the American plutocracy, repressive sexuality and gender roles, and the "slave morality" of bourgeois culture.

Although critical of the socialistic reading of Nietzsche, H. L. Mencken's unashamed version of the unbounded immoralist Übermensch shared a similar vision of the individual who rails against convention. Mencken described the Übermensch as an unyielding, godless, Dionysian aristocrat guided by the gospel of "prudent and intelligent selfishness, of absolute and utter individualism." He argued that "it is only the under-dog . . . that believes in equality. It is only the groveling and inefficient mob that seeks to reduce all humanity to one dead level, for it is only the mob that would gain by such leveling." Once he had sufficiently dethroned Demos, he went on to attack Christian charity. According to Mencken, the Übermensch had the perspicacity to recognize, and the courage to accept, that Christian charity weakened the "race," for it "maintain[ed] the useless at the expense of the strong."[11]

A common vision of the Übermensch as the individual who breaks from the "slave morality" of degrading aspects of modern Christianity, democracy, and capitalism united critics with otherwise warring political sentiments. As two early Nietzsche interpreters expressed this shared concern, "Our present age . . . fosters only degenerate human beings and destroys in their incipiency all movements that give promise of greatness. . . . Everywhere we find only the average man, *das zahme Haustier* [the domesticated animal], *ein Stück Herdenvieh* [one of the cattle], who has no will of his own, but is submissive to the great majority. Everywhere exist proletarian instincts, which render the development of a really superior nature an impossibility." Though some Übermensch supporters might have recoiled from the image of modern society as a safe harbor for "*fin-de-siècle* imbecile[s]" and which likened moderns to "a mangy flock of mediocrity," Nietzsche's philosophy of the higher man worried American interpreters of the Left and the Right with the prospect that Christian charity and democratic egalitarianism fostered a tepid equality among men and valued human uniformity over human greatness.[12]

What made understanding the Übermensch particularly difficult for American observers was what even to call it. There was no definitive translation of the Übermensch; the only two English-language versions of *Zarathustra* available were under sharp attack from philosophers and translators intimate with Nietzsche's philosophy. Scholars wrangled over the accuracy and adequacy of these attempts to translate Nietzsche's term into a word that would make sense to English speakers but remained true to Nietzsche's original meaning. Before Shaw popularized "superman," commentators either defaulted to the original "Übermensch" or opted for "beyond man," the rendering Tille had selected for his 1896 translation. Paul Carus, for one, stressed that translation was no neutral affair, and that philosophical accuracy could not be subordinate to linguistic artistry. He thus sought to stop Tille's "beyond man" dead in its tracks, insisting that "beyond means *jenseits*; and Nietzsche wrote *über*, i.e., superior to, over, or higher than, and the literal translation 'overman' appears to be the best." He likewise rejected "superman" for its "barbaric combination" of Latin and Saxon words.[13] However, Thomas Stockham Baker, a scholar of contemporary German literature and headmaster of a Maryland school for boys, found the construction "superman" appropriate precisely *because* it violated the traditional rules of linguistic construction: "It is convenient, it is even illogical . . . but inasmuch as the idea that it intends to convey has never had a name before, there is no great necessity for logic or a regard either for etymology or precedents."[14] Despite objections, the word *superman* gained traction in the American English vocabulary, and there it stayed, but not without controversy.

Although there were vibrant debates about how best to translate *Übermensch*, all seemed to agree that "man" was the appropriate translation for *Mensch* despite the fact that *Mensch* means "human being." If rendered literally, *Übermensch* would be "over human being."[15] Thus Nietzsche's potentially genderless image of a higher humanity, or at least an image that has the potential to be gendered female, was gendered male in the English language right from the start. It is in part thanks to these slippages in translation that American readers asked, "Did Nietzsche Predict the Superwoman as Well as the Superman?"[16] Nietzsche's barbs about women and feminism certainly did not make an answer in the affirmative axiomatic. One of the most oft-quoted lines—the bit of wisdom from the old woman to Zarathustra: "You are going to women? Do not forget the whip!"—presented some interpretive challenges for the would-be American Überfrau. So too did Zarathustra's pronouncement that "the happiness of man is: I will. The happiness of woman is: he wills." Many feminist readers drawn to Nietzsche were nevertheless repelled by passages that seemed to characterize woman's self-worth as relational, her intellect questionable, and her value to society biological: "Let your hope be: May I give birth to the [Übermensch]!"[17]

There were, however, strategies for feminizing the Übermensch. In order to conclude that "Nietzsche undoubtedly foresaw and welcomed the Superwoman," appreciative female readers were inspired by the vision of the perfected woman as "the mother of the transfigured man of the future."[18] However, fighting such an image of glorified motherhood is precisely what drew Margaret Sanger to the Übermensch. Sanger discovered in Nietzsche's thought both a critical philosophy and an aspirational idea for achieving a woman's right to bodily self-sovereignty. In her speeches and writings, she employed the Übermensch to critique the bankrupt Western morality that undergirded the repression of women by church and state as well as an image of a self worthy of idolatry once all idols were smashed. Feminine chastity, she argued, was an artifact of a desiccated "Christian . . . ascetic ideal," which taught women to hide in shame from their earthly desires. The Übermensch, by contrast, offered an image of "life in its fullness and all that is high, beautiful, and daring."[19] In a 1914 speech on Nietzsche, Sanger argued that he had taught her that "the individual is the original source & constituent of all value."[20] In a journal entry of July that same year entitled "No Gods," she paraphrased a passage from *Zarathustra*: "Alas, brethren [*sic*], that God whom I created was man's work and man's madness, like all gods. Far too many are born. For the superfluous was the State created. Behold how it devoureth them." Sanger found this promise of the liberated female self after God so inspirational that when in 1914 she started *The Woman Rebel*—her newspaper to endorse contraception—she used as its slogan "No Gods, No Masters."[21]

Although Sanger's Übermensch fought against repressive sexual ethics, her image of the perfectly sovereign individual who asserts his (or her) will to power against the mediocre masses reflected the dominant image assimilated into American political and social thought in the early twentieth century. While the figure animated the political imaginations of activists and writers of the Left and the Right, it failed to capture the moral imagination of a number of prominent scholars. The philosopher Josiah Royce, most notably, argued for a vision of the Übermensch as a being striving for self, rather than social, transcendence. Royce argued that the Übermensch was not a fighter against social convention but a moralist who sought to create contingent ideals to guide his ethical commitments without recourse in absolutes. Similarly, the New Humanist classicist Irving Babbitt argued that Nietzsche's battle for mastery was one waged within the self rather than against others. However, as champions of classical ideals that they believed had been lost to moderns, Babbitt and his fellow New Humanists cautioned that antifoundational self-overcoming would lead inexorably to romantic self-abandonment. Although Royce and the New Humanists differed in their assessments of the promises of übermenschian self-transcendence, together they argued that Nietzsche's higher self was best understood as a philosophical rather than a social ideal.

The image of the Übermensch as an oppositional self emerged as the dominant motif during World War I as American political thinkers, philosophers, and journalists increasingly linked it with Bismarck's imperialist blood-and-iron vision of German ascendancy. Although commentators had made much of Nietzsche's "Polish emotionalism" just a few years earlier (discussed in chapter 1), by 1914 they began to interpret him and his vision of the higher self as a window on the German mind. Nietzsche's Übermensch—once celebrated as a crusader for truth, a debunker of superstition, and an iconoclast who placed conscience above convention—now was seen as the martial ideal of imperial Germany. There is not a straight trajectory from London's and Eastman's socialist, Mencken's aristocratic, and Sanger's feminist Übermensch to the image of the Übermensch as a menace to democracy during the war; yet these interpretations are all of one piece in regarding Nietzsche's image of the higher man as one who places his own self above American society as it is, in an effort to remake it into what he alone wills it to be.

## Self-Overcoming and Social Uplift

Given the overwhelming tendency of American thinkers to identify the antidemocratic Übermensch as the imperial ideal of wartime Germany, it is not surprising that *Atlantic Monthly* editor W. Fergus Kernan was taken aback at the discovery of a laudatory essay on Nietzsche written by Josiah Royce among his posthumous papers. "It will perhaps appear strange to many," noted Kernan, that Royce—the esteemed Harvard professor, philosopher of the "Great Community," and vocal proponent of US entry into the war against Germany—"should have found so much, not merely of interest, but of sound doctrine . . . in the philosopher now claimed by modern Germany as its prophet and oracle."[22] For readers familiar with Royce's philosophy, however, the discovery of this article as well as another unfinished essay on Nietzsche among his personal papers should have come as no surprise.[23] Nietzsche's genealogy of ideas as a cumulative process of revision and transvaluation influenced both the method and the spirit of Royce's philosophy of history. Royce imported Nietzsche's concept of ideas as human creations layered with sediments of history and experience. In addition, he learned from Nietzsche that the philosopher must examine the genealogy and application of philosophical concepts such as the Absolute, reason, and loyalty in order to understand their contingent meanings. And in Nietzsche's concept of the Übermensch especially, Royce discovered a model of the naturalized absolute idealism that he believed was vital for the ethical life.

One need not simply search for traces of a Nietzschean sensibility in Royce's idealist thought, however, for Royce himself clearly testified to Nietzsche's impact on his own thinking. In the opening pages of his *Philosophy of Loyalty* (1908), he named Nietzsche as the "philosophical rhapsodist" who had ushered in the intellectual movement in Germany to unearth the human foundations of scientific and religious ideals once considered absolutes. Royce characterized the "restless" and "reforming" spirit of his own generation as one marked by a suspicion of inherited values, an interrogation of "foundations of old beliefs," and a subsequent desire to revise moral traditions. It was Nietzsche's "'transmutation of all moral values'" that "made popular the thesis that all the conventional morality of the past . . . was in principle false, was a mere transition stage of evolution and must be altered to the core." He drew on Nietzsche to give new meaning to the popular phrase "time makes ancient good uncouth," and to come to terms with "the spirit of this modern revolt against moral traditions."[24]

Royce observed that modern reformers had discovered in Nietzsche's thought a source of and justification for their overpowering iconoclastic individualism that threatened to tear the bonds of ethical and communal affiliation. However, he contended that the popular view of Nietzsche's Übermensch as a tireless crusader against social conventions, which was popularized by Shaw, London, and Mencken and bandied about in the popular press, misunderstood Nietzsche's broader vision. The "modern agitator," the "typically restless child of our age," noted Royce, believed that Nietzsche's philosophy demanded the rejection of all ties to the community as debilitating social controls and outworn moral conventions. Challenging the popular interpretation of the Übermensch as a social renegade, Royce suggested that the "individualist, longing to escape, perhaps from his economic cares, perhaps from the marriage bond," is mistaken when he "declare[s] Nietzsche to be his prophet, and set[s] out to be a Superman."[25]

Royce not only rejected this oppositional view of individual identity, he also argued that it found no support in Nietzsche's philosophy. In his estimation, Nietzsche had envisioned the Übermensch as a being whose aim was not to hoist self over society but to achieve self-overcoming (*Überwindung*). He contended that Nietzsche's "will to power" had little to do with "mere brute force," but rather was best understood in a transcendentalist sense of self-mastery. The Übermensch taught the "lesson of [Nietzsche's] experience" of constant physical pain and psychological turmoil:

> If you have any insistent horror, conquer it by facing it and thinking it out. If fate besets you, make what seems fate also appear to you as your own deed. If you have any evil thought, make it a part of your free self by expressing once [and] for all its whole meaning. Do not suppress your weaknesses. Build your strength upon them.

Thus, the real struggle of the heroic individual is not solely to liberate himself from conflict with society, but rather to use the conflict within himself as a source for self-regeneration.[26]

In his effort to assimilate Nietzsche's vision of self-sovereignty into American moral discourse, Royce highlighted the similarities between the Übermensch and the tradition of "ethical Titanism" so central to Western literature and philosophy. As one of the few early twentieth-century American interpreters who observed affinities between Emerson and Nietzsche (though he was unaware of Emerson's influence on Nietzsche), he argued that Nietzsche's aphoristic writings revealed his philosophical inclination to overcome the warring instincts within the self—not by suppressing them but by allowing them their full play. Drawing out the romantic strain in Nietzsche's philosophy, Royce noted, "Like both Emerson and Walt Whitman, Nietzsche feels perfectly free to follow the dialectic of his own mental development, to contradict himself, or, as Walt Whitman said, 'to contain multitudes.'" He argued that Nietzsche's Übermensch also shared qualities with Goethe's Faust and Shelley's Prometheus in perceiving life as a contest between the autonomous individual and the "world of convention, of tradition, or of destiny."[27]

At the same time, Royce argued that Nietzsche's "Titanic ideal" did represent a departure from the tradition of Western individualism. A romantic ideal pressed through Darwinism, Nietzsche's titanism broke from the Divine and, indeed, all timeless moral absolutes. Unlike the iconoclast who "knows who he is and what he wants," Nietzsche's Übermensch represented a "strenuous seeker for selfhood" who "agonizes" over the constitution and aim of his personhood. Without recourse to God, heaven, or first principles, moderns would have to create meaning for themselves "through an imitation of this deliberately created concept of the perfect individual, but still more through a determination restlessly to labor upon the task of creating the concept."[28]

In striving to create meaning anew, Nietzsche's antifoundational Übermensch synthesized the philosophical instrumentalism and romantic individualism that Royce argued characterized the age. In his appraisal of modern thought, Nietzsche had bequeathed to moderns on both sides of the Atlantic "the storm and stress of a reëxamination of the whole problem of truth." As Royce put it,

> Whether you discuss the philosophy of Nietzsche or of mathematics,—whether the *Umwertung aller Werte* or the "class of all classes,"—whether Mr. Russell's "Contradiction" or the *Uebermensch* is in question, ... always the same general issue has sooner or later to be faced. You are involved in some phase of the problem about the nature of truth.[29]

In addition to a "restlessness regarding the very foundations of morality," Royce continued, modern thought was animated by an individualistic "longing to be self-possessed and inwardly free, the determination to submit to no merely external authority." Because man is unwilling or unable to take refuge in the ruins of "doctrinal authority," however, modern thinkers envisioned a sovereign individual who would preside as a self-sufficient creator and arbiter of new truths: "The doer, or perhaps the deed, not only finds, but *is*, the truth."[30] Thus, this individualistic strain in transatlantic instrumentalism viewed truth as something made, not found, and as relative to the individual.

Royce argued that this tension between relativism and individualism was especially acute in the pragmatist philosophy of his friend and Harvard colleague William James. From the perspective of Royce's moral idealism, the post-Darwinian instrumentalism and romantic individualism in James's thought were necessary but insufficient grounds for creating a new ethics in modern life. He argued that James's pragmatic instrumentalism was useful insofar as it was fueled by a critical spirit that helped rescue the study of truth from foundationalism. While it succeeded in providing a valuable contribution to epistemology, by itself James's instrumentalism failed to offer an animating vision of human life. Royce argued that while it may have revealed a procedure for studying truth in terms of consequences, method was no substitute for meaning.

Royce believed that James was a deeply committed moralist like himself, who thought philosophy could be put to work to help transform modern America into what he called the "Beloved Community." But he argued that the Jamesian pragmatism could not get its radical empiricism and romantic ethics to work together. To make his point, Royce turned to Nietzsche. In doing so he employed a strategy of putting Nietzsche and James in dialogue, using the one to interpret the other. In this case, he used a caricature of Nietzsche's theory of truth to characterize James's fusion of relativism and instrumentalism. As Royce put it,

> There is no absolute truth. There is only the truth that you need. . . . Borrow Nietzsche's phraseology. Call the truth of ordinary intellectualism mere *Sklavenwahrheit*. It pretends to be absolute; but only the slaves believe in it. "Henceforth," so some Zarathustra of a new theory of truth may say, "I teach you *Herrenwahrheit*." Credit what you choose to credit. Truth is made for man, not man for truth. Let your life "boil over" into new truth as much as you find such effervescence convenient. When, apart from the constraints of present verification, and apart from mere convention, I say: "This opinion of mine is true," I mean simply: "To my mind, lord over its own needs, this assertion now appears expedient." Whenever my expediency changes, my truth will change.

Ironically, Royce suggested that though Nietzsche himself did *not* hold this view of expedient truths, James did. As Royce quipped, "I hesitate to make accusations which some of my nearest and dearest friends may repudiate as personally injurious." But Nietzsche helped him challenge the warring imperatives in pragmatism. James's pragmatic epistemology tore away the false foundations of palsied certainties, but uncertainty alone, Royce stressed, was not fertile soil for individual growth. And by denying ideals, he concluded, James had also undermined eternal, and therefore all vital, sources of the self.[31]

Though Royce identified a common deconstructive epistemology and a rhapsodical celebration of human autonomy in both Nietzsche and James, he argued that ideals like Nietzsche's Übermensch helped bridge the antifoundational and regenerative tendencies in their thinking. In Royce's naturalized idealism, Nietzsche's concept of the Übermensch exemplified his conception of "loyalty to loyalty"—a commitment to higher ideals without confirmation in moral absolutes.[32] For Nietzsche, as for Royce, "unsettlement" was no "finality": "the seeking Zarathustra desires in the end . . . to define the law of life in terms that shall not be subject to the endless flow." Royce envisioned Nietzsche's Übermensch as one who strove to lift himself above the flux of uncertainty and to define for himself a picture of the higher humanity that would guide his conduct and unify his experiences. He agreed with Nietzsche in his insistence that ideals need not be viewed as magical or supernatural in order to have any power over human imagination. Though the content of ideals is historically and culturally contingent, argued Royce, the struggling to create and realize a higher meaning for one's personhood is an ever-present aspect of human experience. He stressed, "If our philosophy of loyalty is right, Nietzsche was not wrong in this appeal to the superhuman. The superhuman we indeed have always with us. Life has no sense without it."[33]

Based on William James's limited, though telling, references to Nietzsche in his published and unpublished writings, it is not hard to imagine that Royce's observation of their philosophical affinities would have struck a nerve. James's comments on Nietzsche testify to a powerful ambivalence about the German philosopher. He clearly saw the similarities in his and Nietzsche's antimetaphysics. James mentioned Nietzsche briefly in a 1905 letter to Thomas Perry, for example, when he mused, "Every philosopher (W.J., *e.g.*) pretends that all the others are metaphysicians against whom he is simply defending the rights of common sense."[34] He could also, if only in a moment of whimsy, describe himself as an "Übermensch," as he did in a 1904 letter to his wife, Alice, when he told her that he "read Nietzsche . . . and smoked a cigar, 'as an Übermensch.'"[35] And he recognized in Nietzsche another philosopher who emphasized the important role temperament plays in determining one's philosophical views and commitments. But it was likely James's agreement with Nietzsche that philosophy is a confession of the author's temperament that made it so awkward to find himself advancing a view of the nature of moral personhood strikingly similar to that of a philosopher whom he regarded as "pathetic and diseased."[36]

It is difficult to date with precision when James first read Nietzsche, but he was clearly familiar with him in 1892, as evident from his marking on the second flyleaf recto of his copy of *Jenseits von Gut und Böse* (2nd ed., 1891): "Wm. James, Freiburg ... June 1892."[37] He first mentioned him in print in an 1895 review of Max Nordau's *Degeneration*, and his letters record his readings of a handful of works about Nietzsche in the early 1900s.[38] The extensive marginalia in *Jenseits* and *Zur Geneaologie der Moral* (3rd ed., 1894)—the two extant volumes in his personal library—suggest that he read both very closely.[39] The sheer volume of notations (underlines, sidebars) in them makes it difficult to distinguish which ideas most interested him upon reading them. The list of terms he wrote on the right-hand side of the back pastedown of *Jenseits*, however, provides some clues: "Will," "The 'objective' man,'" and "[Nietzsche's] human ideal," among others.[40] But it is the concept set off on its own with an exclamation point on the left pastedown—"Wille zur Macht, 49, 17, 68, 105, 228!"—and the underlined corresponding phrase in the body of the text, "Leben selbst ist Wille zur Macht," that confirm the special significance that this concept had for James.[41]

It is his discussions of Nietzsche's view of moral selfhood that suggest that James grudgingly, if haltingly, shared his belief in the kinds of persons who propel human progress. James read Nietzsche's *On the Genealogy of Morals* in 1900[42] while writing his lectures on the "saintly" versus "worldly" impulses, which later became part of his *The Varieties of Religious Experience* (1902). The striking discussion of the Übermensch (written circa 1900–1901) in his personal notes on ethics (posthumously published) signals James's strong attraction to and ambivalence about Nietzsche's ethical ideal.[43] The piece rehearses an argument straight out of "What Makes a Life Significant?" where James stressed that because we are poor judges of what makes others' lives meaningful, we should not demand their assent to our notions of life. But he stressed that the meanings of life that "make any *genuine vital difference* on a large scale, to the lives of our descendants," are not in one's private ideals or in the rote acceptance of others' but in "the marriage, namely, of some unhabitual ideal, however special, with some fidelity, courage, and endurance; with some man's or woman's pains."[44] It is in response to this very tension in his own vision between private virtue and public good, between the individual's uncoerced imagination and his or her efforts to test its creations in the arena of life, that James called upon the Übermensch.

In his unpublished notes on ethics, James considered the rivalries between what he referred to as individual "high mindedness" and social "prudence." While both make their contributions to society, he wondered whether it is a particular "high minded" type who ultimately propels humanity forward. He described him as the solitary, restless, immoderate "gentleman" who marries his private visions with personal sacrifice and social reality. James wrote, "We stumble on; the übermenschen plant a foot where there is no certain hold; & in the struggle that follows, the whole of us get dragged up after a fashion to the advanced position." James justified this by explaining that what seems immoderate in one age may be the very idea that brings humanity along in the next: the private ideal becomes public good. He recognized that

> with high mindedness inevitably goes cruelty and hardness. But, often as they appear (and in the individual are) features of defect, mere brutal lacks of sensibility, yet they have religious significance; and the servile admiration we all have for the [high-minded] gentleman with the reckless absoluteness of his demands, is a conclusive proof that he is genuinely superior.

James left no doubt where he got this disturbing and yet essential vision of the Übermensch, the individual with defects who nevertheless has religious significance:

> Poor sick Nietzsche has a wholesome meaning in his admiration of the predatory man, who refuses to compromise with the nature of things, leaving that to those of servile destiny. Everyone should be able at *some* conjunctures, to play the gentleman, no matter who gets hurt, no matter what domestic crockery gets broken.—Only afterwards, he mustn't complain![45]

James's quick pivot in the last line might speak to the tension in his own thinking between the sometimes harmonizing, sometimes warring romantic vitalism and instrumentalism, between private visions and public welfare. Or it might suggest how unsavory he found the whole prospect of agreeing with a "sick" philosopher, especially when philosophies are—as he would argue—

expressive of the author's temperament. Perhaps a little of both. But the five-word one-liner made at the end of thirty-eight lines of dramatic language thrusting toward a defense of the Übermensch—like the many aversive comments he would make when invoking Nietzsche—do not suggest that he made light of Nietzsche or his ideas.

The "gentleman" Übermensch crops up once more in James's *The Varieties of Religious Experience*, and with it the same tempered enthusiasm for the vision of striving selfhood he thought it embodied. James read *On the Genealogy of Morals* in the spring of 1900 while preparing his third Gifford Lecture in Edinburgh, which would become part of *Varieties*. His marginalia throughout the third essay, "What Is the Meaning of Ascetic Ideals," in his copy of *Genealogy* demonstrates how he tracked the very genealogy of "saintliness" that he would write about in his book. In discussing in his lecture the "saintly" versus "worldly" impulses, James named Nietzsche the "most inimical critic of the saintly impulses whom I know." He then recited Nietzsche's argument about the historical origins of asceticism found precisely in those heavily underlined passages in his copy of *Genealogy*. Transforming the passages into his own colorful language, James appraised the "biologically useful instinct of welcoming leadership, and glorifying the chief of the tribe." He described the social value of the fear of the towering leader, the rare worthy figure who marries his "conscience" and "will." These are the worldly, "beaked and taloned graspers" who come to symbolize one moral ideal type. He contrasted them with the saints (Nietzsche's ascetics), who are like "tame and harmless barn-yard poultry," inspiring no fear, no reverence, just "contempt." Switching imagery, James once again highlighted the difference between the "saint's type" versus the "gentleman's type," invoking the very immoderate gentleman "Übermensch" he praised in his unpublished notes. "Poor Nietzsche's antipathy is itself sickly enough," noted James, "but we all know what he means, and he expresses well the clash between the two ideals." Thus, in his lecture, in which he was trying to clear a space in modern life for a continued belief in the Divine, James nevertheless threw his weight behind the worldly taloned graspers, arguing that his own "empirical philosophy" encouraged him to do so. According to James (and finding confirmation in Nietzsche), there are no absolute ideal types of saintliness; virtues are relative to the beholder. "There is, in short, no absoluteness in the excellence of sainthood."[46] But more important, empiricism shows that while the saintly type might appeal in theory, in the real world we make ourselves "saintly" saints at our peril. James thus encouraged religious moderns to bring their religion a bit closer to earth.

James gravitated toward the image of the Übermensch, but it nevertheless carried with it disturbing associations of the philosopher whose temperament gave it form. Nary a reference to Nietzsche crops up in James's (at least) ten-year contact with his ideas that does not invoke his sickness. Such references are at their most colorful and generous in *Varieties*, where James described "the mood" of Nietzsche (and Schopenhauer) as marked by "an ennobling sadness," but also by a "peevishness running away with the bit between its teeth." Their "sallies . . . remind one, half the time, of the sick shriekings of two dying rats."[47] Nevertheless, James expressed his sympathy for Nietzsche's unsympathetic attack on asceticism as a moral ideal. And, though halting and uncertain, his descriptions of an Übermensch—the immoderate striver, who can plant a foot in an antifoundational universe where there is no certain hold—indicate the resonance of this image of a higher humanity for him. Though limited and brief, the record of James's engagement suggests that Nietzsche's characterization of the Übermensch fit with his own longing for meaning, for the infinite, and for human progress after Nietzsche declared God dead and James declared Him optional.

James's friend Royce recognized that his own effort to integrate the Übermensch into his naturalized idealism revealed the limitations of Nietzsche's moral vision. Whereas Nietzsche appreciated the "uniqueness of . . . every individual and the genuineness of the duty of every soul to seek its own type of salvation," he failed to appreciate that salvation requires social efficacy. Royce did not see the possibilities that James did in the Übermensch's potential for advancing the progress of the human race. But according to Royce, Nietzsche's concern was the moral "perfection, not of society, not of the masses of men, but of the great individual." In other words, "the great problem of reconciling the unique individual with the world-order is simply not Nietzsche's problem." Royce argued that Nietzsche's philosophy of the Übermensch expressed beautifully the struggle of man in his personal quest to discover what his individuality means for himself. He argued that those searching for a systematic solution to the tension between the free individual and the world of social obligations, conventions, and traditions would have to look elsewhere. For Royce, trying to squeeze a programmatic application out of what he considered an idealist concept not only ran counter to Nietzsche's exquisite vision; it also made little sense. However, he added, one should not "object to the musician because he is unable to carve . . . statues or to build . . . cathedrals."[48]

Throughout the course of the Übermensch's early American career, there were indeed many critics who objected to Nietzsche's vision of the higher individual because he could not carve statues or build cathedrals. Readers took the Übermensch to task because they perceived him to be either a destroyer of truth or a seeker of mastery. Royce understood that Nietzsche had challenged moral realism, but that he also believed in the human necessity for belief. While Nietzsche contended that "morality is not to be measured by a moral yardstick: for there is no absolute morality," he also argued that moral perspectivalism did not mean moral nihilism.[49] For Nietzsche, as for Royce, creating values and meaning without foundations required that "you shall get control over your For and Against and learn how to display [them] in accordance with your higher goal. You shall learn to grasp the sense of perspective in every value judgement."[50] Royce had ears attuned to Nietzsche's "For" and "Against," and thus attempted in his own work to hold nonfoundationalism and idealism in balance. Despite his efforts, however, few American interpreters followed him in his effort to integrate the two aspects of Nietzsche's philosophy into a unified picture of meaning.

## Modern Whirl and Romantic Self-Abandonment

While Josiah Royce was busy imagining the regenerative possibilities embodied in the Übermensch concept, his colleague Irving Babbitt sat across Harvard Yard, writing about the disintegrative tendencies in Nietzsche's philosophy. Even so, there were some commonalities in Royce's and Babbitt's appraisals of Nietzsche. Both believed that Nietzsche's philosophy served as a key contributor to the modern rejection of metaphysical, moral, and rational foundations as the basis for human knowledge and conduct, and both saw it, to varying degrees, as expressions of romanticism. In addition, both were troubled by the overwhelming evidence that, in the words of the historian J. David Hoeveler Jr., "twentieth-century man had lost his bearings."[51] However, while Royce argued that clinging to illusory foundations was not the answer to modern man's rootlessness, Babbitt argued that only by returning to classical ideals could modern man retrieve his moral center. In addition, whereas Royce contended that Nietzsche's constructive Übermensch ideal served as an answer to the deconstructive dimension of pragmatic thought, Babbitt argued that the Übermensch was little more than the culmination of the disintegrative whirl of Nietzsche's antifoundationalism.

As professor of romance languages and literature and of comparative literature at Harvard University, Babbitt garnered a reputation for his antimodernist views as the leader of the small though prominent literary movement known as New Humanism. Together with Paul Elmer More, literary editor of *The Nation* and later professor of Greek and Patristic philosophy at Princeton, and with the assistance of a small coterie of professors affiliated with the movement, including Prosser Hall Frye of the University of Nebraska, Babbitt regarded Nietzsche's philosophy as an example of the Rousseauian romanticism he believed to be the cause of modern moral and intellectual drift.[52] In the early 1910s and 1920s, the New Humanists were among the most visible and vocal opponents of Nietzsche in the academy. The Übermensch surfaces repeatedly as their bête noire—a symbol for the degenerative impulses in romanticism and naturalism that they believed plagued modern life. They viewed the Übermensch as Nietzsche's answer to the gloom, pessimism, and moral purposelessness of modern civilization. Although they sympathized with Nietzsche's diagnosis of the modern condition, they argued that the Übermensch was far from being an antidote to waywardness. Rather, they perceived the Übermensch as both a force promoting and a victim of morbid rootlessness. Without eternal sources of the self, they argued, the modern romance with self-realization led inevitably into self-abnegation.

Babbitt's 1919 study, *Rousseau and Romanticism*, cast Nietzsche as an example of the poverty of modern romanticism as a source for the imaginative arts, as well as for modern morality. The Nietzschean unwarranted regard for the solitary self represented the most recent example of the romantic tradition's botched view of the relationship between the individual and the world. He argued that romantics from Rousseau to Nietzsche had recoiled from the ethically robust and spiritually nourishing ideals of original classicism. In his estimation, Greek classical thought properly emphasized the beauty and value of the universal over the particular, and probability over variability.[53] He argued that the Greeks understood truth as a given—a foundation for timeless standards to guide human thought and conduct. The romantics, conversely, reeled against the imitative ideal as an obstacle to their authenticity. They believed that their individuality lay in self-expression, and that self-expression was to be measured by its distinctiveness, its unpredictability, and its "[violation of] the normal sequence of cause and effect in favor of adventure."[54] The Rousseauian romantic, Babbitt argued, sought not only to discredit intellect in favor of emotion but also to reject all external limitations on himself in favor of a view of his individuality as "infinite." According to Babbitt, Nietzsche recognized the modern romantic tendency to disregard all bounds to human "imagination," "impulse," and "desire." Quoting Nietzsche, he asserted that "proportionateness is strange to us. . . . Our itching is really the itching for the infinite, the immeasurable."[55]

Babbitt went on to argue that Nietzsche's Übermensch stood as the prime example of the modern expressivist's romance with individuality. According to Babbitt, the Übermensch represented the individual who sought to dispense with all "rationalism" and "decorum," all abstract moral and philosophical ideals, in order to "multiply distinctions" between himself and others. Babbitt viewed Nietzsche's Übermensch as an image of the romantic who sets his sense of his own "genius," his perception of his "unique and private self," against all conventions. The Übermensch regards all forms of human sympathy, all efforts to find likeness between himself and his fellow man, as debilitating checks on his will-to-power. "The imagination of the superman," Babbitt wrote, "spurning every centre of control, traditional or otherwise, so cooperates with his impulses and desires as to give them 'infinitude,' that is so as to make them reach out for more and ever for more. The result is a frenzied romanticism." Though he confessed that Nietzsche "can on occasion speak very shrewdly about the evils that have resulted from . . . untrammeled self-expression," he concluded that Nietzsche's Übermensch was caught in the "fatal coil" of the romantic's quest for personal boundlessness.[56]

One of Babbitt's key contributions to the übermenschian discourse was his argument that Nietzsche's ideal type exemplified how modern man "lacks a centre," and that this lack of center was the curse of the "romantic ironist." He argued that Nietzsche's vision of self-overcoming would lead inexorably into an immoral self-abandonment—an abnegation both of the self and of the traditional anchors that bound the individual to eternal truths. Whereas Royce perceived self-overcoming to be a strengthening of the self and one's moral resolve in an uncertain universe, Babbitt interpreted it to be a weakening of the self by succumbing to the whirl of modern lawlessness in the realm of ethics and aesthetics. Borrowing Nietzsche's terminology, he characterized the übermenschian romantic as "the being who must always surpass himself." In his quest for self-overcoming, argued Babbitt, Nietzsche had failed to consider "a choice of direction" for his Übermensch in his "everlasting pilgrimage": "He can conceive of nothing beyond whirling forever on the wheel of change ('the eternal recurrence') without any goal or firm refuge that is set above the flux." Babbitt held that Nietzsche was well aware of the sense of purposelessness that vexed moderns who no longer believed in the existence of God, science, or universal truths. Indeed, he quoted Zarathustra's weary yet defiant observations of modern man's sense of purposelessness:

> Have *I* still a goal? A haven towards which *my* sail is set? A good wind?
> Ah, [only he] who knoweth *whither* he saileth, knoweth what wind is
> good. . . .
>
> Where is *my* home? For it do I ask and seek, and have sought, but
> have not found it. O eternal everywhere, O eternal nowhere, O eternal—
> in vain.[57]

While Babbitt approved of Nietzsche's perceptive description of the drift of the modern romantic, he argued that it was precisely this longing to hoist that which is particular and not representative in the self that exaggerated moderns' sense of estrangement and dislocation.

Moreover, Babbitt asserted that restless moderns' rejection of a moral center resulted in the modern temper of "self-parody" and inescapable "ennui." He accepted Nietzsche's argument that those who would try to live without a clear moral vision and higher ideals would be left with a persistent longing and nostalgia for the psychological security of fixed belief, as well as a newfound irony that mocks their own desire for such comfort. Echoing Nietzsche's argument about the emotional impulse that drives man to seek certainty, Babbitt observed that "the affinity of certain romantic converts for the Church is that of the jelly-fish for the rock." From Rousseau down to Schlegel, romantics had boomeranged away from and back to ritual and authority, but their return to faith was inevitably colored by this mix of ironic distance and self-mockery. Foreshadowing what over a half century later would emerge as a stock idea of postmodernism, Babbitt argued that the (romantic) Nietzschean celebrated his ironic pose as the most exalted of all temperaments. (For Babbitt, however, this was no hearty endorsement of ironic posing: "Like so much else in this movement it is an attempt to give to a grave psychic weakness the prestige of strength.") Romantic irony, Babbitt maintained, thus made an unwholesome reversal of the classical model of virtue. Whereas the Greeks understood that man "should think lightly of himself but should have some conviction for which he is ready to die," the "romantic ironist" is "morbidly sensitive about himself, but is ready to mock at his own convictions."[58]

Babbitt's campaign against the romantic ironist Übermensch received reinforcement from his fellow New Humanist, Paul Elmer More. More presented a vision of the Übermensch as a temperamental philosophical nomad bereft of guiding principles. Though More shared Babbitt's interpretation of Nietzsche as the most recent descendant in a long line of European romantics, he contended that the Übermensch's struggle with self was merely a poetic prelude to his struggle with society.

In two studies, *Nietzsche* (1912) and *The Drift of Romanticism* (1913), More posed his classical dualistic vision of human nature in opposition to what he perceived to be Nietzsche's romantic monism. In More's estimation, there existed in man both a higher and a lower self that struggled for dominance. He characterized the higher self as that aspect of human personality which relies on an "inner check" to external phenomena and strives toward completeness and a unity of all experiences. The lower self, by contrast, is the weaker aspect of the human soul that is conscious of, and thus subject only to, internal instinct and its responses to the flux of the external world. In More's dualistic philosophy of human nature, "true liberation comes only with . . . the consciousness that something within us stands apart from the everlasting flux and from our passions which also belong to the flux."[59] According to him, Nietzsche's egotistic Übermensch conceived of this duality as a struggle between self and society rather than one between his higher and his lower selves. Rather than championing the higher self's aspirations toward restraint and composure, the Übermensch sought to unleash his lower emotive self's will against others.

More argued that Nietzsche's destruction of foundations yielded an image of human nature as ruthless as it was meaningless. Critical of all first and final principles, and steeped in a pessimistic view of the world, Nietzsche "left [the Übermensch] in the hazy uncertainty of the future." According to More, Nietzsche had surveyed the history of Western thought and saw only "futility and purposelessness and pessimistic uncertainty of the values of life." However, because man cannot exist on denials alone, Nietzsche envisioned a model human type who, once "liberated from the herd-law, the false values that have been abolished," would replace beliefs in supernatural ideals with

the values of the rough-and-tumble natural world. More believed that Nietzsche created his Übermensch ideal "by going to Darwinism" and redefining
the "evolutionary struggle for existence" as a struggle for dominance among
competing wills to power. More thus concluded that the Übermensch's protest against idealism led him inexorably into a Darwinian exertion of the will
as an instrument to do battle with the rest of society.[60]

In their common efforts to identify Rousseau as the origin and Nietzsche
as the consequence of the romantic revolt against classicism, the critical New
Humanists failed to notice that the two thinkers were awkward representatives of the alpha and omega of naturalist and instrumental tendencies in
modern thought. By linking Nietzsche with Rousseau and Rousseau with
an unbridled celebration of nature, they overlooked Nietzsche's sustained
critiques of the French thinker—critiques that anticipated their own attacks
on naturalism. Beginning with *The Birth of Tragedy* and culminating in *The
Twilight of the Idols*, Nietzsche repeatedly criticized what he perceived to be
Rousseau's innocent exaltation of nature as paradise. Nature, for Nietzsche,
was neither the model nor the source of egalitarianism and fraternity that
Rousseau believed it to be. Nietzsche emphasized that because nature is rife
with conflict, pain, and ecstasy as well as harmony, balance, and order, human
beings must unleash their rhapsodic Dionysian urges, not as a substitute but
as a counterweight to the Apollonian tendencies toward order and restraint.

Although the New Humanists detected certain romantic and naturalistic
elements in Nietzsche's description of the Übermensch, their constitutional
disdain of everything modern rendered them unable to see that his critical
philosophy anticipated theirs. Unwilling or unable to distinguish Nietzsche's
philosophy from the Rousseauian romanticism that he had taken as his enemy, Babbitt harbored a de-facto opposition to the regenerative idealism that
Royce had identified in Nietzsche's figure. Indeed, Babbitt's claim that "every
doctrine of genuine worth is disciplinary and men in the mass do not desire
discipline" sounds like Nietzsche loosely paraphrased. Although they longed
for discipline in a culture they deemed frivolous and saturated in crude materialism, the New Humanists missed Nietzsche's repeated and strenuous calls
for self-discipline in a decadent world.[61]

Despite the traces of Nietzsche's desire for self-restraint in his Übermensch as in his own life, the New Humanists even read his call to "live dangerously" as a mark of his boundless romanticism. Whereas More viewed the
Übermensch's dictum to "Be hard" as a summons to arms against all social

commitments and historically sanctioned images of the good life, Babbitt saw the figure as one who faced a struggle between the socially inherited and the internally willed aspects of his personality. Babbitt believed the übermenschian drive to overcome the self ultimately bordered on recklessness: "From the perfectly sound premise that man is the being who must always surpass himself, Nietzsche draws the perfectly unsound conclusion that the only way for man thus constantly to surpass himself and so show his infinitude is to spurn all limits and 'live dangerously.'"[62] Though the New Humanists viewed Nietzsche's lust for hardness as primarily a hardness with himself, they argued that the Übermensch's ruthless self-examination and martial existence were merely a form of philosophical boot camp in preparation for the real war he would unleash on others.

Though the New Humanists recognized both the antifoundational and the regenerative aspects of Nietzsche's thought, they argued that his deconstructive epistemology necessarily undermined the constructive elements of philosophy. Without commitment to classical ideals to animate thought and conduct, they insisted, Nietzsche's search for modern self-realization spiraled hopelessly into either a weepy self-abnegation or a reckless self-aggrandizement.

## The Übermensch and the German National Mind

The New Humanists' suspicion that the Übermensch's hardness with himself would be matched—if not surpassed—by his ruthlessness with others began to dominate the American interpretations of Nietzsche during the World War I era. Drawing similarities between the Übermensch's drive for mastery and Germany's quest for sovereignty in Europe, commentators increasingly viewed Nietzsche's philosophy with alarm. In wartime analyses of Nietzsche's thought, his constructive ideal was no longer seen as an organic part of his deconstructive antifoundationalism. Rather, observers plucked the concept from his broader social vision, and treated it as a symbol for the German imperial temper. Whereas once Nietzsche's Übermensch represented an ideological challenge to philosophical ideals and religious customs, now, in the eyes of wartime observers, it posed a live threat to modern civilization.

Soon after Germany's declaration of war on August 1, 1914, the tone of American discussions of Nietzsche's Übermensch shifted dramatically. In both the popular press and scholarly venues, American writers responded with alarm to Germany's unwarranted aggression against neighboring France and neutral Belgium. In this pitched climate, commentators were no longer content to ponder Nietzsche's concept of the self or to examine the inverse relationship between his exalted esteem for the higher man and his low regard of modern society. Instead, observers were keen to uncover the connections between Nietzsche's vision of power and mastery and the imperial designs of modern Germany. Whereas before the war, American commentators debated whether the Übermensch represented the individualist who battled with the lower instincts of the self or with the baser elements of modern society, now critics scouted for the correspondences between Nietzsche's philosophy of self-sovereignty and the German national mind.

George Santayana, Harvard philosopher and former doctoral student of Josiah Royce's, turned Nietzsche-bashing and anti-German sentiment into an art form in his 1916 study, *Egotism in German Philosophy*. Although his book was published during wartime, Santayana said that it was the "fruit of a long gestation."[63] A Spanish-born Catholic atheist, Santayana identified himself "as an outsider" who had "chafed for years under the pressure of a prim, academic idealism," a subjective "egotism," which he believed derived from German intellectual history and had thoroughly saturated American thought and culture. As Santayana put it, he was sickened by the "aroma of German philosophy that has reached my nostrils," a philosophy that privileged "subjectivity in thought and willfulness in morals."[64]

Like the New Humanists, Santayana viewed the romantic subjectivity of modern thought as an impulsive rejection of external authority, and of both the classical and Christian ideals as sources of the self. Like the New Humanists, Santayana maintained that the Übermensch represented a reversion to a primitivism underlying romantic thought. Yet while the New Humanists argued that modern romanticism had a French lineage stemming back to Rousseau, Santayana argued instead that it was the most recent expression of a German idealistic egotism that dated to the Protestant Reformation. Echoing the sentiments of early twentieth-century American Catholic thinkers and clergy, Santayana contended that German Protestantism was an unbridled celebration of individual will and a denial of the authority of the Gospels. He argued that German thinkers from Goethe and Kant down to Nietzsche had inherited Protestantism's rejection of supernaturalism and its "rebellion against mediation in religion, against external authority, and against dogma," to spiritualize what was truly their secular exaltation of the self.[65]

According to Santayana, Nietzsche's philosophy represented the culmination of the egotistic tradition that had ailed German Protestantism and philosophy for so long. He believed that Nietzsche, in his ardent desire to have the Übermensch "transcend humanity," had revealed his commitment to a heroic, abstract, but ultimately illusory view of life. Describing both the thinker and his philosophy in animalistic terms, Santayana claimed that Nietzsche "loved mere life with the pathetic intensity of the wounded beast," and that his Übermensch was "a griffin in soul, if not in body, who instead of labouring hands and religious faith should have eagle's wings and the claws of a lion." Though he agreed with Nietzsche that modern society had grown feeble with shallow optimism and was dissociated from a necessarily tragic view of life, he argued that Nietzsche's vision of the Übermensch was not a viable alternative to the facile modern temper. Like Nietzsche, Santayana contended that "our society is outworn, but hard to renew; the emancipated individual needs to master himself." But how this is to be accomplished, "Nietzsche cannot tell us." While Santayana shared the philosopher's desire for a "nobler race of men," he argued that such a model for humanity already existed in the Christian saints and the ancient Greeks. It was Nietzsche's inherited German egotism reflected in his "wayward imagination," Santayana concluded, that rendered him unable to properly esteem the models of the past.[66]

Despite his own artistic temperament, Santayana was wary of Nietzsche's subjective aestheticism, which viewed art rather than morality as a source of the self. He observed that Nietzsche's worldview, "like that of artists and poets," comprehended experience in aesthetic terms. Although Santayana viewed art as vital to human experience, he believed that it contributed to life only if it was the work of the "trained" artist who had ensured that the lines of a poem or the brushstrokes of a painting corresponded to "prescribed" standards of aesthetic form. In Santayana's estimation, this submission to externally sanctioned ideals was reprehensible to the German philosopher: "To be trained is to be tamed and harnessed, an accession of power detestable to Nietzsche."[67]

Santayana thus identified the Übermensch-artist as a reflection of Nietzsche's aesthetic immoralism. Because Nietzsche mistakenly substituted artistic passions and desires for the whole of aesthetic experience, the Übermensch represented the artist undisciplined by morality. According to Santayana, this figure had no interest in rendering a true picture of the world but desired only to divine an image pleasing to his brutal image of life: "When he praised cruelty, it was on the ground that art was cruel, that it made beauty out of suffering." Santayana recognized Nietzsche's conviction that art, rather than ethics or religion, should be the proper measure and expression of virtue. "Good and evil, we are told, enhance one another, like light and shade in a picture; without evil there can be no good." Therefore Nietzsche's "romantic demand for a violent chiaroscuro . . . blossoms into a whole system of ethics" based on the tastes of a sadist. Santayana argued that Nietzsche would substitute passion for reason and sensibility for principles. The instincts and desires of the Übermensch, he cautioned, would be satisfied only by enhancing contrasts in life as in art.[68]

In dismissing Nietzsche's exaltation of the self merely as a tendency of romantic German idealism, Santayana broke with Royce's vision of the Übermensch that regarded it as a synthesis of naturalistic and romantic elements in Nietzsche's philosophy. He was not, as Royce had argued, an antifoundationalist idealist. Instead, he took Nietzsche's energetic criticism of a-priori idealism simply as an expression of an a-priori idealist mind impatient with ideals it didn't like. Santayana likewise folded his genealogical account of the ways in which religious foundations are historically and culturally constructed into his "naïve" egoism, concluding that Nietzsche rejected religion "on the ground that belief in the existence of God would have made him uncomfortable." Santayana thus concluded that Zarathustra's anguished cry, "If there were Gods, how could I endure not to be one?" was nothing more than evidence of Nietzsche's insatiable German megalomania, rather than a proposition about how to live in a world without foundations.[69]

Santayana concluded that Nietzsche's Übermensch thus drew together all the unsavory tendencies in German egotism: its inclination toward subjectivism, its love of struggle, its emotional aestheticism, and its idealism. Like his predecessors, Nietzsche transformed the insights of early Protestantism about the individual's "inward light" and "absolute duties" into an unbridled celebration of individual "instinct" and "destiny." According to Santayana, Nietzsche carried to new heights German philosophers' delight in luxuriating in the "total relativity of the human mind" and their unwillingness to "peep through the bars of their psychological prison." He claimed that in his unashamed preference for illusion over truth, Nietzsche carried "to its logical conclusion . . . the ultra-romantic and ultra-idealistic doctrine that the very notion of truth or fact is a fiction of the will, invented to satisfy our desire for some fixed point of reference in thought." Seeking no referent to his existence outside the self, the Übermensch thus regarded his will and subjective desires to be divine. He recognized no duty outside the self, and his only sense of obligation was to indulge his biological instincts and aesthetic preferences. In Santayana's estimation, the Übermensch not only wallowed in his subjectivity, he deemed it holy.[70]

## The Übermensch at War and the "Made in Germany" Generation

Although Santayana's concerns about the German mind expressed in *Egotism* predated World War I, his book served as a poetic prelude to the emotional assaults on Nietzsche's Übermensch as well as the anti-Germanism of wartime America. Whether Übermensch enthusiasts or rabid detractors, American writers began to analyze the nineteenth-century thinker in relation to twentieth-century German politics and nationalism, and in doing so significantly heightened the tendencies to read Nietzsche as a spokesperson for a national mindset and his ideas of power as an endorsement of brute force. A tug-of-war ensued between observers who argued that Nietzsche's Übermensch represented the German quest for dominance on the European continent and those who insisted that the kaiser and his armies signified a departure from Nietzsche's vision of a master morality. The discourse on Nietzsche's relationship to Germany signals a watershed in American views of the radical philosopher. Whereas, at the turn of the century, commentators had described Nietzsche alternately as a Polish or a European intellectual, now they had taken to referring to him as a German thinker, and the kaiser and his armies as a conduit for interpreting the contours of the Übermensch.

In the United States as in England, English-speaking critics created a frenzy of speculation about Nietzsche's relationship to German imperial war aims. Drawing on their prewar critiques of the romantic origins of modern relativism and its dangerous consequences for civilization, Irving Babbitt and Paul Elmer More argued that Nietzsche's frenzied irrationalism and celebration of will-to-power had spiraled into German racialist superiority and a "lust of empire."[71] It was so common to view the war as a byproduct of Nietzsche's philosophy of power that one British observer even referred to the war as the "Euro-Nietzschean war."[72] Anti-Nietzsche British tracts crossed the Atlantic, reinforcing the image of the Übermensch as the German imperial ideal.[73] Expressing a view shared by anti-German sloganists, William Archer, a British literary critic who lived in the States, announced, "In a very real sense it is the philosophy of Nietzsche that we are fighting." Archer quoted a passage from *Zarathustra*: "Ye say a good cause will hallow even war? I say unto you it is the good war that halloweth every cause." Nietzsche critics insisted that this passage from "Of War and Warriors," oft-quoted during the war years, was proof positive of his glorification of war. Yet even Archer conceded that Nietzsche's thought was easily misconstrued, admitting that the passage in question might refer to "intellectual rather than physical conflicts." He maintained, however, that "the whole passage has always been, and cannot but be, interpreted as a eulogy of war precisely as it is waged by the Prussian General Staff." Although Archer viewed Nietzsche's philosophy as a justification rather than a cause of the war, he asserted that "the cultured German soldier carries" *Zarathustra* along with *Faust* and the Bible "in his knapsack."[74]

In his taxonomy of German thought, Archer cited passages from Nietzsche's works as examples of the German view of Kultur as a martial ideal and his concept of power as one asserted with iron and sanctified by blood. According to Archer, the Übermensch was both a political and a cultural symbol as well as a representation of the German "eugenic ideal." He noted that it was unclear whether Nietzsche had intended the Übermensch to refer to an individual, "as though all the groaning and travail of creation had no end save the production of a single super-Napoleon," or whether it was a "collective term for a breed or caste, a highly developed variety of the genus 'blond beast'" resulting from a new social order that divided all its subjects into masters and slaves in an effort to perfect the "race." Expressing the prevailing sentiments in England and the United States, Archer argued that both versions of the Übermensch—as a superindividual and a supersociety— reflected the dominant characteristics of "the inordinate self-valuation" and "tribal arrogance" so central to the "German spirit."[75]

This association of Nietzsche's philosophy with German militarism and nationalism during wartime, though widespread, did not go uncontested. Many longtime Nietzsche devotees rallied to defend the philosopher, arguing that holding him accountable for inciting Germany to war was to blame him for precisely those qualities in the German cultural temperament against which he so bitterly protested. One of the strongest objections came from William James's brother-in-law, William Mackintire Salter, himself a prolific writer and speaker on ethics, as well as an early follower of Felix Adler, the German-Jewish founder of the Ethical Culture movement, and the leader of the Society for Ethical Culture of Chicago. Salter, once an aspiring Congregational minister who rejected Christian orthodoxy and turned to Unitarianism before his faith in the "solid grounds for distinctive Christian faith" fully gave way, discovered in Nietzsche a fellow antifoundationalist ethicist who took a higher *humanity*—not a religious tradition's or a national culture's narrow view of it—as his cause.[76] Eager to rescue from wartime vitriol what had been for him Nietzsche's inspirational voluntaristic and aesthetic conception of morality, Salter in 1917 published *Nietzsche the Thinker*, a systematic analysis of the development of his philosophy.[77] Having presented significant portions of the book in earlier articles for popular periodicals and scholarly philosophical and theological journals, Salter could demonstrate that "the book was in substance written before the present European War, and without a thought of such a monstrous possibility."[78] But given the "fashion to connect Nietzsche closely with [the war]," Salter hoped that a book-length study would help portray Nietzsche as a wholesome though challenging ethicist, and make a more forceful intervention into the wartime discourse which charged Nietzsche with an unchecked egoism and will-to-domination expressive of the German national mind.[79]

Throughout the book, Salter presented a philosopher who believed that human greatness was achieved not by lording over others but by a total giving of oneself for their improvement. He emphasized that Nietzsche was "essentially . . . a religious man" without a religion, a searching pilgrim whose "scientific conscience forbade him" to believe in God, but not in the potential grandeur of humankind. His Übermensch, "the final *raison d'être* of the species," was no monster of unbridled passions, but a disciplined and restrained seeker after the "'unexhausted possibilities' of man and our human world." Those possibilities, Salter maintained, were not exemplified in one human type to be stamped on others, but were expressive of his moral "polytheism": "As for himself, [Nietzsche] wants to help all who seek an ideal pattern for their lives simply by showing how to do it; and his greatest joy is in encountering individual patterns that are not like his own." Salter thus emphasized the inconsonance between Nietzsche's pluralistic ethics and the absolutism of imperial Germany while drawing attention to Nietzsche's repeated barbs against the German Empire and Kultur. Insisting that Nietzsche "[felt] so foreign to everything German," his only possible relationship to the impacted morality of the war, Salter maintained, was "as a diagnostician of the general conditions which appear to have given birth to it."[80]

Despite Salter's effort to promote Nietzsche's moral credentials and disassociate him from his alleged influence on German militarism and imperialism, few were as unconvinced of his philosophy's salutary possibilities as the Christian theologians and clergy who were once so reliant on German thought. As long-standing active contributors to American Nietzsche commentary and criticism, now, with the war, Christian commentators moved quickly to affirm his role in cultivating German aggression. Just a few years earlier the same group identified Nietzsche's immoralist Übermensch as a symbol of the "social crisis" and a false prophet who threatened to tear away at modern faith and fellowship; now they argued that he had also undermined faith in a shared Creator by leading Germans away from the transatlantic Christian community that had once united America and Western Europe. They rushed in, echoing the complaint of one Christian observer who argued that Nietzsche's philosophy demonstrated that a primitive "ethics made in Germany" mocked Christian conventions of human solidarity and charity and substituted right with might.[81] Now the excessive worldliness of German Protestantism appeared to be too much of a good thing, as German theologians and clergy saw themselves as functionaries of the German state and had politicized Protestant theology by making it serviceable to the nation's military mission.

Disturbed by the widespread support among German clergy for the war, American Protestant theologians argued that they must reassess their inheritance of and reliance on German scholarship and training, which too easily accommodated Nietzsche's pagan celebration of power. Earlier complaints about Protestant historicism now became Teutonized. Christian commentators argued that what W. H. Griffith Thomas, writing for *Bibliotheca Sacra*, referred to as "German moral abnormality" was evident long before the war.[82] A writer for the *Atlantic Monthly* argued that the path from the early nineteenth-century historicist biblical criticism, to Nietzschean philosophy of power, to German imperialism and militarism was unmistakable: "The inference is inevitable, that, when the leaders of a nation's life in theology and philosophy play skittles with every claim to Divine interest in the affairs of mankind . . . they are not likely to base national conduct upon the immutable and eternal foundations of righteousness."[83]

However, it wasn't enough to point fingers, for the despiritualized view of human affairs that produced the Übermensch and a culture of militarism was also the very culture of rigorous biblical scholarship and training which for generations had been the Rome for American Protestant theologians. The specter of a Teutonized militaristic Übermensch forced liberal theologians not only to reassess their relationship to developments in modern thought but to see how modern thought itself was emblematic of German "moral abnormality." Thomas noted, "It is well known that there is not a single critical position adopted by British, American, and Canadian scholars which did not emanate from Germany." Quick to see the connections between theological naturalism and Nietzschean antifoundationalism, Christian commentators argued that Germany's aggression required them to consider the dangerous consequences of a despiritualized worldview, and thus to rethink their inheritance of German theology.[84]

The tendency to interpret the Übermensch as a reflection of the German moral imagination emerges especially in the writings of American scholars trained in the German academy. The sense of ambivalence about the United States' long-standing relationship to Germany was felt acutely by scholars of the "made in Germany" generation.[85] For American social thinkers, Germany's aggression felt like a renunciation of the intellectual and cultural traditions that they had so admired. In trade, in education, in the social welfare system, and in municipal organization, that country had served as the model social democracy for US social scientists and intellectuals. The degree to which the war felt like a personal betrayal pulsates through their writings. The question that vexed the economist Richard T. Ely and the psychologist G. Stanley Hall was why a "great people" had "gone wrong." According to Ely, it was partly due to the fact that German law had "departed from the moral principles of Kant, and became brutalized by the spreading doctrines of Nietzsche and Treitschke and Bismarck."[86] Likewise, Hall argued that Nietzsche's "focalization on will" had transformed Kant's commitment to duty into a commitment to self. He described Nietzsche as a Darwinist, and argued that his Übermensch was a monster of "hypertrophied egoism," "ruthlessness," and "self-indulgence." The Übermensch appealed to the "ambitions of youth" of a culture driven by the "horror of inferiority" to instinctively fetishize strength and power. Interpreting the war through the new lens of modern psychology, Hall suggested that it represented a therapeutic release from the psychosocial "tensions" brought on by the civilizing process. In their turn toward war as in their romance with Nietzsche's primitive Übermensch, Germans were aching to shed "the superficial veneer of culture" and regress to "things racially old" as a means of moral and spiritual regeneration.[87]

There were indeed other German-trained academics who observed a correlation between Nietzsche's Übermensch and Germany's "national physiognomy." Ralph Barton Perry, Harvard philosopher and biographer of William James, argued that there was "no doubt" that Nietzsche, "whether intentionally or in spite of himself," had deeply influenced the German wartime generation. Perry described the Übermensch as one "who has arrived" and thus can only "sit and meditate upon his own greatness; or walk out upon a balcony and survey with disdain the clamoring multitude below" without concern for the persistent "suffering and failure in the world." The "Nietzschean superman," Perry argued, had come to symbolize German "national self-consciousness," which justified its actions on the world stage simply with "the principle of being one's national self." Because for Nietzsche "absolute morality is a fiction," and there existed no "primary virtues like justice or veracity," the übermenschian state had no regard for laws that were in effect "*only codes*, each particular to a group." Like the Übermensch described in *Zarathustra* who recognizes no standard above the self, Germany felt no obligation to submit herself to the dictates of international law.[88]

In fact, Perry believed that the Übermensch represented an ideational culde-sac for socially minded moderns. He argued that the figure encapsulated all the contrasts and reflected the ambivalences in Nietzsche's thought. Although Nietzsche was critical of Darwin's theory of natural selection, Perry observed a Darwinian element to the Nietzschean view that life is advanced through struggle and contests of power. He argued that while Nietzsche "understood well the wastefulness and fatuousness of war," he also esteemed militarism as an antidote to the softening of modern life. Although Nietzsche held that the entire energies of the masses of society should be directed toward the sole purpose of creating the Übermensch, he also viewed the Übermensch as an island without regard or esteem for the group. And though Nietzsche was a "cosmopolitan" who sought "a certain type of manhood" rather than a "particular race or state," Perry argued that his belief in the moral agent's limitless self-sovereignty fed into Germany's "bloated and arrogant" nationalistic prejudice.[89]

Despite the contradictions in Nietzsche's thought, Perry insisted that Nietzsche deserved admiration. He maintained that while the conflicted aspects of the Übermensch were being played out by Germany on the world stage, Nietzsche's life could be a valuable guide to conduct. Seeking to rescue the philosopher from the philosophy, Perry claimed that he knew of "no

better evidence of this weakness of the Superman than the contrast presented between the Superman and Nietzsche himself." "We feel him, we of
the herd-morality, to be one of us in that he knew hardship and failure, but to
be better than most of us in that he wore himself out for disinterested ends."
Whereas the Übermensch was a Darwinian bully whose "self realization" was
expressed in his domination over others, Nietzsche's commitment to moral
inquiry in the face of relentless personal hardships presented a model of ethical living in a world of uncertainty.[90]

While the commentaries of the "made in Germany" generation reveal a
collective sense of astonishment and dismay at Germany's wartime conduct,
there were those who believed that Americans still had much to learn from
the "German way of thinking." Cognizant that the war had justly soured the
US perception of German political life, the economist Simon Nelson Patten
sought to rescue the German welfare-state model, which he believed was still
worthy of emulation. In contrast to the view of the German Übermensch as a
disintegrative social force, Patten offered a countervision of a "super race," as
reflected in Germany's mechanization, efficiency, and social morality.[91]

According to Patten, the Übermensch, properly understood, represented
a bridge between the American conception of freedom and the German
regard for social organization. He argued that whereas the Anglo-American
mind conceived of liberty as political freedom from tyrants and exploitation,
the German conception of liberty was cultural rather than political, referring
to "the overthrow of religious dogmatism, of ancient superstition, of social
arrogance, of effete traditions, and of conventional morality." Whereas liberty
to the Anglo-American mind was a political concept that has "no content but
freedom from control," the Germans balanced their regard for intellectual
freedom with esteem for social progress. In Patten's estimation, the two cultures had much to learn from each other. By balancing the German appreciation of mechanism with the American love of liberty, both cultures together
could help create a social type superior to the "old individualist." Though
"keen for personal ascendancy," Patten predicted that this German-American
ideological "amalgamation" would "rise through apperception of group loyalty, and gain his ends through mutual aid and social cooperation." According to Patten, the path between the German and the American conception
of liberty represented the "road from the aggressive superman to a super race,
and on this path all races are moving."[92]

Political radicals who had long looked to Germany's social democracy as a beacon for all industrialized societies also sought to defend Nietzsche from the dominant interpretation of his philosophy as the animating idea motivating Germany's war aims.[93] Appropriating the Übermensch ideal for his model of the socialist worker of the world, the radical writer and editor of *The Masses*, Max Eastman, argued that the Übermensch was best conceived of as a cosmopolitan ideal and member of a "Super-Society" that unified workers of all nations. In 1914, Eastman felt, it was especially important to understand that "What Nietzsche Really Taught" was not how to march to the drumbeats of war but why one should be "a great hater of nationalism."[94] Like Perry, he asserted that Nietzsche was a cosmopolitan in love with human greatness in general but of no country or culture in particular. According to Eastman, Nietzsche's commitment was not to the state, which he regarded as little more than an "artificial unit of loyalty." Instead, Nietzsche's ideas proved to be a timely critique of the "'bovine nationalism'" that was stirring both sides of the Atlantic. In his effort to blend Nietzsche's cosmopolitan "poetic celebration of strong men" with his own socialist vision, Eastman appropriated Nietzsche's call for an aristocracy of intelligence, self-discipline, and "eternal sacrifice for posterity" into his vision of a modern society stratified only by strength and merit, rather than hereditary wealth and consolidated power. Insisting that the Übermensch was a martial ideal in the "interest of truth and ideas" rather than a narrow patriotic platform, Eastman sought to replace the German imperial ideal with Nietzsche's cosmopolitan vision of human excellence.[95]

Others joined Eastman in his assessment that Nietzsche's Übermensch was a justification neither of the social status quo nor of the political crisis looming over Europe and the United States. In his 1916 essay on the "theology of militarism," Social Gospeler and pacifist Washington Gladden argued that Nietzsche's philosophy had been wrongly accused of instigating the German view of the state as a "Supreme Being" that recognized no bounds to its imperialist vision except the limits of its own power.[96] Quoting *Human, All Too Human*, Gladden noted that it was Nietzsche himself who had argued that the "highest development of military order and intelligence" will be exhibited when the nation "voluntarily" declares, "'We will break our swords,' and will destroy [our] whole military system,'" adding that disarming "(after having been the most strongly defended) from a loftiness of sentiment—that is the means towards genuine peace." Nietzsche, Gladden averred, was best understood as a psychologist of the militaristic temperament who recognized that states build up armies under the auspices of national defense as a lie to shield their true "lust of conquest." Suggesting that Nietzschean strength referred to self-mastery, Gladden contended that Nietzsche's "doctrine" expounded the Christian motive of "the true inwardness of 'preparedness.'" Challenging the view of Nietzsche as the German imperial mastermind, Gladden affirmed instead, "Have we not found Saul among the prophets?"[97]

Though Gladden's view of Nietzsche as a Hebrew prophet was not unfamiliar to liberal Protestants, now, during the war, it ran counter to the growing perceptions of him as a prophet of German egotism, primitivism, and militarism. However, it exemplified the tendency among readers to comprehend the philosopher in terms familiar to the American moral imagination. Nietzsche's transformation from a Polish aristocrat, to a modern-day Jesus, to a blood-and-iron imperialist testifies to the creative ways in which American interpreters naturalized his Übermensch into American thinking. Thus, while wartime speculations about Nietzsche's Germanness had the immediate effect of establishing him as a *German* thinker in the American mind, they demonstrated how American interpreters appropriated Nietzsche by making him both radically Other and crucially important for articulating the problems of modern thought and morality.

## To Each His Own Übermensch

On the afternoon of May 21, 1924, two University of Chicago students, Richard Loeb and Nathan F. Leopold Jr., took a chisel, a ransom note, and a Nietzsche created in their own image, stepped into a rented Willys-Knight automobile, picked up an unsuspecting fourteen-year-old, Bobby Franks, at random, and brutally murdered him before disposing of his naked body in a marsh. Their defense lawyer, Clarence Darrow, later explained that their motive was "not for money, not for spite; not for hate. They killed as they might kill a spider or a fly, for the experience."[98] The national news picked up the story immediately, publishing the boys' confessions, drawing editorial and comment on everything from their wealthy backgrounds, Jewish families, high IQs, and low moral development. Scientific experts rushed in, including criminologists to comment on forensic evidence, and psychiatrists drawing on new Freudian theories as well as older Lombroso-style ideas about criminality. The *Chicago Tribune* ran as "scientific" sketches of their heads, diagnosing the organic basis of their problems: "sensuous lips," "excessive vanity," "great love of sex," and sexual perversions about the boys contained in the psychiatrists' reports not fit to print.[99] The religious press picked up on the story, with commentators like Billy Sunday blaming the crime on "precocious brains, salacious books, infidel minds," while William Jennings Bryan confirmed his assessment of the moral dangers of modernist ideas.[100] But all the arguments about why these boys would kill tracked back to a common cause: they thought they were Nietzschean supermen.

Darrow had a Houdini-like mind, but even he figured he could not wriggle Nietzsche out of his damaged public reputation after World War I or convince the trial judge of Nietzsche's value (though he himself was an avid Nietzsche reader). But it was his job not to defend Nietzsche but to try to save his clients from the death penalty, as he had entered a guilty plea on their behalf. So Darrow worked creatively within the limited range available to him:

> Your Honor, I have read almost everything that Nietzsche ever wrote. He was a man of a wonderful intellect; the most original philosopher of the last century. . . . More books have been written about him than probably all the rest of the philosophers in a hundred years. More college professors have talked about him. In a way he has reached more people, and still he has been a philosopher of what we might call the intellectual cult. Nietzsche believed that some time the superman would be born, that evolution was working toward the superman.
>
> He wrote that one book, "Beyond Good and Evil," which was a criticism of all moral codes as the world understands them; a treatise holding that the intelligent man is beyond good and evil; that the laws for good and the laws for evil do not apply to those who approach the superman.

During his twelve-hour impassioned defense, Darrow took a number of rangy digressions about Nietzsche, highlighting his worldwide popularity and explaining that the philosopher himself might have been the victim of his own ideas, as he died insane. Darrow hoped to distribute some of the blame to the big publishing houses that printed Nietzsche's works and the libraries that distributed them. He even suggested that the University of Chicago was partly responsible, for it was there that the boys had come into contact with Nietzsche's philosophy. But despite the length of his appeal, and the extended portions devoted to Nietzsche, he did not explain the philosophy, beyond a few broad remarks. Likewise, he did not explain Nietzsche's idea of the Übermensch, the very concept at the center of the controversy. Darrow described it blandly only as "a theory, a dream, a vision," of a higher person beyond conventional moral codes.

But in all Darrow's efforts to show the boys as victims of Nietzsche's philosophy, to suggest that it "destroyed" their lives, he intimated that it was their innocent mistake to think that they were what Nietzsche had in mind. "Nathan Leopold is not the only boy who has read Nietzsche. He may be the only one who was influenced in the way that he was influenced."[101] Though he argued that they were victims, they were so because when they read Nietzsche, they could not help but think that they were reading themselves. Darrow was on to something. For early twentieth-century Americans, the Übermensch was a hazy vision, but it was one they used to see clearly the problems and possibilities of themselves as they came to terms with their modern America.

——————

The naturalization of the Übermensch in the years leading up to and during World War I set the stage for the succeeding career of Nietzsche's heroic image of selfhood in the century to follow. Just as the concept defied national and linguistic boundaries, so too did the Übermensch cross borders of thought that separated Americans of different intellectual interests, moral commitments, and political sensibilities. Interest in the Übermensch moved promiscuously along the political spectrum, served up alternately as a term of derision and affection; it became a charged comment about modern American selfhood that could be enlisted to either skewer or sanction everything from religion to atheism, political progressivism to cultural populism, capitalism to socialism.

New to the war years, however, was the degree to which interpreters effectively severed the destructive and reconstructive aspects of Nietzsche's moral vision as expressed in his Übermensch ideal. Royce had argued that the meaning of Nietzsche's Übermensch could be laid bare only after one synthesized his instrumentalism with his individualism. Likewise, Babbitt and More had argued that the Übermensch fused Nietzsche's romantic naturalism with his quest for power. Though Royce had seen the promises of Nietzsche's challenge to foundations whereas the New Humanists had seen only the perils, they all recognized the dialectic between the deconstructive and the regenerative dimensions in his thought. In Nietzsche's Übermensch they discovered an expression of his contingent idealism and an image of the persistent longing for meaning in a world without foundations.

With the start of World War I, however, the image of the Übermensch as a contingent ideal faded from view. Rather than viewing the figure as an expression of Nietzsche's desire for meaning in a world without absolutes, commentators began to assess it as an artifact of Nietzsche's philosophy of power only. Wartime interpreters popularized the Übermensch as an ideal of sovereignty without holding in balance Nietzsche's idea of truth and meaning in a variable universe. Once commentators could discuss the "Superman," the "Super-Race," and the "Super-Society" without drawing connections back to the philosophy from whence it sprang, the Übermensch proved to be a concept able to accommodate any number of competing moral viewpoints. And once Nietzsche could become a thinker with answers but no questions, and his philosophy a celebration of power rather than a testament to the need for human wonder, the Übermensch's naturalization into American intellectual and cultural life was successfully under way.

# Nietzsche as Educator

> Your true educators and formative teachers reveal to you that the true, original meaning and basic stuff of your nature is something completely incapable of being educated or formed . . . your educators can be only your liberators.
>
> FRIEDRICH NIETZSCHE, "Schopenhauer as Educator" (1874), in *Untimely Meditations*

> We may call ourselves . . . "free-ranging spirits," because we feel the tug towards freedom as the strongest drive of our spirit and, in antithesis to the fettered and firm-rooted intellects, see our ideal almost in an intellectual nomadism.
>
> FRIEDRICH NIETZSCHE, *Human, All Too Human* (1878)

Expressing the sentiments shared by a generation of early twentieth-century American literary radicals and political reformers, the novelist and popular lecturer John Cowper Powys described his lingering romance with Friedrich Nietzsche: "I cannot see a volume of Nietzsche in any shelf without opening it, and . . . [I] cannot open it without feeling, just as [I] did at first, the old fatal intoxication."[1] Preferring imagery more suggestive than mere alcohol, Isadora Duncan likened her first encounter with the nineteenth-century German philosopher to the voluptuous joys of the flesh when she recalled that "the seduction of Nietzsche's philosophy ravished my being."[2] Others described their experience of Nietzsche's philosophy in spiritual terms. Jack London and Eugene O'Neill were two of the many who referred to Nietzsche as their "Christ" and *Thus Spoke Zarathustra* as their "Bible." Throughout the essays, letters, and autobiographies of many young writers who came of age in the early decades of the twentieth century, there is a virtual library of rich imagery for Nietzsche and his thought. He is described as a prophet and a martyr, and his philosophy was portrayed as an intellectual intoxicant, an emotional elixir, and a spiritual astringent, as well as a romp in the hay. Though the metaphors for Nietzsche and his writings are as diverse and colorful as their authors, a theme runs throughout. They described their experience with Nietzsche in deeply intimate terms; indeed, many of them confessed to feeling as though Nietzsche had developed his philosophy expressly for them.

Given this enthusiasm, we have good reason to doubt Henry May's claim that the Nietzsche vogue in America had little impact on radical thinkers who came of age in the prewar United States. As May argues in his magisterial survey of the early twentieth-century cultural rebellion, *The End of American Innocence*, Nietzsche served primarily as "an effective shocker," but on the whole his "German idealism" and "tragic" sensibility were "too alien" to ever be successfully naturalized by the "cheerful" American rebels.[3] May concludes that the loose confederation of "innocent" rebels who were involved in the "little" magazines at this time flirted with—though never fully integrated—Nietzsche's aristocratic sensibility and dark iconoclasm into their thought, and this estimation has persisted.[4]

When one surveys the outpouring of adulation over Nietzsche by the young writers who contributed to the "Chicago Renaissance"; who participated in the traffic of ideas and lovers at Mabel Dodge Luhan's 23 Fifth Avenue salon; who cobbled together their often limited resources to launch experimental "little" magazines like *The Masses*, *The Seven Arts*, and *The New Republic*; and who spent their summers working and playing together in Massachusetts as members of the Provincetown Players, it is easy to see why May viewed the radicals' interest in Nietzsche as an intense but ultimately insubstantial affair.[5] But if part of the intellectual historian's task is to recover the lived experience of historical persons, to try to recapture not only what they thought but how they felt about certain ideas, then perhaps we should start by taking these young writers at their word. In their novels, critical essays, plays, and memoirs, they documented in great detail their first encounters and their ongoing "relationships" with Nietzsche's ideas. If they felt, as they said they did, that Nietzsche was speaking to them personally, then we will get a better understanding of their mental and moral worlds if we actually listen to what they had to say. Their references to Nietzsche's image and ideas provide an opportunity to better understand their vision of the Beloved Community of liberated individuals, and to grasp their conception of their roles as intellectuals in fostering it.

Nietzsche's philosophy exhibited an intense hold on early twentieth-century literary radicals—writer-reformers, experimental artists, and cultural critics—as they sought to come to terms with the problems of modern American life. His arguments for the interpretive and provisional character of human knowledge and beliefs provided them with an approach to the study of cultural and political ideals in America. His writings presented them with a description of Western culture teetering on shaky intellectual and moral foundations that mirrored their own impressions of a modern America that could no longer be supported by its moral and cultural inheritances. Nietzsche emboldened them in their revolt against the stifling genteel sensibility, the psychic bankruptcy of a despiritualized Christianity, and the airy idealism of late nineteenth-century democratic theory. He taught them that their battle with their inheritances was no standard generational revolt of sons against fathers, or New Women against the matriarchal ideal, but rather a full transvaluation of intellectually feeble and yet culturally robust moral absolutes, which had overstayed their welcome in a modernizing America. In his assessment of a will to power underlying all human knowledge and belief, his savage critique of the life-denying impulses in Christian asceticism, and his attack on the "slave morality" of democratic egalitarianism, Nietzsche offered the radicals a method and language for critiquing an American life that they believed had not yet fulfilled its democratic promise.

While the young radicals enlisted Nietzsche's antifoundationalism in their assaults on what they considered a decrepit bourgeois worldview, they also understood that tearing down false idols was no endgame for the serious intellect. The ruins of a toppled past, they learned from Nietzsche, were breeding grounds for despair but no refuge for the modern free spirit. Breaking old idols with the one hand and feverishly gluing them back together with the other was no answer either. The task of the modern thinker instead was to balance the deconstructive with the regenerative, to apply the acids of intellect on debilitating beliefs while employing a playful imagination to contemplate ideals that enliven the spirit. Nietzsche's "gay science" presented these aspiring intellectuals with a new genre of critical philosophy that balanced analytic vivisection with aesthetic creation. Likewise, in Nietzsche's aphorisms, extended essays, and poetic verse, they witnessed a new species of writing that blended the philosophical with the artistic, the sociological with the prophetic, and a hard intellectual hit with a light literary touch. Nietzsche's philosophy became, for them, a model of both literary self-expression and the social efficacy of ideas.

The young writers and reformers read Nietzsche's works through a variety of cultural, economic, and political lenses. Playwrights, novelists, and poets like George Cram Cook, Upton Sinclair, and Kahlil Gibran found in

Nietzsche a romantic model of modern divinity after the "death of God." Socialists including Max Eastman and Hubert Harrison enlisted Nietzsche's theory of "slave morality" to challenge American capitalism, racism, and militaristic nationalism. The literary critic Van Wyck Brooks drew from Nietzsche as he criticized the tepid aesthetics of the American bourgeoisie, while self-identified pragmatists such as William English Walling and Walter Lippmann turned to Nietzsche's romantic instrumentalism as an antidote to modern drift. And figures as diverse as Emma Goldman, H. L. Mencken, and Randolph Bourne mined Nietzsche's texts for his critique of Judeo-Christian asceticism and moral psychology as they attempted to come to terms with the lingering influence of Puritanism on modern American thought.

Whereas Nietzsche's style offered them a model of writing that balanced self-expression and social efficacy, and his ideas a resource for their social thought, Nietzsche's heroic biography represented to the young radicals a model of the independent intellectual life in modern society. When they discovered Nietzsche in the opening decade of the last century, they were adopting for themselves a term new to American political and cultural life: *intellectual*.[6] While the concept of the intellectual as a specifically modern (and necessary) social type was still in formation and its precise social function not yet clear, Nietzsche's own example of the "free-ranging" intellect enabled the young radicals to fill out its contours. His displacement in his own day helped sharpen their grievance with American intellectual life: nowhere did there seem to be a home in modern America for the critical intellect. The theaters of Boston, the big publishing houses of New York, and the newspaper headquarters of the mainstream press seemed too entrenched in the very commercialism an oppositional intellect should critique. And the universities were no better. Rather than a haven in a heartless world of business-driven culture, the universities operated on a new principle of specialization that strangled the life out of higher learning and made it a playground for students who came for credentials and connections but not contemplation.[7]

The grievance went beyond bureaucratic administrators and insouciant students. It was the academic scholar who had made the university an inhospitable home for modern thought. The young radicals believed, with Nietzsche as their guide, that universities produced barren intellectualists—scholars, but not thinkers. When the twenty-four-year-old Nietzsche was appointed professor of classical philology at the University of Basel, he accepted the offer with misgivings. And when his poor health finally caused him to resign his position, his subsequent nomadic years underscored his notion of the intellectual life as necessarily autonomous from institutions. Nietzsche's departure from the university only sharpened his long-standing complaint that German *Wissenschaft* suffered from a lingering metaphysical obsession with absolute truth, as well as a mistaken confidence in a "first cause" or telos of existence. Nietzsche argued that this flawed *Weltanschauung* had created "cramped" specializations within academe, and had produced scholars with a cropped intellectual vision: "Every scholarly book also mirrors a soul that has become crooked."[8] Walling spoke for his fellow radicals when he argued that Nietzsche had demonstrated the impossibility of vital thinking if an intellectual became a scholar "buried among the dry bones of knowledge."[9] And Walter Lippmann pointed out that modernity represented too "big [a] world" for the "little men" of academe, stressing that the universities "were not built for the kind of civilization they are expected to serve."[10]

Nietzsche's biography not only offered a powerful example of the new unaffiliated intellectual, but also showed the young radicals what they were up against. Living the life of the independent thinker, Nietzsche paid the social price in a culture unwilling or unable to appreciate his contribution. But rather than take Nietzsche's own situation as an indication that European intellectual life had some problems of its own, the radicals bleached Nietzsche's grievances with the philistinism and barren scholasticism of its specific references to the nineteenth-century *Kaiserreich*, and used them to rehearse old Emersonian concerns about American democracy's inhospitality toward genius.[11] Nietzsche's marginalization, both theorized and lived, confirmed their fear that the intellectual in an advanced industrial democracy would fare no better. But in using Nietzsche this way, they were engaging in a long-standing ritual of American intellectual life: enlisting a European thinker to think about the problems of American thinking. They bewailed an infertile American culture that failed to nourish native intellect at its roots, and pointed to Nietzsche as an example of the kind of genius they believed America could never cultivate. Many years before members of this generation were "lost" in Europe, they felt at home in Nietzsche, and homeless in modern America.[12]

The literary radicals had many uses for Nietzsche, but their broader aim was singular: Nietzsche helped them think about thinking in modern America. His new moral vocabulary enabled them to articulate their criticisms of and longing for American culture. His writings demonstrated the practical power a mighty pen could yield. And his ideas showed them the ecstasy and agony of a world beyond the good and evil of their religious and moral inheritances. Nietzsche influenced them with both the intellectual life he theorized and the one he lived. Young intellectuals wrote extensively about his persona in an effort to come to terms with the perils and possibilities awaiting the oppositional intellect who longs for a footing in modern democratic culture while tearing up the ground beneath his feet.

## Experiencing Intellect; or, World-Making Words

Nietzsche knew the power of his words. He likened himself to a *"force majeure, a destiny,"* one who sends his words into the world like lightning bolts, causing a "collision of conscience." He imagined that with the stroke of his pen, he was "break[ing] the history of mankind in two. One lives before him, or one lives after him." When these words were written in 1888, just two months before Nietzsche lost his mind, the world had given him no reason to believe that what he had written was true. Yet he got it right. As if the transatlantic Nietzsche vogue at the turn of the century was not enough to ensure his posterity, World War I confirmed that Nietzsche's name would indeed be associated with something "tremendous," "an event without parallel," a monumental "catastrophe."[13]

Before and after the war, American literary radicals portrayed reading Nietzsche as a profoundly life-altering experience. But what they described was very different from the flamethrowers, the scorched earth, and the swarms of terrified boys in gas masks, huddled in muddy trenches, hoping for a quick death when their time came. Rather, for the radicals the power of his words derived from the transformative effect it had on their thinking. Reading his philosophy was so intense because it felt so intimate, because his words grabbed their consciences by the throat, shaking them violently into a new awakened state. But their experience was no mere entertainment; it was also edifying, for it taught them the power of the intellect. When they doubted their value to society as thinkers, when they wondered about the social efficacy of their ideas, reading Nietzsche reminded them what the intellectual could make possible. Nietzsche never took to the streets, never organized a march, never held a position of great authority, never enjoyed great wealth, never had a pulpit (bully or otherwise). And yet he wrote words that made their worlds anew.

In the radicals' estimation, Nietzsche's intellectual force lay in his ideas as well as in his modes of expression. They marvelled at the "most multifarious art of style that has ever been at the disposal of one man,"[14] relishing the experience of his voice as it took on various forms: the flashing insight of his aphorisms, the melodic sound of his verse, the taut logic of his critical essays, and the dithyrambic play of his prose-poetry. These showed that for Nietzsche, the art of criticism was more than the deconstruction of values; it was also a medium for envisioning and creating new images of the possible. In doing so, Nietzsche had dissolved the distinction between the philosopher and the artist. Just as the painter uses color and form to transport the viewer into an imaginative space, Nietzsche invented a language for ideas that, in Lippmann's words, could "bathe" the reader "in suggestion." What made Nietzsche a genius, the young radicals claimed, was that his language enabled the reader to *feel* his ideas. They spoke of Nietzsche's thought as an atmosphere that enveloped the reader.[15]

The sentiment expressed in their descriptions of Nietzsche's poetic way with words, indeed their characterization of Nietzsche as a "poet" or a "poet-philosopher," originated in Emerson's 1844 essay "The Poet," which Nietzsche had read repeatedly throughout his productive years. Emerson described the poet as he who "stands among partial men for the complete man," one who "traverses the whole scale of experience, and is representative of man, in virtue of being the largest power to receive and to impart." Emerson emphatically stressed that the "true poet" is not merely the writer who exhibits "poetical talents" or "industry and skill in metre" but rather the "sayer, the namer," the "sovereign" who "stands on the centre" of his own making. In Emerson's estimation, the work of the poet is to demonstrate the agency of ideas. "Words are also actions," Emerson affirmed, because they have the power to give birth to new possibility. They can do so when the poet dissolves the distinction between creating and representing, art and argument: "For it is not metres, but a metre-making argument, that makes a poem,—a thought so passionate and alive, that, like the spirit of a plant or an animal, it has an architecture of its own, and adorns nature with a new thing."[16]

Emerson's longing for a society of "complete" men and women, his belief that the poet is the full realization of the thinker and the artist in man, helps explain why American socialists and Progressives who cared deeply about social solidarity insisted on Nietzsche as the exemplar of the philosopher-poet. According to the leader of the socialists' "New Intellectuals," William English Walling, socialism is guided by the "prophetic vision" of a fully realized humanity, one that can only be supplied by poets: "For the philosophy that directs our lives, . . . for our vision of the future man toward whom we strive, we are dependent on literature. The great . . . [writer's] ideal is our ideal—of which we had not yet become conscious." In order to achieve this ideal, "the great and central question to be asked is: What kind of man ought to be cultivated, willed, or created. . . . No one has more clearly seized and expressed this problem than Friedrich Nietzsche."[17] The radicals, like Emerson before them, longed for a poet who both addressed and embodied a fully realized humanity. As Max Eastman put it, Nietzsche was that vital poet, who "addressed . . . the soul of man," and whose philosophy—"this colossal sign-post of man's genius"—embodied the intellectual wealth of the commonwealth.[18] The radicals discovered in Nietzsche's writings the affirmative power of the intellect not to adorn society but to *remake* it.

Even strict materialist socialists who focused on bread-and-butter labor issues could turn to Nietzsche for the inspiration to imagine themselves laboring toward a new poetics of humanity. Nowhere do we better see this than with the radical West Indian–American writer Hubert Harrison, founder of the "New Negro" movement. An avid reader of Nietzsche—from his time as a postal worker and freelance editorialist and lecturer in his early twenties through his involvement in the Socialist Party, as a lecturer at the Ferrer Modern School (a hothouse for American Nietzscheanism),[19] and into the 1920s as the intellectual "Father of Harlem Radicalism"—Harrison drew on Nietzsche's philosophy as he hammered out his own. Like so many white aspiring young writers of his day, Harrison discovered in Nietzsche a model of the freelance, freethinking, autonomous intellectual he aspired to become. Although a voracious reader and prolific writer, his own commitment to socialism and his firsthand experience of crushing poverty taught him the material constraints on living the life of the mind. As he put it in a diary entry of 1908,

What a damned powerful modifier of a man's philosophy of life is poverty and the pressure of hunger! If ever I forget this as a starting-point for any scheme of things that I may construct I hope I'll go hungry for three days so that I remember it. . . . I wonder just how much of it went to the making of Nietzsche and Marc [Max] Stirner.

The life of the philosopher and that of the fool are everywhere conditioned . . . by the same three factors: great need, great greed and little faculty. And the need is ever the most prominent. Thus Spake Zarathustra.[20]

Harrison wrote about the material conditions of racial and class exploitation, as he experienced them firsthand. But with books like *Zarathustra*, he could appreciate the vital importance of the intellectual's labor with words and the poetic vision of a new humanity.

The literary radicals discovered the world-making potential of words in their own experiences reading Nietzsche. They not only sensed that his ideas were vivid and alive, they felt as though he were speaking directly to them. Their contact with Nietzsche's ideas made such an indelible mark on them that they recorded with great care what his ideas *felt* like. Their encounters with Nietzsche's writings showed them the effect an active poetic intellect could have in the world. Nietzsche's work demonstrated to them what the thinker can *do*.

Upton Sinclair discovered Nietzsche in an essay by Georg Brandes. Intrigued by what he read, he got hold of *Thus Spoke Zarathustra*. Moved by the experience, he recorded it in his tale of a failed romantic genius and fictionalized autobiography, *The Journal of Arthur Stirling* (1903):

> I have been reading it for two days—reading it in a state of excitement, forgetting everything. Here is a man!—Here is a man! The first night that I read it I kicked my heels together and laughed aloud in glee, like a child. *Oh*, it was so fine! And to find things like this [were] already written, and in the world! Great heavens, it was like finding a gold mine underneath my feet; and I have forgotten all my troubles . . . I have found a man who understands me, a man to be my friend![21]

The writers described their nights reading Nietzsche as preludes to a budding relationship with the philosopher that continued to grow and develop over time. When he was eighteen years old, Eugene O'Neill was introduced to *Thus Spoke Zarathustra* by *Liberty* publisher and anarchist Benjamin Tucker at Tucker's Manhattan bookshop. According to O'Neill, "*Zarathustra* . . . has influenced me more than any book I've ever read. . . . I've always possessed a copy since then and every year or so I reread it and am never disappointed, which is more than I can say of almost any other book."[22] Like O'Neill, many of Nietzsche's writer-readers turned to his books again and again. John Gould Fletcher, the imagist poet and essayist, first came across Nietzsche's *Zarathustra* while he was a student at Harvard: "All through 1904–5 I absorbed it in large doses, reading Nietzsche day after day at the Harvard Union, and dreaming about the superman at night." This intimacy with Nietzsche drew him away from the Christianity of his boyhood and toward poetry, as even the godless "must believe in something"; if there were indeed no God, then it would be up to the poets to create new images of the possible. Reflecting on his path from the Ivy League to his years as an expatriate poet in England, to his forays into regionalist and antimodernist writings, to his Pulitzer Prize for Poetry in 1939, "[Nietzsche], or rather his ghost, controlled very much of my own thinking."[23]

Though it was uncommon for writers to credit Nietzsche with mind control, they readily acknowledged returning to his writings time and again for renewed intellectual inspiration, moral orientation, and psychic sustenance. The young artists who engaged with Nietzsche's texts imagined themselves in dialogue with him as they read along. They feverishly scribbled their responses in the margins of their dog-eared copies of *Human, All Too Human* and *Thus Spoke Zarathustra*. The playwright Susan Glaspell, wife of George Cram Cook and cofounder of the Provincetown Players, described her husband's response. He treasured his "beautiful German edition" of Nietzsche, Glaspell wrote, adding that Nietzsche was a philosopher "to whom [Cook] turned for continuing companionship." But the "companionship" and conversations Cook recorded in his marginalia were not so much with Nietzsche as with himself. In one marginal note (a fragment in the original), he wrote, "Any one who has felt the resonance of something in himself that vibrates to the iron sting of Nietzsche. . . ." Whereas Emerson implored his reader to "trust thyself: every heart vibrates to that iron sting," Cook's marginalia shows how one could identify Nietzsche's voice as the voice of his own conscience. Cook explained how Nietzsche's way with words made this possible: "[He has] great moving new ideas, but it is the passion with which he thinks them and stamps them into words that sets the reader's soul on fire."[24]

If the radicals' encounters with Nietzsche reveal the ways the poet-philosopher could ventriloquize a reader's as-yet-unawakened conscience, they also show how ideas that felt personal radiated socially. Reluctant to keep Nietzsche's message of the unique and autonomous self to themselves, radicals spread the word in their union halls, book clubs, and discussion groups. Cook first introduced Floyd Dell to Nietzsche while the younger aspiring writer worked as a helper on Cook's Iowa farm. There, they picked beets, shucked corn, and talked about Nietzsche. Because they felt that their intellectual exchanges were too precious to leave to chance, they helped found a philosophy discussion group called the Monist Society. The Monists met regularly and "talked all night" about "books, and ideas, and Nietzschean philosophy."[25] And while the Monists enthusiastically discussed Nietzsche in the countryside, members of the Ruskin Club debated his ideas on the bayside. Jack London and Anna Strunsky were two of the members of this socialist group in San Francisco who read Nietzsche and discussed him at their meetings. The ways in which young radicals brought one another into contact with Nietzsche showed how he played a role in fusing the personal with the political. Here was a philosopher who had a reputation for being the prophet of individualism and the destroyer of social bonds who nevertheless brought readers together in a vital exchange of ideas. He showed them how their longing for intellectual autonomy was both a shared sentiment and a sentiment to be shared.

Taking delight in discussing Nietzsche's ideas, the radicals also treasured volumes of his work among their personal possessions, and his books figured prominently in their gifts to one another. In their desire to institute the collective control of the nation's economic production, they shared a thinker who showed them that the real wealth of any commonwealth is its native intellect. Giving a Nietzsche volume to someone symbolized socialist solidarity, as Mabel Dodge Luhan demonstrated when she gave the young IWW organizer Frank Tannenbaum a copy of Nietzsche to bolster his political will as he served a one-year jail term for leading a protest of unemployed workers.[26] A Nietzsche volume or quotation was especially meaningful if given as a sign of romantic affection. Before examining his own unconventional ideas about free love, Floyd Dell rehearsed this political and romantic convention in his autobiographical coming-of-age novel, *Moon-Calf* (1920). When Dell's character, Tom, wants to impress a young actress at a Chicago party, he talks to her about Nietzsche. Later asked how the actress responded to his Nietzschean pick-up line, Tom replies, "She answered me with a quotation from 'Thus Spake Zarathustra.'"[27] Just as young men could use Nietzsche to woo a young woman, women utilized Nietzsche's potent charms themselves. When Ida Rauh, a young Greenwich Village radical, met her future lover and husband, Max Eastman, she introduced him to Nietzsche. Rauh and Eastman read his work together and contemplated free love while they committed to matrimony, and continued to read him on their honeymoon in Europe.[28]

The radicals' own uses of Nietzsche suggested that the poetic intellect was vital in the making of the complete humanity they longed to realize in modern America. Yet they recognized from their experiences of Nietzsche that provocative ideas not only bring people together but also can wrench them apart. That's precisely what Emma Goldman discovered as her fascination with Nietzsche's philosophical anarchism nourished her spirit while wreaking havoc on her relationship with her lover-mentor, Austrian anarchist Ed Brady. Goldman had first read selections from Nietzsche in Reitzel's *Arme Teufel*, and although she was very intrigued, it was not until studying in Vienna in 1895 that she had a chance to systematically read his works. She reveled in her discovery of the "magic of [Nietzsche's] language, the beauty of his vision, [which] carried me to undreamed-of heights." She wanted to share with Brady her "raptures over Nietzsche." But Brady mocked her fascination with "the great poet-philosopher," unwilling to concede that his aristocratic radicalism might have anything to offer philosophical anarchism. They fought over Nietzsche despite Brady's protests that "Nietzsche is not worth it." Feeling "wounded to the heart," Goldman responded, "It isn't Nietzsche, it is you." Brady's failure to understand her intellectual kismet with the German philosopher suggested that he could not understand *her*, thus bringing their tumultuous relationship to a precipitous end.[29]

Although Nietzsche could pose a threat to struggling relationships, he could also heal suffering psyches. Many of the young radicals who were drawn to his philosophy claimed that his affirmation of his fate as self-willed circumstance and his approach to life as an aesthetic experiment enabled them to view their suffering as salutary. In 1905, when Jack London's lover and future wife, Charmian Kittredge, was stricken with neuralgia and a painful abscess in her ear, he sent her volumes of Nietzsche to boost her spirits. London knew the therapeutic powers of Nietzsche firsthand; he had been intimate with Nietzsche's work for years but had only recently begun to read it systematically. So when Kittredge began to sink into despondency, London knew just what to do. "[I h]ave been getting hold of some of Nietzsche," he wrote her. "I'll turn you loose first on his Genealogy of Morals—and after that, something you'll like—Thus Spake Zarathustra." London's prescription worked beautifully. In addition to *Genealogy* and *Zarathustra*, Kittredge read *The Case of Wagner* (1888) and *The Antichrist* (1895), and she "ate them up." In her estimation, London's gift of Nietzsche "accomplished more than any tonic to clear my own surcharged mental atmosphere and set my feet on the road to recovery." There was one passage from *Zarathustra* which spoke to her, so she spoke it to her lover: "At the foot of my height I dwell. How high my summits are? How high, no one hath yet told me. But well I know my valleys."[30]

Indeed, these writers recognized in Nietzsche the author's power to bring readers to a new altitude from which to observe themselves and their surroundings. The intellectual scales the heights, plumbs the depths, and in doing so provides readers with vital perspectives on their experiences. John Cowper Powys's characterization of reading Nietzsche helps to explain many of the writers' attraction to his prose. According to Powys, "the final impression one carries away, after reading Nietzsche, is the impression of 'distinction,' of remoteness from 'vulgar brutality,' from 'sensual baseness,' from the clumsy compromises of the world." Contact with his words, then, provided these radical writers with a new imaginative apparatus, a new range of apprehension. "It may not last, this Zarathustrian mood," conceded Powys. "It lasts with some of us an hour; with some of us a day—with a few of us a handful of years! But while it lasts, it is a rare and high experience. As from an ice-bound promontory stretching out over the abysmal gulfs, we dare to look Creation and Annihilation, for once, full in the face."[31]

Powys's characterization of a trip to Europe in 1912 demonstrates the ways literary radicals welcomed the gravitational pull of Nietzsche's poetic imagination. Traveling the Continent in his "mania for everything connected with Nietzsche," he went to destinations associated with Nietzsche in Florence, Basel, and Seville. But of all the stops along his European tour, Powys's excursion to Nietzsche's Weimar stood out as his most memorable. There he realized an opportunity that the other critics only dreamed of: he made the pilgrimage to the Nietzsche Archive to have tea with Elisabeth Förster-Nietzsche.[32] After the two talked about the philosopher who had meant so much to them, Förster-Nietzsche provided the young cultist with the rare chance to thumb through books in her brother's personal library. "Imagine what I felt when this devoted lady showed me the dead man's books . . . ! There was, I remember, . . . a [French idealist] I had never heard of; but against some eloquent passage of his, in praise of 'the resolute pursuit of the higher truth,' Nietzsche had written in pencil in the margin, several times over, the words: 'in vain'. . . 'in vain'. . . 'in vain.'"[33]

Powys traveled on to Rome, his thoughts now accompanied by a stowaway: Nietzsche's protest against idealism. His marginalia vexed Powys, leaving him despondent and distracted. The very author who had lifted him to the promontory of his Alpine imagination could just as easily send him tumbling down its slopes. Here he had reached the exquisite capital of Western art, yet the notion that the museums and cathedrals housed representations of universal truth and beauty now seemed like empty idealism: "In vain, in vain, in vain!" rang Nietzsche's voice in his ear.[34]

As Nietzsche showed Powys, there was no greater "drama of the human spirit" than the encounter with powerful ideas. Yet the lingering effect of reading Nietzsche taught the radicals also that despite their own desire for authentic experience unmediated by intellectual a prioris, powerful ideas powerfully expressed can beat us to our own experience. However, for Powys this was not a bad deal, for Nietzsche showed what the intellect might make possible for his reader: "My head was . . . full of the hyperborean breath of Nietzsche's imaginations . . . I well remember my exultation . . . with the notion that it would be my destiny one day to give to the world a philosophy as startling and new as that of the author of *Ecce Homo*."[35]

Although Powys and his comrades all harbored ambitions of giving the world a philosophy it could not refuse, none achieved the spectacular success in realizing this dream as did Lebanese-American poet and artist Kahlil Gibran. His 1923 book of prose poems, *The Prophet*, a collection of inspirational aphoristic sermons delivered by the fictional prophet Almustafa, became an instant best seller in the United States. Translated into over twenty languages, it would remain so for the following century, bringing its author international fame.[36] But before millions of readers worldwide found inspiration in Gibran's poetic voice, using his words to guide them through such life events as brises, baptisms, graduations, weddings, and funerals, he came to his quotable insights by way of Nietzsche.

Gibran's lifelong encounter with Nietzsche's writings reveals and clarifies the ways in which Nietzsche's words enacted their world-making potential in the writers who came after him. Gibran's path to Nietzsche was certainly unique among all the writers explored here. Born in Bsharri, Lebanon, in 1883, Gibran moved at age twelve with his mother and three siblings to Boston's South End, a squalid immigrant ghetto. Thus commenced his life of crossings: between East and West, Arabic and English, the Maronite Christianity of his upbringing and the appeal of Islam, his first love, painting and drawing, and his subsequent passion for poetry. Nietzsche's philosophy helped Gibran negotiate these crossings beginning when he first discovered them at age twenty-five.

Gibran's winding path to Nietzsche began in Boston, where his teacher at an art class run by settlement workers discovered his talent for drawing. From there he made his way—as model and muse—into the world of the wealthy turban-wearing, hookah-smoking photographer, publisher, and patron of the arts, Fred Holland Day. In Day's orbit, young Gibran gained exposure to romantic poetry and decadent art while serving as an in-house "Middle Eastern princeling" to the older art lovers swept up in Victorian Orientalism. Though Day provided him with his first venue to exhibit his art in 1904, Gibran eventually found the luster of Boston's Brahmin bohemianism wearing thin and the psychic wages of tokenism heavy. So he departed for Paris in 1908, believing that his path to artistic self-discovery snaked through its boulevards, sidewalk cafes, and museums. He went to study European art but also to find himself. He hoped to begin "a new chapter in the story of my life."[37]

Gibran discovered Nietzsche's philosophy while in Paris. Before doing so, he rejoiced in Parisian life as a living museum of modernist aesthetics. He enjoyed the community around the École des Beaux-Arts, met artists both young and well established, and went every Sunday morning (when admission was free) for devotional worship at the Louvre. It was an intoxicating time—but never more so than when he first encountered Nietzsche's writings. In a dreamy letter he later wrote to a neighbor, "Nietzsche is a great giant—and the more you read him the more you will love him. He is perhaps the greatest spirit in modern times, and his work will outlive many of the things we consider great. Please, p-l-e-a-s-e, read 'Thus Spake Zarathustra' as soon as possible for it is—to me—one of the greatest works of all times." He learned from Nietzsche the transforming potential of words: "What a pen! With one stroke it would create a new world, and with one stroke it would efface old ones, the while dripping beauty, charm and power."[38] He discovered from Nietzsche what his own words could do. Gibran came to start a new chapter in his book of life, and with the discovery of Nietzsche he recognized that he had held the pen in his hand all along.

Gibran returned to the United States and settled in New York, where he continued drawing insights and inspiration from Nietzsche. Like Van Wyck Brooks, Louis Untermeyer, and Waldo Frank, he regularly contributed to James Oppenheim's literary journal, *The Seven Arts*, and like all the Nietzsche-inspired writers who published there he sought to create a socially redemptive art without piety to precursors. As the first *Seven Arts* editorial announced, its writers had "no tradition to continue . . . no school of style to build up," just the "work which is done through a joyous necessity of the writer himself."[39] For Gibran's first book, *The Madman* (1918), written in the shadow of the war, this meant examining the redemptive capacities of art in a broken world. He used the figure of the Nietzschean poet to show that it was the mad genius who was sane, and the war-torn world of national chauvinism and of institutional religion which digs a spiritual grave for the living that was mad. As he described Nietzsche, "What a man! What a man! Alone he fought the whole world in the name of his Superman; and though the world forced him out of his reason in the end, yet did he whip it well. He died a super-man among pygmies, a sane madman in the midst of a world too decorously insane to be mad."[40] Gibran's following book, *The Forerunner* (1920), offered more experiments with Nietzschean language and themes. Whereas Nietzsche celebrated Emerson as a model of the self-begotten self, one who is his own successor, Gibran drew from Nietzsche the model of the self-begotten self who is his own forerunner: "You are your own forerunner, and the towers you have builded are but the foundation of your giant-self. And that self too shall be a foundation." As Nietzsche confirmed for Gibran, "Always have we been our own forerunners, and always shall we be."[41]

After *The Forerunner*, Nietzsche's fount had not yet run dry, and so Gibran followed in 1923 with *The Prophet*. This work announces on every page how Gibran experienced Nietzsche's intellect as a reflection of his own. It follows *Thus Spoke Zarathustra* in heralding the divinity of the self and imploring readers to be their own saviors. It is the story of Almustafa, a prophet who, like Zarathustra, descends to the masses after years in solitude, and gives sermons about self-created virtue, the body as an earthly temple, and the enslaving beliefs of institutional religion. Gibran's prophet, just like Nietzsche's Zarathustra, heralds the coming of a day when the higher soul lives beyond the ethical cage of good and evil: "He who defines his conduct by ethics imprisons his song-bird in a cage." Almustafa also proclaims the meaning of the earth: "Your daily life is your temple and your religion. Whenever you enter into it, take with you your all." Just like Nietzsche's Zarathustra, Gibran's prophet heralds the potential Übermensch in all his readers, those who have the strength and the wisdom to know that "you are good when you are one with yourself."[42]

The parallels continue. Gibran, however, did not believe that he was borrowing from Nietzsche. After all, how could a self that would be its own

Kahlil Gibran's drawing for the cover of *The Prophet* (1923).

forerunner, a self so hostile to slavish utilization of inherited forms, borrow that which can only be created? But because the parallels are so striking, virtually all Gibran commentators feel obliged to explain them. One commentator describes Gibran's relationship with Nietzsche as "so strong that it carried him off his feet and almost uprooted him from his Oriental soil."[43] Gibran's own characterization, however, is more revealing and better echoes the sentiments of the other authors who also were drawn into Nietzsche's world. As he later put it, "Nietzsche took the words out of my mind. He picked the fruit off the tree I was coming to."[44] For Gibran, as for the others, the point wasn't how much he did or did not crib from Nietzsche, but rather how reading Nietzsche made him understand the power of words, the experience of the poet-philosopher. Experiencing Nietzsche's words and wisdom yielded *self-discovery*, not self-abandonment or slavish appropriation. Gibran, like Cook, London, and Goldman before him, understood Nietzsche's exhortation to the liberated intellect as his own conscience announcing its arrival. When Cook reached for Nietzsche's *Ecce Homo* (1908) during a period of personal crisis, he did not think he was beholding Nietzsche so much as beholding the man he, Cook, was coming to be. As he put it, reading *Ecce Homo* freed him to "write of his own."[45] When the encounter with Nietzsche encouraged the young radicals to travel down the road to their own liberated intellect, they believed he could accompany them, but not as compass or guide.

The literary radicals relished the Nietzschean atmosphere both for what it made possible in them and for what it revealed that the writer could make possible in the world. They described their experiences of reading Nietzsche as intoxicating, bracing, challenging, ennobling. But most of all, the experience taught them about the value of ideas as an experience, and words as a vital form of action. Nietzsche taught them the artistry of a strong argument that seeks not to control the reader's mind but to teach it to become itself. Although their enthusiasm for the "poet" Nietzsche often bordered on the ecstatic, it was driven by a serious commitment to the notion that aesthetics and ethics are inseparable. Nietzsche thus affirmed for them their own roles as thinkers who address the whole man, writers who could write in such a way that the readers could *feel* the sting of their own conscience. However, the radicals weren't just drawn to Nietzsche's writings. We come closer to their image of Nietzsche as educator when we consider the figure of Nietzsche himself. When we do so, we learn that when the radicals shared copies of Nietzsche's books with one another, when they celebrated his firestorm of imagery, and when they turned to him as a personal companion, they did so because they believed that in Nietzsche they had found a model of the modern intellect.

## *Imitatio* Nietzsche

While the literary radicals turned to Nietzsche's writings to reflect on American thinking, they also discovered in his own tragic biography a heroic and cautionary tale about the perilous course of the intellectual in the democratic era. They turned to Nietzsche's persona and the trajectory of his career as an example of the new intellectual as modern social type still in formation. The radicals were interested in several aspects of Nietzsche's life and character, including his intellectual independence, his physical condition, his striving for self-sovereignty and self-expression. And they derived meaning from the perceived connections between Nietzsche's genius, his martyrdom, and his madness. Despite the many narratives about Nietzsche's life, these radicals all shared a preoccupation with the persona of the intellectual and his location in the social geography of modern America. The stories they spun were both romantic and sociological, explaining why genius fails, why it requires institutional freedom, what it does for a culture, and what that culture does to him in turn.

Why did American radicals look abroad to examine what Alfred Kazin would later call their "alienation *on* native grounds"?[46] In part, their uses of Nietzsche underscore Kazin's claim that so much of their search for an organic intellectual culture was a rewriting of Emerson's "American Scholar." But perhaps it was Emerson's "Uses of Great Men" (from *Representative Men*, 1850) that they were really rewriting. It wasn't just Nietzsche's ideas that intrigued them, it was his persona—the intellectual Adam, the self-begotten genius, the thinker who was his own forerunner and successor. Nietzsche's philosophy provided them with the means for revolt, but his biography provided them with a narrative of a revolt's personal consequences.

By turning to Nietzsche, these avant-garde writers were participating in the Emersonian practice of looking to Europe for intellectual models. Although Emerson had longed for an America that cultivated its own native intellect, one that no longer feasted off the remains of Europe, his *Representative Men* was a confession that the culture of American democracy may never pull this off. None of his examples of genius in "American Scholar" are

American. After thirteen years in ardent pursuit of the native intellect, he came up empty-handed: none of those whom he classified as great men in history were American either. When Harold Stearns asked in 1921 in his own search for native intellect, *America and the Young Intellectual*, "Where *are* our intellectuals?" he rehearsed a long-standing grievance that in America genius may simply be impossible.[47]

Though their desire to consider their own role as intellectuals in modern America was new, elements of the intellectual apparatus that the literary radicals were working with were not. As they enlisted the figure of Nietzsche to imagine themselves as intellectuals, they did so by working with an eighteenth-century concept of genius. Nineteenth-century European romantics made a cult of genius, but it was their eighteenth-century Enlightenment forerunners who gave the modern concept its form and character. As Carl Pletsch has argued, the late eighteenth-century concept of genius helped bourgeois intellectuals imagine new social roles for themselves as they sought independence from clerical life and aristocratic patronage. Their Enlightenment ideals encouraged them to enthrone humankind as their master, and created new literary roles that aimed to serve humanity rather than God or the aristocracy. The expansion of the late eighteenth-century literary marketplace enabled them to do so, providing thinkers with a degree of financial independence, which in turn afforded them greater intellectual freedom. In Pletsch's assessment, one of the accomplishments of eighteenth-century writers was the creation of new literary genres—in particular, autobiography and biography. This "permitted the public to think about great individuals in entirely new ways"—that is, to think "in terms of genius." Set free from the ties that bound man to his immortal Maker, the genius now embodied the qualities once reserved for God. The genius was considered an "unmoved mover" endowed with the ability to "create *ex nihilo*" and thereby become a "law unto himself." By creating "a new understanding of human greatness," Enlightenment thinkers laid out the framework of a new "social space," which would go on to be occupied by Rousseau, Goethe, and eventually Nietzsche.[48]

There were plenty of European "geniuses" for Americans to turn to, but Nietzsche especially spoke to their romance with independence from institutions and their consequent anxiety of being marginalized. He helped those like Stearns, who sought intellectual freedom yet disliked its consequences: "In our national life to-day the young intellectual speedily finds that *he is not wanted.*"[49] If genius has a history, so too does the hero worship of the alienated genius; and it is this iteration of the young intellectuals' cult of genius that helps explain how the ground for the romance with Nietzsche in the twentieth century was laid in the nineteenth.[50] As we have seen, the early twentieth-century Nietzsche vogue had a broad cultural scope, and was not limited to professional or aspiring thinkers and writers. But for the young intellectuals, it was Nietzsche's role as a freelance philosopher without institutional support, affiliation, or recognition that had particular appeal.

As R. J. Hollingdale argued, the conditions surrounding the failed revolutions of March 1848 helped prepare the way for the European philosopher as "culture star." Germany's state and church authorities succeeded in purging philosophy departments of scholars suspected of subversive intellectual activity. What they did not anticipate, though, is that marginalization from the academy in the post-1848 world would become a badge of intellectual honor. "German philosophy split into two," Hollingdale wrote, into "academic" philosophers who produced bloodless *Wissenschaft* of no intellectual consequence or political import, and "freelance" philosophers who existed "outside and independently of the university." According to Hollingdale, Schopenhauer was the first beneficiary of the turning of the tides. Hostile to and neglected by the philosophic establishment in the first half of the century, the watershed events after 1848 "handed him a public: a German audience" hungry for innovative thought. As the romance with Schopenhauer demonstrates, the philosopher's alienation was now part of his "credentials"; audiences began to take an interest not only in the thinker's ideas but also in his relationship to institutional power. If Schopenhauer was the first beneficiary, then Nietzsche was the second. Thanks to his estrangement, he inhabited a new social space and intellectual type—the freelance philosopher as superstar.[51]

The entwined histories of the concept of genius and intellectual hero worship help to foreground literary radicals' appropriation of his image.[52] In addition, Nietzsche's own writings about genius helped flesh out the still-forming notion of the freelance thinker. He characterized genius as antagonistic to all traditional sources of authority, hence hostile to moral complacency, and he argued that society is equally hostile to it in return. However, Nietzsche also emphasized the geniality of intolerance for the genius. "Mutilation, crippling, [and] a serious deficiency in an organ offers the occasion for an uncommonly successful development of another organ," he argued. "It is in this way one can suppose many a glittering talent to have originated."[53] According to Nietzsche, the formation of a genius requires not just social intolerance but self-sacrifice. The "greatness" of the genius is that "*he expends himself* . . . he uses himself up, he does not spare himself" in his "devotion to an idea, a great cause." While he gives himself freely in the pursuit of a higher aim, society thanks him with its all-too-human "gratitude": it misunderstands him.[54]

Brilliance. Greatness. Alienation. *Genius.* "There is something of Nietzsche in all of us," observed Will Durant in 1917, eager to come to terms with the "lessons" of Nietzsche's intellectual heroism.[55] Though Nietzsche had insisted that future readers not "concern [themselves] about me, but only about the things for which I lived," the young intellectuals believed that for him there was no distinction between the two. After all, as Horace Kallen noted, Nietzsche maintained that "temperaments are the foundations of . . . minds," and that "feelings supply the power and dictate the goals of . . . intellects."[56] As a result, Kallen observed, the things for which he lived were shaped by the things from which he suffered. The literary radicals chronicled in great detail his protracted health problems and his appetites (sexual and otherwise), and surveyed the episodes of his life that they believed foreshadowed his descent into madness. Rather than diagnose Nietzsche's insanity in clinical terms, however, they understood it alternately as the source or consequence of his "genius." Durant likened Nietzsche's genius to a tree of knowledge that tumbled under the "weight and multitude of its own fruit." He found confirmation for this interpretation in a quotation from *Twilight of the Idols,* where Nietzsche claimed that "to perish beneath a load one can neither bear nor throw off . . . that is a philosopher."[57]

The radicals generated competing theories of Nietzsche's insanity, but they all understood it as an example of the martyrdom of modern genius. Many described Nietzsche's madness in mystical terms. George Cram Cook turned to Nietzsche as evidence of how the poet, by virtue of his task, teeters on the edge of insanity. This is so because the poet, like the religious mystic, must push beyond the familiar realm of language and sensation in order to create new forms, images, and ideas to communicate human experience. All poets thus suffer for their "intensity of symbolic thinking," which requires shuttling between the familiar and the unknown in the quest for a new language for experience. But it is the rare genius, like Nietzsche, who makes the ultimate crossing, by imaging the world itself as symbol. Cook asked,

Is that insanity? Whether it is or not may depend on the degree of control the will is able to maintain over the perilous stuff. But whatever it is, it lies at the base of religion. The men in whose minds this kind of thing happens have been the great religious artists, teachers and mystics of mankind. . . .

Not even 'Ecce Homo' is the work of madness, but the partition here between madness and great wit is thin indeed. When he wrote 'Ecce Homo' no control had snapped; the leash still held, but there was a force tugging at the leash. That solitude of spirit which produced the immense tension of Nietzsche, and so his greatest work, endured too long.

According to Cook, Nietzsche pushed his mind toward insanity knowingly and willingly. His madness was no accident, it was martyrdom. Nietzsche "would have been willing to pay the price had he known in advance that it was to be the loss of reason," Cook wrote. He knew that a new world of ideas worth living for would also be worth dying for; mental death was the price. According to Cook, the penalty of madness has always been central to religious mysticism, and it would remain so for secular moderns who struggled against inherited forms but longed for the sense of transcendence they provided.[58]

For radicals like Cook, the lesson of Nietzsche's madness was not simply that mental suffering is an occupational hazard for the modern intellect, but that such suffering has a greater purpose. When Cook wrote that Nietzsche "saved my soul from Tolstoi, Jesus, and Mr. and Mrs. Browning," he was merely emphasizing a common sentiment about the poetic genius's redemptive promise for wayward moderns. The genius requires more than philosophical acumen, literary verve, or clever wit. Talent is a skill, genius is a sacrifice. Nietzsche's life demonstrated how those who came after him benefited from his labors. Cook wrote,

> Into what new and at first terrible environment do inspired men like Nietzsche, insane with truth, plunge and return gasping? In lonely rooms in the cities of men some souls have entered regions more desolate and unadapted to life than the high Arctic—facing there a fate beside which freezing to death is peace. Out there you deal with phases of this fathomless universe you were not made to deal with—you do not inherit powers to do this. The Nietzsches know the danger, yet go, and perish. Likewise the selachians went ashore and perished. Therefore *we* breathe.[59]

Nietzsche's example taught his young American counterparts that even if they were toiling silently in the dark recesses of anonymous cities, with shoulders a little sore, eyes a little strained, and paychecks a little unforthcoming, their labors had a purpose.

The image of the martyred genius thus provided the writers with a romantic, albeit terrifying, model of the fate of the thinker. That Nietzsche may also have "suffered from hereditary syphilis," as Upton Sinclair noted, was beside the point. His mental death, or, as Sinclair put it, the "tragic waste of the greatest genius of modern times," had less to do with his alleged inherited (or contracted) disease that went untreated than with the burdens genius must bear. Sinclair stressed that Nietzsche was "a man who was ill and suffering atrociously. He declared that every year meant for him two hundred days of pain. His view of life is the product of a pain-driven mind, like the ecstasy experienced by martyrs undergoing torture." The object lesson of Nietzsche's collapse was clear: genius suffers. However, if Nietzsche's pain was self-inflicted, his goal wasn't masochism. It was sacrifice. On the title page of his *Mammonart* (1925), Sinclair asked the question burning in the minds of his fellow artists: "Has Genius Served Humanity?" Nietzsche's martyrdom suggested poignantly to them that the answer was "yes." Not only from Nietzsche's philosophy but also from the example of his heroics would the world learn the "strange secrets concerning the possibilities of the human spirit," and his young intellectual admirers the meaning of the intellectual life.[60]

Of all the figures Nietzsche was likened to—modern mystic, Christ, Faust, Prometheus—the one that resonated the most was Nietzsche as a present-day Hamlet. The unfulfilled longings and haunted imagination, which thrust him into madness, recalled the tragic fate that befell Shakespeare's Danish prince. Comparing Nietzsche to Hamlet would remain a perennial feature of Nietzsche interpretation in the United States among thinkers reflecting on the perils of their enterprise.[61] James Huneker provided one of the earliest articulations of this idea when, in 1910, he exclaimed, "Alas! The pathos of Nietzsche's reality. Reality for this self-tortured Hamlet-soul was a spiritual crucifixion and a spiritual tragedy."[62] The image of Hamlet that emerged in this interpretation often resembled the Hamlet that Nietzsche described in *The Birth of Tragedy*. Nietzsche rejected the traditional view of Hamlet as an overly introspective dreamer who drowns in the excess of his own possibilities. "Not reflection, no," Nietzsche argued, it was "*true* knowledge, an insight into the horrible truth" of a "world that is out of joint," that brought about

Hamlet's morbid insanity.[63] Thus, Nietzsche's version of Hamlet's madness and, by extension, the critics' version of Nietzsche's madness emphasized the mental and spiritual costs of fearless moral inquiry. It counseled about the potential dangers awaiting the young thinker who may be inclined to smash false idols or tear away veils of illusion in American culture. Nietzsche's tragic fate demonstrated the perils a Danish prince, a German philosopher, or a young American intellectual faced once he embarked on an all-out search for truth.

Though Nietzsche thought awareness of the truth, not the inability to act, was the root of Hamlet's insanity, the radicals seemed uneasy about Hamlet's psychic paralysis, because it confirmed their concerns about the ineffectual intellectual. They worried about irrelevance as they sensed a gulf between their knowledge of social and economic problems and their ability to transform their knowledge into intelligent action. "We are all Hamlets," Randolph Bourne confessed to a friend, indicating the uneasy kinship he and his friends felt with Shakespeare's character.[64] Van Wyck Brooks agreed that his generation, burdened by the feeling of "internal anarchism," was turning into a "race of Hamlets."[65]

The dangers of too much thinking and too little social action as seen in Hamlet and Nietzsche were especially disturbing to young intellectuals worried that their work as thinkers might have no practical consequence for addressing the problems of modern life. It was bad enough to lose one's mind, but to lose one's relevance was especially disturbing. For Will Durant, a former Ferrer School teacher and socialist activist turned doctoral student of philosophy under John Dewey at Columbia, Nietzsche's example of a life debilitated by thought resonated with young authors like himself, unsure of the social effect of their intellectual labors and worried, if they let their thinking part ways with their doing, that they may have themselves to blame. As philosophy popularizer and author of the perennial best seller *The Story of Philosophy* (1926), Durant would build a lucrative career interrogating Nietzsche as one of his pantheon of philosophical masters. But it was in his 1917 dissertation, "Philosophy and the Social Problem," that he enlisted Nietzsche to consider how the intellectual must integrate his thinking with his doing, in order to rescue philosophy from the thin air of abstraction.

According to Durant, Nietzsche's example wasn't a pleasant one, but its lessons were constructive. Durant noted approvingly that Nietzsche "stood outside our social and moral structure," and suffered the consequences of doing so. However, while his outsider status afforded him a valuable view of the modern condition, it did not demand that he keep his hands clean of it. Durant argued that Nietzsche's "sick" biography was crucial here, not because it appealed to readers' voyeurism but because it helped explain why he went wrong. Nietzsche was a "man sick to the very roots—if you will let me say it, abnormal in sexual constitution; a man not sufficiently attracted to the other sex, because he has so much of the other sex in him." Plenty of authors throughout the century would speculate about Nietzsche's sexuality—his orientation and his undercharged virility—in order to explain why he wrote a compensatory "martial" philosophy, or how his displaced energies fueled his breathless intellectual production. However, Durant's version stressed its particular object "lessons" for young intellectuals. Nietzsche's example demonstrated the effeminacy of the socially passive intellectual: better to have callused palms from manual labor than the neurasthenia of prissy intellectualism. Nietzsche's problem was that he was "abnormally weak in the social instincts," which are crucial for connecting ideas to real world problems, the critical intellectual to community.[66]

The radicals may have agreed that Nietzsche's and Hamlet's estrangement from community contributed to their madness, but not all of them viewed it as such a bad thing. Both Nietzsche and Hamlet exhibited the dangers of the intellectual's "pathos of distance" from the crowd, but they also exhibited its allure. After becoming "intimate with Hamlet," Upton Sinclair began to imagine himself as the modern "Prince of Denmark." "I too was a prince, in conflict with a sordid and malignant world; at least, so I saw myself, and lived entirely in that fantasy."[67] Sinclair later felt sheepish about his sense of distinction, but the concern that the masses misunderstand genius was confirmed by Nietzsche's fate. Though they used the Hamlet figure to chastise themselves for lingering too long in thought and not engaging in action, the avant-garde writers were also skeptical of the very masses that they believed they were addressing. The Hamlet-Nietzsche metaphor for genius revealed their alienation from—and ambivalence toward—the modern democratic public culture they wanted to serve and to lead. The spectacle of Nietzsche laboring in silence, and ultimately collapsing beneath the burden of his refused genius, resonated with a number of intellectuals who perceived themselves as similarly marginalized by an American culture indifferent to their ideas.

As bad as Nietzsche's marginalization during his lifetime had been, it was preferable to his broad reception after his death, the critics argued. Emma

Goldman complained about the philosopher's posthumous notoriety, complaining that "shallow interpreters" balked at "Friedrich Nietzsche, ... that giant mind," only because they had botched his message.[68] But Bourne argued that Nietzsche's posthumous reception evidenced how an indiscriminate public kills genius softly with its *appreciation*. Nietzsche had given him reason to fear not the ignorant masses but the educated philistines who were all too eager to accommodate (and domesticate) radical ideas. Here again, Nietzsche not only endured suffering, he theorized about it. As he wrote in *Untimely Meditations* (1873–76), the cultural philistine "fancies that he is himself a son of the muses and a man of culture," while the great thinker is a *seeker*. The philistine thus thinks he possesses that which the true genius seeks: "a genuine, original ... culture."[69] Bourne identified this as the problem of the American mind—not the cultural hostility to the critical intellect but "the *uncritical hospitality* of current taste." He saw a danger in the sunny gentility that marked American cultural attitudes, which was deadly for the artist. As he put it, "The real enemy is still the genteel tradition which tends to smother the timid experiments of a younger generation that is not satisfied with husks. For the deadly virus of gentility is carried along by an up-to-date cultivated public—small perhaps, but growing—who are all the more dangerous because they are so hospitable." Recognizing the damaging effects of the genteel sensibility on the viability of new ideas, Bourne concluded that "the would-be literary artist needs to be protected not so much from his enemies as from his friends."[70]

Although the radical writers certainly did not desire to emulate Nietzsche's mental collapse, they admired his relentless commitment to his craft and his mission. The figure of Nietzsche served a pedagogical function by showing the uses and abuses of intellect in modern society. His protracted torments taught them that genius suffers but that, as Huneker put it, "suffering makes noble." Nietzsche also demonstrated the perils involved in an intellectual life defined by a pathos of distance. Loneliness and estrangement, the radicals came to believe, may be the price for achieving a critical distance from one's own culture. But while Nietzsche offered a romantic picture of the philosopher-poets they longed to become, so too was he a practical guide for the young writer. As William English Walling observed, "What concerns us is Nietzsche's actual work—that is, not the finished product but the activity itself."[71] Like Nietzsche's early twentieth-century Protestant readers who recoiled from the easy comforts of modern life and sought more strenuous expressions of the faith, the radical writers and artists idealized Nietzsche's martial temperament and his disciplined commitment to his calling. The image of Nietzschean genius thus served as a source for self-flagellation, and gave them good reason to reprimand themselves for their own felt dilettantism. Nietzsche's *Ecce Homo* had served as a manual that instructed how to write well and how to live right. To behold the figure of Nietzsche was to behold a model of *Man Thinking*.

## The "Gay Science" of Cultural Criticism

Nietzsche gave literary radicals reason to doubt "'reason' in philosophy." In *Twilight of the Idols* he wrote,

> You ask me about the idiosyncrasies of philosophers? [It] is their lack of historical sense, their hatred of even the idea of becoming, their Egyptianism. They think they are doing a thing *honour* when they dehistoricize it, *sub specie aeterni* [from the viewpoint of eternity]—when they make a mummy of it. All that philosophers have handled for millennia has been conceptual mummies; nothing actual has escaped from their hands alive. They kill, they stuff, when they worship, these conceptual idolaters—they become a mortal danger to everything when they worship.[72]

Nietzsche's critique of the foundationalist bad habits in Western thought emboldened young American writers who contributed to the early twentieth-century "revolt against formalism" in the arts, and to social and political theory. But they had co-conspirators closer to home as well. Indeed, those drawn to Nietzsche also took an interest in William James's radical empiricism, John Dewey's instrumentalism, Charles Sanders Peirce's "pragmaticism," and Franz Boas's cultural relativism. But it was Nietzsche who showed them how to transform their assaults on foundationalism into a new kind of inquiry. It was, as Brooks, drawing from Nietzsche, referred to it, the "philosoph[y] of the *gaya scienza*," thinking with a "hammer in one hand" and a "divining-rod" in the other, inquiry that simultaneously whacks old idols and imaginatively divines new ones.[73] It was Nietzsche who showed the avant-garde writers a new species of thought that they would come to call cultural criticism.

Literary radicals agreed with Nietzsche that knocking down old values is easy compared to building up new ones. They also understood that tearing down old values *purposefully* is more difficult than it seems. A standard hammer was too blunt an instrument for Nietzschean criticism. Indeed, when Nietzsche explained how to "philosophize with a hammer," he referred to a "hammer as with a tuning fork." The *"grand declaration of war"* on foundationalism, then, commences with "sounding-out" hollow idols.[74] The radicals understood from Nietzsche that the first task of criticism is to "sound out" the cultural wreckage within the modern personality. Before the critic could imagine what kinds of selves "ought to be cultivated, willed, or created," as Walling put it, he must sound out antiquated ideals that have turned into idols.[75]

Nietzsche revealed the power of ideals, but he also demonstrated their historical contingency. His arguments about the historical origins and subsequent inversions of Christian concepts such as good and evil alerted the American writers to the dynamic nature of beliefs. He encouraged them to view such terms as *truth*, *virtue*, and *morality* with great suspicion. If, as Nietzsche argued, moral language is not an expression of universal truth but rather an instrument to serve particular social functions, then it would be their role as critics of American values to investigate how, for example, modern-day Christians and laissez-faire capitalists used words as strongholds to defend or justify their religious traditions and aggrandized wealth.

The young intellectuals were committed to progressive reform and cultural renewal but also to the belief that neither God nor natural law demanded that they be so. In *A Preface to Politics* (1913), Walter Lippmann used Nietzsche's insights to imagine a democratic theory without foundations. To do so, he first sought to demonstrate that political and economic discourse, though grounded in claims of universality, had no such recourse to absolutes. He argued that political commitments, even democratic ones, were informed by human temperament, not by rationality. To understand politics, we should analyze people's psychological longings, their aesthetic tastes, even their irrational impulses, more than the first principles they espouse. Nietzsche had argued that dogmas are no more than "instruments of human purposes." What a culture identifies as moral, therefore, is really just "an effort to find a way of living which men who live it will instinctively feel is good." Lippmann approvingly quoted Nietzsche's claim that "every great philosophy [is an] . . . unconscious autobiography" in his effort to show the subjectivity and contingency of our political ideals.[76]

The problem with American politics, Lippmann argued, was that people clung tenaciously to barren ideals, stock phrases, and abstract theories rather than embraced living realities. Even the realities, though, are often transitory perceptions, not foundational truths. Drawing from Nietzsche's argument about the genealogy of values, Lippmann wrote, "Words, theories, symbols, slogans, abstractions of all kinds are nothing but the porous vessels into which life flows. . . . But our reverence clings to the vessels. The old meaning may have disappeared, a new one come in—no matter, we try to believe there has been no change." He insisted that there is "nothing disastrous in the temporary nature of our ideas." The opposite is true. The risk comes only when we regard them as "final."[77]

Following Nietzsche, Lippmann thus sought to move philosophical inquiry and political debate away from ethical foundations that inhibited practical thought. "What Nietzsche has done here is, in his swashbuckling fashion, to cut under the abstract and final pretensions of creeds." This convinced Lippmann that modern Americans needed to "keep their minds freed from formalism, idol worship, fixed ideas, and exalted abstractions." Although that meant venturing off the firm ground of the eighteenth- and nineteenth-century Enlightenment liberal tradition and into the "topsy-turvyland" of modern reality, Lippmann insisted that any vision of the political must realize that the best it can hope for is one that leaves room for revision.[78] Moral indeterminacy did not mean that we should no longer evaluate our values, but that we should do so by examining them for their aesthetic and experiential dimensions. As Nietzsche had argued in *The Birth of Tragedy*, "The existence of the world is *justified* only as an aesthetic phenomenon."[79] Using this same logic, Lippmann pleaded for evaluating values for "the quality of feeling" they elicit rather than the "conformity to rule" they command. In his own quest for a progressive politics befitting the critics' democratic aspirations, he argued that dogma must be replaced by inquiry, assertions by experiment. He welcomed the provisional and the personal in politics: "Perhaps we shall say with Nietzsche: 'Let the value of everything be determined afresh by you.'"[80]

Such moral indeterminacy could place heavy demands on the individual, however. Indeed, as Emma Goldman admitted, it "urges man to think." While Goldman stressed that "perfect personality" could be realized once moderns liberate their minds from "man-made law" and "truth grown false with age," she also insisted that they would prefer gilding their cages to breaking free of them. Though the masses would be the first to benefit from recognizing how religious and even supposedly democratic ideals espoused in American public life were instruments of internecine terror rather than divine commandments, they were the least likely to do so. The beneficiaries of industrial capitalism manufacture the fictional idol of the free market, for example, but it is the masses who willingly worship it. To demonstrate how the common people were their own tormentors, Goldman went to some of the unlikeliest passages in Nietzsche's writings. She turned, for example, to Nietzsche's maxim, "When you go to woman, take the whip along," to demonstrate how even liberated suffragists couldn't get liberation right. According to Goldman, suffragists grounded their arguments for voting rights on the very outmoded essentialist ideas of female purity and virtue that had subjugated them. If woman is a "purist," Goldman argued, it is only because she has become "bigoted and relentless in her effort to make others as good as she thinks they ought to be." The daily workings of Christian *ressentiment* in American cultural politics showed that though Nietzsche's maxim "is considered very brutal," he accurately "expressed in one sentence the attitude of woman towards her gods."[81]

Perhaps none of the radicals embodied Nietzsche's conception of the dangerous thinker more than Goldman. Certainly, given her 1917 incarceration and subsequent deportation to Russia, none were penalized more harshly for their ideas. Her critique of wartime patriotism as yet another iteration of the masses' slave morality elicited the very response of public morality as weapon of terror that she spent her career protesting. She insisted that patriotism was another manufactured notion of affiliation and obligation that turned one's homeland into a sentimental idol while demanding that the individual submit his labor, if not his life, for the state's aggrandizement.[82]

The hysteria of wartime, however, only dramatized what the radicals perceived as a persistent problem in American thinking: Americans didn't do enough of it. And when Americans did think, it was only in the form of barren ideals and hollow pieties. Although the war snuffed out political debate and reduced public discourse to shrill sloganeering, this merely underscored the radicals' long-standing grievance with a culture they perceived as hostile to free thought and free speech. Disenchanted with modern America's lack of a liberated mindset befitting an advanced industrial democracy, the young intellectuals took cues from Nietzsche's genealogy of values in order to examine the historical sources of the impoverished American mind. A genuinely free personality, a fully realized modern self, they argued, was impossible without a genuinely free mind. Nietzsche had shown how all ideals are historical constructs, a "long succession of masterings and enslavings and deceivings," as Durant put it, which become fossilized as universal truths.[83] Nietzsche's genealogy helped explain what the radicals came to regard as the belated quality of the American intellect, which still preferred the dead relic of a once vital truth to the topsy-turvy land of indeterminacy.

For Hubert Harrison, it was bad enough to have poverty (the result of an exploitative capitalist system) put a lock on your mind, but it was even worse to have your own religion do it. This was, in his view, the most powerful insight Nietzsche's genealogy of the slave morality offered to African Americans. Nietzsche helped him see that African Americans especially should liberate themselves from the "dubious blessings of Christianity," and breathe the larger air of "Freethought." He believed, however, that they were the least likely to do so because "the church saw to it that [Christianity] taught to slaves should stress the servile virtues of subservience and content[ment], and these things have bitten deeply into the souls of black folk." Making matters worse, Harrison argued, the chastened, meek sensibility of Christianity created a timid intellectual "conservatism in [n]egroes." Nietzsche's "slave morality" thus revealed a slave mentality in the African Americans' "sphere of ideas":

> Nietzsche's contention that the ethics of Christianity are the slave's ethics would seem to be justified in this instance. Show me a population that is deeply religious, and I will show you a servile population, content with whips and chains . . . content to eat the bread of sorrow and drink the waters of affliction. The present condition of the Negroes of America is a touching bit of testimony to the truth of this assertion.

It was Nietzsche who helped Harrison explain how Christianity for African Americans conditioned them to glorify "subjugation and subservience," and keep shackles on their minds long after they get rid of them from their bodies. The belief that Christianity provided refuge for, rather than a refutation of, racial inequality, and that it fostered an unwholesome intellectual slavishness among African Americans, emboldened Harrison to break from the church, and to encourage other African Americans to do the same.[84]

For many of the literary radicals, Nietzsche's philosophy offered not only a genealogical approach to the study of contemporary culture but also a couple of archetypes—the *Bildungsphilister* and the "priestly zealot"—to get their inquiries going. Of course, hatred of the American philistine was intense among but not new to them. And while Nietzsche provided a blistering attack of Germany's *Bildungsphilister* (cultural or educated philistine) in *Untimely Meditations*, the radicals could also draw on a lively transnational critique of the cultures of industrialization, starting with Matthew Arnold's popular 1869 indictment of British bourgeois "philistines" and followed in 1874 by *Nation* editor E. L. Godkin's withering critique, "Chromo-Civilization," a condemnation of the American middle class's haughty, pecuniary "pseudo-culture."[85] However, while Godkin was aggrieved with a bourgeoisie that mistook the trappings of wealth for the accomplishments of culture, Nietzsche's criticism focused more pointedly on ideas as a conceit of enlightenment. It was Nietzsche's critique of the educated, but ignorant, collector of modern ideas he doesn't understand that proved most salient.

In an effort to critique the depleted modern American imagination, Van Wyck Brooks took the genealogical turn in his 1915 essay, "'Highbrow' and 'Lowbrow.'" The intellectual style of Nietzsche's cultural philistine provided the bare outlines for Brooks's idea of the effete highbrow, someone who knows how to esteem but not engage ideas. The highbrow views culture as something decorative and feels the need to keep it hygienic, therefore remote, from the messy problems of daily life. The source of Brooks's idea of the lowbrow was closer to home—that is, the American pioneer. The lowbrow represented a style of thought very much of this world—starkly practical, materialistic, and both uninspired by and incapable of speculative thought. Although the two tendencies rarely overlapped, they both conspired against the critical, engaged intellect. For Brooks, the spectacle of these dual tendencies revealed a history of "American mind," either left starving in the barren netherworld between "vaporous idealism and self-interested practicality" or forced to feed off the remains of foreign harvests.[86]

In addition to the nineteenth-century philistine who mistook dead relics for living law, his seventeenth-century predecessor and corollary to Nietzsche's "priestly zealot"—the *Puritan*—seemed to have an insidious effect on American intellectual life. The radicals employed Nietzsche's description of the "life-inimical" "ascetic priest" as they scoured the past for their forefathers and mothers. Nietzsche described these priests as

a self-contradiction: here rules a *ressentiment* without equal, that of an insatiable instinct and power-will that wants to become master not over something in life but over life itself, over its most profound, powerful, and basic conditions; here an attempt is made to employ force to block up the wells of force; here physiological well-being itself is viewed askance, and especially the outward expression of this well-being, beauty and joy; while pleasure is felt and *sought* in ill-constitutedness, decay, pain, mischance, ugliness, voluntary deprivation, self-mortification, self-flagellation, self-sacrifice. All this is in the highest degree paradoxical: we stand before a discord that *wants* to be discordant, that *enjoys* itself in this suffering and even grows more self-confident and triumphant the more its own presupposition, its physiological capacity for life, *decreases*. "Triumph in the ultimate agony": the ascetic ideal has always fought under this hyperbolic sign.

Nietzsche's ascetic priests were "'too good' for this world," and so they sought to penalize those who thought it good enough for them.[87]

While today it is commonplace to bewail the puritanical prudery and provincialism of American culture, the Puritans didn't always have such a bad reputation. Only when early twentieth-century critics like Goldman, Mencken, and Bourne started to excavate the past for the historical conditions conspiring against the free intellect did the modern conception of the Puritan develop. The radicals collapsed Nietzsche's analyses of Christian asceticism and sentimentalism into a critique of the lingering effects of Puritan psychology and piety. While the philistines treated ideas as if they were merely decorative, the Puritan viewed them as disciplinary. In their efforts to find a usable past to critique what they regarded as a culture of rigid moralizing, the radicals discovered the wrathful "Puritan" who policed free thought, hounded liberated spirits, and damaged the free play of personality.

Goldman popularized the latter-day Puritan as the ascetic guardian of public morality who sought to protect young girls' sexuality by denying it. She criticized crusaders who monopolized American sexual ethics by insisting that sexual relations be matrimonial, monogamous, and for the sole purpose of procreation. The problem, as Goldman saw it, was that the crusaders had no ethical grounds for controlling other women's bodies. Her concern, though, was not simply with the modern Puritan's denials of earthly pleasures, but rather the toll that a despiritualized Christian morality—what she referred to as the "narrow puritanic spirit"—takes on the life of the mind. "A spirit which is absolutely blind to the simplest manifestations of life; hence stands for stagnation and decay," she argued, can only produce an intellectual life that is fearful, wrathful, and "steeped in the densest provincialism." Social conservatives were not its only victims. Indeed, social progressives "apparently free from religious and social spooks" are intellectually "as prostrate as the most pious of their kind" before the idol of absolute morality.[88]

Steeped in Nietzsche for over a decade, H. L. Mencken, like Goldman, interpreted the moral austerity and intellectual vacuity of the American mind as "neo-Puritanism," à la Nietzsche. That writers whose politics were so at odds could be so unified in their estimation of Puritanism derived from the plasticity of the image and more from its instrumentality in articulating a shared concern about American anti-intellectualism. In his 1917 essay "Puritanism as a Literary Force," Mencken sought the origins of modern American literature's didactic style, which was devoid of difficult ideas as well as literary nuance, play, or depth. His genealogy of American anti-intellectualism followed many of the same lines as Santayana's and Brooks's. It began with the austere, self-accusing Calvinist of the seventeenth and eighteenth centuries, who lost his dominance with the rise of his nineteenth-century descendant, the philistine, a "trader" or "peasant" in Mencken's version. The philistine is at home in this world but never strays beyond the practical. In fact, neither the Puritan nor the philistine has any sensitivity to the play of ideas, Mencken felt—the Puritan because he fears its seductive powers, the philistine because he is utterly deaf to it. It was during the years between the American Revolution and the Civil War that America began to distinguish itself intellectually as "a paradise of the third-rate," with no "national philosophy" worth speaking of. It was a society dominated by a *Sklavenmoral* of the "spiritually humble," awash in bootstrap politics and commerce, with a paltry "disinherited" intellectual life, the province of scribbling women and "second-rate men."[89]

Then things took a turn for the worse, according to Mencken. After the Civil War, national prosperity led to a "bellicose and tyrannical" new morality, the "*Herrenmoral.*" During the Victorian period, the old Puritanism lost its hold on individual conscience, but its zealotry remained. The once self-accusing sinners in the hands of an angry God were now self-righteous zealots on the prowl for souls to torment. Neo-Puritanism, Mencken argued, explained the modern American:

> His enthusiasm was not for repentance, but for what he began to call service. In brief, the national sense of energy and fitness gradually superimposed itself upon the national Puritanism, and from that marriage sprung a keen *Wille zur Macht*, a lusty will to power. The American Puritan, by

now, was not content with the rescue of his own soul; he felt an irresistible impulse to hand salvation on, to disperse and multiply it, to ram it down reluctant throats, to make it free, universal and compulsory.

Mencken's genealogy showed what was possible when American intellectual history was pressed through Nietzsche's terminology and reassembled by the hands of an angry critic. According to Mencken, the errand into the wilderness had gone terribly awry. From Puritanism to philistinism to a "bellicose" intellectual style that regards its *Sklavenmoral* as "universal and compulsory"—this was American intellectual history. And it explained its intellectual poverty.[90]

With Mencken's relentless war on American anti-intellectualism, it did not take much—maybe a black hat, buckled shoes, and a broad collar—for other young writers to transform Nietzsche's ascetic priest into the ancestor of the modern American Puritan. Summing up what to look for, a writer for *The New Republic* advised,

> Wherever you find a mother imbued with the idea that the will of her child should be broken, there you find a puritan. Wherever you see a legislator obsessed with the idea that the slightest relaxation in the rigidity of the laws and the heaviness of the punishments restraining action will lead to a violent anarchy, there you see a puritan. Wherever you discover a man who despises himself because his healthy, normal feelings do not measure up to the conventions he has been taught to believe in, there you have a puritan. Distrust of normal human life does not now take the form of a belief in infant damnation; it takes the more subtle forms of rigid conventions, of a sense of sin, and of cramping legislation.[91]

Once the impressionistic archetype of the austere, self-righteous premodern Puritan began to take shape, it was relatively easy to survey American society—from the vice campaigns of the Progressive Era through the wartime hysteria to the postwar return to "normalcy"—and discover modern Puritans incapable of free thought and eager to police those who weren't.

This may have been the image of the Puritan that gained traction in the 1920s, but Randolph Bourne insisted that it missed the mark. Bourne agreed that there was a war to be waged in modern America against puritanical influences. But that war was not between fathers and sons, the New Woman and the matriarchal ideal, an intellectual free spirit and Comstockery. It was a war among the instincts of the self. Bourne established his role as "a professional spokesman for the young" in the "Little Renaissance" cultural rebellion before his untimely death at age thirty-two in 1918.[92] With essays like "Youth" (1912), "This Older Generation" (1915), and "Old Tyrannies" (published posthumously in 1919), he revealed himself as a young intellectual who wasn't seeking simply to sound out the idols of his parents but rather to understand how his inheritances played themselves out within his own moral psychology. From his earliest explorations of youthful self-understanding as an undergraduate at Columbia to his last political writings in protest against America's entry into the war, Bourne examined what "a genius like Nietzsche" could teach him about the meaning of the intellectual life.[93]

Bourne felt his affinity with Nietzsche intensely. Hunchbacked, dwarfed from age four by spinal tuberculosis, and with a face misshapen at birth from a forceps delivery, Bourne discovered in Nietzsche a fellow convalescent who embraced his condition with an *Amor Fati*. During the war hysteria, as Nietzsche's philosophy was yoked to German militarism, Bourne used it to critique the "herd instinct" of nationalism at home and imagine a transnational cosmopolitanism that "breathes a larger air."[94] He followed the trends in Nietzsche exegesis, writing acidic reviews of the "denatured Nietzsche" that was emerging in American publications. "It is always a little incongruous to see a great mind expounded by a lesser one," he blanched, "and nowhere is the incongruity more impressive than in the case of Nietzsche. He is too electric, too poetical, too subtle in his insight, too coruscating in his inconsistencies" for his interpreters.[95]

Bourne worried, however, that Nietzsche needed rescuing from his friends more than from his enemies, and he turned to Mencken's Nietzsche-derived critique of American Puritanism as a case in point. Bourne argued that Mencken exemplified the tendency among anti-Puritan "crusaders" to resort to the very morality-based essentialism they set out to destroy. "One wishes Mr. Mencken had spent more time in understanding the depth and subtleties of Nietzsche," Bourne wrote, "and less on shuddering at puritanism as a literary force." Had Mencken done so, Bourne argued, he might have understood that the "attack must be, as Nietzsche made it, on that moralism rather than on its symptoms."[96] According to Bourne, the value of Nietzsche's analysis of the priestly zealotry of Christian slave morality was that it enabled the critic not to ferret out the zealotry of others but to recognize it within one's self. Nietzsche didn't respond to finger-wagging with more of the same, nor did he advocate a simple inversion of slave morality for master morality. Rather, he employed genealogy to demonstrate the relativity of all moral values.

Bourne did agree with Mencken that the archetype of the Puritan was helpful for understanding the grip of moral foundationalism on the American mind. He ruefully acknowledged that the figure of the Puritan was, for moderns, probably more a fantasy than a figure of history, but he also insisted that "if there were no puritans we should have to invent them."[97] According to Bourne, the "Puritan" was a useful fiction for considering the origins of the liberal Protestantism of his middle-class New Jersey childhood, and for analyzing why it no longer served as a spiritual and ethical source for modern America. Drawing from Nietzsche's argument that God is dead, leaving only ritual without belief, Bourne described modern liberal Protestantism as retaining all the ethical trappings of its predecessor while losing its spiritual robustness. "The foundation of this religion [of the older generation] may be religious, but the superstructure is almost entirely ethical. Most sermons of today are little more than pious exhortations to good conduct. By good conduct is meant that sort of action which will least disturb the normal routine of modern middle-class life." "The old Puritan ethics," Bourne added, "which saw in the least issue of conduct a struggle between God and the devil, has become a mere code for facilitating the daily friction of conventional life."[98] Christianity in modern America, he argued, was a regulatory ideal but no longer a religious belief.

Bourne thus enlisted Nietzsche's analysis of the psychology of Christian asceticism while addressing the dominant concern of his own philosophy: the tension between what Brooks called the "free personality" and the "conventional community" in modern America.[99] Nietzsche was helpful to him as he eschewed both the outmoded nineteenth-century ideal of self-reliance and the emerging bureaucratic model of the corporate man. In his critique of Puritanism, Bourne explored how the cardinal virtues of Christianity in despiritualized form discipline but do not ennoble the individual. They may ensure social stability but do nothing to foster interpersonal solidarity. Bourne agreed with Nietzsche that modern ethics had become tired expressions of nineteenth-century sentimentalism: "We have become enfeebled by humanitarianism. . . . Sympathy in place of justice saps the fibre of character and gives free rein to egoistic impulses."[100] Bourne concluded with Nietzsche that sympathy and selflessness do not represent the effacement of the aggrandized self but are rather expressions of it. He argued that even acts of supposed goodwill are really "will to power" strategies, for the act of giving is merely an assertion of our superiority over the person we are supposedly try-ing to help. What troubled Bourne was the prospect that such a conception of moral unilateralism reduced the receiver to a spiritual and material "pau-per," a supplicant to the moral agent's will.[101] The modern Puritan, with his "combination of selfless devotion with self-righteousness," loves "virtue not so much for its own sake as for its being an instrument of his terrorism."[102]

The mistake made by Mencken and other critics of Puritanism, Bourne asserted, was that they focused too much on the trope of the Puritan and not enough on the internal force of despiritualized beliefs. Here, Bourne under-stood Nietzsche's critiques as social theory and moral psychology. When he enlisted Nietzsche to consider the Puritan's will to power in 1917, he decried a "new puritanism [that] will not let us be ends in ourselves, or let personality be the chief value in life." But the power of rigid pieties is that they lodge a "crude assault on the most vulnerable part of other people's souls, their moral sense." Drawing the line of argument straight from Nietzsche, Bourne argued that it is a mistake for his fellow critics to dismiss the Puritan's asceticism as "unnatural," because the entire force of the puritanical belief structure is the way it burrows into the individual's moral psychology and becomes "second-nature." As Bourne put it, the externalized dictates of religion over time be-come naturalized into the believer's entire ethical and psychological gestalt. As a result, "the puritan becomes just as much of a naturalistic phenomenon as the most carnal sinner."[103]

Thus, Bourne suggested that the gay science of sounding out Puritan idols required examining how idols work internally, within one's own psychology. The critique of Puritanism was useful insofar as it examined the ways in which a would-be free personality is necessarily constrained by what comes before it. In a 1915 letter, Bourne remarked that he was "reading Emerson & Nietzsche,"[104] and the influences of both can be seen in his essay "Old Tyran-nies," where he expressed his anxiety of belatedness to a world already fixed into immutable form. "Everything about you is given, ready, constituted, rigid, set up when you arrive. You always think that some day you are going to catch up to this givenness, that you will dominate instead of falling in line." Like Emerson and Nietzsche before him, Bourne was troubled about the prospect of inheritance always having the last word, the prospect that we are always inhibited in ways often invisible to us, either from birth or by our upbring-ing, so that our assertions of self are merely the rattling of our cages. Though

Bourne refused to give in to the myth of the given, he argued that people internalize the dictates of society and only "dimly realize that their outward lives are largely a compulsion of social habit." Although he insisted that "there is nothing fixed about the objects to which society demands conformity," we are trained to be pious to our inherited moral ideals as if they were universal and transcendent. Although we try to outdistance them, we "have never overtaken the given." The net effect, he argued, is that "this divorce between social compulsion and personal desire . . . rarely rises to consciousness." The mistake we make is to think about the individual fighting against society, for the individual we invoke in such a dichotomy "scarcely exists."[105]

Bourne turned to Nietzsche as a philosopher of "personality," a fellow gay scientist who understood the power of illusions to fix themselves into immutable form. And while he shared his fellow radicals' desire to sound out the "cultural wreckage" obstructing the self, he repeatedly insisted with Nietzsche that the most tyrannical of the "old tyrannies" are found *within* the self.[106] In order to cultivate the free modern personality, a culture of genuine intellect, the cultural critic must examine his *own* ideals-turned-idols.

Bourne and his fellow radicals discovered in Nietzsche's philosophy, with its inventive expressions, its genealogical approach, and its concern about the diminished modern personality, a new species of thought they would come to identify as cultural criticism. But they also recognized something familiar in his arguments against absolute truth. They identified striking parallels between Nietzsche's deconstruction of divine and rational foundations, and the pragmatists' challenge to moral and philosophical universals. A number of them had studied under William James at Harvard or John Dewey at Columbia, or had at least followed their work closely; and they had absorbed the idea that truth is plastic and perspectival rather than timeless and absolute. According to the critics, both Nietzsche and the pragmatists sought to reorient philosophy away from idealism, metaphysics, and Darwinian materialism, and toward a closer analysis of personal experience. Both wanted to abandon the notion of mind as a mirror of nature, because, as they argued, no single observer could neutrally and synoptically apprehend the entirety of human experience. Truth was not a finished fact that lay outside human agency but an instrument developed by people as they interacted with their physical and cultural environments. As William English Walling claimed, Nietzsche, along with James and Dewey, stressed the dynamism of an open-ended universe and argued that the validity of ideas must be tested through action. "Nietzsche believes that ... 'we can understand only that which we can do'—certainly the very essence of pragmatism," he wrote.[107]

Lippmann, Walling, and Bourne best expressed this enthusiasm about the parallels between Nietzsche, James, and Dewey. They praised the experimental approach to knowledge and social problems advocated by all three philosophers. And they delighted in the common argument that knowledge is created, not inherited—made, not found. The critics applied this logic to argue that historical knowledge, scientific formulas, and cultural conventions are true only insofar as they are life-affirming and heighten humankind's sense of the possible. In addition, Nietzsche and the pragmatists stressed that man is the maker of his universe. The critics reasoned that if, as Nietzsche had argued, human personality is the product of culture and not of nature or necessity, then modern man's experience of dislocation was the result of a *culture* out of joint. Modern man's feeling of isolation and diminution was a testimony not to some universal human condition but rather to the condition that he had gotten himself into.

This plastic conception of human experience and culture had special appeal among the critics, because it suggested that many of the social and economic problems in modern American life were remediable. It showed them the value of a thinker who could tear down modern Americans' commitment to false foundations, which were inhibiting the promise of democratic pluralism—a Beloved Community of "complete" men and women. But the enthusiasm with which critics embraced this pragmatic understanding of truth and knowledge dimmed as they recognized its limitations, for it failed to provide an animating image of the good life. Instrumentalism alone could not inspire. As critics interested in culture and the human types it socializes, they longed for a view of the world that left room for wonder. The notions of provisional truth and situational ethics were useful strategies for dealing with the mechanics of living, but what they desired above all else was a "prophetic vision" of human existence that was both inspirational and terrifying, sublime and haunting. They wanted a cultural criticism of the hammer, but also of the divining rod.

Bourne articulated this concern most fully, but the sentiment ran through the cultural criticism of all the young radicals. As Bourne wondered in 1917 while watching Dewey enlist pragmatism in defense of the US entry into the war, and his enthusiastic disciples follow in line: where was the divining rod in instrumentalism? Whereas Dewey's pragmatism emphasized the instrumental approach to knowledge, Nietzsche demonstrated that individuals must test their relative conceptions of truth not against the world as it is, but as they will it to be. As the cultural critics argued, ideas that work and concepts that are tested against experience may be true in the pragmatic scheme of things, but it does not mean that they are worthy and ennobling. Speaking for the others, Bourne wrote, "If your ideal is to be adjustment to your situation, in radiant co-operation with reality, then your success is likely to be just that and no more. You never transcend anything. You grow, but your spirit never jumps out of your skin to go on wild adventures." It was precisely this "thirst for more of the intellectual 'war and laughter' that we find Nietzsche calling us to [that] may bring us satisfactions that optimism-haunted philosophies could never bring." For Bourne and many of his fellow radicals, Nietzsche's concept of the will to power picked up where pragmatism left off. It provided a view of man's need to unify his disintegrating experiences. It provided the corrective to an all-too-accommodating instrumentalism and evasive optimism. And it represented a necessary prophetic vision that can "outshoot technique."[108]

## The Modern Intellect and Prophetic Longing

Walter Lippmann summed up the feeling of dislocation in modern life when he wrote, "We are unsettled to the very roots of our being."[109] As the subtitle for his 1914 book, *Drift and Mastery*, suggests, he was "attempt[ing] to diagnose the current unrest" in modern America. Bourne's remark that it was "a book one would have given one's soul to have written" demonstrates how deeply Lippmann's identification of the modern challenges to traditional sources of authority resonated with his contemporaries.[110] His work spoke powerfully to his generation not only because it was a persuasive analysis of the modern forces tearing up the foundations of American society, but because it was a personal confession about how it felt for moderns to have "lost the ties which [had once] bound them" to society and to one another. According to Lippmann, "The rock of ages . . . has been blasted for us": "We have lost authority. We are 'emancipated' from an ordered world. We drift."[111] Although they jubilantly challenged the church's authority, laissez-faire capitalism, liberal political theory, Victorian decorum, and Puritan psychology, the radicals were equally concerned, indeed anxious, about the consequences of toppled truths.

Lippmann's recognition of moderns' loss of roots and their state of moral and psychological drift was echoed by his fellow critics. Van Wyck Brooks worried that American culture had "utterly failed . . . to seize and fertilize" man at his "roots," while Randolph Bourne insisted that "trans-national" cosmopolitanism was not a "policy of drift" but an antidote to the false bonds of wartime panic that masqueraded as patriotism.[112] It is the sentiment expressed in Louis Untermeyer's warning about the blind searching for a path in the darkness after they've pulled down their own sun:

> Lost in the utter dark I stray,
> Seeking in vain the paths I trod;
> And oh, I cannot even pray,
> Because I know there is no God.[113]

This talk of "roots" and "drift" reflects the critics' preoccupation with wayward selfhood in modernity. Their cultural analysis was also mixed with personal confession. Nietzsche's philosophy not only provided them with an analysis of the self in a world without foundations, it captured the psychology of living unmoored from traditional ties. As Nietzsche wrote, "Every great philosophy so far has been: namely, the personal confession of its author and a kind of involuntary and unconscious memoir."[114] While it was Nietzsche the philosopher to whom the critics turned for insights about antifoundationalism, it was Nietzsche the personalist who communicated, in raw and unguarded prose, the intellectual and psychological perils of drift. The "great longing," as Kahlil Gibran put it, is the constant companion of the thinker who seeks to go it alone without absolutes.[115] Nietzsche had shown that we can tear down the celestial staircase but not the need to climb up one.

It is easy to assume that the radicals' enthusiasm for Nietzsche was neo-romantic hero worship, and there were certainly elements of that. There are passages in their writings that read like devotional literature. When Margaret Anderson called Nietzsche the radicals'"prophet" or Agnes Boulton described *Zarathustra* as Eugene O'Neill's "sacred book," it might suggest that the radicals couldn't live in a world after God, so they turned Nietzsche into one.[116] But to view all this enthusiasm as hero worship misses the fuller picture of what Nietzsche meant to the radicals. What they felt they needed more than gods were models of intellect that could educate them about their own roles in modern America. We come closer to their understanding of Nietzsche—the world-making wordsmith, the philosopher-poet-critic, the Hamlet-soul, the gay scientist—when we listen to Bourne's description of the kind of thinker they were looking for:

> Do we not want minds with a touch of the apostolic about them and a certain edge—a little surly, but not embittered—with an intellectual as well as an artistic conscience, with a certain tentative superciliousness towards Demos and an appalling hatred for everything which savors of the bourgeois or the sentimental? Now while everything that is respectable in America seems to be putting its effort, with a sort of joyful perversity, into the technique of destruction, are there no desperate spiritual outlaws with a lust to create?[117]

The radicals discovered in Nietzsche an image of the apostolic thinker that reminded them of what Emerson had had in mind in "Circles" when he claimed, "Beware when the great God lets loose a thinker on this planet. Then all things are at risk."[118] Nietzsche's model was an apostolic thinker who did not hoist himself onto the empty throne of a dead God or offer his own texts as a new New Testament, but rather posed, as Nietzsche had, the momentous question to himself and his readers: "Could you *think* a God?"[119] What they longed for were good models of the antifoundational intellect who helped them tear up the cultural wreckage of their modern America, but also helped them imagine new moral possibilities that could outshoot reality.

The critics searched for—and found—in Nietzsche's radical thought not only an approach to knowledge that wrested truth from the "toothless mouth[s]" of dead gods, but a vision of modern life that inspired transcendence and a feeling of wonder.[120] They gravitated toward Nietzsche's critical insights and poetic vision even though his philosophy did not provide the means for them to create social integration in modern American life. But they realized that it was their job as committed intellectuals to find their path from Nietzsche to the Beloved Community in which they wanted to live.

# Devotions

## *The Letters*

One has to test oneself to see that one is destined for independence and command.... One should not dodge one's tests, though they may be the most dangerous game one could play and are tests that are taken in the end before no witness or judge but ourselves.

Not to remain stuck to a person—not even the most loved—every person is a prison, also a nook.

FRIEDRICH NIETZSCHE, *Beyond Good and Evil* (1886)

Remain faithful to the earth, my brothers.... Let your gift-giving love and your knowledge serve the meaning of the earth.... Out of you, who have chosen yourselves, there shall grow a chosen people—and out of them, the overman. Verily, the earth shall yet become a site of recovery.

FRIEDRICH NIETZSCHE, *Thus Spoke Zarathustra* (1883–85)

I have a terrible fear that one day I will be pronounced *holy*.

FRIEDRICH NIETZSCHE, *Ecce Homo* (1908 [1888])

On Sunday, April 27, 1913, in her Yonkers, New York, home, sixty-seven-year-old Jennie Hintz tried a new way of practicing her piety. She did not need the assistance of clergy, nor did she need to go to church, as she had given up her faith almost a half century earlier. The kind of devotion she experimented with had nothing to do with institutional Christianity, or Jesus, or the sacraments of her youth. It simply required her to put pen to paper and express in unguarded prose what Friedrich Nietzsche meant to her.

Her writing took the form of a long handwritten letter to Nietzsche's sister and literary executor, Elisabeth Förster-Nietzsche, to give thanks and praise for her brother's life and thought. Hintz, a self-described "spinster," introduced herself as a "great admirer of your brother's philosophy and his morals." She explained that she had been reading Nietzsche's works for over a year and a half, starting with *Beyond Good and Evil*, the only Nietzsche volume in her local library at the time. She went on to read "Heinrich Mencken's" monograph before reviewing some studies of his philosophy by British authors and tracking down some more English translations of his works. Hintz also provided Förster-Nietzsche with some details of her life—she was born in Königsburg, moved to Boston at age ten, and now lived in Yonkers with her sister, brother-in-law, and nephew. She said she felt drawn to Nietzsche precisely because "in many points I had already arrived at these truths before *He* expressed them, but I remained mute keeping them for myself." She did so, she explained, because in dealing with people more educated than she, Hintz found she was not listened to or taken seriously. But reading Nietzsche let her know that there was someone she could relate to. Learning about his sickness "brought me to tears," she noted. Hintz continued,

> Had I only known that your brother existed, that *He* had the courage to write his ideas out and to publish them, already in 1887 I could have come to him, stood by his side, and to prove to him that there were people other than his "Lama" [Nietzsche's pet name for his sister], another soul who understood him and in many things could have assisted him. Even given my phobia [*Abscheu*] of the Atlantic Ocean, I would have, for love of him and myself, overcome it, and I would have hurried over with the quickest steamliner and gone to him, to see him, to speak to him, to listen to his lovely voice.

She complained that her voice, unlike the one she imagined Nietzsche had, was like a "foghorn." She therefore desired to, as Nietzsche put it, "preach with a hammer." Hintz could have learned how to do this from Nietzsche directly, if only she could turn back time. Unfortunately, she did not know about Nietzsche until over a decade after his passing. "Can you, honorable Frau and sister, understand my fury against fate?" Hintz asked.[1]

There was so much to tell Förster-Nietzsche, so much to reflect on, that Hintz did not know where to begin. Her longings and frustrations tumbled onto the page. She mentioned a particular poem—Nietzsche's "The Unknown God"—which he coincidentally wrote the very same year that Hintz broke with the church (1863–64). For that reason, the poem had special resonance for her. "With great effort, I've memorized that poem so I could speak it to myself in sleepless nights," she wrote. "It penetrates me, shakes me deeply, how your brother was penetrated and shaken as he wrote it." She told Förster-Nietzsche that she had found in her brother a fellow free spirit frustrated with Christianity, a religion that preached to the masses but seemed to forget the individual: "I find stupidity, sickness, and death or dying are stupidly-conceived things, which I could really do without. Have you ever thought the same? Eternal life is one thing, but eternal life of the individual [—] why aren't we predestined for that? I think this would be the better arrangement [*Einrichtung*]."[2]

Given Nietzsche's importance to her, Hintz expressed her desire to do something for him, namely, to spread the word about him in America. But in order to do that, she would need more of his works, preferably in the original German. She told Förster-Nietzsche that she would buy them if she had more money, but then went on to complain about how financial independence in America, with its constant grind of working and spending, was hard to achieve. Things might have been different, she mused, if only she had "in my younger years attempted to write, my feather to use, perhaps I'd be better off." She did not take herself seriously enough then, simply assuming that everything important had already been said. But now, after reading Nietzsche, she felt emboldened to write on her own. Then the idea came: "Perhaps I'll write about good and evil in F. N.'s philosophy and morals!"[3]

Hintz followed with a second letter two months later, which continued to document her fascination with Nietzsche. It was written in response to Förster-Nietzsche's letter, in which she sent Hintz a picture of Nietzsche and another one of the Nietzsche Archive in Weimar. Hintz expressed her deep gratitude, telling Förster-Nietzsche that the pictures "will be of continuous joy for me." She also hinted that she had hoped for just a little bit more than that, suggesting that she would like Förster-Nietzsche to send some of Nietzsche's works also, "because [they are] terrible to read the English translation." She asked Förster-Nietzsche to send them with all deliberate speed, because "I've already wasted so much time. . . . Because sometimes you don't know how to help yourself the fastest way," she lamented. In her desire to reach Nietzsche straightaway, Hintz confessed how her own life journey had been crooked and confused. "But what is the most direct path? The signposts for it are missing. . . . I fear I might be burdened by blindness and I cannot see the direct path which follows my clear and strong desire for Friedrich Nietzsche's complete writings."[4]

————

Hintz's letters are remarkable, not for any particular longing or grievance she articulated, but for the ways in which they document the sheer range of sentiments voiced by other letter writers to the Nietzsche Archive. Echoing Elise Fincke's 1881 letter expressing her esteem for Nietzsche's writings and her joy in having his writings "edify . . . at their most intimate" [*auf's Innigste erbauen*], Hintz wrote his sister about how his ideas emboldened her to speak her own truths.[5] Like Gustav Dannreuther's 1882 letter asking to "possess a likeness" of Nietzsche, whose writings he repeatedly translated in order to "become more intimate" with his thoughts, Hintz requested a photograph of the author whose poem she repeated to herself in order to experience his experiences.[6] And like Karl Knortz, who in 1882 sent a letter offering his services to publicize Nietzsche's writings, she too stressed her desire to spread the Nietzsche gospel in the United States.[7]

When Hintz sent her letters to the archive in 1913, she was partaking in a devotional practice that was becoming increasingly customary for his American readers. During the 1890s, only a handful of American Nietzsche enthusiasts sent letters to the philosopher, first to Naumburg, where the invalid Nietzsche stayed in the care of his mother and sister, and then to Weimar, where he spent the last three years of his life in a room atop the archive, which Förster-Nietzsche administered up until her death in 1935.[8] By the time this fan mail arrived, Nietzsche was so deranged that he would not have been aware of them. He did not live to see that they were foretastes of the feast to come.

By the time Förster-Nietzsche received Hintz's letter, she was well versed in the unmet desires, cultural grievances, and secret wishes her brother had awakened in his American readers. Though plenty of professional writers and scholars wrote to the archive, Hintz's letter was just one of many from general readers. Fans young and old, male and female, pious and agnostic, from the Left and from the Right, immigrant and native born, sent letters expressing their admiration for Nietzsche. Like Hintz, they requested a picture or an autograph, or simply testified in haunting and exquisite detail how reading his philosophy transformed their views of themselves and their world. They showed how Nietzsche helped them critique the religion of their youth, the intellectual poverty of their democratic culture, and the materialism of their consumer society. They documented the media through which they had access to Nietzsche (identifying translations, compendia, and articles) as well as the places they could find them (such as the local library or antiquarian bookstore). Likewise, many conveyed their devotion to Nietzsche in expressly religious terms, referring to the way "*He*" saved them from despair and how they found new meaning in "*His*" prophetic utterances. And, like Hintz, many expressed their pious regard for him, not simply because he taught them new truths, but because he helped give them the courage to speak theirs.

The majority of extant letters track what we know from published sources; namely, that the fascination with Nietzsche became a growth industry in American intellectual life in the opening years of the new century. Year by year, discussions of Nietzsche's life and thought had increased steadily, studding philosophical journals, popular magazines, political manifestos, Sunday sermons, and public lectures. As we have seen, the fascination with Nietzsche grew to such an extent that observers could, without hyperbole, claim that he caused one of the most significant "intellectual romances"[9] of the early twentieth century, and that "he who will know the *Zeitgeist* must know Nietzsche."[10]

The letters provide an opportunity, rare for intellectual historians, to enter the moral worlds of general readers and hear their longings, their ideas about ideas, and their concerns about the modern forces undermining American intellectual life.[11] Precisely because this mail echoes many of the uses of Nietzsche in published sources, it encourages us to consider how interest in Nietzsche traversed the borders thought to divide American "highbrow" from "middlebrow" and "lowbrow" readers.[12] In the letters to the Nietzsche Archive, all the brows are represented.

Additionally, the letters provide insights into Nietzsche's emergence as a celebrity in American culture—this despite his being neither a singer, nor a dancer, nor an entertainer (in the traditional sense of the word), but an intellectual. He thought for a living. Analyzing the letter writers' attraction to the figure of Nietzsche thus illuminates two central yet unexplored interrelated dimensions of American culture: the contested image of the intellectual and the linkage between the dissemination of ideas and the images of their creators. Whereas the number of historical studies of the culture of celebrity in modern America has increased notably in recent years, research has focused almost exclusively on musical performers and actors.[13] But just as we consider the culture industry and the star system of entertainers and their publics, the letters demonstrate that another important form of celebrity in the United States has been the prophetic thinker. Indeed, the fan mail suggests that Nietzsche occupied a similar space in the American cultural geography. It suggests that the philosopher—this one in particular—was seen as having a special, much-needed authority in modern American society.[14] Readers documented the intimacy of their private experiences reading Nietzsche, and they documented that his appeal lay in his perceived embodiment of his philosophy rather than any particular set of ideas. He showed how philosophy is a way of life and demonstrated how to achieve it. Thus, their Nietzsche—the personalist, the secular savior, and the cultural critic—taught them about the role of the philosopher and the possibilities of philosophy in modern American life.

We might appropriately refer to these letters as "American Nietzsche ephemera," for many of them offer just a snapshot in time and are no longer than a paragraph or two.[15] In most cases, beyond having their names listed in census records and cropping up in tiny obituaries, there is little to nothing left in the public record evidencing the fullness of these letter writers' lives, or the extent to which they incorporated Nietzsche's ideas into their daily conduct. Nevertheless, in their imperfect, fleeting brevity, the letters offer insights about the dynamics involved in the transnational traffic of ideas. As ephemera, they force us to approach the material with a loupe rather than a panoramic lens. In doing so, they remind us about what is at stake in efforts to deprovincialize national intellectual histories. The letters show not only how ideas travel in the world, but also how ideas helped make Americans' moral worlds anew. Each letter, in its own way, gives us some indication of how Nietzsche's ideas made their journey from the historical, cultural, and linguistic contexts of nineteenth-century Germany to those of twentieth-century American culture. In addition, they show how average Americans participated in transnational intellectual and cultural exchanges.[16]

Nietzsche's American fans felt strongly enough about him and his ideas to pour their hearts out onto paper and then send it halfway around the globe. And they did so because by reading Nietzsche they either felt or longed to be "intimate" with him, to borrow a term both Fincke and Dannreuther used in their letters. Those who wrote, as Dannreuther did, to "possess" a photograph or a signature did so because Nietzsche had possessed them. As records of this intimacy and possession, the letters are also testaments of longing. What we see in these unpublished letters mirrors what we have seen in the young literary radicals' fascination with Nietzsche. The only difference is that the radicals got their ideas in print. Though small and incomplete, the letters to the Nietzsche Archive speak to those larger concerns shared by (would-be) professional intellectuals about religious doubt and their questions about inherited sources of intellectual and moral authority in modern Americans' search for meaning. The fan mail suggests that to behold a large-format picture, sometimes we have to start small.

While the letters from Nietzsche's American fans demonstrate his importance as an intellectual celebrity and the ways in which transnational exchange played out in the intimacy of average Americans' moral imaginations, they also encourage us to reconsider the interpretive power of reception history.[17] A passage in Dannreuther's letter helps invoke an all-too-common view of what "reception" studies do: "That I have at least brains enough to enable me to perceive the true greatness of [genius] is at all events something, and compensates me in a measure for the want of such an education as would otherwise have enabled me to preach the gospel of truth myself. My mind is *only receptive, not productive.*"[18] Emerson did not help to show the possibilities of reception when he likewise argued, "We are too passive in the reception of . . . [the writings of genius]. We must not be sacks and stomachs."[19] Despite Janice Radway's insistence that "reading is not eating," and that the consumption metaphor for readership fails to capture the dynamism of textual interpretation, "reception" indeed suggests a vision of the engagement with ideas as if Nietzsche's readers were all just a bunch of "sacks and stomachs."[20] Dannreuther's modesty here was not false, though the letter writers' uses of Nietzsche do suggest that he was mistaken. Nietzsche's readers weren't consumers, and their uses of his ideas demonstrate that the ideas were not ready-made but, rather, made-to-order. Nietzsche's ideas not only made something possible for them, they made something possible in Nietzsche's text and image. Their Nietzsche was never a being but a becoming; he was a product of collaborative meaning-making between text and reader, text and context. As we shall see, by testing various meanings, protesting his protestations, and putting them to work in their own time and place, Nietzsche's letter-writing fans, like American scholars and radical intellectuals before them, took his words and created worlds.

### Nietzsche Possession, Possessing Nietzsche

Given Nietzsche's increasing presence in American intellectual and cultural life, many commentators echoed the sentiment, as one observer in 1910 put it, that he was "in the air."[21] That is how many of the letter writers experienced Nietzsche—as if he were a transcendent spirit. Though their mail documents that shared experience, the letters also remind us that Nietzsche's thought was no mere vapor. Rather, they demonstrate the material dimension of ideas. Because many experienced their initial contact with Nietzsche's philosophy as a transformative experience, they recorded in their correspondence the form in which they first encountered him: as a photograph in a magazine, a name in a newspaper review, or an author whose text was for sale at their local bookshop. The letters testify to the ways in which the embodied forms of ideas take on a psychic value much greater than their monetary one. Letter writers thus commonly referred to their copies of Nietzsche's books as "prize possessions." They shared with Elisabeth Förster-Nietzsche which of her brother's books they owned, which ones they borrowed from a friend or relative, and which ones they hoped to procure.

Many of Nietzsche's American admirers wrote to Förster-Nietzsche in the hope of gaining possession of some precious relic, some tiny piece of the man who, for them, was the lived example of his heroic Übermensch. One of the most common requests was for Nietzsche's signature. In big, bubble-cursive strokes, twelve-year-old John Boogher Jr. of Strafford, Pennsylvania, wrote in 1926, "My Mother loves your brother's writings and I am going to read them when I grow up, but I read all about Friedrich Nietzche [*sic*], in a book that has just been published named 'The Story of Philosophy' by William Durant . . . and I loved it." We can imagine that Boogher wanted to share Nietzsche's autograph with his mom or impress his classmates with it, but he reasoned his request with a simple, unadorned admission that he "would *just love*" to have it: "If you have one I could have I would be so happy."[22]

Others justified their requests for Nietzsche's signature in terms of fulfilling a public service. Stanley Kimmel, editor of *New Orleans Life Magazine*, wrote Förster-Nietzsche in 1927 to inform her that "there are so many admirers of Friedrich Nietzsche here and I count myself among the first." On a trip to Germany a few years earlier, he had hoped for the "pleasure" of visiting the Nietzsche Archive, but lamented that Förster-Nietzsche had been away when he attempted to do so. Now he was following up with a request for some Nietzscheana, yet this time not for himself but on behalf of his magazine. He requested an article about "the great philosopher," in which she might share with his eager American readers some noteworthy "incident in his life that is little known, or that has not been told before." In addition, he asked for "an original photograph, and perhaps a page of some manuscript or letter, or signature" to accompany the article.[23]

Similarly, W. H. Amerland of St. Louis, Missouri, made his 1922 request

John Boogher Jr.'s letter to Elisabeth Förster-Nietzsche, July 29, 1926. Used by permission of the Klassik Stiftung Weimar, Goethe- und Schiller-Archiv, Weimar, Germany.

for a signature by noting that he had no desire to be the beneficiary of this valuable possession, but instead wanted to be a benefactor for others. Nietzsche's signature placed among those of other great men in his treasured autograph collection, he argued, would help memorialize the philosopher for future generations and spread his gospel. "I have just completed the reading of the wonderful works of your brother, Friedrich Nietsche [*sic*], namely 'The Superman' and 'Zarathustra' and I cannot help but feel that his was one of the great spirits of the world." In addition to the autograph, Amerland asked for "any letter or thought that he might have expressed at any time." He informed Förster-Nietzsche that he had been "collecting autographs for nearly twenty years, of world famous men, for the University here and I feel that the list is far from complete without the name of your great brother on that collection." He noted that her brother's works "are becoming more popular each year," and stressed that this memento of the great master "will add to the interest of many in the future generation, to get a touch, as it were, of that great man."[24]

Other admirers sought to commune with Nietzsche's greatness by possessing their very own picture of him. When in 1882 Gustav Dannreuther expressed a desire to "possess a likeness" of Nietzsche, no photographs or drawings of him could be found in American publications. However, by the 1910s, images of Nietzsche were widely available in popular periodicals and books and scholarly journals. American publishers reproduced images of him so that virtually every stage of his life was documented for American audiences. Given the relative ease with which readers in the United States could have access to visual representation of Nietzsche, his "likeness" was likely familiar to them. When they wrote for a photograph or drawing, therefore, it was not to see what their literary hero looked like but to gain possession of a particular image to memorialize him, often with a specific aim. They did not want just any picture but rather one that could bring them closer to him, one that was *authentic*. S. T. Frame of Harvard College made this yearning very clear when he wrote in 1926 to "obtain authentic pictures of Friedrich Nietzsche. I refer especially to the one drawn of him during his last days which portrays him watching the sinking sun from his bed." It is likely that requests coming from academics like Frame were made with specific publication goals in mind. One picture was not enough. He asked whether there were any other "more notable photographs or sketches of Nietzsche" available.[25]

The requests for Nietzsche paraphernalia shed light on the broader context of the longing and desire the philosopher awakened in his readers.[26] In a letter from 1923, Christoph Hofmann of Mt. Vernon, New York, wrote Förster-Nietzsche for information about where he could find "a good picture of your great Herr brother." He explained the earnestness of his request in a lengthy narrative demonstrating his devotion to Nietzsche. Two years earlier, "as a serious student of the 'Gay Science of Zarathustra,' I drew a small circle of healthy disciples around me, and we hold in my library lectures on a small scale on the philosophy of your unique, eternal Herr Brother." In order to fully realize the experience, he and his fellow disciples "mowed through innumerable fine art galleries" on a quest for the perfect picture of Nietzsche "so that we can decorate our reading room with such a holy relic [*Heiligtum*]," but to no avail. Hofmann sought to reassure her that this request was not being made lightly. He added that on behalf of his friends, he also wanted to express their gratitude for her devotion to their suffering saint:

> Please allow me here, honorable madam, to mention that we venerate your honorable person as true holiness, as the only person who already during the lifetime of our only and true master, his tremendous thoughts grasped and comprehended, and stood faithfully to his side. We are fully aware that

without you, your untiring help, the life of your Herr Brother would have been a much more suffering one.

To get a touch of that great man, they sought as well to get a piece of his great sister: "Were we now to have the great fortune to own a picture of you as well, honorable madam, there wouldn't be anything left for us to wish for. Yet I don't even dare to hope for such fulfilled luck."[27]

## Nietzschean Self-Fashioning

If Nietzsche's American devotees wanted to possess a relic of him, it was because he possessed them. They did not simply ask for valuable goods to adorn their lives; they explained how the philosopher they adored had taught them something priceless about the good life. Virtually all letter writers confessed how their encounter with Nietzsche's philosophy either emboldened or chastened them, liberated them from old falsehoods, or saddled them with new moral responsibilities. Helene Bachmüller of Dayton, Ohio, wrote to let Förster-Nietzsche know that her brother had inspired the belief that human greatness was still possible in the modern world. Though unworthy of his greatness, he nevertheless awakened in her a longing for something deeper in herself. Nietzsche, Bachmüller confessed, had saved her from her "own inner emptiness." The "Ohio country" she called home had become "tame and commonplace," filled with lives "trivial and . . . essentially ugly, for they are engrossed with matters of money and motors, not with work or faith or art." She regarded the Methodist church near her house as "vulgar, pretentious." Though disgusted by the offensive mediocrity around her, she was also chagrined by her own limitations: "It would be, probably, impossible for you to imagine anything more superficial than I am." But reading presumably the recently released translation of Förster-Nietzsche's *The Nietzsche-Wagner Correspondence*[28] had exposed Bachmüller to "depths beyond depths, of one great soul striking fire against another great soul, and I became thrilled. I could feel the harmonies and dissonances, the swell and surge of those two glorious beings, and I felt much more that I cannot express." Reading Nietzsche enlivened her to the possibility "for a companionship that would stimulate, that would deepen, that would give me Tiefen [depth]." Nietzsche strengthened her resolve that "all my life I will hold on to my hunger, if I never manage to have a soul, at any rate I will remain, by hook or crook, aware of it and I will desire one all my life, I will not accept substitutes."[29]

In Bachmüller, we see an example of how a reader used Nietzsche's philosophy to explain herself to herself. Nietzsche had given her justification for, and a language to articulate, her feelings of displacement and disaffection in a world that seemed content with ugly compromises. His philosophy gained traction in readers yearning for individuality as well as belonging. In their desire for self-understanding, they fashioned their own version of Nietzsche as the exemplar of individuality and a new self in that image.

Though George E. Nitzsche of Philadelphia did not express Bachmüller's sense of debased surroundings, his letter similarly shows a self longing for exaltation and connection. It was, quite literally, *Nietzsche* to whom he sought to cleave himself: "My name, as you will see from the above letterhead, is one of the few Nitzsches in America—probably the only one. Unfortunately my grandparents, in a legal document, left out the 'e,' and the error was perpetuated. However, I am proud of the name, and that probably my ancestors came from the same stock as you and your illustrious brother." In an effort to sketch out the possible trunk of their mutual family tree, Nitzsche went on to tell the woman he hoped was a not-so-distant cousin about the Moravian and Bohemian roots of their people, and how his branch of the Ni(e)tzsche family immigrated to Pennsylvania in 1739. Though centuries and an ocean separated them, he hoped "to possess a specimen of [Nietzsche's] handwriting and his autograph, and also a copy of your own biography of your illustrious brother, with an autographed inscription in your handwriting"—just a few mementos of the thinker whom he hoped was in his blood.[30]

When placed with the letters sent by people with surnames like Schreiner, Jessen, Marx, Von Hagen, and Wilm, Nitzsche's imagining himself as a relative of Nietzsche's underscores that a disproportionate number of the letter writers were of German heritage. However, the sheer dominance of German Americans among the letter writers cannot alone tell us whether Nietzsche had some special appeal to them that was distinct from other American readers' experience. They did express concerns related specifically to German speakers (or those with German surnames who thought they should be). They asked for original editions because the English translations were so poor, inquired where they could find good English translations because their German was so poor, or expressed embarrassment that their ability to write their letters in their mother tongue was not what it used to be. They certainly did emphasize Nietzsche's German *Kultur*, *Bildung*, or *Weltanschauung*. But so did American readers who weren't German, and with the same degree of fervor. Bachmüller's and Nitzsche's letters, for example, demonstrate that Nietzsche's philosophy gained traction in readers yearning for belonging, and it is not hard to imagine that one of those feelings of affiliation was the sense of a shared cultural heritage with Nietzsche. But Nietzsche's more dominant appeal lay in how he sanctioned readers' feelings of radical otherness—feelings that traversed ethnic, racial, class, and gender divides. As Werner Sollors reminds us, "In America, casting oneself as an outsider may in fact be considered a dominant cultural trait."[31]

Already in 1896, well before the Nietzsche vogue broke in the United States, Francis Langer of Pittsburgh documented in two long, hand-written letters to Förster-Nietzsche how American readers could simultaneously exalt and identify with her brother. "No work in world literature has bound [*gefesselt*] me more than [*Also Sprach Zarathustra*]," Langer wrote. "Now I read nothing but Nietzsche.... Your brother is the greatest assassin in literature." Langer requested a "larger picture of him to put in a frame," to commemorate the figure of his reverence. But he also asked for a picture of Nietzsche "from his early years," likely because he felt he could relate: "I was born in the same year [as him]."[32] Perhaps because Langer imagined shared life experiences, he demanded to know why no one had stepped in to forestall his doom: "Why didn't you, dear madam, take better care of him?" He persisted, "Are you honestly reporting everything about his current state?" and wanted to know "does he have moments of clarity?" Clearly frustrated with the feeling that he did not have all the facts about Nietzsche's condition, Langer also worried that reports of Nietzsche's suffering state were true. Didn't anyone realize, he wanted to know, that the "genius is like a big child and has to be cared for like a big child[?] [One] who writes those works needs a spiritual diet and needs a personal physician like Bismarck, who would be his therapist and keep him in check." If the reports about Nietzsche were true, and if this heroic thinker was allowed to languish, Langer would have handled things differently: "If I was his brother right after the attack, after the hopelessness [of the situation] was apparent, I would have helped him to die [*zum Herzensstillstand befördert*]."[33]

Feelings of radical otherness went hand-in-hand with a strong affinity for Nietzsche's life and thought, and assumed many forms. John I. Bush of Duluth, Minnesota, believed that he was Nietzsche's philosophy realized. On December 9, 1919, he sent the first of three missives to Förster-Nietzsche announcing his good tidings:

Dear Madam:

I beg to inform you that I am here, who "is evil enough" (see: Thus Spake Zarathustra, Chapter, Old and New Tables, Aphorism seven by: Friedrich Wilhelm Nietzsche, your beloved deceased brother).

May you hereby have the consolation and delight to have lived long enough to know that the visions, prophesies, and hopes of your brother have been fulfilled to the very letter; for the author of this scribbling is the very man prognosticated in the said volume.

Very resp. John I. Bush ("A Strange figure from the North." "A man without disgust;" "And One who is evil enough")[34]

When a week went by without receiving a jubilant response from the Nietzsche Archive, Bush followed up with a telegram (apparently transcribed by a non-English speaker on the receiving end in Germany): "Are your living yet one who is evil enough[,] john bush."[35] So inconceivable it was that Förster-Nietzsche might be ignoring his extraordinary revelation, Bush seemed to think that the only reason for her silence was that she was dead. Why else wouldn't she respond to the American Übermensch? So he sent an aggrieved third attempt at contact on January 26, 1920, in which he could barely contain his exasperation:

Dear Gentlemen:

I, the undersigned, do beg humble to inquire: Does the Elisabeth-Förster Nietzsche, (the sister of the late Fried. W. Nietzsche) live yet? I would greatly appreciate if some one connected with Nietzsche archives will kindly answer the above query. Just one word will suffice, please. Comply with this small request and oblige.

Enclosed, please, find self addressed envelope for reply. As it is inconvenient to remit postage, I neglected that part of my obligation, but hope that you will incur in that trifle expense.

Thanking you in advance, I remain.
Very resp. John I. Bush . . .[36]

Though Bush's felt connection to Nietzsche's Übermensch was less abashed than that experienced by most others, the ways in which he put Nietzsche's philosophy to work for his self-fashioning was a strategy common to all of Nietzsche's readers. They used the philosopher's terms and aspects of his life to describe themselves to themselves. And yet the varieties of the selves fashioned suggest that the distinctions between reception and production, and between readership and authorship, are blurry at best. Despite the readers' sense that "Nietzsche" happened to them, we do better to see how *they* happened to Nietzsche. The "Nietzsches" put to work for readers' self-creation were as varied and complex as the readers who pressed them into service.

Bush's reading himself into Nietzsche's texts may have been a bit extreme, but it was not an anomalous reaction to the works. While readers sought to draw meaning from Nietzsche's concepts, they also drew details into their hazy contours. Some readers, like Bush, apparently thought that interpreting Nietzsche's ideas was a straightforward affair. Others, however, seem to have recognized the tensions and instabilities in Nietzsche exegesis. In an undated letter, Edward Evans of New Brunswick, New Jersey, wrote as if demanding assistance in interpreting the following passage from *Zarathustra*:

> "Why so hard?" the kitchen coal once said to the diamond. "After all, are we not close kin?"
>
> Why so soft? O my brothers, thus I ask you: are you not after all my brothers? . . .
>
> Only the noblest is altogether hard. This new tablet, O my brothers, I place over you: *become hard!*[37]

Nietzsche's exhortation to self-hardening inspired Evans to speculate on the fragility of such an enterprise, while, perhaps, revealing his own:

Let Nietzsche ask himself if he will marry for all eternity ___ the Diamond absolute—will marry for all eternity one who is the charcoal absolute? . . . Let him ask himself, that is—if the Diamond is made in any other way than by charcoal? And if he says "yes"—then the charcoal out of its pure, its absolute, Love—or Hate?—of the Diamond is ready to pass out into the pure blackness of darkness whence it came—No, No, No, not so, not so! Let the charcoal vibrate up [with] dazzle of the Diamond![38]

It is unclear whether Evans was offering his interpretation or pleading for clarification, but what his cryptic letter underscores is how readers used Nietzsche's words to imagine new moral and intellectual worlds for themselves. Though reading for authorial intent is often a risky enterprise, especially in a rambling fragment, Evans's letter is one of the many examples of how readers gravitated to certain passages, identified them as essential, and put them in motion as they sought to come to terms with themselves and their world.

No better do we see how Nietzsche's readers used his words to make sense of their worlds than in the four extant letters sent to the archive by Elmer Schreiner of California, Pennsylvania, from 1920 to 1924. Schreiner's letters demonstrate how many Nietzsche admirers not only tussled with a particular concept or passage from his works but also used Nietzsche's philosophy to make sense of, and to give meaning to, a variety of their life's experiences. For Schreiner, there was nothing "in all the world . . . quite so good and beautifully true, than the philosophy of Friedrich Nietzsche." He alternately quoted him—as "your brother said once . . ."[39]—or invoked him—"How often I thought of your brother . . ."[40]—to interpret his joys and disappointments. As Schreiner contemplated his lost passion for his schoolwork and his feeling that he "no longer could endure doing that which in me was dead," he recalled one of Nietzsche's letters to Richard Wagner in which he wrote, "I am still chained to my dog kennel, the University."[41] The degree to which Schreiner delighted in seeing the world through "His" eyes is reflected in the name he gave his daughter: "Nizza," after Nice, France—not only because she was born there but, even more so, because almost a half century earlier Nietzsche had given birth there to his *Zarathustra*, book three, and "perhaps also because your brother said 'In Nice one could often see me dancing.'"[42]

Sometimes the tiniest detail tells the greatest story, as we see with Schreiner's capitalized *H* in "His." Similarly, Hintz repeatedly capitalized (and underlined) *He* (Er) for her invocations of Nietzsche.[43] The reason so many readers sought to fashion themselves with his language and after his image is that, as Dr. Hellmut Marx of Rochester, Minnesota, expressed it, Nietzsche was "more of a great Spirit, than . . . a human being."[44] The strong religious imagery found in so many of his his admirers' letters demonstrates that felt spiritual dimension of American Nietzsche devotion.

## Nietzsche Pilgrimage

Readers like Schreiner demonstrated their devotion to Nietzsche in a variety of forms, but a common way of doing so was to travel to the Nietzsche Archive to meet his sister, look at his personal library, and see the room where he spent the last years of his life. Some of the letters refer to actual visits to the archive, while others refer to trips in the planning stages and travel plans aborted or delayed. Jossie Farmer, a "lady correspondent" with an American newspaper who was interested in writing an article about Nietzsche, maintained in 1923 that she was "very anxious" to come see the archive firsthand.[45] While there is no record that Farmer actually made the journey, the series of letters from Otto Manthey-Zorn, a professor of German at Amherst College and later the author of *Dionysus: The Tragedy of Nietzsche* (1956), confirms that he did, and struck up a cordial friendship with Förster-Nietzsche in the first of several visits. In an undated Christmas card, he confessed that of all the stops in his recent European tour, "the most beautiful time was in Weimar" with her at the archive.[46]

Expeditions both realized and unrealized provide a fuller view of the modes of the American Nietzsche exchange. They remind us that when ideas move readers, they do so both in mind and in body. Nietzsche's American readers went to a bookstore. They went to a library. They visited a Nietzsche shrine in their friend's reading room. And they made the transatlantic voyage to Germany. The discussions of travels to the archive suggest, then, that a one-way view of transnational reception tells only part of the story of the Atlantic crossings of Nietzsche. Not only did Nietzsche's texts travel to the United States *with* ideas, but Americans likewise traveled to Germany *for* them.

Perhaps more significant than the readers' desire to visit the archive in Weimar was the language with which they expressed it. Nietzsche admirers who longed to see the archive for themselves often cast this desire in the language of religious devotion. Edwards Bobo Murray, an American at the university in Heidelberg, wrote in 1910 to inform Förster-Nietzsche that he hoped to "make a special 'pilgrimage' to the Nietzsche Archive before returning to America."[47] Gottfried Betz, a professor of German at Columbia University who had corresponded with Förster-Nietzsche a number of times and visited her at the archive, told her, "Your home has become my holy place of pilgrimage!"[48]

The two letters in 1910 from Lydia Lois Tilley of Norfolk, Virginia, demonstrate the eagerness with which Nietzsche's American devotees sought to draw nearer to him. In her first letter, Tilley introduced herself to Förster-Nietzsche as a "very humble admirer of the glorious work of your great brother," one who will be "sailing shortly for the Fatherland with the hope of meeting you and of visiting the Nietzsche Archives as one of the chief incentives to my journey."[49] When she did not hear back from Förster-Nietzsche, she sent an anxious follow-up letter from Eisenach, Germany, a month later:

> Having received no reply to my letter from America to you I feel confident either it or your answer has gone astray.... I am more anxious to visit your home than any other place in Germany and it is the goal of my trip.... I trust that I am not greatly presumptuous and that if I am you will forgive me in your great love for your brother, and your exquisite appreciation of his work. I place his achievement in a class with Goethe's and wish to come as to a shrine. If I may do so ... it will be a pleasure and privilege I can never forget. I realize the great favor I am requesting and I do not do so lightly.[50]

The degree to which Nietzsche's fans longed to come into contact with him is demonstrated in Elmer Schreiner's 1920 trip to not only the archive but also Röcken, to see Nietzsche's birthplace: "the room ... in which your dear brother was born, also your father's study, and the old kitchen."[51] The trip proved so transformative, he informed Förster-Nietzsche, that it inspired his next book project: "'A Nietzsche Pilgrimage.' It's a little book with around eight or nine thousand words, just a tribute to Nietzsche for Nietzscheans."[52]

## Pathos of Distance from Democratic Culture

The transatlantic travels of Nietzsche texts and American Nietzsche devotees documented in letters demonstrate that the traffic of ideas flows in both directions. They show how both Nietzsche's ideas and ideas about Nietzsche traversed national borders thought to distinguish "American" from "German" and "European" intellectual life, consequently encouraging us to rethink the integrity of our national narratives regarding thought and culture. The letters alone suggest that because a German thinker proved inspirational to so many readers in the United States, efforts among American historians to deprovincialize the study of US intellectual history are much needed. The letters—though short, fragmentary, and ephemeral—testify to some larger idea transfers shaping twentieth-century American intellectual life. The flow of Nietzsche texts from Germany to America, the letters from America to Germany asking for a Nietzsche autograph, the honored requests sent in return, and Americans' trips to Weimar certainly help us to consider the ways in which moral outlooks and social concerns in the United States have been forged through cross-cultural exchange, transmission, modification, and transformation. In doing so, we see the value of breaking down static concepts such as "foreign thought," "organic ideas," "German theories," and "American worldviews."

But before we too zealously embrace the artificiality of constructs like "American" and "German" or "foreign" and "organic," or too quickly give in to our enthusiasm for cultural hybridization, creolization, and betwixt and between-ness, we should not forget the power such perceived differences had in shaping the lived experiences of the people we study. As these letters show, many readers' ideas about what is "us" and what is "them" were hardened, not softened, in the friction of this movement. The letters, in their own small way, tell a bigger story about how the transnational traffic of Nietzsche's image and ideas helped puncture and rebuild, traverse and reconstitute intellectual borders between the United States and Germany.

One of the most common concerns raised by the letter writers that reveals the flow and rupture involved in transnationalism is the issue of English translations of Nietzsche's works.[53] Their steady commentary on bad or unavailable translations reminds us of the centrality of language to the story. American readers asked Förster-Nietzsche about available English-language editions or complained about them, while others offered their services to translate Nietzsche for an American audience. Some of the letters, on their own, seem perfectly innocuous, such as the letter from Preston Barba of Muhlenberg College in Allentown, Pennsylvania, who wrote about his anthology of German poetry, which "included a selection from Nietzsche's poetry, including a short sketch of his life, in the hopes that it brings American students closer to Nietzsche as lyrical poet."[54] Although bitter contestations about *what* Nietzsche wrote occurred throughout the century, none of the letter writers would have taken issue with the fan who averred that Nietzsche's works contain "the most glorious German that we have, perhaps the most illuminating language that ever was written or spoken."[55]

Understandably, then, because commentators deemed Nietzsche's writing so inventive, they complained about the available translations, which failed to capture his artistry. The philosopher James Taft Hatfield of Northwestern University informed Förster-Nietzsche in 1913 that the university library owned "only the English translations of Nietzsche, wherein so much of his wonderful style is missing."[56] Because so much of the original German had been lost in translation, those able to read that language, like Christoph Hofmann, signaled how important it was for native English speakers to set the original against the translation. Hofmann stated that his "indignation" at both German and English editions being hard to find "knows no boundaries. I personally consider myself lucky to own the complete works in both languages, but many of my friends would like to do the same."[57]

In many of the letters from American authors, scholars, and translators interested in assisting with the Nietzsche Archive's ongoing efforts to make Nietzsche's texts available to English-speaking audiences, we see Förster-Nietzsche's business acumen at work as well as the complicated legal and financial issues involved in the international publication and distribution of texts. Together with many of her own letters, those sent to the archive reveal her constant striving to find American Nietzsche acolytes willing to contact American publishing houses about undertaking translations of her brother's works, or of her own books about her brother. She cajoled and she threatened, playing one eager translator against another. There was always one more edition of her brother's biography, another collection of her brother's letters, or an expanded version of her own memoirs that she wanted to see published in English. But in all this epistolary traffic, aside from the focus on the business end of translations, is a shared concern about getting Nietzsche's prose into English worthy of the original.

It is this concern about the troubles of translation that serves as the leitmotif of a series of over twenty extant letters to Förster-Nietzsche from Herman George Scheffauer. An American writer and critic then living in Berlin, Scheffauer wrote a few short articles on Nietzsche for American literary reviews and translated a few of Nietzsche's poems. In virtually every letter, he discussed the inadequacies of the available translations and warned about how difficult it would be to find the right talent for a Nietzsche translation: "In many [translations] the style or spirit of your great brother isn't matched." German-born translators, he cautioned, even those with the most exquisite mastery of English, cannot quite capture it. He warned, "A poet can and must be translated only by other poets. Translation in general is often an abominable thing. There are so few good translators that can achieve what an artist can!"[58] Scheffauer questioned both the translatability of German into English as well as the subtlety of American English altogether. Referring to the prospect of having someone translate Förster-Nietzsche's biography of her brother, *Becoming Nietzsche* (*Der werdende Nietzsche*), he lamented that "there are even so few native-born Americans who have the mastery to translate into classical English."[59] But the alternative, he warned, was even more unacceptable: "If the translator is . . . a foreigner, whose mother tongue is not English, the result is often totally atrocious, despite the best intentions and dedication to the task. . . . It would naturally be an unending pity, were the deep, poetic language of your brother's not to be rendered in a fully worthy English."[60]

Why all the turmoil surrounding translation? Why did the letter writers complain about English renderings that missed the mark? Was there really no native German or English speaker who could bridge the distance between American audiences and Nietzsche, between America and Germany, between "us" and "them"? These questions were not limited to the letters. Indeed, the questions about how best to translate Nietzsche into English echo long-standing debates carried on elsewhere in American reviews, essays, and books throughout the century. From the first English translations of Nietzsche in 1896 through Walter Kaufmann's midcentury translations (discussed in chapter 5), American commentators bickered and protested over translation issues large and small. What is an adequate English equivalent for *Übermensch*— "beyond man," "superman," or "overman"? What is a better rendering of *Umwertung aller Werte*—"transmutation" or "transvaluation of all values"? Is *Zur Genealogie der Moral* "On the Genealogy of Morals," "On the Genealogy of Morality," "Towards the Genealogy of Morals," or none of the above? Observers worried about everything ranging from whether translations of Nietzsche's poems needed to rhyme to the proper placement of a comma. Every new rendering unleashed a minor furor. But when concerns flared up in the letters and beyond, they were never simply about piety to standard English or *Hochdeutsch* as such. They were not simply about language, they were about fit: Can Nietzsche's poetic German ever be adequately captured in English? Are language and culture so thoroughly embedded in each other that even if we could get the words right, we would still lose their meaning? Wafting like an unpleasant vapor throughout these quarrels is a nagging concern: can the American mind grasp what this German had to say? Echoing concerns expressed by the first wave of American commentators on Nietzsche translation, contestations over language always tipped on the question of the potential incommensurability between the German and English languages, between German *Kultur* and American culture.

Additional letters from the archive do not address translations but nevertheless help provide some insight about which concerns may have fed this fire. Each shows how readers turned to Nietzsche not to break down the perceived borders between German and American intellectual life but to ensure their integrity. Though we might be tempted to view the vibrancy of Nietzsche's posthumous American career as a sign of long-standing, salutary transnational intellectual exchanges and mutuality, many of Nietzsche's American readers saw just the opposite. They turned to Nietzsche, not because they thought he could make something possible for the pedestrian American intellect, but precisely because, in their view, he couldn't. A letter from Scheffauer explained how he drew from Nietzsche as he contemplated writing a book called *The Spirit of America Today*. That spirit, he argued, betrayed "the old, noble, when also narrow Puritanism I admire so much, even if it was philistine and hostile to art. But it brought forth beautiful and exalted types. Alas, the types of today! Absolute degeneration and wildness—a wild hedonism, mechanization, herd morality. If only your eternal brother were here to give his verdict over today's America."[61] Similarly, Gottfried Betz of Columbia University used his letters to Förster-Nietzsche to reflect on the differences between German and American intellectual and cultural life: "Our wealth is inconceivable. We can buy the whole world, but no intellectual treasures. Their value is at the lowest level in America. What can you do with character [*Gemüt*], beauty, and a finely-educated mind? . . . Business and the stupidest, mindless recreations fill the life of the American. . . . Whoever confesses other ideals is an exception."[62]

That Nietzsche's philosophy could shrink the distance between German and American culture was the last thing on many of his American readers' minds. Though they were reading Nietzsche in the United States, they never thought his philosophy would find refuge here, nor did they desire it. They simply wanted more of Nietzsche, more of the German pathos of distance, more of his philosophy with which to shield themselves from the crude, anti-intellectual mob mentality of American life. Just as we see variations of hero worship among professional intellectuals, so too do we see fears of American anti-intellectualism deeply burrowed into the imagination of general readers, who wrote to the archive. The letters thus document that moral inquiry and reverence for ideas, even if as a stick to beat corporate capitalism or mass culture with, knew no distinction from one "brow" to the next.

This desire for the Nietzschean pathos of distance is especially apparent in the 1915 letter from Theodore Van Derlyn, a self-professed "Nietzschean devotee," who informed Förster-Nietzsche that he was writing a Nietzschean-inspired critique of the mediocrity of man in the masses. With Nietzsche as his model, Van Derlyn was composing "*Aristocracy, A Book for the Highest Type of Americans.*" He explained about the toll modern American democracy was taking on the nation's elevated souls. "It is obviously plain to you how democratic [America] is. With every new immigrant it becomes even more democratic, so democratic in fact, that for a thinking person it stirs up his bile when he imagines that it might go on like this. The old aristocracy is extinct, lying fully eroded in the grave of United States history." To make matters worse, now the "recognized standard of the American society is the [plutocratic] 'ultra fashionable set' . . . [who] use no sense, have no soul, no reason, no character, nothing, except a peacock-like egocentricity, and above all, money, lots of money." But, thanks to her brother, all was not lost. Like Nietzsche, Van Derlyn had "been altogether neglected from everyone, because only a few understand me. The world praises or damns, understanding it does very seldom." He confessed to Förster-Nietzsche that because his "soul was deeply moved by the spirit of Nietzsche," he "felt a calling" to resist the poverty of modern American cultural life.[63]

Much like Hintz's letters of 1913, which demonstrate the various ways in which American fans enlisted Nietzsche's image and ideas to contemplate themselves and critique their country, T. D. Kriton's of September 1933 brings together quite vividly the major leitmotifs of American Nietzsche devotion. The two-page typed letter from the San Francisco–based Kriton—a pseudonym for Timokheon Dimilriou Kourkoulakis, which demonstrates how a Nietzschean could also use Plato's "Crito" ("Kriton" in German) for self-fashioning—exalts a prophetic Nietzsche as the timeless savior of modern humanity and a timely critic of a world out of kilter. He began by telling Förster-Nietzsche,

"The life of your brother, was, the life of a Christ's, pure and great. No man suffered what he did on account of his convictions, not even Jesus Christ." He informed Förster-Nietzsche that he, a Greek American who had immigrated to the United States as a child, believed that Nietzsche, and the German people from which he came, were, like him, the true descendants of the Hellenic spirit. He flashed back to 1914, when "THUS SPAKE ZARATHUSTRA came to me like a thunderbolt of Zeus from Olympos." When the United States entered the "unjust war on Germany" in 1917, Kriton opted for "incarceration" rather than bearing arms against these "True Greeks." He was "disgusted" with American literature, which produced only junk writers—none worthy of her brother—with one possible exception: H. L. Mencken.[64] He then moved from his critique of botched American culture to contrast it with his esteemed Germany and Italy. "I only hope that America [might someday] produce ... writers like this type of Mencken, then America will be in a place to show her savior, as Italy and Germany." That these lines were written in 1933 can only suggest that Hitler's rise to power confirmed Kriton's view of American culture. He concluded by thanking Förster-Nietzsche's brother for having graced world history with his timeless and timely "Philosophy and Life."[65]

Packed as it is with the major themes running through virtually all the American fan mail sent to the Nietzsche Archive, Kriton's letter reveals how general readers—young and old, male and female, from Pittsburgh to San Francisco—made and remade Nietzsche in their own image. Scholars, writers, and general readers like Kriton all lent a hand in putting their Nietzsche—whether the personalist companion, secular saint, or cultural critic—to work on themselves and their America. They were not empty "sacks and stomachs" but active participants who collaborated with Nietzsche to make meaning of and for themselves and of their world. For Kriton in particular, Nietzsche-as-Hellenic-Christ helped him fill in the contours of his own Greek-American identity, helped him articulate why he felt so distant from American culture, and helped him hammer out his political ideas. His use of Nietzsche shows how the philosopher's ideas moved through time and space and were reconstituted every time a new reader got ahold of one of his books. Kriton, as did the other letter writers, considered Nietzsche's books among his prized possessions. By writing to procure additional works, an "original" photograph, or a swatch of his handwriting, his admirers sought a tangible record of the author whose ideas demonstrated practical power in their lives.

The only reason they wanted to possess some Nietzscheana, however, was because he possessed them.

And although Kriton's letter shows how such ephemera are records of modern American longing, they also document the transnational circumnavigation of ideas. Though Nietzsche's philosophy made the transatlantic journey to the United States, though it traversed the perceived borders between German and American thought and culture, though it pierced Kriton at his most intimate, it also enabled this American citizen to reconstitute national, political, and cultural distinctions, which he regarded as essential. And finally, we see how images of Nietzsche the thinker—for Kriton it was Nietzsche as *Hellenic* (not Hebraic) martyr, for others it was Nietzsche the genius, the secular savior, and the suffering saint—influenced the ways in which his readers naturalized his ideas into their moral worlds.

There are risks involved in making Kriton's two-page epistle carry more interpretive weight than it can bear. Can a typo-ridden, eccentric letter really tell us anything of broader significance for understanding Nietzsche's importance in the making of modern American thought? My belief is that it does, precisely because it speaks to the ways in which a variety of Americans both took part in and resisted the implications of transnational intellectual exchanges. In addition, it shows how Nietzsche worked by making the designation "average" no longer meaningful to his readers as a term of self-description. Even for those who came to Nietzsche with a sense of being human, all too human, he showed them a pathos of distance from everyday values—whether of the church, the marketplace, or the civics lesson—that helped them sharpen their sense of distinction in themselves, enabling them to feel their own particularity. And the letter shows how Nietzsche's readers yearned for a philosophy that harmonized thinking and doing. They turned to Nietzsche as a philosopher-prophet who worked not by issuing instructions for conduct but by serving as a guide to becoming. If they were unable to anchor their beliefs in timeless universals, they could at least cleave to a thinker who had learned to live without them.

# Dionysian Enlightenment

*One thing is needful.*—To "give style" to one's character—a great and rare art! It is practiced by those who survey all the strengths and weaknesses of their nature and then fit them into an artistic plan until every one of them appears as art and reason and even weaknesses delight the eye. Here a large mass of second nature has been added; there a piece of original nature has been removed—both times through long practice and daily work at it. . . . It will be the strong and domineering natures that enjoy their finest gaiety in such constraint and perfection under a law of their own.

FRIEDRICH NIETZSCHE, *The Gay Science* (1882)

From the earliest years of the Nietzsche vogue up until our own time, Nietzsche has never fallen out of fashion. But there were periods in American life when he fell out of favor. The years leading up to World War II through the immediate postwar period represent a notable case in point. Though interpreters wrangled over the competing views of Nietzsche's "immoralism," the apparent ease with which Germany had employed his philosophy in support of its blood-and-iron imperialism during World War I continued to put all sympathetic appraisals of him on the defensive. Beginning in the late 1920s, US observers of Italian politics noted that even after the mass devastation of war on the European continent, the romance with Nietzsche had not waned; Benito Mussolini now claimed the mantle of Nietzscheism.[1] But it was not until Hitler's rise to power in the early 1930s that American public sentiment about Nietzsche began to cool considerably. Though the connections between Italian fascism and German Nazism were not clear, their mutual exaltation of Nietzsche helped Americans identify their common roots and complementary worldviews. Mussolini left no doubt about the importance of Nietzsche to both powers: "I am sure that he is the most impressive and influential author of modern Europe."[2] The story was too familiar: Nietzsche bequeathed a philosophy of raw power in the absence of moral absolutes and

"Mussolini's Three Political Saints; Machiavelli, Mazzini, and Nietzsche Influence the Thought of Italy's 'Man of Destiny.'" *New York Times*, February 15, 1925.

a brutal agenda for remaking modern Europe. If he was the philosophical spirit of German imperialism during World War I, now he had become the philosophical mastermind of totalitarianism.

Given the popular press's image of *Zarathustra* as the Ur-text of European totalitarianism, and the academy's general disregard for him, it was hard to imagine that Nietzsche's philosophy had much of a future in American intellectual life. Commentators in the United States sympathetic to Nietzsche worked hard to redeem his damaged reputation after World War I. After his being linked to a *second* world war, however, few were willing to try it again. But one Harvard graduate student in philosophy stepped forward: Walter Kaufmann. Much as we may prefer to believe that ideas spread because of their essential worth or their inherent aptness at a particular historical moment, the case of Nietzsche in postwar America shows how one relatively obscure scholar can usher in a momentous shift in intellectual styles and concerns.

A German émigré who taught at Princeton University as a philosophy professor from 1947 until his death in 1980, Kaufmann catapulted to prominence after the 1950 publication of his *Nietzsche: Philosopher, Psychologist, Antichrist*. From 1950 to 1974, the book went through four editions, and from its first printing onward established its hegemony in Nietzsche studies. Many regard it as the single most important—certainly the most popular—study of the German philosopher ever written in any language. Throughout his career, Kaufmann presided over the English-language Nietzsche industry, advocating for or recommending against the publication of new Nietzsche studies, and reviewing new scholarship in the field. Not the least of Kaufmann's accomplishments was his translation of all but three of Nietzsche's published works, including *Thus Spoke Zarathustra, Twilight of the Idols*, and *The Antichrist* in *The Portable Nietzsche* in 1954; *Beyond Good and Evil* and *The Birth of Tragedy* in 1966; *On the Genealogy of Morals* (with R. J. Hollingdale) in 1967; and *The Gay Science* in 1974. For the last half century, English-speaking readers of Nietzsche have been, first and foremost, readers of Kaufmann's Nietzsche. However, it was also his *Nietzsche* that paved the way for the renewed interest in translations of the German philosopher's works and provided readers with an interpretive context for them. In the words of one prominent Nietzsche scholar, Tracy Strong, the "power of Kaufmann's [book on and translations of Nietzsche] effectively gave him . . . control over Nietzsche studies in America. . . . His was the only opinion that would always be sought." At least up until his death in 1980, "Kaufmann's Nietzsche was *the* Nietzsche for American and British studies."[3]

The longevity of Kaufmann's hegemony in English-language Nietzsche studies is remarkable enough. Even more astonishing is that he managed to revitalize Nietzsche's American career when he did, for the conservative postwar era can only be described as a most inauspicious intellectual climate for the renaissance of such a radical thinker.[4] Indeed, during and immediately after World War II, Friedrich Nietzsche was persona non grata in American intellectual life. While commentators in the wartime popular press charged Nietzsche with crimes against humanity, professors at the university offered him no refuge. With the increasing dominance of the Anglo-American analytic tradition in philosophy departments, scholarly philosophers had little incentive to study a thinker long considered recklessly impressionistic, unsystematic, and hostile to truth. Kaufmann thus had to reckon with an American Nietzsche who enjoyed a reputation alternately as a prophet, poet, or pariah, but not a serious philosopher.[5] Given Nietzsche's infamy beyond the academy and his perceived irrelevance within it, it is no wonder that when Kaufmann was writing his Nietzsche manuscript at Princeton, one of his colleagues wondered why he would bother: "I thought Nietzsche was dead as a doornail."[6] Nietzsche was not dead, but he was widely considered an abomination to American readers at midcentury, and it was Kaufmann's study that helped bring a redeemed Nietzsche back to life.

———

How did Kaufmann do it? How did he transform a "dead as a doornail" nineteenth-century German thinker into an indispensable philosopher for postwar American life? A close look at his monumental *Nietzsche* reveals his strategies for rescuing the German philosopher from his damaged reputation after the war and for establishing him, for the first time, as a thinker worthy of serious study in the United States. Whereas isolated academics had worked with Nietzsche's ideas in the past, it is only after Kaufmann that broad interest in him as a thinker emerged in the American academy. Contrary to the dominant views of Nietzsche, which deemed him an aberration from the Western tradition, Kaufmann sought to establish Nietzsche as both a critic of, and an important interlocutor with, the major philosophers within it. Likewise, he presented a towering thinker uniquely poised to address many of the pressing intellectual concerns of the cold war era: anxieties about the psychic costs and social dangers of mass society, hostility to collectivist ideologies, and longing for new sources of redemption after the horrors of the recent past. So while Kaufmann presented Nietzsche as a thinker who raised universal questions about the meaning of the good life, he also put Nietzsche's texts to work to answer them.

Kaufmann also employed Nietzsche to address what he regarded as the impoverished status of philosophy in midcentury American life. In his estimation, the "parting of the ways" in transatlantic philosophy that split continental European and English-speaking philosophers into two antagonistic groups hampered the proper reception of Nietzsche in American universities and damaged moral inquiry in general.[7] Rather than ascribe Nietzsche to either the Continental or the Anglo-analytic tradition, Kaufmann sought to extend the reach of Nietzsche's significance by demonstrating how his philosophy resonated with both. Moreover, if Nietzsche could negotiate the intellectual tensions within professional philosophy, so too could he extend the reach of scholarship to a broader public. As Bruce Kuklick has noted, after World War II, "philosophy in the United States was at a low ebb," when the impulse toward increased specialization created "an inward-looking organization that had its own set of professional questions and that seldom reached out to the wider culture."[8] Kaufmann thus offered Nietzsche as a rare philosopher able to bridge the increasingly distinct moral worlds of midcentury specialists and general readers. Ironically, while consciously using Nietzsche as a weapon within professional philosophical debates about the accessibility of scholarship, Kaufmann created a Nietzsche who transcended scholarly discourse altogether.

For Kaufmann, the only honest account of Nietzsche's philosophy, much like Nietzsche's own vision of his *Thus Spoke Zarathustra*, must be "a book for all and none" (Ein Buch für Alle und Keinen), a book that expanded the availability of his ideas without making them cheap and easy.[9] But the challenges of writing a book that made Nietzsche's philosophy broadly accessible without sacrificing its subtlety and complexity was certainly not lost on him. Kaufmann handily accomplished his first aim by employing certain structural and rhetorical strategies in his book. Interpretive struggles, for example, do not loom large in the text despite his extensive engagement with (primarily German-language) Nietzsche scholarship.[10] When Kaufmann took issue with previous interpretations, he largely consigned his disputes to the footnotes, leaving the body of his text free to engage Nietzsche directly. In addition, he consistently employed language describing Nietzsche exegesis as perfectly straightforward and uncomplicated, if only readers would actually *read* Nietzsche's works (preferably in their entirety and in the original German). Kaufmann loaded his pages with affirmations that Nietzsche's positions were "unquestionably," "singularly unequivocal," and "abundantly plain," and that apparently dissonant arguments in his writings were "entirely at one" with one another when put in their proper context.[11] The problem with Kaufmann's own presentation of a Nietzsche who did not contradict himself, whose language was literary but "perfectly clear" in meaning—a fully reasonable and harmonious Nietzsche accessible to the enlightened everyman—was that Kaufmann, like his Nietzsche, believed that the capacity for intellectual enlightenment was not universal: "Some people are more favored by nature than others."[12]

Examining Kaufmann's *Nietzsche* in the context in which it initially appeared and in the discourses for which it was appropriated over the course of its four editions is crucial for understanding both how and why a redeemed image of Nietzsche captured the imagination of American readers in the 1950s, '60s, and early '70s.[13] By providing a historicized analysis of his interpretive strategies, this chapter will demonstrate the inadequacy of the current estimation of Kaufmann's work. Though there is general agreement that he performed a minor miracle in making Nietzsche palatable to leery American audiences in the conservative atmosphere of the postwar United States, his critics argued that he did so by taking great interpretive liberties to clean up Nietzsche's act.[14] Scholars generally agree that in order to distance Nietzsche from Nazism, Kaufmann transformed Nietzsche into a charming and inoffensive *salonfähig* existentialist, erasing the darker elements of his philosophy of power and neutralizing his attacks on liberal ideals. Thus, instead of providing a serious reckoning with one of the world's greatest philosophers of power, Kaufmann presented a "King-Kong-in-chains . . . under heavy sedation."[15]

The significance of Kaufmann's *Nietzsche* for historians lies not in its adequacy as an exegesis of Nietzsche's thought but in the ways in which it both reflected and shaped so many of the dominant intellectual and cultural concerns of the period. A historicized reading of this text demonstrates that the common charge that his interpretation is little more than a veiled attempt to rescue Nietzsche from the Nazis misses the mark. While Kaufmann undoubtedly sought to distance Nietzsche from the compromised political uses of his philosophy, he did so as part of a larger philosophical project to reappraise the question of intellectual influence altogether. Furthermore, Kaufmann did not turn Nietzsche into an existentialist, as his critics often assert, but used Nietzsche's philosophy to awaken American readers to European existentialism, with which they were largely unfamiliar.[16] And while he highlighted Nietzsche's existential (or "experimental") qualities, so too did he underscore the Enlightenment, empirical, and pragmatic dimensions of his philosophy. Kaufmann's innovation, then, was to draw out Nietzsche's unexpected harmony with the full range of competing philosophical, sociological, and cultural discourses of the period, and in so doing transform him into the monumentally creative inventor of a "Dionysian [E]nlightenment."[17]

## Walter Kaufmann, German Émigrés, and Nietzsche as Hitler's Exile

The bare outlines of Kaufmann's early intellectual biography are instructive, for they help in part to account for his remarkable fluency in both German and English, and his unique ability to render Nietzsche in terms meaningful to a broad American audience.[18] However, placing Kaufmann's biography in the larger context of the mass migration of German-speaking exiles fleeing Nazism makes clear the fuller dimension of his work. The sometimes subtle, sometimes distinct harmonies and differences in their life stories and their perspectives on Nietzsche yield insights into why Kaufmann's particular interpretation would be acclaimed most fully into midcentury American thought and culture.

Walter Arnold Kaufmann was born in 1921 in Freiburg, Germany, to a Protestant father and a Jewish mother. As he later recounted his religious trajectory, he was a practicing Protestant until age eleven, when he decided that he no longer believed in the Trinity and therefore wanted to convert to Judaism, assuming it to be "the religion for people who believed in God, but not in Christ or the Holy Ghost."[19] Because under German law a child could not convert until the age of twelve, Kaufmann had to wait until his next birthday to become a Jew. In those intervening months, Hitler rose to power, which added to his parents' concern about their son's intentions. It was during this time that Kaufmann first learned that his father had converted from Judaism to Lutheranism in his twenties.[20] Kaufmann later prepared for his bar mitzvah under the instruction of Rabbi Leo Baeck (whose German-language works Kaufmann would later translate into English for American audiences) and studied with him while a student at the Hochschule für die Wissenschaft des Judentums in Berlin. He completed a semester in rabbinical studies at the Lehranstalt[21] before immigrating to the United States in 1939 at age eighteen with the intention of becoming a rabbi.[22]

Kaufmann enrolled at Williams College, and after only two years graduated with honors in philosophy and religion. Though intensely interested in his religious studies, as the war broke out he had what he later described as a "mystical experience": "In the most intense despair I suddenly saw that I had deceived myself for years: I had believed. At last the God of tradition joined the Holy Ghost and Christ."[23] Having abandoned his religious quest but not his fervent pursuit of truth, Kaufmann began his graduate work in philosophy at Harvard in 1941. He trained there until 1944, when he interrupted his studies to serve in the US Air Force and Military Intelligence in Austria and Germany. While in Berlin he came across the complete works of Nietzsche. He decided, despite—or perhaps because of—Nietzsche's reputation on both sides of the Atlantic as a proto-Nazi, a romantic racialist, and an extravagant literary figure (anything but a serious philosopher), that he would write his doctoral dissertation on Nietzsche's contributions to Western philosophy. This decision likely raised the eyebrows of his professors back at Harvard, because, as Kaufmann later recalled, their department was dominated by Anglo-analytic philosophy and openly hostile to the speculative nature of German philosophy. After returning to Harvard, Kaufmann wrote his dissertation, "Nietzsche's Theory of Values," in one year (1947) under C. I. Lewis and then left for Princeton, where he revised it for publication and commenced his role as a leading authority in Anglo-European Nietzsche studies and as a translator and interpreter of Continental philosophy for American audiences.

The hazy outlines of Kaufmann's early biography and the role it played in his particular vision of Nietzsche come into greater focus when we consider him as part of the mass exodus of German-speaking intellectuals, scientists, and artists who fled Nazism from 1933 through the early 1940s. One of the National Socialists' immediate aims after Hitler became chancellor in January 1933 was to root out all intellectual and literary figures whose scholarship and artistic accomplishments they deemed insufficiently "Aryan," including socialists, "cultural Bolsheviks," and, above all, Jews. In April 1933, the Nazis passed the Civil Service Law (Gesetz zur Wiederherstellung des Berufsbeamtentums), leading to the expulsion of more than a thousand scholars from academic positions. A month later, the Nazi-dominated German Student League organized a nationwide campaign "Against the Un-German Spirit"—massive book burnings of writers including Marx, Freud, Hesse, and Kafka. Speaking at a Berlin rally as master of ceremonies, Minister of Propaganda Joseph Goebbels welcomed the end of "the age of extreme Jewish intellectualism."[24] Over the following years, an estimated half million intellectuals were purged by the Nazis; more than a third of them took refuge in the United States, and roughly two-thirds of them were Jewish.

Alone, the roll of names of refugees who took part in this unprecedented intellectual and cultural transfer is astonishing. Included among the thousands of émigrés were social theorists and political philosophers Herbert Marcuse, Max Horkheimer, Leo Strauss, Hannah Arendt, Franz Neumann, and Hans Morgenthau; psychoanalysts Erich Fromm, Erik Erikson, and Wilhelm Reich; philosophers Karl Löwith and Ernst Cassirer; and the theologian Paul Tillich. Though most of them arrived at the height of the Depression—a period marked by political isolationism, anti-Semitism, and anti-immigrant nativism—their erudition, training, and, in many cases, international reputation spared them some of the resentment that typically greeted exiles. Nevertheless, all—even the ones who in time managed to build (or rebuild) a vibrant intellectual life in America—testified to difficulties in acclimatizing to a new culture, language, and institutions, and in healing from the ever-present feelings of rupture and loss involved in forced exile. As Hannah Arendt put it in an uncharacteristically personal account, "We Refugees," in the *Menorah Journal* in 1943, "We lost our home, which means the familiarity of daily life. We lost our occupation, which means the confidence that we are of some use in this world. We lost our language, which means the naturalness of reaction, the simplicity of gestures, the unaffected expression of feelings," and instead became "outlaws" in a "topsy-turvy world."[25]

Despite Kaufmann's shared background and circumstance with the other prominent émigrés, his participation in this well-documented episode in American intellectual life has been overlooked. Because he came as a nineteen-year old student while the intellectuals typically considered part of this transfer were adults and in many cases had well-established careers, it is easy to see why his story does not fold easily into collective biographies of German intellectual exiles in the United States. But like the others, Kaufmann was an intellectual exile who, as an aspiring rabbi, had no choice but to flee. In addition, like many of the other émigrés, he eventually established himself as a prominent scholar and a major force in American intellectual life. Also like the others, Nietzsche was a central figure in his intellectual coming of age and in the ongoing development of his thought. He shared their interest in Nietzsche's effort to unmoor moral foundations, their firsthand experience of the Nazism that worshipped Nietzsche, and their broad agreement that Nietzsche was no proto-Nazi. If Germany gave Americans reason to worry that Nietzsche's philosophy prepared the way for mass slaughter, it also provided them with a cohort of extraordinary thinkers, themselves victims of the very regime for which Nietzsche was blamed, who attempted to persuade them otherwise. The émigrés shared a very different Nietzsche from the one celebrated as the official philosopher of the Nazis; indeed, their Nietzsche was Hitler's forced exile.

The harmonies between Kaufmann's and the older émigrés' fascination with Nietzsche are striking. First, like Kaufmann, despite their diverse training and temperaments, these exiles expressed a deep intellectual debt to him. Leo Strauss, like so many of the older exiles who studied Nietzsche in the 1920s when renewed interest in his radical historicism and moral perspectivalism filtered into virtually every register of Weimar German intellectual and cultural life, began reading the philosopher as a student, and continued to do so, even single-mindedly into adulthood. "Nietzsche so dominated and charmed me between my 22nd and 30th years," Strauss wrote, "that I literally believed everything I understood of him."[26] Thomas Mann, with the benefit of a much lusher psychological repertoire at his disposal, expressed his reverence teetering on devotion equally unreservedly. Consummated in the figure of Adrian Leverkühn in his masterwork *Doktor Faustus* (1947), Nietzsche served as Mann's personal "saint of immoralism," whose life and writings influenced him from the 1890s into his American exile. He appreciated Nietzsche's holy dandyism, drew inspiration from his psychological self-vivisection and his conception of the artist as knower, modeled his own effort to sanctify himself as a lyrical and tragic *Gesamtkunstwerk* on Nietzsche's, and found consolation for his own sacralization of the aesthetic life in Nietzsche's claim that "the goal of humanity . . . lies not at its end, but in its highest representatives." From his early twenties onward, Mann believed that integrating "Nietzsche's criticism of culture and his stylistic artistry [was] the first order of importance in . . . my life."[27]

As with Kaufmann, many of the other émigrés' major works testify to Nietzsche's animating presence in their thought. Though their approaches to and conclusions about Nietzsche are varied and complex, they, like Kaufmann, drew insights from his antifoundational philosophy as they assessed the ramifications of living in a world after God. The social scientists enlisted Nietzsche's psychological concepts as they sought to understand, as the psychoanalyst Erich Fromm put it, modern man's psychological drive to "escape from freedom," while the humanists reckoned with Nietzsche's forebodings about nihilism that feeds off the corpse of God.[28]

Like so many of the other émigrés, Kaufmann reassessed his religious views in light of Nietzsche's assaults on them. Lutheran theologian Paul Tillich brought with him in 1933 a Nietzsche burrowed deep in his theological self-understanding. It was Nietzsche's *Zarathustra* that Tillich had turned to as a twenty-nine-year old military chaplain with the German army stationed in France, to make sense of the unspeakable death and carnage around him. Nietzsche helped him see that in man's worship of false institutions the "God of theism" was dead, because modern man, in his arrogance, had killed Him. Throughout the 1920s and into his exile in the United States, Tillich continued to draw from Nietzsche as he encouraged other searching moderns to "shak[e] . . . the foundations" of official religion grown sinful from its separation from "the Ground of Being," the "Protestant Principle" to challenge any institutional authority against speaking for religious absolutes, the "Courage to Be" free of a hollow piety, and to reach for the "God above the God of theism."[29] Though Kaufmann would later come to express doubts about Tillich's use of Nietzsche for Christian apologetics, he shared with him the certainty that the Nazis' visions of secular transcendence did *not* exemplify the Nietzschean task of finding meaning beyond meaninglessness. Expressing a sentiment shared by the exiles, the philosopher Karl Löwith argued in his 1949 study, *Meaning and History*, that their own experiences had proved Nietzsche right. The notion that the universe is guided by providential design or natural law of progress was forever bankrupt: "All this is now past because it has conscience against it."[30]

Viewing Kaufmann's *Nietzsche* against the backdrop of German émigrés also influenced by the philosopher enables us to see that he was not alone in his effort to deny the Nazis their claim to his legacy. This is apparent in their collective effort to inoculate Nietzsche against charges of anti-Semitism.[31] Kaufmann's own strategy for doing so involved attributing all notions about Nietzsche's negative estimation of Jews and Judaism to his sister, Elisabeth. Her 1885 marriage to the prominent German anti-Semite Bernhard Förster, founder of a Teutonic colony in Paraguay and later an enthusiastic supporter of the Nazis, made Kaufmann's job of blaming her somewhat easier. Together with head archivist Max Oehler, who joined the Nazi Party in 1931, Elisabeth Förster-Nietzsche viewed serving National Socialism as an official function of the Nietzsche Archive.[32] "We are drunk with enthusiasm," she effused in 1933, "because at the head of our government stands such a wonderful, indeed phenomenal, personality like our magnificent Chancellor Adolf Hitler."[33]

Once he highlighted Förster-Nietzsche's anti-Semitism, Kaufmann built his case for Nietzsche's innocence by emphasizing the philosopher's "powerful ambivalence" about his little sister. He loved her because of her devotion to him, but he was often aggrieved by all the ways she "embodied the narrowness . . . and the deeply unchristian Christianity" of the warped culture of the Kaiserreich.[34] Ambivalence escalated to disgust when he learned of her marriage to Förster. Witness, for example, his letter to her in 1887 in which he wrote, "One of the greatest stupidities you have committed—for yourself and for me! Your association with an anti-Semitic chief expresses a foreignness to *my* whole way of life which fills me ever again with ire or melancholy." To this Kaufmann added Nietzsche's hatred of "Anti-Semitic Teutonism," which played a central role in his break from Wagner, and loaded his text with selections from Nietzsche's published writings and personal letters that showed his disdain for anti-Semitism as another expression of nineteenth-century German ignorance and chauvinism. Kaufmann quoted Nietzsche's last letter to his friend Franz Overbeck: "Just now I am having all anti-Semites shot."[35]

Though other émigrés' commentaries of Nietzsche's estimation of Jews and Judaism were more nuanced, they uniformly insisted that *anti-Semite* was too crude a term to describe him. Hannah Arendt, the German exile regarded as the leading authority on totalitarianism and modern anti-Semitism, sought to separate both Nietzsche and the tradition of European high culture that was his heritage from the web of historical conditions leading to modern European anti-Semitism and make them both "above any such suspicion."[36] In his *Behemoth* (1942), one of the earliest comprehensive social scientific studies of the Nazi regime, Frankfurt School political scientist Franz Neumann argued that Nazism lacked not only a clear political theory or even a coherent ideology but also any understanding of Nietzsche's position on the Jews: "But Nietzsche was no Anti-Semite and every attempt to stamp him as such must end in failure. . . . Nietzsche denounced Anti-Semitism as mere jealousy."[37]

If there were striking harmonies between Kaufmann's and the other émigrés' biographies and interest in Nietzsche, there were also deep dissonances, which help distinguish Kaufmann's Nietzsche from theirs. Indeed, it is these differences that help account for why Kaufmann's version of the philosopher was uniquely poised to enjoy the widespread resonance in American culture that it did. The older émigrés came with their Nietzsche, while Kaufmann formulated his in the context of his American studies. When the older émigrés utilized Nietzsche to reappraise their personal situations, or to protest the horrors committed in his name, they did so by looking back to a Nietzsche who was part of their own German identity, a part of their German past, a part of their homeland, which was no longer their home. Though Kaufmann, too, associated Nietzsche with the German philosophical culture from which he came, his relationship with him began where he began—as a US citizen, a new scholar for a new world. And though Kaufmann was neither innocent nor naïve, the Nietzsche he formed in his mind was a Nietzsche in his own image of the young thinker with no history at his back.

No better do we see these contrasts between the émigrés' Nietzsche and the newly constituted one of Kaufmann than by considering the most extreme expression of the exiled Nietzsches of this period: Theodor Adorno's. Of all the other émigrés mentioned above, none were more influenced by Nietzsche, and none drew as consistently on his ideas as Adorno. And yet in almost every respect, his Nietzsche bore little resemblance to Kaufmann's. In 1944, when a twenty-three-year old Kaufmann was discovering in Nietzsche a theorist of the absolute moral autonomy and self-sufficiency he sought for himself, Adorno was using Nietzsche to show that the liberal romance with autonomy was just another fiction of modernity's bourgeois-administered world. He had made his way to the United States in 1938 from Geneva and Oxford after he and his fellow Institute for Social Research colleagues were purged from their posts in Frankfurt in 1933. After limited success in New York, he relocated with his Frankfurt School friend and mentor Max Horkheimer to the Pacific Palisades in California. It was there, under the bright sunny skies of Los Angeles, that Adorno and Horkheimer composed their decidedly un-sunny monumental Nietzschean critique of modernity titled *Dialectic of Enlightenment* (1944).[38]

In *Dialectic*, Adorno and Horkheimer drew heavily on Nietzsche's critique of the Enlightenment to challenge the conventional view of its legacies as progress. The Enlightenment's unwarranted esteem for human rationality, they argued, did not simply lead to the "disenchantment of the world"—it sowed the seeds of its own destruction. By exalting the limitless power of instrumental rationality, the Enlightenment cultivated an ideology in which nothing lay beyond the power of human apprehension, domination, and administration. The "administered world" of Nazism, then, represented the realization, not the abandonment, of the Enlightenment: the "Enlightenment is totalitarian." According to Adorno and Horkheimer, though Nietzsche would not have known the modern coinage *totalitarian*, he clearly "recognized the dialectic of enlightenment" animating its worldview. Much to their horror, what Nietzsche had attacked as Enlightenment violence masked as order, and sadism as compassion, was not limited to European fascism but also could be found in what they termed the American "culture industry." Writing just a few miles outside Hollywood, they claimed that in advanced industrial capitalism, culture became a commodity that aimed to entertain, not elevate, and in doing so, purposefully dulled modern man's consciousness of himself and blinded him to the gross inequities around him. The culture industry of American capitalism, as in German Nazism, produced utterly counterfeited personalities, incapable of independent thoughts and desires. Even human personality had become an example of the administered logic of late modernity, of the "Enlightenment as Mass Deception."[39]

During Adorno's American exile, with his unremitting feeling of loss of ground, Nietzsche's "negative dialectics"[40] offered him whatever modicum of existential and intellectual traction he could find. From the moment he arrived in the United States in 1938, he always felt himself to be a displaced European, booted out of a vertical cultural world that had provided him with his sense of moral and aesthetic orientation. Never at home in America, Adorno was both ill-disposed and unwilling to make the necessary accommodations to a society that to him seemed devoid of history, overfed on mindless popular amusements, and undernourished by the life of the mind. Struggling to make a life in a culture and language he found inhospitable, Adorno observed that "every intellectual in emigration is, without exception, mutilated," because "his language has been expropriated, and the historical dimension that nourished his knowledge, sapped."[41] His years in American exile did very little to soften his views of the United States. At the first opportunity, he went home to Germany in 1949. After a brief return to the United States in 1953, he packed his bags and left for good.

Adorno's Nietzschean narrative of the dangerous triumph of Enlightenment thinking forms a distinct leitmotif in his writing in America through the 1940s and early '50s.[42] Throughout his major works of the period, he used Nietzsche to question the vantage point from which the engaged but oppositional critic of "official culture" can get a footing—not ground already colonized by the very culture it seeks to critique. This was the persistent problem that haunted Adorno throughout his time in exile. Where can the thinker think *his* thoughts, and not counterfeited ones; adopt *his* moral posture, without posturing a vacated morality? "To write poetry after Auschwitz is barbaric," he concluded in 1949. What made it barbaric, Adorno argued, was not its escapism from the dark realities of an instrumental world but because it *could not* escape from its totalizing brutality. He asked how, after the Holocaust, can we even be sure that our thinking is our thinking, and not the thinking of our administered modernity?[43]

This was Adorno's Nietzschean "negativism,"[44] one that had virtually no audience in American intellectual life in the 1950s and '60s. Adorno's Nietzsche is the most extreme example of the sorrows and sufferings of the older exiles' Nietzsche. Certainly, so idiosyncratic a thinker as Adorno cannot be made representative of all the other émigrés. But the extremity with which his negativist Nietzsche registered their psychic dislocations, their loss, their anguish, and their fury with a world turned upside down poses a crucial backdrop for understanding why Kaufmann's Nietzsche made the easy headway into mid-century American culture that it did. As we shall see, in almost every respect Kaufmann's Nietzsche is a counter-Nietzsche to Adorno's. Adorno's negativist Nietzsche was forced from a settled life and clear career path in Germany. Kaufmann's Nietzsche was formulated while a student in America. Adorno's Nietzsche relentlessly criticized the Enlightenment. Kaufmann's Nietzsche exemplified its unrealized promises. Adorno's Nietzsche thought the rational self parroted instrumental virtues. Kaufmann's Nietzsche considered the rational self the seat of all morality. For Adorno, Nietzsche was above all a homeless dialectician who would have never succumbed to unity as "stylized barbarity," while Kaufmann's Nietzsche was a "*dialectical monist*," whose ideas and literary style all tracked back to a unified whole.[45] Whereas the other émigrés' Nietzsche made more inroads than Adorno's, none accomplished this feat as completely and comprehensively as Kaufmann's. In the suffocating environment of cold war culture, Americans were ready for a liberating thinker who helped them breathe larger air. Kaufmann's Nietzsche offered them that: a philosopher of a Dionysian Enlightenment, not a totalitarian one.

## Nietzsche as Problem Thinker

Throughout his study, Kaufmann sought to make clear his agenda to reverse all trends in Nietzsche interpretation on both sides of the Atlantic, which cast him as either a Darwinist, a romantic, or a "wayward disciple" of Schopenhauer. Most of all, he wanted to establish Nietzsche as a serious philosopher. Kaufmann insisted that it was high time that Nietzsche be afforded his rightful "place in the grand tradition of Western thought." In order to demonstrate that Nietzsche was "a major historical event" in the Western tradition, Kaufmann argued that it was necessary to put him in dialogue with the appropriate interlocutors: Socrates, Plato, Luther, Kant, Hegel, and Goethe. In fact, Kaufmann maintained that Nietzsche was best understood as an Enlightenment figure. Similar to Kant's "motto" for the Enlightenment, "Have the courage to avail yourself of your own understanding" (Sapere aude!), Nietzsche defined his philosophical quest as the pursuit of intellectual self-sovereignty. "'*One thing is needed*'—namely, 'that a human being attain satisfaction with himself,' recreate himself, and become a 'single one' by giving style to his character."

According to Kaufmann, though Nietzsche may have "lost the optimism of some of the men of the Enlightenment," he spoke the same message of liberation and self-reliance, though not to "mankind" as Kant had done, but rather to "single human beings." If Nietzsche had lost the Enlightenment faith in mankind, he still shared the Enlightenment belief in man.[46]

Kaufmann recognized that making room for Nietzsche in the pantheon of great Western philosophers required that he first establish the coherence of Nietzsche's vision. In order to achieve this aim, he argued that rigorous study of Nietzsche's ideas reveals a reasoned philosophy of "self-perfection." Kaufmann thought that despite Nietzsche's reputation for making "self-contradictory" claims in his writings, when placed in the larger context of his philosophy, his ideas about power, self-sovereignty, and intellectual integrity exhibited a synthetic unity. He argued that any inconsistencies or ambiguities in Nietzsche's claims were more apparent than real. Because Nietzsche stridently "denounced" the romantics' "protest 'against reason, enlightenment,'" and above all, what he regarded as the "ambiguity" in their writing, Kaufmann warned that reading Nietzsche as a romantic would falsely identify him "with what he fought." He stressed that Nietzsche's "intentions are singularly unequivocal, and he was not one to sit on both sides of the fence at once. Insofar as he had a 'dual nature,' he was ever seeking to overcome it. . . . Self-overcoming, not ambiguity, is the key to Nietzsche."[47]

In arguing for the coherence of Nietzsche's ideas, Kaufmann recognized that he also needed to account for Nietzsche's curious aphoristic style. In Kaufmann's estimation, readers found it difficult to understand Nietzsche because (not despite the fact that) he was such a remarkable writer. Kaufmann warned his readers that "Nietzsche's books are easier to read but harder to understand than those of almost any other thinker." But he insisted that Nietzsche was more than a great stylist. In fact, Nietzsche admonished writers who let style trump substance. He criticized what he called "literary decadence," where meaning resides in flashes of insight but not in the text as a whole. If the dots do not connect, then all we have got—as Nietzsche put it—is an "anarchy of atoms."[48] Indeed, critics had long charged that Nietzsche wrote in aphorisms because he could not think straight. Throughout the first half of the century, they recognized his literary skill and his searing intellect, but they insisted that aphorism was unfit for serious philosophy. He thus used Nietzsche's own criticism of literary decadence to inoculate him against this

Undated photograph of Walter Kaufmann. Princeton University Archives Department of Rare Books and Special Collections, Princeton University Library. Used by permission of Princeton University Library.

very charge. According to Kaufmann, Nietzsche proved that philosophy can be produced with lightning strikes.

Kaufmann defended Nietzsche's use of aphorism by arguing that it was the necessary means for him to radically revise both the mode and the purpose of philosophical inquiry. He argued that aphorisms were crucial to Nietzsche's pluralistic project, for they let him come at the question of life from as many different angles as possible. In addition, he argued that Nietzsche's aphorisms served as thought experiments, provisional hypotheses to test new visions of the good life in a contingent universe. He characterized both Nietzsche's theory of knowledge and the form he used to express it by introducing the terms *experimental* and *existential*. By this, Kaufmann meant that questions about truth, beliefs, and nature are valuable only insofar as they are relevant to one's way of life. For Nietzsche, philosophy is "not a finished and impersonal system, but a passionate quest for knowledge, an unceasing series of courageous experiments—small experiments, lacking in glamour and apparent grandeur, yet so serious that we cannot dodge them." Only those problems which grow out of real experience and not out of the philosopher's logic games or his desire for a metaphysical map of the universe are worthy of consideration. For Kaufmann, Nietzsche's existentialism is best understood when we consider him to be a "problem-thinker," not a "system-thinker," and that his use of aphorism was his way of "'living through' each problem." By insisting that aphorism is not an abandonment but a realization of the serious inquiry into the problems of living, that it is not an "anarchy of atoms" but an experimental form for a philosophy of life, Kaufmann connected the dots: "Life does indeed reside in the whole of Nietzsche's thinking and writing, and there is a unity which is obscured, but not obliterated, by the apparent discontinuity in his experimentalism."[49]

Kaufmann's *Nietzsche* appeared when the immediate postwar American "vogue of French existentialism" was at its height, as was the demand for a coherent explication of it. In popular magazines from *Time* and *Life* to *Vogue* and *Harper's Bazaar*, a flurry of articles carried dispatches from abroad, translated excerpts of the existentialists, and printed photographic portraits of Sartre, de Beauvoir, and Camus, heralding existentialism as an intriguing new philosophical fashion. The coverage noted a new philosophy, appropriate to the uncertainties of modern times, which dealt with man's questioning of the conditions of his own existence, his desires for infinitude in a world of limits, and the quest for meaning in the face of an indifferent universe. In response to the German occupation of their country during World War II, French thinkers were forced underground into bohemian nightclubs and cafes as well as into a kind of inner immigration. In the face of untimely death, they instated a philosophy demanding an accounting of human life. Americans read that this philosophy was not merely a way of thinking, an inauthentic set of ideas divorced from matters of life. Rather, it was a complete way of life that infused thinking with doing, making moral claims with acting on them; and it even came with its own paraphernalia—expatriated jazz, cigarettes, and dark clothing. To postwar American observers, the cultural messages wafting out of the smoke-filled cafes of Paris were alluring, yet confusing.[50]

Kaufmann marshaled that curiosity about existentialism to show Nietzsche's role in setting the terms for its emergence as a particular mode of modern inquiry as well as to use Nietzsche to tie it back to larger leitmotifs in Western philosophical thought. But he did so cautiously, introducing readers to concerns and styles of thought that he only occasionally defined as existentialist. He described "the urgency of [Nietzsche's] task": after the death of God, when divine explanations are untenable and naturalistic explanations fail to give human experience any dignity or meaning, the solitary individual must confront his awesome aloneness in an indifferent universe.[51] Nihilism is no option, for it is simply a retreat into worn-out habits of thought characterized by the conviction that the world is only meaningful if it has *one* meaning. Kaufmann tentatively and even cautiously defined these elements of Nietzsche's thought as existential. It is worth noting that these elements were the very features of European existentialism that he would import to America six years later, when he became the ambassador for a fully synthesized treatment of it in *Existentialism from Dostoyevsky to Sartre* (1956).[52] In 1950, however, Kaufmann was still working out the contours of existentialism and Nietzsche's role in it. The vital connection between Nietzsche and the later existentialists was their common desire for a philosophy that affirmed life and thus rejected nihilism as a form of inauthentic existence: "Not only the use of the word *Existenz*, but the thought which is at stake, suggests [that what Nietzsche had in mind] is particularly close to what is today called *Existenzphilosophie*. Man's fundamental problem is to achieve true 'existence.'" He does so by refusing to view his "existence" in a contingent universe as nothing "more than just another accident."[53]

American reviewers enthusiastically greeted Kaufmann's effort to establish Nietzsche as a philosopher worthy of serious examination. In scholarly journals and the popular press, commentators described Kaufmann's study as a "revelation," "one of those rare works that no student of modern thought can afford to ignore," and "one of the best expositions of Nietzsche's philosophy," noting that one of his greatest achievements was that he made Nietzsche make sense.[54] Positive as the initial reviews had been, Kaufmann likely suspected that it would be difficult to persuade academic philosophers of Nietzsche's value. At midcentury, the rift that had been growing since the late nineteenth century between Anglo-American and Continental thought was as wide as ever.

Anglo-American philosophers had grown increasingly suspicious of the speculative nature of the metaphysics associated with German idealism. Beginning in the 1930s and continuing well into the 1950s, analytic philosophy, particularly logical positivism, dominated most major philosophy departments in the United States. Analytic philosophers came to view the aims of philosophy as akin to those of the sciences, and thus sought to narrow the range of philosophical inquiry to raise only those questions that could produce verifiable results. Instead of examining what makes a life significant, analytic philosophers asked: What do we mean when we refer to something as true? What kind of truth claims can be verified? When is a belief warranted? Consequently, they came to view language as the primary realm in which propositions could be adequately tested for their truth value, and so logical positivism came to focus almost exclusively on specific terms and definitions that comprised particular truth claims. In doing so, logical positivists developed a bare-bones though highly technical discourse as the medium appropriate to investigate truth. Because they considered only verifiable claims meaningful, analytic philosophers ultimately sought to move philosophical inquiry away from its traditional association with literature, art, and theology.[55]

Meanwhile, as Anglo-American philosophy increasingly emulated the sciences, philosophy on the European continent was extending its reach, employing literary, artistic, and psychological discourses to examine the experience of modern man. Continental thinkers continued to examine the full range of human experience—individual identity, modern anxiety, and longing for transcendence—in order to draw a more complete picture of man. However, because of this broadly humanistic scope, the ideas of Husserl, Heidegger, Jaspers, and Sartre were deemed insufficiently "philosophical" for serious study in most American philosophy departments.[56]

This rift between the two distinct cultures of philosophy on either side of the Atlantic made it difficult for any single philosopher to speak to the concerns of a broad reading audience. But Kaufmann considered Nietzsche just the thinker to bring existentialism and analytic philosophy, Europe and America, into dialogue with each other. On the one hand, Nietzsche exhibited the "temper" of existentialism. According to Kaufmann, he blended philosophy and psychology, examined the consequences of the death of God for modern man, and drew from literary sources in his cultural criticism. On the other hand, Nietzsche also exhibited a "positivistic streak": his rejection of metaphysics, his empiricism, and his attention to the uses of language all demonstrated his affinity with analytic philosophers.[57] In pulling these two strains together in Nietzsche, Kaufmann also showed their unexpected harmonies. Despite the antagonisms between them, both sought to dispel illusions masquerading as truth and to question false necessities, and desired "to bring philosophy down to earth."[58] As Kaufmann later expressed his zeal for Nietzsche's redemptive possibilities for midcentury philosophy in his introduction to *The Portable Nietzsche* (1954), "Nietzsche is the . . . best bridge between positivism and existentialism." With "German and Romance philosophy and Anglo-American 'analysis'. . . completely out of touch with each other," Kaufmann argued that Nietzsche could help reestablish "some bond between what are now two completely divergent branches of modern thought." He did not miss the irony that "Nietzsche, once stupidly denounced as the mind that caused the First World War, might well become a major aid to international understanding."[59]

Given Nietzsche's compromised reputation both in the profession and among a broader reading audience, Kaufmann was likely concerned that his Nietzsche as intellectual ambassador was not one for whom his readers were primed. And yet, in his estimation, this was the "real" Nietzsche, the one who had been obscured by years of ill-informed interpretations: Nietzsche as Darwinist, Nietzsche as romantic, Nietzsche as poet. By first returning Nietzsche to the context of the Western philosophical tradition and then elucidating the ways in which his form expressed the substance of his philosophical experimentalism, Kaufmann effectively demonstrated that the dots could connect: Nietzsche's ideas were not an aberration from the main lines of Western philosophy. Nietzsche made sense.

## Nietzsche and the Nazis

Not content simply to establish the unity of Nietzsche's thought, Kaufmann sought to dismantle the legend of Nietzsche as warmonger. Already before World War I, readers on both sides of the Atlantic had interpreted Nietzsche's martial language and his critique of Christian "slave morality" as a celebration of militarism. His claims for the death of God, and thus the absence of any divine, transhistorical arbiter of universal values, underscored their view that for him might makes right. Kaufmann set out to challenge the hawkish interpretation of Nietzsche's "will to power" by demonstrating that it is expressed not by overtaking others but by "overcoming" (Überwindung) the self. And yet because Nietzsche's conception of power appeared to be a celebration of unbridled ruthlessness against others, his vibrant posthumous career as a philosopher of war raised the stakes.

Nietzsche's reputation barely had time to recover from its association with the First Cause of World War I when another world-historical catastrophe struck. The apprehension about the antidemocratic, racialist Übermensch crystallized during the 1930s as Americans witnessed the rise of Nazism and fascism in Europe. In the years leading up to the war, US commentators in both the scholarly and the popular press began interpreting Nazism's emphasis on the Aryan race as an expression of Nietzsche's "blonde beast" and "master morality," which recognized no law above the will to power. While the Nazis had incorporated a number of thinkers and artists from the pantheon of towering German intellectual and cultural figures as their forerunners, including Luther, Fichte, Herder, Goethe, and Wagner, it was Nietzsche whom they believed was the architect of their political, racial, and social *Weltanschauung*. With increasing revulsion, US newspapers reported on the spectacles of the "Nietzscheanization" of German politics. Without exception, the dispatches were alarming. Over the course of the 1930s, American readers confronted articles drawing connections between "Nietzsche and the Crisis," announcing that "Nietzsche Held Nazis' Prophet in War on Christ," and warning that developments in Europe were proving Nietzscheism to be the most "serious enemy" of modern Christianity.[60] "I Married a Nazi!" reported an American woman, whose once-happy marriage to a German was now destroyed by his Nietzschean hatred for all things Christian and democratic, while "Pagan Customs Revived for Nazi Weddings" quoted the passages from *Zarathustra* mandated as part of the neopagan Nazi wedding ceremonies.[61] In 1943, *New York Times* readers learned that Hitler had sent Mussolini a specially bound edition of the complete works of Nietzsche for his sixtieth birthday. Though some popular accounts of the Nazification of Nietzsche wondered if the Nazis had gotten Nietzsche quite right, the press did note how his rejection of bourgeois values, democracy, and Christian sympathy made their enlistment of him easy. Could anyone dispute how trippingly Nietzsche's rhetoric, such as "democracy is the historic form of the decay of the State" and praise for the "the magnificent blond brute, avidly rampant for spoil and victory" flowed from Nazi tongues and through bullhorns at National Socialist conventions (Reichsparteitagen) and marches?[62]

Though Kaufmann would have had his work cut out for him simply taking on the Nietzsche image in the popular press, it was the 1941 authoritative study of the philosopher's life and thought by Harvard intellectual historian (and later American Historical Association president) Crane Brinton that demanded the fullest response. Throughout the 1940s, Brinton's book, which argued that Nietzsche's philosophy was the inspiration for Nazism, emerged as the authoritative interpretation of Nietzsche. Thus, in order to challenge the claim that Nietzsche was a forerunner of the Nazis, Kaufmann had to take on Brinton. Blending biography and reception history, Brinton's *Nietzsche* focused on the competing twentieth-century applications of Nietzsche's philosophy. He surveyed Nietzsche's reputation and distinguished two opposing cults: the "gentle" and the "tough" Nietzscheans. He admitted that this "frankly dualistic device," this "neat conceptual polarity," was a pretty simplistic way of distinguishing tendencies in thought inspired by such a complicated thinker. But Brinton made no apologies for his dualism; he believed that it accurately distilled two opposing views of Nietzsche's philosophy. The gentle Nietzscheans, he argued, believed that for all his tough rhetoric, Nietzsche was a wholesome moralist who simply wanted to hold nineteenth-century Western societies to higher standards of beauty, truth, and goodness. Bemused by the great lengths to which gentle Nietzscheans had gone in order to turn Nietzsche into a "man of good will," Brinton concluded that they had whitewashed Nietzsche beyond all recognition. "The tough Nietzscheans," by contrast, "have had rather easier going," finding all sorts of evidence in Nietzsche's writings that he had nothing but contempt for others. Their Nietzsche "was the [D]ionysian rebel, the unashamed pagan, the joyous fighter" who unapologetically advocated cruelty against the "bewildered herd." According to Brinton, the "tough" Nietzscheans got him right. So, Brinton concluded, Nietzsche worshipped unbridled strength; the Nazis worshipped tyranny and violence; thus, the Nazis were tough Nietzscheans. Therefore, "were Nietzsche alive now . . . he would be a good Nazi."[63]

Kaufmann detected that because the image of Nietzsche as a forerunner of the Nazis was so dominant, Brinton let himself off the hook from trying to make his arguments persuasive. Kaufmann recognized, for example, Brinton's slack use of Nietzsche's "alleged glorification of war" to make his case.[64] He conceded that Nietzsche made many contradictory and therefore confusing statements about the source and expression of human power. Despite Nietzsche's remark that "'*we shall shatter the sword*.'. . . *To disarm while being the best armed*, out of an *elevation* of sensibility—that is the means to *real* peace," Zarathustra's exhortation that "you should love peace as a means to

Adolf Hitler's visit to the Nietzsche Archive, Weimar, Germany, 1934. As reprinted in Crane Brinton, *Nietzsche* (1941).

new wars—and the short peace more than the long" suggested to many that "Nietzsche was a fascist."[65] According to Kaufmann, the tensions in Nietzsche's competing claims about war were more apparent than real. Brinton, like all interpreters who read Nietzsche as a philosopher of war, had consistently taken his remarks out of context. Placing them back in the context of his "repudiation of Christ," Kaufmann averred, revealed that for Nietzsche, "war is classed with the altruism of the weak who find in it an escape from their hard task of self-perfection."[66] According to Kaufmann's Nietzsche, warfare is not an expression of true power but rather an admission of its absence.

Kaufmann undoubtedly sought to create a picture of Nietzsche that stood in stark contrast to this "blood red" image of Nietzsche the Nazi. When we consider the hostile intellectual climate in the United States to all things German in general and the compromised status of Nietzsche's reputation in particular, it is not difficult to understand Kaufmann's determination to distinguish Nietzsche from the Nazis. But his effort in this regard was part of a much broader aim: namely, to separate Nietzsche from the issue of his intellectual and political influence altogether. In 1950, Nietzsche was not just famous—or, rather, infamous—for his influence on Nazism, he was also famous for his imprint on a wide array of intellectual, cultural, and political movements in Europe. Kaufmann argued that it was absurd to interpret Nietzsche by way of his influence on modern thought, because, at least in Germany, "hardly any educated German after 1900 was not 'influenced' somehow by Nietzsche." As he made clear, given the questionable uses to which Nietzsche's philosophy had been put, it was undeniable that "Nietzsche's thought ha[d] been obscured rather than revealed by its impact."[67] Furthermore, he argued that causal claims in intellectual history are problematic, not the least because such claims tend to be asserted, not demonstrated: "Historical causation is extremely complex and cannot be dealt with adequately by the mere assertion of an influence." For Kaufmann, Nietzsche's posthumous career was case in point: thinkers and texts can be influential because they are so misunderstood.[68]

Kaufmann's insistence that it was ludicrous to study Nietzsche by way of his influence is borne out by his book's earliest reviewers. Some of them, chagrined by his deft handling of Nietzsche's ideas, were even willing to admit that they were part of the problem. Walter Cerf acknowledged that he had irresponsibly taken at face value "generally accepted ideas about Nietzsche without bothering to winnow the chaff from the wheat, thus helping to spread gossip about [Nietzsche's] work."[69] The confession by Crane Brinton in his assessment of Kaufmann's book for the *Saturday Review of Literature* in 1951 is even more startling. He began by poking fun at the flawed US scholarship on Nietzsche's ideas and conceded that his was no better: "I myself . . . brought out a brief [it was 266 pages] and, I admit, rather ill-tempered analysis of Nietzsche in which I found some of his ideas congruous with those of the Nazis, and Nietzsche himself a somewhat unpleasantly pathetic intellectual." Throughout his study, Kaufmann consistently took issue with Brinton's interpretations, and Brinton, in turn, used his book review as a platform to tone down or qualify his claims from a decade earlier. He praised the "compact richness of [Kaufmann's] book," noting the subtlety with which Kaufmann synthesized Nietzsche's ideas while "avoid[ing] the tendency to put Nietzsche back together too neatly." By granting that Kaufmann made "the best case for" a revisionist interpretation of Nietzsche's martial claims, Brinton seemed willing to question his own version of the philosopher as a demented and decadent proto-Nazi. He noted approvingly that Kaufmann's study was "one of the very best books on Nietzsche I have seen."[70]

More generally, Kaufmann's energetic effort to free Nietzsche's philosophy from its influence on subsequent thinkers and movements exemplifies what can be regarded as his broader vision of the history of intellectuals and ideas. What we see in his aim to excavate an unmediated Nietzsche is the sentiment that the worth of any great thinker cannot and should not be measured by his influence. Influence is simply what happens when important ideas are set in motion. To account for the inner workings of influence—the way one person affects another, the way an idea bounces off other ideas, the way a philosophy paves its way through human history—requires first and foremost a conviction that one can distinguish cause from effect. According to Nietzsche, belief in causation was simply a metaphysical hangover of a worn-out belief in objectivity.

Kaufmann's desire to distinguish the "real" Nietzsche from what he perceived to be the traffic of questionable appropriations of his ideas expresses a thoroughly Nietzschean view that in a world without foundations, without God, without a telos, without transhistorical truth—in other words, without some kind of universal confirmation of human meaning—influence is no measure of value.[71] In his treatment of Nietzsche's philosophy, great ideas need no external justification, just as the great übermenschian individual needs no confirmation from others that his existence is of value. Great thinkers and great ideas justify themselves.

## Nietzschean Experimentalism and Jamesian Pragmatism

Though Kaufmann wrote his *Nietzsche* primarily for an American English-speaking audience, he very selectively engaged with thinkers and traditions within the intellectual life of his adopted country. There are significant omissions from the American intellectual context—in particular his failure to address Ralph Waldo Emerson's profound impact on Nietzsche from the time that he was a teenager. Kaufmann later discussed Nietzsche's interest in Emerson in his 1974 introduction to *The Gay Science*, and though he catalogued in some detail Nietzsche's engagement with Emerson's ideas, he blandly dismissed the notion that the two philosophies had much in common without explanation.[72] He did, however, make glancing references to other important figures in American thought, including George Santayana, William Salter, Josiah Royce, and Arthur Lovejoy, and he noted that the genealogy of the Nazis' racial policies could be traced to Madison Grant and Lothrop Stoddard's racialist theories. Yet Kaufmann's engagement with the American pragmatists, William James in particular, demonstrates his familiarity with relevant discourses and his interest in considering their affinities with Nietzsche's thought. Though he only occasionally invoked James, his comparison of Nietzschean "experimentalism" and Jamesian pragmatism is crucial, for it enabled him to reintroduce readers to Nietzsche's philosophical challenges to foundationalism in terms recognizable to those familiar with similar efforts in American thought. Kaufmann explored their similarities while underscoring their differences. In doing so, he participated in what by then was, and would continue to be, a long-standing practice in American Nietzsche interpretation. By comparing Nietzsche with James and Dewey, his text invited the question: why turn to the German Nietzsche when, in James and Dewey, Americans already have American pragmatists?

It was Brinton who provided Kaufmann with the occasion to draw the link between Nietzsche and James. Kaufmann rightly observed that Brinton had drawn his "gentle" versus "tough" dualism from William James's "tender-minded" versus "tough-minded" classification of styles of thought in *Pragmatism* (1907). But Kaufmann easily dismissed Brinton's categorization of "gentle" and "tough" Nietzsche interpreters, arguing that it failed to capture the subtlety of Nietzsche's philosophy, or even to account for the taxonomy of the varieties of "Nietzschean" interpretation. First, he insisted that the term *Nietzschean* made no sense. Nietzsche repeatedly scorned anyone who would follow another master. As he himself put it, "One repays a teacher badly if one always remains a pupil only." Nietzsche's philosophy repudiated the very idea of intellectual discipleship: "A 'Nietzschean'... whether 'gentle' or 'tough,' is in a sense a contradiction in terms: to be a Nietzschean, one must not be a Nietzschean."[73] According to Kaufmann, fidelity to Nietzsche's ideas required understanding him in the terms in which he would have understood himself.

While Kaufmann objected to James's typology of philosophical personalities, he recognized parallels between Nietzsche's and James's shared conviction that a philosopher's temperament conditions his philosophical views. Nietzsche contended that all philosophy is autobiography, while James argued similarly that a "philosophy is the expression of a man's intimate character."[74] Kaufmann once again highlighted the distinction in what James referred to as "two types of mental make-up"[75]—namely, the two personality types that color a philosopher's outlook: "tough" and "tender." Nevertheless, he remained skeptical: why only two? Whereas Nietzsche insisted that a philosopher must never stop interrogating his own subjective tendencies, James,

Kaufmann maintained, simply "urg[es] us to accept his." According to Kaufmann, "A critic may marvel how 'pluralism' is abandoned so suddenly and how radically unempirical is the claim that there are only two philosophies to choose from: James' [tough] and Royce's [tender]." For Kaufmann, James's dualism was inadequate for understanding the varieties of human personality in a pluralistic universe.[76]

Though Kaufmann argued that Nietzsche was critical of simple dualisms, he shared James's and Dewey's appreciation of the *dialectical* qualities within human thought and personality. Kaufmann asserted that Nietzsche consistently argued against a dualistic understanding of reason and passion, rationalism and empiricism, and that this was a criticism he shared with the pragmatists. Nietzsche showed both the affective dimensions of thought and, likewise, the rational dimensions of feeling, examining how thought and passion were not opposed but rather how, through conditioning, rationality becomes a matter of instinct: "The truly rational man subjects all opinions to rational consideration, because this has become his second nature." Kaufmann argued that Nietzsche's examination of how modes of thinking and feeling are the products of conditioning, and conversely, how ways of viewing the world become instinct, converged with the pragmatists. But he also asserted Nietzschean priority: Nietzsche's ideas are what "later became known as the James-Lange theory" and "strikingly [anticipate] John Dewey's *Human Nature and Conduct*."[77]

Similarly, Kaufmann drew parallels between Nietzsche's experimentalism and pragmatism by arguing that both shared similar epistemological assumptions.[78] He retraced their common heritage in Darwin. Whereas once the intellect was regarded as something "eternal," now, after Darwin, philosophers on both sides of the Atlantic "had to be accounted for in terms of evolution." Accordingly, Nietzsche and the pragmatists recognized that the intellect "originated in time" as an "instrument" in the struggle for survival. Both likewise drew from Kant's insistence that the mind can apprehend phenomena but not ultimate reality. By fusing Darwin and Kant, both philosophies came to view one's "truths" not as accurate descriptions of the world but simply as "statements which 'work' and thus fit us for survival." Kaufmann argued that both Nietzschean experimentalism and pragmatism ruled out all forms of philosophical inquiry which were not directly relevant to the problems of living. His description of Nietzsche's experimentalism here could easily be used to characterize pragmatism:

Experimenting involves testing an answer by trying to live according to it. . . . [And yet] the decision to live according to [the] answers is . . . not an afterthought. The problem itself is experienced deeply, and only problems that are experienced so deeply are given consideration. Only problems that present themselves so forcefully that they threaten the thinker's present mode of life lead to philosophic inquiries.

Both James and Nietzsche stressed this criterion of urgency; the philosopher's inquiry is valuable only insofar as its answers have concrete consequences for living.[79]

In an effort to parse out how Nietzsche reconciled the painful experiences that such an experimental life could yield, Kaufmann turned once again to James. He argued that in posing philosophical inquiry as an experiment, both James and Nietzsche sought answers that would enable the individual to come into an authentic relationship with the universe. In Kaufmann's opinion, both viewed joy and pain as necessarily intertwined. He quoted at length a passage from "The Dilemma of Determinism" in order to express James's longing to escape the halcyon utopias of modern man's moral imagination. In it, James noted the "strange paradox" of modern man's yearning for happiness unburdened by pain:

> Everybody must at some time have wondered at the strange paradox of our moral nature, that, although the pursuit of outward good is the breath of its nostrils, the attainment of outward good would seem to be its suffocation and death. Why does the painting of any paradise or utopia, in heaven or on earth, awaken such yearnings for . . . escape? . . . To our crepuscular natures, born for the conflict, the Rembrandtesque Chiaroscuro, the shifting struggle of the sunbeam in the gloom, such pictures of light upon light are vacuous and expressionless, neither to be enjoyed nor understood. If *this* be the whole fruit of the victory, we say . . . better lose than win the battle, or at all events better ring down the curtain before the last act of the play, so that a business that began so importantly may be saved from so singularly flat a winding up.[80]

According to Kaufmann, James's "insipid creatures" suffocated by the bland mediocrity of their longing for easy comforts are reminiscent of Nietzsche's "last man." Quoting *Zarathustra*, he noted, "One herd: each wants the same, each is the same—and whoever feels different goes voluntarily into an asylum."[81] Kaufmann thus used James to make Nietzsche's point: coming into an authentic relationship with the universe does not mean arriving at a pure state of pleasure absent of suffering. For Kaufmann's Nietzsche, pleasure and pain are equally part of the chiaroscuro of living; both are crucial components for the power of self-mastery.

While Kaufmann highlighted significant similarities between Nietzsche and James, he argued that Nietzsche's experimentalism was a better means than James's pragmatism for achieving the vibrant chiaroscuro that both thinkers so desperately sought. He characterized James's pragmatism as a form of utilitarianism that regards a belief as true if it is useful for the person who holds that belief. In his reading of James's "right to believe," an idea is true if it helps us to make our way in the world.[82] Kaufmann asserted that Nietzsche would have rejected (what Kaufmann once again identified as) the subtle a prioris inherent in James's thinking. Measuring beliefs in terms of their utility requires that from the outset, we have a presumption of what is useful. If beliefs are deemed true if they meet our needs, then from where do those needs arise in the first place? For Nietzsche, truth can be indifferent to our needs; he argued repeatedly that we should not presume that the world was made for us. For this reason, Kaufmann argued, Nietzsche would have stridently rejected the presumption "that what is useful . . . must be true." For Nietzsche, even a belief that is necessary for life may be false: just because one cannot bear the idea that God does not exist does not give God the right to exist.[83] Kaufmann, likewise, contended that Nietzsche differed from the pragmatists, for even though he too held that "the intellect is an instrument, its figments should be frankly labeled as fictions." Indeed for Nietzsche, "'appearance, error, deception, dissimulation, delusion, self-delusion' all aid life; life 'has always shown itself to be on the side of the most unscrupulous *polytropoi*.'"[84] In this regard, Kaufmann deemed Nietzsche a truer pluralist than James, for he widened the field for experience.

In Kaufmann's estimation, an even more significant reason for Nietzsche's rejection of utilitarianism was his fundamental assertion that the will to power, not the will to life, was the prime motor of human experience. Thus, Kaufmann argued that Nietzsche would have rejected James's pragmatism on the same grounds that he rejected Darwinism. For Nietzsche, neither comfort in the world, nor sheer survival, were the endgames. Both versions of adapting to the environment—whether passively, in a Darwinian sense, or actively, in a Jamesian sense—were equally flawed, for both required that man remain a supplicant to the whims of a dynamic universe indifferent to his existence. Nietzsche maintained that creating meaning should never be a collaborative project. In a world without any universal confirmation of human values, the higher man alone must become his own legislator of values. According to Kaufmann's Nietzsche, sickness and health, pain and joy, truth and fiction are the raw materials for the higher man to harness in his quest for self-mastery. Power, not survival, is the measure of man. And true power is the ability to employ, not just overcome, pain. Kaufmann concluded that "Nietzsche scorns any utilitarian or pragmatic approach to truth," insisting that "truth may spell discomfort and suffering—but renouncing truth for that reason would be a sign of weakness." According to Kaufmann, Nietzsche argued that the sovereign individual seeks truth precisely because it is not salutary to life. As Nietzsche put it, "The strength of a spirit might be measured according to how much of the 'truth' he would be able to stand." His *Amor Fati*, then, is no passive acceptance of fate; it is the power to create a life that one would willingly accept again and again. As Kaufmann put it, "Man wants power more than life."[85]

In using Jamesian pragmatism to understand Nietzschean experimentalism, Kaufmann employed a long-standing American strategy for analyzing Nietzsche's philosophy. By comparing him to the pragmatists, Kaufmann rendered Nietzsche's moral claims and the theory of knowledge on which they were based in terms familiar to American audiences. Though he did not seek too tight a fit, he suggested that Nietzsche's formulations "antedate" and "prove his historical priority" to whatever is of value in the pragmatists' theory of knowledge or their insights into human psychology.[86] His analysis thereby addressed a leitmotif in Nietzsche's American reception. To the question of why turn to Nietzsche's experimentalism, when in the pragmatists we have our own, Kaufmann answered: Nietzsche came first, and Nietzsche was a subtler thinker.

But for Kaufmann there was an even more important point. Seeing the full range of the substance and style of Nietzsche's philosophy helps cast the particularity of his vision of power in bold relief. In Kaufmann's telling, all of Nietzsche's experiments track back to a vision of true power only achievable through individual autonomy. Nietzschean power, he argued, had nothing to do with brute force or with power over others. The truly powerful individual rejects all forms of political, religious, and ideological affiliation; he refuses to borrow meaning from *or* to legislate values for others. Power is the standard of one's values, and these standards can never be confirmed by others. The truly powerful individual does not seek to hurt others; he is indifferent to them. "Only the weak need to convince themselves and others of their might by inflicting hurt: the truly powerful are not concerned with others but act out of a fullness and an overflow." This fullness, Kaufmann argued, is achieved not by overcoming others but rather by the "will to overcome *one-self*." He asserted that true power in the Nietzschean sense is the willingness and ability to harness the chaos within the self, to perfect the self according to laws of its own making, to refuse nature a free hand by disciplining one's impulses in such a way as to—as Nietzsche put it—"give 'style' to [one's] character." "Instead of relying on heavenly powers to redeem him, to give meaning to his life, and to justify the world," the self-sovereign individual "gives meaning to his own life by achieving [a] perfection" authored and realized by him alone.[87]

## Counter-Dionysian Enlightenments

Kaufmann's *Nietzsche* was a big book, a testament to its author's even bigger aspirations to get Nietzsche heard in America. Like Nietzsche, Kaufmann believed that readers can ultimately hear only that which they have ears for. But given his own ear, sensitive to the nuances of English and German, keenly attuned to the subtle differences and similarities in the worlds of thought embedded in them, Kaufmann's Nietzsche helped American readers at midcentury to hear their own concerns and to think about their own thinking. He presented them with a Nietzsche of unmistakable unity and clarity, unimpressed with physical manifestations of power, scornful of ideologies—a thinker who was not just rational but reasonable. His Nietzsche forced them to think about the ways moderns had made themselves sick by scrounging for nourishment in the decomposing idols of thought and belief. And he embodied the quest to break free of narrow commitments and find universals once again. But this time, he would do so not under the sheltering sky of religion or atop firm empirical grounds but in the trustworthy foundations of the authentically thinking, problem-solving self. Kaufmann's great achievement was that in his reconstituted Nietzsche, he constituted a thinker whom a variety of midcentury readers—sociologists, literary critics, philosophers, theologians, and political revolutionaries—could put to work in their own fashion. He created a Nietzsche who cut into, and in turn reshaped, American cold war culture. The many curious Counter-Enlightenments of Kaufmann's Dionysian Enlightenment exemplify what Nietzsche's own *Zarathustra* had shown: a book for all and none makes for interesting history.

One of Kaufmann's achievements lay in the ways in which he rendered a Nietzsche who could speak in so many of the different cultural registers of the day. His portrait of an independent thinker averse to *Massenmenschen* and ideological orthodoxies could be easily put to work alongside the varieties of 1950s sociological, political, and literary criticism. His *Nietzsche* appeared the same year as David Riesman's *The Lonely Crowd*, the classic sociological critique of the emergence of the "other-directed" American personality type, and echoed similar concerns about the modern man who seeks approval rather than autonomy.[88] Similarly, Kaufmann's Nietzsche harmonized with the Nietzsche of the emergent anticommunist Right, who shared concerns about the danger of modern man's conformism. No better do we see this than in the conservative critic and poet Peter Viereck's *The Unadjusted Man* (1956), which argued that "Nietzsche will always remain relevant as the first great writer to proclaim unadjustedness as the form heroism takes in a mechanized mass-society." Viereck used a very Kaufmann-esque Nietzsche to diagnose the characterological deficits of midcentury Americans, to exhort them to "preserve the inner life" and to appreciate that liberty is fundamentally achieved as an "inner psychological liberty."[89] This Nietzsche—the cultural physician of the inner life—who understands the importance of the human *cultural* grounds of freedom, moved easily from the anti-Stalinist Right to the anti-Stalinist Left, and informed the criticism of Lionel Trilling. In 1950, Trilling presented a Nietzsche who helped him articulate his own exhaustion with collectivist ideologies and his cautious rapprochement with American culture, and identified the "liberal imagination"—what Nietzsche helped him to see as "life's continuous evaluation of itself"—as the only preserve of genuine freedom. Like Kaufmann, he sought to distinguish this "Nietzsche [as] the *real* one, not the lay figure of cultural propaganda."[90]

Kaufmann's *Nietzsche* helped cultivate a growing interest in European existentialism in America, and established him in his next role as a major midwife of this new style of thought.[91] Six years later, in *Existentialism from Dostoyevsky to Sartre* (1956), he drew on the features of thought he had introduced in *Nietzsche*—man's examination of the conditions of his own existence, his alternating feelings of psychic thrownness and givenness in an anonymous and indifferent universe, and the dissatisfaction with academic philosophical

systems in their unwillingness to pose these kinds of questions. In it, he provided many English-speaking readers with their first exposure to European
thinkers, including Heidegger, Sartre, Camus, and Jaspers, many of whom, up
until that time, had not been translated into English. Kaufmann's treatment
of existentialism and his claims for Nietzsche's role in it had huge popular appeal. As George Cotkin has observed, "Hardly a college student in the 1960s
could be found without a dog-eared copy of Walter Kaufmann's [*Existentialism*]."[92] In his anthology, Kaufmann sought to present Nietzsche as a crucial
forerunner of existentialism while insisting that he was too rich a thinker to
be understood only in this vein. Likewise, he sought to show that the most
salient features of existentialism were not the more prominent postwar ones,
which lingered on morbid thoughts of dread and death, but the ones apparent
in Nietzsche's more universal and timeless "perfervid individualism."[93] But it
wouldn't be long before Kaufmann would realize how difficult it was to make
Nietzsche a forerunner of existentialism but not an existentialist, a timely
thinker who must remain untimely.[94]

At base, this was a fundamental tension within Kaufmann's text that he
was unable to fully resolve. He clearly hoped his Nietzsche would be palatable
to American readers, but not as a literary cocktail to cap off the evening. But
that is precisely what began to happen after the book's publication in 1950.
Kaufmann may not have recognized how easily his own Nietzsche paved the
way for the one who would emerge in the imaginations of middle-class teen-
agers itching to break free from their parents' suburban cocoons, and would
confirm the quiet desperation of their organization-men fathers, pressed into
a smooth mediocrity at the firm and bored by the tame rhythms of bourgeois
marriage. But Hugh Hefner surely helped him see the connection. In his
editorial for the first issue of *Playboy* magazine in December of 1953, which—
with a beautiful, buxom Marilyn Monroe on the cover—flew off the shelves
and sold almost 54,000 copies, Hefner suggested how men in a period of
cultural conservativism and conformity could put the new Nietzsche to work
for a little transgressive fun:

> If you're a man between the ages of 18 and 80, PLAYBOY is meant for you.
> If you like your entertainment served up with humor, sophistication and
> spice, PLAYBOY will become a very special favorite . . . a pleasure-primer
> styled to the masculine taste. . . . We like our apartment. We enjoy mixing
> up cocktails and an *hors d'oeuvre* or two, putting a little mood music on the

phonograph and inviting in a female acquaintance for a quiet discussion on Picasso, Nietzsche, jazz, sex.[95]

Kaufmann had tried to present a Nietzsche, like Zarathustra, for everyone and no one: accessible, but not ready-made; coherent, but not convenient. But the quick success of his *Nietzsche* might have suggested to him how difficult that would be. He wanted Nietzsche to be a problem thinker, but the problem of how bored white-collar men could spice up their sex lives was likely not what he had in mind.

Another discourse that Kaufmann's *Nietzsche* both prepared American readers for and found itself in dialogue with over the course of the 1950s and '60s was the small but highly visible "Death of God" movement in American theology. Kaufmann later took some credit for the "paradoxical attempt to base a new theology" on his chapter in *Nietzsche* addressing "The Death of God" and his later Nietzsche translations dealing with relevant themes, but he "took no pride" in his "progeny."[96] His treatment of the death of God emphasized that it was to be understood as "an attempt at a diagnosis of contemporary civilization, not a metaphysical speculation about ultimate reality." He was insistent on this point. Nietzsche's claim about the death of God was not a way of sneaking another metaphysics through the back door: "It demands no more than that we agree not to invoke God to cut short discussion." Nietzsche was a disciple of truth, understanding the moral obligation to go it alone without any metaphysical accounting of the universe. However, Kaufmann's Nietzsche recognized that this was no unqualified liberation but rather, for many, would lead to nihilism. Kaufmann argued that Nietzsche's explorations of the death of God represent his "greatest and most persistent problem," namely "whether universally valid values and a meaningful life are at all possible in a godless world."[97]

Within a decade of its initial publication, the "greatest and most persistent problem" of Kaufmann's *Nietzsche* became the focal point and rallying cry of a small but visible group of American religious thinkers, who came to be known as "Death of God" theologians. Drawing on the religious existentialism of Paul Tillich, the ethics of Dietrich Bonhoeffer, and even the Neo-Orthodoxy of Karl Barth, these liberal theologians sought to examine whether Christian views of the universe were still tenable after the horrors of World War II. Though they came from different Protestant denominations and applied different kinds of analyses, collectively they faced the awful prospect that the notion of God as all-loving, all-powerful, all-knowing could not be reconciled with the monumental suffering of the death camps, or the atomic hell unleashed on the people of Hiroshima and Nagasaki. The varieties of radical theology moved between claims that God outside human history has never existed to arguments that the traditional languages for describing God need a dramatic overhaul so that they can be more meaningful to modern minds. Though George Burman Foster had anticipated many of the major themes of death of God theology already in 1906 with his *Finality of the Christian Religion*, the terrors of the recent past gave the notion of the death of God a more widespread sense of its efficacy and urgency. But it also led to a forgetting that these were the very Nietzschean issues taken up by radical American Protestant theology over a half century earlier.[98]

Nietzsche's presence in this 1960s discourse is most apparent in the work of Thomas J. J. Altizer, professor of Bible and religion at Emory University and the leading light of death of God theology. Altizer's "Gospel of Christian Atheism" was no cheeky appeal to antireligionists, but a deeply theological argument about how the death of God is fundamental to the Christian message. Altizer turned to Nietzsche to understand how the birth of Christianity was instantiated in Christ's death. It was the self-sacrifice of the living God for his people. The death of God was no divine abandonment of his creation, Altizer contended, but the ultimate redemptive act on its behalf. Nietzsche's claims helped modern Christians understand how God works in the world, how Christianity "entered time and history" and became a "'world-affirming' religion"—how death became life.[99] "It is precisely the acceptance of Nietzsche's proclamation of the death of God that is the real test of a contemporary form of faith," Altizer argued.[100]

If these liberal theologians understood the death of God as an event in human history, their overnight notoriety in 1966 showed how it was also a media event in American popular culture. For it was the April 8, 1966, cover of *Time* magazine, which boldly asked, "Is God Dead?" that catapulted death of God theology into the limelight. Never before in *Time*'s forty-three-year history had the editors run a cover without an illustration or photograph. However, in their search for a work of art "suggesting a contemporary idea of God," they came up empty-handed.[101] It turned out that the three words—"Is God Dead?" in bright red letters set against a stark black background—said it all. The issue, which sympathetically portrayed the theologians' ideas, had the highest newsstand sales in more than twenty years, and brought in the largest

"Is God Dead?" Cover of *Time*, April 8, 1966.

crop of letters to the editor in the magazine's history. The article admitted how curious such a question might seem in a culture where institutional churches were strong, and polls showed that 97 percent of the population professed a belief in God. But it also raised the question whether America's pews might really just be "filled on Sunday with practical atheists—disguised nonbelievers who behave during the rest of the week as if God did not exist."[102]

Just a little over a month later, *Time*'s publisher announced that "FEW TIME stories have created so much stir and comment," noting how the issue already had become a prop in Sunday sermons and ignited a firestorm of debate in newspaper columns, radio and television programs, and religious and lay periodicals nationwide. The editor insisted that any pious outrage could only have come from those who had not gotten past the cover, for "TIME's positive view of God permeated the story."[103] The article was a search, as the title noted, for the "hidden God" in a fallen world, not a claim for God's absence. But this spoke directly to Kaufmann's complaint with the theology itself. Just as the radical theologians had done, the *Time* article answered its probing of Christianity with eschatological affirmations. This outcome explains why Kaufmann later disparaged death of God theology as a "predictably stillborn" project, and questioned the uses of Nietzsche for Christian apologetics—but he understood his role in opening the discursive space, which helped to make the movement possible.[104]

One important strain of the death of God theology not mentioned by *Time* in 1966 was its relevance for Jewish self-understanding after the Holocaust. In that same year, the rabbi and theologian Richard Rubenstein offered his wrenching Nietzschean confession of Jewish faith in his *After Auschwitz* (1966). Though his exploration is shot through with references to Nietzsche, Rubenstein adopted the moniker "death of God theology" much more reluctantly than his Christian counterparts. Like Kaufmann, he would vigorously seek to demonstrate that Nietzsche was no anti-Semite, insisting that Nietzsche's significance for modern Jews was not that he caused their plight, but that he helped them understand it. Neither Kaufmann nor Rubenstein was effective, though, in shutting off this concern, which would continue to accompany all American Nietzsche interpretation moving forward.

According to Rubenstein, however, Nietzsche's crucial insight for modern Jews was that he helped them to see something latent in their own faith and history: the Jew as eternal wanderer. Rubenstein not only argued that Auschwitz simply laid bare the terrible vision Nietzsche presented of a world adrift, of a people cut loose from the anchors of faith and scripture as hallmarks of modernity, but also asserted that this was part of the Jews' diasporic experience, deep in their own history. Furthermore, unlike Christians, Jews had been *theological* wanderers all along: their messiah never came. In this regard, the Christian theologians were the latecomers to what Jews had known throughout their history. Thus, for Rubenstein, the Jew as spiritual and psychic wanderer, ever adrift, was an image deeply part of their ever-present, ever-tenuous existence in the world. But in this regard, Rubenstein argued,

Jews had continued relevance for the modern world in their role as witnesses to history, and in their representative function of modern exile: "Life is exile. . . . The Jewish situation, like so many Jewish gestures, exaggerates what is common to all men."[105] Indeed, the ineluctable power of this Nietzschean image of Jewish nomadism cut across religious and secular divides and helps explain what Daniel Bell recognized as Nietzsche's resonance for secular Jewish intellectuals. It is what Bell, in the shattered world of 1946 described in his moving *Jewish Frontier* essay, "A Parable of Alienation," which led off with a Nietzsche epigraph: "Woe to him who has no home." For Bell, Nietzsche helped illustrate the plight of the wandering Jew as a metaphor for the necessary alienation of the modern Jewish intellectual: "The deepest impulses urge us home. But where are we to go?" For Bell as for Rubenstein, Jews could no longer take refuge in ideology, in tradition, or even in Zionism. Nietzsche had shown them that latent in their Judaism, even after the death of God, one remains a Jew, and that radical homelessness was that givenness of being a Jew. Now, after the Holocaust, Bell affirmed, the Jew can only keep on living as he had always had to live: "in permanent tension and as a permanent critic."[106]

The effectiveness of Kaufmann's effort to bring Nietzsche to American audiences can be seen in the sheer range of the counter-Enlightenments it ushered in. No better do we see this than in the journey of Kaufmann's Nietzsche from an anti-ideological, apolitical thinker to a revolutionary for social justice. Throughout the 1960s and into the early 1970s, Kaufmann's book remained the authoritative text on the German philosopher, popularizing Nietzsche among a new generation of readers disenchanted with US military intervention in Vietnam, aggrieved by the inauthenticities of bourgeois culture, and frustrated that even after the accomplishments of the civil rights movement, the fight for racial equality was far from over.[107] Kaufmann's Nietzsche toppled illusions while creating new ideals worthy of human imagination; he promised readers a way to balance their dismay over the poverty of human institutions with their belief in the promise of humanity. It is this emphasis on individual authenticity and a commitment to the *true* truth—and not the official morality—of bankrupt institutions that made its way from student unions to the streets, from marches and be-ins into jail cells. Kaufmann provided an opening in American culture for a new generation of readers to enlist Nietzsche to work out the meaning of their own existences while fighting to dignify those of others.

Frustrated with what they regarded as the slow and uneven progress of the nonviolent civil rights movement, Huey P. Newton and Bobby Seale drafted their Black Panther Party platform and program in 1966, and with it a new vision of how Nietzsche could become a source of power for black self-determination and liberation. In his autobiography, *Revolutionary Suicide* (1973), Newton cited Nietzsche's writings on power, Christian morality, and a de-divinized humanity as exerting "a great impact on the development of the Black Panther philosophy." Nietzsche's ideas were instrumental, Newton argued, in "raising consciousness" among African Americans about themselves and their America. "When I read [Kaufmann's translation of] Nietzsche's *The Will to Power*, I learned much from a number of his philosophical insights. This is not to say that I endorse all of Nietzsche, only that many of his ideas have influenced my thinking."[108] Reminding his reader that the Black Panther ideology was as much a philosophy as it was a political and economic program, and that it was as committed to changing people's minds as it was their material conditions, Newton enlisted Nietzsche to consider the soft power of ideas in the fight for racial justice.

The ways in which he did that reveal how Kaufmann's Nietzsche helped Newton see a philosopher who could challenge the morality of modern America, the lingering mindset of Jim Crow, and Christian other-worldliness as sources of black oppression. He offered a Nietzsche who encouraged a self who could listen to its inner voice and not mistake the white man's voice for his own conscience. Nietzsche could teach African Americans to no longer be supplicants to "vacated mythologies" about an open society or black racial inferiority.[109] Thus, for example, Newton transfigured *Thus Spoke Zarathustra* to animate his vision of an America after the death of the "white man's . . . God." He stressed that the slogan "All Power to the People" was more than something catchy to shout at marches or to inscribe on Black Panther Party memos. Instead, it expressed quite explicitly a "metaphysical" claim about "man as God," animating the Panthers' vision for the movement.[110]

Newton's "metaphysics" are shot through with Nietzsche's ideas about the promise of a redeemed humanity in a de-divinized America. In Newton's re-telling of the genealogy of the slave morality, the dispossessed may have been filled with *ressentiment*, but they marshaled that ill-will effectively by describing themselves and their oppressors anew. He argued that this could teach Black Panthers to understand how words had no fixed meaning that tracked an Absolute reality, but rather were simply historical calcifications of the human will to power. Using Nietzsche, Newton could examine how and why certain terms entered American English—such as *black* to describe African Americans—in order to constrain meaning and subjugate a people. But he also showed how, in their variability, they could be co-opted and reinscribed as an affirmation. He demonstrated how finding a new word, *pig*, to describe an old enemy—a cop—enabled African Americans to reevaluate the value of those who sought to strip them of theirs. Likewise, he followed Nietzsche's critique of Christian asceticism and other-worldliness as he explained its degrading effect on African Americans from the time of slavery to the present. Echoing Zarathustra's plea to forget the fantasies of redemption in a great hereafter and *"remain faithful to the earth,"* Newton sought "to convince Black people that their rewards were due in the present, that it was in their power to create a Promised Land *here and now.*" He believed with Nietzsche that the idea of "God" was a damaging historical fiction which reduced man's sense of power and self-worth: "The more he attributes to God, the more inferior he becomes," Newton concluded.[111] Nietzsche thus helped him topple illusions and find the "truth" African Americans could speak to white power.

And yet, here Newton's "metaphysics" moves with, then pivots against, Kaufmann's antimetaphysical Nietzsche. In Newton's version of the slave morality, Nietzsche had shown how "in the beginning the Christians were weak, but they understood how to make the philosophy of a weak group work for them." Then, just as "Nietzsche pointed out that [moral redescription] had been used to good effect by the Christian against the Romans," Newton argued, so too might African Americans' redescription of the police by calling them "pigs," for example, force their oppressors to see themselves from the perspective of their "victims," who experience them as "brutal" and "grotesque." He thus offered Nietzsche's genealogy as a narrative of triumph and a blueprint for African-American victory in the fight against oppression. In addition, Newton's Nietzsche argued that man should strive to make man his God, rather than prostrate himself to a fictive one. However, for Kaufmann that meant striving for the Übermensch—an as-yet unrealized higher humanity, while for Newton that meant striving for the God in one another. "If you believe that man is the ultimate being, then you will act according to your belief," argued Newton. "Your attitude and behavior toward man is a kind of religion in itself, with high standards of responsibility."[112] His reformulation of Nietzsche, then, stressed the *social responsibility* that comes with endowing one's self and one's fellowmen with reverence and awe. What he refers to as the "metaphysical sense" of "power to the people," was deeply, unmistakably *social*. If Newton's God was dead, all the better, then, for realizing the *truth* of human obligation.

For Kaufmann as for Newton, Nietzsche's philosophy was one crucial resource for digging out from under false universals, if only to excavate more deeply the foundations of the thinking self. Doing so, of course, was not easy. Certainly not for Newton, who recognized that it demanded "revolutionary suicide," of himself and all his fellow freedom fighters, so many of whom had been taken down in the struggle for racial justice. Indeed, Newton invoked Nietzsche's "arrow of longing for another shore" as an image of the perilous aim to shoot over the abyss of racism to achieve not mere justice but something more sublime: a redemption self-achieved. But as Newton reminds us, only that which is worth dying for is also worth living for: the great authority of moral and intellectual self-sovereignty.[113]

Kaufmann may not have recognized his apolitical Nietzsche turned political revolutionary, his criticisms of slave morality transfigured into an endorsement of it, or his explanations about the death of God transformed into the basis of a new social ethics. And yet like Kaufmann, Newton's analysis of the variability of truth is not an endorsement of a thoroughgoing relativism or nihilism. Neither Newton nor Kaufmann saw in Nietzsche a philosopher who endorsed a view that any truth goes. Their reading of Nietzschean perspectivalism sought to view the world perspectivally, to get the perspective on human values *right*. What we see in Newton's and in Kaufmann's Nietzsche is the commitment to a particular perspective *knowing*. For Kaufmann, as for Newton, truth may not be absolute, but the moral center holds.

## Kaufmann's Nietzsche for All and None

In his effort to reformulate Nietzsche's will to power as the strength for self-sovereignty, Kaufmann argued that it was not the basis of a political program. He insisted that "Nietzsche begs his readers to keep in mind that he does not write to endorse a course of action. His [philosophy] wants to stimulate *thought*, 'nothing else'... it is meant for people 'to whom thinking is a *delight*, nothing else.'" Kaufmann's Nietzsche embodied the philosopher of the *vita contemplativa*, for whom contemplation was itself a vital, life-affirming activity. He used aphorisms to experiment with or "live through" propositions for living, but the life he envisioned was the life of the self-creating individual.

Though Nietzsche used muscular language, though he worshipped Dionysus, though he exalted power, he did so, Kaufmann tells us, as an invitation to
"self-realization." Nietzsche talked hard talk, not because he approved of the
vitalist's hardness against others so much as the "hardness of the creator who
creates himself."[114] Throughout his study, Kaufmann repeatedly emphasized
that Nietzschean power, properly understood, is the ability to go it alone.

As an exegesis of Nietzsche's philosophy, Kaufmann's interpretation
certainly has its limitations. His image of Nietzsche as a Goethean figure
struggling for authentic selfhood fails to capture the philosopher's repeated
emphasis on the warring instincts in, not the unified mastery of, the self. In
addition, by severing his work from the question of influence, Kaufmann's
study presents a picture of Nietzsche as timeless, hence impervious to histo-
ricization. And by casting Nietzsche as an apolitical thinker indifferent to the
manifestations of will to power outside the self, Kaufmann's interpretation
makes the untenable claim that an individual's power has no consequences
for others. Kaufmann admirably rejected dualism as a failure of imagination
in an antifoundational world, and yet his retreat into monism is equally problematic. However, while Kaufmann's *Nietzsche* may have its flaws, it is crucial
for understanding why, when it first appeared in 1950 and was reprinted three
times during the volatile 1960s, American readers welcomed his autonomous,
self-reliant, enlightened Dionysus as a "revelation."

Throughout the postwar period, Kaufmann's Nietzsche proved to be an
indispensable seer, critic, and educator. Beginning with *Nietzsche* in 1950 and
for the following three decades, Kaufmann continued to cultivate an audience
for Nietzsche's philosophy among English-speaking readers with a steady
output of Nietzsche translations, intellectual histories, surveys of contemporary philosophy, and studies on religion, tragedy, and literature, of which
Nietzsche's intellectual self-sovereignty served as the continual leitmotif. The
existential tenors in Kaufmann's interpretation are indeed pronounced. Yet to
detect only those dimensions in his *Nietzsche* is to miss the real innovation as
well as the historical significance of his work. Rather than narrow Nietzsche's
range to place him within the province of existentialism, Kaufmann consistently drew out his ecumenicalism. By reinforcing Nietzsche's philosophical
balancing act between his Dionysian "fullness of overflow" of his intellectual
and moral resources and his "Enlightened" self-restraint and self-sovereignty,
Kaufmann insisted that Nietzsche's writings not only contributed to but improved the best features of Western moral philosophy.

Later in his life, when reflecting on the role of the philosopher, it was not Emerson whom Kaufmann invoked but Nietzsche, when he insisted that the best a philosopher can do in a world after God is to work by provocation. In Kaufmann's estimation, because "no one way is the best way of life for all," the philosopher's "noblest duty is to lead others to think for themselves."[115] The goal of philosophy, he argued, is not agreement but "diversity," not answers but critical conversation. Shortly thereafter, a young analytic philosopher by the name of Richard Rorty would join the ranks of the Princeton philosophy faculty, and there he would take up Kaufmann's Nietzschean quest for conversation. But as the "death of God" of the 1960s gave way to the "death of the author" movement of the 1970s and '80s, Rorty found himself engaged with Nietzschean interlocutors very different from Kaufmann—French theorists like Jacques Derrida—who had grave doubts about even the possibilities for conversation. Rorty too would come to argue that conversation—and contributing to the proliferation of languages with which to conduct it— was philosophy's signal contribution. And though neither he nor the deconstructionist and poststructuralist Nietzsches with whom he conversed prized agreement or even thought it possible, they could agree on one thing: the days of the "unmistakable," "unequivocal," enlightened Dionysian Nietzsche were over. And so too the possibilities of a Nietzschean center that holds.

# Antifoundationalism on Native Grounds

What, then, is truth? A mobile army of metaphors, metonyms, and anthropomorphisms—in short, a sum of human relations, which have been enhanced, transposed, and embellished poetically and rhetorically, and which after long use seem firm, canonical, and obligatory to a people: truths are illusions about which one has forgotten that this is what they are; metaphors which are worn out and without sensuous power; coins which have lost their pictures and now matter only as metal, no longer as coins.

    FRIEDRICH NIETZSCHE, "On Truth and Lie in an Extra-Moral Sense" (1873)

You shall learn to grasp the sense of perspective in every value judgment—the displacement, distortion and merely apparent teleology of horizons and whatever else pertains to perspectivism ... and the whole intellectual loss which every For, every Against costs us. You shall learn to grasp the *necessary* injustice in every For and Against, injustice as inseparable from life, life itself as *conditioned* by the sense of perspective and its injustice.

    FRIEDRICH NIETZSCHE, *Human, All Too Human* (1878)

There is no "being" behind doing, effecting, becoming; "the doer" is merely a fiction added to the deed—the deed is everything.

    FRIEDRICH NIETZSCHE, *On the Genealogy of Morals* (1887)

Jacques Derrida rarely found himself speechless, and certainly not on occasions for which he was commissioned to speak. But after accepting an invitation to the University of Virginia in 1976 to give a series of lectures on the US Declaration of Independence and the French Declaration of the Rights of Man and of the Citizen in honor of the Bicentennial of the American founding, Derrida surprised his audience with an apology: "I beg your pardon, but it will be impossible for me to speak to you this afternoon ... about what I was engaged to deal with." He admitted that he found the prospect of subjecting the Declaration of Independence to a "'textual' analysis" "intimidating." But before he abandoned his commissioned experiment, he briefly gave it a try, and in terms that would be increasingly familiar to the ever-increasing American audience for his deconstructive criticism. He questioned the source of authority and the representational function of the signatures on the declaration, arguing that independence—indeed the very subject of the "we" announcing its independence—did not exist prior to, but rather was instantiated in, the act of signing. Founding documents such as the Declaration of Independence do not report an autonomy or independence already present, but instead perform autonomy and independence in the very act of announcing them. Though Derrida asserted that the "signature invents the signer" and the speech act of "we" creates its own subjectivity, he remained frustrated by the question of origins: "How is a State made or founded, how does a State make or found itself?" What, in other words, are the foundations of foundings?[1]

By figuratively tapping his tuning fork on the founding document of the American nation, Derrida gestured the ways in which deconstruction could be an experiment not only with rhetorical and literary value but also with political implications: "Do I dare, here, in Charlottesville, recall the *incipit* of your Declaration?" He then abruptly abandoned the experiment. "Nothing," he confessed, "had prepared me for it." In fact, he did have preparation, though not *for* such an interpretive task so much as *against* it. After all, for decades Derrida had been steeped in an author whom he understood to have warned against the hunt for origins, and mistaking findings for foundings. So instead of keeping his promise, he informed his audience that he would "mak[e] it easier on myself, falling back on subjects which are closer . . . to me."[2] Indeed, he fell back on the very author who counseled against the very commemorative exercise he had agreed to undertake. Derrida did not lecture on the Declaration of Independence. He lectured instead on Friedrich Nietzsche.

Did Derrida's American hosts think his lectures on Nietzsche were a colossal bait-and-switch tactic? Did they think he was being impertinent to suggest that they listen to his lecture "with one or the other sort of ear ([as] everything comes down to the ear you are able to hear me with)"?[3] No, for he gave them what they wanted, or at least, certainly what they had come to expect. In Charlottesville he delivered deconstruction at work. For Derrida, following Nietzsche, the hunt for origins had come to an end, because origins are simply that which we ourselves create, and then impute meaning after the fact. We *found* foundings, we do not find them. Likewise, when we read Nietzsche, as Derrida would do in his analysis of *Ecce Homo*, we can no longer expect to locate the author, or his intended meanings, in the text. When we do, we enlist a rough-and-ready proper name, "Nietzsche," to do the work for us. By drawing from Nietzsche's ideas about language, extending the implications of his "death of God" to the "death of the author," and showing the utter instability in the simplest acts of reading, Derrida offered a new textualist Nietzsche, who left "traces" of dissimulation in his wake.[4] The readings of Nietzsche's texts, like the readings of the Declaration of Independence, Derrida argued, are never static. But as "there is nothing outside of the text," as he put it in *Of Grammatology* (1967), there is no escaping the endless movement, vitality, and terror of meaning-making when all the world's a text, and yet its Author is dead.[5]

Derrida may have broken his promise to his Charlottesville hosts to lecture on the Declaration of Independence, but in his reasons for doing so he in fact participated in what, by 1976, was a long-standing practice in American intellectual life: he thought about America by thinking with Nietzsche. Indeed, he thought about American independence from Europe by using a European thinker to do so. And yet the methods by which he did this seemed radically new and unfamiliar. And that was what made them so ineluctably fascinating—they comprised a wholly novel way of thinking about truth and meaning, and with it a new way of thinking about America. American observers were increasingly coming to know this new style of thought as *postmodernism*, a general term to encapsulate new interpretive modes from France, specifically deconstruction and poststructuralism.[6] The drama of its ideas, the celebrity of its spokespeople, gave allure to the notion that French postmodernism brought Nietzschean antifoundationalism to the United States, and with it a host of intellectual and moral problems the country did not have before. What got lost in much of the thrill and horror of the "new French" Nietzsche was that the language and methodologies were new, but the reckoning with antifoundationalism was not. Although Nietzschean-inspired French philosophy and literary criticism played a significant role in cultivating new academic and popular audiences for the German philosopher, they comprised an important, but not the only, source of American engagements with Nietzschean antifoundationalism. Indeed, even the engagements with

French theory—by using it to think about American thinking in relation to Continental thought—demonstrate the ways in which Americans had long come to terms with antifoundationalism on their native grounds.

———

Walter Kaufmann may have reopened the floodgates of Nietzsche interpretation in postwar America, but he did not control its subsequent canals, streams, and eddies. One of those channels became known as the "French Nietzsche," the "New Nietzsche," and the "New French Nietzsche," though all these names broadly refer to the academic surge of interest in postmodernism that began in languages and literature departments in the 1970s, and moved into various cultural studies programs and departments during the 1980s.[7] This Nietzsche believed that tearing at universal truth did not stop until one tore up the foundations of the knowing self. He was not a moralist who believed in individual autonomy but rather a linguist, a genealogist who examined the linguistic, social, and political structures that construct and restrict it. And he was the intellectual force behind what Jean-François Lyotard described as the "postmodern condition": an "incredulity toward metanarratives" in history, morals, and the self.[8] Though many French theorists exerted a powerful influence on postmodern American thought, it was primarily the force of the writings and the personas of Jacques Derrida and his former mentor, Michel Foucault, that had the greatest impact, and gave luster to the notion of the French First Cause of the American postmodern reading of Nietzsche.[9]

It was during this period that a flood of scholarship produced by "French Nietzscheans" poured into the US academy.[10] First came a number of high-profile gatherings, including the two-day conference on structuralism, "Languages of Criticism and the Sciences of Man," at the Johns Hopkins University in October 1966, where the most anticipated scholars were the philosophers, linguistic theorists, and psychoanalysts from France. There in Baltimore they broke into a critical landscape—as Edward Said would later describe it—"of quite amazing intellectual and theoretical poverty."[11] They brought with them their common admiration for Nietzsche, who, according to the conference organizers, had "now come to occupy the central position that, since the thirties . . . was held by the Gallic Hegel."[12] The real showstopper was the young Jacques Derrida, who with his "Structure, Sign, and Play in the Discourse of the Human Sciences" upended the entire premise of the conference, arguing that structuralism was rooted in a flawed Eurocentric logocentrism. The English coinage *poststructuralism* would not begin to circulate for a few more years, but, as François Cusset has observed, "the Americans present at Johns Hopkins in 1966 realized that they had just attended the live performance of its public birth."[13] The 1975 "Schizo-Culture" conference at Columbia University was another high-visibility event that featured French theorists, most notably Michel Foucault, who profiled their Nietzschean-inspired theories of cultural deviance and transgression, adding to the visibility of "the reception of Nietzsche's texts in America, travelling on a French ticket."[14]

A number of books and newly founded journals facilitated the transfer, presenting the "New Nietzsche" as an antifoundationalist revelation from France.[15] A 1977 collection of essays, *The New Nietzsche: Contemporary Styles of Interpretation*, edited by David B. Allison, introduced a French-inspired, postphenomenological linguistic and cultural theorist who, in all his guises, assaulted the "subject" and "univocal meaning," and "no longer promise[d] a final aim, goal, or purpose" for interpretation. Now the death of God, long familiar to American readers, would be made unfamiliar with its new application as the death of "traditional logocentric hierarchy," while the will to power would be transcribed as the will to interpret texts. As Allison made clear, such a volume was not limited to any "particular orthodoxy," though he offered a clear rebuke of what it *will not* do: "It certainly does *not* consist in one more pointless series of oversimplifications, biographical anecdotes, or convenient summaries—a tradition to which the English-speaking audience has long ago become accustomed." This new antifoundationalist Nietzsche, Allison argued, was as yet "*unheard of*" in America.[16]

Similarly, the 1978 issue of *Semiotext(e)*, "Nietzsche's Return," introduced a French "Fred," who offered "an incessant critique of Unity, Self, continuity, stability, etc.—like so many variations on a theme. No. Not really, really variations in search of a theme." Fronting essays by French thinkers Gilles Deleuze, Jean-Francois Lyotard, and Pierre Klossowski along with a few Americans, most notably the composer John Cage, James Leigh's introduction announced that they had come to "Free Nietzsche" from Kaufmann's (weakening) grip. "So how does it happen that we are announcing Nietzsche's return? Are we . . . trying to horn in on Walter Kaufmann's territory? . . . Or are we simply cashing in on a trend—attempting to transplant a (more or less) Gallic version of the philosopher who has certainly become the most-frequently-quoted-German in Paris?" Readers were encouraged to help identify the causes of

From "My Life," comic in "Nietzsche's Return," special issue of *Semiotext(e)*, 1978. Used by permission of the publisher.

the new Nietzsche surge by filling out a questionnaire identifying themselves as "disciples," "rightful heirs," or "crass profiteers" and sending it directly to Kaufmann at Princeton.[17] The pages contain images of Nietzsche's mustache from every angle, an eight-page comic replete with depictions of Nietzsche and his sister involved in a series of incestuous escapades, a cigarette-smoking, postcoital Nietzsche contemplating how "women are the only private property that has complete control over its owner," and drawings of the philosopher as a capped, flying superman and a mustachioed King Kong.[18]

Adding currency to the notion that recent Nietzsche-inspired French theory marked a temporal as well as an intellectual watershed for American readers, the 1981 special issue of the postmodern journal *boundary 2* asked, "Why Nietzsche Now?" reciting the increasingly common refrain that Nietzschean antifoundationalism had introduced a radically new discourse to America.[19] In the preface to the issue published in book form, the editor, Daniel T. O'Hara, could now characterize Gallic Heideggerian hermeneutics, Derridean deconstruction, and Foucauldian genealogy of power as the three forms of the "postmodern appropriation of Nietzsche." Why Nietzsche *now* in "our supposedly postmodern time?" Because, as these new strains of antifoundationalism show, Nietzsche was the "prophet of an ironic perception of the worthlessness at the heart of *culture*."[20]

While the force of the writings and the personas of Derrida and Foucault propelled them to celebrity status in the United States, their uses of Nietzschean antifoundationalism helped cultivate important homegrown academic celebrities as well. Two who employed French readings of Nietzsche to great effect were Eve Kosofsky Sedgwick and Judith Butler. They drew on a quotation from Nietzsche's *On the Genealogy of Morals*—a text that had formed the mainstay of American Nietzsche interpretations—but which, thanks to their effort to identify power relations masked as a stable subject, took on new resonance in the 1980s: "There is no 'being' behind doing, effecting, becoming; 'the doer' is merely a fiction added to the deed—the deed is everything."[21] In *Epistemology of the Closet* (1992), Sedgwick employed a Nietzschean hermeneutic to challenge compulsory dualisms in human sexuality, in order to examine how notions of desire have been encoded with damaging epistemes, thereby showing how his antiessentialism was essential for queer theory.[22] Likewise, in *Gender Trouble* (1990), Judith Butler transformed Foucault's Nietzsche-inspired challenge to the "metaphysics of substance" as the

The infirm Nietzsche in the summer of 1899, one year before his death. Photograph by Hans Olde. As reprinted in Daniel T. O'Hara, ed., *Why Nietzsche Now?* (1985).

basis of her assault on the "foundationalist fictions" of gender. According to Butler, Nietzsche helped show how gender categories were not "natural" but "contested sites of meaning," discursive spaces in which identity is performed within or against social norms. "We might state as a corollary [to Nietzsche]: There is no gender identity behind the expressions of gender; that identity is performatively constituted by the very 'expressions' that are said to be its results."[23]

While Sedgwick and Butler enlisted newer French readings of Nietzsche in their campaigns against essentialism as expression of Eurocentric gender anxieties, they participated in what by the 1990s was established cultural practice to use Nietzsche to challenge false necessities restricting female and sexual liberation. Though the discourses were unmistakably new and indeed penetrated more deeply into the foundations of the self, the reckoning with the selfhood in a world without universals was already well established in American Nietzschean interpretation.

Nevertheless, as the startling news emanated from the academy that professors were instructing their students that crucial Western conceptions of the moral subject were nothing more than white male apologetics, conservative cultural commentators responded with alarm. The growing thunder on the Right heightened drama around a postmodern Nietzsche, whose ideas challenged the truthfulness of truth. Conservatives regarded his philosophy as an exogenous pathogen infecting young Americans' hearts and minds. Giving voice to frustrations with the American academy and popular culture of the growing lyrical Right in the 1980s and '90s, Allan Bloom provided a blistering attack on the "Nietzscheanization" of the academy in *The Closing of the American Mind* (1987). He articulated a growing grievance among conservatives that it was bad enough to have the spectacle of the counterculture's constant carnival migrate from the be-ins and student protests of the sixties to the popular culture of the seventies and eighties, but it was worse to have this kind of political theater migrate to the academy. Bloom railed against the "*value* relativism" he believed left-wing professors were peddling to their students, eager for Nietzsche's authoritative license of their moral licentiousness.[24] The problem with the democratic mind of the late twentieth century, Bloom lamented, was not that it was closed, but that it was too radically open, too indiscriminate to understand Nietzsche's subtle moral criticism and his warnings about nihilism. Arguments against relativism in the academy were long in evidence from Irving Babbitt's complaint against Nietzschean romanticism in the early decades of the century and Robert Maynard Hutchins's attacks on the "rudderless rabbits" of progressive education in the 1930s. But by pinning them on a new postmodern Nietzsche whom he described as a corrupting "foreign influence" with "alien views and alien tastes," Bloom contributed to the broader discourse on both the Right and the Left that the reckoning with foundationalism was a new moral problem, a wholly foreign notion to American thought and culture.[25]

Critics of the growing lyrical Right picked up on this narrative. Roger Kimball, in a later postscript to his attack on the relativist antihumanism in the humanities, *Tenured Radicals* (1990), described how the odd alloy between relativism and identity politics in the humanities had turned the university classroom into a "swamp yawn[ing] open before us, ready to devour everything. The best response to all this—and finally the only serious and effective response—is not to enter these murky waters in the first place." As Kimball put it, "As Nietzsche observed, we do not refute a disease. We resist it."[26]

While Bloom helped advance an argument that the implications of Nietzschean-inspired "pop relativism" posed a grave threat to the mission

Illustration by Jay Cotton in George Scialabba, "Thoroughly Modern Friedrich," *Village Voice*, August 19, 1986. Used by permission of the artist.

of the academy, he argued that the consequences were much worse for the American "soul."[27] Originally titled *Souls without Longing*, Bloom's *Closing* sought to make clear that while Nietzsche's antifoundationalism paved the way for modern nihilism, he was also a theorist who—unlike his American progeny—understood its consequences for the human spirit. At the core, the outrage generated over the "Nietzscheanization" of the liberal arts was not just that the academy no longer trained students to adjudicate moral claims, but that it was undermining moral claims altogether, cultivating new generations of Americans with no belief in—or capacity for—intellectual and moral perfectionism.

This concern lay at the heart of *The End of History and the Last Man* (1992), a best seller by Bloom's former Cornell undergraduate classics student, Francis Fukuyama. Because one of the book's premises was that American liberal democracy and capitalism were proving to be the "final form of human government," critics alternately lauded and derided it as a piece of triumphalist Americana. In Fukuyama's view, these reactions wholly missed his larger point. While he indeed argued that world history was leading to the US political economy, as confirmed by the fall of the Berlin Wall and the collapse of the Soviet Union, this alone did not capture the "deeper and more profound question . . . [about] the goodness of liberal democracy itself." He stressed that "Nietzsche's greatest fear was that the 'American way of life' should become victorious," and one of the book's aims was to explain why these fears were warranted. He used Nietzsche's characterization of democracy as the triumph of slave morality to frame the book; drew chapter titles and used epigraphs from Nietzsche's *Will to Power*, *Thus Spoke Zarathustra*, and "The Use and Abuse of History"; and took Nietzsche's cautionary diagnosis of the slovenly "last men" to characterize the "typical citizen of a liberal democracy." What mattered more than the survival of liberal democracy, Fukuyama maintained, was whether it was *worthy* of survival. Nietzsche prophesied that once the logic of Western civilization ran its course, a few rare Übermenschen would emerge who could live without traditional morality and overcome—even embrace—an uncertain universe. But the "last men" would be there too at the end of history, perfectly content to keep their heads low and cling to their bankrupt morality. Fukuyama lamented that modern Americans were already showing evidence of this insidious contentment, too willing to settle for goodness, no longer capable of striving for greatness, a little too satisfied with liberal freedoms, and a lot too complacent to strive for the distinction, valor, and honor that make liberal freedom worth it. What they were missing was a noble *thymos*, a Greek word meaning "spiritedness," something akin to the desire for distinction. For Fukuyama, the problem wasn't relativism as such. It was what individual Americans would make of their relative goods.[28]

This was the warning of the "real" Nietzsche, a "new" Nietzsche, as yet unheard of in America. Fukuyama followed in his mentor's footsteps, and another American Nietzschean best seller was born. Thus at the height of Nietzsche's popularity as a French-speaking postmodernist, he got his Nietzsche to speak Greek, and in doing so establish his bona fides as the father of modern American conservatism. Fukuyama proclaimed a new Nietzsche utterly foreign to American ways of thinking, but he is the silenced Nietzsche, the one in whom the "Right found its most brilliant spokesman."[29]

French-inspired postmodern discourses drew out the antifoundational implications of Nietzsche's philosophy. They provided new languages and theories to explore the processes of and possibilities for meaning-making after the accounts on every last vestige of moral, epistemological, and metaphysical foundationalism had been closed. They inspired enthusiasts, who saw these foreclosures as the necessary opening for American thought, while drawing the ire of others, who saw them as a foreclosing of the American mind. But as Americans came to terms with a "new" Nietzsche, they did so in ways that were long part of American reckonings with him. They used him as a way to come to terms with the epistemic, moral, and cultural grounds of American thought, always already assessed not only in relation to absolutes but in relation to Europe. Elements of this antifoundational interpretation were new, but Nietzsche's presence in American thought and culture was not. What was old in this period was the ways in which American readers of Nietzsche used him to come to terms with antifoundationalism on native grounds.

What was also drowned out in the *Sturm und Drang* surrounding the arrival of a "new French" Nietzsche in the 1970s, '80s, and '90s was important contributions to Nietzschean discourse that were neither new nor forged along the lines of deconstruction or poststructuralism. Indeed, three of the most prominent thinkers of the period, who were important Nietzschean interlocutors—the literary theorist Harold Bloom and philosophers Richard Rorty and Stanley Cavell—emphasized that antifoundationalism had formed an important part of American thought. They drew on familiar discourses of Nietzsche as one who assailed nihilism even more passionately than he assailed truth. But they turned to Nietzsche not simply to reckon with his ideas but to examine how doing so enabled Americans to think about their own thinking. They presented a Nietzsche who, in their view, harmonized with sources of American antifoundationalism, precisely because he had heard that very antifoundationalism in Emerson (and which Emerson passed on to William James and John Dewey). As we shall see, Bloom, Rorty, and Cavell turned to Nietzsche, not to turn away from antifoundational elements in American thought, but to face them in Emerson and his pragmatist children. These three irrepressibly unique voices nevertheless brought familiar elements back. They turned to Nietzsche, just as Nietzsche had turned to Emerson, to consider their native intellect in relation to one across the Atlantic, to long for a "home" for foundationless philosophy, and to reinstate a philosophy that inquires, how do I live? yet also asks, how do I know?—questions especially crucial in a world without foundations.

## Harold Bloom: The Quest for Emersonian Priority

On the morning of his seventy-fifth birthday on July 11, 2005, Harold Bloom sat down to reflect on his imprint on literary criticism for an afterword to *The Salt Companion to Harold Bloom*, a large collection of appreciation and commentary. The editors opened the volume with the undeniable claim that "Harold Bloom is the most famous living literary critic in the English-speaking world," while also noting that Bloom nevertheless consistently presented himself as a "solitary voice, ignored by an academic audience who should—but never will—listen."[30] True to this characterization, Bloom closed the volume with a confession about the necessary loneliness of the *longue durée* career "ranting against cant," calling out the academic fashions that changed names but not their "outrages to humane aestheticism," which he witnessed over half a century from his professorship at Yale University. No surprise, he thought, that the editors had chosen to "compile a giant Invectorium" of his reception in the academy. Equally plausible, though, would have been an invectorium of his own decades-long *agon*—the term he used to define literary influence and exchange—which he both theorized about and enacted with historical poets and contemporary critics. Then Bloom offered an important clue to his theory of—and a view of his own—influence: "Nietzsche taught that every spirit must unfold itself in fighting." Nietzsche had likewise imparted on Bloom the haunting and exquisite vision of the eternal recurrence of the same. Better to embrace than protest one's life path with an *Amor Fati*. Nietzsche had taught that although the human will can do many things, it cannot will *backward*. No matter—Bloom wouldn't have wanted it to: "I am glad I cannot have my days again, since indeed I would repeat the same mistakes: the same enemies, the same misguided kisses. Error about life, Nietzsche says, is necessary for life."[31] Bloom's invocation of Nietzsche as he looked back on his life as a critic reflected how he had used the German philosopher to constitute his literary self. For over forty years of prodigious literary output, when Harold Bloom thought about Harold Bloom, or about the dynamics of aesthetic creation, he often thought about Nietzsche.[32]

Over the long arc of his career, as he engaged in his agonistic battles with scholarly trends in the academy, Bloom drew from Nietzsche as a theorist of intellectual belatedness and indebtedness and an exemplar of the poetic burden of the critic. Whether challenging the New Critics' overspiritualization of criticism and its insistence on the hermetic closure of texts in the 1960s; deconstructionists' radical despiritualization of criticism and celebration of radical indeterminacy with the "death of the author" in the 1970s; or the move from literary criticism to cultural studies, and with it the politicization of texts by their cultural studies offspring in the 1980s and '90s, Bloom upbraided the literary critic as knower of truth. In his view, his precursors approached texts as if they could be certain of their meaning, while his contemporaries and their students approach texts with a certainty that there was no meaning whatsoever. But in Bloom's estimation, both kinds of literary critics are bedeviled by the same problem: they may have questions, but they have no quest. Both seek knowledge, but not wisdom. Already as a graduate student at Yale in 1951, Bloom read Nietzsche's "On the Uses and Disadvantages of History for Life," and took it as clear instruction of what to look out for in academic criticism: "swarm of historical neuters [who] will always be in their place, ready to consider the author through their long telescopes." Resentful critics, weak readers, may have the "most astonishing works" before them, but all they can produce is an "echo" in the "form of 'criticism,'" "though the critic never dreamed of the work's possibility a moment before." Nietzsche troubled Bloom with his image of impotent criticism that begets nothing other than another criticism, and one that has no "influence in the true sense—an influence on life and action."[33]

Bloom recognized that his antihistoricism and insistence on literary greatness was out of step with the major moves in the academy. But he believed that even in a world without eternals, there were some extraordinary, singular voices that had a shot at "secular immortality": "Time, which destroys us, reduces what is not genius to rubbish." Even the call for a scholarship that aspires to something eternal smacked of an unholy holiness frowned upon in the late twentieth-century academy. But for Bloom this did not matter. He had learned from Nietzsche long ago that the only voice that can speak with any authority is the one that invokes no authority other than the self. "At seventy-one, a literary critic has learned that he can speak only for himself, and not for what is fashionable, so let me begin by dismissing 'French Nietzsche.'. . . I will consider only what Nietzsche has done, and goes on doing, for me."[34] What Nietzsche did for Bloom was bring him to his insights about the anxieties of intellectual belatedness as he would come to wrestle with it on his own. What the Continental critics had missed, and Nietzsche's Emersonian insights had shown, was that criticism at its best is a form of wisdom literature—signposts to the divinity in our all-too-human humanity. For Bloom, Emerson's ephebe, Nietzsche, showed American criticism a way out of Continental deconstruction and back to its native priority. Before the Continental naysayers, there was *Emerson*.

_____

*The Anxiety of Influence* (1973) marks the beginning of Bloom's career as literary critic superstar as well as his deep engagement with Nietzsche to rewrite rhetorical criticism. In what was his slimmest and yet most ambitious and controversial volume to date, Bloom insisted that it was high time that critics "give up the failed enterprise of seeking to 'understand' any single poem as an entity in itself," and to consider the source of poetic meaning, which is no longer believed to be cleaved to the words on the page. Meaning, he argued, is generated in the workings of literary tradition. However, for Bloom this tradition was not to be understood as the passing of poetic norms from one poet to the next, but rather a psychic field of anxieties in which the later poet wrestles with his precursor. Contrary to the traditional view of influence as the power an earlier poet asserts on a later one, Bloom described it as the *descendant's* response to the fear of being constrained, conditioned, or even erased by his ancestor, by the anxiety that his ancestor has beaten him to his own best thoughts. Though no poet can tolerate belatedness, Bloom argued, only the "weaker talents idealize," whereas the "strong poets," the "figures of capable imagination," can willfully misread their precursor and "appropriate for themselves."[35]

Nietzsche looms large in *Anxiety of Influence* as a genealogist of the imagination, a critical historian of the anxiety of influence, and himself an ancestor-become-God who made everyone in his wake belated to him. Bloom made his own debt to Nietzsche clear: "Nietzsche and Freud are, so far as I can tell, the prime influences upon the theory of influence presented in this book." While Freud enabled Bloom to listen for defense mechanisms at work in the creative process, "Nietzsche is the prophet of the antithetical [whose] *Genealogy of Morals* is the profoundest study available to me of the revisionary and ascetic strains in the aesthetic temperament." Bloom's theories of poetic will and of the history of romantic psychology, and his language of the poetic "latecomer," were all drawn from Nietzsche's protest against Hegelianism.[36] He quoted Nietzsche from "On the Uses and Disadvantages of History for Life": "The belief that one is a late-comer in the world is, anyhow, harmful and degrading; but it must appear frightful and devastating when it raises our late-comer to godhead, by a neat turn of the wheel, as the true meaning and object of all past creation, and his conscious misery is set up as the perfection of the world's history."[37] Bloom saw Nietzsche's protest as one against Hegel, but also against feelings of belatedness in himself. Nietzsche's embodiment of his own theory showed self-hatred at work: the latecomer does not just idolize the self anticipated by a precursor, he loathes him as well. Bloom knew that the story of how creative poets "have suffered other poets" wasn't pretty. But it was the very perversity of "the enchantment of incest" that yielded strong poetry.[38]

As Bloom would later recall, his theory of influence got its "starting-point" in Nietzsche's 1872 fragment "Homer's Contest," in which he valorized the ancient Greeks' perpetual striving, contest, and one-upmanship as the source of their health and vigor.³⁹ But it is the fuller treatment of the salutary implications of belatedness in Nietzsche's essay "'Guilt,' 'Bad Conscience,' and the Like" from *On the Genealogy of Morals* from 1887 that dominates Bloom's discussion. According to Bloom, Nietzsche's appraisal of the history of "the guilt of indebtedness" is a prelude to any serious "philosophy of composition," for it confirms Nietzsche's observation that "there is perhaps nothing more terrible in man's earliest history than his mnemotechnics." In Bloom's strong rereading of this essay, though Nietzsche associated memory with pain, guilt with debt, and memory of one's ancestors with the latecomer's agnostic striving, he missed the powerful implications of his own genealogy of moral psychology. Whereas Nietzsche's later writings testify to the "sickness of bad conscience" caused by the sublimated resentment of indebtedness, he also showed how it was necessary for fostering feelings of tribal belonging, and for turning one's ancestors into gods—an essential development, Nietzsche argued, in the "human creation of gods."⁴⁰ According to Bloom, Nietzsche linked the "hideous pain" of memory of the ancestor with illness, "but an illness," as Nietzsche put it, "as pregnancy is an illness."⁴¹ As Bloom would come to repeatedly emphasize in his subsequent works, because Nietzsche was himself haunted by belatedness, he insisted that "forgetfulness . . . is a property of all action."⁴² However, latent in his very own conception of memory was the demonstration of why it was so crucial: Nietzsche had shown that memory is the motive force of meaning. Memory is the sickness *necessary* for birthing imagination, human piety, and ideas of transcendence. One's own origins matter. They are the inferno from which all human meaning comes.

In 1973, American readers would have come to expect that a discussion of Nietzsche might entail some unseemly elements. But to find *Emerson* in a book drenched in a language of thundering pathos, darkness, and resentment might have come as a surprise. Yet it was the Emerson of *Anxiety of Influence* (whom Bloom paired with Nietzsche as a "great [denier] of anxiety-as-influence"⁴³) who understood the simple law of compensation in all matters human: "Nothing is got for nothing."⁴⁴ Though in later books Bloom would emphasize their relationship as one of father and son, precursor and ephebe, in *Anxiety of Influence* Nietzsche is his prime theorist of strong poets, and Emerson the exemplar. The late Emerson of "Fate" could accept the high cost of achieving oneself for one's self as "Beautiful Necessity," and yet do so with a magnanimity of which only a "liberating god" like himself was capable.⁴⁵ While he understood the valuable weight of necessity, he also exhibited a welcoming impertinence to it: "You think me the child of my circumstance: I make my circumstance."[46] This "swerve"[47] in Emerson, between necessity and freedom, ancestral origins and self-begetting, is what Bloom would identify as Emerson's "American sublime," and it would be that very sublimity which Bloom would increasingly come to distinguish from "the anti-humanistic plain dreariness of all those developments in European criticism."[48]

Throughout the 1970s and early '80s, from the remaining works of his tetralogy on poetic influence[49] and his theoretical studies of revisionism,[50] Bloom continued to draw on Nietzsche the moral psychologist who theorized thinking and wondered about the function of criticism when meanings are unstable. He continued to draw on Nietzsche, together with Derrida, Paul de Man, J. Hillis Miller, and Geoffrey Hartman, as a member of the "Yale School," the first wave of deconstructive literary criticism in the United States. Though Bloom was an important midwife to deconstructive theories, editing and contributing to their American manifesto, *Deconstruction and Criticism* (1979), and was widely identified as a major figure in this "Hermeneutical Mafia,"[51] his emphasis on human subjectivity created in dialogue with, but not endemic to, discourse made him an odd fit. As Hartman explained in his preface to the volume, though Bloom, like his more epistemologically oriented fellow theorists, "understand[s] Nietzsche when he says 'the deepest pathos is still aesthetic play,' [he has] a stake in that pathos: its persistence, its psychological provenance. For [him] the ethos of literature is not dissociable from its pathos."[52] Though he shared with his fellow Yale critics a common ancestor in Nietzsche, an interpreter of interpretation who challenged the notion of a primordial referent to which words in a text or speech attach meaning, his commitment to a common project with the others was the most tenuous and fleeting.

Already in the very theoretical works for which he was associated with deconstructionists, Bloom used his Nietzsche to critique theirs. He understood himself as an heir of Nietzsche, too, and recognized that "we share . . . Nietzsche's suspiciousness: who *is* the interpreter anyway, and precisely *what* power does he seek to gain over the text?"[53] But precisely because of their shared inheritance, he had to disaggregate his reading of Nietzsche from the Continental theorists' Nietzsche, even if that required turning them and their arguments into "pragmatic" tropes to distinguish his views from theirs.[54]

Though very much a theorist of reading, unlike Continental critics, who discussed readers and texts, Bloom typically employed the language of poets and poems. He did so in what he regarded as the Nietzschean sense of "the primordial poem of mankind"—the figuration for all human experience.[55] For Bloom, however, the poet existed before the poem. He agreed that literature helps form the self, and that was indeed one of the best reasons anyone should ever pick up a book. But he argued that the self was never purely a linguistic construction. He viewed the psyche as prior to and yet impossible without imaginative literature (and imagined forebears). Consequently, Bloom had his quarrels with "our theoretical critics [who] have become negative theologians," rejecting "all Gallic modes of recent interpretation because they dehumanize poetry and criticism."[56] He thus posed his critic as imaginative poet engaged in the "primal scene of instruction" against Derrida's critic as theorist of the "scene of writing."[57] For Bloom, the most crucial element in that scene of instruction was the very "subject" erased by deconstruction. "A poetic 'text,' as I interpret it, is not a gathering of signs on a page, but is a psychic battlefield upon which authentic forces struggle for the only victory worth winning, the divinating triumph over oblivion."[58] Though many of his Continental critics and friends took exception to his characterizations of their work, they likely would have conceded to him that they did not think divination was part of the literary critic's vocation.

Bloom appropriated Nietzsche to distinguish his vision of literary criticism as a form of wisdom literature, as compensation and consolation in a cosmos that is nothing more and nothing less than poetic. He characterized deconstructionists as "negative theologians," whose nihilism left nothing at stake in literary interpretation, quite literally proving Emerson's theory of compensation that nothing was got for nothing. It was efforts like the one in his friend and colleague Paul de Man's book *Allegories of Reading* (1979), in which de Man called off the search for an "extralinguistic referent or meaning," that led Bloom to conclude that deconstructionists had called off all quests altogether.[59] They theorized theorizing, with no ambition that it got them anywhere, because they believed that if there was no one way to go, there must be nowhere to go. (Better to "will *nothingness* than *not* will," as Nietzsche had challenged nihilists.[60]) In the Derridean-inspired focus on language and texts and "nothing outside the text," they missed Nietzsche's warning in *Twilight of the Idols*: "That for which we find words is something already dead in our hearts."[61]

Bloom agreed with the deconstructionists that texts are neither self-contained units of meaning nor transcripts of a higher reality. He insisted that insofar as they are "written by men," they take on meaning only when the critic reads them as testaments of human desires and longings by an author wrestling with his inheritance as he seeks his own voice.[62] "Literature is not merely language; it is also the will to figuration, the motive for metaphor that Nietzsche once defined as the desire to be different, the desire to be elsewhere."[63] He argued that deconstructionism aped the traditional foundationalism it set out to dismantle. Although Bloom had his tropes, as did the deconstructionists, he argued that they used a "trope of a demiurgical entity named 'Language'" much like the "traditionalist trope of the Imagination as a kind of mortal god endlessly doing our writing for us."[64] Likewise, he argued that they privileged epistemology, which ran counter to the moral and aesthetic stances in Nietzsche's oeuvre. According to Bloom, an epistemological stance "is no more or less literary, no more or less a trope. . . . What can a trope provoke except a trope . . . only the troping of a prior trope, or of the concept of trope itself."[65] Nietzsche may have appreciated how tropes are necessary fictions, but Bloom argued that they were nothing more than provisional "hedges against 'interpretive anarchy.'" This was not to endorse a science of tropology; what mattered to him and Nietzsche was not the theory of the trope but its ability to claim more life. By turning criticism into an "epistemology of tropes" rather than an art of loving and fearing literature, the deconstructionists' talk of play and endless signifying was at best a contact sport where knees are skinned and eyes blackened, but no blood is drawn, no lives are at stake.[66] What was missing in deconstruction, Bloom complained, was a fundamental love of literature, of reading. Without reverence, there are no stakes. Bloom insisted repeatedly that the deconstructionists' strategies for deciphering meaning turned criticism into a bloodless sport with no life to gain, because it had nothing to lose.

But the most grievous problem with deconstructionists, Bloom argued, was that they were heirs of Nietzsche's biggest mistakes, not his most salient insights. He traced their errors to Nietzsche's essay "'Guilt,' 'Bad Conscience,' and the Like" from *On the Genealogy of Morals*, the very text that was so instrumental to his own theory of composition. Some of the errors of poststructuralism, he argued, tracked back to Foucault, who had appropriated the weaker aspects of Nietzsche's genealogy, which separated meaning and purpose, origins and utility, in the history of values. Other errors tracked back to Derrida's emphasis on Nietzsche's claim that behind every custom is merely a sign-chain of new interpretations which are arbitrarily jumbled together as a product of chance. But it was this very text that, from *Anxiety of Influence* forward, formed the core of Bloom's own criticism. The difference, in Bloom's view, was that Foucault and Derrida missed what Bloom believed he recognized, that "the prestige of origins is a universal phenomenon, against which a solitary de-mystifier like Nietzsche struggled in vain." Though Nietzsche tried to deny origins their prestige, he nevertheless accounted for why they have it. And though he resisted their authority, he knew, better than his predecessors, that "all sacred history . . . was against him, and sacred history has a way of prevailing even in ages and societies where the sacred appears largely through displacement."[67]

Indeed, Nietzsche's own example of tracing the origins—and not just the subsequent genealogy—of bad conscience, his own reckoning with the power of mnemotechnics, where meaning is generated by the hideous pain of memory, went missing altogether in deconstruction: "How . . . meaning ever gets started . . . is quite unanswerable upon deconstructive terms." This was Nietzsche's great *moral* and *aesthetic* contribution, wholly obliterated in what Bloom regarded as the excessive historicism of poststructuralism in particular, where every stance an author makes in a text can be traced "home" to a political, social, or economic context. "Criticism and poetry are not primarily political, social, economic or philosophical processes," Bloom insisted. "They are barely epistemological events."[68] Nor was criticism a science, "not even a 'human science,' and it is not a branch of philosophy. . . . The theory of poetry, like all criticism, is an art, a teachable and useful art, and its true criteria are poetic. . . . *It must be strong*, with the strength of usurpation, of persistence, of eloquence."[69] This is the part of meaning that the deconstructionists take from Nietzsche, and in doing so take literary criticism in the wrong direction, Bloom argued. As he put it,

> And we have discovered no way as yet to evade the insights of Nietzsche, which are more dangerously far-reaching even than those of Freud. . . . Yet Nietzsche's "perspectivism," which is all he can offer us as alternative to Western metaphysics, is a labyrinth more pragmatically illusive than the illusions he would dispel. One need not be religious in any sense or intention, or inclined to any degree of theosophy or occult speculation, still to conclude that meaning, whether of poems or of dreams, of any text, is

excessively impoverished by a Nietzsche-inspired deconstruction, however scrupulous.[70]

Though Bloom thought these were *bad* (not strong) misreadings of Nietzsche, given Nietzsche's aversion to his own greatest spiritual insights, he began, bit by bit, to cede the trope of Nietzsche, but not his demands that in a world without foundations, poetic images of the possible are all we have to justify ourselves. At once he could disparage the "flood of post-Nietzschean philosopher-critics" while praising Nietzsche's notion that aestheticism is "the only justification for our readings and unreadings, of the poets and of ourselves."[71] He would take issue with "Nietzsche-inspired deconstruction" but not Nietzsche's poetics of pain, in which meaning is driven by the horrible trauma of memory, and the desire to transfigure it. During Bloom's years as the resident fuddy-duddy among the high priests of negative theology, he would increasingly toss off references to the "excessively despiritualized [criticism] by the followers of the school of Deconstruction, the heirs of Nietzsche,"[72] which, in the context of his own consistent uses of Nietzsche's ideas, made no sense. His Nietzsche did not endorse the view of texts as a mobile army of metaphors, but rather warned that words alone are dead artifacts, relics of an "it was," not psychic fields of an *I becoming*. Bloom gave little reason to think that the deconstructionists' "Nietzsche" was the right Nietzsche, certainly not the best one, but that was okay, because the German ephebe pointed to the wisdom of his American precursor, who wasn't prone to such mistakes. Nietzsche showed how Emerson made them all belated.

Before Nietzsche, before his Continental descendants, there was *Emerson*. For Bloom, America already had its "interior orator," who spoke America's truths. Nietzsche's genius was the ability to hear this American voice. As Bloom put it, Americans will "never know our own knowing" without knowing how Emerson gave voice to the terrors and the joys of a self without God, meaning without absolutes, a present without a past, a shot at transcendence without eternity.[73] It was the voice of a man, not a text, struggling with the myth (but also the psychic appeal) of givenness, longing for release from the tyrannies of the past, and reckoning with inherited language as "tomb of the muses" and "fossil poetry." Emerson understood that readers can turn to works of the intellect and imagination not in the hope of instruction but for provocation, and to read them so that *they* may be read. It was Emerson who anticipated the problems involved in his own effort to unhinge meaning from absolutes, the sublime from eternity, and himself from God. Emerson sought to transform being into becoming, refusing the "it was" with the *I becoming*. He argued that in a world without givens, man must be his own Namer: "Speak your latent conviction, and it shall be the universal sense." While Nietzsche contemplated the primordial poem of mankind, Emerson considered how America might best be conceived as a work of human imagination and creation: "America is a poem in our eyes."[74] Bloom described Emerson as giving voice to the "American swerve," where "tradition is denied its last particle of authority, and the voice that is great within us rises up":

> Life only avails, not the having lived. Power ceases in the instant of repose; it resides in the moment of transition from a past to a new state, in the shooting of the gulf, in the darting of an aim.[75]

Bloom learned from Emerson that "power is an affair of crossings, of thresholds or transitional moments, evasions, substitutions, mental dilemmas resolved only by arbitrary acts of will." For Bloom, this was no epistemology of tropes, no rhetorical philosophy, but a poetic criticism of the strong misread. It is one without foundations, but one in which "every fall is a *fall forward*, neither fortunate nor unfortunate, but *forward*, without effort, impelled to the American truth, which is that the stream of power and wisdom flowing in as life is eloquence. Emerson *is* the fountain of our will because he understood that, in America, in the evening-land, eloquence *had* to be enough. The image of voice is the image of influx, of the Newness, but always it knowingly is a broken image, or image of brokenness."[76] For Bloom, Emerson's voice is the voice of American "knowing." Emerson's voice did not speak a language of debunking, demystifying, or de-idealizing, but one of circles, ever moving outward from the striving self. Emerson wrote of circles knowing that they have no center. In a world without a center, the only source of authority, of meaning, is the self-begotten self. Emerson showed that this is no easy task, but a heavy "American burden."[77] But Emerson, like Nietzsche, instructed all latecomers that "nothing is got for nothing."

Bloom's Nietzsche did for America what Emerson said genius should do: enable it to hear its own thoughts with a renewed sense of their alienated majesty. Once Nietzsche alerted Bloom to the anxieties of belatedness, and showed his own antithetical strategies for resisting false authorities outside the self, in history, in an inherited intellectual tradition, his Nietzsche also enabled America to hear its own inner orator. In looking for logocentricism, American criticism forgot that voice, not text, is America's knowing. According to Bloom, until Americans know their Emerson, their primordial knowing, they won't understand the "American difference." Just as "Emerson's American Gnosis denies our belatedness by urging us not to listen to tradition," Bloom argued that for Americans to know their knowing, they must know Emerson.[78]

## Richard Rorty: Fusing the Horizons between Nietzsche and the Pragmatists

What do Leon Trotsky and wild orchids have to do with each other? This was the burning question that occupied the fifteen-year-old Richard Rorty as he began his studies at the University of Chicago in 1946. The grandson of Social Gospel theologian Walter Rauschenbusch and the only son of two anti-Stalinist socialist writers, James Rorty and Winifred Rauschenbusch, he grew up imbibing his family's commitment to social justice. But he also had a "private, weird, snobbish" fascination with the wild orchids near his New Jersey home. Though he could not see what these exquisite, though "socially useless" flowers had to do with his socialist politics, he figured that is what college would be for: to give him access to a transcendent view of the world that would enable him to, in the words of Yeats, "hold reality and justice in a single vision."[79]

For someone on a quest for certainty, he picked the perfect program. The Hutchins College at Chicago was imbued with the neo-Aristotelianism of the school's president, Robert Maynard Hutchins, and philosophers Mortimer Adler and Richard McKeon. Rorty also studied (alongside Allan Bloom) with the political philosopher and German émigré Leo Strauss. He was thus enveloped in an austere but affirming environment of scholars certain about moral certainty. "This sounded pretty good to my 15-year-old ears," he recalled. "For moral and philosophical absolutes sounded a bit like my beloved orchids—numinous, hard to find, known only to a chosen few." He set out to be a Platonist for the next five years, but his efforts to squeeze Trotsky and his orchids into a single moral framework wasn't working. It did not help that he came to question Platonism altogether—was it to provide irrefutable arguments, quiet all doubts, prove why one a priori was better than another? But what made matters worse was the neo-Thomist solution of resolving a contradiction by drawing a distinction. That might enable philosophers to demonstrate their great skills at slicing arguments with mental paring knives, but Rorty came to doubt that applying the intellect like cutlery would make him "either wise or virtuous." After five years, he gave up on the project of finding a "fabled place" of a universal standpoint. And though he would go off to Yale for a Ph.D. in philosophy, he did not leave behind his question of "what, if anything, philosophy is good for."[80]

Though he began his career in the late 1950s as an analytic philosopher, Rorty would come to discover in antifoundationalism the possibility of answering the question. It would help him see that what much of the Western philosophical tradition had long been good at—grounding its claims in moral absolutes—was not working very well anymore. John Dewey would help him understand that sometimes the best thing philosophy can do is *not* resolve intellectualist dilemmas, but to, as Dewey put it, "get over them."[81] Similarly, Friedrich Nietzsche would help persuade him that one of the "idiosyncrasies of philosophers" is that the absolutes they think they are handling are nothing more than "conceptual mummies."[82] Dewey and Nietzsche shared the view that philosophy is neither a tribunal of reason nor a secular religion, but a way of showing moderns how to manage life without them.

In his landmark study, *Philosophy and the Mirror of Nature* (1979), Rorty followed suit by exploring the foundationalist fictions at work in modern epistemology. He focused specifically on the futility of the notion of the "mind as a great mirror" of nature, which seeks accurate representation of the world. Though the main figures of this study were Dewey, Heidegger, and Wittgenstein, Rorty enlisted Nietzsche and James as fellow antirepresentationalists, who shared the criticism of the Kantian notion of "'grounding,'" "culture," and "knowledge-claims." Rorty found in all these thinkers allies in his campaign to demonstrate that knowledge is nothing more and nothing less than a "social practice," and any effort to prove the contrary simply persisted in the illusion that we are discovering when we are really creating, knowing when we are simply putting ideas to work, copying a transcript of the world when we are really just coping with life.[83] According to Rorty, in their quest for certainty, most professional philosophers—analytic philosophers especially—were mere puzzle-workers in an intellectual and cultural paradigm that had long outlived its usefulness. He thus began slowly identifying his project as the unrealized promise of "pragmatism," and spent the remainder of his career attempting to reinstate pragmatism as an alternative to epistemological and metaphysical foundationalism. He proposed that pragmatism could make philosophical inquiry timely again by enabling philosophy to get over its outmoded zeal for timelessness.

From the early 1980s up until his death in 2007, Rorty was an advocate for pragmatist antifoundationalism who was recognized nationally and internationally as a preeminent American philosopher, a "towering" public intellectual in American life and "one of the world's most influential . . . thinkers." However, as his appreciative readers among academics across the disciplines as well as a general audience grew, so too did an ever-lengthening queue of opponents to his enterprise.[84] He took his lumps from all sides: philosophers and scientists who marveled at his unwillingness to acknowledge that proof, not persuasion, is the best way to back up truth claims; conservatives who were repelled by his breezy denials of religion; and leftists who were aghast at what they regarded as the political complacency and quietism of his social theory. But many of Rorty's most potent critics came not from those who opposed pragmatism but from those who sought to defend it. Rather than praise Rorty for helping to "make pragmatism intellectually respectable," beginning in the early 1980s, many philosophers and intellectual historians interested in pragmatism have—as Richard Bernstein put it—"view[ed] him as the villain in the story . . . [one] who betray[ed] the tradition he is always invoking."[85] Speaking for a range of Rorty's readers who envisioned themselves within (or appreciative commentators on) the American classical pragmatic tradition, James Kloppenberg characterized Rorty's pragmatism as "An Old Name for Some New Ways of Thinking."[86]

A major source of concern among his pragmatist critics was the ease with which Rorty made pragmatism encapsulate antihumanist, antiliberal strains of thought, like Nietzsche's, which were so at odds with the American philosophers' moral commitments. The concerns went beyond mere nomenclature, as none would deny Rorty's claim that *pragmatism* has, from its beginnings, been "a vague, ambiguous, and overworked word."[87] Rorty himself recognized that Nietzsche's philosophy was altogether devoid of the "spirit of social hope" so essential for the American pragmatists. But for Rorty, the similarities between Nietzsche's and the American pragmatists' epistemology were similar enough to justify defining them as part of a coherent philosophical movement. Indeed, it was *because* of these similarities that he used Nietzsche to build a case for the philosophical rigor of the classical pragmatists in the early 1980s. In *Consequences of Pragmatism* (1982), Rorty launched his first full-scale effort to reinstate the promise of the pragmatic theory of truth, to get a fresh hearing for James and Dewey, two "neglected" writers in analytic philosophy, by drawing out their strong affinities with Nietzsche's "more fashionable" philosophy (as it was at the time, thanks to his Princeton colleague Walter Kaufmann's efforts). Despite the popular conception of American pragmatism as a "provincial" and "outdated philosophical movement," Rorty underscored the similarities between Nietzsche's and the pragmatists' notion of truth as something contingent and provisional.[88] He thus leveraged Nietzsche's capital for the American pragmatists much in the same way that European philosophers and social theorists would begin to do on the other side of the Atlantic: "Nietzsche [was] the figure who did most to convince European intellectuals of the doctrines which were purveyed to Americans by James and Dewey."[89] In this way, Rorty began reinstating pragmatism by presenting Nietzsche as a "German pragmatist," arguing that Nietzsche and James, in particular, "feed each other lines[;] their metaphors rejoice in one another's company," and describing Dewey as a Nietzsche without "sneers."[90]

Despite the occasional patriotic gesture to proclaim pragmatism "the chief glory of our country's intellectual tradition," over the course of the 1980s and '90s, Rorty persistently emphasized the epistemological affinities among Nietzsche, James, and Dewey.[91] In doing so, he presented a thoroughly *heimatlosen* Nietzsche, and thus a cosmopolitan pragmatism, both of which eluded national distinctions between "us" and "them," "organic" thought and "foreign ideas," "American" and "Continental" antifoundationalism. In fusing the horizons, he offered a vision of both Nietzsche and pragmatism, which was indifferent to national origins, and which sought to loosen the tight fit between epistemological and political commitments.

Because Nietzsche emerged as such a central figure in Rorty's writings, there was, of course, plenty of opportunity to let him do solo work. Rorty presented Nietzsche as a perspectivalist and an antiessentialist, an "edifying philosopher" who opens "space . . . for the sense of wonder," and a "Prophet of Diversity" who helped Rorty envision a society in which "creative self-destiny" is treasured.[92] He became one of Rorty's standard models to show the promise of the philosopher who resists specialization and refuses to identify "philosophy" as a separate *Fach*, which must keep itself hygienic from literature, psychology, and social criticism. Most significantly, he was Rorty's "strong poet," one who exalted a world after God in which truth is understood as nothing more than a contingent metaphor.[93] It was this Nietzsche who helped Rorty imagine a postphilosophical culture. As he put it, "A culture in which Nietzschean metaphors were literalized would be one which took for granted that philosophical problems are as temporary as poetic problems. . . . [Such a culture] would let us see the poet, in the generic sense of the maker of new words, the shaper of new languages, as the vanguard of the species."[94] Rorty's Nietzsche was one such maker of new words and, therefore, a maker of new worlds. Indeed, he regarded Nietzsche's philosophy as so monumental and transformative for the history of thought that he periodized intellectual history into "pre-Nietzschean" and "post-Nietzschean" philosophy.[95] For Rorty, Nietzsche made words, and Nietzsche made history.

One of the histories Nietzsche contributed to was the history of pragmatism. Rorty argued, following René Bertholet's 1911 *Un romantisme utilitaire*, that pragmatists' ideas (along with Bergson, Poincaré, and some of the Catholic modernists) grew out of the same late nineteenth-century transatlantic ferment in philosophy that traced its roots to German romanticism and the utilitarianism of British evolutionary theory.[96] Not only did their attempted synthesis of nineteenth-century romanticism and utilitarianism constitute a coherent historical intellectual movement, Rorty argued, they also played an important role in his own "Pragmatist's Progress." In his "semiautobiographical narrative," Rorty described the young "Seeker after Enlightenment" who comes across mounds of thorny dualisms and realizes, in Deweyian fashion, they "can be dispensed with." The next "early stage of Enlightenment comes when one reads Nietzsche and begins thinking of all these dualisms as just so many metaphors for the contrast between an imagined state of total power, mastery and control and one's own present impotence." But Rorty did not stop there. "A further state is reached when, upon rereading *Thus Spake Zarathustra*, one comes down with the giggles." It is not clear if giggling is an essential part of the initiation process, whether he was giggling because, this time around, he saw how his first reading was a little too hot and heavy, or whether Rorty simply wanted to make the point that the "final stage" of pragmatic awareness is when one realizes the these are not "stages in the ascent" but "contingent results of encounters with various books which happened to fall into one's hands."[97] In any event, for Rorty, both historically and personally speaking, Nietzsche, James, and Dewey could all meaningfully be understood as participating in the cosmopolitan conversation of pragmatism.

In *Contingency, Irony, and Solidarity* (1989), perhaps thanks to his success in rehabilitating pragmatism, Rorty temporarily stopped using "pragmatism" as a name for tendencies in thought emerging in Western philosophy since Nietzsche or to describe the German philosopher himself. And yet it is important to see how he enlisted Nietzsche in this book to understand both what it tells us about his notions of pragmatism and Nietzsche's relevance for it. It also helps explain why his effort to fuse the horizons between Nietzsche and American pragmatism—while unfusing them between private virtues and public commitments (between wild orchids and Trotsky)—were so contested.

In works that followed, Nietzsche and James reappear as partners in a transatlantic conversation; but in this volume, the American pragmatists receive little attention, leaving more room for a new coterie of writers from Europe. In *Contingency, Irony, and Solidarity*, Nietzsche takes center stage, sharing scenes and engaging in conversations with Mill, Freud, Proust, and Heidegger about the contingency of selfhood, language, and community. The leitmotif of these conversations is that the world gives us no moral leitmotif. And according to Rorty, it is Nietzsche who got this conversation going: "It was Nietzsche who first explicitly suggested that we drop the whole idea of 'knowing the truth.'" Rorty drew on the newly popular passage (and one of cardinal importance to deconstructionists) from "On Truth and Lie in an Extra-Moral Sense" to provide a "definition of truth as a 'mobile army of metaphors' [which] amounted to saying that the whole idea of 'representing reality' by means of language, and thus the idea of finding a single context for all human lives, should be abandoned."[98]

In Rorty's conception of irony, the consequences of contingency are on full display. He suggested that although a world without foundations yields uncertainty, it need not yield fear or despair. Though it means we must go it alone without metaphysical comforts, it also promises what Rorty referred to as "freedom as the recognition of contingency." For his Nietzsche, recognition of contingency fosters irony, which Rorty defined quite simply as the acceptance that there is no single transcript for the universe. He believed that Nietzsche fully embodied and embraced this ironic perspective—this view that because no individual can invoke a higher authority to defend his moral vocabulary against another's, he need not try to do so either; no one's metaphors can be, or need to be, "final vocabularies" for another's. Final vocabularies, in Rorty's estimation, are words like *true, good, right*, and *beautiful*, and words like *God, Christ, science*, and *the church*. These are words that—precisely when used as recourse to authority—have "no noncircular argumentative recourse."

These words "are as far as [one] can go with language; beyond them there is only helpless passivity or a resort to force." The ironist avoids such a muddle by recognizing that his vocabulary "is [not] closer to reality than others," nor that "it is in touch with a power not [himself]."[99] As Rorty pointed out, this doesn't mean that the ironist does not inherit or borrow others' vocabularies. He just does not think that the vocabularies he has inherited or borrowed help lay the universe bare or break through to transcendent meaning. It also does not mean that he stops speaking with others; it just means that he does not speak *for* others.

Perhaps Nietzsche's greatest influence on Rortyian contingency was the implication of his conception of truth for conceptions of the self. Before Nietzsche, philosophers predicated their philosophical investigations on a flawed conception of man. They envisioned "man"—as Nietzsche put it—as an "*aeterna veritas*," something that remains constant in the midst of all flux, as a sure measure of things.[100] With Nietzsche, Rorty argued, things changed. Nietzsche had insisted that man is not a static being, but rather is constantly in the process of becoming. He demonstrated to Rorty that today's selves are as provisional and contingent as today's truths. According to Rorty, Nietzsche demonstrated that when we track down the sources of the self, we do not make our way to divine intervention or materialist necessity; we simply find our way to those animating beliefs and ideas that either we have put there ourselves (if we are strong poets), or others have put there for us (if we are not).

Rorty thus employed Nietzsche to illustrate the ironist's quest to divest himself of all final vocabularies and to "replace" them with "self-made contingencies." He seeks to self-create in the absence of self-discovery. In Rorty's view, Nietzsche's dictum to become "who one actually is" can be misleading, for it "does not mean 'who one actually was all the time' but 'whom one turned oneself into in the course of creating the taste by which one ended up judging oneself.'" Nietzsche embodied the Rortyian ironist: one who engaged in "self-redescription" without a predestined resting place, redescription that does not try to "surmount time and chance, but to use them" for the purpose of greater autonomy. But while Rorty viewed him as an exemplar of the necessary quest for self-perfection, he argued—following Heidegger, who criticized Nietzsche for "relapsing into metaphysics"—that he loses sight of his own best perspectivalist insights, since he sought not just *a* perfected self but *the* perfected self, not just *a* beautiful self as a work of art, but a *sublime* self, one which, in its historical grandeur, surpassed all perspectives. According to Rorty, here is where we see the rub between Nietzsche's instrumentalism and romanticism. Unlike Royce, who thought Nietzsche synthesized the two to greater effect than James, Rorty argued that he fared no better. "As long as he is busy relativizing and historicizing his predecessors," Nietzsche is on "firm" antifoundational ground, Rorty maintained. But as soon as he forgets that the self can never achieve a "privileged perspective on itself," when he thinks he can get to a purely realized essential self, "*pure* self-creation, pure spontaneity, he forgets all about his perspectivalism."[101]

Nietzsche played an equally significant role in Rorty's formulation of solidarity, precisely *because*—not despite the fact—he had nothing much good to say about it. Rorty identified him as antiliberal, but argued that it had nothing to do with his antifoundationalism. Rorty's James was as much an antifoundationalist as Nietzsche, though he envisioned a different kind of freedom that comes with the recognition of contingency. Unlike Nietzsche, who believed that contingency fostered greater autonomy, James believed that it enabled better community. Similar to Nietzsche's perspectivalism, James had emphasized the "blindness in human beings." He argued that because there is no common denominator for human experience, we do not always get the "peculiar ideality" of our neighbor's beliefs and longings.[102] Indeed, we are often sometimes downright blind to it. However, for James, unlike for Nietzsche, this recognition has a chastening effect, humbling us, and making us *more* fit to live in a liberal community. He believed that this blindness reminds us that none of us have exclusive claims to moral authority, because moral authority is not exclusive.

Thus, Rorty recognized important differences between Nietzsche's and the American pragmatists' conception of contingency: one emphasized autonomy, the other solidarity. While Rorty invoked Nietzsche as an exemplar of irony, he readily confessed that his philosophy would not be the one he would turn to for inspiration about human solidarity. Instead, his Nietzsche was the exemplar of "what private perfection—a self-created, autonomous, human life—can be like." Dewey, by contrast, represented one of Rorty's "fellow citizens" rather than an exemplar. The difference for Rorty was that Dewey wrote as part of a "social effort" to "make our institutions and practices more just and less cruel." Rorty flatly asserted that Nietzsche's ironic self-perfection had "nothing in particular to do with questions of social policy" and therefore had nothing in particular to do with Dewey's political progressivism. Here Rorty and his pragmatist critics could agree. Nietzsche and the

American pragmatists wrote their work in two very different "spirits": one of social disinterest and even hostility, the other of social hope.[103]

But this was the very point of *Contingency, Irony, and Solidarity*. It was the reason, no matter what angle of vision he strove for since age fifteen, Rorty could not get Trotsky and the wild orchids in one view. He could fuse the horizons of Nietzsche and the pragmatists, but he "got over" trying to fuse the ways in which they might be put to work in building a liberal society. The differences in Nietzsche's antihumanist temperament and Dewey's progressive one were important insofar as they demonstrated why we need different authors, different moral vocabularies, for getting what we want. We need our writers on self-perfection *and* our writers on social harmony. That each cannot do the work of the other presents no inconsistency, because "we shall only think of these two kinds of writers as *opposed* if we think that a more comprehensive philosophical outlook would let us hold self-creation and justice, private perfection and human solidarity, in a single vision." But after all, it was Nietzsche, James, and Dewey who argued that once we are ready to drop all philosophies with mirrors, so too can we "drop the demand for a theory which unifies the public and private."[104]

Here Rorty arrived at his no-man's-land between public commitments and private longings that his pragmatist critics found so objectionable. Because of his willingness to drop the demand for synthesis between public and private, and his unwillingness to draw firm distinctions between Nietzsche's and the American pragmatists' antifoundationalism, he dropped the necessary connection between instrumentalism and democracy that Dewey, in particular, took as the hallmark of his philosophy. By unfusing the horizons between public and private, Rorty jettisoned the "spirit of social hope" that James and Dewey saw as essential to pragmatism. He affirmed that while they wrote in such a spirit, and so did he, Nietzsche did not; James and Dewey were as convinced of the promises of a liberal society as Nietzsche was of its perils. Whereas Nietzsche sought to create a self that would be a work of art, Dewey sought to create "a society that would . . . be a work of art."[105] But according to Rorty, within the context of their ideas about contingency, these are differences in temperament alone. They are individual differences, not examples of national intellectual physiognomies; personal idiosyncrasies, not competing foundations of antifoundationalism. Rorty asserted that they expressed nothing more than the authors' competing sensibilities about the way a society might look after it has gotten over moral absolutes.

Rorty contended that though Nietzsche and Dewey, especially, had very different temperaments, their competing visions of the good life indeed had something very much in common: *both are rooted in the authors' lapse into metaphysics*. For Nietzsche, it was his assumption that socialization was "antithetical to something deep within us," and therefore "that human solidarity goes when God and his doubles go."[106] But why, Rorty asked, should solidarity go any more than social atomism? Nietzsche gives us no reason to believe that he was on to something here. Quite the opposite, for when he lapsed into antihumanistic sentiments, he simply belied his own insight that *there is nothing deep down within us*, except that which we put there ourselves. Whenever Nietzsche spewed his muck against humanism, liberalism, and democracy, it might be unpleasant for American readers, but according to Rorty, they need not see it as anything but his occasional bad bedside manner. "Nietzsche's contempt for democracy," he averred, "was an adventitious extra, inessential to his overall philosophical outlook."[107] Nietzsche's assertions that without Christian foundationalism, all the humanistic ideals in its wake would or should go, were nothing more than a bad theory of human nature from a very good philosopher on the contingency of all things human.[108]

But Rorty did not let Dewey off the hook. Dewey, he argued, smuggled in essentialist claims about democracy when, as he often did, he emphasized experience as the empirical test demonstrating that "democracy . . . [is] the precondition for the . . . [harmonious] solution of social problems."[109] He maintained that Dewey turned metaphysical anytime he argued that there are necessary preconditions for *anything*, especially for solving social problems. He rejected Dewey's implication that there are particular "relations given . . . in experience[, for] . . . a notion of 'givenness' . . . is just one more 'dogma of empiricism.'"[110] And so, in a similar vein, Rorty shrugged off his critics' complaint that Dewey would never have made Rorty's distinction between the private and the public self. He noted one critic's objection that "Dewey . . . thinks that the 'possession of a sense of the common good is required for individual self-realization.'" But as Rorty insisted, it is one thing to say that having our lives bound up with and responsible for others gives *most* of us a feeling of fulfillment, but it is quite another (and quite inconsonant with his instrumentalism) to say that it is "required" for self-realization.[111] So there was no reason, he argued, for us to incorporate Nietzsche's dismissive claims about democracy any more than Dewey's defenses of it. Neither Nietzsche nor Dewey gives us reason to assume that American liberalism cannot go it alone without metaphysics, or an American way of life without foundationalist fictions.

Rorty did not think Nietzsche's pragmatism made the world safe for totalitarianism. Nor did he think that James and Dewey made the world safe for democracy. And yet he insisted that this should not stop anyone from trying to give the world new metaphors for the promise of a life in a "liberal utopia."[112] Even in his impassioned appeal to a renewed leftist patriotism in *Achieving Our Country* (1998)—his most extensive exploration of the relationship between pragmatism and American democracy—he argued that there is no necessary fit between pragmatism and politics. He still thought there was no way to philosophically justify America. But he did think pragmatists could help persuade, not prove, that the vision of a just, tolerant America with no "frame of reference" was worth the human effort it would require to realize it.[113] There was just no way to ever "back up" such a vision.[114] But according to Rorty, following Nietzsche and his fellow pragmatists, Americans need not try to. For it is only once they stop trying to *back up* their claims for solidarity, and instead move *forward* with new visions of the possible, that they might achieve their America.

## Stanley Cavell: Nietzsche, Emerson, and American Philosophy Finding Its Way Home

"No matter how many people tell you the connection [between Emerson and Nietzsche] exists," observed Stanley Cavell, "you forget it, and you can't believe it, and not until you begin to have both voices in your ears do you recognize what a transfiguration of an Emerson sentence sounds like when Nietzsche rewrites it."[115] Surveying the mindscape of postwar American philosophy in 1995, Cavell began to wonder why it seemed that Emerson's "decisive philosophical importance for Nietzsche evidently *cannot* be remembered by philosophers."[116] "Remembered" suggests that this erasure stemmed from forgetting, not ignorance.[117] And if philosophers forgot, it is likely because they did not care. Though Nietzsche after Kaufmann came to attract growing attention in postwar academic American philosophy,[118] Emerson hadn't yet found his Kaufmann among professional philosophers. During philosophy's establishment as an academic field in the mid-nineteenth century, he was already dismissed as too romantic and antiscientific; by the time analytic philosophy emerged as the dominant force in academic philosophy in the 1930s, he wasn't regarded as philosophically barren so much as not regarded at all.[119]

Emerson's absence from academic philosophy might have been more shocking to Cavell had he not been trained in the academic culture that ignored him. After receiving his bachelor's degree in music from Berkeley in 1946 and then abandoning his postgraduate studies in musical composition at Juilliard, Cavell began studying philosophy and psychology at UCLA before starting his graduate training in philosophy at Harvard University. He entered Harvard in the early 1950s—a time when the philosophy program, like most of the major graduate training programs—was steeped in logical positivism, but his training there also coincided with a semester-long visit in the spring of 1955 by J. L. Austin, a philosopher of language at Oxford. Austin's insights on what we *do* with words—how our utterances are themselves *acts*—stressed the notion that the ordinary should be the domain of philosophy. Thus, Cavell came to learn about what constituted legitimate philosophy—positivism's strict empiricism and vision of philosophy as the science of knowledge and Austin's Oxford orientation toward clarifying ordinary speech, the two dominant modes of Anglo-analytic philosophy as they crossed paths at Harvard. Though at odds, both would instruct students like Cavell that philosophy was not a guide to morality, beauty, or wisdom; its proper role was neither to edify nor inspire, but to clarify knowledge claims. It was in this kind of environment that a graduate student could get himself into trouble for suggesting that movies, or theater, or literature—the sources Cavell would later gravitate toward—might have something to offer philosophical inquiry.[120] Despite its radical antimetaphysical posture, analytic philosophy was proudly ascetic—in, but not of, the world. In a philosophical climate that insisted that philosophy was *improved*, not imperiled, by foreclosing moral inquiry, it is no wonder, then, that Emerson—a thinker who asked, how should I live? without once subjecting *how* or *live* to linguistic analysis—would have had no resonance for Cavell.

In time, Cavell would come to discover Emerson's possibilities for ordinary language philosophy, but not before he learned how to use Nietzsche as an interlocutor with Austin and Wittgenstein on the role of philosophy. Nietzsche was an early influence on Cavell, one who helped him consider his profession "a desert of thought (they make a desert and call it a clearing)." Though he believed it was right and salutary for modern philosophy to press our words to test if they can, in locutionary practice, carry their own interpretive freight, he learned first from Austin, then from Wittgenstein, that the aim was not to remove our words from the everyday world to do so, but to restore them to their most ordinary meanings. "Wittgenstein speaks of philosophical procedures as bringing words back from their metaphysical to their everyday use—as if our words are *away*, not at home, and as if it takes the best efforts of philosophy to recognize when and where our words have strayed into metaphysics." There's a burden in the revelation that we have "been away [from] our words."[121] That recognition would, as Zarathustra instructed, keep philosophers *"faithful to the earth,"* keep them conversant not only with all kinds of moral discourse but with movies, literature, and the arts—the stuff of everyday life. Exploring the ordinary as something forgotten or lost might help us see our words "with a certain alienated majesty," and might enable us to restore the exceptional in the everyday, the sublime in the commonplace.[122] It wasn't until he discovered "the Nietzschean connection" in the 1970s that Cavell "began to draw ever closer to Emerson."[123] It took discovering Nietzsche to see how Emerson was asking *his* questions about philosophy restored to the everyday, a philosophy come home.

If ever there was an American thinker who thought about how Nietzsche brings Americans back to their Emerson, how reading foreign texts can return a prodigal philosophical culture to its forgotten founding (or rather, *finding*), it was Cavell. But for him the passion for learning from Nietzsche's passion for Emerson was not driven by a quest for intellectual precedence, a chest-thumping claim of American priority. Nor was it a source of consternation so much as a "topic of separate and abiding interest" for him over the course of his long career, enabling him to both contemplate and engage in philosophical practices—indeed a view of philosophy itself—long banished from professional philosophy.[124] If Emerson is insufficiently philosophical for professional philosophers, then on what grounds do philosophers consider thought "philosophical"? If they are the same grounds as those for the European traditions, then why are they—or must they be?—the same grounds for America? If all that counts as philosophy is that which we have inherited, does that mean, Cavell wondered, that "America never expressed itself philosophically? Or has it[?]"[125]

But how does one look for what might be an absence? (Indeed, the history of American engagements with Nietzsche is a history of American readers asking the same question.) What are the grounds to look for American philosophy? Cavell came to recognize these questions as those animating Emerson's essay "Experience" (1844) when he asked on behalf of a new American culture, "Where do we find ourselves?" For Cavell, the power of the longing, uncertainty, and frustration throbbing in that question was unleashed in what he regarded as Nietzsche's direct response to it. In *On the Genealogy of Morals*, Cavell found Nietzsche's answer to Emerson: "We have never sought ourselves—how could it happen that we should ever *find* ourselves?" Indeed, Cavell argued that the entire passage in *Genealogy* in which Nietzsche lamented that "men of knowledge" are especially unknown to themselves because they are strangers to their own thinking was intimately in dialogue with Emerson's "Experience." He thus presented the "circuit" of concerns between the two authors, finding in Nietzsche a direct "transcription of something Emerson means."[126] Though each spoke with a singular voice, both issued a similar warning that the search for a genuine philosophy must not be cut short by the assumption that it will be found on firm ground. Thus, Nietzsche's clear assaults on epistemological and moral foundationalism enabled Cavell to hear what Emerson himself might have been looking for: a philosophy without an inheritance, without a past—a philosophy that conceives itself not as a body of knowledge but rather as a way of life. Not man's thought but *Man Thinking*—the making of a philosophy without foundations.

Long before Cavell discovered in Nietzsche a midwife of Emersonian philosophy who helped bring America back "home" to its thinking, he found him to be a philosopher who challenged the very enterprise of professional philosophy in which Cavell found himself. In "Existentialism and Analytic Philosophy" (1964), he argued that Nietzsche sought to restore the discipline to the Platonic and Aristotelian view that it is not a body of knowledge but rather a mode of inquiry which "itself exacts a mode of life."[127] Nietzsche argued that for the modern philosopher who believes his enterprise is to apprehend pristine, absolute truth, his mode of life is asceticism. In *Must We Mean What We Say?* (1969), his first full-length study of ordinary language philosophy, Cavell drew on Nietzsche's ascetic ideal as he examined how it carried on in modern analytic philosophy's self-conception. For one, he saw how modern philosophers' view of themselves and their enterprise can be seen in the "masks" they adopt and the "audience" they believe they are speaking to. For the modern ascetic philosopher, believing he speaks on behalf of truth causes him to adopt the "traditional mask of the Knower; that is, as the only form in which he could carry authority." But if the modern analytic Knower's policy is to renounce the moral and aesthetic elements of man's daily life as unworthy of philosophical examination, who constitutes the "we" of philosophy? Nietzsche's discussion of "the problem of audience" in *The Birth of Tragedy* enabled Cavell to push this further: to whom are the ascetic Knower's truths addressed? If the answer is the technical specialist and not the ordinary man, the problems of philosophy and not the problems of life, then perhaps, Cavell wondered with Nietzsche, this esotericism is "the late version of one of philosophy's most ancient betrayals—the effort to use philosophy's name to put a front on beliefs rather than to face the source of assumption, or of emptiness, which actually maintains them."[128]

In *The Claim of Reason* (1979), Cavell drew on Nietzsche's death of God to reinstate skepticism as a way to consider how modern philosophy might know itself better. The problem for Cavell was that modern philosophy had become too committed to a notion that truth is not in the here and now, not in the daily workings of life, but *elsewhere*, either in absolutes outside human history or rooted in inheritances from Europe. He continued to wonder, as he had put it earlier, whether our efforts to make "beelines" to the absolute "[have] to do with our efforts first to create and then to destroy our Gods. Nietzsche said we will have to become Gods ourselves to withstand the consequences of such deeds."[129] Cavell argued that Nietzsche's skepticism offered crucial epistemological insights for modern analytic philosophy. He had shown that efforts to shun moral questions rested on the false epistemological assumption that the gap between the mind and the world could be closed up. According to Cavell,

> I remarked that traditional philosophy, so far as this enters the Anglo-American academic tradition, fails to take this gap seriously as a real, a practical problem. It has either filled it with God or bridged it with universals which *insure* the mind's collusion with the world; or else it has denied, on theoretical grounds, that it *could* be filled or bridged at all. I think this is something Nietzsche meant when he ridiculed philosophers for regarding life "as a riddle, as a problem of knowledge" ... implying that we question what we cannot fail to know in order not to seek what it would be painful to find out. This, of course, does not suggest that skepticism is trivial; on the contrary it shows how profound a position of the mind it is. Nothing is more human than the wish to deny one's humanity, or to assert it at the

expense of others. But if that is what skepticism entails, it cannot be combated through simple "refutations." The idea that a philosophical position can simply be "refuted" is one that Nietzsche *also* ridicules.[130]

In Cavell's reading of Nietzsche, his tragic skepticism does not welcome limitlessness by denying absolutes; it shows the cost of modern philosophy tethered to them. By insisting on truths as that which close up epistemological gaps, it offers a God of certainty situated elsewhere in time and space, awaiting our arrival. But by thinking *in time*, we unhinge knowing from the expectation that it will carry us back to a foundation. By abandoning the notion that inquiry must converge on certainty in order for its concepts to be deemed truthful, we open the possibility that our most pressing truths are the ones experienced in those painful gaps in our here and now, between ourselves and others, our ideals and our daily lives. In emphasizing the irremediable distance between our words and our worlds, Nietzschean skepticism brings us to our presentness, back to *our* problems, which are not just epistemological but also moral.

Nietzsche's strenuous insistence on viewing truths as *ours* in the immediacy of our own time and place—and his assertion that the uncertainties of the everyday are caused not by a failure to grasp truths but by a failure to recognize them as our truths—became Cavell's initiating nudge to bring him home to these questions in American philosophy. He could recognize in Nietzsche the same impulse at play in America's "pre-philosophical moment, measured in American time, [which] occurred before the German and the English traditions of philosophy began to shun one another."[131] In turn, he could hear Nietzsche's concern that the disconnects between self and other, and between word and world, cannot be filled by science, logic, or God. We do not close them up, grafting pathways over ruptures, but rather domesticate our thinking in our everyday.

Cavell identified Nietzsche as the primary Continental author who enabled him to see Emerson's "American Scholar" (1837)—a text in which Emerson was "*thinking* about the idea of thinking"—in terms that spoke to the concerns of modern-day analysts. Certainly a study in epistemology, it was also a moral meditation on how to restore thinking to life, epistemology to moral inquiry, and the authority of truths which speak to—and do not shout down—the authority in our own experiences. It was Emerson's recognition, picked up by Nietzsche, that when we think our thinking needs absolutes and elsewheres, we are *not yet thinking*. For Emerson, the only way to think was to do so, as Cavell put it, "aversive[ly]," pushing against all inheritances as shortcuts to false foundations that will root us in origins and carry us up to God or across the Atlantic to Europe.[132] Nietzsche shared this inclination to turn against the "it was" of inherited truths, to reject all predetermined conditions for thought, and to view truths as being created in the process of thinking itself.

For Cavell, Emerson's pivot away from inheritances did not mean that he had no use for other texts or authors. Quite the opposite. It meant that he put a very high premium on what Cavell referred to as philosophy's *responsiveness* to other philosophies, other ideas, other propositions—a crucial feature of moral inquiry without foundations. Cavell identified this as the virtue of perfectionism: philosophy that enlivens others not through instruction but through provocation. He noted the sense of wonder: "When one mind finds itself or loses itself in another, time and place seem to fall away—not as if history is transcended but as if it has not begun." Nietzsche enabled Cavell to see how the perfectionist's apparently excessive regard for his own spiritual well-being is indeed a study in "how to manage individuation, its economy, the power that goes into passiveness.... The distinction between private and public, subjective and objective, a feast for metaphysical and moral dispute, becomes the daily fare of democracy." By striving for the claims of the "unattained self," one cultivates the responsiveness to the needs of others. Perfectionism in an Emersonian and Nietzschean sense, then, is less an ideal than a practice. The practice of perfectionism is the practice of striving to be forerunners of ourselves, and exemplars for one another of the grandeur that striving can yield. Emerson called for the discovery that "each philosopher ... has only done for me, as by a delegate, what one day I can do for myself." Returning ourselves to our future selves, our selves not yet achieved, is what a Nietzschean-inscribed Emersonian perfectionism does for us. "Perfectionist thinking is a response to the way's being lost."[133]

A Nietzsche who thinks with Emerson, whose thinking brings alive what has for too long been repressed in the American philosopher, enabled Cavell to perceive the differences in the metaphors of ground when used by Emerson and Nietzsche (here Nietzsche is more "Emersonian" than "European"), as opposed to those used by Heidegger or Derrida. When Emerson asks in "Experience," "Where do we find ourselves?" he answers neither in exuberance nor in anguish: "It is very unhappy, but too late to be helped, the discovery we have made that we exist. That discovery is called the Fall of Man....I am ready to die out of nature and be born again into this new yet unapproachable America."[134] Nietzsche helped Cavell to discover in Emerson not a cheerful pantheist but a deadly serious philosopher who knows humans are not coddled by the universe but are instead "thrown for a loss." This language of loss in Emerson hauntingly anticipates (post-)modern Continental thought. It points to the felt need of European philosophers after Hegel to either accept or destroy "the completed edifice of philosophy as . . . necessary, unified foundation."[135] It is the vigorous rejection of foundationalism Cavell saw in Derrida. He maintained, "If I lived from a culture, call it France, the chief city of which had for some five centuries been producing world-historical literature, and which knew it, and fed the same samples of it to all the young who will occupy public positions, I would doubtless also be thinking of . . . excavation or deconstruction in which to have my own thoughts."[136]

Cavell's Emerson explored the absence of grounds, too. But what for Derrida was loss of ground was for Emerson a loss of something never there, an edifice he never had. "Here in North America," Cavell argued, "room comes first, and it is always doubtful . . . whether our voices, without echo, can make it to one another across the smallest fields."[137] In exploring the particularity of Emersonian antifoundationalism, Cavell asked,

> What happens to philosophy if its claim to provide foundations is removed from it—say the founding of morality in reason or in passion, of society in a contract, of science in transcendental logic, of ideas in impressions, of language in universals or in a formalism of rules? Finding ourselves on a certain step we may feel the loss of foundation to be traumatic, to mean the ground of the world falling away, the bottom of things dropping out, ourselves foundered, sunk on a stair. But on another step we may feel this idea of (lack of) foundation to be impertinent, an old thought for an old world.[138]

If, as Nietzsche instructed, knowledge exacts a mode of life, then the reverse is also true: a mode of life exacts a knowledge. In Emerson, antifoundationalism is that American way of life. Emersonian antifoundationalism is not a theory, it is a way of thinking and living in a world without foundations. It is not deconstructive, because it recognizes that the "edifices" of philosophy were not there to inherit or destroy. From a European past America cannot domesticate, Emerson moves toward a New World of men (and women) thinking, finding their way in the everyday, the here and now, a culture ready to be "born again."[139]

Following Emerson, modern Americans do not inherit philosophical problems that belong to a philosophical culture that is not theirs, but they can *achieve* that inheritance if it gets them back to the selves they are to become. Cavell achieved his Emerson by putting him in constant dialogue with Nietzsche. His Emerson and his Nietzsche finish each other's thoughts. And they do so, most significantly, when both are thinking about thinking without foundations. For Cavell, it was the "Nietzsche-Emerson" connection that helped him pivot back to an Emerson he had not yet discovered. But the pivot was not, nor did he think it should be, a single move. It was (and is) movement back and forth, to see and unsee what we have considered the province and possibility of philosophy in America. For Cavell, this was not about enlisting Nietzsche to give Emerson capital in American philosophy. He did not use Nietzsche or Heidegger to authenticate the philosophy of Emerson and Thoreau but rather to understand how "America's search for philosophy continues, by indirection, Columbus's great voyage of indirection, refinding the West by persisting to the East." It is an American philosophy that moves by "indirection" toward, and then averting from (and thus taking with), its European interlocutors. "Others take Emerson to advise America to ignore Europe," Cavell observed. "To me his practice means that part of the task of discovering philosophy in America is discovering terms in which it is given to us to inherit the philosophy of Europe."[140]

As Cavell argued, Emerson's effort to go without foundations "could not have presented itself as a stable philosophical proposal before the configuration of philosophy established by the work of the later Heidegger and the later Wittgenstein," both of whom were heirs of Nietzsche. In addition, if philosophy's virtue is its responsiveness to other philosophies, then American philosophy is enhanced, not compromised, by texts that can be representatives for it. But these texts must be interlocutors against which American philosophy averts itself again and again. Nietzsche showed in Emerson the notion that roads of inquiry are not laid on firm ground. This was a new way of thinking about the open road, and the American "philosopher as the hobo of thought."[141]

Is *this* "American" philosophy? Or perhaps the only kind of philosophy Cavell thinks can find a home in America? According to him, what is meant by philosophy, in Emerson's day and in ours, has been heavily inflected by European philosophers and philosophizing, sources that inform but do not necessarily speak in a voice expressive of American experience. Nietzsche is one of those voices. Though an antifoundational philosopher knows there are no metaphysical maps of the universe, he can still ask for directions. Sometimes we need a foreigner to help us find our way home.

## Thinking about American Thinking

Harold Bloom, Richard Rorty, and Stanley Cavell used Nietzsche to engage in a century-long practice: thinking about American thinking. Though they embraced Nietzsche's explorations of radical indeterminacy, perspectivalism, and heterogeneity of all knowledge and beliefs, they rejected a Nietzsche narrowly concerned with the assault on logocentrism, and argued instead for a more expansive, edifying role for philosophy once it had finally given up its foundational apologetics and its quest for technical specialization. Though conversant with the poststructuralist and deconstructive discourses ushered in with the arrival of the "new French" Nietzsche, they employed these new discourses to draw out elements of an American Nietzsche present in the United States throughout the twentieth century. Their Nietzsche harkened back to earlier philosophical interpretations which understood that in a world without foundations, our views of truth, language, and the self are not mirrors of reality but useful fictions to explore new avenues of discovery, new sources of wonder.

Bloom, Rorty, and Cavell, each in their own way, also used Nietzsche to come to terms with American thinking in relation to European thought. Whereas Rorty enlisted Nietzsche to consider the untapped promises of pragmatist antifoundationalism, Bloom and Cavell used him to reconsider Emersonian prophetic antifoundationalism. But all turned to Nietzsche in order to turn back to expressions of antifoundationalism on American native grounds. Whether to emphasize an "American Difference," as Bloom had done; to "get over" national distinctions in philosophy, as Rorty had done; or to consider that notions of what is "American" and "Continental" are created in the friction of transatlantic engagements, as Cavell had done, all demonstrate powerfully that the "family romance" of antifoundationalism has always extended beyond the nation.

Together these philosophers reconceived the American "home" not as a place but as a process. Though Bloom stressed the prestige of origins, what their uses of Nietzsche show is that it matters less where an idea comes from than where it takes the reader. They argued that America can find itself by *founding* (not finding) itself thinking with other thinkers. And they enacted the ways in which American readers over the century found themselves and their America not yet achieved every time they found themselves thinking with Nietzsche.

What they discovered in the process was the varieties of American antifoundationalism long part of America's knowing. Nietzsche helped them consider how philosophy once looked and might look again, when the role of the philosopher is to be the exemplar of the self who instructs by provocation. They rediscovered the possibilities of an American philosophy that seeks individual meaning without recourse to nature or necessity, a philosophy that never abandons the humanistic promises while reckoning with the unmistakable perils of antifoundationalism. A philosophy not just of the hammer, but of the divining rod as well. In doing so, they showed a new-old way of coming to terms with meaning in a world without foundations. They believed, as so many before them had, that a world "after Nietzsche" need not be a world without wonder. While Nietzsche provided (post-)modern Americans with neither compass nor guide for the moral life, he also demonstrated to them that a life without meaning is not a life worth living.

# Nietzsche Is Us

O my soul, I gave you back the freedom over the created and uncreated; and who
knows, as you know, the voluptuous delight of what is yet to come? . . .
O my soul, I taught you the contempt that does not come like the worm's gnaw-
ing, the great, the loving contempt that loves most where it despises most. . . .
O my soul, I took from you all obeying, knee-bending, and "Lord"-saying; I
myself gave you the name "cessation of need" and "destiny.". . .
O my soul, I poured every sun out on you, and every night and every silence and
every longing: then you grew up like a vine. . . .
O my soul, your smile longs for tears and your trembling mouth for sobs. "Is not
all weeping a lamentation? And all lamentation an accusation?". . .
Thus spoke Zarathustra.

FRIEDRICH NIETZSCHE, "On the Great Longing," in
*Thus Spoke Zarathustra* (1883–85)


Allan Bloom made for an unlikely American celebrity. A classics scholar who
taught at the University of Chicago as a professor in the Committee on Social Thought, he established his academic reputation with significant translations and commentaries on Plato's *Republic* and Rousseau's *Émile*. A Mid-
western gay Jewish atheist, he had an insatiable appetite for luxury to rival his
delight in the pleasures of knowledge: European oil paintings and Oriental
rugs to adorn his Chicago apartment, fine watches and exclusive clothing to
adorn himself, and classic texts to line his office like erotic totems. Decades
of chain-smoking gave a gravelly base to his baritone voice, which lingered
over words in a searching manner before tumbling into an avalanche of quick
periphrastic sentences, cut short by pauses for deep breaths. Though more
mannered than pugilistic, his every sentence was an argument, every question
an assertion. With each passing year as a professor in the academy, he felt the
gulf widening between his esteem for learning and his students' yawning indifference to it. After Bloom articulated his grievances in a withering report
on contemporary American college students for the conservative journal *The
National Review* in 1982, his friend and colleague Saul Bellow, knowing that

he had more holy fury and highbrow ribaldry coiled within him, persuaded him to let it unfurl in a full-length book.[1] He took his friend's advice, and in 1987, to his, Bellow's, and his publishers' astonishment, *The Closing of the American Mind* vaulted into the number-one slot on the *New York Times* Best Seller list in nonfiction, becoming the second-best-selling hardback book of 1987.[2]

*Closing of the American Mind* generated a firestorm of interest in newspapers, magazines, and journals of opinion all along the political spectrum. George F. Will praised it as the "How-To Book for the Independent," while Garry Wills dismissed it as "grim, humorless and vindictive."[3] Martha Nussbaum marveled at Bloom's "un-Socratic," "undemocratic vistas," concluding that his appeal to the authority of the ancients was "extremely odd in view of the insistence of every great ancient philosopher on the priority of rational argument to traditional authority."[4] Wondering why Bloom's book should have such appeal, Benjamin Barber asked, "Why are Americans so anxious to welcome a book that claims they can't read, so willing to accept a polemic that excoriates their literary intelligence?"[5] Though many offered answers, one thing was certain, noted a reporter for *Entertainment Weekly*: "Bloom was the right crank at the right time. His book was originally titled *Souls Without Longing*, but it turned out that the nation was really longing for a kick in the pants from a soul without mercy."[6]

It might have felt like a kick in the pants, but according to his preface Bloom intended the book to be "a meditation on the state of our souls" from the vantage point of a teacher in higher education. The state, he insisted, was not good, and Nietzsche's dominating influence on American intellectual and cultural life was to blame. Bloom traced the entrance of Nietzsche's philosophy to his own German-émigré professors at the University of Chicago, who brought with them Nietzsche's terrible insights about the bankruptcy of universal, transcendent truth in Western thought and morality. That was all well and good when the academy was committed to teaching students how to work through difficult ideas. But as his philosophy made its way from the academy of the 1940s and 1950s into the radicalized and politicized culture of the 1960s, and from the cloistered seminar to the American marketplace, it became transfigured into a blank check for late twentieth-century American "value relativism." "On enchanted American ground the tragic sense has little place," Bloom asserted, insisting that "rootless cosmopolitanism of the revolutions of the Left" threw down just enough fertile soil to nourish Nietzsche's assaults on universals, but not the moral reckoning they required. In a pluralist culture trying to find common moral and intellectual ground where the *pluribus* can find its *unum*, Nietzsche's claims that God was a grotesque human fiction, values descriptions with no correspondence to moral absolutes, and truths a cloak for power underwrote the cultural revolutions of the 1960s, which not only gave up on the vision of wholeness animating the American democratic experiment, but deemed it unworthy. "Suddenly a new generation that had not lived off inherited value fat" took relativism as its new idol. "We are a bit like savages who, having been discovered and evangelized by missionaries, have converted to Christianity without having experienced all that came before and after the revelation." Unable to understand the context from which the ideas came or the consequences for their own lives, contemporary Americans had adopted an unwholesome, lighthearted, and softheaded "nihilism with a happy ending."[7] Bloom's diagnosis of the state of America's souls confirmed, as he put it, the "*overwhelming* influence of Nietzsche on *everything* in *our* life": "Nietzsche is *us*."[8]

Bloom's Nietzsche was not only the cause of America's problems but also its best diagnostician. For an author so critical of relativism's ill effects, Bloom gave little discussion to the virtue of moral absolutes. This is because he lamented not the loss of absolutes as such, but the loss of striving that comes with a belief in absolutes, the belief that truth is possible. He believed it was in the interstices between uncertainty and the belief that certainty is attainable that independent, vital thinking occurs. What Bloom called for was not the *truth* of texts, but the pleasures of the text, for he worried that the "notion of books as companions" was utterly "foreign" to students trained to think that there is no great beyond. For him, this is what the academy as an "experiment in excellence" should make possible.[9] He placed less emphasis on handing down truths than on fostering the drive to attain them.

Bloom's Nietzsche understood that urgency. His "works are a glorious exhibition of the soul of a man" who understood the awesome responsibility and demand for intellectual creativity that comes with indeterminacy. Bloom drew from Nietzsche the alarm of the "great spiritual bleeding" that occurs with relativism as the resting point of inquiry:

> I fear that spiritual entropy or an evaporation of the soul's boiling blood is taking place, a fear that Nietzsche thought justified and made the center of all his thought. He argued that the spirit's bow was being unbent and

risked being permanently unstrung. Its activity, he believed, comes from culture, and the decay of culture meant not only the decay of man in this culture but the decay of man simply. This is the crisis he tried to face resolutely: the very existence of man as man, as a noble being. . . . Today's select students know so much less, are so much more cut off from the tradition, are so much slacker intellectually. . . . The soil is ever thinner, and I doubt whether it can now sustain the taller growths.[10]

There is little indication in the book that Bloom cared about common ground. He wanted transcendence. He wanted independent thinking without the crutch of ideas hardened into ideology. He gave no evidence that he cared where the inquiry ended, but he did care whether the human conditions were good enough for the journey to even get started.

One of the reasons Bloom found himself an accidental public intellectual in 1987 was not because his arguments about American intellectual life or about Nietzsche were new, but because they fit seamlessly into discourses long part of the American intellectual tradition. The introductory distillation of Bloom's 1987 *Wilson Quarterly* essay, "How Nietzsche Conquered America," explained that "ideas have consequences. They also have pedigrees. But by the time an idea gains wide acceptance, its origins may be murky, even invisible."[11] The same can be said of Bloom's own thesis. Indeed, the entire anatomy of his lament—the assessment of the dangers of moral and epistemological relativism, the diagnosis of the American mind as infected by challenging European ideas, the criticism of anti-intellectualism, and the worry that Americans lack an agonized conscience necessary for penetrating thought and for wrestling with moral problems—brought him into conversation with generations of American commentators worried about the same. Certainly, his conclusion that Nietzsche had warned of the consequences of his own challenge to moral foundations, but that America was just too intellectually lean to get the profundity of it, was not new. Even Bloom's animating question, though not feigned, had a long history. When he asked, wide-eyed, "Why, then, could *ideas* so contrary to American *ideals* so easily take root?" he was posing a question that had been raised repeatedly over the century.[12] And each time it was raised—whether by liberal Protestant ministers wondering why the pews were thinning out on Sundays, liberal humanists who regarded antifoundationalism as a European problem, or conservative commentators astonished that such an antidemocratic thinker was co-opted by the Left—the questioners were thrown off course by looking for *elsewheres* rather than into their own interest in Nietzsche. Bloom, like so many others, argued that Nietzsche's centrality to American thought would not be such a bad thing, if Americans knew their Nietzsche as he did.

If there is one aspect, especially, that shows how dramatically unexceptional and therefore powerfully representative Bloom's *Closing of the American Mind* was, it is the ways in which it expressed reverence for the Nietzschean longing that he feared was in short supply in America. Bloom's esteem for Nietzsche is unmistakable. Nietzsche was a cultural relativist, but he "recognized the terrible intellectual and moral risks involved" in challenging absolutes. Bloom's Nietzsche understood that the pursuit of self-transcendence is the basis of culture. He had shown Bloom that the exhaustion of values required individuals to turn to themselves to generate new ones: "The self must be a tense bow. It must struggle with opposites rather than harmonize them. . . . The self must also bring forth arrows out of its longing. Bow and arrow, both belonging to man, can shoot a star into the heavens to guide man." Bloom thus admired Nietzsche for the way he turned to the resources in himself to fight the nihilistic implications of his own relativism. Although Nietzsche heralded the death of God, he nevertheless "restored something like the soul to our understanding of [modern] man."[13]

Bloom was right—Nietzsche had become the American "us," though not in the way he thought about his influence but instead in the way he enacted it. His engagement with Nietzsche is a testament of longing, like so many earlier American appropriations of Nietzsche. His sense of the personal Nietzsche, *his* Nietzsche against a culture that would never understand him, that pathos of distance, has, in fact, been the American Nietzsche. Bloom's posture here as the lonely thinker in a land of pygmies is one adopted by many before him. It was one adopted by Nietzsche. And it was one adopted, on many occasions, by Nietzsche's own first philosophical love, Emerson.

For Bloom, if Americans are to know their knowing, they must know how Nietzsche has been at once a cultural hero and an invisible intellectual force. Bloom made an impassioned claim for the critical, yet quiet importance of ideas: "as Nietzsche said, 'the greatest deeds are thoughts,' that 'the world revolves around the inventors of new values, revolves silently.'" His point is not a "know-nothing response to foreign influence" but rather the call for a "heighten[ed] awareness of where we must look if we are to understand what we are saying and thinking." Bloom thought that Nietzsche exerted a stultifying influence on the American mind. When Bloom called on Americans "to think through the meaning of the intellectual dependency that has led us to such an impasse," though, he did not realize that he was in fact enacting an American way of knowing Nietzsche, or an Emersonian way of thinking: these could have been words straight out of Emerson's "American Scholar."[14]

Intellectual historians may quibble, as they should, about the accuracy of Bloom's diagnosis of late twentieth-century American intellectual and cultural life. They can certainly take issue with his history; Nietzsche's impact on American thought and culture began before Bloom's German-émigré professors were born. For those who are also teachers, they can challenge him on the consequences of Nietzschean relativism in the classroom. And they can question how ecumenical his vision of the thinking life was, or whether an educator who spoke so disparagingly of his students could care for them in a way that would cultivate, not condemn, their intellects. Nietzsche, who took Emerson as his educator, understood what an education after absolutes might look like. It would provoke, not instruct, young souls to shoot arrows of longing over the yawning *ressentiment* of intellectual belatedness, and over the abyss of antifoundationalism. That longing, from Emerson to Nietzsche and indeed down to Bloom, is a longing worth longing for.

Writing a book can be the most solitary of enterprises. And yet, in my case, it was possible only through the persistent support of colleagues, friends, family, and research institutions along the way. Thanks to the intellectual and material sustenance they have given me, working on this project has been a not-so-lonely labor of love.

This book got its start while I was a doctoral student in history at Brandeis University. One does not often see the words *Doktorvater* and *friend* paired in the same sentence, and yet, from early on, James Kloppenberg has been both for me. While working with him as a graduate student and in the years since, Jim has provided me with an incomparable scholarly model for coming to terms with the past through careful study of ideas and their contexts. He has emboldened me intellectually, inspired me with his extraordinary range, and sustained me with his warm enthusiasm and encouragement. Rudolph Binion is responsible for getting me to think about Nietzsche in historical perspective in his graduate course on European thought and culture. Rudy always wondered why I would study American intellectual life when I was, in his view, condemned to starve within it. Though he never managed to persuade me to remake myself as a Europeanist, thanks to his broad knowledge and his ear for the nuance of an argument, he helped guide me early on in this study. The words at my disposal are not adequate to describe what Richard Wightman Fox and Jane Kamensky have meant to this project. This is especially humbling, as it is from these two gifted historians and dear friends that I learned the rewards of bringing a literary imagination to historical scholarship. To read their comments on a draft or their rapid-response e-mails, or simply to talk with them, is to be bathed in the rich possibilities of language. I would consider it a great accomplishment if I have managed to put to good use even a hint of their model of eloquence in this book, and their model of friendship in my life.

I have had the great fortune of having not one but two wonderful history departments welcome me into their fold, and provide me with colleagues who offered me their scholarly expertise and warm friendship. At the University of Miami, Edward Baptist, Richard Godbeer, Joshua Greenberg,

Mary Lindemann, Michael Miller, Guido Ruggiero, and Erica Windler read earlier portions of the manuscript, showing how high thoughts and hearty laughter can go hand in hand. The move to the University of Wisconsin–Madison history department came during the final years of writing the book. I am grateful to have so many wonderful neighbors on the fourth- and fifth-floor history wing of the Mosse Humanities Building. I want to pay especial tribute to the following colleagues for their critical interventions in the manuscript, my state of mind, or both: Suzanne Desan, Frank M. Glover, Francine Hirsch, Pernille Ipsen, William Jones, Stephen Kantrowitz, Rudy Koshar, Gerda Lerner, Florencia Mallon, Tony Michels, David McDonald, William Reese, Stanley Schultz, David Sorkin, Steve Stern, Sarah Thal, Lee Wandel, André Wink, and the late Jeanne Boydston. Without the help and good humor of the history department staff, I cannot even begin to imagine how I would have stayed afloat these last few years. A heartfelt thank you is in order to Amy Schultz, Nicole Hauge, Teri Tobias, Carrie Tobin, Leslie Abadie, Scott Burkhardt, John Persike, Mike Burmeister, and Jane Williams for the innumerable tangible and intangible ways that they have swooped in with assistance. Charles L. Cohen's steady feedback and guidance have improved the quality of the manuscript and its author's quality of life in ways I can scarcely explain but will never forget. Thank you, Chuck, for serving patiently as my in-house mentor, editor, and wise counsel, and for never once making me feel guilty about asking for a little help from your searing intellect at a moment's notice. And thank you, most of all, for being you.

A number of research institutions provided me with generous funding for carrying out this project. Fellowships from the Berlin Program for Advanced German and European Studies and the Gottlieb Daimler and Karl Benz Stiftung first brought me to Germany, financed my early research at the Nietzsche Archive, and brought me into contact with German scholars and scholars of Germany who helped me to think critically about the transatlantic contours of the project. A Harvard University fellowship supported my research and gave me access to the incomparable resources of the Harvard University library system, while the Charlotte W. Newcombe Fellowship of the Woodrow Wilson Institute provided me with the necessary support to allow me to devote a full year to writing. As for negotiating the sometimes warring demands of teaching and scholarship, the National Endowment for the Humanities and the Graduate Schools at the University of Miami and the University of Wisconsin–Madison gave me the precious gift of summers devoted to the book, while the Center for European Studies at Madison generously financed additional travel to the Nietzsche Archive in Weimar. And for a subvention for the publication of this book from the University of Wisconsin–Madison Provost's Office and the Graduate School, I extend my sincere gratitude.

A Visiting Scholars Program fellowship at the American Academy of Arts and Sciences generously provided me with the time, resources, and stimulating atmosphere for working on early revisions of the manuscript. The magnanimous invitation to participate in the Charles Warren Center's "American Intellectuals and the Culture of the Atlantic World" seminars offered me an additional circle of superb historians, whose company and conversation improved this manuscript in ways large and small. For helping to give shape and substance to this project, my sincere thanks to both communities of scholars in Cambridge, most especially Carol Anderson, Carrie Tirado Bramen, Charles Capper, Chip Colwell-Chanthaphonh, Robert Chodat, Jenny Davidson, Dean Grodzins, David Hall, Elizabeth Lyman, Jennifer Marshall, Alexandra Oleson, Jason Puskar, Jeffrey Sklansky, Sarah Song, Lisa Szefel, and Sharon Weiner.

I wish I could single out by name each and every helpful and patient librarian on both sides of the Atlantic who helped me track down obscure books and century-old periodicals with tiny print runs. What's clear is that I cannot go without expressing my deep and abiding gratitude to the extraordinary staff of the Klassik Stiftung Weimar at the Goethe- and Schiller-Archive, who facilitated my research over the course of many trips as I worked my way through the Nietzsche Archive collections. For assisting me as I made research arrangements, helping me to creatively navigate the sources to find letters from the States, showing me how to crack the code of *Sütterlin*, indulging me in my occasional bursts of jubilation upon discovering a new letter, and for sharing with me the sheer fun of this detective work, I sincerely thank Karin Ellermann, Barbara Hampe, Silke Henke, Marita Prell, Hedwig Völkerling, and Susan Wagner. I must also express my great appreciation of Erdmann von Wilamowitz-Moellendorf of the Klassik Stiftung Weimar at the Herzogin Anna Amalia Bibliothek, who provided me with his expert guidance in examining Nietzsche's Emerson volumes, found Nietzsche photographs from his Schulpforta days, and alerted me to the growing curiosity about the Nietzsche-Emerson connection in European scholarship.

The opportunity to present my work to different scholarly communities at crucial stages in the research enabled me to test new ideas and showed me the range of audiences for the book. I want to thank the members of the New York Area Seminar in Intellectual and Cultural History, most especially Richard Wolin and Jerrold Seigel, for their invitation to present my research on Nietzsche's image in American culture at an early stage in its conceptualization. Richard was then, and has continued to be, an invaluable source of advice and understanding, while Jerrold kindly offered crucial feedback about Nietzsche's philosophy in the context of Western philosophies of the self. The late John Patrick Diggins made sure that I showed up for my talk properly nourished on Caesar salad and a breadstick and appropriately enlivened by his stories recounting his favorite American Nietzscheans at an unforgettable lunch at the Century Club. And while I'm remembering with fondness the largesse of New York–based intellectual historians, I must turn to the late Tony Judt, for his invitation to participate in the Remarque Institute's Kandersteg Seminar in 2007. I will never forget the magic of those days of stimulating conversations, and I am deeply thankful for the lasting friendships that grew out of them. I am grateful to the American History program at Brandeis, not only for outfitting me with an incomparable training for this line of work, but also for welcoming me back to Olin-Sang to give the Ray Ginger Lecture. And my deep gratitude extends to Nick Witham, for the invitation to present my work at the conference "American Ideas in Context" at the University of Nottingham, which enabled me, more recently, to think anew about American thinking.

Participation in the 2009 "Ideas in Motion" workshop at the Shelby Cullom Davis Center for Historical Studies at Princeton University put me in the orbit of a remarkable group of scholars, similarly working on themes in intellectual reception. I am especially grateful to Daniel T. Rodgers and Anson Rabinbach, for asking me to join this conversation; Thomas Bender and Nadia Urbinati, for their astute, incisive reading of my paper; Suzanne Marchand and Eric Weitz, for their bolstering comments and enlivening conversation; and Richard King, who nourished this project with his range of expert knowledge on so many of the book's subjects, and its author with his ennobling encouragement.

The University of Wisconsin–Madison Center for the Humanities' "First Book" Program funded by the Mellon Foundation provided me with an invigorating seminar devoted to my manuscript, and an embarrassment of riches in scholarly feedback during the late stages of revision. I want to thank the center's director, Sara Guyer, and its administrators, Michael Goodman and Sandy Nuzback, for making this event possible. My gratitude extends to my Madison colleagues who generously read and commented on the entire manuscript: Russ Castronovo, Chuck Cohen, Rudy Koshar, David McDonald, Lou Roberts, Ivan Soll, and David Zimmerman, and to Julia Mickenberg for coming on board at the last minute to add her voice to the discussion. I do not know how to properly thank Jackson Lears and Robert Westbrook for agreeing to come to Madison in the dead of winter, for reading the manuscript down to the very marrow of its bones, for their trademark brilliance, and for their sage advice for completing the project. I hope my lifelong gratitude will do. While no one book could adequately incorporate the competing insights, methodological interventions, and suggestions for revision of so large and diverse a focus group of scholars, their feedback helped draw out the manuscript's strengths and make whatever shortcomings remain less serious.

Many scholars, colleagues, and friends were instrumental at various stages of the book's development. When the project was just getting started, I was fortunate to have the constructive feedback and nurturing companionship of Caroline Fisher, Jennifer Green, Jonathan Hansen, Darra Mulderry, Tulasi Srinivas, and Andrea Volpe. My early research in Germany benefited from the instructive insights of Lauren Applebaum, Karin Goihl, Dietrich Hermann, Molly Wilkinson Johnson, Sabine Kriebel, Lisa Vanderlinden, and Peter Vogt. For their encouraging conversations and suggestions for fruitful avenues of inquiry, I thank Casey Blake, Lawrence Buell, David Engerman, Daniel Horowitz, Hans Joas, and Robert Holub. The manuscript benefited immeasurably from the critical commentary on various portions of it and the all-purpose intellectual magnanimity of Paul Boyer, Steve Cantley, George Cotkin, Michael Gomez, Andrew Hartman, David Pickus, Jeffrey Sklansky, and Robert Westbrook. I will forever be grateful to Jonathan Levy for the psychic boost given to me by his unsolicited e-mail, enthusiastically responding to a previously published article discussing an earlier version of ideas presented here. While conversations with and feedback from Sian Hunter, Alison Kallet, and Rob Tempio were instrumental in helping me to conceptualize the scope of and audience for the book, Erin Clune, Jeanine Magill, Ronit Stahl, Kent Williams, and Rachel White helped improve various portions of the manuscript with their finely tuned eyes, steady hands, and agility wielding an editor's scalpel. The research assistance that Neal Davidson and

Sarah Rous provided in the late stages of the manuscript helped ensure that bibliographies were up-to-date, census records were sufficiently mined, and notations drawn from William James's Nietzsche volumes were spot on. "Research assistance" fails to adequately capture what Vaneesa Cook has meant to this project during the last, long stretch of book revisions. An indefatigable researcher, a quick study, and a careful reader, Vaneesa has graced this project with her steady input and her steadying presence. It may seem that my gratitude doth runneth over a bit, but there's really no way to properly thank those who have offered their seemingly inexhaustible supply of tough-minded and tender-hearted feedback on the project, and their glorious fellowship with its author. Here I have in mind Daniel Greene, Matthew Hale, Kristen Joiner, Kristin Phillips-Court, Martin Woessner, and Lisa Szefel. I am not sure that I am deserving of the sustained intellectual engagement and camaraderie of so many remarkable thinkers, writers, and human beings. But I am surely grateful that I got them.

Nary a day goes by that I don't thank my lucky stars for bringing Douglas Mitchell to this project, and for Doug's help in bringing this book into the world. His immediate interest in and loyalty to my vision helped me figure out my course and stay on it. Simply having Doug on board made me think that the project was worthwhile; I hope that what I've pulled off here is something that makes him proud. This book has been blessed to have landed at the University of Chicago Press, not just because of Doug, but because of the extraordinary team he plays on. My deep thanks as well to Tim McGovern, for his upbeat assistance in shepherding the project through publication; Levi Stahl, for his broad conception of the book; and Sandy Hazel, for her sensitive ear for prose, her careful scrutiny of mine, and her much-needed expert advice throughout the editing process. Derek Gottlieb deserves praise for his great skills in the art of indexing. And the anonymous reviewers for the press deserve my deep gratitude for their extensive commentary and illuminating suggestions, which made this a better book than it otherwise would have been.

There are two crucial people who, in very different ways, opened the world of intellectual history to me. It was from my undergraduate professor at the University of Rochester, Christopher Lasch, that I discovered the phrase "intellectual history," and first gained access to its rewards and challenges. Professor Lasch (I was too young to know him as "Kit") first brought me to a number of the thinkers in this study and taught me how to read them with the focused intensity they deserve. Though I am not sure what he would think of how I put his instruction and example to use, I am certain that my imagining his penetrating insights about what I have written here has helped me to improve it. A decade before this book ever took shape, death took the body of my grandmother, Ida Lavine Weyman, long after Alzheimer's disease claimed her mind. But her influence marks every page herein. Like a good southern lady, Nannie Ida never let on about the torrent of unfilled existential longings and philosophical questions stirring inside her, but thankfully, her bookshelf did. It was in her private library that I, as child, discovered Will Durant's *Story of Philosophy* and her many portable companions of the "great philosophers." We never had our chance to talk philosophy: I was too little and she was too reticent. But I cannot help but think that she is the real force behind my gravitation to it.

I turn now to the other members of my family, who would be justified in thinking that apologies, not thanks, are in order here. Whatever whiff of quiet civility or *Gemütlichkeit* there was in our homes, I owe to my in-laws, Albert and Erika Rosenhagen. With every move—from Dresden to Marburg to Miami to Madison—they showed up time and again to paint, saw, scrub, rake, cook, diaper babies' bottoms, and, best of all, goad their daughter-in-law onward. Though they always showed esteem for this odd existence and praised the sacrifices scholars make for their work, their occasional raised eyebrow or carefully worded exhortation to not forget the "life" part of the "life of the mind" reminded me, at crucial moments, that the great thing about straight-talking parents-in-law is that they're not required to love you unconditionally. Erika's existential allergy to doubt and second-guessing regularly served as a tonic to my mental atmosphere and fortified me as a scholar-writer-mother. To my siblings, Hal Ratner, Sari Judge, and Marni Whelan; their spouses, Jeanine Magill, Michael Judge, and Kyle Whelan; and my beautiful niece and nephews, thank you for your unending warmth and good humor, for tolerating my late arrivals to and early departures from holiday gatherings, and for loving me through my unlovely moments of fatigue. I am especially indebted to my big sister Sari, for her persistent guiding wisdom and grounding pragmatism, and to my grandmother Anne Ratner for never failing to ask when I was going to "graduate."

This book is dedicated to my parents, not only for affirming me over the long course of its production, but also for showing me, by their example, the rewards of fervent dedication to one's work. I am so very grateful for Phillip

Ratner's delight in his daughter's calling, and for my stepmother, Ellen Ratner, who, thanks to her broad reading tastes, alerted me every time Nietzsche's name popped up in one of her novels or magazines. I do not know whether admiration quite does the trick for expressing my feelings for my mother throughout this process. Though a social worker, Miriam Lavine Ratner graciously moonlit (without compensation) as the book's editor, proofreading and commenting on virtually every word in every version of this project, from its inception to its completion. For every late-night session in which she offered me her steady companionship, for every time during her busy schedule she set aside her work to let me talk through an idea or test a new formulation, and, most of all, for generously letting me believe that she actually enjoyed all the demands I placed on her, I remain everlastingly indebted to her.

It is fitting that I turn now to mention the three people most precious in this process, while trying to drown out the impressively loud background noise created by two of them. This project has placed very big demands on two very small people, Amelie Charlotte and Jonah Friedrich Rosenhagen. And yet for reasons I will never understand but will always remember, they managed to bear them with an exuberant love of life and contagious lightness of spirit that carried their mom through. Then there is Ulrich, without whom the process of book writing would have been neither possible nor tolerable. A witness to the initial spark of the project, a steady co-conspirator fanning its flames, and a smart survivalist who knew when it was time to encourage his *Frau* to tamp out glistening intellectual embers and shut down her computer for the night, Ulrich has been my rock and refuge. Somehow he always knew when I needed to be gently reminded about the requirements of his work and scholarship, and when I needed to forget them. For this and so much more, I admire him, adore him, and praise the heavens for him. Together with Amelie and Jonah, he has taught me that love is a foundation that need never be questioned.

# Prologue

1 Friedrich Nietzsche, as quoted in R. J. Hollingdale, *Nietzsche: The Man and His Philosophy*, rev. ed. (Cambridge: Cambridge University Press, 1999), 132.

2 Elise Fincke to Friedrich Nietzsche, 1881, in *Briefwechsel: Kritische Gesamtausgabe* III.2, ed. Giorgio Colli and Mazzino Montinari (Berlin: Walter de Gruyter, 1975–2004), 204 (hereafter noted as *KGB*); this and all other translations are mine unless otherwise indicated. All epigraphs are drawn from the Nietzsche translations listed in the bibliography.

3 Friedrich Nietzsche to Elise Fincke, March 20, 1882, in ibid., III.1, 181.

4 Friedrich Nietzsche (note on back side of letter from Elise Fincke to Nietzsche, 1881), Klassik Stiftung Weimar, Goethe- und Schiller-Archiv, Weimar, Germany (GSA hereafter), 71/BW48.

5 Gustav Dannreuther to Friedrich Nietzsche, May 29, 1882, in *KGB* III.2, 256.

6 Friedrich Nietzsche, *The Gay Science* (1882), trans. Walter Kaufmann (New York: Vintage Books, 1974), 303. On perspectives of America in European thought, see James W. Ceaser, *Reconstructing America: The Symbol of America in Modern Thought* (New Haven, CT: Yale University Press, 1997), and Melvin Lasky, "America and Europe: Transatlantic Images," and Marcus Cunliffe, "European Images of America," in *Paths of American Thought*, ed. Arthur M. Schlesinger Jr. and Morton White (New York: Houghton Mifflin, 1963), 465–514. The specifically German conceptions of America are discussed in Dan Diner, *America in the Eyes of the Germans: An Essay on Anti-Americanism* (Princeton, NJ: Markus Wiener, 1996), and Paul C. Weber, *America in Imaginative German Literature in the First Half of the Nineteenth Century* (New York: Columbia University Press, 1926).

7 Friedrich Nietzsche, *Sämtliche Werke: Kritische Studienausgabe*, ed. Giorgio Colli and Mazzino Montinari (Berlin: Walter de Gruyter, 1999), 9, 7 [229], 365 (hereafter noted as *KSA*); Friedrich Nietzsche to Paul Rée, June 1877, in *KGB* II.5, 246; Nietzsche, *KSA* 9, 7 [100], 338.

8 Nietzsche, *Gay Science*, 258–59.

9 Friedrich Nietzsche, *Human, All Too Human* (1878), trans. R. J. Hollingdale (Cambridge: Cambridge University Press, 1996), 132. In 1884 Nietzsche wondered whether "the Americans get used up too fast—perhaps they only appear a future world power" (Nietzsche, *KSA*, 11, 26 [247], 215).

10 Friedrich Nietzsche to Franz Overbeck, December, 24, 1883, in *KGB* III.1, 463.

11 Ralph Waldo Emerson, *The Journals and Miscellaneous Notebooks of Ralph Waldo Emerson*, vol. 8, ed. William Gilman and J. E. Pearsons (Cambridge, MA: Har-

vard University Press, Belknap Press, 1970), 368. See also Ralph Waldo Emerson, "Prospects," in *The Early Lectures of Ralph Waldo Emerson*, vol. 3, ed. Robert E. Spiller and Wallace E. Williams (Cambridge, MA: Harvard University Press, Belknap Press, 1970), 368.

12 Nietzsche slightly modified the wording in his German translation. The original from Emerson's essay "History" (1841) reads, "To the poet, to the philosopher, to the saint, all things are friendly and sacred, all events profitable, all days holy, all men divine" (Ralph Waldo Emerson, "History," from *Essays: First Series* (1841), in *The Collected Works of Ralph Waldo Emerson*, vol. 2, ed. Alfred R. Ferguson and Jean Ferguson Carr [Cambridge, MA: Harvard University Press, Belknap Press, 1979], 8). The notion of treating every joy, ache, and pain as if they were self-willed and personally beneficial later formed the basis of Nietzsche's "Amor Fati." It also became a way he understood the task of the philosopher. On Christmas of 1882, Nietzsche wrote Franz Overbeck, "If I do not discover the alchemists' trick of turning . . . excrement into *gold*, I am lost.—Thus I have the *most beautiful* opportunity to prove that for me 'all experiences are profitable, all days holy, and all human beings divine'!!!!" (Friedrich Nietzsche to Franz Overbeck, December 25, 1882, *KGB* III.1, 312).

13 Ralph Waldo Emerson, "Fate," from *The Conduct of Life* (1860), in *The Collected Works of Ralph Waldo Emerson*, vol. 6, ed. Douglas Emory Wilson (Cambridge, MA: Harvard University Press, Belknap Press, 2003), 1.

14 Friedrich Nietzsche to Carl von Gersdorff, September 24, 1874, *KGB* II.3, 258; Ludwig Marcuse, "Nietzsche in America," *South Atlantic Quarterly* 50 (July 1951): 332.

15 Harold Bloom, *Genius: A Mosaic of One Hundred Exemplary Creative Minds* (New York: Warner Books, 2002), 195.

16 Friedrich Nietzsche, *Twilight of the Idols* (1889), in *"Twilight of the Idols" and "The Anti-Christ,"* trans. R. J. Hollingdale (New York: Penguin, 1990), 86.

17 Nietzsche, *Gay Science*, 146; Nietzsche, *KSA*, 9, 12 [151], 602.

18 On the periodization of Nietzsche's works, see Keith Ansell Pearson, "Friedrich Nietzsche: An Introduction to His Life, Thought, and Work," in *A Companion to Nietzsche*, ed. Pearson (Malden, MA: Blackwell, 2006), 1–21; Linda L. Williams, *Nietzsche's Mirror: The World as Will to Power* (Lanham, MD: Rowman and Littlefield, 2001), 3; and Ruth Abbey, *Nietzsche's Middle Period* (New York: Oxford University Press, 2000), xi–xvii. Abbey points out that it was Lou Andreas-Salomé who first popularized the tripartite schema in *Friedrich Nietzsche in seinen Werken* (1894; Redding Ridge, CT: Black Swan Books, 1988).

19 The most complete study of Emerson's influence on Nietzsche is George J. Stack, *Nietzsche and Emerson: An Elective Affinity* (Athens: Ohio University Press, 1992). The systematic study of Nietzsche's interest in Emerson commenced with Eduard Baumgarten's research in the Nietzsche Archive in the 1930s, which he published later under "Mitteilungen und Bemerkungen über den Einfluss Emersons auf Nietzsche," *Jahrbuch für Amerikastudien* 1 (1956): 93–152. Other

important contributions to scholarship on Nietzsche's uses of Emerson include Herwig Friedl, "Emerson and Nietzsche: 1862–1874," in *Religion and Philosophy in the United States of America*, ed. Peter Freese (Essen: Die Blaue Eule Verlag, 1987), 1:267–87; Stanley Hubbard, *Nietzsche und Emerson* (Basel: Verlag für Recht und Gesellschaft, 1958); Hermann Hummel, "Emerson and Nietzsche," *New England Quarterly* 19 (March 1946): 63–84; Rudolf Schottlaender, "Two Dionysians: Emerson and Nietzsche," *South Atlantic Quarterly* 39 (July 1940): 330–43; Thomas H. Brobjer, *Nietzsche and the "English": The Influence of British and American Thinking on His Philosophy* (Amherst, NY: Humanity Books, 2008), 155–66; Vivetta Vivarelli, "Nietzsche und Emerson: Über einige Pfade in Zarathustras metaphorischer Landschaft," *Nietzsche Studien* 16 (1987): 227–63; and the essays in the special issue "Emerson/Nietzsche," edited by Michael Lopez, of *ESQ: A Journal of the American Renaissance* 43 (1997). On Emerson's influence on German thought, see Julius Simon, *Über Emersons Einfluss in Deutschland (1851–1932)* (Berlin: Junker & Dünnhaupt, 1937), and Luther S. Luedtke, "German Criticism and Reception of Ralph Waldo Emerson" (PhD diss., Brown University, 1971).

20  He owned the following Emerson texts: Ralph Waldo Emerson, *Die Führung des Lebens* [The Conduct of Life]*: Gedanken und Studien*, trans. E. S. v. Mühlenberg (Leipzig: Steinacker, 1862); Ralph Waldo Emerson, "Historic Notes of Life and Letters in Massachusetts," *Atlantic Monthly*, October 1883, 529–43; Ralph Waldo Emerson, *Neue Essays* [Letters and Social Aims], trans. Julian Schmidt (Stuttgart: Abenheim, 1876); Ralph Waldo Emerson, *Über Goethe und Shakespeare: Aus dem Englischen nebst einer Kritik der Schriften Emersons von Hermann Grimm* (Hannover: Rümpler, 1857); and Ralph Waldo Emerson, *Versuche* [Essays], ed. G. Fabricius (Hannover: C. Meyer, 1858). See Brobjer, *Nietzsche and the "English,"* 159–60, 282–83.

21  Brobjer, *Nietzsche and the "English,"* 162, 293–325.

22  Friedrich Nietzsche, *Werke in drei Bänden*, vol. 3, ed. Karl Schlechta (München: Carl Hanser Verlag, 1954–56), 106–7.

23  Nietzsche to Gersdorff, *KGB* II.3, 258.

24  Baumgarten, "Mitteilungen und Bemerkungen," 110, 112.

25  George Kateb, *Emerson and Self-Reliance* (Thousand Oaks, CA: Sage, 1995), xxix.

26  Friedl, "Emerson and Nietzsche," 267–68, 283.

27  Ralph Waldo Emerson, *Representative Men* (1850), in *The Collected Works of Ralph Waldo Emerson*, vol. 4, ed. Douglas Emory Wilson (Cambridge, MA: Harvard University Press, Belknap Press 1987), 4.

28  Nietzsche, autobiographical fragment from 1868/69, in *Werke in drei Bänden*, 3:151.

29  On Nietzsche's Schulpforta experiences, see Carl Pletsch, *Young Nietzsche: Becoming a Genius* (New York: Free Press, 1991), 46–62; Curtis Cate, *Friedrich Nietzsche* (Woodstock, NY: Overlook Press, 2005), 17–39; and Hollingdale, *Nietzsche,* 18–27.

30  Nietzsche, *Werke in Drei Bänden*, 3:75.

31  On Nietzsche's changing relationship to—and ideas about—Christianity from his Schulpforta years onward, see Jörg Salaquarda, "Nietzsche and the Judeo-

Christian Tradition," in *The Cambridge Companion to Nietzsche*, ed. Bernd Magnus and Kathleen M. Higgins (Cambridge: Cambridge University Press, 1996), 90–118; and Thomas Brobjer, "Nietzsche's Changing Relation with Christianity: Nietzsche as Christian, Atheist, and Antichrist," in *Nietzsche and the Gods*, ed. Weaver Santaniello (Albany: State University of New York Press, 2001), 137–58.

32 Friedrich Nietzsche, *Friedrich Nietzsche: Werke und Briefe; Historisch-Kritische Gesamtausgabe*, vol. 2, ed. Hans Joachim Mette (Munich: Beck, 1933), 68 (hereafter noted as *HKG*).

33 Nietzsche, *Werke in Drei Bänden*, 3:151. On Nietzsche's adolescent crisis and his retreat into Germania, see Pletsch, *Young Nietzsche*, 51–58.

34 Brobjer, *Nietzsche and the "English,"* 155.

35 Nietzsche, *HKG* 2:221.

36 Friedrich Nietzsche, "Fate and History: Thoughts," in *The Nietzsche Reader*, ed. Keith Ansell Pearson and Duncan Large (Malden, MA: Blackwell, 2006), 14.

37 Ralph Waldo Emerson, "Quotation and Originality," from *Letters and Social Aims* (1875), in *The Collected Works of Ralph Waldo Emerson*, vol. 8, ed. Joel Myerson (Cambridge, MA: Harvard University Press, Belknap Press, 2010), 94, 107.

38 Herwig Friedl not only makes this point but shows Emerson's importance for Nietzsche as he began working out his philosophical concerns and concepts. Friedl, "Emerson and Nietzsche."

39 Nietzsche, "Fate and History," 12–13.

40 Emerson, "Fate," 5.

41 Nietzsche, "Fate and History," 14.

42 Emerson, "Fate," 5.

43 Nietzsche, "Fate and History," 14.

44 Emerson, "Fate," 26.

45 Nietzsche, "Fate and History," 14.

46 Emerson, "Fate," 2.

47 Nietzsche, "Fate and History," 14.

48 Emerson, "Fate," 26.

49 Ibid., 25, 17.

50 Nietzsche, "Freedom of Will and Fate," 16–17. Nietzsche quoted this line from the opening poem to Emerson's "Fate" from his copy of the German translation by E. S. von Mühlenberg: "Immer ist der Gendanke vereint[,] Mit dem Ding, das als sein Ausdruck erscheint." Emerson's original reads, "For the prevision is allied[,] Unto the thing so signified."

51 Emerson, "Fate," 26.

52 Nietzsche, "Fate and History," 12–13. "This one fact the world hates, that the soul *becomes*": "Self-Reliance," from *Essays: First Series*, in *Collected Works of Ralph Waldo Emerson*, 2:40.

53 Nietzsche, "Fate and History," 12–13.

54 Nietzsche, *HKG* 2:334.

55 Eduard Baumgarten made this discovery. Nietzsche wrote "Ecce Homo" in the

margins of his copy of "Spiritual Laws" next to the following passage, which he underlined: "It will certainly accept your own measure of your doing and being, whether you sneak about and deny your own name, or whether you see your work produced to the concave sphere of the heavens, one with the revolution of the stars. [The same reality pervades all teaching.] The man may teach by doing, and not otherwise" (Baumgarten, "Mitteilungen und Bemerkungen," Table III, 142).

56  Nietzsche, *KSA*, vol. 14, pp. 476–77.

57  Walter Kaufmann, translator's introduction to Nietzsche, *Gay Science*, 10–11.

58  Emerson, "Fate," 16; Friedrich Nietzsche, "On the Uses and Disadvantages of History for Life" (1874), in *Untimely Meditations*, trans. R. J. Hollingdale and ed. Daniel Breazeale (Cambridge: Cambridge University Press, 1997), 62; Emerson, "Fate," 14; Nietzsche, "On the Uses and Disadvantages," 106.

59  Emerson, "Power," in *Conduct of Life*, 28; Nietzsche, *Beyond Good and Evil* (1886), trans. Walter Kaufmann (New York: Vintage, 1989), 203.

60  Emerson, "Self-Reliance," 40.

61  Nietzsche, "On the Uses and Disadvantages of History for Life," 62.

62  Emerson, "Divinity School Address" (1838), in *The Collected Works of Ralph Waldo Emerson*, vol. 1, ed. Alfred R. Ferguson (Cambridge, MA: Harvard University Press, Belknap Press, 1971), 84; Nietzsche, *Gay Science*, 181.

63  Ralph Waldo Emerson, "Compensation" (1841), in *The Collected Works of Ralph Waldo Emerson*, 2:69; Nietzsche, *Twilight of the Idols*, 33.

64  Baumgarten, "Mitteilungen und Bemerkungen," 105.

65  Friedrich Nietzsche to Carl von Gersdorff, April 7, 1866, *HKG* 2:960.

66  Nietzsche, *Twilight of the Idols*, 76–77.

67  Emerson, "History," 2:13 (in the original, Emerson refers to "intellectual nomadism"); Nietzsche, *Human, All Too Human*, 6.

68  Nietzsche, "Schopenhauer as Educator" (1874), in *Untimely Meditations*, 193.

69  Ibid., 129; Emerson as quoted in ibid.

70  By way of introduction, Knortz sent Nietzsche two of his own books he hoped would interest him: one on Walt Whitman, and another on contemporary American poetry. Karl Knortz, *Amerikanische Gedichte der Neuzeit* (Leipzig: Wartig, 1883), and Karl Knortz, *Walt Whitman: Vortrag* (New York: Vorträge des Gesellig Wissenschaftlichen Vereins, no. 14, 1886).

71  Friedrich Nietzsche to Karl Knortz, June 21, 1888, in *Selected Letters of Friedrich Nietzsche*, trans. and ed. Christopher Middleton (Chicago: University of Chicago Press, 1960), 298–99. For the letter in the original German, see *KGB* III.5, 339–41.

72  Friedrich Nietzsche to Ernst Wilhelm Fritzsch, April 14, 1888, in *KGB* III.5, 296; Nietzsche to Reinhart von Seydlitz, May 13, 1888, ibid., 314; and Nietzsche to Malwida von Meysenbug, July 1888, ibid., 378. Other letters include Nietzsche to Heinrich Köselitz, May 17, 1888, ibid., 315–17; Nietzsche to Carl Fuchs, July 29, 1888, ibid., 374–76; and Nietzsche to Emily Fynn, August 11, 1888, ibid., 387.

73  Nietzsche, *KSA*, 9, 12 [68], 588.

# Introduction

1 Sigmund Zeisler, "Nietzsche and His Philosophy," *Dial*, October 1, 1900, 219.

2 Despite Nietzsche's importance for the course of twentieth-century American thought and culture, his impact has received little systematic attention from historians. Two important exceptions are the Nietzsche reception studies by Hays Steilberg and Melvin Drimmer. Both scholars take a traditional approach to reception history by focusing on the influence of Nietzsche's ideas on prominent intellectuals. See Hays Alan Steilberg, *Die amerikanische Nietzsche-Rezeption von 1896 bis 1950* (Berlin: Walter de Gruyter, 1996), and Melvin Drimmer, "Nietzsche in American Thought, 1895–1925" (PhD diss., University of Rochester, 1965). An excellent collection of essays about Nietzsche's influence on particular thinkers and writers is Manfred Pütz, ed., *Nietzsche in American Literature and Thought* (Columbia, SC: Camden House, 1995).

3 On the history of antifoundationalism in Western philosophy, see Tom Rockmore and Beth J. Singer, eds., *Antifoundationalism Old and New* (Philadelphia: Temple University Press, 1992).

4 Several histories have dealt with aspects of the twentieth-century challenge to foundationalism. The two classic studies are Morton White, *Social Thought in America: The Revolt against Formalism* (1949; rev. ed., Boston: Beacon, 1957), on the American context, and H. Stuart Hughes, *Consciousness and Society: The Reorientation of European Social Thought, 1890–1930* (New York: Knopf, 1958), for the European one. Edward A. Purcell Jr., *The Crisis of Democratic Theory: Scientific Naturalism and the Problem of Value* (Lexington: University Press of Kentucky, 1973), deals with the effect of relativist thinking on the social sciences and legal and democratic theory; James Kloppenberg examines the transatlantic networks among *via media* philosophers and social thinkers in *Uncertain Victory: Social Democracy and Progressivism in European and American Thought, 1870–1920* (New York: Oxford University Press, 1986), and Merle Curti, *Human Nature in American Thought: A History* (Madison: University of Wisconsin Press, 1980), examines how the late nineteenth-century "discovery" of the dynamic unconscious upset theorists' stable categories of human nature. For studies that examine the challenge to foundationalism in American philosophy, see Robert B. Westbrook, *John Dewey and American Democracy* (Ithaca, NY: Cornell University Press, 1991); Bruce Kuklick, *A History of Philosophy in America, 1720–2000* (Oxford: Oxford University Press, 2001); and Cornel West, *The American Evasion of Philosophy: A Genealogy of Pragmatism* (Madison: University of Wisconsin Press, 1989). On the influence of challenges to foundationalism in higher education in general and the social sciences in particular, see Dorothy Ross, ed., *Modernist Impulses in the Human Sciences, 1870–1930* (Baltimore: Johns Hopkins University Press, 1994); Peter Novick, *That Noble Dream: The "Objectivity Question" and the American Historical Profession* (Cambridge: Cambridge University Press, 1988); and Julie A. Reuben, *The Making of the Modern University: Intellectual Transformation and the*

*Marginalization of Morality* (Chicago: University of Chicago Press, 1996). For histories that look at the cultural responses to the reorientation in social thought, see Jackson Lears, *No Place of Grace: Antimodernism and the Transformation of American Culture, 1880–1920* (New York: Pantheon Books, 1981), and George Cotkin, *Reluctant Modernism: American Thought and Culture, 1880–1900* (New York: Twayne, 1992).

5  Analyzing the uses of his troubled biography provides a window onto a central yet unexplored dimension of American cultural life: the contested image of the intellectual. An important study that specifically considers the persona of the philosopher (albeit in early modern Europe) is Conal Condren, Stephen Gaukroger, and Ian Hunter, eds., *The Philosopher in Early Modern Europe: The Nature of a Contested Identity* (Cambridge: Cambridge University Press, 2006).

6  By examining the steady traffic of commentary about Nietzsche's person, and analyzing how conceptions of the philosopher consistently mediated the interpretations of his writings, this book bridges intellectual and cultural history, and shows the need for a more comprehensive understanding of the relationship between a thinker's ideas and his or her popular persona. On the figure and celebrity of the literary author, see Loren Glass, *Authors Inc.: Literary Celebrity in the Modern United States, 1880–1980* (New York: New York University Press, 2004), and David Haven Blake, *Walt Whitman and the Culture of American Celebrity* (New Haven, CT: Yale University Press, 2006).

7  Reception histories that yield an integrated narrative about the national or cultural context under consideration include James W. Ceaser, *Reconstructing America: The Symbol of America in Modern Thought* (New Haven, CT: Yale University Press, 1997); Richard Wightman Fox, *Jesus in America: Personal Savior, Cultural Hero, National Obsession* (New York: Harper San Francisco, 2004); David Armitage, *The Declaration of Independence: A Global History* (Cambridge, MA: Harvard University Press, 2007); Caroline Winterer, *Mirror of Antiquity: American Women and the Classical Tradition, 1750–1900* (Ithaca, NY: Cornell University Press, 2007); and Steven Biel, *American Gothic: A Life of America's Most Famous Painting* (New York: Norton, 2006). A helpful survey of contributions to reception theory is James Machor and Philip Goldstein, eds., *Reception Study from Literary Theory to Cultural Studies* (New York: Routledge, 2001). This aspect of my study directly addresses some central concerns of historians of books and readers. Two classic studies that connect the thought in books to the stuff of life are Carlo Ginzburg's *The Cheese and the Worms: The Cosmos of a Sixteenth-Century Miller*, trans. John Tedeschi and Anne Tedeschi (Baltimore: Johns Hopkins University Press, 1980), and Robert Darnton, "Readers Respond to Rousseau: The Fabrication of Romantic Sensitivity," in *The Great Cat Massacre: And Other Episodes in French Cultural History* (1984; New York: Basic Books, 1999), 215–56. For a collection of insightful meditations on the experience of reading and the interpretive agency of readers, see Alberto Manguel, *A History of Reading* (New York: Viking, 1996).

8  Jackson Lears makes a bold and powerful case for examining history as a history

327

of longing in his *Rebirth of a Nation: The Making of Modern America, 1877–1920* (New York: HarperCollins, 2009). I discuss opening intellectual history to the study of the affective dimensions of intellectual transfer in "Conventional Iconoclasm: The Cultural Work of the Nietzsche Image in Twentieth-Century America," *Journal of American History* 93 (December 2006): 728–54. On the romantic sources of Nietzschean longing, see Bernard Yack, *The Longing for Total Revolution: Philosophical Sources of Social Discontent from Rousseau to Marx and Nietzsche* (Princeton, NJ: Princeton University Press, 1986), and George S. Williamson, *The Longing for Myth in Germany: Religion and Aesthetic Culture from Romanticism to Nietzsche* (Chicago: University of Chicago Press, 2004). Works especially sensitive to the emotional dynamics involved in reading are Janice Radway, *Reading the Romance: Women, Patriarchy, and Popular Literature* (Chapel Hill: University of North Carolina Press, 1991); Barbara Sicherman, *Well-Read Lives: How Books Inspired a Generation of American Women* (Chapel Hill: University of North Carolina Press, 2010); and Wayne Booth, "Implied Authors as Friends and Pretenders," in *The Company We Keep: An Ethics of Fiction* (Berkeley: University of California Press, 1988), 169–98.

9   Important studies that view developments in American intellectual and cultural life from a transnational or global perspective include Kloppenberg, *Uncertain Victory*; Daniel T. Rodgers, *Atlantic Crossings: Social Politics in a Progressive Age* (Cambridge, MA: Harvard University Press, Belknap Press, 1998); Paul Gilroy, *Black Atlantic: Modernity and Double-Consciousness* (Cambridge, MA: Harvard University Press, 1993); Larry J. Reynolds, *European Revolutions and the American Literary Renaissance* (New Haven, CT: Yale University Press, 1988); Leslie Butler, *Critical Americans: Victorian Intellectuals and Transatlantic Liberal Reform* (Chapel Hill: University of North Carolina Press, 2007); Penny Von Eschen, *Race against Empire: Black Americans and Anticolonialism, 1937–1957* (Ithaca, NY: Cornell University Press, 1997); Anthony Heilbut, *Exiled in Paradise: German Refugee Artists and Intellectuals in America, from the 1930s to the Present* (1983; Berkeley: University of California Press, 1997); Martin Jay, *The Dialectical Imagination: A History of the Frankfurt School and the Institute for Social Research, 1923–1950* (1973; Berkeley: University of California Press, 1996); and George Cotkin, *Existential America* (Baltimore: Johns Hopkins University Press, 2003). For a recent discussion of transnational history, see "AHR Conversation: On Transnational History," *American Historical Review* 3 (December 2006): 1441–64.

10  Nietzsche's American career thus tracks the history of the idea of anti-intellectualism in American life. I discuss the origins and early career of this trope in my "Anti-Intellectualism as Romantic Discourse," *Daedalus: Journal of the American Academy of Arts and Sciences* 138 (Spring 2009): 41–52. On American anti-intellectualism, see Richard Hofstadter, *Anti-Intellectualism in American Life* (New York: Knopf, 1963); Susan Jacoby, *Age of American Unreason* (New York: Pantheon, 2008); and Jacques Barzun, *House of Intellect* (New York: Harper, 1959).

For an important reminder that American intellectuals aren't the only ones who worry that they live in a culture indifferent to their labors, see Stefan Collini, *Absent Minds: Intellectuals in Britain* (Oxford: Oxford University Press, 2006).

11 And yet it is the sheer diversity of "Nietzsches" within each of these national contexts that makes anything more than a few sweeping generalizations well-nigh impossible. For studies of Nietzsche in diverse national contexts, see Patrick Bridgwater, *Nietzsche in Anglosaxony: A Study of Nietzsche's Impact on English and American Literature* (Leicester, UK: University of Leicester Press, 1972); Steven E. Aschheim, *The Nietzsche Legacy in Germany, 1890–1990* (Berkeley: University of California Press, 1992); R. Hinton Thomas, *Nietzsche in German Politics and Society, 1890–1918* (Manchester: Manchester University Press, 1983); David S. Thatcher, *Nietzsche in England, 1890–1914: The Growth of a Reputation* (Toronto: University of Toronto Press, 1970); Christopher E. Forth, *Zarathustra in Paris: The Nietzsche Vogue in France, 1891–1918* (De Kalb: Northern Illinois University Press, 2001); Thomas Harrison, ed., *Nietzsche in Italy* (Stanford, CA: Stanford University Press, 1988); Gonzalo Sobejano, *Nietzsche en España* (Madrid: Editorial Grados, 1967); and Bernice Glatzer Rosenthal, ed., *Nietzsche in Russia* (Princeton, NJ: Princeton University Press, 1986).

12 On cultural stratification in twentieth-century American intellectual life, see Joan Shelley Rubin, *The Making of Middlebrow Culture* (Chapel Hill: University of North Carolina Press, 1992); Joan Shelley Rubin, "The Scholar and the World: Academic Humanists and General Readers in Postwar America," in *The Humanities and the Dynamics of Inclusion Since WWII*, ed. David Hollinger (Baltimore: Johns Hopkins University Press, 2006), 73–103; Lawrence Levine, *Highbrow/Lowbrow: The Emergence of Cultural Hierarchy in America* (Cambridge, MA: Harvard University Press, 1988); Janice Radway, *A Feeling for Books: Book-of-the-Month Club, Literary Taste, and Middle-Class Desire* (Chapel Hill: University of North Carolina Press, 1997); Andrew Ross, *No Respect: Intellectuals and Popular Culture* (New York: Routledge, 1998); Paul R. Gorman, *Left Intellectuals and Popular Culture in Twentieth-Century America* (Chapel Hill: University of North Carolina Press, 1996); and Herbert Gans, *Popular Culture and High Culture: An Analysis and Evaluation of Taste* (New York: Basic Books, 1974). This aspect of my study directly addresses some central concerns of historians of the book. See Robert Darnton, *The Business of the Enlightenment: A Publishing History of the* Encylopédie, *1775–1800* (Cambridge, MA: Harvard University Press, 1979). For reviews of the field, see Robert Darnton, "What Is the History of Books?," in *Books and Society in History*, ed. Kenneth E. Carpenter (New York: R. R. Bowker, 1983), 3–26; G. Thomas Tanselle, *The History of Books as a Field of Study* (Chapel Hill: University of North Carolina Press, 1981); Cathy N. Davidson, "Towards a History of Books and Readers," *American Quarterly* 40 (March 1988): 7–17; and David D. Hall, "Readers and Reading in America: Historical and Critical Perspectives," *American Antiquarian Society Proceedings* 103 (1993): 337–57.

13 For the original articulation of "imagined communities," see Benedict Anderson, *Imagined Communities: Reflections on the Origin and Spread of Nationalism* (London: Verso, 1983).

## Chapter One

1 Wilbur M. Urban, "Metaphysics and Value," in *Contemporary American Philosophy: Personal Statements*, ed. George P. Adams and William P. Montague (New York: Russell & Russell, 1962), 2:358–59 (italics added). Urban's discovery of Nietzsche echoes Nietzsche's discovery of Arthur Schopenhauer. Nietzsche came across Schopenhauer's *The World as Will and Representation* (1818) in a secondhand bookshop in Leipzig in 1865 when he was a 21-year-old student. He bought the book on impulse, took it home, and upon reading it immediately recognized Schopenhauer's transformative implications for his thinking. For Nietzsche's account of this discovery, see Friedrich Nietzsche, *Werke in Drei Bänden*, 3:133–34.

2 Although his study focuses primarily on German-trained economists and social scientists, Rodgers's *Atlantic Crossings* provides an excellent portrait of young American academics in the German academy at the turn of the last century. For the nineteenth-century influence of German scholarship on American thinkers, see Carl Diehl, *Americans and German Scholarship, 1770–1870* (New Haven, CT: Yale University Press, 1978). Studies that discuss the role of the German research university as a model for American higher education and disciplines include Laurence R. Veysey, *The Emergence of the American University* (Chicago: University of Chicago Press, 1965); Dorothy Ross, *The Origins of American Social Science* (Cambridge: Cambridge University Press, 1991); and Jurgen Herbst, *The German Historical School in American Scholarship: A Study in the Transfer of Culture* (Ithaca, NY: Cornell University Press, 1965). On the appeal of the German university and the public status of German scholars, see Burton Bledstein, *The Culture of Professionalism: The Middle Class and the Development of Higher Education in America* (New York: Norton, 1976), chaps. 7 and 8.

3 Urban, "Metaphysics and Value," 358–59. In addition to stumbling across Nietzsche's *On the Genealogy of Morals*, Urban also discovered a copy of Alexius Meinong's *Psychologische-ethische Untersuchung zur Wertheorie* (1894), which taught him about the psychological dimension of value formation.

4 Ibid., 357.

5 For discussions of nineteenth-century positivism in the physical and human sciences, see Klaus Christian Köhnke, *The Rise of Neo-Kantianism: German Academic Philosophy between Idealism and Positivism*, trans. R. J. Hollingdale (Cambridge: Cambridge University Press, 1991); Ross, ed., *Modernist Impulses in the Human Sciences*; Bruce Kuklick, *The Rise of American Philosophy* (New Haven, CT: Yale University Press, 1977) and *A History of Philosophy in America*; and Daniel J. Wilson, *Science, Community, and the Transformation of American Philosophy, 1860–1930* (Chicago: University of Chicago Press, 1990).

6   Urban, "Metaphysics and Value," 359.

7   Nietzsche's battle with poor health is recounted in Cate, *Friedrich Nietzsche*;
    Rüdiger Safranski, *Nietzsche: A Philosophical Biography*, trans. Shelley Frisch (New
    York: Norton, 2002); and Hollingdale, *Nietzsche: The Man and His Philosophy*.
    Already during his lifetime, medical doctors speculated that the cause of his most
    serious ailments and the source of his ultimate psychic collapse was syphilis. For
    a short history of, and argument for, the syphilis theory, see Deborah Hayden,
    *Pox: Genius, Madness, and the Mysteries of Syphilis* (New York: Basic Books,
    2003), 172–99.

8   Friedrich Nietzsche to Ernst Schmeitzner, February 13, 1883, in *KGB*, III.1, [375],
    327–28. This and other episodes in Nietzsche's publication history are recounted
    in William H. Schaberg, *The Nietzsche Canon: A Publication History and Bibliogra-
    phy* (Chicago: University of Chicago Press, 1995).

9   For Nietzsche's early reception in Germany up to 1918, see Richard Frank Krum-
    mel, *Nietzsche und der Deutsche Geist*, 2 vols. (1974; Berlin: Walter de Gruyter,
    1983).

10  Georg Brandes's lectures were published in Germany two years later under the
    title "Aristokratischer Radikalismus: Eine Abhandlung über Friedrich Nietzsche,"
    *Deutsche Rundschau* 63 (April 1900): 52–89.

11  Brandes established his reputation with his four-volume encyclopedic survey,
    *Main Currents in the Literature of the Nineteenth Century* (1872–85), which was
    translated into English in 1906.

12  George Brandes to Friedrich Nietzsche, November 26, 1887, in *KGB* III.6, 120;
    and Nietzsche to Brandes, December 2, 1887, in *KGB* III.5, 206.

13  *How to Philosophize with a Hammer* is the subtitle of Nietzsche's *Twilight of the
    Idols* (1889).

14  Friedrich Nietzsche, *Ecce Homo* (1908), in *"On the Genealogy of Morals" and "Ecce
    Homo,"* trans. Walter Kaufmann (New York: Vintage Books, 1989), 333.

15  Friedrich Nietzsche to Heinrich Köselitz, December 31, 1888, in *KGB* III.5,
    567. For just a sampling of the many letters Nietzsche signed with variations
    of "Nietzsche Caesar," "Dionysus," and "The Crucified" which he sent in late
    December 1888 through early January 1889, see Friedrich Nietzsche to August
    Strindberg, December 31, 1888, in *KGB* III.5, 567–68; Friedrich Nietzsche to Ca-
    tulle Mendès, January 1, 1889, in *KGB* III.5, 571; and Friedrich Nietzsche to Meta
    von Salis, January 3, 1889, in *KGB* III.5, 572.

16  Franz Overbeck to Heinrich Köselitz, January 15, 1889, in *Friedrich Nietzsche:
    Chronik in Bildern und Texten*, compiled for the Stiftung Weimarer Klassik by
    Raymond J. Benders and Stephan Oettermann (Munich: Carl Hanser Verlag;
    Vienna: Deutschen Taschenbuch Verlag, 2000), 732.

17  On Förster-Nietzsche, see Heinz Frederick Peters, *Zarathustra's Sister: The Case
    of Elisabeth and Friedrich Nietzsche* (New York: Crown, 1977), and Carol Diethe,
    *Nietzsche's Sister and the Will to Power: A Biography of Elisabeth Förster-Nietzsche*
    (Urbana: University of Illinois Press, 2003). For a history of the Nietzsche

Archive, see David Marc Hoffmann, *Zur Geschichte des Nietzsche-Archivs* (Berlin: Walter de Gruyter, 1991).

18  On the early Nietzsche reception in Germany, see Aschheim, *The Nietzsche Legacy in Germany*, and Thomas, *Nietzsche in German Politics and Society*. On the early Nietzsche reception in France, see Forth, *Zarathustra in Paris*, and in England, see Dan Stone, *Breeding Superman: Nietzsche, Race and Eugenics in Edwardian and Interwar Britain* (Liverpool: Liverpool University Press, 2002).

19  Bakewell would later return as their colleague before moving on to professorships at the University of California and Yale University.

20  Charles M. Bakewell, "Nietzsche: A Modern Stoic," *Yale Review* 5 (October 1915): 67.

21  Urban, "Metaphysics and Value," 358.

22  Emma Goldman noted Reitzel's importance for facilitating American exposure to European radical thought. She described him as a "brilliant writer" and his *Arme Teufel* as "the one German paper in the States that kept its readers in contact with the new literary spirit in Europe." Goldman, as quoted in Randall P. Donaldson, *The Literary Legacy of a "Poor Devil": The Life and Work of Robert Reitzel (1849–1898)* (New York: Lang, 2002), 50–51.

23  Eugene O'Neill to Benjamin De Casseres, June 22, 1927, in *Selected Letters of Eugene O'Neill*, ed. Travis Bogard and Jackson R. Bryer (New Haven, CT: Yale University Press, 1988), 245–46. For more on Tucker's function as O'Neill's intellectual broker, see Stephen A. Black, *Eugene O'Neill: Beyond Mourning and Tragedy* (New Haven, CT: Yale University Press, 1999). John Patrick Diggins credits Tucker's bookstore, which also introduced O'Neill to Max Stirner and Arthur Schopenhauer, as encouraging the "Germanic turn" in his early philosophical-anarchist thinking. See Diggins, *Eugene O'Neill's America: Desire under Democracy* (Chicago: University of Chicago Press, 2007), 62.

24  In 1917, Mencken described Huneker as "the first to see the rising star of Nietzsche." H. L. Mencken, *A Book of Prefaces* (New York: Knopf, 1917), 162.

25  On Reitzel, see Ulrike Heider, *Der "Arme Teufel": Robert Reitzel vom Vormärz zum Haymarket* (Bühl-Moos: Elster, 1986), and Richard Oestreicher, "Robert Reitzel, Der Arme Teufel," in *The German-American Radical Press: The Shaping of a Left Political Culture, 1850–1940*, ed. Elliott Shore, Ken Fones-Wolf, and James P. Danky (Urbana: University of Illinois Press, 1992), 145–67.

26  "Last of the Anarchists," *New York Times*, November 14, 1887, 1. For a transcript of the eulogy, see Robert Reitzel, "Am Grabe," in *Des "Armen Teufel": Gesammelte Schriften*, ed. Max Baginski (Detroit: Reitzel Klub, 1913), 142–44.

27  Robert Reitzel, "Predigten aus der Neuen Bibel: *Also Sprach Zarathustra*, VIII," *Der Arme Teufel*, October 29, 1892, 385; Reitzel, "Predigten aus der Neuen Bibel, I," *Der Arme Teufel*, September 17, 1892, 337; Reitzel, "Predigten aus der Neuen Bibel, V," *Der Arme Teufel*, October 15, 1892, 369; and Reitzel, "Predigten aus der Neuen Bibel, I," *Der Arme Teufel*, September 17, 1892, 337.

28  On Tucker's role in American anarchism, see Wendy McElroy, *The Debates of*

*Liberty: An Overview of Individualist Anarchism* (Lanham, MD: Rowman and Littlefield, 2003), 1–16, and Frank H. Brooks, *The Individualist Anarchists: An Anthology of* Liberty, *1881–1908* (New Brunswick, NJ: Transaction, 1994).

29  Benjamin Tucker, "Freer Banking vs. Greenbackism," *Liberty*, October 1, 1892, 3.

30  Benjamin Tucker, "A Radical Publication Fund," *Liberty*, June 17, 1893, 2.

31  Tucker, "Freer Banking vs. Greenbackism."

32  George Schumm was also German-American anarchist Max Baginski's brother-in-law, a later biographer of Tucker, and a major translator of German-language anarchist texts, such as John Henry Mackay's *The Anarchists* in 1891 and Max Stirner's *The Ego and Its Own* in 1907. On Schumm see Paul Avrich, *Anarchist Voices: An Oral History of Anarchism in America* (Princeton, NJ: Princeton University Press, 1995).

33  Nietzsche, as quoted in "Extracts from the Works of Nietzsche," *Liberty*, December 17, 1892, 4.

34  Nietzsche, as quoted in "Religion and Government," *Liberty*, January 7, 1893, 1.

35  A very direct example of this is how a passage from Nietzsche excerpted in *Liberty* inspired John Badcock Jr.'s 1894 lecture, "Slaves to Duty," which Tucker later published as part of his radical publications. Badcock drew from Nietzsche his assertion that one's own conscience, when too beholden to external authorities, isn't his own. Badcock concluded that all forms of "duty"—religious, economic, political, and familial—are slavery. Echoing Nietzsche, he argued, "The believer in duty . . . will either be enslaved by the crafty, or by what he calls his 'conscience.'. . . Circumstances change, and your moral codes won't stand the test. In place of duty I put—nothing. Superstitions never want replacing, or we should never advance to freedom. Waste not your energies, but turn them *all* to your own advantage." Badcock, *Slaves to Duty* (New York: Benjamin R. Tucker, 1906), 37. On Nietzsche as Badcock's inspiration, see Tucker's note in *Liberty*, November 17, 1894, 4.

36  Benjamin Tucker, "Aphorisms from Nietzsche," *Liberty*, July 1899, 6n.

37  Benjamin Tucker, "On Picket Duty," *Liberty*, December 1897, 1.

38  Nietzsche, as quoted in "Aphorisms from Nietzsche," 6.

39  Benjamin Tucker, *Instead of a Book by a Man Too Busy to Write One: A Fragmentary Exposition of Philosophical Anarchism, Culled from the Writings of Benj. R. Tucker* (New York: B. R. Tucker, 1897), 14.

40  *Liberty's* masthead read, "Not the Daughter but the Mother of Order."

41  E. Horn, as translated in "The Liberty of Egoism," *Liberty*, April 7, 1894, 7.

42  George Schumm, "Friedrich Nietzsche," *Book Reviews* 3 (February 1896): 275–80.

43  James Huneker to H. L. Mencken, April 11, 1916, in *The Letters of James Gibbons Huneker*, ed. Josephine Huneker (New York: Charles Scribner's Sons, 1922), 211.

44  James Huneker to Elisabeth Förster-Nietzsche, September 1904, GSA 72/BW3475.

45  H. L. Mencken, *Book of Prefaces*, 163–64.

46  H. L. Mencken, introduction to James Huneker, *Essays by James Huneker* (1929; reprint, New York: AMS Press, 1976), xi.

**47** James Huneker, "Friedrich Nietzsche," *Musical Courier* 41 (September 5, 1900): 19.

**48** James Huneker, "Nietzsche the Rhapsodist," in *Overtones: A Book of Temperaments* (New York: Charles Scribner's Sons, 1904), 117, 131–32.

**49** Huneker, "Friedrich Nietzsche," 18–19.

**50** Huneker, *Letters*, 213.

**51** For *The Pathos of Distance*, Huneker used a Nietzsche quotation on the requirements of genius as the book's epigraph to describe himself to himself: "convictions are prisons . . . new ears for new music. New eyes for the most remote things . . . the pathos of distance." Huneker, *The Pathos of Distance* (New York: Charles Scribner's Sons, 1913).

**52** Huneker, *Letters*, 213.

**53** James Huneker, *Egoists: A Book of Supermen* (New York: Charles Scribner's Sons, 1909), 257; Huneker, "Nietzsche the Rhapsodist," 126; Huneker, *Egoists*, 238–39.

**54** James Huneker, *Steeplejack* (New York: Charles Scribner's Sons, 1918–20), 2:191. For an excellent biography of the short-lived *M'lle New York*, see David Weir, *Decadent Culture in the United States: Art and Literature against the American Grain, 1890–1926* (Albany: State University of New York Press, 2008), 42–47.

**55** Huneker, *Steeplejack*, 2:190.

**56** Vance Thompson, "Boyesen-Brandes-Nietzsche," *M'lle New York*, October 1895, 43.

**57** Ibid., 44.

**58** Vance Thompson, "Leader," *M'lle New York*, November 1898, 1–2. As David Weir put it, "What Thompson apparently wished for was a rejuvenation of American culture through an infusion of foreign influence, not the actual presence of 'foreigners' on American soil." Weir, *Decadent Culture in the United States*, 47.

**59** Vance Thompson, "The Doomed Republic," *M'lle New York*, August 1895, 6–8.

**60** Thompson, "Leader," 1.

**61** Vance Thompson, "Democracy Is Bankrupt," *M'lle New York*, August 1895, 9–14.

**62** "F. W. Nietzsche," *Bookman: A Journal of Literature and Life*, October 1900, 99–100.

**63** "Friedrich Wilhelm Nietzsche," *Popular Science Monthly*, October 1900, 668; "F. W. Nietzsche," *Outlook*, September 8, 1900, 94.

**64** "Prof. Nietzsche Dead," *New York Times*, August 26, 1900, 7.

**65** William L. Alden, "London Literary Letter," *New York Times Saturday Review*, September 22, 1900, BR16.

**66** The publication history of the first translations is recounted in Thatcher, *Nietzsche in England*. Alexander Tille's Darwinist read of Nietzsche can be seen in his study, *Von Darwin bis Nietzsche: Ein Buch Entwicklungsethik* (Leipzig: C. G. Naumann, 1895). On Tille's efforts as a transnational ambassador of Nietzsche, see Stefan Manz, "Translating Nietzsche, Mediating Literature: Alexander Tille and the Limits of Anglo-German Intercultural Transfer," *Neophilologus* 91 (January 2007): 117–34.

**67** "A Philosophic 'Mr. Hyde,'" *Nation*, June 11, 1896, 459.

68 Charles M. Bakewell, "Review of *The Philosophy of Friedrich Nietzsche*," *Philosophical Review* 10 (May 1901): 327.

69 "Was Nietzsche a Madman or a Genius?," 641.

70 "The Greatest European Event since Goethe," *Current Literature* 43 (July 1907): 65.

71 Advertisement for Tille and Common, trans., *Collected Works of Nietzsche* (London: Henry & Co., 1896); GSA, 72/BW2368.

72 Ernest Antrim and Heinrich Goebel, "Friedrich Nietzsche's Uebermensch," *Monist* 9 (July 1899): 571. For a critique of Americans' belated adaptations of European zeitgeists, see popular-science writer Edwin E. Slosson's "The Philosopher with the Hammer," *Independent* 65 (September 24, 1908): 693–97.

73 "Will Nietzsche Come into Vogue in America?," *Current Literature* 49 (July 1910): 65.

74 Havelock Ellis, "The Genius of Nietzsche," reprint from *Weekly Critical Review*, April 30, 1903, in *Views and Reviews* (London: Desmond, Harmsworth, 1932), 147–48. Likewise, Huneker thought it a "pity" that *Der Fall Wagner* [*The Case of Wagner*], one of the last books Nietzsche wrote as madness closed in on him, was among the first books translated for English readers. Though he noted that it is an "extraordinary" book containing "flashes of dazzling fugitive ideation," Huneker confessed that it was "too fantastic, too ill-balanced" to set the proper tone for understanding Nietzsche's philosophy as a whole. See Huneker, "Nietzsche the Rhapsodist," 11–12.

75 "A Philosophic 'Mr. Hyde,'" 460.

76 William Wallace, "Thus Spake Zarathustra: A Book for All and None," *International Journal of Ethics* 7 (April 1897): 369.

77 G. R. T. Ross, "Beyond Good and Evil," *International Journal of Ethics* 18 (July 1908): 518.

78 F. C. S. Schiller, "Nietzsche and His Philosophy," *Book Buyer* 13 (August 1896): 408. Vance Thompson described Nietzsche as the "outlawed count of Poland," while James Huneker emphasized his "Polish individualism." Vance Thompson, *French Portraits* (Boston: Richard Badger, 1900), 222, and Huneker, "Friedrich Nietzsche," 18–20. The presence of Schiller's reviews in American publications reminds us of the transnational dimension of US commentary about Nietzsche. Whereas the first English translators hailed from England, a number of the scholarly interpretations published in American publications were written by British academics or by Germans in translation, and indeed even the early popularization of the "superman" was thanks, in part, to Irishman George Bernard Shaw's *Man and Superman* (1903).

79 "A Philosophic 'Mr. Hyde,'" 460.

80 "New Revelations of Nietzsche," *Current Literature* 40 (June 1906): 644; "New Light on Nietzsche and His Friends," *Current Literature* 50 (June 1911): 638; and Herbert L. Stewart, "Some Criticisms of the Nietzsche Revival," *International Journal of Ethics* 19 (July 1909): 443.

81 "Anti-Morality of Fr. Nietzsche," *New York Times*, January 4, 1908, BR4; Alfred Rau, "Nietzsche's Morality," *New York Times Saturday Review of Books*, January 18, 1908, BR32.

82 Grace Neal Dolson, *The Philosophy of Friedrich Nietzsche* (New York: Macmillan, 1901), iv, 102.

83 Joseph Jacobs, "Works of Friedrich Nietzsche," *New York Times*, May 7, 1910, BR8.

84 Victor S. Yarros, "Theoretical and Practical Nietzscheism," *American Journal of Sociology* 6 (March 1901): 682.

85 Huneker, "The New English Nietzsche," in *Pathos of Distance*, 320–21.

86 Camillo Von Klenze, "A Philosopher Decadent," *Dial*, June 16, 1897, 356.

87 Schiller, "Nietzsche and His Philosophy," 407–8.

88 On the interdependence of developments in the history of philosophy and the competing personas of philosophers, see Condren et al., *The Philosopher in Early Modern Europe*. The essays here draw connections between the ideas about philosophy as an intellectual activity and the kinds of persons who undertake those activities.

89 Zeisler, "Nietzsche and His Philosophy," 219.

90 "The Most Revolutionary System of Thought Ever Presented to Men," *Current Literature* 40 (March 1906): 282.

91 Nietzsche, *Ecce Homo*, 323.

92 H. L. Mencken, *The Philosophy of Friedrich Nietzsche* (Boston: Luce, 1908), 28.

93 Willard Huntington Wright, a fellow *Smart Set* contributor, also argued that Nietzsche's books are a commentary on his personality in his 1915 study of Nietzsche's philosophy, *What Nietzsche Taught* (New York: B. W. Huebsch, 1915).

94 H. L. Mencken, as quoted in Marion Elizabeth Rodgers, *Mencken: The American Iconoclast* (New York: Oxford University Press, 2005), 105.

95 H. L. Mencken, as quoted in Carl Bode, *Mencken* (Carbondale: Southern Illinois University Press, 1969), 54.

96 H. L. Mencken, *George Bernard Shaw: His Plays* (Boston: Luce, 1905).

97 Mencken, *The Philosophy of Friedrich Nietzsche*, 9. Mencken's obsession with intelligence as a quality missing in modern America can be seen in the title of his first magazine venture, *The Smart Set*, which bore on its masthead of the first issue of September 1914, "one civilized reader is worth a thousand boneheads."

98 These quotations are from the 1913 revised edition: H. L. Mencken, *Friedrich Nietzsche* (Boston: Luce, 1913), 288.

99 Mencken, *The Philosophy of Friedrich Nietzsche*, 118.

100 Ibid., 3, 4, 48, 58.

101 Huneker, *Egoists*, 240, 243.

102 Huneker, "Friedrich Nietzsche," 19.

103 "Was Nietzsche a Madman or a Genius?," 641.

104 "Interesting Revolutionary Theories from a Writer Now in a Madhouse," *New York Times*, March 5, 1898, RBA158.

105 Hays Steilberg, "First Steps in the New World: Early Popular Reception of Nietz-sche in America," in Pütz, *Nietzsche in American Literature and Thought*, 22–23.

106 William James, Review of *Degeneration*, by Max Nordau (New York: Appleton, 1895), in *Essays, Comments, and Reviews* (Cambridge, MA: Harvard University Press, 1987): 507–8. For appreciative treatments of Nordau, see Aline Gorren, "The New Criticism of Genius," *Atlantic Monthly*, December 1894, 794–800, and "A Philosophic 'Mr. Hyde,'" 459. For an earlier American medical opinion, which similarly drew a connection between Nietzsche's physical state and his philoso-phy, see George M. Gould, *Biographical Clinics* (Philadelphia: P. Blakiston's Son, 1904), vol. 2. Gould, a physician, argued that Nietzsche developed his aphoristic style while walking because he was physically unable to be stationary at a desk for long periods due to his illnesses. Unlike Nordau, Gould argued that Nietzsche's ability to produce his philosophy in the face of his debilitating illnesses was noth-ing short of heroic.

107 George Mosse, introduction to *Degeneration*, by Max Nordau (1895; New York: H. Fertig, 1968), xvi. On Nordau, see Michael Stanislawski, *Zionism and the Fin de Siècle: Cosmopolitanism and Nationalism from Nordau to Jabotinsky* (Berkeley: University of California Press, 2001).

108 Nordau, *Degeneration*, 415, 451, 416, 445–46, 432.

109 Elisabeth Förster-Nietzsche, *Das Leben Nietzsches*, 2 vols. (Leipzig: Naumann, 1895). Elisabeth Förster-Nietzsche, *The Life of Nietzsche*, vol. 1, *The Young Nietz-sche*, trans. Anthony Ludovici (New York: Sturgis and Walton, 1912), and *The Life of Nietzsche*, vol. 2, *The Lonely Nietzsche*, trans. P. Cohn (New York: Sturgis and Walton, 1915).

110 Förster-Nietzsche, *The Life of Nietzsche*, 2:v. Förster-Nietzsche's authority as Nietzsche interpreter received sanction and assistance from American interpret-ers. In an appreciative review of her Nietzsche biography, James Taft Hatfield, professor of philosophy at Northwestern University and correspondent of Förster-Nietzsche's, described her as "the most consistent advocate and furtherer of her brother's mission, [who] is at her very best in this intimate story of the life she knew so well." William Barry likewise acknowledged that it is "from the minute details given of her family by Madame Förster-Nietzsche [that] we owe our knowledge" of Nietzsche. And James Huneker described her as "a good-looking intellectual lady, devoted to the memory of her brother and writing much about him." James Taft Hatfield, "The Younger Life of Friedrich Nietzsche," *Dial*, September 1, 1912, 127; William Barry, "The Ideals of Anarchy," *Littel's Living Age* 211 (December 1896), 618; and Huneker, *Steeplejack*, 2:224.

111 Elisabeth Förster-Nietzsche, *The Lonely Nietzsche*, v; *The Young Nietzsche*, 71–72, 82; *Lonely Nietzsche*, 294; *Young Nietzsche*, vii.

112 Paul Carus, *Philosophy as a Science* (Chicago: Open Court, 1909), 1; Paul Carus, *Friedrich Nietzsche and Other Exponents of Individualism* (Chicago: Open Court, 1914), 1.

113 See, for example, Paul Carus's critique of pragmatism, *Truth on Trial* (Chicago: Open Court, 1911).

114 Paul Carus, "Immorality as a Philosophic Principle," *Monist* 9 (July 1899): 581. This article was reprinted and expanded in his *Friedrich Nietzsche and Other Exponents of Individualism* (1914).

115 Carus, "Immorality as a Philosophical Principle," 596.

116 Ibid., 596–97n.

117 Carus's reading of Nietzsche photographs reveals the perceived realism of late-Victorian photographic portraiture. On mimesis and artifice in late nineteenth-century photography, see Miles Orvell, *The Real Thing: Imitation and Authenticity in American Culture, 1880–1940* (Chapel Hill: University of North Carolina Press, 1989), and Bevis Hillier, *Victorian Studio Photographs* (Boston: David R. Godine, 1976).

118 Paul Carus, "Friedrich Nietzsche," *Monist* 17 (April 1907): 247–48; reprinted in Carus, *Friedrich Nietzsche and Other Exponents*, n.p.

119 Carus, *Friedrich Nietzsche and Other Exponents*, 65–66.

120 Ibid., 64.

121 On Freud's visit to Clark University, see Nathan G. Hale Jr., *The Beginnings of Psychoanalysis in the United States, 1876–1917*, vol. 1 of *Freud and the Americans* (New York: Oxford University Press, 1971), 1:1–22. On the early Americanization of Freud, see F. H. Matthews, "The Americanization of Sigmund Freud: Adaptations of Psychoanalysis before 1917," *Journal of American Studies* 1 (1967): 39–62. For an example of how early Freud readers in the 1910s used Nietzsche's psychological theories to interpret his, see Emily Hamblen, *Friedrich Nietzsche and His New Gospel* (Boston: R. G. Badger, 1911).

122 Johannes Broene, "The Philosophy of Friedrich Nietzsche," *American Journal of Religious Psychology and Education* 4 (March 1910): 78–79, 131. Broene thought Nietzsche a great "object lesson" for modern psychologists but a danger to young minds in formation: "No boy or girl should be allowed to read Nietzsche. . . . To let the immature read Nietzsche is like pulling up a plant to see if its roots are growing" (ibid., 165). On Broene's assessment of Nietzsche as a misguided humanist, see Johannes Broene, "Nietzsche's Educational Ideas and Ideals," *Educational Review* 37 (January 1909): 55–70.

123 Louise Collier Willcox, "Nietzsche: A Doctor for Sick Souls," *North American Review* 194 (November 1911): 773, 770.

124 Ibid., 768, 766.

125 "Will Nietzsche Come into Vogue in America?," 65. See also the characterization two years earlier that Nietzsche's "name constantly appears in all sorts of connections . . . and those who have once fallen under his spell are not likely to escape it," in "Some American Criticisms of Nietzsche," *Current Literature* 44 (February 1908): 295.

126 Wilbur Urban, review of *Nietzsche, the Thinker*, by William M. Salter, *Philosophical Review* 27 (May 1918): 307–8.

# Chapter Two

1 Friedrich Nietzsche, *The Antichrist* (1895), in *"Twilight of the Idols" and "The Anti-Christ,"* trans. R. J. Hollingdale (New York: Viking Penguin, 1990), 181, 140, 175, 161, 178, 161, 178.

2 Nietzsche, *Ecce Homo*, 326.

3 On the late nineteenth-century intellectual challenges to Protestantism's theological authority, see Bruce Kuklick, *Churchmen and Philosophers: From Jonathan Edwards to John Dewey* (New Haven, CT: Yale University Press, 1985): 191–261; and James Campbell, *A Thoughtful Profession: The Early Years of the American Philosophical Association* (Peru, IL: Open Court, 2006), 1–38.

4 Roy Rozenzweig, *Eight Hours for What We Will* (Cambridge: Cambridge University Press, 1983), 57; William Leach, *Land of Desire: Merchants, Power, and the Rise of a New American Culture* (New York: Pantheon, 1993), 135, 144; E. Brooks Holifield, *God's Ambassadors: A History of Christian Clergy in America* (Grand Rapids, MI: William B. Eerdmans, 2007), 145–82; and R. Laurence Moore, "Religion, Secularization, and the Shaping of the Culture Industry in Antebellum America," *American Quarterly* 41 (June 1989): 216–42.

5 James Turner, *Without God, Without Creed: The Origins of Unbelief in America* (Baltimore: Johns Hopkins University Press, 1986).

6 Shailer Mathews, *The Faith of Modernism* (New York: Macmillan, 1924), 4, 2, 4. On the broad transformations in liberal Protestant theology, see Gary Dorrien, *The Making of American Liberal Theology.* Vol. 2, *Idealism, Realism, and Modernity (1900–1950)* (Westminster: John Knox Press, 2003).

7 E. Brooks Holifield, *Theology in America: Christian Thought from the Age of the Puritans to the Civil War* (New Haven, CT: Yale University Press, 2005), 506–7.

8 Rev. James Lindsay, "A Critical Estimate of Nietzsche's Philosophy," *Bibliotheca Sacra* 72 (January 1915): 67.

9 Charles Lerch, "Nietzsche Madness," *Bibliotheca Sacra* 69 (January 1912): 71–87.

10 The initial American religious appropriation of Nietzsche tracked closely with the German, mostly Protestant, reception of Nietzsche as a movement within the faith to reinvigorate institutional Christianity, largely because theology and philosophy in the United States up until World War I were strongly influenced by German theology and philosophy. It contrasts starkly with the Russian religious reception, which, by and large, found its most visible contributors among un-churched intellectual and artistic "God-Seekers" longing for religious experience. On the religious reception in Germany, see Aschheim, *The Nietzsche Legacy in Germany*, and Peter Köster, "Nietzsche-Kritik und Nietzsche Rezeption in der Theologie des 20 Jahrhunderts," *Nietzsche-Studien* 10/11 (1981/1982): 615–85. On the religious reception in Russia, see Rosenthal, ed., *Nietzsche in Russia*, 51–145, and Nel Grillaert, *What the God Seekers Found in Nietzsche: The Reception of Nietzsche's Übermensch by Philosophers of the Russian Religious Renaissance* (Amsterdam: Rodopi, 2008).

11   William R. Sorley, *Recent Tendencies in Ethics* (Edinburgh: W. Blackwood and
     Sons, 1904), 32; "The Christian Reply to Nietzsche," *Current Literature* 45 (July
     1908): 64; and J. L. Raschen, "The Apostle of the Superman," *Methodist Review*,
     May 1910, 385.

12   As David Hollinger has shown, historians' varied uses of *modernism* exhibit a
     similar conceptual elusiveness. See his "The Knower and the Artificer," *American
     Quarterly* 39 (Spring 1987): 37–55. See also Ann Douglas, "Periodizing the Ameri-
     can Century: Modernism, Postmodernism, and Postcolonialism in the Cold War
     Context," *Modernism/Modernity* 5 (September 1998): 71–98; and for the varieties
     of meanings of *modern*, see its entry in *New Keywords: A Revised Vocabulary of
     Culture and Society*, ed. Tony Bennett and Lawrence Grossberg et al. (Malden,
     MA: Blackwell, 2005), 219–23.

13   R. C. Schiedt, "Nietzsche and the Great Problems of Modern Thought,"
     *Reformed Church Review* 16 (April 1912): 148. See also his "Ernst Haeckel and
     Friedrich Nietzsche: First Part," *Reformed Church Review* 12 (January 1908):
     29–48, and "Ernst Haeckel and Friedrich Nietzsche: Second Part," *Reformed
     Church Review* 12 (April 1908): 213–34.

14   On the correspondence between scientific developments and religious reform, see
     John Hedley Brooke, "The Parallel between Scientific and Religious Reform,"
     chap. 3 in *Science and Religion: Some Historical Perspectives* (Cambridge: Cam-
     bridge University Press, 1991).

15   The most common strategy among Protestants for reconciling the Christian
     faith with scientific theories that proposed a dynamic universe was to perceive
     divine creation as an ongoing relationship between God and nature, and to view
     interpretation and experimentation as the only way to uncover that relationship.
     For the influence of philosophy on biblical criticism, see Walter H. Conser, *God
     and the Natural World: Religion and Science in Antebellum America* (Columbia:
     University of South Carolina Press, 1993), and Theodore Dwight Bozeman, *Prot-
     estants in an Age of Science: The Baconian Ideal and Antebellum American Religious
     Thought* (Chapel Hill: University of North Carolina Press, 1977). The mid- to
     late-century response to Darwinism is especially crucial. As Frederick Gregory
     has argued, historians have overstated the immediate impact of Darwinism on
     nineteenth-century Protestantism. He argues that Darwin's theories simply
     renewed ongoing religious debates about the relationship of scientific discoveries
     to biblical historicity and chronology. See his essay, "The Impact of Darwinian
     Evolution on Protestant Theology in the Nineteenth Century," in *God and Na-
     ture: Historical Essays on the Encounter between Christianity and Science*, ed. David
     C. Lindberg and Ronald L. Numbers (Berkeley: University of California Press,
     1986), 369–90. For the turn-of-the-century view of the pursuit of knowledge
     as a religious directive, see David Hollinger, "Justification by Verification: The
     Scientific Challenge to the Moral Authority of Christianity in Modern America,"
     in *Religion and Twentieth-Century American Life*, ed. Michael Lacey (New York:
     Cambridge University Press, 1989), 116–35.

**16** George S. Patton, "Beyond Good and Evil," *Princeton Theological Review* 6 (July 1908): 393, 394, 428, 411.

**17** Charles C. Everett, "Beyond Good and Evil: A Study of the Philosophy of Friedrich Nietzsche," *New World* 8 (December 1898): 690, 688.

**18** J. Kenneth Mozley, "Modern Attacks on Christian Ethics," *Living Age* 257 (May 9, 1908): 353.

**19** Thomas Cary Johnson, *Some Modern Isms* (Richmond, VA: Presbyterian Committee of Publication, 1919), 152, 170, 173, 190, 192.

**20** Patton, "Beyond Good and Evil," 392–93.

**21** Nietzsche, *Twilight of the Idols*, 33.

**22** P. A. Forde, "Is Dogma Out of Date?," *American Catholic Quarterly Review*, January 1915, 22.

**23** Rev. P. M. Northcote, "The Catholic Apologist," *American Catholic Quarterly Review*, January 1923, 5.

**24** Rev. Thomas J. Gerrard, "Modern Theories and Moral Disaster," *Catholic World*, July 1912, 433.

**25** Northcote, "Catholic Apologist," 5, 1. See also V. Cathrein, "Ethics," *The Catholic Encyclopedia*, ed. Charles G. Herbermann et al. (New York: Robert Appleton, 1909), 5:561; A. A. McGinley, "The Testimony of Science to Religion," *Catholic World*, November 1900, 235–36; and Rev. Thomas J. Gerrard, "Eugenics and Catholic Teaching," *Catholic World*, June 1912, 292. The task of identifying the dangers of secular knowledge fell to lay Catholics as well. A prominent example can be found in Harry Thurston Peck, professor of Latin and literature at Columbia University and editor-in-chief of the popular literary magazine *Bookman*, who diagnosed the Protestant quest for secular knowledge as the source of Nietzsche's madness. Peck, "A Mad Philosopher," *Bookman*, September 1898, 25–32. On Catholic thought in the Progressive era, see Thomas E. Woods Jr., *The Church Confronts Modernity: Catholic Intellectuals and the Progressive Era* (New York: Columbia University Press, 2004).

**26** M. D. Petre, "Studies on Friedrich Nietzsche: A Life Militant," *Catholic World*, December 1905, 317–30; M. D. Petre, "Studies on Friedrich Nietzsche: The Poet," *Catholic World*, January 1906, 516–26; M. D. Petre, "Studies on Friedrich Nietzsche: Nietzsche the Anti-Moralist," *Catholic World*, February 1906, 610–21; M. D. Petre, "Studies on Friedrich Nietzsche: The Superman," *Catholic World*, March 1906, 773–84; M. D. Petre, "Studies on Friedrich Nietzsche: Nietzsche the Anti-Feminist," *Catholic World*, May 1906, 159–70; M. D. Petre, "Studies on Friedrich Nietzsche: Nietzsche the Anti-Christian," *Catholic World*, June 1906, 345–55.

**27** Mencken, *Friedrich Nietzsche*, 295.

**28** Petre, "Nietzsche the Anti-Moralist," 618–20.

**29** Pope Pius X, *Pascendi dominici gregis: On the Doctrine of the Modernists*, encyclical letter, September 8, 1907, http://www.papalencyclicals.net/Pius10/p10pasce.htm (accessed January 2010). For an excellent account of the modernist controversy, as well as a historical perspective on the church's resistance to subjectivist thinking, see Gabriel Daly, *Transcendence and Immanence: A Study in Catholic Modernism and Integralism* (Oxford: Clarendon Press, 1980). Also useful on Catholic modernism is Michele Ranchetti, *The Catholic Modernists: A Study of the Religious Reform Movement 1864–1907*, trans. Isabel Quigly (London: Oxford University Press, 1969). For a helpful survey on Catholicism in America that views the early twentieth-century controversy from an American perspective, see James Hennesey, *American Catholics: A History of the Roman Catholic Community in the United States* (New York: Oxford University Press, 1981).

30  George H. Derry, "Unlocking the Medieval Mind," *America* 17 (September 15, 1917): 579; F. Aveling, "The Neo-Scholastic Movement," *American Catholic Quarterly Review* 31 (January 1906): 33.

31  Petre, "A Life Militant," 317.

32  Petre, "Nietzsche the Anti-Moralist," 620.

33  Petre, "Nietzsche the Anti-Feminist," 162 and, quoting Nietzsche, 165.

34  Petre, "Nietzsche the Anti-Christian," 355.

35  On Petre's modernist views, see Clyde F. Crews, "Maude Petre's Modernism," *America* 144 (May 16, 1981): 403–6. For Petre's assessment of Catholic modernism, see M. D. Petre, *Modernism: Its Failure and Its Fruits* (London: T. C. & E. C. Jack, 1918).

36  A similar argument is made by Catholic atheist (and self-described "aesthetic Catholic") George Santayana in his *Egotism in German Philosophy* (1916; London: J. M. Dent & Sons, 1939), which is discussed in chapter 3.

37  Joseph B. Jacobi, "The Nietzschean Idea and the Christian Ideal—Superman and Saint," *American Catholic Quarterly Review* 41 (July 1916): 489, 491.

38  James Martin Gillis, *False Prophets* (New York: Macmillan, 1925), 88–89. For a useful discussion of Gillis's long career as a public figure, see Richard Gribble, *Guardian of America: The Life of James Martin Gillis, CSP* (New York: Paulist Press, 1998).

39  Gillis, *False Prophets*, 100, 186, 187, 191, 184.

40  Petre, "A Life Militant," 330.

41  William R. Hutchison, *The Modernist Impulse in American Protestantism* (Cambridge, MA: Harvard University Press, 1976), 145.

42  William Adams Brown, *Is Christianity Practicable?* (New York: Charles Scribner's Sons, 1919), 95.

43  Shailer Mathews, *The Gospel and the Modern Man* (New York: Macmillan, 1910), 251.

44  Walter Rauschenbusch, *Christianity and the Social Crisis* (New York: Macmillan, 1907), 315–16.

45  Walter Rauschenbusch, as quoted in Christopher H. Evans, *The Kingdom is Always but Coming: A Life of Walter Rauschenbusch* (Grand Rapids, MI: William B. Eerdmans, 2004), 309.

46  H. Richard Niebuhr, *The Kingdom of God in America* (1937; Middletown, CT: Wesleyan University Press, 1988), 193.

**47** Rauschenbusch, *Christianity and the Social Crisis*, 342.

**48** Francis Greenwood Peabody, "The Practicability of the Christian Life," *Harvard Theological Review* 6 (April 1913): 129.

**49** Ibid.; Lyman Abbott, "Are the Ethics of Jesus Practicable?," *Biblical World* 17 (April 1901): 256–64; Brown, *Is Christianity Practicable?*

**50** Mathews, *Gospel and the Modern Man*, 240.

**51** Francis Greenwood Peabody, "Ethics and the Social Question," in *The Approach to the Social Question: An Introduction to the Study of Social Ethics* (New York: Macmillan, 1909), 96–135.

**52** Abbott, "Are the Ethics of Jesus Practicable?," 258, 256.

**53** Francis Greenwood Peabody, *Jesus Christ and the Christian Character* (1905; New York: Macmillan, 1913), 161, 154, 156, 159–60.

**54** Peabody, *Approach to the Social Question*, 113, 116–18.

**55** Mathews, *Gospel and the Modern Man*, 249.

**56** Vida Dutton Scudder, *Socialism and Character* (Boston: Houghton Mifflin, 1912), 26, 6, 50, 3. On Scudder's theological vision, see Peter J. Frederick, *Knights of the Golden Rule: The Intellectual as Social Reformer in the 1890s* (Lexington: University Press of Kentucky, 1967), 113–40, and Lears, *No Place of Grace*, 209–15. Not all Christian Socialists agreed with Scudder's assessment of Nietzsche's value as a moral guide. For an example of a critical rejection of Nietzchean ethics, see Christian Socialist and Crozier Theological Seminary church historian Henry C. Vedder's *Socialism and the Ethics of Jesus* (New York: Macmillan, 1912). On Vedder see Dwight A. Honeycutt, *Henry Clay Vedder: His Life and Thought* (Atlanta: Baptist History and Heritage Society, 2008).

**57** Scudder, *Socialism and Character*, 298.

**58** Vida Dutton Scudder, *On Journey* (New York: E. P. Dutton, 1937).

**59** Scudder, *Socialism and Character*, 43, 33–36.

**60** Ibid., 298, 205–6, 299.

**61** Mathews, *Gospel and the Modern Man*, 270–71.

**62** Edwin Dodge Hardin, "Nietzsche's Service to Christianity," *American Journal of Theology* 18 (October 1914): 546.

**63** Rev. Robert S. Loring, *Thoughts from Nietzsche* (Milwaukee: Printed for Free Distribution by Members of the Milwaukee Unitarian Church, 1919), 3–4.

**64** Jacobi, "The Nietzschean Idea," 472–73.

**65** Lears, *No Place of Grace*, 45, 177–78.

**66** For the "feminine" origins of the turn-of-the-century Protestant romance with muscularity, see Ann Douglas, *The Feminization of American Culture* (1977; New York: Doubleday, 1988), and Barbara Welter, "The Feminization of American Religion, 1800–1860," in her *Dimity Convictions: The American Woman in the Nineteenth Century* (Athens: Ohio University Press, 1976): 83–102. On the longing for masculine piety and iconography in Victorian culture, see Norman Vance, *The Sinews of the Spirit: The Ideal of Christian Manliness in Victorian Literature and Religious Thought* (Cambridge: Cambridge University Press, 1985). Clifford Putney's *Muscular Christianity: Manhood and Sports in Protestant America, 1880–1920* (Cambridge, MA: Harvard University Press, 2001), demonstrates the pervasiveness of the religious crisis by arguing that it took various cultural forms in Progressive Era America.

67 John Neville Figgis, *The Will to Freedom; or, The Gospel of Nietzsche and the Gospel of Christ* (London: Longmans, Green, 1917), 92, 313.

68 Ibid., 316, 309, 315, 312, 313.

69 Lindsay, "A Critical Estimate of Nietzsche's Philosophy," 75.

70 John M. Warbeke, "Friedrich Nietzsche, Antichrist, Superman, and Pragmatist," *Harvard Theological Review* 2 (July 1909): 378–79.

71 Hardin, "Nietzsche's Service to Christianity," 548–49.

72 Loring, *Thoughts from Nietzsche*, 28.

73 Ibid., 29–30.

74 Warbeke, "Friedrich Nietzsche," 375.

75 Loring, *Thoughts from Nietzsche*, 7.

76 Figgis, *Will to Freedom*, 74.

77 Hardin, "Nietzsche's Service to Christianity," 551, 550.

78 Warbeke, "Friedrich Nietzsche," 381. For a recent study on the correspondences between Jesus and Nietzsche, see John M. Quigley, *The Superman of Nazareth: Towards a More Jesuan Christianity after Nietzsche* (Sussex: Book Guild, 2000). Like his liberal Protestant predecessors almost a century earlier, Quigley was "knocked off" his "conventional Christian perch by Nietzsche's captivating masterpiece." He describes his study—the culmination of fifty years of intermittent Nietzsche readings—as an effort to "arrange a pact between Christ and *Zarathustra*" (ibid., xi).

79 Lindsay, "A Critical Estimate of Nietzche's Philosophy," 78. For a similar charge against the immanence of the Übermensch personality, see Mozley, "Modern Attacks," 362; and Lerch, "Nietzsche Madness," 87.

80 Loring, *Thoughts from Nietzsche*, 24–25.

81 Figgis, *Will to Freedom*, 129.

82 George Burman Foster, "The Prophet of a New Culture," *Little Review* 1 (March 1914): 14.

83 For more on Foster's biography and the controversies surrounding him, see Alan Gragg, *George Burman Foster: Religious Humanist*, Perspectives in Religious Studies (Danville, VA: Association of Baptist Professors of Religion, 1978). For an excellent treatment of Foster's life and thought, see Dorrien, *Making of American Liberal Theology*, 156–81.

84 George Burman Foster, *The Finality of the Christian Religion* (Chicago: University of Chicago Press, 1906), xii, 185, 177. On Foster's modernism and prefiguration of the 1960s "death of God" movement in theology, see Harvey Arnold, "Death of God—'06," *Foundations* 10 (October–December 1967): 331–53.

85 William Rainey Harper, as quoted in Dorrien, *Making of American Liberal Theology*, 156.

86 George Burman Foster, as recalled by Shailer Mathews in Mathews, *New Faith for Old: An Autobiography* (New York: Macmillan, 1936), 68.

87 Foster, *Finality of the Christian Religion*, 260, 187.

88 "Ministers' Meeting," *Standard* 53 (March 10, 1906): 841–42; see also "The Foster Incident," *Standard* 53 (February 24, 1906): 706; Johnston Myers, "About the Protest," *Standard* 53 (March 24, 1906): 894; and "Dr. George B. Foster Replies to His Critics," *Standard* 53 (April 14, 1906): 573–75.

89 George Burman Foster, *The Function of Religion in Man's Struggle for Existence* (Chicago: University of Chicago Press, 1909), xi, 142–43.

90 "Baptists after Row Expel Prof. Foster," *New York Times*, June 22, 1909, 3. The *New York Times* reported Foster's insistence that his religious inquiries were in defense of the church. "Foster Still a Baptist," *New York Times*, June 9, 1909, 5. "George Burman Foster," s.v. in *Dictionary of Heresy Trials in American Christianity*, ed. George H. Shriver (Westport, CT: Greenwood Press, 1997), 142–49.

91 The Library Board in Davenport, Iowa, for one, refused to buy Foster's *Finality of the Christian Religion*. Unlucky for the library's board, George Cram Cook, Floyd Dell, Susan Glaspell, and the other outspoken members of the Monist Society (who will be discussed in chapter 4) were among its patrons. Outraged by the board's decision, the writers launched a letter-writing campaign to protest its attempt to deny them access to Foster's vital new ideas about religion. Susan Glaspell, *The Road to the Temple* (New York: Frederick A. Stokes, 1927), 193.

92 George Burman Foster, "Longing," *Little Review* 1 (October 1914): 25.

93 Foster, *Function of Religion*, 63.

94 Foster, "Prophet of a New Culture," 14.

95 Ibid., 17, 15.

96 Foster, "Longing," 23.

97 Foster, *Function of Religion*, 22, 170.

98 George Burman Foster, "The New Loyalty," *Little Review* 1 (July 1914): 24–25.

99 Foster, *Function of Religion*, 184.

100 Foster, "Man and Superman," *Little Review* 1 (April 1914): 7.

101 Foster, "Prophet of a New Culture," 15.

102 His university lectures on Nietzsche were published posthumously as George Burman Foster, *Friedrich Nietzsche* (New York: Macmillan, 1931).

103 Ibid., 211–12.

104 W. C. A. Wallar, "A Preacher's Interest," *American Journal of Theology* 19 (January 1915): 89–90.

105 Ibid., 90.

106 "Will to freedom" and "will to love" are Figgis's expressions.

## Chapter Three

1 On Goethe in nineteenth-century American literature and culture, see Maxine Grefe, *"Apollo in the Wilderness": An Analysis of the Critical Reception of Goethe in*

*America, 1806–1840* (New York: Garland, 1988), and John Paul von Grueningen, "Goethe in American Periodicals from 1860–1900" (PhD diss., University of Wisconsin, 1931). A useful source on the British reception of Faust is William Frederic Hauhart, "The Reception of Goethe's Faust in England in the First Half of the Nineteenth Century" (PhD diss., Columbia University, 1909). On the broader context of German imaginative literature in American culture, see Lynne Tatlock and Matt Erlin, *German Culture in Nineteenth-Century America: Reception, Adaptation, Transformation* (Rochester, NY: Camden House, 2005).

2  Johann Wolfgang von Goethe, *Faust* (1808), part 1 (Munich: Hugo Schmidt Verlag, 1923), 31.

3  Goethe, *Faustus from the German of Goethe*, trans. Samuel Taylor Coleridge, ed. Frederick Burwick and James C. McKusick (Oxford: Oxford University Press, 2007), 12. So did Francis Leveson Gower in his 1823 translation (London: Murray, 1823).

4  Goethe, *Faust*, trans. Abraham Hayward (London: Edward Moxon, 1838), 21. Anna Swanwick's translation, which went through several reprintings until 1914, rendered it "demigod" as well. Goethe, *Faust*, trans. Anna Swanwick (London: George Bell and Sons, 1870).

5  Goethe, *Faust: A Tragedy*, trans. Bayard Taylor (1871; Boston: Houghton, Mifflin, 1898) 22. Percy Bysshe Shelley in 1832 and Captain Knox again in 1841 also opted for "superhuman." Goethe, *Faust, A Tragedy*, trans. Captain Knox (London: John Olliver, 1841), 51, and Goethe, as translated by Percy Bysshe Shelley, *The Works of Percy Bysshe Shelley in Verse and Prose*, ed. Henry Buxton Forman, vol. 7 (London: Reaves and Turner, 1880), 322.

6  Friedrich Nietzsche, *Thus Spoke Zarathustra* (1883–85), trans. Walter Kaufmann (New York: Modern Library, 1995), 12–13.

7  Kuno Francke, Harvard professor of German art and literature, recognized the Goethean origins of Nietzsche's Übermensch, arguing that it was originally "Goethe who [had] impressed upon German life the Superman motif." In his estimation, Nietzsche and Wagner, two of the "representative men" of nineteenth-century German literature, expressed "something Faustlike and . . . Meisterlike" in their "Goethean gospel of salvation through ceaseless striving," their exaltation of "strenuousness," their experimental view of life, and their "undaunted striding from experience to experience . . . in their ever-renewed efforts to round out their own being." According to Francke, the "spectacle" of "this tradition of striving" was the defining characteristic of the "German spirit." See Francke, *The German Spirit* (New York: Henry Holt, 1916), 65–66. Much of Francke's writings (especially during wartime) focused heavily on different national traits of mind, regularly distinguishing the "German" from the "American" mind.

8  John H. Mecklin, "The Tyranny of the Average Man," *International Journal of Ethics* 28 (January 1918): 240–52; Charles Zueblin, *Democracy and the Overman* (New York: B. W. Huebsch, 1910); and Lothrop Stoddard, *The Revolt against*

*Civilization: The Menace of the Under Man* (New York: Charles Scribner's Sons, 1922).

9 George Bernard Shaw, *Man and Superman* (Cambridge, MA: Harvard University Press, 1903).

10 For London's naturalist reading of Nietzsche, see John E. Martin, "Martin Eden, a London Superman Adventurer: A Case Study of the Americanization of European Ideology," in *Die amerikanische Literatur in der Weltliteratur: Themen und Aspekte*, ed. Claus Uhlig and Volker Bischoff (Berlin: E. Schmidt, 1982), 218–30, and Katherine M. Little, "The 'Nietzschean' and the Individualist in Jack London's Socialist Writings," *Amerikastudien* 22 (1977): 309–23.

11 Mencken, *Friedrich Nietzsche*, 102, 105–6, 108.

12 Antrim and Goebel, "Friedrich Nietzsche's Uebermensch," 566–67; Huneker, *Egoists*, 167.

13 Carus, "Immorality as a Philosophical Principle," 588–89; Carus, "Friedrich Nietzsche," 231.

14 Thomas Stockham Baker, "What Is the Superman?," *Independent* 65 (December 1908): 1615. As a Germanist, he spent the early part of his career examining the influence of German romanticism in American culture (*Lenau and Young Germany in America* [1897]) and tracking the contemporary German literary scene for American audiences (he published Gerhart Hauptmann's play *The Sunken Bell* with Henry Holt in 1900). See also Thomas Stockham Baker, "Contemporary Criticism of Friedrich Nietzsche," *Journal of Philosophy, Psychology, and Scientific Methods* 4 (July 18, 1907): 406–19.

15 This was the conclusion of Nietzsche's most important twentieth-century translator, Walter Kaufmann, though he believed that "over human being" lost the music of *Übermensch* and so opted for "overman" in his popular midcentury translations.

16 "Did Nietzsche Predict the Superwoman as Well as the Superman?," *Current Literature* 43 (December 1907): 643–44.

17 Nietzsche, *Thus Spoke Zarathustra*, 66–67.

18 "Did Nietzsche Predict the Superwoman as Well as the Superman?," 644. See also "A Feminist Disciple of Nietzsche," *Current Opinion* 54 (January 1913): 47–48.

19 Margaret Sanger, journal entry of November 3–4, 1914, as quoted in David M. Kennedy, *Birth Control in America* (New Haven, CT: Yale University Press, 1970), 14. See also Ellen Chesler, *Woman of Valor: Margaret Sanger and the Birth Control Movement in America* (1992; New York: Simon and Schuster, 2007).

20 Margaret Sanger, "Frederick Nietzsche," Margaret Sanger Papers, US Library of Congress, Washington, DC (LCM 130:356); online at http://www.nyu.edu/projects/sanger/webedition/app/documents/show.php?sangerDoc=143705.xml (accessed June 27, 2009).

21 Margaret Sanger, *Selected Papers of Margaret Sanger*, ed. Esther Katz (Urbana: University of Illinois Press, 2003), 1:78–79.

22 W. Fergus Kernan, editorial introduction to Josiah Royce, "Nietzsche," *Atlantic Monthly*, March 1917, 321.

**23** Josiah Royce, "The Teachings of Friedrich Nietzche" [*sic*], HUG 1755.5, box 97, Josiah Royce Papers, Harvard University Archives, Cambridge, MA.

**24** Josiah Royce, *The Philosophy of Loyalty* (1908; Nashville: Vanderbilt University Press, 1995), 3–4. James Russell Lowell is the original author of the quotation "Time makes ancient good uncouth." See James Russell Lowell, "The Present Crisis," in *Early Poems of James Russell Lowell*, ed. Nathan Haskell Dole (1892; New York: Thomas Y. Crowell, 1898), 203.

**25** Josiah Royce, "The Moral Burden of the Individual," in *The Problem of Christianity*, ed. John E. Smith (Chicago: University of Chicago Press, 1968), 117.

**26** Royce, *Philosophy of Loyalty*, 41; Royce, "Nietzsche," 327.

**27** Royce, "Nietzsche," 321–22.

**28** Ibid., 322, 324.

**29** Josiah Royce, "The Problem of Truth in the Light of Recent Discussion," in *William James and Other Essays on the Philosophy of Life* (1911; Freeport, NY: Books for Libraries Press, 1969), 190.

**30** Royce, *Philosophy of Loyalty*, 4; Royce, "The Problem of Truth," 196, 198–99.

**31** Royce, "The Problem of Truth," 230–31.

**32** Though Royce consistently took jabs at his friend's fusion of relativism and individualism while he was alive, after his death Royce began to view James's "Will to Believe" as he viewed Nietzsche's will to power, as an example of this contingent absolute idealism. See Josiah Royce, "William James and the Philosophy of Life," in Royce, *William James and Other Essays on the Philosophy of Life*, 3–45. For an analysis of the distinction between James's pragmatism and Royce's "Absolute Pragmatism," see Bruce Kuklick, *Josiah Royce: An Intellectual Biography* (1972; Indianapolis: Hackett, 1985), 119–35.

**33** Royce, "Nietzsche," 324; Royce, *Philosophy of Loyalty*, 177.

**34** William James to Thomas Sargeant Perry, August 24, 1905, in *The Letters of William James*, ed. Henry James (Boston: Atlantic Monthly Press, 1920), 2:232–33.

**35** William James, "Calendar," in *The Correspondence of William James*, ed. Ignas K. Skrupskelis and Elizabeth M. Berkeley (Charlottesville: University Press of Virginia, 2002), 10:614.

**36** William James to Alice Howe Gibbens, May 12, 1910, in ibid., 12:510.

**37** William James's personal copy of Friedrich Nietzsche, *Jenseits von Gut und Böse*, 2nd ed. (Leipzig: C. G. Naumann, 1891), WJ760.25, Houghton Library, Harvard University, Cambridge, MA.

**38** William James, review of *Degeneration*, by Max Nordau, in James, *Essays, Comments, and Reviews* (Cambridge, MA: Harvard University Press, 1987), 508. For example, he mentions reading Emile Faguet's *En lisant Nietzsche* (1903) in 1905 and Julius Goldstein's appreciative 1902 *Mind* article on Nietzsche. William James to Alice Howe Gibbens James, March 14, 1905, in *Correspondence*, 10:567, and William James to Julius Goldstein, June 1, 1910, in ibid., 12:540.

**39** In addition to his copy of *Jenseits*, Houghton Library possesses James's copy of

Friedrich Nietzsche, *Zur Genealogie der Moral*, 3rd ed. (Leipzig: C. G. Naumann, 1894), AC85 J2376 Zz894n.

40  James's copy of Nietzsche, *Jenseits*, Houghton Library, Harvard University.

41  Because I have been unable to identify additional documentation that indicates when James first read *Beyond Good and Evil*, I am unable to track whether he indeed read the phrase in 1892 (four years before he wrote "Will to Believe" in 1896), read it after 1896 and noted a parallel, or simply found the phrase and/or idea provocative and drew no associations with his own work.

42  William James to Elizabeth Glendower Evans, April 13, 1900, in *Correspondence*, 9:188. The letter was written from the "Costebelle Hotel" in France. On the title page of his copy of *Genealogie*, James wrote "Wm. James Hotel Costebelle." A week later, he wrote to Alice Smith from Costebelle, France: "What Saints' lives I have been reading of late!—material for Gifford lectures" (William James to Alice Smith, April 17, 1900, in ibid., 190).

43  William James, "Notes on Ethics III," in *Manuscript Essays and Notes*, ed. Ignas K. Skrupskelis (Cambridge, MA: Harvard University Press, 1988), 312–13.

44  William James, "What Makes a Life Significant," in *Talks to Teachers on Psychology: And to Students on Some of Life's Ideals* (1899; Cambridge, MA; Harvard University Press, 1983), 154. The original lecture was given at Bryn Mawr College in 1892.

45  James, "Notes on Ethics III," 312–13.

46  William James, *The Varieties of Religious Experience: A Study in Human Nature* (1902; New York: Longmans, Green, 1911), 371–75.

47  Ibid., 38.

48  Royce, "Nietzsche," 328, 322, 327–28.

49  Friedrich Nietzsche, *Daybreak* (1881), trans. R. J. Hollingdale (Cambridge: Cambridge University Press, 1996), 139.

50  Nietzsche, *Human, All Too Human*, 9.

51  J. David Hoeveler Jr., *The New Humanism: A Critique of Modern America* (Charlottesville: University Press of Virginia, 1977), 3.

52  As J. David Hoeveler Jr. demonstrates in his study of New Humanism, only a small group of university professors either identified themselves as New Humanists or supported the movement's positions up until the late 1920s. Babbitt and More were the key figures in the movement. In addition to Frye, Stuart Sherman of the University of Illinois, Frank Jewitt Mather Jr. and Kenyon Cox of Princeton, and later Norman Foerster of the University of North Carolina contributed to the movement at the end of the 1920s. It is, indeed, somewhat awkward to refer to the positions of such a small group of thinkers as comprising a movement. However, though their numbers were few, the two leading New Humanists gained an undeniable visibility for their ideas because of their positions at prominent universities and because of More's control of the literary voice at the *Nation*, a key journal of opinion in the first decades of the twentieth century. In addition,

their ideas do form a consistent body of thought that not only swam against the naturalist and pragmatic currents of their day but, as Hoeveler persuasively argues, also influenced the Southern Agrarian, Neo-Orthodoxy, and New Conservativism movements.

53 Babbitt lauded Greek classicism as the best classicism to emulate. He argued that the romantics mistook the purely formalist aspects of seventeenth-century "neoclassicism" for true classical thought. Romanticism, he contended, was simply an inversion of neoclassicism: "Because the neo-classicist held the imagination lightly as compared with good sense the romantic rebels were led to hold good sense lightly as compared with imagination. The romantic view in short is too much the neo-classical view turned upside down." Irving Babbitt, *Rousseau and Romanticism* (Boston: Houghton Mifflin, 1919), 14.

54 Ibid., 4.

55 Ibid., 250, 198–99.

56 Ibid., 199, 245, 198.

57 Ibid., 263, 245, 246, 260, 261 (the last from Nietzsche, *Thus Spoke Zarathustra*, as quoted in Babbitt).

58 Ibid., 263, 251, 263. Babbitt quoted Zarathustra's warning about the lure of fixed beliefs even for nonbelievers: "To such unsettled ones as thou, seemeth at last even a prisoner blessed. Didst thou ever see how captured criminals sleep? They sleep quietly, they enjoy their new security. . . . Beware in the end lest a narrow faith capture thee, a hard rigorous delusion! For now everything that is narrow and fixed seduceth and tempteth thee" (from Nietzsche, *Thus Spoke Zarathustra*, as quoted in Babbitt, *Rousseau and Romanticism*, 263). Babbitt's campaign against the romantic ironist Übermensch received reinforcement from his fellow New Humanist Prosser Hall Frye in *Romance and Tragedy* (1922). Although Frye viewed Nietzsche's philosophy as an attack on social cohesion, he argued that the disintegrative tendencies were balanced by Nietzsche's reconstructive vision of the Übermensch, who attempted to view the world and self as an "aesthetic product." Nietzsche, he argued, had reasoned that the world could not have been the "work of a moral being," but rather that "its origin is explicable by an artist-creator alone." Without foundations for the self, Frye maintained, the Nietzschean moral free agent has no option but to view the self as if it were a work of art. Prosser Hall Frye, *Romance and Tragedy* (1922; Lincoln: University of Nebraska Press, 1961), 116, 123.

59 Paul Elmer More, *The Drift of Romanticism* (Boston: Houghton Mifflin, 1913), 255, 263.

60 Paul Elmer More, *Nietzsche* (Boston: Houghton Mifflin, 1912), 71, 61, 68.

61 Babbitt, *Rousseau and Romanticism*, 24.

62 Ibid., 250–51.

63 George Santayana, *Egotism in German Philosophy* (1916; London: J. M. Dent & Sons, 1940), 5. Indeed, he had taken German "transcendental" subjectivity to task

in his classical formulation of the American mind, "The Genteel Tradition in American Philosophy" of 1911.

64 Ibid., 5, 3, 7, 6. On Santayana's long-standing ambivalence toward German thought and culture, see Kenneth M. Price, "George Santayana and Germany: An Uneasy Relationship," in *Germany and German Thought in American Literature and Cultural Criticism*, ed. Peter Freese (Essen: Verlag die Blaue Eule, 1990), 159–69, and John McCormick, *George Santayana: A Biography* (New York: Knopf, 1987). On Santayana as social critic, see Robert Dawidoff, *The Genteel Tradition and the Sacred Rage: High Culture vs. Democracy in Adams, James, and Santayana* (Chapel Hill: University of North Carolina Press, 1992).

65 Santayana, *Egotism in Philosophy*, 28.

66 Ibid., 137–38, 143.

67 Ibid., 137, 126.

68 Ibid., 131–32.

69 Ibid., 136, 134.

70 Ibid., 13–14, 28.

71 Paul Elmer More, "The Lust of Empire," *Nation*, October 22, 1914, 493–95; and Irving Babbitt, "The Breakdown of Internationalism. Part I and II," *Nation*, June 17 and June 24, 1915, 677–80, 704–6. Babbitt's dispute with romanticism is already apparent in his *Literature and the American College* (Boston: Houghton Mifflin, 1908) and *The New Laokoon: An Essay on the Confusion in the Arts* (Boston: Houghton Mifflin, 1910).

72 As quoted in James Joll, "The English, Friedrich Nietzsche and the First World War," in *Deutschland in der Weltpolitik des 19 und 20 Jahrhunderts*, ed. Imanuel Geiss and Bernd Jürgen Wendt (Düsseldorf: Bertelsmann Universitätsverlag, 1973), 305.

73 For the tendency to view the Übermensch as a philosophical distillation of the "German mind," and the German mind as an expression of the unbridled quest for power, see Edmund McClure, *Germany's War-Inspirers, Nietzsche and Treitschke* (New York: E. S. Gorham, 1915); J. H. Muirhead, *German Philosophy in Relation to the War* (London: J. Murray, 1915); and Ernst Barker, *Nietzsche and Treitschke: The Worship of Power in Modern Germany* (Oxford: Oxford University Press, 1914).

74 William Archer, "Fighting a Philosophy," *North American Review* (January 1915): 44, 39, 32. See also William Archer, *501 Gems of German Thought* (London: T. Fisher Unwin, 1916). Wartime sales of *Zarathustra* underscore Archer's claim that the soldier in the trenches as well as the bourgeoisie in their parlors turned to Nietzsche for inspiration. According to H. F. Peters, forty thousand copies of *Zarathustra* were sold in 1917. See Peters, *Zarathustra's Sister: The Case of Elisabeth and Friedrich Nietzsche* (New York: Crown, 1977), 279. Robert G. L. Waite notes that a "wartime edition" of *Zarathustra* "was specially printed, bound in durable field-gray, and sold to tens of thousands of German soldiers." See Robert G. L. Waite, *The Psychopathic God: Adolf Hitler* (New York: Basic Books, 1977), 279.

75  Archer, "Fighting a Philosophy," 42, 43; Archer, *501 Gems*, xvi–xvii.

76  William Mackintire Salter, *The Fiftieth Anniversary of the Ethical Movement, 1876–1926* (New York: D. Appleton, 1926), 39.

77  William Mackintire Salter, *Nietzsche the Thinker: A Study* (1917; New York: Frederick Unger, 1968). Salter presented the development of Nietzsche's thought in stages—his early enthusiasm for Schopenhauer and Wagner, his middle "critical" period, and his final "constructive" phase, in which he sought to create a "comprehensive world-view." Salter, *Nietzsche*, 98, 149.

78  Salter, *Nietzsche*, xxvii. Already in a 1912 *Nation* editorial, Salter presented a vision of Nietzsche's restrained ethical and aesthetic "individualism," foreshadowing what would become the main leitmotif of the book: "The truth is, Nietzsche is a moralist, not of instinct and impulse, but of culture and discipline all along the line." Salter, "Nietzsche's Individualism," *Nation*, April 11, 1912, 361.

79  Salter, *Nietzsche*, xxvii. Though Salter's *Nietzsche* received a number of generally appreciative reviews, his book neither exerted demonstrable influence on wartime commentary nor altered the terms of debate. For notable reviews, see Will Durant, review of *Nietzsche The Thinker: A Study*, by William M. Salter, *Political Science Quarterly* 33 (June 1918): 266–68; Herbert L. Stewart, "An Exposition of Nietzsche," *American Journal of Theology* 24 (April 1920): 309–14; and H[orace] M. Kallen, review of *Nietzsche the Thinker: A Study*, by William M. Salter, *Harvard Theological Review* 13 (July 1920): 306–10.

80  Salter, *Nietzsche*, 340, 350, 416, 396, 397, 24, xxvii.

81  Chauncey Brewster, "Ethics Made in Germany," *North American Review* 201 (March 1915), 398.

82  W. H. Griffith Thomas, "German Moral Abnormality," *Bibliotheca Sacra* 76 (January 1919): 84–104.

83  Joseph H. Odell, "Peter Sat by the Fire Warming Himself," *Atlantic Monthly*, February 1918, 147.

84  Thomas, "German Moral Abnormality," 103. See also W. H. Griffith Thomas, "Germany and the Bible," *Bibliotheca Sacra* 72 (January 1915): 49–66.

85  G. Stanley Hall, foreword to *The Problems and Lessons of the War*, ed. George H. Blakeslee (New York: G. P. Putnam's Sons, 1916), xi.

86  Richard T. Ely, *The World War and Leadership in a Democracy* (New York: Macmillan, 1918), 4, 174.

87  Hall, foreword to Blakeslee, *Problems and the Lessons of the War*, xiv, xv, xxiii. For Hall's own longing for racial regeneration, see Gail Bederman, *Manliness and Civilization: A Cultural History of Gender and Race in the United States, 1880–1917* (Chicago: University of Chicago Press, 1995).

88  Ralph Barton Perry, *The Present Conflict of Ideals: A Study of the Philosophical Background of the World War* (London: Longmans, Green, 1918), 9, 150, 171; Ralph Barton Perry, *The Free Man and the Soldier: Essays on the Reconciliation of Liberty and Discipline* (New York: Charles Scribner's Sons, 1916), 61; and Perry, *Present*

*Conflict of Ideals*, 155. On German-American intellectuals during World War I, see Phyllis Keller, *States of Belonging: German-American Intellectuals and the First World War* (Cambridge, MA: Harvard University Press, 1979).

89 Perry, *Present Conflict of Ideals*, 162, 168, 171. Perry's assessment would not go uncontested. Observing how Nietzsche's criticisms of German culture did not fold easily into an endorsement of it, a writer for the *New York Times* noted, "It is [Nietzsche's Übermensch] which is supposed to have had so much influence upon the aristocracy of Germany and to have made them regard themselves as a race of Superman. This would be, indeed, strange, since Nietzsche regarded the Germans as the type of Philistine and subservient class against which his Superman had to struggle." Likewise, Nietzsche viewed with "contempt" the "boastings of German 'Kultur.'" Joseph Jacobs, "Nietzsche's Life and Work," *New York Times Review of Books*, April 4, 1915, sec. 6, p. 1.

90 Perry, *Present Conflict of Ideals*, 171; Perry, *Free Man and the Soldier*, 59.

91 Simon Nelson Patten, "The German Way of Thinking," *Forum* 54 (July 1915): 26.

92 Ibid., 22, 26.

93 For an example of the radical effort to dissociate Nietzsche's philosophy from German imperialism, see "Nietzsche on War," *Mother Earth*, October 1914, 260–64.

94 Max Eastman, "What Nietzsche Really Taught," *Everybody's Magazine*, November 1914, 703. For an additional commentary on Nietzsche's cosmopolitanism, see poet Hart Crane's "The Case against Nietzsche," *Pagan*, April–May 1918, 34–35.

95 Max Eastman, *"Understanding Germany: The Only Way to End War" and Other Essays* (New York: Mitchell Kennerley, 1916), 110, 61, 62, 65, 68. Eastman's appraisal of Nietzsche's cosmopolitanism and his critique of nationalism find support in Thomas Bailey, "Nietzsche as a Tonic in War Time," *Sewanee Review* 26 (July 1918): 364–74.

96 Gladden suggested that the linkage between Nietzsche and the war had been made by those who either hadn't read or hadn't properly understood Nietzsche. And this Gladden knew from firsthand experience. Just a year earlier, he had written a letter to the *New York Times* in which he claimed that Nietzsche had inspired the German people to war. A week later, Emily Hamblen responded with a letter in which she argued that Gladden had misinterpreted Nietzsche's writings by reading them literally rather than as poetry. Gladden followed with a response of his own, conceding that he had used the "slovenly method" of quoting Nietzsche from secondary sources. A year later, he completely reversed his position on Nietzsche in "The Theology of Militarism" (Gladden, *The Forks of the Road* [New York: Macmillan, 1916]). Washington Gladden, "Nietzsche on Peace," *New York Times*, March 21, 1915, sec. 1; Gladden, letter to the editor, *New York Times*, April 15, 1915, p. 12; Emily S. Hamblen, "Nietzsche Defended," *New York Times*, April 4, 1915, sec. 6. Quotation is from Gladden, letter to the editor, 12; also in Gladden, *Forks of the Road*, 74.

97  Gladden, "The Theology of Militarism," 83, 85.

98  Clarence Darrow, *Clarence Darrow's Plea for the Defense of Loeb and Leopold (August 22, 23, 25)* (Girard, KS: Haldeman-Julius, 1925), 17.

99  From phrenological diagrams of Leopold's and Loeb's heads; see reproductions in *Chicago Daily Tribune*, July 28, 1924, 3. On the scientific theories as evidence during the trial, see Paula Fass, "Making and Remaking an Event: The Leopold and Loeb Case in American Culture," *Journal of American History* 80 (December 1993): 919–51. On the murder and trial, see Hal Higdon, *The Crime of the Century: The Leopold and Loeb Case* (New York: G. P. Putnam's Sons, 1975); Maureen McKernan, *The Amazing Crime and Trial of Leopold and Loeb* (1924; New York: Signet, 1957); and Gilbert Geis and Leigh Bienen, *Crimes of the Century: From Leopold and Loeb to O. J. Simpson* (Boston: Northeastern University Press, 1998).

100  Billy Sunday, as quoted in *Chicago Herald and Examiner*, June 5, 1924, 3. Bryan's campaign against Nietzschean "Darwinian" doctrines had already begun shortly after the war. See William Jennings Bryan, "Brother or Brute?," *Commoner* 20 (November 1920): 11. But if the murder of Bobby Franks was not enough to convince him of the dangers of Nietzsche, Darrow's defense of the boys did, and he used it in his prosecution at the Scopes Trial of 1925: "Because Leopold and Loeb read Nietzsche . . . and adopted his philosophy as a superman, he was not responsible for taking human life. That's the doctrine they are trying to bring in here with the evolution theory." Bryan, as quoted in Genevieve Forbes Herrick and John Origen Herrick, *The Life of William Jennings Bryan* (Chicago: Kessinger Publication, 2005), 357.

101  Darrow, *Clarence Darrow's Plea*, 44–45, 48, 47, 45.

## Chapter Four

1  John Cowper Powys, *Enjoyment of Literature* (New York: Simon and Schuster, 1938), 468.

2  Isadora Duncan, *My Life* (New York: Boni and Liveright, 1927), 141.

3  Henry F. May, *The End of American Innocence: A Study of the First Years of Our Own Time, 1912–1917* (New York: Knopf, 1959), 206, 209.

4  For a characterization of the radicals as innocents, see Leslie Fishbein, *Rebels in Bohemia: The Radicals of the Masses, 1911–1917* (Chapel Hill: University of North Carolina Press, 1982).

5  For surveys of many of the intellectuals treated in this chapter, see Christine Stansell, *American Moderns: Bohemian New York and the Creation of a New Century* (New York: Metropolitan Books, 2000); Brenda Murphy, *The Provincetown Players and the Culture of Modernity* (Cambridge: Cambridge University Press, 2006); Casey Nelson Blake, *Beloved Community: The Cultural Criticism of Randolph Bourne, Van Wyck Brooks, Waldo Frank, and Lewis Mumford* (Chapel Hill: University of North Carolina Press, 1990); Suzanne W. Churchill and Adam McKible, eds., *Little Magazines & Modernism: New Approaches* (Aldershot, UK: Ashgate,

2007); Ann Douglas, *Terrible Honesty: Mongrel Manhattan in the 1920s* (New York: Noonday Press, 1997); Ross Wetzsteon, *Republic of Dreams: Greenwich Village, the American Bohemia, 1910–1960* (New York: Simon and Schuster, 2002); and James Gilbert, *Writers and Partisans: A History of Literary Radicalism in America* (1968; New York: Columbia University Press, 1992).

6  The most valuable histories of the concept of the modern intellectual in America remain Christopher Lasch, *The New Radicalism in America, 1889–1963: The Intellectual as a Social Type* (New York: Norton, 1965), and Thomas Bender, *New York Intellect: A History of Intellectual Life in New York City, from 1750 to the Beginnings of Our Own Time* (New York: Knopf, 1987). It has been often asserted—though to my knowledge, neither sufficiently supported nor refuted—that William James first brought the term *intellectual* into American English after it was employed in France during the Dreyfus Affair in the 1890s. On James as the importer of *intellectual*, see George Cotkin, *William James: Public Philosopher* (Baltimore: Johns Hopkins University Press, 1990), 124, and Ross Posnock, "The Politics of Pragmatism and the Fortunes of the Public Intellectual," *American Literary History* 3 (1991): 566–87. On the Dreyfus Affair origins of the concept of the modern intellectual, see Christopher E. Forth, "Intellectuals, Crowds, and the Body Politics of the Dreyfus Affair," *Historical Reflections/Réflexions Historiques* 24 (Spring 1998): 63–92; Raymond Williams, "Intellectual," in *Keywords: A Vocabulary of Culture and Society* (London: Fontana, Croom, Helm, 1976), 169–71; Jeremy Jennings and Tony Kemp-Welch, "The Century of the Intellectual: From the Dreyfus Affair to Salman Rushdie," in *Intellectuals in Politics: From the Dreyfus Affair to Salman Rushdie*, ed. Jennings and Kemp-Welch (New York: Routledge, 1997), 1–21.

7  On early twentieth-century young aspiring writers' quest for intellectual independence, see Steven Biel, *Independent Intellectuals in the United States, 1910–1945* (New York: New York University Press, 1992).

8  Nietzsche, *Gay Science*, 322.

9  William English Walling, *The Larger Aspects of Socialism* (New York: Macmillan, 1913), 107.

10  Walter Lippmann, *Drift and Mastery* (1914; Madison: University of Wisconsin Press, 1985), 93.

11  The classic formulation of anti-intellectualism in America is Hofstadter, *Anti-Intellectualism in American Life*. On the romantic origins of the critique of anti-intellectualism, see my "Anti-Intellectualism as Romantic Discourse," *Daedalus: Journal of the American Academy of Arts and Sciences* 138 (Spring 2009): 41–52. For an excellent reminder that the lament of anti-intellectualism is not exclusive to America, see Stefan Collini, *Absent Minds: Intellectuals in Britain* (Oxford: Oxford University Press, 2006).

12  For the collective biography of the lost generation, see Malcolm Cowley, *Exile's Return: A Literary Odyssey of the 1920s* (1934; New York: Viking, 1951). The classic work on the modern literary quest for native culture is Alfred Kazin, *On Native*

*Grounds: An Interpretation of Modern American Prose Literature* (1942; San Diego: Harvest, 1995).

13   Nietzsche, *Ecce Homo*, 333, 326, 333, 326, 333.

14   Ibid., 265.

15   Lippmann, *Drift and Mastery*, 175. For a contemporary academic assessment of Nietzsche as an artist-philosopher who enabled the reader to "feel" his ideas, see Louis William Flaccus, *Artists and Thinkers* (New York: Longmans, Green, 1916), 161–200.

16   Ralph Waldo Emerson, "The Poet" (1844), from *Essays: Second Series*, in *The Collected Works of Ralph Waldo Emerson*, vol. 3, ed. Joseph Slater (Cambridge, MA: Harvard University Press, Belknap Press, 1983), 4–6.

17   Walling, *Larger Aspects of Socialism*, 191–92.

18   Max Eastman, "What Nietzsche Really Taught," *Everybody's Magazine*, November 1914, 704; Max Eastman, "Nietzsche, Plato and Bertrand Russell," *Liberator*, September 1920, 6.

19   Will Durant (the school's principal), and Emma Goldman, Margaret Sanger, Upton Sinclair, and Jack London (all affiliated with the school) were self-described Nietzscheans.

20   Hubert Harrison, as quoted in Jeffrey Perry, *Hubert Harrison: The Voice of Harlem Radicalism, 1883–1918* (New York: Columbia University Press, 2009), 82. On socialists' self-understanding as creative and critical thinkers, and their conception of socialism as an intellectual movement, see Robert Rives La Monte, *Socialism: Positive and Negative* (Chicago: Charles H. Kerr, 1914).

21   Upton Sinclair, *The Journal of Arthur Stirling* (New York: D. Appleton, 1903), 211.

22   Eugene O'Neill to Benjamin De Casseres, June 22, 1927, in *Selected Letters of Eugene O'Neill*, ed. Travis Bogard and Jackson R. Bryer (New Haven, CT: Yale University Press, 1988), 245–46. For more on Tucker's function as O'Neill's intellectual broker, see Stephen A. Black, *Eugene O'Neill: Beyond Mourning and Tragedy* (New Haven, CT: Yale University Press, 1999).

23   John Gould Fletcher, *Life Is My Song* (New York: Farrar and Rinehart, 1937), 20–21; and John Gould Fletcher, *Selected Letters of John Gould Fletcher* (Fayetteville: University of Arkansas Press, 1996), 233. For descriptions of the "intoxicating" experience of reading the "poet" Nietzsche for young writers and artists coming of age in the 1920s, see Burton Rascoe, *A Bookman's Daybook* (New York, Horace Liveright, 1929); Burton Rascoe, *Prometheans: Ancient and Modern* (New York: G. P. Putnam's Sons, 1933); and Burton Rascoe, *Before I Forget* (Garden City, NY: Doubleday Doran, 1937).

24   Susan Glaspell, *The Road to the Temple* (New York: Frederick A. Stokes, 1927), 138; George Cram Cook, as quoted in ibid.

25   Floyd Dell, *Moon-Calf* (New York: Knopf, 1920), 295. On the Monist Society and the Davenport intellectuals, see Linda Ben-Zvi, *Susan Glaspell: Her Life and Times* (New York: Oxford University Press, 2005).

**26** Mabel Dodge Luhan, *Movers and Shakers* (1936; Albuquerque: University of New Mexico Press, 1984), 153.

**27** Dell, *Moon-Calf*, 318.

**28** Milton Cantor, *Max Eastman* (New York: Twayne, 1970), 45.

**29** Emma Goldman, *Living My Life* (1931; New York: Dover Publications, 1970), 1:172, 193–95.

**30** Charmian London, *The Book of Jack London* (New York: Century, 1921), 2:31–32.

**31** John Cowper Powys, *Visions and Revisions: A Book of Literary Devotions* (1915; London: Macdonald, 1955), 158. That they valued Nietzsche's artistry does not mean that they aped his style. Powys is case in point. A lush, prolix, extravagant wordsmith who let images somersault their way through his gargantuan novels, he clearly harbored none of Nietzsche's ambitions "to say in ten sentences what everyone else says in a book" (Nietzsche, *Twilight of the Idols*, 115).

**32** John Cowper Powys, *Autobiography* (1934; Hamilton, NY: Colgate University Press, 1968), 431, 386–99. James Huneker was another American critic who made the pilgrimage to the Nietzsche Archive in Weimar in 1904. He sparked a cordial friendship with Elisabeth Förster-Nietzsche, and the two corresponded for years to come. It is not clear whether H. L. Mencken ever met with Förster-Nietzsche personally, but the two exchanged letters for over two decades. Other notable American scholars who had correspondences with Förster-Nietzsche are William Salter and Johannes Broene.

**33** Ibid., 398–99. For an excellent study that seeks to move marginalia away from the margins of intellectual history and literary theory, see H. J. Jackson, *Marginalia: Readers Writing in Books* (New Haven, CT: Yale University Press, 2001).

**34** Ibid., 403.

**35** Ibid., 432, 395.

**36** On Gibran's life and thought, see Robin Waterfield, *Prophet: The Life and Times of Kahlil Gibran* (New York: St. Martin's Press, 1998); Suheil Bushrui and Joe Jenkins, *Kahlil Gibran: Man and Poet* (Boston: One World, 1998); and Mikhail Naimy, *Kahlil Gibran: A Biography* (New York: Philosophical Library, 1950).

**37** Kahlil Gibran, *Kahlil Gibran: A Self-Portrait*, trans. Anthony R. Ferris (New York: Citadel Press, 1959), 22.

**38** Kahlil Gibran, as quoted in Naimy, *Kahlil Gibran*, 124, 119.

**39** "Editorials," *Seven Arts* 1 (November 1916): 53.

**40** Gibran, as quoted in Naimy, *Kahlil Gibran*, 119.

**41** Kahlil Gibran, *The Forerunner* (1920; London: Heinemann Press, 1963), 7.

**42** Kahlil Gibran, *The Prophet* (1923; New York: Knopf, 1986), 77, 78, 64.

**43** Naimy, *Kahlil Gibran*, 142.

**44** Gibran, as quoted in Virginia Hilu, ed., *Beloved Prophet: The Love Letters of Kahlil Gibran and Mary Haskell and Her Private Journal* (New York: Knopf, 1972), 137.

**45** George Cram Cook, as quoted in Glaspell, *Road to the Temple*, 171. Cook discovered in the superman ideal an image of "the human future," in particular, "a new

Messiah . . . one for whom humanity must sacrifice itself, as a parent for a child."
This messiah was an earthly savior, a "Son of Man" instead of the son of God who
would signal the future of economic justice and social solidarity (ibid., 205).

46 Kazin, preface to *On Native Grounds*, xxiii–xxiv.

47 Harold Stearns, *America and the Young Intellectual* (New York: George Doran,
1921), 46.

48 Pletsch, *Young Nietzsche*, 1–3, 8, 7, 5.

49 Stearns, *America and the Young Intellectual*, 21.

50 Another strand of this genealogy certainly goes back to Thomas Carlyle's *On
Heroes, Hero-Worship, and the Heroic in History* (1841), which expressed the very
nineteenth-century Victorian sentimentality that Nietzsche found so despicable.
Despite Nietzsche's effort to distance himself from Carlyle's romantic celebration
of genius as well as from his view that "great men" are the agents of human history, he is consistently likened to Carlyle. A now classic example of this comparison can be found in Eric Bentley, *A Century of Hero-Worship* (1944; Boston:
Beacon, 1957).

51 R. J. Hollingdale, "The Hero as Outsider," in *The Cambridge Companion to
Nietzsche*, ed. Bernd Magnus and Kathleen M. Higgins (Cambridge: Cambridge
University Press, 1996), 73–75. Though Emerson was a successful example of
what we today would call a "public intellectual," who cultivated an intellectual
life without the institutional support of the church or the academy, it wasn't until
later, in the 1930s and 1940s, that radicals turned their attention to native sons
and daughters. For Emerson as public intellectual, see Lawrence Buell, *Emerson*
(Cambridge, MA: Harvard University Press, Belknap Press, 2003), and Linck
Johnson, "Emerson: America's First Public Intellectual?," *Modern Intellectual History* 2 (April 2005): 135–51.

52 Hollingdale's theory about the implication of 1848 for the subsequent sociology
of ideas and intellectuals is also useful for historicizing Nietzsche's attraction to
Schopenhauer (before souring on him) and his lifelong emulation of Goethe and
Emerson.

53 Nietzsche, *Human, All Too Human*, 111.

54 Nietzsche, *Twilight of the Idols*, 109.

55 Will Durant, *Philosophy and the Social Problem* (New York: Macmillan, 1917), 173.

56 Horace Kallen, "Nietzsche—Without Prejudice," *Dial*, September 20, 1919, 252.

57 Durant, *Philosophy and the Social Problem*, 178; Nietzsche, as quoted in ibid.

58 George Cram Cook, quoted in Glaspell, *Road to the Temple*, 170–71.

59 Ibid., 171, 197–98.

60 Upton Sinclair, "The Overman," in *Mammonart: An Essay in Economic Interpretation* (Pasadena, CA: Published by the author, 1924), 291.

61 The Nietzsche-Hamlet image would continue to animate Nietzsche interpretation throughout the century. Thomas Mann's characterization indicates the image
often invoked: "It is a tragic pity for an overloaded, overcharged soul which was
only called to knowledge, not really born to it and, like Hamlet, was destroyed

by it; for a dainty, fine, good soul for which love was a necessity, which inclined toward noble friendship and was never meant for loneliness, the aloneness of a criminal; for a spirituality at first deeply pious, entirely prone to reverence, bound to religious tradition, which was dragged by fate practically by the hair into a wild and intoxicated prophesy of barbaric resplendent force, of stifled conscience, of evil, a state devoid of all piety and raging against its very own nature." Thomas Mann, *Nietzsche's Philosophy in the Light of Contemporary Events* (Washington, DC: Library of Congress, 1947), 4.

62  Huneker, *Egoists*, 255.

63  Friedrich Nietzsche, *The Birth of Tragedy* (1872), in *"The Birth of Tragedy" and "The Case of Wagner,"* trans. Walter Kaufmann (New York: Vintage Books, 1967), 60.

64  Randolph Bourne to Carl Zigrosser, November 16, 1913, quoted in *The Letters of Randolph Bourne: A Comprehensive Edition*, ed. Eric J. Sandeen (Troy, NY: Whitston, 1981), 172–73.

65  Van Wyck Brooks, "The Critics and Young America," in *Criticism in America: Its Function and Status*, ed. Irving Babbitt (New York: Harcourt, Brace, 1924), 145.

66  Durant, *Philosophy and the Social Problem*, 173–74.

67  Upton Sinclair, *The Autobiography of Upton Sinclair* (New York: Harcourt, Brace & World, 1962), 45.

68  Emma Goldman, preface to *"Anarchism" and Other Essays* (1910; Port Washington, NY: Kennikat Press, 1969), 50.

69  Nietzsche, *Untimely Meditations*, 7, 9.

70  Randolph Bourne, "Traps for the Unwary," in *The Radical Will: Selected Writings, 1911–1918*, ed. Olaf Hansen (New York: Urizen Books, 1977), 481. Though Bourne was committed to a vision of the democratic artist, he confessed his lack of faith in democratic taste.

71  Huneker, *Egoists*, 241; Walling, *Larger Aspects of Socialism*, 194.

72  Nietzsche, *Twilight of the Idols*, 45.

73  Van Wyck Brooks, introduction to Randolph Bourne, *"The History of a Literary Radical" and Other Essays* (New York: B. W. Huebsch, 1920), xiii, xxxiii.

74  Nietzsche, *Twilight of the Idols*, 32.

75  Walling, *Larger Aspects of Socialism*, 192.

76  Walter Lippmann, *A Preface to Politics* (New York: Mitchell Kennerley, 1913), 235, 200, 234 (Nietzsche, as quoted in Lippmann).

77  Ibid., 169, 236.

78  Ibid., 235, 202, 235.

79  Nietzsche, *The Birth of Tragedy*, 22.

80  Lippmann, *Preface to Politics*, 200, 245.

81  Goldman, *"Anarchism" and Other Essays*, 56, 61, 56, 81, 201 (Nietzsche, as quoted in Goldman), 209, 201–2.

82  Ibid., 133–150.

83  Durant, *Philosophy and the Social Problem*, 173.

84  Hubert Harrison, "On a Certain Conservatism in Negroes," in *The Negro and the*

*Nation* (New York: Cosmo-Advocate, 1917), 42, 44. It is a reprint with modifications of his article "The Negro a Conservative: Christianity Still Enslaves the
Minds of Those Whose Bodies It Has Long Held Bound," *Truth Seeker*, September 12, 1914, 41–47.

85 E. L. Godkin, "Chromo-Civilization," *Nation*, September 24, 1874, 201–2.

86 Van Wyck Brooks, "'Highbrow' and 'Lowbrow,'" in *America's Coming of Age* (New
York: B. W. Huebsch, 1915), 9, 34.

87 Friedrich Nietzsche, *On the Genealogy of Morals* (1887), in *"On the Genealogy of
Morals" and "Ecce Homo,"* trans. Walter Kaufmann and R. J. Hollingdale (New
York: Vintage Books, 1989), 117–18.

88 Emma Goldman, "Victims of Morality," in *Red Emma Speaks: Selected Writings
and Speeches*, ed. Alix Kates Shulman (New York: Random House, 1972), 127–28.

89 H. L. Mencken, "Puritanism as a Literary Force," in *A Book of Prefaces* (New York:
Knopf, 1917), 210–11, 235, 211, 213.

90 Ibid., 233, 236, 237.

91 F. B. Kaye, "Puritanism, Literature, and War," *New Republic*, December 15, 1920, 65.

92 Max Lerner, "Randolph Bourne and Two Generations," *Twice a Year* 5 (Fall–
Winter 1940): 58.

93 Randolph Bourne, review of Paul Elmer More, *Nietzsche* (1911), *Journal of Philosophy, Psychology and Scientific Methods* 9 (August 15, 1912): 471.

94 Randolph Bourne, "The State," in *Radical Will*, 363; and Randolph Bourne,
"Trans-National America," in ibid., 259.

95 Randolph Bourne, "Denatured Nietzsche," *Dial*, October 12, 1917, 389.

96 Randolph Bourne, "H. L. Mencken," in *Radical Will*, 474.

97 Randolph Bourne, "The Puritan's Will to Power," in ibid., 301.

98 Randolph Bourne, "This Older Generation," in ibid., 161.

99 Brooks, "The Critics and Young America," 136.

100 Randolph Bourne, "Paul Elmer More," in *Radical Will*, 468.

101 Bourne, "This Older Generation," 163.

102 Bourne, "The Puritan's Will to Power," 304.

103 Ibid., 301–302, 305, 302.

104 Randolph Bourne to Elizabeth Shepley Sergeant, August 30, 1915, in *The Letters of
Randolph Bourne*, 325.

105 Randolph Bourne, "Old Tyrannies," in *Radical Will*, 169–72.

106 Bourne, "Trans-National America," 255; Bourne, "Old Tyrannies," 169.

107 Walling, *Larger Aspects of Socialism*, 203. For an excellent discussion of Nietzsche
as an "important reference point" for Bournian and Rortian pragmatism, see
John Pettegrew, "Lives of Irony: Randolph Bourne, Richard Rorty, and a New
Genealogy of Critical Pragmatism," in *A Pragmatist's Progress?: Richard Rorty and
American Intellectual History*, ed. Pettegrew (Lanham, MD: Rowman & Little-
field, 2000), 103–34.

108 Randolph Bourne, "Twilight of Idols," in *Radical Will*, 344, 347, 344.

109 Lippmann, *Drift and Mastery*, 92.

110 Randolph Bourne, quoted in William E. Leuchtenburg, introduction to ibid., 1.

111 Lippmann, *Drift and Mastery*, 100, 16, 111.

112 Brooks, "The Critics and Young America," 118; Bourne, "Trans-National America," 260.

113 Louis Untermeyer, "The Heretic," *Moods* 1 (March 1909): 144.

114 Nietzsche, *Beyond Good and Evil*, 13.

115 Kahlil Gibran, "The Great Longing," from *The Madman* (1918), in *The Collected Works* (New York: Everyman's Library, 2007), 41.

116 Margaret Anderson, ed., *The Little Review Anthology* (New York: Hermitage House, 1953), 18; Margaret Anderson, *My Thirty Years War* (New York: Covici, Friede, 1930), 48; Agnes Boulton, *Part of a Long Story* (New York: Doubleday, 1958), 61.

117 Randolph Bourne, "Traps for the Unwary," in *Radical Will*, 483–84.

118 Ralph Waldo Emerson, "Circles," from *Essays: First Series*, in *Collected Works of Ralph Waldo Emerson*, 2:183.

119 Nietzsche, *Thus Spoke Zarathustra*, 86.

120 Ibid., 72.

## Interlude

1 Jennie E. Hintz to Elisabeth Förster-Nietzsche, April 27, 1913, GSA 72/BW 2311. All letters cited below are from this collection unless otherwise noted.

2 Ibid.

3 Ibid.

4 Jennie E. Hintz to Elisabeth Förster-Nietzsche, June 18, 1913, GSA 72/BW 2311.

5 Elise Fincke to Friedrich Nietzsche, in *KGB* III.2, 204.

6 Gustav Dannreuther to Friedrich Nietzsche, in ibid., 255–56.

7 Only Nietzsche's response of June 21, 1888, is extant. See Nietzsche to Knortz, June 21, 1888, in Middleton, ed., *Selected Letters of Friedrich Nietzsche*, 298–99. Knortz sent additional letters to Elisabeth Förster-Nietzsche in 1895, 1896, and 1905. GSA 72/BW 2822.

8 On Förster-Nietzsche, see Peters, *Zarathustra's Sister*, and Diethe, *Nietzsche's Sister and the Will to Power*. For a history of the Nietzsche Archive, see Hoffmann, *Zur Geschichte des Nietzsche-Archivs*.

9 "Will Nietzsche Come into Vogue in America?," 65.

10 Antrim and Goebel, "Friedrich Nietzsche's Uebermensch," 571.

11 On the popularization of philosophy in America, see Cotkin, *Existential America*, and George Cotkin, "Middle-Ground Pragmatists: The Popularization of Philosophy in American Culture," *Journal of the History of Ideas* 55 (April 1994): 283–302. On the popularization of philosophy in postwar France, see Tamara Chaplin, *Turning on the Mind: French Philosophers on Television* (Chicago: University of Chicago Press, 2007).

12 For the history of cultural stratification in twentieth-century American intellec-

tual life, see Rubin, *The Making of Middlebrow Culture*; Levine, *Highbrow/Low-brow*; Radway, *A Feeling for Books*; and Gans, *Popular Culture and High Culture*.

13   On the culture of celebrity, see Charles L. Ponce de Leon, *Self-Exposure: Human Interest Journalism and the Emergence of Celebrity in America, 1890–1940* (Chapel Hill: University of North Carolina Press, 2002) and *Fortunate Son: The Life of Elvis Presley* (New York: Hill and Wang, 2007). On the relationship between stars and their fans, see Erika Doss, *Elvis Culture: Fans, Faith, and Image* (Lawrence: University Press of Kansas, 1999), and Daniel Cavicchi, *Tramps Like Us: Music and Meaning among Springsteen Fans* (New York: Oxford University Press, 1998). On the concept of stardom, see Richard Dyer, *Stars* (London: British Film Institute, 1998). For a longer history of American spectatorship, see Richard Butsch, *The Making of American Audiences: From Stage to Television, 1750–1990* (Cambridge: Cambridge University Press, 2000).

14   Though Nietzsche the *philosophical* celebrity raises different questions than do literary celebrities, the growing scholarship on the latter (and the paucity of scholarship on the former) helps signpost some of the issues relevant here. See Glass, *Authors Inc.*, and Blake, *Walt Whitman and the Culture of American Celebrity*.

15   Altogether I have examined letters from approximately seventy people. Some wrote just a single letter. The most correspondence from a single American is twenty-one letters. The shortest correspondence is a single telegram, and the longest is ten handwritten pages. Except in rare instances, the archive has no record of Förster-Nietzsche's responses. The only way to glean this information is from cases in which a single person wrote multiple letters, some of which either thank her for her response or question why she hasn't responded. The archive also has no record indicating how many letters arrived from the United States, or what proportion of the total incoming letters the extant ones in their collection represent.

16   For an excellent study on middle-class Americans' role in transnational consumption, see Kristin Hoganson, *Consumers' Imperium: The Global Production of American Domesticity, 1865–1920* (Chapel Hill: University of North Carolina Press, 2007).

17   Examples of reception studies that yield broader cultural and political histories include Robert Darnton, *The Great Cat Massacre: And Other Episodes in French Cultural History* (1984; New York: Basic Books, 1999); Aschheim, *The Nietzsche Legacy in Germany*; Ceaser, *Reconstructing America*; Fox, *Jesus in America*; Armitage, *The Declaration of Independence*; and Winterer, *Mirror of Antiquity*.

18   Dannreuther to Nietzsche, *KGB* III.2, 256–57 (italics added).

19   Emerson, "Uses of Great Men," in *Representative Men*, 4:8.

20   Janice A. Radway, "Reading Is Not Eating: Mass-Produced Literature and the Theoretical, Methodological, and Political Consequences of a Metaphor," *Book Research Quarterly* 2 (Fall 1986): 7–29. For more works on reception history, see Philip Goldstein and James L. Machor, eds., *New Directions in American Recep-*

*tion Study* (New York: Oxford University Press, 2008). For a history of reception theory (both philosophical and literary), see Robert C. Holub, *Reception Theory: A Critical Introduction* (London: Metheun, 1984). On the difference between what a text means versus what a text does, see Stanley E. Fish, "Literature in the Reader: Affective Stylistics," in *Reader-Response Criticism: From Formalism to Post-Structuralism*, ed. Jane P. Tompkins (Baltimore: Johns Hopkins University Press, 1980), 70–100.

21 Joseph Jacobs, quoted in "Will Nietzsche Come into Vogue in America?," 65.

22 John Boogher Jr. to Elisabeth Förster-Nietzsche, July 29, 1926, GSA 72/BW 609.

23 Stanley Kimmel to Elisabeth Förster-Nietzsche, June 1, 1927, GSA 72/BW 3821.

24 W. H. Amerland to Elisabeth Förster-Nietzsche, March 30, 1922, GSA 72/BW 61. Amerland provided Förster-Nietzsche with the inventory of signatures in his collection, including Victor Hugo, Charles Darwin, Ralph Waldo Emerson, Albert Einstein, Bismarck, Abraham Lincoln, and George Washington. Frau Förster-Nietzsche did not oblige him with a signature. In a letter dated May 19, 1922, a staff member of the archive wrote Amerland to inform him that the bylaws of the Nietzsche Archive foundation did not permit "one single line" of Friedrich Nietzsche's handwriting to be given away. Nonetheless, there are several occasions in which Förster-Nietzsche did just that. Nietzsche Archive to William H. Amerland, May, 19, 1922, Minnesota Historical Society, William Amerland Papers, A.A512, box 2. Seasoned autograph collectors recognized that a signature alone would not do. Charles Gallup of Coxsackie-on-Hudson, New York, wrote Förster-Nietzsche in December 1914 to acquire not only an autograph of her "late and lamented" brother but also "some impersonal note or letter [of Nietzsche's], signed" as well as a note of authenticity from Förster-Nietzsche for his "rather famous collection." The signature of the philosopher of authenticity surely had to be authentic. Charles Gallup to Elisabeth Förster-Nietzsche, December 4, 1914, GSA 72/BW 1568. We have no record of her response to Gallup's request.

25 S. T. Frame to the Nietzsche Archive, September 14, 1926, GSA/BW 1448. I have been unable to locate any publication by Frame on Nietzsche, so it is unclear whether the archive replied to his request or if he ever published anything on Nietzsche.

26 Other requests included information about where they could find a specific Nietzsche publication, details about a local Nietzsche Society, and one of his musical compositions. In 1924, Stephen D. Parrish, a lawyer from Richmond, Kentucky, wrote, "I am very much interested in the study of Nietzsche,—his life and life-work," and asked to whom the "Nietzsche Society" awarded its annual prize on the topic of "The Individual and the Community." Stephen D. Parrish to Nietzsche Society, Weimar, July 21, 1924, GSA 72/BW 4050.

27 Christoph J. Hofmann to Elisabeth Förster-Nietzsche, February 28, 1923, GSA 72/BW 2384.

28  Elisabeth Förster-Nietzsche, ed., *The Nietzsche-Wagner Correspondence*, trans. Caroline Kerr (New York: Boni and Liveright, 1921).

29  Helene Bachmüller to Elisabeth Förster-Nietzsche, January 5, 1922, GSA 721/BW 131.

30  George E. Nitzsche to Elisabeth Förster-Nietzsche, October 16, 1931, GSA 72/BW 3872. Förster-Nietzsche replied to Nitzsche, sending him her book with an inscription but no autograph. In a reply dated January 4, 1932, Nitzsche thanked her for the book and told her, "I understand that the autographs of your famous brother should stay intact." George E. Nitzsche to Elisabeth Förster-Nietzsche, January 4, 1932, GSA 72/BW 3872.

31  Werner Sollors, *Beyond Ethnicity: Consent and Descent in American Culture* (New York: Oxford University Press, 1986), 31.

32  Francis Langer to Elisabeth Förster-Nietzsche, January 16, 1896, GSA 72/BW 3074.

33  Francis Langer to Elisabeth Förster-Nietzsche, September 8, 1896, GSA 72/BW 3074.

34  John I. Bush to Elisabeth Förster-Nietzsche, December 9, 1919, GSA 72/BW 816.

35  John I. Bush to Elisabeth Förster-Nietzsche, December 16, 1919, GSA 72/BW 816.

36  John I. Bush to Nietzsche Archive, January 26, 1920, GSA 72/BW 816.

37  Nietzsche, *Thus Spoke Zarathustra*, 214.

38  Edward Evans to Nietzsche Archive, n.d., GSA 72/BW 254.

39  Elmer Schreiner to Elisabeth Förster-Nietzsche, December 8, 1921, GSA 72/Schreiner.

40  Elmer Schreiner to Elisabeth Förster-Nietzsche, December 20, 1924, GSA 72/Schreiner.

41  Ibid; Nietzsche, as quoted in ibid.

42  Schreiner to Förster-Nietzsche, December 8, 1921.

43  Hintz to Förster-Nietzsche, April 27, 1913, and June 18, 1913.

44  Hellmut Marx to Elisabeth Förster-Nietzsche, March 3, 1929, GSA 72/BW 3434.

45  Jossie Farmer to Elisabeth Förster-Nietzsche, January 17, 1923, GSA 72/BW 142a.

46  Otto Manthey-Zorn to Elisabeth Förster-Nietzsche, n.d., GSA 72/BW 3401.

47  Edwards Bobo Murray to Elisabeth Förster-Nietzsche, April 1, 1910, GSA 72/BW 3752. See also Melker Johnson, who thanked Förster-Nietzsche for his time "studying" in the Nietzsche Archive. Melker Johnson to Elisabeth Förster-Nietzsche, August 8, 1929, GSA 72/BW Johnson. For other references to archive visits, see Detlev Jessen to Elisabeth Förster-Nietzsche, September 2, 1903; March 23, 1904; December 15, 1908; May 12, 1911; June 14, 1911; and December 13, 1911, GSA 72/BW 2568 (Jessen refers to his visit as "the best time of my life"); J. A. C. Hildner to Elisabeth Förster-Nietzsche, November 6, 1925 (who justifies the visit by informing her that as a professor of German literature at the University of Michigan, he had been teaching *Zarathustra* and *Ecce Homo* to filled classes), GSA 72/BW 2299; W[alter?] Wadepuhl to Max Oehler, June 20, 1932, GSA 72/

BW 1776; and Helene Mueller Schlenkkopf to Elisabeth Förster-Nietzsche, n.d. (in which she refers to a trip she made with "American Professors [male and female]" through Carl Schurz Travels, 1934), GSA 101/BW 197.

48 Gottfried Betz to Elisabeth Förster-Nietzsche, July 12, 1927, GSA 72/BW 457.

49 Lydia Lois Tilley to Elisabeth Förster-Nietzsche, June 7, 1910, GSA 72/BW 5503.

50 Lydia Lois Tilley to Elisabeth Förster-Nietzsche, July 7, 1910, GSA 72/BW 5503.

51 Elmer Schreiner to Elisabeth Förster-Nietzsche, June 24, 1920, GSA 72/ Schreiner.

52 Schreiner to Förster-Nietzsche, December 8, 1921. It is unclear whether Schreiner ever wrote the book; I have not been able to find record of its publication.

53 For the story of the first translations, see Thatcher, *Nietzsche in England*. On the difficulties of translating Nietzsche for the English speaker, see Frank McEachran, "On Translating Nietzsche into English," *Nietzsche-Studien* 6 (1977): 295–99. A synopsis of the major Nietzsche translations can be found in Raymond Hargreaves, "Friedrich Nietzsche, 1844–1900," in *Encyclopedia of Literary Translations into English*, ed. Olive Classe (Chicago: Fitzroy Dearborn, 2000), 2:1001–5.

54 Preston A. Barba to Elisabeth Förster-Nietzsche, January 11, 1927, GSA 72/ BW 158.

55 Marx to Förster-Nietzsche, March 3, 1929.

56 James Taft Hatfield to Elisabeth Förster-Nietzsche, January 8, 1913, GSA 72/BW 2080. In the letter he explained, "It is well-known that the pearl of the venerable Harvard University library is a dedicated edition of Goethe's works.... Would it be too much to ask, when I make the request of you to send your published edition of the works [of Nietzsche] with a signed dedication 'for the library of Northwestern University'?"

57 Hofmann to Förster-Nietzsche, February 28, 1923.

58 Herman George Scheffauer to Elisabeth Förster-Nietzsche, June 3, 1924, GSA72/BW Scheffauer.

59 Herman George Scheffauer to Elisabeth Förster-Nietzsche, October 30, 1924, GSA 72/BW Scheffauer.

60 Herman George Scheffauer to Elisabeth Förster-Nietzsche, December 1, 1924, GSA 72/BW Scheffauer.

61 Herman George Scheffauer to Elisabeth Förster-Nietzsche, June 14, 1924, GSA 72/BW Scheffauer.

62 Gottfried Betz to Elisabeth Förster-Nietzsche, October 28, 1926, GSA 72/ BW 457.

63 Theodore N. Van Derlyn to Elisabeth Förster-Nietzsche, December 12, 1915, GSA 72/BW 972.

64 T. D. Kriton to Elisabeth Förster-Nietzsche, September 1933, GSA 72/BW 2951. Kriton dedicated his (1935 [1931]) English translation of E. Roidis's *Papissa Joanna* to H. L. Mencken, for whom he had "sincere respect."

65 Ibid.

## Chapter Five

1 Allanson Shaw, "Mussolini's Three Political Saints: Machiavelli, Mazzini, and Nietzsche Influence the Thought of Italy's 'Man of Destiny,'" *New York Times*, February 15, 1925, SM9; William Kilborne Stewart, "The Mentors of Mussolini," *American Political Science Review* 22 (November 1928): 843–69; and Leonard Woolf, *Quack, Quack!* (New York: Harcourt, Brace, 1935).

2 Benito Mussolini, as quoted in Thomas A. O'Hara, "Nietzsche and the Crisis," *Commonweal*, March 13, 1936, 537.

3 Tracy Strong, *Friedrich Nietzsche and the Politics of Transfiguration* (1975; exp. ed., Urbana: University of Illinois Press, 2000), 312–13, original emphasis.

4 On the conservative intellectual climate of 1950s America, see Richard Pells, *The Liberal Mind in a Conservative Age: American Intellectuals in the 1940s and 1950s* (New York: Harper & Row, 1985); Purcell, *The Crisis of Democratic Theory*, 235–66; and John McCumber, *Time in the Ditch: American Philosophy and the McCarthy Era* (Evanston, IL: Northwestern University Press, 2001).

5 Hays Steilberg makes this point in his *Die amerikanische Nietzsche-Rezeption von 1896 bis 1950* (Berlin: Walter de Gruyter, 1996).

6 Walter Kaufmann, *Nietzsche: Philosopher, Psychologist, Antichrist* (1950; Princeton, NJ: Princeton University Press, 1974), vii; reference is to the 1974 edition.

7 Michael Friedman, *A Parting of the Ways: Carnap, Cassirer, and Heidegger* (Chicago: Open Court, 2000).

8 Bruce Kuklick, *A History of Philosophy in America, 1720–2000*, 227. See also Bruce Kuklick, "Philosophy and Inclusion in the United States, 1929–2001," in Hollinger, *Humanities and the Dynamics of Inclusion*, 159–88.

9 Nietzsche, *Thus Spoke Zarathustra*.

10 On Kaufmann's interest in the German intellectual tradition, see Ivan Soll, "Walter Kaufmann and the Advocacy of German Thought in America," *Paedagogica Historica* 33 (1997): 117–33.

11 Kaufmann, *Nietzsche*, 269, 252, 266, 264; these and all subsequent references are to the 1950 edition unless otherwise indicated.

12 Ibid., 249–50.

13 There were four editions of Kaufmann's *Nietzsche* over a twenty-four-year period: a second edition was issued in 1956; a third edition, revised and enlarged, in 1968; and a fourth edition in 1974.

14 Indeed, in recent years it has become—as the historian David Pickus puts it—the "industry standard" to characterize Kaufmann's treatment of Nietzsche as a highly problematic apologia of a philosopher regarded as an important intellectual source for Nazism. For an excellent analysis of contemporary Kaufmann criticism, see David Pickus, "The Walter Kaufmann Myth: A Study in Academic Judgment," *Nietzsche-Studien* 32 (2003): 226–58.

15 Robert Ackermann, "Current American Thought on Nietzsche," in *Nietzsche Heute: Die Rezeption seines Werkes nach 1968*, ed. Sigrid Bauschinger, Susan L.

Cocalis, and Sara Lennox (Bern: Francke Verlag, 1988), 129–36; quotation is from p. 129. Though Ackermann does not refer to Kaufmann by name, he refers more broadly to the postwar "translation and commentary" of which Kaufmann was the most prominent figure. For commentary on Kaufmann, see Aschheim, *The Nietzsche Legacy in Germany*, 315; Michael Tanner, "Organizing the Self and the World," *Times Literary Supplement*, May 16, 1986, 519; Walter Sokel, "Political Uses and Abuses of Nietzsche in Walter Kaufmann's Image of Nietzsche," *Nietzsche-Studien* 12 (1983): 436–42; Gregory Bruce Smith, *Nietzsche, Heidegger and the Transition to Postmodernity* (Chicago: University of Chicago Press, 1996), 69; Richard Wolin, *The Seduction of Unreason: The Intellectual Romance with Fascism from Nietzsche to Postmodernism* (Princeton, NJ: Princeton University Press, 2004), 27–62, 32; and Peter Bergmann, "The Anti-Motif," in *Nietzsche, "The Last Antipolitical German"* (Bloomington: Indiana University Press, 1987), 1–8.

16 For the American reception of French existentialism, see Ann Fulton, *Apostles of Sartre: Existentialism in America, 1945–1963* (Evanston, IL: Northwestern University Press, 1999). For a broader study of the varieties of existential thought in the United States both before and after Sartre, see George Cotkin, *Existential America* (Baltimore: Johns Hopkins University Press, 2003).

17 Walter Cerf, review of *Nietzsche: Philosopher, Psychologist, Antichrist*, by Walter Kaufmann, *Philosophy and Phenomenological Research* 12 (December 1951): 287.

18 As there is no extant collection of Kaufmann's personal papers except for a small manuscript collection at Princeton University, the following biographical information is drawn from two essays on Kaufmann by Ivan Soll, professor of philosophy at University of Wisconsin–Madison and former graduate student of Kaufmann's at Princeton University: "Walter Kaufmann and the Advocacy of German Thought in America," and Ivan Soll, "Walter Arnold Kaufmann," in *American National Biography*, ed. John A. Garraty and Mark C. Carnes (New York: Oxford University Press, 1999), 403–5; Kaufmann's autobiographical remarks in his prologue to *The Faith of a Heretic* (Garden City, NY: Doubleday, 1961), x; and "An Interview with Walter Kaufmann," with Trude Weiss-Rosmarin, *Judaism* 30 (Winter, 1981): 120–28.

19 Walter Kaufmann, "The Faith of a Heretic," *Harper's Magazine*, February 1959, 33.

20 Kaufmann later contended that his decision to convert was neither a protest against the Nazis nor a nostalgic embrace of his heritage, but based solely on religious grounds.

21 Formerly the Hochschüle für die Wissenschaft des Judentums; the Nazis changed the name in 1934.

22 There is a vast literature on the German intellectual émigrés. Those offering some of the most comprehensive views of the impact on the American intellectual climate include Anthony Heilbut, *Exiled in Paradise: German Refugee Artists and Intellectuals in America, from the 1930s to the Present* (1983; Berkeley: University of California Press, 1997); Jarrell C. Jackman and Carla M. Borden, eds., *The Muses Flee Hitler: Cultural Transfer and Adaptation, 1930–1945* (Washington, DC:

Smithsonian Institute Press, 1983); Claus-Dieter Krohn, *Intellectuals in Exile: Refugee Scholars and the New School for Social Research* (Amherst: University of Massachusetts Press, 1993); Martin Jay, *The Dialectical Imagination: A History of the Frankfurt School and the Institute of Social Research, 1923–1950* (Berkeley: University of California Press, 1973); H. Stuart Hughes, *The Sea Change: The Migration of Social Thought, 1930–1965* (New York: Harper and Row, 1975); and Ehrhard Bahr, *Weimar on the Pacific: German Exile Culture in Los Angeles and the Crisis of Modernism* (Berkeley: University of California Press, 2007).

23  Kaufmann, "Faith of a Heretic," 33.

24  Joseph Goebbels, as quoted by Louis P. Lochner; reprinted in Jeremy Noakes and Geoffrey Pridham, eds., *Nazism, 1919–1945*, vol. 2, *State, Economy and Society 1933–1939* (Exeter: University of Exeter Press, 1998), 401.

25  Hannah Arendt, "We Refugees," *Menorah Journal*, January–March 1943, 69, 77.

26  Leo Strauss, as quoted in Laurence Lampert, *Leo Strauss and Nietzsche* (Chicago: University of Chicago Press, 1996), 5. Strauss brought with him his "furtive" interest in Nietzsche when he arrived in the United States in 1937, and incorporated his philosophy into his teaching of political science at the New School for Social Research from 1938 to 1948, as well as at the University of Chicago for the next two decades. Strauss's reading of Nietzsche's conception of illusion as necessary for life, his attack on nineteenth-century historicism, his ideas of the contrasting moral sources of theism and secular rationalism as well as his embodiment of the genuine philosopher, informed to varying degrees the major contrasting conceptions animating his thought: the difference between esoteric and exoteric textual meaning, natural right and historicism, "Athens versus Jerusalem," and the image of the genuine philosopher's salutary pathos of distance from conventional relativistic science. In *Natural Right and History* (1953), Strauss argued that Nietzsche's attack on nineteenth-century historicism demanded a parting of the ways between a superficial understanding of relativism and a deeper grasp of it, which he believed Nietzsche had: "According to Nietzsche, the theoretical analysis of human life that realizes the relativity of all comprehensive views and thus depreciates them would make human life itself impossible, for it would destroy the protecting atmosphere within which life or culture or action is alone possible. Moreover, since the theoretical analysis has its basis outside of life, it will never be able to understand life. The theoretical analysis of life is noncommittal and fatal to commitment, but life means commitment. To avert the danger to life, Nietzsche could choose one of two ways: he could insist on the strictly esoteric character of the theoretical analysis of life—that is, restore the Platonic notion of the noble delusion—or else he could deny the possibility of theory proper and so conceive of thought as essentially subservient to, or dependent on, life or fate. If not Nietzsche himself, at any rate his successors adopted the second alternative" (Leo Strauss, *Natural Right and History* [Chicago: University of Chicago Press, 1953], 26).

Strauss considered Nietzsche, like himself, one of the rare modern philosophers who chose the first alternative. Though Strauss is an important figure in the revival of political philosophy, and a significant gateway for the postwar appropriation of Nietzsche for conservative political thought, his prime influence on American Nietzsche interpretations was as a teacher and philosophical figurehead to his "Straussian" students and adherents, including Allan Bloom and Bloom's student Francis Fukuyama. Bloom and Fukuyama emerged as two of the most prominent interpreters of Nietzschean neoconservatism in the 1980s and '90s, and are discussed in chapter 6 and the epilogue. On Nietzsche's centrality in Strauss's political philosophy, see Lampert, *Leo Strauss and Nietzsche*; Shadia B. Drury, *The Political Ideas of Leo Strauss* (1988; New York: Palgrave Macmillan, 2005); and Catherine Zuckert, "Strauss's Return to Premodern Thought," in *The Cambridge Companion to Leo Strauss*, ed. Stephen B. Smith (Cambridge: Cambridge University Press, 2009), 119–36.

27 Mann, *Nietzsche's Philosophy in the Light of Contemporary Events*, 19, 17; and Thomas Mann, *Thomas Mann: Briefe 1937–1947*, ed. Erika Mann (Frankfurt: S. Fischer, 1963), 23.

28 Erich Fromm, *Escape from Freedom* (New York: Farrar & Rinehart, 1941).

29 Paul Tillich, *The Shaking of the Foundations* (New York: Charles Scribner's Sons, 1948); Paul Tillich, *The Protestant Era*, trans. James Luther Adams (Chicago: University of Chicago Press, 1948), 161; and Paul Tillich, *The Courage to Be* (New Haven, CT: Yale University Press, 1952), 189–90.

30 Karl Löwith, *Meaning in History: The Theological Implications of the Philosophy of History* (1949; Chicago: University of Chicago Press, 1962), v.

31 While Nietzsche's Jewish and non-Jewish interpreters in Germany tried to reconcile his competing claims on Jews and Judaism, in the United States the interest in Nietzsche's position only first emerged as a subject of significant interest during this period. Though there are instances of American interpreters interested in his conception of Hebraism and Hellenism in modern culture, or curious whether the slave morality was instantiated already in Judaism or only came about in its early Christian morphology, it took the Nazis' increasing moves from anti-Semitic rhetoric to exterminationist action for Americans to take notice of the potentials for anti-Semitism (or, conversely, latent philo-Semitism) in Nietzsche's texts. But over the course of the 1940s, the connections crystallized, making what decades earlier was not an issue for most American Nietzsche commentators become, by 1950, critically important for Kaufmann.

32 Martha Zapata Galindo, *Triumph des Willens zur Macht: Zur Nietzsche-Rezeption im NS-Staat* (Hamburg: Argument, 1995), 186.

33 Elisabeth Förster-Nietzsche, as quoted in H. F. Peters, *Zarathustra's Sister: The Case of Elisabeth and Friedrich Nietzsche* (New York: Crown, 1977), 220; on the archive's role in uniting Nietzsche and National Socialism, see Aschheim, *Nietzsche Legacy*, 239–40.

34 Kaufmann, *Nietzsche*, 39.

35 Nietzsche to Förster-Nietzsche, quoted in ibid., 40; Kaufmann, ibid; and Nietzsche to Franz Overbeck, quoted in ibid.

**36** Hannah Arendt to Karl Jaspers, March 4, 1961, in *Hannah Arendt/Karl Jaspers Correspondence, 1926–69*, ed. Lotte Köhler and Hans Saner (New York: Harcourt Brace, 1992), 166. While Arendt was not alone in exculpating Nietzsche from Nazi genealogy, her effort to fully exempt German culture from suspicion stood opposed to other theorists, who saw Nazism as developing within the antibourgeois, anti-Semitic, idealist elements in German thought. See Steven E. Aschheim, *Culture and Catastrophe: German and Jewish Confrontations with National Socialism and Other Crises* (New York: New York University Press, 1996), chap. 1. As Richard Wolin has shown, Arendt and her fellow exiles who studied with Martin Heidegger—Karl Löwith, Hans Jonas, and Herbert Marcuse—calibrated their ideas about totalitarianism and German anti-Semitism in response to his support of Nazism. On the Heideggerian dialectic in German-Jewish émigré thought, see Richard Wolin, *Heidegger's Children: Hannah Arendt, Karl Löwith, Hans Jonas, and Herbert Marcuse* (Princeton, NJ: Princeton University Press, 2001).

**37** Franz Neumann, *Behemoth: The Structure and Practice of National Socialism, 1933–1944* (1942; rev. ed., Toronto: Oxford University Press, 1944), 127–28.

**38** On Adorno's years in the United States, see David Jenemann, *Adorno in America* (Minneapolis: University of Minnesota Press, 2007).

**39** Max Horkheimer and Theodor Adorno, *Dialectic of Enlightenment* (1944), trans. John Cumming (New York: Continuum, 2002), 3, x, 6, 44, 120. Although now considered one of the most impressive works published by any of the exiled émigrés, and indeed one of the most important treatises in twentieth-century philosophy and cultural studies, when *Dialectic of Enlightenment* was first published (in German) in New York in 1944, it was not until the New Left slowly rediscovered Adorno in the 1960s that his philosophical works began to make an impact on American thought. See Martin Jay, "Adorno in America," in *Permanent Exiles: Essays on the Intellectual Migration from Germany to America* (New York: Columbia University Press, 1986), 127–29.

**40** Theodor Adorno, *Negative Dialectics* (1966), trans. E. B. Ashton (London: Routledge, 1973). For a marvelous reflection on the difficulties involved in translating Adorno's German into English, see Ashton's "Translator's Note," ix–xv.

**41** Theodor Adorno, *Minima Moralia: Reflections from Damaged Life* (1951), trans. E. F. N. Jephcott (London: Verso, 2002), 33.

**42** The one exception was his most social-scientific work (and also the one most widely received), *The Authoritarian Personality* (1950).

**43** Theodor Adorno, "Cultural Criticism and Society," in *Prisms* (1955), trans. Samuel and Shierry Weber (Cambridge, MA: MIT Press, 1981), 34.

**44** Theodor Adorno, "Wagner, Nietzsche, and Hitler," *Kenyon Review* 9 (Winter 1947): 161.

**45** Horkheimer and Adorno, *Dialectic*, 128; and Kaufmann, *Nietzsche*, 206; original emphasis.

**46** Kaufmann, *Nietzsche*, vii, 368; original emphasis.

**47** Ibid., 320, 7, 14–15. Contrary to the dominant tendency in German Nietzsche interpretation to read Nietzsche as a romantic (most notably Karl Joel and Ernst Bertram), Kaufmann consistently argued that the "superficial" similarities between Nietzsche's and the German romantics' literary styles, subjectivity, and aestheticism masked their profound differences in their moral outlooks. For Kaufmann's effort to underscore distinctions between "Dionysian" and romantic ethics and aesthetics, see his discussions on 101–3, 113–17, 282–84, 327–29, and 333–37.

48 Ibid., 52; Nietzsche, as quoted in ibid., 53.

49 Ibid., 68, 61, 69–70.

50 Cotkin, *Existential America*, 91–104.

51 Kaufmann, *Nietzsche*, 141.

52 Kaufmann's *Existentialism from Dostoyevsky to Sartre* (New York: Meridian Books, 1956) provided English readers with their first exposure to European thinkers, including Heidegger, Sartre, and Camus, who had not been translated into English up until that time. The interest in a specifically French existentialism would quickly be eclipsed by the success of Kaufmann's *Nietzsche*, which set the terms for his own anthology in 1956, as well a flurry of other major efforts, including, most notably, Kurt Reinhart's *The Existentialist Revolt* (1952) and William Barrett's *Irrational Man* (1958).

53 Kaufmann, *Nietzsche*, 133.

54 Francis Strickland, "Weird Genius," *Christian Century*, May 2, 1951, 561; Ernst Koch, "Review of Walter Kaufmann, *Nietzsche*," *Modern Language Journal* 37 (January 1953): 60; and H. R. Smart, "Review of Walter Kaufmann, *Nietzsche*," *Philosophical Review* 61 (January 1952): 125.

55 On the midcentury developments in professional philosophy in the United States, see Kuklick, *A History of Philosophy in America*; Friedman, *Parting of the Ways*; Soll, "Walter Kaufmann and the Advocacy of German Thought," 117–21; and McCumber, *Time in the Ditch*.

56 For observations about the continental divide in philosophy, see William Barrett's introductory remarks in his *Irrational Man: A Study in Existential Philosophy* (New York: Doubleday Anchor, 1958), 3–19.

57 Kaufmann, *Nietzsche*, 422 (1974 edition).

58 Kaufmann, *Existentialism*, 51.

59 Walter Kaufmann, ed. and trans., *The Portable Nietzsche* (New York: Viking Press, 1954), 18–19.

60 O'Hara, "Nietzsche and the Crisis," 539; and John Evans, "Nietzsche Held Nazis' Prophet in War on Christ," *Chicago Daily Tribune*, May 4, 1935, 23.

61 Margaret Porter Reinke, "I Married a Nazi!: American Girl's Romance Wrecked by Hitlerism," *Chicago Daily Tribune*, February 26, 1939, G4; and Sigrid Schultz, "Pagan Customs Revived for Nazi Weddings: Blood Purity Is Stressed," *Chicago Daily Tribune*, May 1, 1938, G11.

62 Ruth Adler, "Speaking as One Superman to Another," *New York Times*, October 17, 1943, SM27.

63 Crane Brinton, *Nietzsche* (Cambridge, MA: Harvard University Press, 1941), 184–85, 230.

64 Kaufmann, *Nietzsche*, 337.

65 Nietzsche, *Human, All Too Human*, 380; Kaufmann, *Nietzsche*, 338.

66 Kaufmann, *Nietzsche*, 295, 339.

67 Ibid., 364, 366, vii.

68 Walter A. Kaufmann, "Goethe and the History of Ideas," *Journal of the History of Ideas* 10 (October 1949): 511. In addition to presenting two dramatically different images of Nietzsche's philosophy, Kaufmann's and Brinton's studies offered two competing approaches to the history of ideas. Kaufmann, a philosopher, and Brinton, a historian in the years when *Geistesgeschichte* (intellectual history) was first coming into formation in the United States and a founding editor of the *Journal of the History of Ideas*, offered two very opposed visions of where (and how) to apprehend the agency of ideas—either in authorial intent or influence, or in intellectual production or cultural reception. In an article (drawn from his forthcoming book) titled "The National Socialists' Use of Nietzsche," published in the first volume of the *Journal of the History of Ideas* in 1940, Brinton noted, "The *Journal of the History of Ideas* will inevitably in these days have to occupy itself much with the questions centered round the great problem of the relation between ideas—especially more or less abstract ideas—and the rest of what goes on in this world. We may here be permitted to leave this larger problem unconsidered, and ask ourselves what *use* the German National Socialists have made of Nietzsche" (Crane Brinton, "The National Socialists' Use of Nietzsche," *Journal of the History of Ideas* 1 [April 1940]: 131; original emphasis).

69 Cerf, review of *Nietzsche*, 287.

70 Crane Brinton, "Heir of Socrates?," *Saturday Review of Literature*, January 13, 1951, 32–33.

71 According to Kaufmann, there was one feature of Nietzsche's posthumous influence (which he referred to as "Nietzsche's Heritage") worthy of consideration: "Nietzsche as Educator." But even here, Nietzsche educated his reader to "become who you are!" In other words, the only "influence" Nietzsche could have on a reader that would be true to his philosophy was, ironically, to convince the reader to not be convinced by his ideas. See Kaufmann, "Nietzsche's Heritage," in *Nietzsche*, 361–68.

72 If one of Kaufmann's consistent aims as a Nietzsche interpreter was to establish his relevance for modern philosophy, then given Emerson's virtual absence from academic philosophy both in 1950 when Kaufmann wrote *Nietzsche* and through 1974 when he wrote his half-hearted introduction to his *Gay Science* translation, it is not surprising that he had little incentive to press deeper into this discussion.

73 Kaufmann, *Nietzsche*, 352.

74 William James, as quoted in ibid., 59.

75 William James, "The Present Dilemma in Philosophy," in *Pragmatism: A New*

*Name for Some Old Ways of Thinking* (1907; Cambridge, MA: Harvard University Press, 1975), 13.

76 Kaufmann, *Nietzsche*, 59n. In "The Present Dilemma in Philosophy," from which Kaufmann drew James's distinction between the tough-minded and the tender-minded personality, James poked fun at the "brutal caricature" of his own "barbaric distinction," admitting that it was nothing more than a conceptual convenience for examining tendencies in thought. It was clearly no endorsement of philosophical "toughness." In Kaufmann's effort to show Nietzsche's value over James's, he missed not one but two beats, for he not only failed to recognize James's insistence that neither tough nor tender fully satisfies, but also ignored James's point here, which was to critique the very systematic thinking that Nietzsche found so problematic.

77 Ibid., 204, 235, 204.

78 Kaufmann stressed, however, that with the exception of Charles Peirce's philosophy, Nietzsche's formulations predated those of the other pragmatists. Though Kaufmann noted the similarity between Nietzsche and the American pragmatists, he made no claim for influence.

79 Ibid., 66, 68.

80 William James, as quoted in Kaufmann, *Nietzsche*, 240; original emphasis. For James's strenuous rejection of pleasure as the endgame of human experience and his longing to experience life *"in extremis,"* see James, "What Makes a Life Significant," 646–48.

81 Kaufmann, *Nietzsche*, 240.

82 William James, as quoted in ibid., 67.

83 Kaufmann, *Nietzsche*, 311–12. For the competing views of the role of God in Nietzsche's and James's thinking, see Cotkin, *William James: Public Philosopher*, 103.

84 Kaufmann, *Nietzsche*, 312–14.

85 Ibid., 314–15.

86 Ibid., 67.

87 Ibid., 167, 173, 246, 285; original emphasis.

88 Though Riesman's other-directed Americans have strong elements of Nietzsche's last men from *Zarathustra*—those who seek comfort in frictionless consensus in the status quo—it was the anthropologist Ruth Benedict's appropriation of Nietzsche's *Birth of Tragedy* that informs his "inner-directed" and "other-directed" typologies. In *Patterns of Culture* (1934), Benedict used this Nietzschean typology to distinguish between New Mexican Pueblos' peaceful, conformist, orderly "Apollonian" cultural personality and the raucous, sensualist, self-glorifying "Dionysian" cultural personality of the Kwakiutls of the northwest coast. Though primarily a study of native North American cultures, Benedict reflected on how these patterns could be seen in American culture more generally. She argued that culture in the United States of the 1930s reflected the downside of Apollonianism, where "eccentricity is more feared than parasitism. . . . The fear of being different

is the dominating motivation." In "Americans and Kwakiutls," chapter 11 of *The Lonely Crowd*, Riesman similarly lamented that in a culture which prided itself on sturdy individualism, Americans were nevertheless Apollonians. Though Americans think of themselves as a culture of "rivalrous Kwakiutl Indian chiefs," the truth is that in their desires for conformism and easy evasions from conflict, and their preferences to being likable fellows rather than great men, they are more like the other-directed, "peaceable, cooperative Pueblo agriculturalists." In Riesman, we see the curious journey of ideas—a view of ancient Greeks mediated by a nineteenth-century German, applied by an American anthropologist to describe Native Americans, in turn appropriated by an American sociologist to describe postwar American culture. Ruth Benedict, *Patterns of Culture* (1934; New York: Mariner Books, 2005), 273; David Riesman with Nathan Glazer and Reuel Denney, *The Lonely Crowd: A Study of the Changing American Character* (1950; New Haven, CT: Yale University Press, 2001), 225.

89 Peter Viereck, *The Unadjusted Man: A New Hero for Americans; Reflections on the Distinction between Conforming and Conserving* (Boston: Beacon Press, 1956), 63, 3.

90 Lionel Trilling, *The Liberal Imagination: Essays on Literature and Society* (1950; New York: New York Review of Books, 2008), 197, 195, emphasis added.

91 Kaufmann clearly placed more emphasis on the Continental rather than the analytic dimensions of Nietzsche's thought, and indeed his claims for Nietzsche's relevance for analytic philosophers are largely gestured, not demonstrated. However, they opened the doors for Nietzsche's entry into analytic philosophy. The first full-scale effort to examine Nietzsche's anticipation of analytic themes was Arthur Danto's *Nietzsche as Philosopher* (1965), which argued that Nietzsche's philosophical nihilism (simply a dramatic rejection of the correspondence theory of truth), his emphasis on language, and his method aimed—much like modern positivism—to *undermine* philosophical propositions, not refute them. Unsurprisingly, Kaufmann later criticized Danto for turning Nietzsche into a narrow linguistic analyst.

92 Cotkin, *Existential America*, 1. Cotkin examines Kaufmann's impact on the "canon of existentialism," noting the huge appeal of his volume: over the course of the next twelve years it went through twenty-eight printings (147).

93 Kaufmann, *Existentialism*, 11.

94 On Kaufmann's anthology, see David Pickus, "Paperback Authenticity: Walter Kaufmann and Existentialism," *Philosophy and Literature* 34 (April 2010): 17–31. For Kaufmann's own reflections on the American reception of European existentialism, see Walter Kaufmann, "The Reception of Existentialism in the United States," *Midway* 9 (Summer 1968): 97–126.

95 Hugh Hefner, editor's comment, *Playboy*, December 1953.

96 Walter Kaufmann, "Preface to the 1972 Edition," in *Critique of Religion and Philosophy* (1958; Princeton, NJ: Princeton University Press, 1978), xv–xvi.

97 Kaufmann, *Nietzsche*, 78, 81.

98 There was great variety among those classed as "death of God" theologians.

Temple University theologian and ordained minister Paul Van Buren, trained in linguistic analysis, sought to rule out all "God talk" that appealed to unverifiable beliefs while trying to find a way to interpret the gospel that did not invoke transcendence. In his major book, *The Death of God: The Culture of Our Post-Christian Era* (1961), Gabriel Vahanian, theologian and sociologist of religion at Syracuse University, argued that for the modern mind, the notion of a sacred world was lost, but not moderns' capacity for experiencing the deity. William Hamilton, who trained with Reinhold Niebuhr and was influenced by the ethics of Dietrich Bonhoeffer, sought dramatic reconceptualizing of Christianity as ethical action with no foundations in absolutes, where Christian faith serves not as a ground of moral truth but as a guide to human conduct. In the bibliography of Thomas Altizer and William Hamilton's *Radical Theology and the Death of God* (1966) is an extensive list of works that pertain to the development of radical theology, including those of Ludwig Feuerbach, David Friedrich Strauss, Leo Tolstoy, and even modern figures like Joseph Wood Krutch and George Santayana, but no George Burman Foster. Thomas J. J. Altizer and William Hamilton, eds., *Radical Theology and the Death of God* (Indianapolis: Bobbs-Merrill, 1966), 193–202.

99  Thomas J. J. Altizer, "Theology and the Death of God," in ibid., 102.

100  Thomas J. J. Altizer, "America and the Future of Theology," in ibid., 11.

101  "A Letter from the Publisher," *Time*, April 8, 1966; online at http://www.time .com/time/magazine/article/0,9171,835257,00.html (accessed May 1, 2010). See also William Grimes, "John T. Elson, Editor Who Asked 'Is God Dead?' at *Time* Dies at 78," *New York Times*, September 18, 2009; online at http://www.nytimes .com/2009/09/18/business/media/18elson.html (accessed May 1, 2010).

102  "Toward a Hidden God," *Time*, April 8, 1966; online at http://www.time.com/ time/magazine/article/0,9171,835309,00.html (accessed February 28, 2011).

103  "A Letter from the Publisher," *Time*, May 20, 1966; online at http://www.time .com/time/magazine/article/0,9171,835548,00.html (accessed May 1, 2010).

104  Kaufmann, preface to the 1972 edition, in *Critique of Religion and Philosophy*, xvi.

105  Richard Rubenstein, *After Auschwitz: Radical Theology and Contemporary Judaism* (Indianapolis: Bobbs-Merrill, 1966), 220.

106  Daniel Bell, "A Parable of Alienation," *Jewish Frontier*, November 1946, 12, 18–19.

107  Kaufmann's *Nietzsche* was reprinted in 1968 and 1974. For Nietzsche's role among the "semiofficial authors" of the counterculture, see Philip Beidler, *Scriptures for a Generation: What We Were Reading in the '60s* (Athens: University of Georgia Press, 1994).

108  Huey P. Newton, *Revolutionary Suicide* (New York: Harcourt Brace Jovanovich, 1973), 163.

109  Huey P. Newton, "The Mind Is Flesh," in *The Huey P. Newton Reader*, ed. David Hilliard and Donald Weise (New York: Seven Stories Press, 2002), 324.

110  Newton, *Revolutionary Suicide*, 168–69.

111  Nietzsche, *Thus Spoke Zarathustra*, 13; Newton, *Revolutionary Suicide*, 168–69.

112  Newton, *Revolutionary Suicide*, 168.

113  Ibid., 332; Nietzsche, as quoted in ibid.

114  Kaufmann, *Nietzsche*, 217, 133, 130.

115  Kaufmann, "Faith of a Heritic," 38–39.

## Chapter Six

1  Jacques Derrida, "Declaration of Independence," *New Political Science* 15 (1986): 7, 10, 13.

2  Ibid., 11, 7, 13. For the complete 1976 University of Virginia lectures, see Jacques Derrida, *Otobiographies: L'enseignement de Nietzsche et la politique du nom propre* (Paris: Éditions Galilée, 1984).

3  Jacques Derrida, "Otobiographies: The Teaching of Nietzsche and the Politics of the Proper Name," trans. Avital Ronell, in Derrida *The Ear of the Other: Otobiography, Transference, Translation*, ed. Christie V. McDonald (New York: Schocken Books, 1985), 4.

4  Roland Barthes first formulated the concept "death of the author." See Roland Barthes, "Death of the Author," in *Image, Music, Text*, trans. Stephen Heath (New York: Hill and Wang, 1977), 142–48.

5  Jacques Derrida, *Of Grammatology*, trans. Gayatri Chakravorty Spivak (Baltimore: Johns Hopkins University Press, 1976), 158.

6  For the purpose of clarity in this chapter, I will refer to the broader term *postmodernism*, which is typically the general rubric used to encapsulate both modes of interpretation, except in cases when distinguishing deconstruction or poststructuralism is necessary for specificity. For reappraisals of Nietzsche's philosophy in light of postmodernism, see Clayton Koelb, ed., *Nietzsche as Postmodernist: Essays Pro and Contra* (Albany: SUNY Press, 1990).

7  On the history of French theory in the United States, see François Cusset, *French Theory: How Foucault, Derrida, Deleuze, & Co. Transformed the Intellectual Life of the United States*, trans. Jeff Fort (Minneapolis: University of Minnesota Press, 2008). On the history of developments in academic literary studies, see Vincent B. Leitch, *American Literary Criticism from the Thirties to the Eighties* (New York: Columbia University Press, 1988), and Gerald Graff, *Professing Literature: An Institutional History* (Chicago: University of Chicago Press, 1987).

8  Jean-François Lyotard, *The Postmodern Condition: A Report on Knowledge*, trans. Geoff Bennington and Brian Massumi (Minneapolis: University of Minnesota Press, 1984), xxiv.

9  On Nietzsche's influence on poststructuralism, see Alan D. Schrift, *Nietzsche's French Legacy: A Genealogy of Poststructuralism* (New York: Routledge, 1995).

10  Sylvère Lotringer, "Doing Theory," in *French Theory in America*, ed. Sylvère Lotringer and Sande Cohen (New York: Routledge, 2001), 141.

11  Edward Said, "The Franco-American Dialogue," in *Traveling Theory: France and the United States*, ed. Ieme van der Poel, Sophie Bertho, and Ton Hoenselaars (Madison, NJ: Fairleigh Dickinson University Press, 1999), 136.

12 The conference proceedings were published as *The Structuralist Controversy: The Languages of Criticism and the Sciences of Man*, ed. Richard Macksey and Eugenio Donato (Baltimore: Johns Hopkins University Press, 1970); the quotation is from p. xviii.

13 Cusset, *French Theory*, 31. Indeed, the continued use of the language of "birth" and "new" and "French" to discuss the poststructuralist Nietzsche shows the ineluctable appeal of origins, even among those most suspicious of them.

14 Sylvère Lotringer and Sande Cohen, "Introduction: A Few Theses on French Theory in America," in Lotringer and Cohen, *French Theory in America*, 7. For an excellent examination of the "Schizo-Culture" conference's role in importing French theory to the academy and American counterculture, see Joanna Pawlik, "'Various Kinds of Madness': The French Nietzscheans inside America," *Atlantic Studies* 3 (October 2006): 225–44.

15 Notable journals that would become ports of entry for French intellectuals' engagement with Nietzsche include *Diacritics* at Cornell in 1971, *Critical Inquiry* at University of Chicago in 1974, *Glyph* at Johns Hopkins in 1976, *Social Text* at Duke in 1979, and *Semiotext(e)*, the brainchild of Sylvère Lotringer, a student of Barthes who took up a professorship at Columbia. Cusset, *French Theory*, 59–65.

16 David B. Allison, ed., *The New Nietzsche: Contemporary Styles of Interpretation* (1977; Cambridge, MA: MIT Press, 1985), xxiv, x, ix.

17 James Leigh, introduction to "Nietzsche's Return," *Semiotext(e)* 3 (1978): 4–5.

18 Quotation is attributed to Nietzsche in Max von Avillez, "My Life," *Semiotext(e)*, 154. This comic is based on a book attributed to Nietzsche, reportedly written during his institutionalization in a Jena insane asylum in the early 1890s, and published posthumously as *My Sister and I* by Boar's Head Books in New York in 1951.

The comic opens with a wink and a nod to that "very authentic book," as the book was widely considered a forgery, thanks in large part to Walter Kaufmann's challenges to its authenticity in two widely circulated early reviews (Avillez, "My Life," 150). See Walter Kaufmann, "Nietzsche and the Seven Sirens," *Partisan Review* 19 (May/June 1952): 372–76; and Kaufmann, review of *My Sister and I*, by Friedrich Nietzsche, trans. Oscar Levy, *Philosophical Review* 65 (January 1955): 152–53. For an effort to reconsider its authenticity, see Walter Stewart, "*My Sister and I*: The Disputed Nietzsche," *Thought* 61 (1986): 321–35; and for an effort to maintain that it is a hoax, see R. J. Hollingdale, review of *My Sister and I*, by Nietzsche, trans. Levy, *Journal of Nietzsche Studies* (Autumn 1991): 95–102.

19 "Why Nietzsche Now?," Symposium in *boundary 2, a journal of postmodern literature* 9/10 (Spring/Fall 1981).

20 Daniel T. O'Hara, preface to *Why Nietzsche Now?* (Indianapolis: Indiana University Press, 1985), viii, vii, x. Cornel West's contribution to the *boundary 2* issue, "Nietzsche's Prefiguration of Postmodern American Philosophy," examined Nietzsche's anticipation of what West called the new "postmodern American" philosophy of W. V. Quine, Nelson Goodman, Wilfred Sellars, Thomas Kuhn, and Richard Rorty. According to West, Nietzsche "prefigured" all the moves

thought to be new in American postmodernism—"the move toward anti-realism or conventionalism in ontology," "the move toward the demythologization of the Myth of the Given or anti-foundationalism," and "the move toward the detranscendentalization of the subject or the dismissal of the mind as a sphere of inquiry." The problem, West argued, was that American postmodernists took only the first three Nietzschean moves, but not the last and most important "countermovement"—an effort to overcome the nihilism ushered in with evasions of foundationalism. West thus used Nietzsche, drawing from his *Will To Power*, to criticize American postmodern philosophy as "hanging in limbo, as a philosophically critical yet culturally lifeless rhetoric mirroring a culture . . . permeated by the scientific ethos, regulated by racist, patriarchal, capitalist norms, and pervaded by debris of decay." This search for antifoundationalism—which takes a "countermove" to overcome its nihilism—formed the basis of West's pathbreaking study of American pragmatism in *The American Evasion of Philosophy* (1989). The language changed slightly, the cast of characters was extended, and his interests in an antifoundationalism that can be put to use in the fight for social justice were explained. But now it is *Emerson*—an "organic intellectual" who "prefigures the dominant themes of American pragmatism"—who "enacts an intellectual style of cultural criticism that permits and encourages American pragmatists to swerve from mainstream European philosophy." Though he observed that "like Friedrich Nietzsche, Emerson is first and foremost a cultural critic obsessed with ways to generate forms of power," West was not interested in the pattern of transnational antifoundationalist dialogue so much as the "prophetic pragmatism" in the "American grain." Nevertheless, his earlier characterization of Nietzsche's attempt to overcome traditional metaphysics, his antiepistemological stance, and his "countermovements" all prefigure his characterizations of American pragmatism: Nietzsche's "moves" became Emersonian "evasions," and Nietzsche's "countermoves," Emerson's "prophecy." By the logic of West's own definition, he might have considered Nietzsche as organic an American intellectual as Emerson (West, "Nietzsche's Prefiguration of Postmodern American Philosophy," 241–42, 265; Cornel West, *The American Evasion of Philosophy: A Genealogy of Pragmatism* [Madison: University of Wisconsin Press, 1989], 11, 9, 211, 239).

21 Nietzsche, *On the Genealogy of Morals*, 45. The surge of interest in this quotation, which was widely available in English translation since the beginning of the twentieth century but had never inspired significant interest or commentary, helps chart the emergence of new uses of Nietzschean antiessentialism, which track closely with the emergence of postmodernism. *Jenseits von Gut und Böse* was first available as volume 12 of Oscar Levy's *Complete Works of Friedrich Nietzsche* (1909).

22 Eve Kosofsky Sedgwick, *Epistemology of the Closet* (Berkeley: University of California Press, 1992).

23 Judith Butler, *Gender Trouble: Feminism and the Subversion of Identity* (1990; New York: Routledge, 1999), 33, 6, 43, 33.

24 Allan Bloom, *The Closing of the American Mind: How Higher Education Has Failed*

*Democracy and Impoverished the Souls of Today's Students* (New York: Simon and Schuster, 1987), 217, 141. I discuss Bloom's work more extensively in the epilogue.

25  Milton Mayer, *Robert Maynard Hutchins: A Memoir* (Berkeley: University of California Press, 1993), 186; Bloom, *Closing of the American Mind*, 152, 148.

26  Roger Kimball, *Tenured Radicals: How Politics Has Corrupted Our Higher Education* (1990; 3rd ed., Chicago: Ivan R. Dee, 2008), 304.

27  Bloom, *Closing of the American Mind*, 144.

28  Francis Fukuyama, *The End of History and the Last Man* (New York: Avon Books, 1992), xi, xxi, 310, xxii, 162.

29  Ibid., xxii.

30  Graham Allen and Roy Sellars, "Preface: Harold Bloom and Critical Responsibility," in *The Salt Companion to Harold Bloom* (Cambridge: Salt, 2007), xiii.

31  Harold Bloom, afterword to *Salt Companion to Harold Bloom*, 487–89.

32  On Bloom's uses of Nietzsche, see Daniel O'Hara, "The Genius of Irony: Nietzsche in Bloom," in *The Yale Critics: Deconstruction in America*, ed. Jonathan Arac et al. (Minneapolis: University of Minneapolis Press, 1983), 109–32, and Hubert Zapf, "Elective Affinities and American Differences: Nietzsche and Harold Bloom," in Pütz, *Nietzsche in American Literature and Thought*, 337–55. On the development of Bloom's criticism, see David Fite, *Harold Bloom: The Rhetoric of Romantic Vision* (Amherst: University of Massachusetts Press, 1985).

33  Harold Bloom, *The Anxiety of Influence: A Theory of Poetry* (1973; 2nd ed., New York: Oxford University Press, 1997), 49. Bloom not only used Nietzsche to criticize the narrow specialization of scholarly criticism, he followed his lead in producing criticism that flouted academic conventions. He demonstrated his love of literature by expressing his disdain for scholarly apparatus: no footnotes, bibliographies, or indices.

34  Bloom, *Genius*, 814, 194.

35  Bloom, *Anxiety of Influence*, 43, 5.

36  Ibid., 8.

37  Friedrich Nietzsche, as quoted in ibid., 55.

38  Bloom, ibid., 94–95.

39  Bloom, *Genius*, 195.

40  Bloom, *Anxiety of Influence*, 117–18.

41  Ibid., 117; Nietzsche, *On the Genealogy of Morals*, 88.

42  Nietzsche, as quoted in Bloom, *Anxiety of Influence*, 55.

43  Bloom, ibid., 50.

44  Ralph Waldo Emerson, as quoted in ibid., 102.

45  Bloom, ibid., 107.

46  Emerson, as quoted in ibid., 103.

47  Harold Bloom, *Agon: Towards a Theory of Revisionism* (New York: Oxford University Press, 1982), 171.

48  Bloom, *Anxiety of Influence*, 103, 12–13.

49  Harold Bloom, *A Map of Misreading* (1975; 2nd ed., Oxford: Oxford University

Press, 2003); Harold Bloom, *Kabbalah and Criticism* (New York: Continuum, 1975); and Harold Bloom, *Poetry and Repression: Revisionism from Blake and Stevens* (New Haven, CT: Yale University Press, 1976).

50 Bloom, *Agon*; Harold Bloom, *The Breaking of the Vessels* (Chicago: University of Chicago Press, 1982).

51 William H. Pritchard, "The Hermeneutical Mafia; or, After Strange Gods at Yale," *Hudson Review* 28 (Winter 1975–76): 601–10.

52 Geoffrey Hartman, preface to *Deconstruction and Criticism*, by Harold Bloom, Paul de Man, Jacques Derrida, Geoffrey H. Hartman, and J. Hillis Miller (London: Continuum, 1979), ix.

53 Bloom, *Breaking of the Vessels*, 3.

54 Bloom, *Agon*, 31.

55 Harold Bloom, introduction to Bloom, ed., *Friedrich Nietzsche* (New York: Chelsea House, 1987), 6.

56 Bloom, *Map of Misreading*, 29; Bloom, *Breaking of the Vessels*, 29.

57 Bloom, "The Primal Scene of Instruction," in *Map of Misreading*, 41–62; Jacques Derrida, "Freud and the Scene of Writing," in *Writing and Difference*, trans. Alan Bass (Chicago: University of Chicago Press, 1978), 196–231.

58 Bloom, *Poetry and Repression*, 2.

59 Paul de Man, *Allegories of Reading: Figural Language in Rousseau, Nietzsche, Rilke, and Proust* (New Haven, CT: Yale University Press, 1979), 106.

60 Nietzsche, *On the Genealogy of Morals*, 163.

61 Friedrich Nietzsche, as quoted in the epigraph to Harold Bloom's *Shakespeare: The Invention of the Human* (New York Riverhead Books, 1998).

62 Bloom, *Anxiety of Influence*, 43.

63 Harold Bloom, *The Western Canon: The Books and School of the Ages* (New York: Riverhead Books, 1994), 11.

64 Bloom, *Agon*, 43.

65 Bloom, *Breaking of the Vessels*, 30–31.

66 Bloom, *Agon*, 43, 37.

67 Bloom, *Map of Misreading*, 46–47.

68 Bloom, *Agon*, 43, 41.

69 Bloom, *Breaking of the Vessels*, 25.

70 Bloom, *Map of Misreading*, 85.

71 Bloom, *Breaking of the Vessels*, 39–40.

72 Bloom, *Map of Misreading*, 85, 79.

73 Bloom, *Agon*, 178.

74 Emerson, as quoted in Bloom, *Breaking of the Vessels*, 73, 33, 73.

75 Bloom, *Agon*, 171; Emerson, as quoted in ibid.

76 Emerson, as quoted in ibid.; Bloom, ibid., 172.

77 Bloom, *Map of Misreading*, 167.

78 Bloom, *Agon*, 32, 177.

79 Richard Rorty, *Philosophy and Social Hope* (New York: Penguin, 1999), 6–8.

80 Ibid., 8, 10–11. For Rorty's intellectual biography, see Neil Gross, *Richard Rorty: The Making of an American Philosopher* (Chicago: University of Chicago Press, 2008), and Casey Nelson Blake, "Private Life and Public Commitment: From Walter Rauschenbusch to Richard Rorty," in Pettegrew, *A Pragmatist's Progress?*, 85–101.

81 John Dewey, "The Influence of Darwinism on Philosophy," in *The Essential Dewey: Pragmatism, Education, and Democracy*, ed. Larry Hickman and Thomas M. Alexander (Bloomington: Indiana University Press, 1998), 1:44.

82 Nietzsche, *Twilight of the Idols*, 45.

83 Richard Rorty, *Philosophy and the Mirror of Nature* (Princeton, NJ: Princeton University Press, 1979), 12, 4, 96.

84 Russell Berman, as quoted in John Sanford, "Richard M. Rorty, Distinguished Public Intellectual, Dead at 75," *Stanford Report*, June 11, 2007; Patricia Cohen, "Richard Rorty, Contemporary Philosopher, Dies at 75," *New York Times*, June 11, 2007.

85 Richard Bernstein, "The Conflict of Narratives," in *Rorty and Pragmatism: The Philosopher Responds to His Critics*, ed. Herman J. Saatkamp Jr. (Nashville: Vanderbilt University Press, 1995), 62.

86 James T. Kloppenberg, "Pragmatism: An Old Name for Some New Ways of Thinking?," *Journal of American History* 83 (June 1996): 100. There is an industry of Rorty criticism, but the additional sources particularly helpful in framing Rorty's engagements with Nietzsche include Matthew Festenstein and Simon Thompson, eds., *Richard Rorty: Critical Dialogues* (Cambridge: Polity, 2001); Alan Malachowski, ed., *Reading Rorty: Critical Responses to "Philosophy and the Mirror of Nature" (and Beyond)* (Cambridge: Basil Blackwell, 1990); West, *The American Evasion of Philosophy*; and Robert Westbrook, "A Dream Country," in *Democratic Hope: Pragmatism and the Politics of Truth* (Ithaca, NY: Cornell University Press, 2005), 139–74.

87 Richard Rorty, *Consequences of Pragmatism: Essays 1972–1980* (Minneapolis: University of Minnesota Press, 1982), 160. Indeed, intellectual historians and philosophers have used *pragmatism* to include not only Charles Sanders Peirce (who himself, in a countermove, referred to "pragmaticism"), William James, John Dewey, Horace Kallen, and Sidney Hook, but also Ralph Waldo Emerson, Reinhold Niebuhr, and Lionel Trilling (as Cornel West did), and Jane Addams and Alain Locke (as Louis Menand did), to characterize a tremendously diverse set of individual thinkers with varying commitments ranging from epistemology to moral philosophy to social theory. As Bernstein reminds us, even Peirce, James, and Dewey had a "conflict of narratives" about the founding and development of pragmatism. West, *American Evasion of Philosophy*; Louis Menand, *The Metaphysical Club: A Story of Ideas in America* (New York: Farrar, Straus and Giroux, 2001); Bernstein, "The Conflict of Narratives," 59.

88 Rorty, *Consequences of Pragmatism*, 160–61, xvii.

89 Richard Rorty, *Essays on Heidegger and Others: Philosophical Papers* (Cambridge:

Cambridge University Press, 1991), 2:2. Georg Simmel is quoted as saying that pragmatism was "the part of Nietzsche which the Americans adopted." Simmel, as quoted in Hans Joas, "American Pragmatism and German Thought," in *Pragmatism and Social Theory* (Chicago: University of Chicago Press, 1993), 99.

90 Rorty, *Philosophy and Social Hope*, 269; Richard Rorty, *Contingency, Irony, and Solidarity* (Cambridge: Cambridge University Press, 1989), 39; and Rorty, *Essays on Heidegger and Others*, 2. On Rorty's role in reinstating pragmatism to American philosophy, see Kuklick, *A History of Philosophy in America*, 275–80. For a sense of how pragmatism looked like a forgotten historical episode in American thought in 1980 to a discerning intellectual historian (just two years before Rorty's *Consequences of Pragmatism*), see David Hollinger, "The Problem of Pragmatism in American History," *Journal of American History* 67 (June 1980): 88–107. On the resurgence of pragmatism in social, political, and legal theory, see Morris Dickstein, ed., *The Revival of Pragmatism: New Essays on Social Thought, Law, and Culture* (Durham, NC: Duke University Press, 1998).

91 Rorty, *Consequences of Pragmatism*, 160.

92 Rorty, *Philosophy and the Mirror of Nature*, 369–70; Richard Rorty, "Ein Prophet der Vielfalt," *Die Zeit*, September 19, 2007 (orig. pub. August 24, 2000); online at http://www.zeit.de/2000/35/200035_nietzsche_rorty.xml (accessed March 10, 2011). On Rorty and Nietzsche, see Daniel Shaw, "Rorty and Nietzsche: Some Elective Affinities," *International Studies in Philosophy* 21 (1989): 3–14.

93 Rorty drew his concept of the "strong poet" from Harold Bloom's *Anxiety of Influence* (1973). Rorty and Bloom referred to each other's works beginning with Rorty's first reference to *Anxiety* in *Philosophy and the Mirror of Nature* (1979). Rorty employed Bloom's notion of literature as a "primal scene of instruction" from Bloom's *Map of Misreading* (1975), and continued to quote him in his subsequent works. Bloom, in turn, began employing Rorty's language for pragmatism—though to articulate the *differences* between American and Continental criticism—in *Agon* (1982). He also dedicated his *Where Shall Wisdom Be Found?* (2004) to Rorty.

94 Rorty, *Contingency, Irony, and Solidarity*, 20.

95 Rorty, *Essays on Heidegger and Others*, 1. Here, Rorty enacts Nietzsche's claim that he "breaks the history of mankind in two. One lives before him, or one lives after him" (Nietzsche, *Ecce Homo*, 333).

96 Richard Rorty, "Pragmatism as Romantic Polytheism," in *Philosophy as Cultural Politics* (Cambridge: Cambridge University Press, 2007), 4:27–41.

97 Rorty, *Philosophy and Social Hope*, 133.

98 Rorty, *Contingency, Irony, and Solidarity*, 27.

99 Ibid., 46, 73. Rorty's "final vocabularies" are reminiscent of James's "magic words" (see William James, "What Pragmatism Means," in *Pragmatism: A New Name for Some Old Ways of Thinking*, 27–44). In *Contingency, Irony, and Solidarity*, Rorty described the ironist as a "strong poet"; in *Philosophy and the Mirror of Nature*, he

identified him as an "edifying philosopher" (as opposed to a "systematic philosopher"). The terms have changed, but the notion has stayed the same: the ironic, edifying, strong poet "dread[s] the thought that his vocabulary should ever be institutionalized" (Rorty, *Philosophy and the Mirror of Nature*, 369). It is worth noting that each time these typologies are invoked, Nietzsche is cited as an example.

100   Nietzsche, *Human, All Too Human*, 12.

101   Rorty, *Contingency, Irony, and Solidarity*, 98–99, 106–7. An important influence on Rorty's view of the Nietzschean self as a work of art is Alexander Nehamas, *Nietzsche: Life as Literature* (Cambridge, MA: Harvard University Press, 1985).

102   William James, as quoted in Rorty, *Contingency, Irony, and Solidarity*, 38.

103   Rorty, ibid., xiv, 99.

104   Ibid., xiv, xv.

105   Richard Rorty, "Nietzsche and the Pragmatists," *New Leader*, May 19, 1997, 9.

106   Rorty, *Contingency, Irony, and Solidarity*, xiv; Rorty, *Consequences of Pragmatism*, 207.

107   Rorty, "Pragmatism as Romantic Polytheism," 31.

108   For a further development of this argument, see Rorty, "Nietzsche and the Pragmatists," 9.

109   Hilary Putnam, "A Reconsideration of Deweyian Democracy," in *The Pragmatism Reader: From Peirce through the Present*, ed. Robert B. Talisse and Scott F. Aikin (Princeton, NJ: Princeton University Press, 2011), 331.

110   Richard Rorty, "Dewey between Hegel and Darwin," in Saatkamp, *Rorty and Pragmatism*, 2.

111   Richard Rorty, "Response to Matthew Festenstein," in Festenstein and Thompson, *Richard Rorty*, 221.

112   Rorty, *Contingency, Irony, and Solidarity*, xvi.

113   Richard Rorty, *Achieving Our Country: Leftist Thought in Twentieth-Century America* (Cambridge, MA: Harvard University Press, 1998), 20.

114   Rorty, *Contingency, Irony, and Solidarity*, 197.

115   Stanley Cavell, as quoted in Giovanna Borradori, *The American Philosopher: Conversations with Quine, Davidson, Putnam, Nozick, Danto, Rorty, Cavell, MacIntyre, and Kuhn*, trans. Rossana Crocitto (Chicago: University of Chicago Press, 1994), 132.

116   Stanley Cavell, *Philosophical Passages: Wittgenstein, Emerson, Austin, Derrida* (Cambridge: Blackwell, 1995), 95.

117   For an excellent introduction to the efforts to overcome this amnesia, see Michael Lopez, "Emerson and Nietzsche: An Introduction," in "Emerson/Nietzsche," special issue, *ESQ*: 1–35.

118   Two important ways Nietzsche entered specifically American analytic thought include Danto, *Nietzsche as Philosopher* and John T. Wilcox, *Truth and Value in Nietzsche: A Study of His Metaethics and Epistemology* (Ann Arbor: University of Michigan Press, 1974).

119   Kuklick, *The Rise of American Philosophy*, 7–10, 46–47, 102.

120 On Cavell's recollections of his graduate years at Harvard, see Stanley Cavell, *A Pitch of Philosophy: Autobiographical Exercises* (Cambridge, MA: Harvard University Press, 1996).

121 Stanley Cavell, *Themes Out of School: Effects and Causes* (Chicago: University of Chicago Press, 1988), 199, 33–34.

122 Nietzsche, *Thus Spoke Zarathustra*, 13; Emerson, "Self-Reliance," 2:27.

123 Cavell, as quoted in Borradori, *The American Philosopher*, 131.

124 Cavell, *Philosophical Passages*, 95.

125 Stanley Cavell, *The Senses of Walden* (1972; exp. ed., Chicago: University of Chicago Press, 1992), 33. On Cavell's framing of these questions, see James Conant, "Cavell and the Concept of America," in *Contending with Stanley Cavell*, ed. Russell B. Goodman (Oxford: Oxford University Press, 2005), 55–81.

126 Stanley Cavell, *This New Yet Unapproachable America: Lectures after Emerson after Wittgenstein* (Albuquerque, NM: Living Batch Press, 1989), 25 (Emerson, as quoted in Cavell), 24–25 (Nietzsche, as quoted in Cavell), 25.

127 Stanley Cavell, "Existentialism and Analytic Philosophy," *Daedalus: Journal of the American Academy of Arts and Sciences* 93 (Summer 1964): 961.

128 Stanley Cavell, *Must We Mean What We Say?* (New York: Charles Scribner's Sons, 1969), 112, 157, xxviii. Cavell would continue to consider that the different cultural personae of the philosopher could reflect different intellectual ideals: "Austin was committed to the manners, even the mannerisms, of an English professor the way a French intellectual is committed to seeming brilliant. It is the level at which an American thinker or artist is likely to play dumb, I mean undertake to seem like a hick, uncultivated. These are all characters in which authority is assumed, variations I suppose of the thinker's use—as unmasked by Nietzsche—of the character of the sage" (Cavell, *Themes Out of School*, 29).

129 Cavell, *This New Yet Unapproachable America*, 25; Cavell, *Must We Mean What We Say?*, 162.

130 Stanley Cavell, *The Claim of Reason: Wittgenstein, Skepticism, Morality, and Tragedy* (Oxford: Oxford University Press, 1979), 109.

131 Cavell, *The Senses of Walden*, xiv.

132 Stanley Cavell, *Conditions Handsome and Unhandsome: The Constitution of Emersonian Perfectionism* (Chicago: University of Chicago Press, 1990), 33.

133 Ibid., 41, 31, 49, 54 (Emerson, as quoted in Cavell), 55.

134 Emerson, as quoted in Cavell, *This New Yet Unapproachable America*, 90.

135 Cavell, ibid., 90, 108.

136 Stanley Cavell, "The Division of Talent," *Critical Inquiry* 11 (June 1985): 531.

137 Ibid., 531.

138 Cavell, *This New Yet Unapproachable America*, 109.

139 Emerson, as quoted in ibid., 91.

140 Cavell, *This New Yet Unapproachable America*, 109, 70.

141 Ibid., 116.

# Epilogue

1  Allan Bloom, "Our Listless Universities," *National Review*, December 10, 1982, 1537–48.

2  William Goldstein, "The Story behind the Best Seller: Allan Bloom's *Closing of the American Mind*," *Publishers Weekly*, July 3, 1987, 25.

3  George Will, "A How-To-Book for the Independent," *Washington Post*, July 30, 1987, A19; Garry Wills, as quoted in Michael Miner, "Wrestling in the Halls of Academe/Digging for Meaning," *Chicago Reader*, online at http://www.chicagoreader.com/chicago/wrestling-in-the-halls-of-academedigging-for-meaning/Content?oid=902427 (accessed July 20, 2010).

4  Martha Nussbaum, "Undemocratic Vistas," *New York Review of Books*, November 5, 1987, 21.

5  Benjamin Barber, "The Philosopher Despot," *Harper's Magazine*, January 1988, 61.

6  Tim Appelo, "Legacy: Allan Bloom," *Entertainment Weekly*, October 23, 1992; online at http://www.ew.com/ew/article/0,20183503,00.html (accessed March 6, 2011).

7  Allan Bloom, *The Closing of the American Mind: How Higher Education Has Failed Democracy and Impoverished the Souls of Today's Students* (New York: Simon and Schuster, 1987), 19, 141, 151, 202, 151, 156, 147.

8  "Allan Bloom Discusses the 'Difficulty of Nietzsche' 1," Youtube, http://www.youtube.com/watch?v=a8QxMe16b38&feature=fvst (accessed July 5, 2010).

9  Bloom, *Closing of the American Mind*, 62, 50.

10  Ibid., 198, 51.

11  Allan Bloom, "How Nietzsche Conquered America," *Wilson Quarterly* 11 (Summer 1987): 80.

12  Ibid., 92.

13  Bloom, *Closing of the American Mind*, 203, 198, 207.

14  Ibid., 148, 152, 156.

## Primary Sources

ARCHIVAL MATERIALS

Förster-Nietzsche/Nietzsche-Archiv Collections. Klassik Stiftung Weimar, Goethe- und Schiller-Archiv, Weimar, Germany.

Josiah Royce Papers. Harvard University Archives, Cambridge, MA.

Nietzsche's Personal Library. Klassik Stiftung Weimar, Herzogin Anna Amalia Bibliothek, Weimar, Germany.

William James Collection. Houghton Library, Harvard University, Cambridge, MA.

FRIEDRICH NIETZSCHE'S WRITINGS

*Friedrich Nietzsche: Werke und Briefe; Historisch-Kritische Gesamtausgabe.* Vol. 2, edited by Hans Joachim Mette. Munich: Beck, 1983.

*Nietzsche Briefwechsel: Kritische Gesamtausgabe.* Edited by Giorgio Colli and Mazzino Montinari. 25 vols. Berlin: Walter de Gruyer, 1975–2004.

*Sämtliche Werke: Kritische Studienausgabe.* Edited by Georgio Colli and Mazzino Montinari. 15 vols. Berlin: Walter de Gruyter, 1999.

*Werke in drei Bänden.* Edited by Karl Schlechta. 3 vols. Munich: Carl Hanser Verlag, 1954–56.

ENGLISH TRANSLATIONS OF NIETZSCHE'S WORKS

*The Antichrist.* Translated with an introduction by H. L. Mencken. New York: Knopf, 1920.

*Beyond Good and Evil.* Translated by Walter Kaufmann. New York: Vintage Books, 1989.

*Beyond Good & Evil.* Translated by Helen Zimmern. New York: Macmillan, 1907.

*"The Birth of Tragedy" and "The Case of Wagner."* Translated by Walter Kaufmann. New York: Vintage Books, 1967.

*The Complete Works of Friedrich Nietzsche.* Edited by Oscar Levy. 18 vols. New York: Macmillan, 1909–13.

*Daybreak.* Translated by R. J. Hollingdale. Cambridge: Cambridge University Press, 1996.

*The Gay Science.* Translated by Walter Kaufmann. New York: Vintage Books, 1974.

*"On the Genealogy of Morals" and "Ecce Homo."* Translated by Walter Kaufmann and R. J. Hollingdale. New York: Vintage Books, 1989.

*Human, All Too Human.* Translated by R. J. Hollingdale. Cambridge: Cambridge University Press, 1996.

*The Nietzsche Reader.* Edited by Keith Ansell Pearson and Duncan Large. Malden, MA: Blackwell, 2006.

*The Portable Nietzsche.* Translated, edited, and with an introduction by Walter Kaufmann. New York: Viking, 1954.

*Selected Letters of Friedrich Nietzsche.* Edited by Oscar Levy. New York: Macmillan, 1921.

*Selected Letters of Friedrich Nietzsche.* Translated and edited by Christopher Middleton. Chicago: University of Chicago Press, 1960.

*Thus Spoke Zarathustra.* Translated and with a preface by Walter Kaufmann. New York: Modern Library, 1995.

*"Twilight of the Idols" and "The Anti-Christ."* Translated by R. J. Hollingdale. New York: Penguin, 1990.

*Untimely Meditations.* Translated by R. J. Hollingdale. Edited by Daniel Breazeale. Cambridge: Cambridge University Press, 1997.

*The Will to Power.* Edited by Walter Kaufmann. Translated by Walter Kaufmann and R. J. Hollingdale. New York: Vintage Books, 1968.


BOOKS AND ARTICLES

Abbott, Lyman. "Are the Ethics of Jesus Practicable?" *Biblical World* 17 (April 1901): 256–64.

Abraham, Gerald. *Nietzsche.* New York: Macmillan, 1933.

Adams, Maurice. "The Ethics of Tolstoy and Nietzsche." *International Journal of Ethics* 11 (October 1911): 82–105.

Adler, Ruth. "Speaking as One Superman to Another." *New York Times,* October 17, 1943, SM27.

Adorno, Theodor. *Minima Moralia: Reflections from Damaged Life.* Translated by E. F. N. Jephcott. 1951. London: Verso, 2002.

———. *Negative Dialectics.* Translated by E. B. Ashton. 1966. London: Routledge, 1973.

————. *Prisms.* Translated by Samuel and Shierry Weber. 1967. Cambridge, MA: MIT Press, 1981.

————. "Wagner, Nietzsche and Hitler." *Kenyon Review* 9 (Winter 1947): 155–62.

Adorno, Theodor, Else Frenkel-Brunswik, Daniel Levinson, and Nevitt Sanford. *The Authoritarian Personality.* New York: Harper & Row, 1950.

Allison, David B., ed. *The New Nietzsche: Contemporary Styles of Interpretation.* 1977. Cambridge, MA: MIT Press, 1985.

Altizer, Thomas J. J. *The Gospel of Christian Atheism.* Philadelphia: Westminster Press, 1966.

Altizer, Thomas J. J., and William Hamilton, eds. *Radical Theology and the Death of God.* Indianapolis: Bobbs-Merrill, 1966.

Anderson, Margaret. *My Thirty Years War.* New York: Covici, Friede, 1930.

————, ed. *The Little Review Anthology.* New York: Hermitage House, 1953.

Antrim, Ernest, and Heinrich Goebel. "Friedrich Nietzsche's Uebermensch." *Monist* 9 (July 1899): 563–71.

Archer, William. "Fighting a Philosophy." *North American Review* 201 (January 1915): 30–44.

————. *501 Gems of German Thought.* London: T. Fisher Unwin, 1916.

Arendt, Hannah. *Hannah Arendt/Karl Jaspers Correspondence, 1926–69.* Edited by Lotte Köhler and Hans Saner. Translated by Robert and Rita Kimber. New York: Harcourt Brace, 1992.

————. "We Refugees." *Menorah Journal,* January–March 1943, 69–77.

Aveling, F. "The Neo-Scholastic Movement." *American Catholic Quarterly Review* 31 (January 1906): 19–33.

Babbitt, Irving. "The Breakdown of Internationalism. Part I and II." *Nation* 100 (June 17 and June 24, 1915): 677–80, 704–6.

————. *Literature and the American College.* Boston: Houghton Mifflin, 1908.

————. *The New Laokoon: An Essay on the Confusion in the Arts.* Boston: Houghton Mifflin, 1910.

————. *Rousseau and Romanticism.* Boston: Houghton Mifflin, 1919.

Badcock, John, Jr. *Slaves to Duty.* New York: Benjamin R. Tucker, 1906.

Bailey, Thomas. "Nietzsche as a Tonic in War Time." *Sewanee Review* 26 (July 1918): 364–74.

Baker, Thomas Stockham. "Contemporary Criticism of Friedrich Nietzsche." *Journal of Philosophy, Psychology and Scientific Methods* 4 (July 18, 1907): 406–19.

———. "What Is the Superman?" *Independent* 65 (December 1908): 1613–16.

Bakewell, Charles M. "Nietzsche: A Modern Stoic." *Yale Review* 5 (October 1915): 66–81.

———. "The Philosophy of War and Peace." *Bookman*, May 1917, 225–30.

———. "Review of *The Philosophy of Friedrich Nietzsche.*" *Philosophical Review* 10 (May 1901): 327.

———. "The Teachings of Friedrich Nietzsche." *International Journal of Ethics* 9 (April 1899): 314–31.

———. "The Tragic Philosopher." *Saturday Review of Literature*, April 24, 1926, 733–35.

Barker, Ernst. *Nietzsche and Treitschke: The Worship of Power in Modern Germany.* Oxford: Oxford University Press, 1914.

Barrett, William. *Irrational Man: A Study in Existential Philosophy.* New York: Doubleday Anchor, 1958.

Barry, William. "Friedrich Nietzsche." In *Heralds of Revolt: Studies in Modern Literature and Dogma*, 343–78. London: Hodder and Stoughton, 1904.

———. "The Ideals of Anarchy." *Littel's Living Age* 211 (December 1896): 616–36.

Barthes, Roland. "Death of the Author." In *Image, Music, Text*, translated by Stephen Heath, 142–48. New York: Hill and Wang, 1977.

Beck, Lewis White. "Philosophy in War Time." *Journal of Philosophy* 39 (January 29, 1942): 71–75.

Bell, Daniel. "A Parable of Alienation." *Jewish Frontier*, November 1946, 12–19.

Benedict, Ruth. *Patterns of Culture.* 1934. New York: Mariner Books, 2005.

Benn, Alfred M. "The Morals of an Immoralist—Friedrich Nietzsche." *International Journal of Ethics* 19 (October 1908, January 1909): 1–23, 192–211.

Bentley, Eric. *A Century of Hero-Worship: A Study of the Idea of Heroism in Carlyle and Nietzsche.* 1944. Boston: Beacon, 1957.

Berg, Leo. *The Superman in Modern Literature.* Philadelphia: John C. Winston, 1917.

Blakeslee, George H., ed. *The Problems and Lessons of the War.* New York: G. P. Putnam's Sons, 1916.

"Blaming Nietzsche for It All." *Literary Digest*, October 17, 1914, 743–44.

Bloom, Allan. *The Closing of the American Mind: How Higher Education Has Failed Democracy and Impoverished the Souls of Today's Students.* New York: Simon and Schuster, 1987.

———. "How Nietzsche Conquered America." *Wilson Quarterly* 11 (Summer 1987): 80–93.

———. "Our Listless Universities." *National Review*, December 10, 1982, 1537–48.

Bloom, Harold. *Agon: Towards a Theory of Revisionism.* New York: Oxford University Press, 1982.

———. *The Anxiety of Influence: A Theory of Poetry.* 1973. 2nd ed., New York: Oxford University Press, 1997.

———. *The Breaking of the Vessels.* Chicago: University of Chicago Press, 1982.

———, ed. *Friedrich Nietzsche.* New York: Chelsea House, 1987.

———. *Genius: A Mosaic of One Hundred Exemplary Creative Minds.* New York: Warner Books, 2002.

———. *Kabbalah and Criticism.* New York: Continuum, 1975.

———. *A Map of Misreading.* 1975. 2nd ed., Oxford: Oxford University Press, 2003.

———. *Poetics of Influence.* New Haven, CT: Schwab, 1988.

———. *Poetry and Repression: Revisionism from Blake and Stevens.* New Haven, CT: Yale University Press, 1976.

———. *Shakespeare: The Invention of the Human.* New York: Riverhead Books, 1998.

———. *The Western Canon: The Books and School of the Ages.* New York: Riverhead Books, 1994.

Bloom, Harold, Paul de Man, Jacques Derrida, Geoffrey H. Hartman, and J. Hillis Miller. *Deconstruction and Criticism.* London: Continuum Group, 1979.

Boas, George. "Germany from Luther to Nietzsche." In *The Major Traditions of European Philosophy*, chap. 8. New York: Harper and Brothers, 1929.

Bourne, Randolph. "Denatured Nietzsche." *Dial*, October 12, 1917, 389–91.

———. *"The History of a Literary Radical" and Other Essays.* Edited with an introduction by Van Wyck Brooks. 1920. New York: S. A. Russell, 1956.

———. *The Letters of Randolph Bourne: A Comprehensive Edition.* Edited by Eric J. Sandeen. Troy, NY: Whitston, 1981.

———. *The Radical Will: Selected Writings, 1911–1918.* Preface by Christopher

Lasch. Selection and introductions by Olaf Hansen. New York: Urizen Books, 1977.

———. "Randolph Bourne: Letters (1913–1914)." *Twice a Year* 5–6 (Fall–Winter 1940, Spring–Summer 1941): 76–90.

———. Review of *Nietzsche*, by Paul Elmer More. *Journal of Philosophy, Psychology and Scientific Methods* 9 (August 15, 1912): 471–73.

———. *Untimely Papers*. New York: B.W. Huebsch, 1919.

Brandes, Georg. "Aristokratischer Radikalismus: Eine Abhandlung über Friedrich Nietzsche." *Deutsche Rundschau* 63 (April 1900): 52–89.

———. *Friedrich Nietzsche*. New York: Macmillan, 1914.

Brann, Henry Walter. "Hegel, Nietzsche, and the Nazi Lesson." *Humanist* 12 (1952): 11–115, 179–82.

———. "A Reply to Walter Kaufmann." *Journal of the History of Philosophy* 3 (October 1965): 246–50.

Brewster, Chauncey. "Ethics Made in Germany." *North American Review* 201(March 1915): 398–401.

Brinton, Crane. "Heir of Socrates?" *Saturday Review of Literature*, January 13, 1951, 32–33.

———. "The National Socialists' Use of Nietzsche." *Journal of the History of Ideas* 1 (April 1940): 131–50.

———. *Nietzsche*. Cambridge, MA: Harvard University Press, 1941.

Broene, Johannes. "Nietzsche's Educational Ideas and Ideals." *Educational Review* 37 (January 1909): 55–70.

———. "The Philosophy of Friedrich Nietzsche." *American Journal of Religious Psychology and Education* 4 (March 1910): 68–170.

Brooks, Hildegard. "Friedrich Nietzsche's Philosophy." *Book Reviews* 6 (May 1898): 11–14.

Brooks, Van Wyck. *America's Coming of Age*. New York: B. W. Huebsch, 1915.

———. *The Confident Years, 1885–1915*. New York: E. P. Dutton, 1952.

———. "The Critics and Young America." In *Criticism in America: Its Function and Status*, edited by Irving Babbitt, 116–51. New York: Harcourt, Brace, 1924.

———. *Days of the Phoenix: The Nineteen-Twenties I Remember*. New York: Dutton, 1957.

———. *The Writer in America*. New York: Dutton, 1953.

Brown, William Adams. *Is Christianity Practicable?* New York: Charles Scribner's Sons, 1919.

Bryan, William Jennings. "Brother or Brute?" *Commoner* 20 (November 1920): 11–12.

Butler, Judith. *Gender Trouble: Feminism and the Subversion of Identity.* 1990. New York: Routledge, 1999.

"Cannonading the Temple of Nietzsche." *Current Literature* 47 (December 1909): 818–24.

Carus, Paul. "Friedrich Nietzsche." *Monist* 17 (April 1907): 231–51.

———. "Immorality as a Philosophic Principle." *Monist* 9 (July 1899): 572–616.

———. *Friedrich Nietzsche and Other Exponents of Individualism.* Chicago: Open Court, 1914.

———. *Philosophy as a Science.* Chicago: Open Court, 1909.

Cathrein, V. "Ethics." In *The Catholic Encyclopedia*, edited by Charles G. Herbermann et al., 5:556–66. New York: Robert Appleton, 1909.

Cavell, Stanley. *Cities of Words: Pedagogical Letters on a Register of the Moral Life.* Cambridge, MA: Harvard University Press, Belknap Press, 2004.

———. *The Claim of Reason: Wittgenstein, Skepticism, Morality, and Tragedy.* Oxford: Oxford University Press, 1979.

———. *Conditions Handsome and Unhandsome: The Constitution of Emersonian Perfectionism.* Chicago: University of Chicago Press, 1990.

———. "The Division of Talent." *Critical Inquiry* 11 (June 1985): 519–38.

———. *Emerson's Transcendental Etudes.* Stanford, CA: Stanford University Press, 2003.

———. "Existentialism and Analytic Philosophy." *Daedalus: Journal of the American Academy of Arts and Sciences* 93 (Summer 1964): 946–74.

———. *Must We Mean What We Say?* New York: Charles Scribner's Sons, 1969.

———. *Philosophical Passages: Wittgenstein, Emerson, Austin, Derrida.* Cambridge: Blackwell, 1995.

———. *Philosophy the Day after Tomorrow.* Cambridge, MA: Harvard University Press, Belknap Press, 2005.

———. *A Pitch of Philosophy: Autobiographical Exercises.* Cambridge, MA: Harvard University Press, 1996.

———. *The Senses of Walden.* 1972. Chicago: University of Chicago Press, 1992.

———. *Themes Out of School: Effects and Causes.* Chicago: University of Chicago Press, 1988.

————. *This New Yet Unapproachable America: Lectures after Emerson after Wittgenstein*. Albuquerque, NM: Living Batch Press, 1989.

Cerf, Walter. "Philosophy and This War." *Philosophy of Science* 9 (April 1942): 166–82.

————. Review of *Nietzsche, Philosopher, Psychologist, Antichrist*, by Walter Kaufmann. *Philosophy and Phenomenological Research* 12 (December 1951): 287–91.

"The Christian Reply to Nietzsche." *Current Literature* 45 (July 1908): 64–65.

"The Christianization of Nietzsche's 'Blond Beast.'" *Current Literature* 51 (September 1911): 5–10.

Collins, James. *The Existentialists: A Critical Study*. Chicago: Henry Regnery, 1952.

Common, Thomas. "Nietzsche's Works in English." *Nation*, March 29, 1906, 259.

Cook, George Cram. *The Chasm*. New York: Frederick A. Stokes, 1911.

————. *Greek Coins*. New York: George H. Doran, 1925.

————. "Socialism the Issue in 1912." *Masses* 2 (July 1912): 7.

Cowley, Malcolm. *Exile's Return: A Literary Odyssey of the 1920s*. 1934. New York: Viking, 1951.

Crane, Hart. "The Case against Nietzsche." *Pagan* 4 (April–May 1918): 31–35.

Cushman, Herbert Ernst. "Friedrich Nietzsche." In *A Beginner's History of Philosophy*, vol. 2, *Modern Philosophy*, 375–76. 1911. Rev. ed., Boston: Houghton Mifflin, 1918.

Danto, Arthur C. *Nietzsche as Philosopher*. New York: Macmillan, 1965.

Darrow, Clarence. *Clarence Darrow's Plea for the Defense of Loeb and Leopold (August 22, 23, 25)*. Girard, KS: Haldeman-Julius, 1925.

————. *The Story of My Life*. New York: C. Scribner, 1932.

Davis, Helen E. *Tolstoy and Nietzsche*. New York: New Republic, 1929.

de Huszar, George. "The Essence of Nietzsche." *South Atlantic Quarterly* 18 (1944): 368–74.

————. "Nietzsche's Theory of Decadence and the Transvaluation of All Values." *Journal of the History of Ideas* 6 (July 1945): 259–72.

Dell, Floyd. *Homecoming: An Autobiography*. New York: Farrar and Rinehart, 1933.

————. *Moon-Calf*. New York: Knopf, 1920.

de Man, Paul. *Allegories of Reading: Figural Language in Rousseau, Nietzsche, Rilke, and Proust*. New Haven, CT: Yale University Press, 1979.

————. "Genesis and Genealogy in Nietzsche's *The Birth of Tragedy*." *Diacritics* 2 (Winter 1972): 44–53.

Derrida, Jacques. "Declarations of Independence." *New Political Science* 15 (1986): 7–15.

————. "Freud and the Scene of Writing." In *Writing and Difference*, translated by Alan Bass, 196–231. Chicago: University of Chicago Press, 1978.

————. *Of Grammatology*. Translated by Gayatri Chakravorty Spivak. Baltimore: Johns Hopkins University Press, 1976.

————. "Otobiographies: The Teaching of Nietzsche and the Politics of the Proper Name." Translated by Avital Ronell, 1–40. In *The Ear of the Other: Otobiography, Transference, Translation*. Edited by Christie McDonald. New York: Schocken Books, 1985.

Derry, George H. "Unlocking the Medieval Mind." *America* 17 (Sept. 15, 1917): 579–80.

Descaves, P., and Jean Bloch. "Nietzsche the Good European." *Living Age*, August 14, 1926, 355–58.

Dewey, John. Foreword to *Tolstoy and Nietzsche*, by Helen E. Davis. New York: New Republic, 1929.

————. *German Philosophy and Politics*. New York: Henry Holt, 1915.

————. "The Influence of Darwinism on Philosophy." In *The Essential Dewey: Pragmatism, Education, and Democracy*, vol. 1, edited by Larry Hickman and Thomas M. Alexander, 39–45. Bloomington: Indiana University Press, 1998.

————. "The Tragedy of the German Soul." *New Republic*, December 9, 1916, 155–156.

————. "On Understanding the Mind of Germany." *Atlantic Monthly*, February 1916, 251–62.

Dhons, Illian. "About Nietzsche." *Little Review* 1 (April 1914): 19–24.

"Did Nietzsche Cause the War?" *Educational Review* 48 (November 1914): 353–57.

"Did Nietzsche Predict the Superwoman as Well as the Superman?" *Current Literature* 43 (December 1907): 643–44.

Dolson, Grace Neal. *The Philosophy of Friedrich Nietzsche*. New York: Macmillan, 1901.

"Dr. George B. Foster Replies to His Critics." *Standard* 53 (April 14, 1906): 573–75.

Duncan, Isadora. "Dionysian Art." *Dionysian* 1 (October 1914): 1–4.

———. *My Life*. New York: Boni and Liveright, 1927.

Durant, Will. *Nietzsche: Who He Was and What He Stood For*. Girard, KS: Haldeman-Julius, 1923.

———. "Philosophy and the Social Problem." PhD diss., Columbia University, 1917.

———. *Philosophy and the Social Problem*. New York: Macmillan, 1917.

———. Review of *Nietzsche, the Thinker*, by William M. Salter. *Political Science Quarterly* 33 (June 1918): 266–68.

———. *Socialism and Anarchism*. New York: Mother Earth Publishing Association, 1914.

———. *The Story of Nietzsche's Philosophy*. Little Blue Books 19. Girard, KS: Haldeman-Julius, 1925.

———. *The Story of Philosophy*. New York: Simon and Schuster, 1926.

Duvall, Trumbull. "Life Is a Task to Be Done—Not Understood. Schopenhauer and Nietzsche." Chap. 15 in *Great Thinkers: The Quest of Life for Its Meaning*. New York: Oxford University Press, 1937.

Eastman, Max. "Nietzsche, Plato, and Bertrand Russell." *Liberator*, September 1920, 5–10.

———. "A Note on Nietzsche." *Everybody's Magazine*, January 1915, 60–68.

———. *"Understanding Germany: The Only Way to End War" and Other Essays*. New York: Mitchell Kennerley, 1916.

———. "What Nietzsche Really Taught." *Everybody's Magazine*, November 1914, 703–4.

Eckstein, Walter. "Discussion by Walter Eckstein." *Journal of the History of Ideas* 6 (July 1945): 304–6.

———. "Friedrich Nietzsche in the Judgement of Posterity." *Journal of the History of Ideas* 6 (June 1945): 310–24.

———. "Friedrich Nietzsche and Modern Germany." *Standard* 31 (1944): 44–50.

"Editorials." *Seven Arts* 1 (November 1916): 52–56.

Edman, Irwin. "The Nietzsche the Nazis Don't Know." *New York Times*, October 15, 1944.

"The Education of the Superman." *Current Literature* 44 (January 1908): 73–74.

Eliot, T. S. Review of *The Philosophy of Nietzsche*, by A. Wolf. *International Journal of Ethics* 26 (April 1916): 426–27.

Elkin, William Baird. "The Kultur of Germany: The Worship of the 'Superman' as Taught by Nietzsche." In *The Great Events of the Great War*, edited by George F. Horne, 1:21–43. New York: Little and Ives, 1920.

Ellis, Edith M. O. "Nietzsche and Morals." *Forum* 44 (October 1910): 425–38.

———. *Three Modern Seers*. New York: M. Kennerley, 1910.

Ellis, Havelock. "Friedrich Nietzsche." *Savoy* 1 (April, July, August 1896): 79–94, 68–82, 57–63.

———. "The Genius of Nietzsche." *Weekly Critical Review*, April 30, 1903. In *Views and Reviews*, 147–53. London: Desmond, Harmsworth, 1932.

Ely, Richard T. *The World War and Leadership in a Democracy*. New York: Macmillan, 1918.

Emerson, Ralph Waldo. *The Collected Works of Ralph Waldo Emerson*. Edited by Alfred R. Ferguson et al. 9 vols. Cambridge, MA: Harvard University Press, Belknap Press, 1971–.

———. *The Early Lectures of Ralph Waldo Emerson*. Vol. 3. Edited by Robert E. Spiller and Wallace E. Williams. Cambridge, MA: Harvard University Press, Belknap Press, 1970.

———. *The Journals and Miscellaneous Notebooks of Ralph Waldo Emerson*. Vol. 8. Edited by William Gilman and J. E. Pearsons. Cambridge, MA: Harvard University Press, Belknap Press, 1970.

Evans, John. "Nietzsche Held Nazis' Prophet in War on Christ." *Chicago Daily Tribune*, May 4, 1935, 23.

Everett, Charles C. "Beyond Good and Evil: A Study of the Philosophy of Friedrich Nietzsche." *New World* 8 (December 1898): 684–703.

———. "Beyond Good and Evil." In *Essays Theological and Literary*, 99–129. Boston: Houghton Mifflin, 1901.

"Extracts from the Works of Nietzsche." *Liberty*, December 17, 1892, 4.

"A Feminist Disciple of Nietzsche." *Current Opinion* 54 (January 1913): 47–48.

Figgis, John Neville. *The Will to Freedom; or, The Gospel of Nietzsche and the Gospel of Christ*. London: Longmans, Green, 1917.

Fletcher, John Gould. *Life Is My Song*. New York: Farrar and Rinehart, 1937.

———. *Selected Letters of John Gould Fletcher*. Fayetteville: University of Arkansas Press, 1996.

Fogel, Philip H. "Nietzsche's Jewish Obsession." *Sewanee Review* 23 (October 1915): 449–57.

Forde, P. A. "Is Dogma Out of Date?" *American Catholic Quarterly Review*, January 1915, 22–32.

Forster, Charles Hancock. "Thus Spake Zarathustra—Against Democracy." *Overland Monthly* 70 (September 1917): 284–87.

Förster-Nietzsche, Elisabeth. *The Lonely Nietzsche*. Translated by P. Cohn. Vol. 2 of *The Life of Nietzsche*. New York: Sturgis and Walton, 1915.

———. "Nietzsche, France, and England." *Open Court* 34 (February 1920): 147–54.

———, ed. *The Nietzsche-Wagner Correspondence*. Translated by Caroline Kerr. New York: Boni and Liveright, 1921.

———. "Wagner and Nietzsche: The Beginning and End of Their Friendship." *Musical Quarterly* 4 (July 1918): 466–89.

———. *The Young Nietzsche*. Translated by Anthony Ludovici. Vol. 1 of *The Life of Nietzsche*. New York: Sturgis and Walton, 1912.

Foster, George Burman. "Art and Life." *Little Review* 1 (April 1914): 19–24.

———. "The Bestowing Virtue." *Little Review* 1 (January 1915): 25–31.

———. *The Finality of the Christian Religion*. Chicago: University of Chicago Press, 1906.

———. *Friedrich Nietzsche*. New York: Macmillan, 1931.

———. *The Function of Religion in Man's Struggle for Existence*. Chicago: University of Chicago Press, 1909.

———. "A Hard Bed." *Little Review* 1 (February 1915): 39–45.

———. "Longing." *Little Review* 1 (October 1914): 22–26.

———. "Man and Superman." *Little Review* 1 (April 1914): 3–7.

———. "The New Loyalty." *Little Review* 1 (July 1914): 22–31, 66.

———. "Nietzsche and the Great War." *Sewanee Review* 28 (April 1920): 139–51.

———. "Nietzsche and Wagner." *Sewanee Review* 32 (January 1924): 15–29.

———. "The Nietzschean Love of Eternity." *Little Review* 1 (September 1914): 25–30.

———. "Noise." *Little Review* 1 (November 1914): 32–39.

———. "Personality." *Little Review* 1 (December 1914): 40–45.

———. "The Prophet of a New Culture." *Little Review* 1 (March 1914): 14–18.

———. "The Schoolmaster." *Little Review* 2 (March 1915): 26–30.

———. "The Will to Live." *Little Review* 1 (June 1914): 23–27.

"The Foster Incident." *Standard* 53 (February 24, 1906): 706.

Foucault, Michel. *The Foucault Reader*. Edited by Paul Rabinow. New York: Pantheon, 1984.

Fouillee, Alfred. "The Ethics of Nietzsche and Guyea." *International Journal of Ethics* 13 (October 1902): 13–27.

———. "Nietzsche and Darwinism." *International Monthly* 3 (September 1901): 134–65.

Francke, Kuno. *The German Spirit*. New York: Henry Holt, 1916.

"Friedrich Wilhelm Nietzsche." *Popular Science Monthly*, October 1900, 668.

Fromm, Erich. *Escape from Freedom*. New York: Farrar & Rinehart, 1941.

Frye, Prosser Hall. "Nietzsche." *Midwest Quarterly* 2 (July 1915): 312–42.

———. *Romance and Tragedy*. 1922. Lincoln: University of Nebraska Press, 1961.

Fukuyama, Francis. "The End of History?" *National Interest* 16 (Summer 1989): 3–18.

———. *The End of History and the Last Man*. New York: Avon Books, 1992.

"F. W. Nietzsche." *Bookman: A Journal of Literature and Life*, October 1900, 99–100.

Gerrard, Rev. Thomas J. "Eugenics and Catholic Teaching." *Catholic World*, June 1912, 289–304.

———. "Modern Theories and Moral Disaster." *Catholic World*, July 1912, 433–45.

Gibran, Kahlil. *The Forerunner*. 1920. London: Heinemann Press, 1963.

———. *The Madman*. 1918. In *The Collected Works*, 1–48. New York: Everyman's Library, 2007.

———. *Kahlil Gibran: A Self-Portrait*. Translated by Anthony R. Ferris. New York: Citadel Press, 1959.

———. *The Prophet*. 1923. New York: Knopf, 1986.

Gillis, James Martin. *False Prophets*. New York: Macmillan, 1925.

———. "Nietzsche." *Catholic World*, May 1924, 226–34.

Gilman, Benjamin Ives. "Nietzsche's Melancholia." *Johns Hopkins Alumni Magazine*, January 1920, 129–35.

Gilman, Lawrence. "Two Supermen." *North American Review* 216 (August 1922): 259–72.

Gladden, Washington. *The Forks of the Road*. New York: Macmillan, 1916.

———. Letter to the editor. *New York Times*, April 15, 1915, 12.

———. "Nietzsche and Christianity." *New York Times*, April 15, 1915, 12.

———. "Nietzsche on Peace." *New York Times*, March 21, 1915, sec. 1.

———. "The Theology of Militarism." Chap. 6 in *The Forks of the Road*.

Glaspell, Susan. *The Road to the Temple*. New York: Frederick A. Stokes, 1927.

Godkin, E. L. "Chromo-Civilization." *Nation*, September 24, 1874, 192–205.

Goethe, Johann Wolfgang von. *Faust*. Part 1. 1808. Munich: Hugo Schmidt Verlag, 1923.

———. *Faust*. Translated by Abraham Hayward. London: Edward Moxon, 1838.

———. *Faust*. Translated by Anna Swanwick. London: George Bell and Sons, 1870.

———. *Faust: A Drama in Verse*. Translated by Francis Leveson Gower. London: Murray, 1823.

———. *Faust: A Tragedy*. Translated by Captain Knox. London: John Olliver, 1841.

———. *Faust: A Tragedy*. Translated by Bayard Taylor. 1871. Boston: Houghton Mifflin, 1898.

———. *Faustus from the German of Goethe*. Translated by Samuel Taylor Coleridge. Edited by Frederick Burwick and James C. McKusick. Oxford: Oxford University Press, 2007.

———. "Scenes from the Faust of Goethe." Translated by Percy Bysshe Shelley. In *The Works of Percy Bysshe Shelley in Verse and Prose*, vol. 7, edited by Henry Buxton Forman. London: Reaves and Turner, 1880.

Goldman, Emma. *"Anarchism" and Other Essays*. 1910. Port Washington, NY: Kennicat Press, 1969.

———. "The Failure of Christianity." *Mother Earth*, April 1913, 41–43.

———. *Living My Life*. Vol. 1. 1931. New York: Dover Publications, 1970.

———. *Red Emma Speaks: Selected Writings and Speeches*. Edited by Alix Kates Shulman. New York: Random House, 1972.

Gorren, Aline. "The New Criticism of Genius." *Atlantic Monthly*, December 1894, 794–800.

Gould, George M. *Biographical Clinics*. Vol. 2. Philadelphia: P. Blakiston's Son, 1904.

———. "Eyestrain and Civilization." *American Medicine*, October 10, 1903.

———. "The Origin of the Ill Health of Nietzsche." *Biographic Clinics* 2 (1903): 285–322.

Gray, J. Glenn. "Heidegger Evaluates Nietzsche." *Journal of the History of Ideas* 14 (April 1953): 304–9.

"The Greatest European Event since Goethe." *Current Literature* 43 (July 1907): 65–67.

Gregg, Frederick James. "The War among the Intellectuals: Is Nietzsche to Blame for the Chaos in Europe? Or Treitschke? Or Carlyle?" *Vanity Fair*, December 1914, 45, 82.

Grene, Marjorie. *Dreadful Freedom: A Critique of Existentialism.* Chicago: University of Chicago Press, 1948.

———. *Introduction to Existentialism.* Chicago: University of Chicago Press, 1959.

Halevy, Daniel. *The Life of Nietzsche.* New York: Macmillan, 1911.

Hamblen, Emily S. *Friedrich Nietzsche and His New Gospel.* Boston: R. G. Badger, 1911.

———. *A Guide to Nietzsche.* Little Blue Books. Girard, KS: Haldeman-Julius, 1923.

———. *How to Understand the Philosophy of Nietzsche.* Little Blue Books 11. Girard, KS: Haldeman-Julius, 1919.

Hardin, Edwin Dodge. "Nietzsche's Service to Christianity." *American Journal of Theology* 18 (October 1914): 545–52.

Harrison, Hubert. *The Negro and the Nation.* New York: Cosmo-Advocate, 1917.

Hatfield, James Taft. "Christianity's Fiercest Antagonist." *Dial*, September 2, 1915, 144–46.

———. "The Younger Life of Friedrich Nietzsche." *Dial*, September 1, 1912, 127–29.

Hefner, Hugh. Editor's comment. *Playboy*, December 1953.

Heller, Otto. "Friedrich Nietzsche: A Study in Exaltation." In *Prophets of Dissent: Essays on Masterlinck, Strindberg, Nietzsche, and Tolstoy*, 109–60. New York: Knopf, 1918.

Hess, Mary Whitcomb. "The Nazi Cult of Nietzsche." *Catholic World*, January 1943, 434–37.

Hitch, Marcus. "Marxian versus Nietzschean." *International Socialist Review* 10 (May 1910): 1021–27.

Horkheimer, Max, and Theodor Adorno. *Dialectic of Enlightenment.* Translated by John Cumming. 1944. New York: Continuum, 2002.

Huneker, James. "The Case of Dr. Nordau." *Forum* 54 (November 1915): 571–87.

———. *Egoists: A Book of Supermen*. New York: Charles Scribner's Sons, 1909.

———. *Essays by James Huneker*. 1929. Reprint, New York: AMS Press, 1976.

———. "Friedrich Nietzsche." *Musical Courier* 41 (September 5, 1900): 18–20.

———. "Friedrich Nietzsche." *New York Sun*, January 12, 1908: 8.

———. "Friedrich Nietzsche's Teachings." *Musical Courier* 34 (May 6, 1896): 21–23.

———. *Iconoclasts*. New York: Charles Scribner's Sons, 1905.

———. *Ivory, Apes and Peacocks*. New York: Charles Scribner's Sons, 1915.

———. *The Letters of James Gibbons Huneker*. Edited by Josephine Huneker. New York: Charles Scribner's Sons, 1922.

———. "A Literary Scandal." *New York Sun*, May 3, 1908: 8.

———. *Melomaniacs*. New York: Charles Scribner's Sons, 1902.

———. *Mezzotints in Modern Music*. New York: Charles Scribner's Sons, 1899.

———. "Nietzsche's Apostacy." *New York Sun*, September 21, 1908: 4.

———. *Overtones: A Book of Temperaments*. New York: Charles Scribner's Sons, 1904.

———. *Painted Veils*. New York: Boni and Liveright, 1920.

———. *The Pathos of Distance*. New York: Charles Scribner's Sons, 1913.

———. *Steeplejack*. 2 vols. New York: Charles Scribner's Sons, 1918–20.

———. *Unicorns*. New York: Charles Scribner's Sons, 1917.

———. *Variations*. New York: Charles Scribner's Sons, 1921.

———. *Visionaries*. New York: Charles Scribner's Sons, 1905.

———. "The Will to Suffer." *New York Sun*, November 29, 1908: 8.

Jacobi, Joseph B. "The Nietzschean Idea and the Christian Ideal." *American Catholic Quarterly Review* 41 (July 1916): 463–91.

James, William. *The Correspondence of William James*. Edited by Ignas K. Skrupskelis and Elizabeth M. Berkeley. 12 vols. Charlottesville: University Press of Virginia, 2002.

———. *Essays, Comments, and Reviews*. Cambridge, MA: Harvard University Press, 1987.

———. *Letters of William James*. Vol. 2. Edited by Henry James. Boston: Atlantic Monthly Press, 1920.

———. *Manuscript Essays and Notes*. Edited by Ignas K. Skrupskelis. Cambridge, MA: Harvard University Press, 1988.

———. *Pragmatism: A New Name for Some Old Ways of Thinking*. New York: Longman Green, 1907. Cambridge, MA: Harvard University Press, 1975.

———. *Talks to Teachers on Psychology: and to Students on Some of Life's Ideals*. 1899. Cambridge, MA: Harvard University Press, 1983.

———. *The Varieties of Religious Experience: A Study in Human Nature*. 1902. New York: Longmans, Green, 1911.

Johnson, Thomas Cary. *Some Modern Isms*. Richmond, VA: Presbyterian Committee of Publication, 1919.

Johnston, G. A. "German Philosophy in Relation to the War." *International Journal of Ethics* 26 (October 1915): 121–31.

Johnston, Mercer. "First Impressions of Nietzsche." In *Patriotism and Radicalism*, 77–122. Boston: Sherman, French, 1917.

Kallen, H[orace] M. "The Lyric Philosopher." *Journal of Philosophy, Psychology and Scientific Methods* 7 (October 27, 1910): 589–94.

———. "Nietzsche—Without Prejudice." *Dial*, September 20, 1919, 251–52.

———. "Remarks on R. B. Perry's Portrait of William James." *Philosophical Review* 46 (January 1937): 68–78.

———. Review of *Nietzsche the Thinker: A Study*, by William M. Salter. *Harvard Theological Review* 13 (July 1920): 306–10.

Kaufmann, Walter, ed. and trans. *Basic Writings of Nietzsche*. New York: Random House, 1968.

———. *Critique of Religion and Philosophy*. New York: Harper and Brothers, 1958. Princeton, NJ: Princeton University Press, 1978.

———. *Existentialism from Dostoyevsky to Sartre*. New York: Meridian Books, 1956.

———. "Existentialism, New and Old." *New York Times*, July 30, 1967, 204.

———. "The Faith of a Heretic." *Harper's Magazine*, February 1959, 33–39.

———. *The Faith of a Heretic*. Garden City, NY: Doubleday, 1961.

———. Foreword to *Frau Lou*, by Rudolph Binion. Princeton, NJ: Princeton University Press, 1968.

———. *From Shakespeare to Existentialism*. New York: Doubleday, 1960.

———. *The Future of the Humanities*. New York: Reader's Digest Press, 1977.

———. "Goethe and the History of Ideas." *Journal of the History of Ideas* 10 (October 1949): 503–16.

———. "Nietzsche and Existentialism." *Symposium* 28 (Spring 1974): 7–16.

———. *Nietzsche: Philosopher, Psychologist, Antichrist*. Princeton, NJ: Princeton University Press, 1950.

———. *Nietzsche: Philosopher, Psychologist, Antichrist*. 1950. Princeton, NJ: Princeton University Press, 1974.

———. "Nietzsche's Admiration for Socrates." *Journal of History of Ideas* 9 (October 1948): 472–91.

———. "Nietzsche and the Seven Sirens." *Parisian Review* 19 (May–June 1952): 372–76.

———. "The Reception of Existentialism in the United States." *Midway* 9 (Summer 1968): 97–126.

———. Review of *My Sister and I*, by Friedrich Nietzsche. Translated by Oscar Levy. *Philosophical Review* 65 (January 1955): 152–53.

———. *Tragedy and Philosophy*. Garden City, NY: Doubleday, 1968.

Kaye, F. B. "Puritanism, Literature, and War." *New Republic*, December 15, 1920, 65.

Kennedy, J. M. *The Quintessence of Nietzsche.* New York: Duffield, 1910.

Klenze, Camillo von. "A Philosopher Decadent." *Dial*, June 16, 1897, 356–59.

Knortz, Karl. *Amerikanische Gedichte der Neuzeit*. Leipzig: Wartig, 1883.

Koch, Ernst. "Review of Walter Kaufmann, *Nietzsche*." *Modern Language Journal* 37 (January 1953): 60.

Kohn, Hans. "The Eve of German Nationalism (1789–1812)." *Journal of the History of Ideas* 12 (April 1951): 256–84.

———. *The Mind of Germany*. New York: 1960.

La Monte, Robert Rives. *Socialism: Positive and Negative*. Chicago: Charles H. Kerr, 1914.

"Leader." *M'lle New York*, November–December 1898, 82, 89–91, 198.

Leigh, James. Introduction. In "Nietzsche's Return," special issue, *Semiotext(e)* 3 (1978): 4–5.

Lerch, Charles. "Nietzsche Madness." *Bibliotheca Sacra* 69 (January 1912): 71–87.

Lerner, Max. "Randolph Bourne and Two Generations." *Twice a Year* 5 (Fall–Winter 1940): 54–78.

Levy, Oscar. *The Idiocy of Idealism*. London: H. Hodge, 1940.

———. "Mussolini Says: 'Live Dangerously.'" *New York Times*, November 9, 1924.

———. "Nietzsche and the Crisis: Reply." *Commonweal* 24 (1936): 78.

———. "Nietzsche to Mussolini." *New York Times*, August 22, 1943, 4, 8.

Libby, Walter. "Two Fictitious Ethical Types." *International Journal of Ethics* 18 (July 1908): 466–75.

Lindsay, James. "A Critical Estimate of Nietzsche's Philosophy." *Bibliotheca Sacra* 72 (January 1915): 67–82.

———. "Eugenics and the Doctrine of the Superman." *Eugenics Review*, January 1916, 247–62.

Lippmann, Walter. *Drift and Mastery*. 1914. Madison: University of Wisconsin Press, 1985.

———. *A Preface to Politics*. New York: Mitchell Kennerley, 1913.

Lloyd, J. William. "The Case of Nietzsche." *Modern School* 3, 4 (February, March, April, May, June–July, September 1917): 176–79, 195–200, 233–36, 246–49, 12–17, 82–87.

Lochner, Louis P. "The Goebbels Diaries 1942–43." In *Nazism 1919–1954*. Vol. 2, *State, Economy and Society, 1933–39: A Documentary Reader*, ed. Jeremy Noakes and Geoffrey Pridham, 207–8. Exeter, UK: University of Exeter Press, 1998.

London, Charmian. *The Book of Jack London*. Vol. 2. New York: Century, 1921.

London, Jack. *The Call of the Wild*. New York: Macmillan, 1903.

———. "How I Became a Socialist." *Comrade* 2 (March 1903): 122–23.

———. *The Iron Heel*. New York: Macmillan, 1907.

———. *Martin Eden*. New York: Macmillan, 1909.

———. *"Revolution" and Other Essays*. New York: Macmillan, 1910.

———. *The Sea Wolf*. New York: Macmillan, 1904.

———. "Wanted: A New Law of Development." *International Socialist Review* 3 (August 1902): 65–78.

———. *War of the Classes*. New York: Regent Press, 1905.

Loring, Robert S. *Thoughts from Nietzsche*. Milwaukee: Printed for Free Distribution by Members of the Milwaukee Unitarian Church, 1919.

Lowell, James Russell. "The Present Crisis." In *Early Poems of James Russell Lowell*, edited by Nathan Haskell Dole. 1892. New York: Thomas Y. Crowell, 1898.

Löwith, Karl. *From Hegel to Nietzsche: The Revolution in Nineteenth-Century Thought*. Translated by David E. Green. New York: Holt, Rinehart and Winston, 1964.

———. *Meaning in History: The Theological Implications of the Philosophy of History*. 1949. Chicago: University of Chicago Press, 1962.

———. "Nietzsche's Doctrine of Eternal Recurrence." *Journal of the History of Ideas* 6 (July 1945): 273–84.

Luhan, Mabel Dodge. *Movers and Shakers*. 1936. Albuquerque: University of New Mexico Press, 1984.

Lyotard, Jean-François. *The Postmodern Condition: A Report on Knowledge*. Translated by Geoff Bennington and Brian Massumi. Minneapolis: University of Minnesota Press, 1984.

Mann, Thomas. *Doctor Faustus: The Life of the German Composer Adrian Leverkühn, as Told by a Friend*. Translated by H. T. Lowe-Porter. 1948. New York: Vintage Books, 1971.

———. "German Letter." *Dial*, July 1928, 56–58.

———. *Nietzsche's Philosophy in the Light of Contemporary Events*. Washington, DC: Library of Congress, 1947.

———. *"Past Masters" and Other Papers*. New York: 1933.

———. *Thomas Mann: Briefe 1937–1947*. Edited by Erika Mann. Frankfurt: S. Fischer, 1963.

Manthey-Zorn, Otto. *Dionysus: The Tragedy of Nietzsche*. Amherst, MA: Amherst College Press, 1956.

———, ed. and trans. *Nietzsche: An Anthology of His Work*. New York: Washington Square Press, 1964.

Marcuse, Ludwig. "Nietzsche in America." *South Atlantic Quarterly* 50 (July 1951): 330–39.

———. "Was Nietzsche a Nazi?" *American Mercury*, December 1944, 737–40.

Mather, Frank. "Nietzsche in Action." *Unpopular Review* 3 (January–March 1915): 31–42.

Mathews, Shailer. *The Faith of Modernism*. New York: Macmillan, 1924.

———. *The Gospel and the Modern Man*. New York: Macmillan, 1910.

———. *New Faith for Old: An Autobiography*. New York: Macmillan, 1936.

McClure, Edmund. *Germany's War-Inspirers, Nietzsche and Treitschke*. New York: E. S. Gorham, 1915.

McGinley, A. A. "The Testimony of Science to Religion." *Catholic World*, November 1900, 235–40.

McGovern, William. *From Luther to Hitler: The History of Fascist-Nazi Political Philosophy*. New York: Houghton Mifflin, 1941.

Mecklin, John H. "The Tyranny of the Average Man." *International Journal of Ethics* 28 (January 1918): 240–52.

Mencken, H. L. *A Book of Prefaces*. New York: Knopf, 1917.

———. *Friedrich Nietzsche*. 1913. New Brunswick, NJ: Transaction, 1997.

———. *George Bernard Shaw: His Plays*. Boston: Luce, 1905.

———. *The Gist of Nietzsche*. Boston: Luce, 1910.

———. *Letters of H. L. Mencken*. Edited by Guy J. Forgue. New York: Knopf, 1961.

———. "The Literary Heavyweight Champion." *Smart Set*, March 1910, 155–57.

———. "The Mailed Fist and Its Prophet." *Atlantic Monthly*, November 1914, 602–4.

———. "Nietzscheans." *Baltimore Sun*, November 3, 1910.

———. *The Philosophy of Friedrich Nietzsche*. Boston: Luce, 1908.

———. "The Prophet of the Superman." *Smart Set*, March 1912, 153–58.

———. "What About Nietzsche?" *Smart Set*, November 1909, 153–57.

Mills, Lawrence. "Zarathustrian Analogies in Daniel, Revelations, and in Some Other Books of the Old and New Testaments." *Monist* 17 (1907): 23–32.

"Ministers' Meeting." *Standard* 53 (March 10, 1906): 841–42.

"The Modern Assault on the Christian Virtues." *Current Literature* 47 (July 1909): 68–70.

More, Paul Elmer. *The Drift of Romanticism*. Boston: Houghton Mifflin, 1913.

———. "The Lust of Empire." *Nation*, October 22, 1914, 493–95.

———. "Nietzsche." *Nation*, September 21 and 28, 1911, 259–62, 284–87.

———. *Nietzsche*. Boston: Houghton Mifflin, 1912.

———. "Nietzsche in England." *Nation*, June 12, 1913, 589–90.

Morgan, George A. *What Nietzsche Means*. Cambridge, MA: Harvard University Press, 1941.

Mosse, George L. "The Mystical Origins of National Socialism." *Journal of the History of Ideas* 22 (January–March 1961): 81–96.

"The Most Revolutionary System of Thought Ever Presented to Men." *Current Literature* 40 (March 1906): 282–84.

Mozley, J. Kenneth. "Modern Attacks on Christian Ethics." *Living Age* 257 (May 9, 1908): 353–62.

Mügge, M. A. "Eugenics and the Superman: A Racial Science, and a Racial Religion." *Eugenics Review* 1 (April 1909–January 1910): 184–93.

———. *Friedrich Nietzsche.* New York: Brentano, 1915.

Muirhead, J. H. *German Philosophy in Relation to the War.* London: J. Murray, 1915.

Myers, Johnston. "About the Protest." *Standard* 53 (March 24, 1906): 894.

Nehamas, Alexander. *Nietzsche: Life as Literature.* Cambridge, MA: Harvard University Press, 1985.

Neumann, Franz L. *Behemoth: The Structure and Practice of National Socialism, 1933–1944.* [1942]. Toronto: Oxford University Press, 1944.

"The New Edition of Nietzsche." *Critic* 33 (September 1898): 202–3.

"New Life of Nietzsche." *Bookman*, August 1912, 573–74.

"New Light on Nietzsche and His Friends." *Current Literature* 50 (June 1911): 628–40.

"New Revelations of Nietzsche." *Current Literature* 40 (June 1906): 644–46.

Newton, Huey P. "The Mind Is Flesh." In *The Huey P. Newton Reader*, edited by David Hilliard and Donald Weise. New York: Seven Stories Press, 2002.

———. *Revolutionary Suicide.* New York: Harcourt Brace Jovanovich, 1973.

Nicolas, M. P. *From Nietzsche Down to Hitler.* London: W. Hodge, 1938.

Niebuhr, H. Richard. *The Kingdom of God in America.* 1937. Middletown, CT: Wesleyan University Press, 1988.

"Nietzsche—the Antichrist." *Current Literature* 44 (April 1908): 404–7.

"Nietzsche Breviary." *Bookman*, October 1898, 153.

"Nietzsche and His Philosophy." *Current Literature* 20 (October 1896): 299–300.

"Nietzsche Interest." *Bookman*, November 1907, 246.

"Nietzsche, The New Idol." *Mother Earth*, February 1913, 409–11.

"Nietzsche on War." *Mother Earth*, October 1914, 260–64.

"Nietzsche's Death." *Outlook* 66 (September 8, 1900): 94

"Nietzsche's Letter." *New York Times*, March 23, 1901, Books, 19.

"Nietzsche's Philosophy." *Athenaeum*, November 7, 1896, 632–33.

"Nietzsche's Swan Song." *Current Literature* 46 (March 1909): 297–98.

Nordau, Max. *Degeneration*. 1895. New York: H. Fertig, 1968.

Northcote, Rev. P. M. "The Catholic Apologist." *American Catholic Quarterly Review*, January 1923, 1–14.

"Not Up On Nietzsche." *Literary Digest*, November 7, 1914, 260–64.

Nussbaum, Martha. "Undemocratic Vistas." *New York Review of Books*, November 5, 1987, 20–26.

O'Brien, Conor Cruise. "The Gentle Nietzscheans." *New York Review of Books*, November 5, 1970, 12–16.

Odell, Joseph H. "Peter Sat by the Fire Warming Himself." *Atlantic Monthly*, February 1918, 145–54.

O'Hara, Daniel T. Preface to *Why Nietzsche Now?* Indianapolis: Indiana University Press, 1985.

O'Hara, Thomas. "Nietzsche and the Crisis." *Commonweal*, March 13, 1936, 537–39.

O'Neill, Eugene. *Complete Plays of Eugene O'Neill*. New York: Literary Classics of the United States, 1988.

———. *Selected Letters of Eugene O'Neill*. Edited by Travis Bogard and Jackson R. Bryer. New Haven, CT: Yale University Press, 1988.

"The Pathological Aspects of Nietzsche's Superman." *Current Literature* 44 (May 1908): 551–53.

Patten, Simon Nelson. "The German Way of Thinking." *Forum* 54 (July 1915): 18–26.

Patton, George S. "Beyond Good and Evil." *Princeton Theological Review* 6 (July 1908): 392–436.

Peabody, Francis Greenwood. *The Approach to the Social Question: An Introduction to the Study of Social Ethics*. New York: Macmillan, 1909.

———. *Jesus Christ and the Christian Character*. 1905. New York: Macmillan, 1913.

———. "The Practicability of the Christian Life." *Harvard Theological Review* 6 (April 1913): 129.

Peck, Harry Thurston. "A Mad Philosopher." *Bookman*, September 1898, 25–32.

Perkins, J. R. "What Christianity Has to Say on the Subject." *Christian Century* 34 (1917): 13–14.

Perry, Ralph Barton. *The Free Man and the Soldier: Essays on the Reconciliation of Liberty and Discipline*. New York: Charles Scribner's Sons, 1916.

———. *The Moral Economy*. New York: Macmillan, 1909.

———. "Pragmatism in Italy and Germany." In *The Thought and Character of William James*, chap. 34. Cambridge, MA: Harvard University Press, 1948.

———. *The Present Conflict of Ideals: A Study of the Philosophical Background of the World War*. London: Longmans, Green, 1918.

Petre, M[aude] D. *Modernism: Its Failure and Its Fruit*. London: T. C. & E. C. Jack, 1918.

———. "Studies on Friedrich Nietzsche: A Life Militant." *Catholic World*, December 1905, 317–30.

———. "Studies on Friedrich Nietzsche: Nietzsche the Anti-Christian." *Catholic World*, June 1906, 345–55.

———. "Studies on Friedrich Nietzsche: Nietzsche the Anti-Feminist." *Catholic World*, May 1906, 159–70.

———. "Studies on Friedrich Nietzsche: Nietzsche the Anti-Moralist." *Catholic World*, February 1906, 610–21.

———. "Studies on Friedrich Nietzsche: The Poet." *Catholic World*, January 1906, 516–26.

———. "Studies on Friedrich Nietzsche: The Superman." *Catholic World*, March 1906, 773–84.

"A Philosophic 'Mr. Hyde.'" *Nation*, June 11, 1896, 459–60.

Podach, Erich. *The Madness of Nietzsche*. London: Putnam, 1931.

Porter Reinke, Margaret. "I Married a Nazi!: American Girl's Romance Wrecked by Hitlerism." *Chicago Daily Tribune*, February 26, 1939, G4.

Powys, John Cowper. *Autobiography*. 1934. Hamilton, NY: Colgate University Press, 1968.

———. *Enjoyment of Literature*. New York: Simon and Schuster, 1938.

———. *Visions and Revisions: A Book of Literary Devotions*. 1915. London: Macdonald, 1955.

Pritchard, William H. "The Hermeneutical Mafia; or, After Strange Gods at Yale." *Hudson Review* 28 (Winter 1975–76): 601–10.

Rascoe, Burton. *Before I Forget*. Garden City, NY: Doubleday Doran, 1937.

———. *A Bookman's Daybook*. New York: Horace Liveright, 1929.

———. *Prometheans: Ancient and Modern*. New York: G. P. Putnam's Sons, 1933.

Rauschenbusch, Walter. *Christianity and the Social Crisis*. New York: Macmillan, 1907.

Reinhardt, Kurt. *The Existential Revolt: The Main Themes and Phases of Existentialism*. New York: Frederick Unger, 1952.

Reitzel, Robert. *Des "Armen Teufel": Gesammelte Schriften*. Edited by Max Baginski. Detroit: Reitzel Klub, 1913.

———. "Predigten aus der Neuen Bibel: *Also Sprach Zarathustra*, I." *Der Arme Teufel*, September 17, 1892, 337–38.

———. "Predigten aus der Neuen Bibel: *Also Sprach Zarathustra*, V." *Der Arme Teufel*, October 15, 1892, 369–70.

———. "Predigten aus der Neuen Bibel: *Also Sprach Zarathustra*, VIII." *Der Arme Teufel*, October 29, 1892, 385–86.

"Religion and Government." *Liberty*, January 7, 1893, 1.

Reuter, Gabriele. "A Meeting with Nietzsche." *Living Age* 310 (August 13, 1921): 393–94.

Riesman, David, with Nathan Glazer and Reuel Denney. *The Lonely Crowd*. 1950. New Haven, CT: Yale University Press, 2001.

"Roman Catholic Appreciation." *Current Literature* 41 (August 1906): 198–200.

"The Roots of Decadence." *Outlook* 54 (September 12, 1898): 475–76.

Rorty, Richard. *Achieving Our Country: Leftist Thought in Twentieth-Century America*. Cambridge, MA: Harvard University Press, 1998.

———. *Consequences of Pragmatism: Essays 1972–1980*. Minneapolis: University of Minnesota Press, 1982.

———. *Contingency, Irony, and Solidarity*. Cambridge: Cambridge University Press, 1989.

———. "Dewey between Hegel and Darwin." In *Rorty and Pragmatism: The Philosopher Responds to His Critics*, edited by Herman J. Saatkamp Jr., 1–15. Nashville: Vanderbilt University Press, 1995.

———. "Ein Prophet der Vielfalt." *Die Zeit*, August 24, 2000, 41.

———. *Essays on Heidegger and Others: Philosophical Papers*. Vol. 2. Cambridge, MA: Harvard University Press, 1991.

———. "Nietzsche and the Pragmatists." *New Leader*, May 19, 1997, 9.

———. *Philosophy and the Mirror of Nature*. Princeton, NJ: Princeton University Press, 1979.

———. *Philosophy and Social Hope*. New York: Penguin, 1999.

———. "Pragmatism as Romantic Polytheism." In *Philosophy as Cultural Politics*, 4:27–41. Cambridge: Cambridge University Press, 2007.

Ross, G. R. T. "Beyond Good and Evil." *International Journal of Ethics* 18 (July 1908): 517–18.

Royce, Josiah. *The Hope of the Great Community.* New York: Macmillan, 1916.

———. "The Moral Burden of the Individual." In *The Problem of Christianity*, edited by John E. Smith, chap. 3. Chicago: University of Chicago Press, 1968.

———. "Nietzsche." *Atlantic Monthly*, March 1917, 321–31.

———. *The Philosophy of Loyalty.* 1908. Nashville: Vanderbilt University Press, 1995.

———. *William James and Other Essays on the Philosophy of Life.* 1911. Freeport, NY: Books for Libraries Press, 1969.

Rubenstein, Richard. *After Auschwitz: Radical Theology and Contemporary Judaism.* Indianapolis: Bobbs-Merrill, 1966.

Salter, William M. "William M. Salter" and "The Basis of the Ethical Movement." In *The Fiftieth Anniversary of the Ethical Movement: 1876–1926*, edited by Felix Adler, 37–43, 44–50. New York: D. Appleton, 1926.

———. "An Introductory Word on Nietzsche." *Harvard Theological Review* 6 (October 1913): 358.

———. "Nietzsche's Individualism." *Nation*, April 11, 1912, 361.

———. "Nietzsche's Madness." *Nation*, October 6, 1910, 313.

———. "Nietzsche's Superman." *Journal of Philosophy, Psychology and Scientific Methods* 12 (1915): 421–38.

———. *Nietzsche the Thinker: A Study.* 1917. New York: Frederick Unger, 1968.

———. "Nietzsche and the War." *International Journal of Ethics* 27 (April 1917): 357–79.

Sanger, Margaret. *Margaret Sanger: An Autobiography.* New York: W. W. Norton, 1938.

———. *The Pivot of Civilization in Historical Perspective.* Edited by Michael W. Perry. 1922. Seattle: Inkling Books, 2001.

———. *The Selected Papers of Margaret Sanger: The Woman Rebel, 1900–1928.* Vol. 1. Edited by Esther Katz. Urbana: University of Illinois Press, 2003.

———. *Woman and the New Race.* New York: Brentano's, 1921.

Santayana, George. *Egotism in German Philosophy.* 1916. London: J. M. Dent & Sons, 1940.

———. "The Genteel Tradition in American Philosophy." In *Winds of Doctrine*, 186–215. London: J. M. Dent, 1913.

———. "Philosophical Heresy." *Journal of Philosophy, Psychology and Scientific Methods* 12 (October 14, 1915): 561–68.

———. "Philosophic Sanction of Ambition." *Journal of Philosophy, Psychology and Scientific Methods* 12 (March 4, 1915): 113–16.

Scheffauer, Herman. "A Correspondence between Nietzsche and Strindberg." *North American Review* 198 (1913): 197–205.

———. "Nietzsche the Man." *Edinburgh Review* 218 (July 1913): 163–79.

Schiedt, R. C. "Ernst Haeckel and Friedrich Nietzsche." In two parts. *Reformed Church Review* 12 (January and April 1908): 29–48, 213–34.

———. "Nietzsche and the Great Problems of Modern Thought." *Reformed Church Review* 16 (April 1912): 145–76.

Schiller, F. C. S. "Nietzsche and His Philosophy." *Book Buyer*, August 1896, 406–9.

———. "On Nietzsche Translations." *Nation*, April 26, 1906, 343.

———. "The Philosophy of Friedrich Nietzsche." *Quarterly Review* 218 (January 1913): 148–67.

Schultz, Sigrid. "Pagan Customs Revived for Nazi Weddings: Blood Purity Is Stressed." *Chicago Daily Tribune*, May 1, 1938, G11.

Schuman, Frederick L. "The Political Theory of German Fascism." *American Political Science Review* 28 (April 1934): 210–32.

Schumm, George. "Friedrich Nietzsche." *Book Reviews* 3 (February 1896): 275–80.

Scudder, Vida Dutton. *On Journey*. New York: E. P. Dutton, 1937.

———. *Socialism and Character*. Boston: Houghton Mifflin, 1912.

Sedgwick, Eve Kosofsky. *Epistemology of the Closet*. Berkeley: University of California Press, 1992.

Seldes, Gilbert. "Nietzsche after an Interval." *New Republic*, August 12, 1925, 320–21.

Shaw, Allanson. "Mussolini's Three Political Saints: Machiavelli, Mazzini, and Nietzsche Influence the Thought of Italy's 'Man of Destiny.'" *New York Times*, February 15, 1925, SM9.

Shaw, Charles Gray. "Emerson the Nihilist." *International Journal of Ethics* 25 (October 1914): 68–86.

Shaw, George Bernard. "Giving the Devil His Due." *Saturday Review*, May 13, 1899, Supplement, iii.

———. "Letter on Nietzsche." *ES*, April 15, 1898, 27.

———. *Man and Superman*. Cambridge, MA: Harvard University Press, 1903.

———. "Nietzsche in English." *Saturday Review*, April 11, 1896, 373–74.

Sinclair, Upton. *The Autobiography of Upton Sinclair*. New York: Harcourt, Brace & World, 1962.

———. *The Journal of Arthur Stirling*. New York: D. Appleton, 1903.

———. *My Lifetime in Letters*. Columbia: University of Missouri Press, 1958.

———. "The Overman." In *Mammonart: An Essay in Economic Interpretation*, 291–94. Pasadena, CA: Published by the author, 1924.

Sinclair, Upton, and Jack London, eds. *The Cry for Justice*. Philadelphia: John C. Winston, 1915.

Singer, Edgar. "Friedrich Nietzsche." In *Modern Thinkers and Present Problems*, 183–210. New York: Holt, 1923.

Slosson, Edwin. "The Philosopher with the Hammer." *Independent* 65 (1908): 693–97.

Smith, Lewis Worthington. "Ibsen, Emerson, and Nietzsche: The Individualists." *Popular Science Monthly*, February 1911, 147–57.

"Some American Criticisms of Nietzsche." *Current Literature* 44 (February 1908): 295–96.

Sorely, William R. *Recent Tendencies in Ethics*. Edinburgh: W. Blackwood and Sons, 1904.

Stace, Walter. *The Destiny of Modern Man*. New York: Reynal and Hitchcock, 1941.

Stampfer, Friedrich. "Nazism: Its Spiritual Roots." In *European Ideologies*, edited by Felix Gross, 763–804. New York: Philosophical Library, 1948.

Stearns, Harold. *America and the Young Intellectual*. New York: George Doran, 1921.

Steiner, Rudolf. "Friedrich Nietzsche: Ein Kampfer gegen Seine Zeit." *Philosophical Review* 5 (January 1896): 100.

Stewart, Herbert L. "An Exposition of Nietzsche." *American Journal of Theology* 24 (April 1920): 309–14.

———. "Some Criticisms of the Nietzsche Revival." *International Journal of Ethics* 19 (July 1909): 427–43.

Stewart, William Kilborne. "The Mentors of Mussolini." *American Political Science Review* 22 (November 1928): 843–69.

Stoddard, Lothrop. *The Revolt against Civilization: The Menace of the Under Man*. New York: Charles Scribner's Sons, 1922.

Strauss, Leo. *Natural Right and History*. Chicago: University of Chicago Press, 1953.

Strickland, Francis. "Weird Genius." *Christian Century*, May 2, 1951, 561.

Stringer, Arthur. "The Superman." *Forum* 44 (October 1910): 463.

"Superman." *Living Age* 273 (June 29, 1912): 782–87.

"Superman in Germany." *Christian Science Monitor*, November 15, 1948, 18.

Thayer, William Roscoe. *The Collapse of the Superman*. Boston: Houghton Mifflin, 1918.

———, ed. *Germany vs. Civilization*. Boston: Houghton Mifflin, 1916.

———, ed. *Out of Their Own Mouths*. New York: D. Appleton, 1917.

Thilly, Frank. "Nietzsche and the Ideals of Modern Germany." *Philosophical Review* 25 (March 1916): 188–92.

———. "The Philosophy of Friedrich Nietzsche." *Popular Science* 67 (1905): 707–27.

Thomas, W. H. Griffith. "German Moral Abnormality." *Bibliotheca Sacra* 76 (January 1919): 84–104.

———. "Germany and the Bible." *Bibliotheca Sacra* 72 (January 1915): 49–66.

Thompson, Vance. "Boyesen-Brandes-Nietzsche." *M'lle New York*, October 1895, 43–45.

———. "Democracy Is Bankrupt." *M'lle New York*, August 1895, 9–14.

———. "The Doomed Republic." *M'lle New York*, August 1895, 1–7.

———. Editorial. *M'lle New York*, August 1895, 1.

———. *French Portraits*. Boston: Richard Badger, 1900.

———. "Leader." *M'lle New York*, November 1898, 1–3.

Tillich, Paul. *The Courage to Be*. New Haven, CT: Yale University Press, 1952.

———. *The Protestant Era*. Translated by James Luther Adams. Chicago: University of Chicago Press, 1948.

———. *The Shaking of the Foundations*. New York: Charles Scribner's Sons, 1948.

"Toward a Hidden God." *Time*, April 8, 1966, 82–87.

"Tragedy of a Thinker." *Macmillan Magazine*, December 1899, 106–13.

Trilling, Lionel. *Beyond Culture: Essays on Literature and Learning*. New York: Viking, 1965.

———. *The Liberal Imagination: Essays on Literature and Society*. 1950. New York: New York Review of Books, 2008.

———. *The Moral Obligation to Be Intelligent: Selected Essays*. Edited by Leon Wieseltier. New York: Farrar, Straus and Giroux, 2000.

———. *Sincerity and Authenticity*. Cambridge, MA: Harvard University Press, 1972.

Trotter, W. F. "The Works of Friedrich Nietzsche." *International Journal of Ethics* 7 (January 1897): 258–60.

Tucker, Benjamin. "Aphorisms from Nietzsche." *Liberty*, July 1899, 6.

———. "Freer Banking vs. Greenbackism." *Liberty*, October 1, 1892, 3.

———. *Instead of a Book by a Man Too Busy to Write One: A Fragmentary Exposition of Philosophical Anarchism, Culled from the Writings of Benj. R. Tucker*. New York: B. R. Tucker, 1897.

———. "On Picket Duty." *Liberty*, December 3, 1892, 1.

———. "On Picket Duty." *Liberty*, December 1897, 1.

———. "A Radical Publication Fund." *Liberty*, June 17, 1893, 2.

Tupper, Frederick. "The Avatar of the Hun." *Nation*, June 21, 1917, 729–30.

Untermeyer, Louis. *From Another World*. New York: Harcourt, Brace, 1939.

———. "The Heretic." *Moods* 1 (March 1909): 144.

Urban, Wilbur M. *The Intelligible World: Metaphysics and Value*. Westport, CT: Greenwood Press, 1977.

———. "On Intolerables: A Study in the Logic of Valuation." *Philosophical Review* 24 (September 1915): 477–500.

———. "Knowledge of Value and the Value-Judgement." *Journal of Philosophy, Psychology and Scientific Methods* 13 (December 1916): 673–87.

———. "Metaphysics and Value." In *Contemporary American Philosophy: Personal Statements*, edited by George P. Adams and William P. Montague, 2:356–84. New York: Russell & Russell, 1962.

———. "The Nature of the Community: A Defense of Philosophic Orthodoxy." *Philosophical Review* 28 (November 1919): 547–61.

———. "Ontological Problems of Value." *Journal of Philosophy, Psychology and Scientific Methods* 14 (June 1917): 309–27.

———. "Origin and Value." *Philosophical Review* 32 (September 1923): 451–69.

———. "Progress in Philosophy in the Last Quarter Century." *Philosophical Review* 35 (March 1926): 93–123.

———. "The Relation of the Individual to the Social Value Series." *Philosophical Review* 11 (March 1902): 303–9.

———. Review of *Nietzsche the Thinker*, by William M. Salter. *Philosophical Review* 27 (May 1918): 303–9.

———. "Tubal Cain: The Philosophy of Labor." *Atlantic Monthly*, December 1912, 789.

———. "What Is the Function of a General Theory of Values?" *Philosophical Review* 17 (January 1908): 42–62.

Vahanian, Gabriel. *The Death of God: The Culture of Our Post-Christian Era.* New York: George Braziller, 1961.

Vedder, Henry C. *Socialism and the Ethics of Jesus.* New York: Macmillan, 1912.

Viereck, George S. "Humanizing the Superman." *International* 7 (May 1913): 120–21.

Viereck, Peter. *The Unadjusted Man: A New Hero for Americans; Reflections on the Distinction between Conforming and Conserving.* Boston: Beacon Press, 1956.

Voegelin, Eric. "Nietzsche, the Crisis and the War." *Journal of Politics* 6 (May 1944): 177–212.

Walker, James. *The Philosophy of Egoism.* Denver: K. Walker, 1905.

Wallace, William. "Thus Spake Zarathustra: A Book for All and None." *International Journal of Ethics* 7 (April 1897): 360–69.

Wallar, W. C. A. "A Preacher's Interest in Nietzsche." *American Journal of Theology* 19 (January 1915): 74–91.

Walling, Anna Strunsky. "Nietzsche." *New Review* 3 (August 1915): 166–67.

———. "Emma Goldman in Washington." *Mother Earth*, May 1916, 517–18.

Walling, William English. *The Larger Aspects of Socialism.* New York: Macmillan, 1913.

———. *Progressivism and After.* New York: Macmillan, 1914.

———. *Socialism as It Is.* New York: Macmillan, 1912.

Warbeke, John M. "Friedrich Nietzsche, Antichrist, Superman, and Pragmatist." *Harvard Theological Review* 2 (July 1909): 366–85.

"Was Nietzsche a Madman or a Genius?" *Current Literature* 44 (June 1908): 641–44.

Watt, Lewis. "Nietzsche, Tolstoi, and the Sermon on the Mount." *Catholic World*, August 1920, 577–89.

West, Cornel. *The American Evasion of Philosophy: A Genealogy of Pragmatism.* Madison: University of Wisconsin Press, 1989.

———. *The Cornel West Reader.* New York: Basic Civitas Books, 1999.

———. "Nietzsche's Prefiguration of Postmodern American Philosophy." In *Why Nietzsche Now?* edited by Daniel T. O'Hara, 241–69. Indianapolis: Indiana University Press, 1985.

"What Is the Superman?" *Current Literature* 46 (February 1909): 176–77.

"What Might Makes Right?" *Independent* 77 (October 19, 1914): 79–80.

"Why Nietzsche Now?" Symposium in *boundary 2, a journal of postmodern literature* 9/10 (Spring/Fall 1981).

Will, George F. "A How-To-Book for the Independent." *Washington Post*, July 30, 1987, A19.

Willcox, Louise Collier. "Nietzsche: A Doctor for Sick Souls." *North American Review* 194 (November 1911): 765–74.

Williams, Herbert P. "Nietzsche's Works in English." *Nation*, February 22, 1906, 157.

"Will Nietzsche Come into Vogue in America?" *Current Literature* 49 (July 1910): 65–68.

Wood, James N. *Democracy and the Will to Power.* With an introduction by H. L. Mencken. New York: Knopf, Free Lance Books, 1922.

Woolf, Leonard. *Quack, Quack!* New York: Harcourt, Brace, 1935.

"The Works of Friedrich Nietzsche." *Literary World* 27 (October 3, 1896): 326–27.

Wright, Willard Huntington. *What Nietzsche Taught.* New York: B. W. Huebsch, 1915.

Yarros, Victor S. "Theoretical and Practical Nietzscheism." *American Journal of Sociology* 6 (March 1901): 682–94.

———. "What Shall We Do with the State? I." *American Journal of Sociology* 25 (March 1920): 572–83.

Zangwill, Israel. *The Melting Pot.* New York: Macmillan, 1914.

Zeisler, Sigmund. "Nietzsche and His Philosophy." *Dial*, October 1, 1900, 219–22.

Zueblin, Charles. *Democracy and the Overman.* New York: B. W. Huebsch, 1910.

## Secondary Sources

Abbey, Ruth. *Nietzsche's Middle Period.* New York: Oxford University Press, 2000.

Allen, Gay Wilson. *Waldo Emerson: A Biography.* New York: Viking Press, 1981.

Allen, Graham, and Roy Sellars. *The Salt Companion to Harold Bloom.* Cambridge: Salt, 2007.

Anderson, Benedict. *Imagined Communities: Reflections on the Origin and Spread of Nationalism.* London: Verso, 1983.

Andreas-Salomé, Lou. *Friedrich Nietzsche in Seinen Werken.* 1894. Redding Ridge, CT: Black Swan Books, 1988.

Ansell Pearson, Keith, ed. *A Companion to Nietzsche.* Malden, MA: Blackwell, 2006.

———. *Nietzsche Contra Rousseau: A Study of Nietzsche's Moral and Political Thought.* Cambridge: Cambridge University Press, 1991.

Appelo, Tim. "Legacy: Allan Bloom." *Entertainment Weekly*, October 23, 1992. Online at http://www.ew.com/ew/article/0.20183503,00.html (accessed March 6, 2011).

Armitage, David. *The Declaration of Independence: A Global History.* Cambridge, MA: Harvard University Press, 2007.

Arnold, Harvey. "Death of God—'06." *Foundations* 10 (October–December 1967): 331–53.

Aschheim, Steven E. *Culture and Catastrophe: German and Jewish Confrontations with National Socialism and Other Crises.* New York: New York University Press, 1996.

———. *The Nietzsche Legacy in Germany, 1890–1990.* Berkeley: University of California Press, 1992.

Avrich, Paul. *Anarchist Voices: An Oral History of Anarchism in America.* Princeton, NJ: Princeton University Press, 1995.

Bahr, Ehrhard. *Weimar on the Pacific: German Exile Culture in Los Angeles and the Crisis of Modernism.* Berkeley: University of California Press, 2007.

Bannister, Robert C. *Social Darwinism: Science and Myth in Anglo-American Social Thought.* Philadelphia: Temple University Press, 1979.

Barber, Benjamin. "The Philosopher Despot." *Harper's Magazine*, January 1988, 61–65.

Barclay, David E., and Elisabeth Glaser-Schmidt, eds. *Transatlantic Images and Perceptions: Germany and America since 1776.* Washington, DC: German Historical Institute, 1997.

Barzun, Jacques. *House of Intellect.* New York: Harper, 1959.

Baumgarten, Eduard. "Mitteilungen und Bemerkungen über den Einfluss Emersons auf Nietzsche." *Jahrbuch für Amerikastudien* 1 (1956): 93–152.

Bauschinger, Sigrid, Susan L. Cocalis, and Sara Lennox, eds. *Nietzsche Heute: Die Rezeption seines Werkes nach 1968.* Bern: Francke Verlag, 1988.

Bederman, Gail. *Manliness and Civilization: A Cultural History of Gender and Race in the United States, 1880–1917.* Chicago: University of Chicago Press, 1995.

Beidler, Philip. *Scriptures for a Generation: What We Were Reading in the '60s.* Athens: University of Georgia Press, 1994.

Bender, Thomas. *New York Intellect: A History of Intellectual Life in New York City, from 1750 to the Beginnings of Our Own Time.* New York: Knopf, 1987.

Benders, Raymond J., and Stephan Oettermann, comps. *Friedrich Nietzsche: Chronik in Bildern und Texten.* Munich: Carl Hanser Verlag; Vienna: Deutschen Taschenbuch Verlag, 2000.

Bennett, Tony, and Lawrence Grossberg et al., eds. *New Keywords: A Revised Vocabulary of Culture and Society.* Malden, MA: Blackwell, 2005.

Ben-Zvi, Linda. *Susan Glaspell: Her Life and Times.* New York: Oxford University Press, 2005.

Bergmann, Peter. *Nietzsche, "The Last Antipolitical German."* Bloomington: Indiana University Press, 1987.

Berkowitz, Peter. *Nietzsche: The Ethics of an Immoralist.* Cambridge, MA: Harvard University Press, 1995.

Biel, Steven. *American Gothic: A Life of America's Most Famous Painting.* New York: Norton, 2006.

———. *Independent Intellectuals in the United States, 1910–1945.* New York: New York University Press, 1992.

Black, Stephen A. *Eugene O'Neill: Beyond Mourning and Tragedy.* New Haven, CT: Yale University Press, 1999.

Blake, Casey Nelson. *Beloved Community: The Cultural Criticism of Randolph Bourne, Van Wyck Brooks, Waldo Frank, and Lewis Mumford.* Chapel Hill: University of North Carolina Press, 1990.

———. "The Young Intellectuals and the Culture of Personality." *American Literary History* 1 (Fall 1989): 510–34.

Blake, David Haven. *Walt Whitman and the Culture of American Celebrity.* New Haven, CT: Yale University Press, 2006.

Bledstein, Burton. *The Culture of Professionalism: The Middle Class and the Development of Higher Education in America.* New York: Norton, 1976.

Bluhm, Heinz. "Nietzsche's Early Religious Development." *GR* 11 (1936): 164–83.

———. "Nietzsche's Religious Development as a Student at the University of Bonn." *PMLA* 52 (1937): 880–91.

———. "Nietzsche's Religious Development as a Student at the University of Leipzig." *Journal of English and German Philosophy* 41 (1942): 490–507.

Bode, Carl. *Mencken.* Carbondale: Southern Illinois University Press, 1969.

Booth, Wayne. "Implied Authors as Friends and Pretenders." In *The Company We Keep: An Ethics of Fiction,* 169–98. Berkeley: University of California Press, 1988.

Borradori, Giovanna. *The American Philosopher: Conversations with Quine, Davidson, Putnam, Nozick, Danto, Rorty, Cavlle, MacIntyre, and Kuhn.* Translated by Rossana Crocitto. Chicago: University of Chicago Press, 1994.

Boulton, Agnes. *Part of a Long Story.* New York: Doubleday, 1958.

Bozeman, Theodore Dwight. *Protestants in an Age of Science: The Baconian Ideal and Antebellum American Religious Thought.* Chapel Hill: University of North Carolina Press, 1977.

Brennan, Stephen C., and Stephen R. Yarbrough. *Irving Babbitt.* Boston: Twayne, 1987.

Brennecke, Detlev. "Die blond Bestie: Vom Misverstaendnis eines Schlagworts." *Nietzsche-Studien* 5 (1976): 113–45.

Bridgwater, Patrick. *Nietzsche in Anglosaxony: A Study of Nietzsche's Impact on English and American Literature.* Leicester, UK: University of Leicester Press, 1972.

Brobjer, Thomas H. *Nietzsche and the "English": The Influence of British and American Thinking on His Philosophy.* Amherst, NY: Humanity Books, 2008.

Brooke, John Hedley. *Science and Religion: Some Historical Perspectives.* Cambridge: Cambridge University Press, 1991.

Brooks, Frank H. *The Individualist Anarchists: An Anthology of* Liberty, *1881–1908.* New Brunswick, NJ: Transaction, 1994.

Brown, David S. *Richard Hofstadter: An Intellectual Biography.* Chicago: University of Chicago Press, 2006.

Buell, Lawrence. *Emerson*. Cambridge, MA: Harvard University Press, Belknap Press, 2003.

Bushrui, Suheil, and Joe Jenkins. *Kahlil Gibran: Man and Poet*. Boston: One World, 1998.

Butler, Leslie. *Critical Americans: Victorian Intellectuals and Transatlantic Liberal Reform*. Chapel Hill: University of North Carolina Press, 2007.

Butsch, Richard. *The Making of American Audiences: From Stage to Television, 1750–1990*. Cambridge: Cambridge University Press, 2000.

Cadello, James Peter. "Nietzsche in America: The Spectrum of Perspectives, 1895–1925." PhD diss., Purdue University, 1990.

Campbell, James. *A Thoughtful Profession: The Early Years of the American Philosophical Association*. Peru, IL: Open Court, 2006.

Cantor, Milton. *Max Eastman*. New York: Twayne, 1970.

Carey, John J. "Letters to Thomas Altizer." In *The Death of God Debate*, edited by Jack Lee Ice and John J. Carey. Philadelphia: Westminster Press, 1967.

Cate, Curtis. *Friedrich Nietzsche*. Woodstock, NY: Overlook Press, 2005.

Cavicchi, Daniel. *Tramps Like Us: Music and Meaning among Springsteen Fans*. New York: Oxford University Press, 1998.

Ceaser, James W. *Reconstructing America: The Symbol of America in Modern Thought*. New Haven, CT: Yale University Press, 1997.

Chaplin, Tamara. *Turning on the Mind: French Philosophers on Television*. Chicago: University of Chicago Press, 2007.

Chapman, A. H. "The Influence of Nietzsche on Freud's Ideas." *British Journal of Psychiatry* 166 (1995): 251–53.

Chesler, Ellen. *Woman of Valor: Margaret Sanger and the Birth Control Movement in America*. 1992. New York: Simon and Schuster, 2007.

Churchill, Suzanne W., and Adam McKible, eds. *Little Magazines & Modernism: New Approaches*. Aldershot, UK: Ashgate, 2007.

Collini, Stefan. *Absent Minds: Intellectuals in Britain*. Oxford: Oxford University Press, 2006.

Collins, H. P. *John Cowper Powys, Old Earth Man*. London: Barrie and Rockliff, 1966.

Conant, James. "Emerson as Educator." In "Emerson/Nietzsche," special issue, *ESQ: A Journal of the American Renaissance* 43 (1997): 181–206.

Condren, Conal, Stephen Gaukroger, and Ian Hunter, eds. *The Philosopher in Early Modern Europe: The Nature of a Contested Identity*. Cambridge: Cambridge University Press, 2006.

Conser, Walter H. *God and the Natural World: Religion and Science in Antebellum America*. Columbia: University of South Carolina Press, 1993.

Cotkin, George. *Existential America*. Baltimore: Johns Hopkins University Press, 2003.

———. "Middle-Ground Pragmatists: The Popularization of Philosophy in American Culture." *Journal of the History of Ideas* 55 (April 1994): 283–302.

———. *Reluctant Modernism: American Thought and Culture, 1880–1900*. New York: Twayne, 1992.

———. *William James: Public Philosopher*. Baltimore: Johns Hopkins University Press, 1990.

Crews, Clyde F. "Maude Petre's Modernism." *America* 144 (May 16, 1981): 403–6.

Crockett, Clayton. Introduction to *Secular Theology: American Radical Theological Thought*, edited by Clayton Crockett. New York: Routledge, 2001.

Crunden, Robert M. *American Salons: Encounters with European Modernism, 1885–1917*. New York: Oxford University Press, 1993.

Curti, Merle. *Human Nature in American Thought: A History*. Madison: University of Wisconsin Press, 1980.

Cusset, François. *French Theory: How Foucault, Derrida, Deleuze, & Co. Transformed the Intellectual Life of the United States*. Translated by Jeff Fort. Minneapolis: University of Minnesota Press, 2008.

Dakin, Arthur H. *Paul Elmer More*. Princeton, NJ: Princeton University Press, 1960.

Daly, Gabriel. *Transcendence and Immanence: A Study in Catholic Modernism and Integralism*. Oxford: Clarendon Press, 1980.

Darnton, Robert. *The Business of Enlightenment: A Publishing History of the Encyclopédie, 1775–1800*. Cambridge, MA: Harvard University Press, 1979.

———. *The Great Cat Massacre: And Other Episodes in French Cultural History*. 1984. New York: Basic Books, 1999.

———. "What Is the History of Books?" In *Books and Society in History*, edited by Kenneth E. Carpenter, 3–26. New York: R. R. Bowker, 1983.

Davidson, Cathy N. "Towards a History of Books and Readers." *American Quarterly* 40 (March 1988): 7–17.

Dawidoff, Robert. *The Genteel Tradition and the Sacred Rage: High Culture vs. Democracy in Adams, James, and Santayana*. Chapel Hill: University of North Carolina Press, 1992.

Dickstein, Morris, ed. *The Revival of Pragmatism: New Essays on Social Thought, Law, and Culture*. Durham, NC: Duke University Press, 1998.

Diehl, Carl. *Americans and German Scholarship, 1770–1870*. New Haven, CT: Yale University Press, 1978.

Diethe, Carol. *Nietzsche's Sister and the Will to Power: A Biography of Elisabeth Förster-Nietzsche*. Urbana: University of Illinois Press, 2003.

Diggins, John Patrick. *Eugene O'Neill's America: Desire under Democracy*. Chicago: University of Chicago Press, 2007.

———. "From Pragmatism to Natural Law: Walter Lippmann's Quest for the Foundations of Legitimacy." *Political Theory* 19 (November 1991): 519–38.

Diner, Dan. *America in the Eyes of the Germans: An Essay on Anti-Americanism*. Princeton, NJ: Markus Wiener, 1996.

Donaldson, Randall P. *The Literary Legacy of a "Poor Devil": The Life and Work of Robert Reitzel (1849–1898)*. New York: Lang, 2002.

Dorrien, Gary. *The Making of American Liberal Theology*. Vol. 2, *Idealism, Realism, and Modernity (1900–1950)*. Louisville: Westminster/John Knox Press, 2003.

Doss, Erika. *Elvis Culture: Fans, Faith, and Image*. Lawrence: University Press of Kansas, 1999.

Douglas, Ann. *The Feminization of American Culture*. 1977. New York: Doubleday, 1988.

———. *Terrible Honesty: Mongrel Manhattan in the 1920s*. New York: Noonday Press, 1996.

———. "Periodizing the American Century: Modernism, Postmodernism, and Postcolonialism in the Cold War Context." *Modernism/Modernity* 5 (September 1998): 71–98.

Drimmer, Melvin. "Nietzsche in American Thought, 1895–1925." PhD diss., University of Rochester, 1965.

Drinnon, Richard. *Rebel in Paradise: A Biography of Emma Goldman*. Chicago: University of Chicago Press, 1961.

Drury, Shadia B. *The Political Ideas of Leo Strauss*. 1988. New York: Palgrave Macmillan, 2005.

Dyer, Richard. *Stars*. London: British Film Institute, 1998.

Evans, Christopher H. *The Kingdom Is Always but Coming: A Life of Walter Rauschenbusch.* Grand Rapids, MI: William B. Eerdmans, 2004.

Fass, Paula. "Making and Remaking an Event: The Leopold and Loeb Case in American Culture." *Journal of American History* 80 (December 1993): 919–51.

Festenstein, Matthew, and Simon Thompson, eds. *Richard Rorty: Critical Dialogues.* Cambridge: Polity, 2001.

Fink, Leon. *Progressive Intellectuals and the Dilemmas of Democratic Commitment.* Cambridge, MA: Harvard University Press, 1997.

Fish, Stanley E. "Literature in the Reader: Affective Stylistics." In *Reader-Response Criticism: From Formalism to Post-Structuralism,* edited by Jane P. Tompkins, 70–100. Baltimore: Johns Hopkins University Press, 1980.

Fishbein, Leslie. *Rebels in Bohemia: The Radicals of the Masses, 1911–1917.* Chapel Hill: University of North Carolina Press, 1982.

Fite, David. *Harold Bloom: The Rhetoric of Romantic Vision.* Amherst: University of Massachusetts Press, 1985.

Flaccus, Louis William. *Artists and Thinkers.* New York: Longmans, Green, 1916.

Forth, Christopher E. "Intellectuals, Crowds, and the Body Politics of the Dreyfus Affair." *Historical Reflections/Réflexions Historiques* 24 (Spring 1998): 63–92.

———. *Zarathustra in Paris: The Nietzsche Vogue in France, 1891–1918.* De Kalb: Northern Illinois University Press, 2001.

Fox, Richard Wightman. *Jesus in America: Personal Savior, Cultural Hero, National Obsession.* New York: Harper San Francisco, 2004.

Frederick, Peter J. *Knights of the Golden Rule: The Intellectual as Social Reformer in the 1890s.* Lexington: University Press of Kentucky, 1967.

Frenzel, Ivo. *Nietzsche.* Hamburg: Rowohlt, 1966.

Freud, Sigmund. *An Autobiographical Study.* Translated by James Strachey. New York: Norton, 1935.

Friedl, Herwig. "Emerson and Nietzsche: 1862–1874." In *Religion and Philosophy in the United States of America.* Vol. 1, edited by Peter Freese, 267–87. Essen: Die Blaue Eule Verlag, 1987.

———. "Fate, Power, and History in Emerson and Nietzsche." In "Emerson/Nietzsche," special issue, *ESQ: A Journal of the American Renaissance* 43 (1997): 267–93.

Friedman, Michael. *A Parting of the Ways: Carnap, Cassirer, and Heidegger.* Chicago: Open Court, 2000.

Fulton, Ann. *Apostles of Sartre: Existentialism in America, 1945–1963.* Evanston, IL: Northwestern University Press, 1999.

Furniss, Norman F. *The Fundamentalist Controversy, 1918–1931.* New Haven, CT: Yale University Press, 1954.

Galindo, Martha Zapata. *Triumph des Willens zur Macht: Zur Nietzsche-Rezeption im NS-Staat.* Hamburg: Argument, 1995.

Gans, Herbert. *Popular Culture and High Culture: An Analysis and Evaluation of Taste.* New York: Basic Books, 1974.

Geis, Gilbert, and Leigh Bienen. *Crimes of the Century: From Leopold and Loeb to O. J. Simpson.* Boston: Northeastern University Press, 1998.

Gelb, Arthur, and Barbara Gelb. *O'Neill.* New York: Simon and Schuster, 1962.

Gilbert, James. *Writers and Partisans: A History of Literary Radicalism in America.* 1968. New York: Columbia University Press, 1992.

Gilman, Sander. *Difference and Pathology: Stereotypes of Sexuality, Race, and Madness.* Ithaca, NY: Cornell University Press, 1985.

Gilroy, Paul. *Black Atlantic: Modernity and Double-Consciousness.* Cambridge, MA: Harvard University Press, 1993.

Ginzburg, Carlo. *The Cheese and the Worms: The Cosmos of a Sixteenth-Century Miller.* Translated by John Tedeschi and Anne Tedeschi. Baltimore: Johns Hopkins University Press, 1980.

Gitlin, Todd. "Postmodernism: The Stenography of Surfaces." *New Perspectives Quarterly,* Spring 1989, 55–59.

Glass, Loren. *Authors Inc.: Literary Celebrity in the Modern United States, 1880–1980.* New York: New York University Press, 2004.

Goldstein, Philip, and James L. Machor, eds. *New Directions in American Reception Study.* New York: Oxford University Press, 2008.

Goldstein, William. "The Story behind the Best Seller: Allan Bloom's *Closing of the American Mind.*" *Publishers Weekly,* July 3, 1987, 25.

Golomb, Jacob. *Nietzsche, Godfather of Fascism? On the Uses and Abuses of a Philosophy.* Princeton, NJ: Princeton University Press, 2002.

Goodman, Russell B., ed. *Contending with Stanley Cavell.* Oxford: Oxford University Press, 2005.

Gorman, Paul R. *Left Intellectuals and Popular Culture in Twentieth-Century America.* Chapel Hill: University of North Carolina Press, 1996.

Graff, Gerald. *Professing Literature: An Institutional History.* Chicago: University of Chicago Press, 1987.

Gragg, Alan. "George Burman Foster." In *Dictionary of Heresy Trials in American Christianity*, edited by George H. Shriver, 142–49. Westport, CT: Greenwood Press, 1997.

———. *George Burman Foster: Religious Humanist.* Perspectives in Religious Studies. Danville, VA: Association of Baptist Professors of Religion, 1978.

Grefe, Maxine. *"Apollo in the Wilderness": An Analysis of the Critical Reception of Goethe in America, 1806–1840.* New York: Garland, 1988.

Gregory, Frederick. "The Impact of Darwinian Evolution on Protestant Theology in the Nineteenth Century." In *God and Nature: Historical Essays on the Encounter between Christianity and Science*, edited by David C. Lindberg and Ronald L. Numbers, 369–90. Berkeley: University of California Press, 1986.

Gribble, Richard. *Guardian of America: The Life of James Martin Gillis, CSP.* New York: Paulist Press, 1998.

Grillaert, Nel. *What the God-Seekers Found in Nietzsche: The Reception of Nietzsche's Übermensch by Philosophers of the Russian Religious Renaissance.* Amsterdam: Rodopi, 2008.

Gross, Neil. *Richard Rorty: The Making of an American Philosopher.* Chicago: University of Chicago Press, 2008.

Groth, J. H. "Wilamowitz-Möllendorf on Nietzsche's Birth of Tragedy." *Journal of the History of Ideas* 11 (April 1950): 179–90.

Gullace, Giovanni. "The Pragmatist Movement in Italy." *Journal of the History of Ideas* 23 (January–March 1962): 91–105.

Hadot, Pierre. *Philosophy as a Way of Life: Spiritual Exercises from Socrates to Foucault.* Malden, MA: Blackwell, 1995.

Hale, Nathan G., Jr. *The Beginnings of Psychoanalysis in the United States, 1876–1917.* Vol. 1 of *Freud and the Americans.* New York: Oxford University Press, 1971.

———. *The Rise and Crisis of Psychoanalysis in the United States, 1917–1985.* Vol. 2 of *Freud and the Americans.* New York: Oxford University Press, 1995.

Hall, David D. "Readers and Reading in America: Historical and Critical Perspectives." *American Antiquarian Society Proceedings* 103 (1993): 337–57.

Hanighen, Frank C. "Vance Thompson and *M'lle New York*." *Bookman*, September 1932, 78–84.

Hargreaves, Raymond. "Friedrich Nietzsche, 1844–1900." In *Encyclopedia of Literary Translations into English*, edited by Olive Classe, 2:1001–5. Chicago: Fitzroy Dearborn, 2000.

Harrison, Thomas, ed. *Nietzsche in Italy*. Stanford, CA: Stanford University Press, 1988.

Hathaway, Lillie V. *German Literature in the Mid-Nineteenth Century in England and America as Reflected in the Journals, 1840–1914*. Boston: Chapman and Grimes, 1935.

Hauhart, William Frederic. "The Reception of Goethe's Faust in England in the First Half of the Nineteenth Century." PhD diss., Columbia University, 1909.

Hayden, Deborah. *Pox: Genius, Madness, and the Mysteries of Syphilis*. New York: Basic Books, 2003.

Heider, Ulrike. *Der "Arme Teufel": Robert Reitzel vom Vormärz zum Haymarket*. Bühl-Moos: Elster, 1986.

Heilbut, Anthony. *Exiled in Paradise: German Refugee Artists and Intellectuals in America, from the 1930s to the Present*. 1983. Berkeley: University of California Press, 1997.

Hennesey, James. *American Catholics: A History of the Roman Catholic Community in the United States*. New York: Oxford University Press, 1981.

Herbst, Jurgen. *The German Historical School in American Scholarship: A Study in the Transfer of Culture*. Ithaca, NY: Cornell University Press, 1965.

Herrick, Genevieve Forbes, and John Origen Herrick. *The Life of William Jennings Bryan*. Chicago: Kessinger Publication, 2005.

Higdon, Hal. *The Crime of the Century: The Leopold and Loeb Case*. New York: G. P. Putnam's Sons, 1975.

Higham, John. "The Matrix of Specialization." In *The Organization of Knowledge in Modern America, 1860–1920*, edited by Alexandra Oleson and John Voss, 3–18. Baltimore: Johns Hopkins University Press, 1976.

Hillier, Bevis. *Victorian Studio Photographs*. Boston: David R. Godine, 1976.

Hills, Matt. *Fan Cultures*. London: Routledge, 2002.

Hilu, Virginia, ed. *Beloved Prophet: The Love Letters of Kahlil Gibran and Mary Haskell and Her Private Journal*. New York: Knopf, 1972.

Hobson, Fred. *Mencken: A Life*. New York: Random House, 1994.

Hoeveler, J. David, Jr. *The New Humanism: A Critique of Modern America, 1900–1940*. Charlottesville: University Press of Virginia, 1977.

———. *The Postmodernist Turn: American Thought and Culture in the 1970's.* New York: Twayne, 1996.

Hoffman, Frederick J. *Freudianism and the Literary Mind.* Baton Rouge: Louisiana State University Press, 1945.

———. "Philistine and Puritan in the 1920s." *American Quarterly* 1 (Autumn 1949): 247–263.

Hoffman, Frederick, Charles Allen, and Carolyn Ulrich. *The Little Magazine: A History and a Bibliography.* Princeton, NJ: Princeton University Press, 1946.

Hoffmann, David Marc. *Zur Geschichte des Nietzsche-Archivs.* Berlin: Walter de Gruyter, 1991.

Hofstadter, Richard. *Anti-Intellectualism in American Life.* New York: Knopf, 1963.

———. *Social Darwinism in American Thought.* 1944. Rev. ed. New York: George Braziller, 1959.

Hoganson, Kristin. *Consumers' Imperium: The Global Production of American Domesticity, 1865–1920.* Chapel Hill: University of North Carolina Press, 2007.

Holifield, E. Brooks. *God's Ambassadors: A History of Christian Clergy in America.* Grand Rapids, MI: William B. Eerdmans, 2007.

———. *Theology in America: Christian Thought from the Age of the Puritans to the Civil War.* New Haven, CT: Yale University Press, 2005.

Hollingdale, R. J. *Nietzsche: The Man and His Philosophy.* Rev. ed. Cambridge: Cambridge University Press, 1999.

———. Review of *My Sister and I,* by Friedrich Nietzsche, trans. Oscar Levy. *Journal of Nietzsche Studies* (Autumn 1991): 95–102.

Hollinger, David A., ed. *The Humanities and the Dynamics of Inclusion after World War II.* Baltimore: Johns Hopkins University Press, 2006.

———. "Inquiry and Uplift: Late-Nineteenth-Century American Academics and the Moral Efficacy of Scientific Practice." In *The Authority of Experts: Studies in History and Theory,* edited by Thomas L. Haskell, 142–56. Bloomington: Indiana University Press, 1984.

———. "Justification by Verification: The Scientific Challenge to the Moral Authority of Christianity in Modern America." In *Religion and Twentieth-Century American Life,* edited by Michael Lacey, 116–35. New York: Cambridge University Press, 1989.

————. "The Knower and the Artificer." *American Quarterly* 39 (Spring 1987): 37–55.

————. "The Problem of Pragmatism in American History." *Journal of American History* 67 (June 1980): 88–107.

Holub, Robert C. *Reception Theory: A Critical Introduction.* London: Metheun, 1984.

Honeycutt, Dwight A. *Henry Clay Vedder: His Life and Thought.* Atlanta: Baptist History and Heritage Society, 2008.

Hoslett, Schuyler. "The Superman in Nietzsche's Philosophy and in Goethe's Faust." *MFDU* 31 (1939): 294–300.

Hubbard, Stanley. *Nietzsche und Emerson.* Basel: Verlag für Recht und Gesellschaft AG, 1958.

Hughes, H. Stuart. *Consciousness and Society: The Reorientation of European Social Thought, 1890–1930.* New York: Knopf, 1958.

————. *The Sea Change: The Migration of Social Thought, 1930–1965.* New York: Harper & Row, 1975.

Hummel, Hermann. "Emerson and Nietzsche." *New England Quarterly* 19 (March 1946): 63–84.

Hutchison, William R. "Liberal Protestantism and the 'End of Innocence.'" *American Quarterly* 15 (Summer 1963): 126–39.

————. *The Modernist Impulse in American Protestantism.* Cambridge, MA: Harvard University Press, 1976.

Jackman, Jarrell C., and Carla M. Borden, eds. *The Muses Flee Hitler: Cultural Transfer and Adaptation, 1930–1945.* Washington, DC: Smithsonian Institute Press, 1983.

Jackson, H. J. *Marginalia: Readers Writing in Books.* New Haven, CT: Yale University Press, 2001.

Jacoby, Susan, *The Age of American Unreason.* New York: Pantheon, 2008.

Janz, Curt Paul. *Friedrich Nietzsche Biographie in drei Bänden.* Munich: Hanser, 1978–79.

Jaspers, Karl. *Nietzsche and Christianity.* Translated by E. B. Ashton. Chicago: Regnery, 1961.

————. *Nietzsche: An Introduction to the Understanding of His Philosophical Activity.* Translated by Charles F. Wallraff and Frederick J. Schmitz. 1965. Baltimore: Johns Hopkins University Press, 1997.

Jay, Martin. "Adorno in America." In *Permanent Exiles: Essays on the Intel-*

*lectual Migration from Germany to America*, 120–37. New York: Columbia University Press, 1986.

———. *The Dialectical Imagination: A History of the Frankfurt School and the Institute for Social Research, 1923–1950*. 1973. Berkeley: University of California Press, 1996.

Jenemann, David. *Adorno in America*. Minneapolis: University of Minnesota Press, 2007.

Jennings, Jeremy, and Tony Kemp-Welch, eds. *Intellectuals in Politics: From the Dreyfus Affair to Salman Rushdie*. New York: Routledge, 1997.

Joas, Hans. *Pragmatism and Social Theory*. Chicago: University of Chicago Press, 1993.

Johnson, Linck. "Emerson: America's First Public Intellectual?" *Modern Intellectual History* 2 (April 2005): 135–51.

Johnson, Pauline. "Nietzsche Reception Today." *Radical Philosophy* 80 (1996): 24–33.

Joll, James. "The English, Friedrich Nietzsche and the First World War." In *Deutschland in der Weltpolitik des 19 und 20 Jahrhunderts*, edited by Imanuel Geiss and Bernd Jürgen Wendt, 287–306. Düsseldorf: Bertelsmann Universitätsverlag, 1973.

Jones, Ernest. *Sigmund Freud: Life and Work*. Vol. 3. London: Hogarth Press, 1953–57.

Kateb, George. *Emerson and Self-Reliance*. Thousand Oaks, Ca: Sage, 1995.

Kaufmann, LeRoy. "The Influence of Friedrich Nietzsche on American Literature." PhD diss., University of Pennsylvania, 1963.

Kazin, Alfred. *On Native Grounds: An Interpretation of Modern American Prose Literature*. 1942. San Diego: Harvest, 1995.

Keller, Phyllis. *States of Belonging: German-American Intellectuals and the Frist World War*. Cambridge, MA: Harvard University Press, 1979.

Kellogg, Walter G. "Harry Thurston Peck." *American Mercury*, September 1933, 83–88.

Kennedy, David M. *Birth Control in America*. New Haven, CT: Yale University Press, 1970.

Kimball, Roger. *Tenured Radicals: How Politics Has Corrupted Our Higher Education*. 1990. 3rd ed., Chicago: Ivan R. Dee, 2008.

King, Richard. *The Party of Eros: Radical Social Thought and the Realm of Freedom*. 1972. Chapel Hill: University of North Carolina Press, 2009.

Kloppenberg, James T. *Uncertain Victory: Social Democracy and Progressivism in European and American Thought, 1870–1920*. New York: Oxford University Press, 1986.

———. "Pragmatism: An Old Name for Some New Ways of Thinking?" *Journal of American History* 83 (June 1996): 100–138.

Koelb, Clayton, ed. *Nietzsche as Postmodernist: Essays Pro and Contra*. Albany: State University of New York Press, 1990.

Köhnke, Klaus C. *The Rise of Neo-Kantianism: German Academic Philosophy between Idealism and Positivism*. Translated by R. J. Hollingdale. Cambridge: Cambridge University Press, 1991.

Köster, Peter. "Nietzsche-Kritik und Nietzsche Rezeption in der Theologie des 20 Jahrhunderts." *Nietzsche-Studien* 10/11 (1981/1982), 615–85.

Krohn, Claus-Dieter. *Intellectuals in Exile: Refugee Scholars and the New School for Social Research*. Translated by Rita and Robert Kimber. Amherst: University of Massachusetts Press, 1993.

Krummel, Richard Frank. *Nietzsche und der Deutsche Geist*. 2 vols. Berlin: Walter de Gruyter, 1974, 1983.

Kuklick, Bruce. *Churchmen and Philosophers: From Jonathan Edwards to John Dewey*. New Haven, CT: Yale University Press, 1985.

———. *A History of Philosophy in America, 1720–2000*. Oxford: Oxford University Press, 2001.

———. *Josiah Royce: An Intellectual Biography*. 1972. Indianapolis: Hackett, 1985.

———. *The Rise of American Philosophy*. New Haven, CT: Yale University Press, 1977.

Lampert, Laurence. *Leo Strauss and Nietzsche*. Chicago: University of Chicago Press, 1996.

Lasch, Christopher. *The New Radicalism in America, 1889–1963: The Intellectual as a Social Type*. New York: Knopf, 1965.

Leach, William. *Land of Desire: Merchants, Power, and the Rise of a New American Culture*. New York: Pantheon, 1993.

Lears, Jackson. *No Place of Grace: Antimodernism and the Transformation of American Culture, 1880–1920*. New York: Pantheon Books, 1981.

———. *Rebirth of a Nation: The Making of Modern America, 1877–1920*. New York: HarperCollins, 2009.

Leitch, Vincent B. *American Literary Criticism from the Thirties to the Eighties*. New York: Columbia University Press, 1988.

Levine, Lawrence. *Highbrow/Lowbrow: The Emergence of Cultural Hierarchy in America*. Cambridge, MA: Harvard University Press, 1988.

Little, Katherine M. "The 'Nietzschean' and the Individualist in Jack London's Socialist Writings." *Amerikastudien* 22 (1977): 309–23.

Lopez, Michael, ed. "Emerson/Nietzsche." Special issue, *ESQ: A Journal of the American Renaissance* 43 (1997).

Lotringer, Sylvère, and Sande Cohen, eds. *French Theory in America*. New York: Routledge, 2001.

Luebke, Frederick C. *Bonds of Loyalty: German-Americans and World War I*. De Kalb: Northern Illinois University Press, 1974.

Luedtke, Luther S. "German Criticism and Reception of Ralph Waldo Emerson." PhD diss., Brown University, 1971.

Machor, James, and Philip Goldstein, eds. *Reception Study from Literary Theory to Cultural Studies*. New York: Routledge, 2001.

Macksey, Richard, and Eugenio Donato, eds. *The Structuralist Controversy: The Languages of Criticism and the Sciences of Man*. Baltimore: Johns Hopkins University Press, 1970.

Magnus, Bernd. "Nietzsche Today: A View from America." *International Studies in Philosophy* 15 (1983): 95–103.

———. "Nietzsche and Postmodern Criticism." *Nietzsche-Studien* 18 (1989): 301–16.

Magnus, Bernd, and Kathleen M. Higgins, eds. *The Cambridge Companion to Nietzsche*. Cambridge: Cambridge University Press, 1996.

Malachowski, Alan, ed. *Reading Rorty: Critical Responses to "Philosophy and the Mirror of Nature" (and Beyond)*. Cambridge: Basil Blackwell, 1990.

Manguel, Alberto. *A History of Reading*. New York: Viking, 1996.

Manz, Stefan. "Translating Nietzsche, Mediating Literature: Alexander Tille and the Limits of Anglo-German Intercultural Transfer." *Neophilologus* 91 (January 2007): 117–34.

Marcuse, Ludwig. "Nietzsche in America." *South Atlantic Quarterly* 50 (July 1951): 330–39.

Martin, John E. "Martin Eden, a London Superman Adventurer: A Case Study of the Americanization of European Ideology." In *Die amerikanische Literatur in der Weltliteratur: Themen und Aspekte*, edited by Claus Uhlig and Volker Bischoff, 218–30. Berlin: E. Schmidt, 1982.

Matthews, F. H. "The Americanization of Sigmund Freud: Adaptations of Psychoanalysis before 1917." *Journal of American Studies* 1 (1967): 39–62.

Matthiessen, F. O. "Irving Babbitt." In *Responsibilities of the Critic: Essays and Reviews*, edited by John Rackliffe, 161–65. New York: Oxford University Press, 1952.

May, Henry F. *The End of American Innocence: A Study of the First Years of Our Own Time, 1912–1917*. New York: Knopf, 1959.

Mayer, Milton. *Robert Maynard Hutchins: A Memoir*. Berkeley: University of California Press, 1993.

Mazlish, Bruce. "Freud and Nietzsche." *Psychoanalytic Review* 55 (1968): 360–75.

McCarraher, Eugene. "Heal Me: 'Personality,' Religion, and the Therapeutic Ethic in Modern America." *Intellectual History Newsletter* 21 (1999): 31–40.

McClay, Wilfred M. *The Masterless: Self & Society in Modern America*. Chapel Hill: University of North Carolina Press, 1994.

McCormick, John. *George Santayana: A Biography*. New York: Knopf, 1987.

McCumber, John. *Time in the Ditch: American Philosophy and the McCarthy Era*. Evanston, IL: Northwestern University Press, 2001.

McEachran, Frank. "On Translating Nietzsche into English." *Nietzsche-Studien* 6 (1977): 295–99.

McElroy, Wendy. *The Debates of Liberty: An Overview of Individualist Anarchism*. Lanham, MD: Rowman & Littlefield, 2003.

———, ed. *Liberty, 1881–1908: A Comprehensive Index*. St. Paul, MN: Michael E. Coughlin, 1982.

McGrath, William J. *Dionysian Art and Populist Politics in Austria*. New Haven, CT: Yale University Press, 1974.

McKernan, Maureen. *The Amazing Crime and Trial of Leopold and Loeb*. 1924. New York: Signet, 1957.

Menand, Louis. *The Metaphysical Club: A Story of Ideas in America*. New York: Farrar, Straus and Giroux, 2001.

Miller, James. "The Prophet and the Dandy: Philosophy as a Way of Life in Nietzsche and Foucault." *Social Research* 65 (1998): 871–96.

Moore, R. Laurence. "Religion, Secularization, and the Shaping of the Culture Industry in Antebellum America." *American Quarterly* 41 (June 1989): 216–42.

Morgan, Bayard Quincy. *A Critical Bibliography of German Literature in English Translation, 1481–1927*. 2nd ed. Stanford, CA: Stanford University Press, 1938.

Murphy, Brenda. *The Provincetown Players and the Culture of Modernity.* Cambridge: Cambridge University Press, 2005.

Naimy, Mikhail. *Kahlil Gibran: A Biography.* New York: Philosophical Library, 1950.

Nevin, Thomas. *Irving Babbitt: An Intellectual Study.* Chapel Hill: University of North Carolina Press, 1984.

Nicholls, R. A. "The Beginnings of the Nietzsche Vogue in Germany." *Modern Philology* 56 (August 1958): 24–37.

Nolte, Ernst. *Nietzsche und der Nietzscheanismus.* Frankfurt am Main: Propylaen, 1990.

Novick, Peter. *That Noble Dream: The "Objectivity Question" and the American Historical Profession.* Cambridge: Cambridge University Press, 1988.

O'Hara, Daniel. "The Genius of Irony: Nietzsche in Bloom." In *The Yale Critics: Deconstruction in America,* edited by Jonathan Arac, Wlad Godzich, and Wallace Martin, 109–32. Minneapolis: University of Minneapolis Press, 1983.

Orvell, Miles. *The Real Thing: Imitation and Authenticity in American Culture, 1880–1940.* Chapel Hill: University of North Carolina Press, 1989.

Pawlik, Joanna. "'Various Kinds of Madness': The French Nietzscheans inside America." *Atlantic Studies* 3 (October 2006): 225–44.

Pells, Richard. *The Liberal Mind in a Conservative Age: American Intellectuals in the 1940s and 1950s.* New York: Harper & Row, 1985.

Perry, Jeffrey. *Hubert Harrison: The Voice of Harlem Radicalism, 1883–1918.* New York: Columbia University Press, 2009.

Persons, Stow, ed. *Evolutionary Thought in America.* New Haven, CT: Yale University Press, 1950.

Peters, H. F. *Zarathustra's Sister: The Case of Elisabeth and Friedrich Nietzsche.* New York: Crown, 1977.

Pettegrew, John, ed. *A Pragmatist's Progress?: Richard Rorty and American Intellectual History.* Lanham, MD: Rowman & Littlefield, 2000.

Pickus, David. "Paperback Authenticity: Walter Kaufmann and Existentialism." *Philosophy and Literature* 34 (April 2010): 17–31.

———. "The Walter Kaufmann Myth: A Study in Academic Judgment." *Nietzsche-Studien* 32 (2003): 226–58.

Pletsch, Carl. *Young Nietzsche: Becoming a Genius.* New York: Free Press, 1991.

Pochmann, Henry A. *German Culture in America: Philosophical and Literary Influences, 1600–1900.* Madison: University of Wisconsin Press, 1957.

Ponce de Leon, Charles L. *Fortunate Son: The Life of Elvis Presley*. New York: Hill and Wang, 2007.

———. *Self-Exposure: Human Interest Journalism and the Emergence of Celebrity in America, 1890–1940*. Chapel Hill: University of North Carolina Press, 2002.

Posnock, Ross. "The Politics of Pragmatism and the Fortunes of the Public Intellectual." *American Literary History* 3 (1991): 566–87.

Price, Kenneth M. "George Santayana and Germany: An Uneasy Relationship." In *Germany and German Thought in American Literature and Cultural Criticism*, edited by Peter Freese, 159–69. Essen: Verlag die Blaue Eule, 1990.

Purcell, Edward A., Jr. *The Crisis of Democratic Theory: Scientific Naturalism and the Problem of Value*. Lexington: University Press of Kentucky, 1973.

Putnam, Hilary. "A Reconsideration of Deweyan Democracy." In *The Pragmatism Reader: From Peirce through the Present*, ed. Robert B. Talisse and Scott F. Aikin, 331–52. Princeton, NJ: Princeton University Press, 2011.

Putney, Clifford. *Muscular Christianity: Manhood and Sports in Protestant America, 1880–1920*. Cambridge, MA: Harvard University Press, 2001.

Pütz, Manfred, ed. *Nietzsche in American Literature and Thought*. Columbia, SC: Camden House, 1995.

Quigley, John M. *The Superman of Nazareth: Towards a More Jesuan Christianity after Nietzsche*. Sussex: Book Guild, 2000.

Rabinbach, Anson. *In the Shadow of Catastrophe: German Intellectuals between Apocalypse and Enlightenment*. Berkeley: University of California Press, 1997.

Radway, Janice. *A Feeling for Books: Book-of-the-Month Club, Literary Taste, and Middle-Class Desire*. Chapel Hill: University of North Carolina Press, 1997.

———. "Reading Is Not Eating: Mass-Produced Literature and the Theoretical, Methodological, and Political Consequences of a Metaphor." *Book Research Quarterly* 2 (Fall 1986): 7–29.

———. *Reading the Romance: Women, Patriarchy, and Popular Literature*. Chapel Hill: University of North Carolina Press, 1984.

Ranchetti, Michele. *The Catholic Modernists: A Study of the Religious Reform Movement, 1864–1907*. Translated by Isabel Quigly. London: Oxford University Press, 1969.

Ratner-Rosenhagen, Jennifer. "Anti-Intellectualism as Romantic Discourse." *Daedalus: Journal of the American Academy of Arts and Sciences* 138 (Spring 2009): 41–52.

———. "Conventional Iconoclasm: The Cultural Work of the Nietzsche Image in Twentieth-Century America." *Journal of American History* 93 (December 2006): 728–54.

Reichert, Herbert W. "The Present Status of Nietzsche: Nietzsche Literature in the Post-War Era." *Monatshefte* 51 (March 1959): 103–20.

Reichert, Herbert, and Karl Schlechta, eds. *The International Nietzsche Bibliography.* 1960. Chapel Hill: University of North Carolina Press, 1968.

Reuben, Julie A. *The Making of the Modern University: Intellectual Transformation and the Marginalization of Morality.* Chicago: University of Chicago Press, 1996.

Reynolds, Larry J. *European Revolutions and the American Literary Renaissance.* New Haven, CT: Yale University Press, 1988.

Richardson, Robert D., Jr. *Emerson: The Mind on Fire.* Berkeley: University of California Press, 1995.

Rockmore, Tom, and Beth J. Singer, eds. *Antifoundationalism Old and New.* Philadelphia: Temple University Press, 1992.

Rodgers, Daniel T. *Atlantic Crossings: Social Politics in a Progressive Age.* Cambridge, MA: Harvard University Press, Belknap Press, 1998.

Rodgers, Marion Elizabeth. *Mencken: The American Iconoclast.* New York: Oxford University Press, 2005.

Rosenthal, Bernice Glatzer, ed. *Nietzsche in Russia.* Princeton, NJ: Princeton University Press, 1986.

Rosenzweig, Roy. *Eight Hours for What We Will: Workers and Leisure in an Industrial City, 1870–1920.* Cambridge: Cambridge University Press, 1983.

Ross, Andrew. *No Respect: Intellectuals and Popular Culture.* New York: Routledge, 1998.

Ross, Dorothy, ed. *Modernist Impulses in the Human Sciences, 1870–1930.* Baltimore: Johns Hopkins University Press, 1994.

———. *The Origins of American Social Science.* Cambridge: Cambridge University Press, 1991.

Rubin, Joan Shelley. *The Making of Middlebrow Culture.* Chapel Hill: University of North Carolina Press, 1992.

Rusk, Ralph L. *The Life of Ralph Waldo Emerson.* New York: C. Scribner, 1949.

Saatkamp, Herman J., Jr. *Rorty and Pragmatism: The Philosopher Responds to His Critics.* Nashville: Vanderbilt University Press, 1995.

Safranski, Rüdiger. *Nietzsche: A Philosophical Biography.* Translated by Shelley Frisch. New York: Norton, 2002.

Said, Edward. "The Franco-American Dialogue." In *Traveling Theory: France and the United States,* edited by Ieme van der Poel, Sophie Bertho, and Ton Hoenselaars, 134–56. Madison, NJ: Fairleigh Dickinson University Press, 1999.

Santaniello, Weaver, ed. *Nietzsche and the Gods.* Albany: State University of New York Press, 2001.

Schaberg, William H. *The Nietzsche Canon : A Publication History and Bibliography.* Chicago: University of Chicago Press, 1995.

Schacht, Richard. "Nietzsche and Nihilism." *Journal of the History of Philosophy* 11 (January 1973): 65–90.

———. "Nietzsche's Gay Science; or, How to Naturalize Cheerfully." In *Reading Nietzsche,* edited by Robert C. Solomon and Kathleen M. Higgins, 68–86. Oxford: Oxford University Press, 1988.

———. "Philosophy as Linguistic Analysis: A Nietzschean Critic." *Philosophical Studies* 25 (1973): 153–71.

Schlesinger Arthur M., Jr., and Morton White, eds. *Paths of American Thought.* Boston: Houghton Mifflin, 1963.

Schottlaender, Rudolf. "Two Dionysians: Emerson and Nietzsche." *South Atlantic Quarterly* 39 (July 1940): 330–43.

Schrift, Alan D. *Nietzsche's French Legacy: A Genealogy of Poststructuralism.* New York: Routledge, 1995.

Schwab, Arnold T. *James Gibbons Huneker: Critic of the Seven Arts.* Stanford, CA: Stanford University Press, 1963.

Schwarke, Christian. *Jesus kam nach Washington: Die Legitimation der amerikanischen Demokratie aus dem Geist des Protestantismus.* Gütersloh: Gütersloher Verlag, 1991.

Shaw, Daniel. "Rorty and Nietzsche: Some Elective Affinities." *International Studies in Philosophy* 21 (1989): 3–14.

Shore, Elliott, Ken Fones-Wolf, and James P. Danky, eds. *The German-American Radical Press: The Shaping of a Left Political Culture, 1850–1940.* Urbana: University of Illinois Press, 1992.

Sicherman, Barbara. *Well-Read Lives: How Books Inspired a Generation of American Women*. Chapel Hill: University of North Carolina Press, 2010.

Simon, Julius. *Über Emersons Einfluss in Deutschland (1851–1932)*. Berlin: Junker & Dünnhaupt, 1937.

Smith, Barry, ed. *European Philosophy and the American Academy*. La Salle, IL: Hegeler Institute, 1994.

Smith, Gregory Bruce. *Nietzsche, Heidegger and the Transition to Postmodernity*. Chicago: University of Chicago Press, 1996.

Smith, Steven B., ed. *The Cambridge Companion to Leo Strauss*. Cambridge: Cambridge University Press, 2009.

Snider, Nancy V. "An Annotated Bibliography of English Works on Friedrich Nietzsche." PhD diss., University of Michigan, 1962.

Sobejano, Gonzalo. *Nietzsche en España*. Madrid: Editorial Gredos, 1967.

Sokel, Walter. "Political Uses and Abuses of Nietzsche in Walter Kaufmann's Image of Nietzsche." *Nietzsche-Studien* 12 (1983): 436–42.

Soll, Ivan. "Walter Kaufmann and the Advocacy of German Thought in America." *Paedagogica Historica* 33 (1997): 117–33.

Sollors, Werner. *Beyond Ethnicity: Consent and Descent in American Culture*. New York: Oxford University Press, 1986.

Solomon, Robert C., ed. *Nietzsche: A Collection of Critical Essays*. Garden City, NY: Anchor Press, 1973.

Stack, George J. *Nietzsche and Emerson: An Elective Affinity*. Athens: Ohio University Press, 1992.

——— "Nietzsche's Influence on Pragmatic Humanism." *Journal of the History of Philosophy* 20 (1982): 369–406.

Stambaugh, Joan. *Nietzsche's Thought of Eternal Return*. Baltimore: Johns Hopkins University Press, 1972.

Stanislawski, Michael. *Zionism and the Fin de Siècle: Cosmopolitanism and Nationalism from Nordau to Jabotinsky*. Berkeley: University of California Press, 2001.

Stansell, Christine. *American Moderns: Bohemian New York and the Creation of a New Century*. New York: Henry Holt, Metropolitan Books, 2000.

Steel, Ronald. *Walter Lippmann and the American Century*. Boston: Little, Brown, 1980.

Steilberg, Hays Alan. *Die amerikanische Nietzsche-Rezeption von 1896 bis 1950*. Berlin: Walter de Gruyter, 1996.

Stewart, Walter. "*My Sister and I*: The Disputed Nietzsche." *Thought* 61 (1986): 321–25.

Stone, Dan. *Breeding Superman: Nietzsche, Race and Eugenics in Edwardian and Interwar Britain*. Liverpool: Liverpool University Press, 2002.

Strong, Bryan. "Images of Nietzsche in America, 1900–1970." *South Atlantic Quarterly* 70 (Autumn 1971): 575–94.

Strong, Tracy B. *Friedrich Nietzsche and the Politics of Transfiguration*. 1975. Exp. ed. Urbana: University of Illinois Press, 2000.

Susman, Warren. *Culture as History: The Transformation of American Society in the Twentieth Century*. New York: Pantheon Books, 1973.

Tanner, Michael. *Nietzsche*. Oxford: Oxford University Press, 1994.

Tanselle, G. Thomas. *The History of Books as a Field of Study*. Chapel Hill: University of North Carolina Press, 1981.

Tatlock, Lynne, and Matt Erlin. *German Culture in Nineteenth-Century America: Reception, Adaptation, Transformation*. Rochester, NY: Camden House, 2005.

Taubeneck, Steven. "Nietzsche in North America: Walter Kaufmann and After." Translator's afterword to *Confrontations: Derrida/Heidegger/Nietzsche*, by Ernst Behler, 159–77. Stanford, CA: Stanford University Press, 1991.

Thatcher, David S. *Nietzsche in England, 1890–1914: The Growth of a Reputation*. Toronto: University of Toronto Press, 1970.

Thomas, R. Hinton. *Nietzsche in German Politics and Society, 1890–1918*. Manchester: Manchester University Press, 1983.

Tolzmann, Don Heinrich. *The German-American Experience*. Amherst, MA: Humanity, 2000.

Turner, James. *Without God, Without Creed: The Origins of Unbelief in America*. Baltimore: Johns Hopkins University Press, 1986.

Vance, Norman. *The Sinews of the Spirit: The Ideal of Christian Manliness in Victorian Literature and Religious Thought*. Cambridge: Cambridge University Press, 1985.

Van der Will, Wilfried. "Nietzsche in America: Fashion and Fascination." *History of European Ideas* 11 (1989): 1015–23.

Veysey, Laurence R. *The Emergence of the American University*. Chicago: University of Chicago Press, 1965.

Vivarelli, Vivetta. "Nietzsche und Emerson: Über einige Pfade in Zarathustras metaphorischer Landschaft." *Nietzsche Studien* 16 (1987): 227–63.

Von Eschen, Penny. *Race against Empire: Black Americans and Anticolonialism, 1937–1957.* Ithaca, NY: Cornell University Press, 1997.

Von Grueningen, John Paul. "Goethe in American Periodicals from 1860–1900." PhD diss., University of Wisconsin, 1931.

Von Petzold, Gertrud. "Nietzsche in englisch-amerikanischer Beurteilung bis zum Ausgang des Weltkrieges." *Anglia* 53 (1929): 134–217.

Waite, Robert G. L. *The Psychopathic God: Adolf Hitler.* New York: Basic Books, 1977.

Waterfield, Robin. *Prophet: The Life and Times of Kahlil Gibran.* New York: St. Martin's Press, 1998.

Watson, James R., ed. *Portraits of American Continental Philosophers.* Bloomington: Indiana University Press, 1999.

Weber, Paul C. *America in Imaginative German Literature in the First Half of the Nineteenth Century.* New York: Columbia University Press, 1926.

Weir, David. *Decadent Culture in the United States: Art and Literature against the American Grain, 1890–1926.* Albany: State University of New York Press, 2008.

Weiss-Rosmarin, Trude. "An Interview with Walter Kaufmann." *Judaism* 30 (Winter, 1981): 120–28.

Welter, Barbara. "The Feminization of American Religion, 1800–1860." In *Dimity Convictions: The American Woman in the Nineteenth Century,* 83–102. Athens: Ohio University Press, 1976.

Westbrook, Robert B. *Democratic Hope: Pragmatism and the Politics of Truth.* Ithaca, NY: Cornell University Press, 2005.

———. *John Dewey and American Democracy.* Ithaca, NY: Cornell University Press, 1991.

Wetzsteon, Ross. *Republic of Dreams: Greenwich Village, the American Bohemia, 1910–1960.* New York: Simon and Schuster, 2002.

White, Morton. *Social Thought in America: The Revolt against Formalism.* 1949. Rev. ed., Boston: Beacon, 1957.

Wiebe, Robert H. *The Search for Order, 1877–1920.* 1967. New York: Hill and Wang, 1994.

Wilcox, John T. *Truth and Value in Nietzsche: A Study of His Metaethics and Epistemology.* Ann Arbor: University of Michigan Press, 1974.

Williams, Linda. *Nietzsche's Mirror: The World as Will to Power.* Lanham, MD: Rowman and Littlefield, 2001.

Williams, Raymond. *Keywords: A Vocabulary of Culture and Society*. London: Fontana, Croom, Helm, 1976.

Williamson, George S. *The Longing for Myth in Germany: Religion and Aesthetic Culture from Romanticism to Nietzsche*. Chicago: University of Chicago Press, 2004.

Wilson, Daniel J. *Science, Community, and the Transformation of American Philosophy, 1860–1930*. Chicago: University of Chicago Press, 1990.

Winterer, Caroline. *Mirror of Antiquity: American Women and the Classical Tradition, 1750–1900*. Ithaca, NY: Cornell University Press, 2007.

Woessner, Martin. "Being Here: Heidegger in America." PhD diss., City University of New York, 2006.

Wolin, Richard. *Heidegger's Children: Hannah Arendt, Karl Löwith, Hans Jonas, and Herbert Marcuse*. Princeton, NJ: Princeton University Press, 2001.

———. *The Seduction of Unreason: The Intellectual Romance with Fascism from Nietzsche to Postmodernism*. Princeton, NJ: Princeton University Press, 2004.

Woods, Thomas E., Jr. *The Church Confronts Modernity: Catholic Intellectuals and the Progressive Era*. New York: Columbia University Press, 2004.

Yack, Bernard. *The Longing for Total Revolution: Philosophical Sources of Social Discontent: From Rousseau to Marx and Nietzsche*. Princeton, NJ: Princeton University Press, 1986.